PENGUIN CLASSICS

MOZART
A LIFE IN LETTERS

WOLFGANG AMADEUS MOZART, who was born at Salzburg, Austria, on 27 January 1756, is ranked among the most famous, and the most popular, of all composers. A child prodigy, he toured western Europe between 1763 and 1771, with later trips to Vienna, Munich, Mannheim and Paris. After his break with the Archbishop of Salzburg in 1781, Mozart took up permanent residence in Vienna, where he became a successful freelance composer and performer. The author of masses, symphonies, serenades, concertos, operas, string quartets and other works in virtually every genre of the time, he died prematurely at the age of thirty-five, on 5 December 1791.

CLIFF EISEN teaches at King's College London. He has published widely on late eighteenth-century music and on Mozart in particular, including the Mozart article for the revised *New Grove Dictionary of Music and Musicians* (2001). In addition, he has edited two volumes of *Mozart Studies* (1991 and 1997) as well as the *Cambridge Mozart Encyclopedia* (2005 with Simon P. Keefe). His current research projects include a monograph on Mozart and biography, an annotated translation of Hermann Abert's classic *W. A. Mozart* (1919–23) and a study of the musicals of Frank Loesser.

STEWART SPENCER was born in Yorkshire and studied Modern Languages at Oxford. He taught Medieval German Literature at the University of London and has subsequently worked as a translator. He is the editor, with Barry Millington, of *Selected Letters of Richard Wagner* (1987), *Wagner in Performance* (1992) and *Wagner's Ring of the Nibelung: A Companion* (1993). He has translated books on Wagner, Liszt, Mozart and Bach and has published numerous articles on Wagner.

MOZART

A Life in Letters

Edited by CLIFF EISEN
Translated by STEWART SPENCER

PENGUIN BOOKS

PENGUIN BOOKS

Published by the Penguin Group
Penguin Books Ltd, 80 Strand, London WC2R ORL, England
Penguin Group (USA) Inc., 375 Hudson Street, New York, New York 10014, USA
Penguin Group (Canada), 90 Eglinton Avenue East, Suite 700, Toronto, Ontario, Canada M4P 2Y3
(a division of Pearson Penguin Canada Inc.)
Penguin Ireland, 25 St Stephen's Green, Dublin 2, Ireland
(a division of Penguin Books Ltd)
Penguin Group (Australia), 250 Camberwell Road, Camberwell, Victoria 3124, Australia
(a division of Pearson Australia Group Pty Ltd)
Penguin Books India Pvt Ltd, 11 Community Centre, Panchsheel Park, New Delhi – 110 017, India
Penguin Group (NZ), 67 Apollo Drive, Mairangi Bay, Auckland 1310, New Zealand
(a division of Pearson New Zealand Ltd)
Penguin Books (South Africa) (Pty) Ltd, 24 Sturdee Avenue, Rosebank, Johannesburg 2196, South Africa

Penguin Books Ltd, Registered Offices: 80 Strand, London WC2R ORL, England

www.penguin.com

First published in Penguin Classics 2006
1

Chronology, introduction and editorial material copyright © Cliff Eisen, 2006
Translation copyright © Stewart Spencer, 2006
All rights reserved

The moral right of the editor and translator has been asserted

Set in 11.25/12.75 pt Monotype Fournier
Typeset by Rowland Phototypesetting Ltd, Bury St Edmunds, Suffolk
Printed in Great Britain by Clays Ltd, St Ives plc

ISBN-13: 978-0-141-44146-7
ISBN-10: 0-141-44146-1

Contents

Chronology

1756 *27 January* Mozart is born in Salzburg.

1761 Learns to play short keyboard pieces and composes his first work, the andante K1a.

1762 His father Leopold Mozart takes him and his elder sister, Nannerl, to perform for Elector Maximilian III Joseph of Bavaria in Munich, and for Emperor Francis I and Empress Maria Theresa in Vienna.

1763–6 The whole family tours modern-day Germany, France, England, Holland, Belgium and Switzerland, and the children perform for King Louis XV of France and King George III of Britain, among others. Composes several sonatas for keyboard and violin, symphonies and arias.

1767–8 Travels to Vienna where he composes symphonies, an *opera buffa*, *La finta semplice*, and a singspiel, *Bastien und Bastienne*.

1769 Appointed unpaid third concertmaster in the Salzburg court music establishment.

1769–73 Travels three times to Italy with Leopold; composes the operas *Mitridate, re di Ponto* (1770) and *Lucio Silla* (1772) and two serenatas, *Ascanio in Alba* (1771) and *Il sogno di Scipione* (1772), several symphonies and his first string quartets (K80 and K155–160). Visits Vienna between mid-July and mid-September 1773; composes six string quartets (K168–173).

1774 Travels to Munich in December for the premiere of his opera, *La finta giardiniera*.

1775–6 Remains in Salzburg; composes several serenades, four violin concertos, three piano concertos, divertimentos for strings and horns and the serenata, *Il re pastore*.

1777 Composes the piano concerto K271; resigns from Salzburg court service and travels with his mother, Maria Anna, to Munich, Augsburg and Mannheim, where he falls in love with the singer Aloysia Weber.

1778–9 Visits Paris where he composes several well-received works but fails to make significant professional headway; his mother dies on 3 July 1778. Returns unwillingly to Salzburg where he has been reappointed to court service as court and cathedral organist with increased pay. Is rejected by Aloysia. Composes the 'Paris' symphony K297, the concerto for flute and harp K299, the keyboard and violin sonatas K301–306 and the keyboard sonata K310.

1779–80 In Salzburg; composes symphonies, serenades, masses and other church works. Receives commission to write an *opera seria* for the Munich court theatre.

1781 *Idomeneo* premiered in Munich on 29 January; called to Vienna, where he has a falling out with Archbishop Hieronymus Colloredo and is finally dismissed from court service on 8 June. Establishes himself as a freelance performer and composer; commissioned to write a German opera, *Die Entführung aus dem Serail*, and publishes six keyboard and violin sonatas (K296, K376–380).

1782 *Die Entführung* performed on 16 July; marries Constanze Weber, Aloysia's sister, on 4 August. Compositions include three piano concertos (K413–415), the 'Haffner' symphony K385 and a string quartet (K387).

1783 First child, Raimund Leopold, born but dies two months later; visits Salzburg with Constanze (July–October). Composes 'Linz' symphony K425, keyboard sonatas K330–332, two string quartets (K421, 428).

1784 Gives numerous subscription and private concerts; joins Masonic lodge. Second child, Carl Thomas, is born. Composes six piano concertos (K449–459), quintet for piano and winds K452, keyboard sonatas K333 and K457, and string quartet K458 ('Hunt').

1785 Visit of Leopold Mozart to Vienna (February–April); Mozart gives successful concert series and performs at the Burgtheater. Compositions include the serenade for winds K361, the string quartets K464 and 465, three piano concertos (K466, 467 and 482), several songs, a piano quartet (K478) and a violin sonata (K481).

1786 Opera *Le nozze di Figaro* premiered at the Burgtheater on 1 May. Third child, Johann Thomas Leopold, is born and dies. Other compositions include three piano concertos (K488, 491 and 503); the 'Prague' symphony K504, the 'Skittles' trio K498, the 'Hoffmeister' quartet K499 and the concert aria *Ch'io mi scordi di te* K505.

1787 Travels twice to Prague for performances of *Le nozze di Figaro* (January) and the premiere of his opera *Don Giovanni* (October). Leopold Mozart dies on 28 May. Other works include the string quintets K515 and 516, *Eine kleine Nachtmusik* K525, the violin sonata K526 and several songs. Fourth child, Theresia Constanzia Adelheid, is born; she survives six months.

1788 *Don Giovanni* premiered in Vienna (7 May); faced with financial problems, Mozart begins to borrow money from his Masonic brother, Michael Puchberg. Composes three symphonies (K543, 550 and 551 'Jupiter'), three piano trios (K542, 548 and 564) and the divertimento for string trio K563.

1789 Travels to Dresden, Leipzig, Potsdam and Berlin with artistic but not financial success. Composes two keyboard sonatas (K570, 576), a string quartet (K575) and the clarinet quintet K581. Fifth child, Anna Maria, is born and dies.

1790 Opera *Così fan tutte* premiered on 26 January in Vienna; in October, Mozart attends the coronation of Emperor Leopold II in Frankfurt. Other compositions include the string quartets K589 and 590, and the string quintet K593.

1791 Sixth child, Franz Xaver Wolfgang, is born. Mozart travels to Prague for the premiere of his *opera seria*, *La clemenza di Tito*, commissioned to celebrate the coronation of Leopold II as king of Hungary; German opera *Die Zauberflöte* premieres in Vienna on 30 September. During the summer begins work on a Requiem, which is left incomplete on his death. Other works include the motet *Ave verum corpus* (K618) and the clarinet concerto K622. Falls ill in November and dies suddenly, probably from rheumatic inflammatory fever, on 5 December at the age of thirty-five.

Introduction

Two hundred and fifty years on, Wolfgang Amadeus Mozart – child prodigy, performer par excellence, universally admired composer, tragic Romantic artist and cultural icon – continues to fascinate musicians and music lovers alike. Along with Wagner, Mozart is probably the most written about composer in history. And more than any other composer, he has been featured in documentaries, movies, novels, television commercials and pop culture generally. Everyone seems to know something about Mozart, even if it is only the story of his final illness and early death at the age of thirty-five.

As a cultural icon, however, Mozart is also subject to the whims and fancies of any particular time and any particular place – the story that is told of his life is as much a reflection of its teller as of Mozart himself. Nevertheless, all biographies of Mozart, whatever their points of view or interpretative strategies, are based on the same documentary sources: the composer's autographs, contemporary accounts of his life and works, and a rich family correspondence, including letters not only between Wolfgang and his father Leopold, but also between Leopold and his friends in Salzburg. In fact, the Mozart family correspondence, some twelve hundred letters written between 1756 and 1791, is more extensive than that of any earlier composer, and of many later ones as well. As such, it offers a unique insight into the family dynamics, Mozart's relationship with his father and friends and lovers, the moving death of his mother in Paris in 1778, his compositional method (particularly with regard to the operas *Idomeneo* and *Die Entführung aus dem Serail*) and the events of his everyday life. To be sure, the letters can be read in any number of ways. Yet they remain the primary source for setting the biographical record straight and they allow Mozart and his father to speak in their own voices – or rather in a variety of voices, depending on the person they were addressing and the reason for writing.

In a single volume of this kind, it is not possible to include all of the family's letters. And they can never tell the complete life. Not only do they refer to people and events now lost from the historical record, but there are long stretches where no correspondence survives, chiefly when the family was all together in Salzburg. A further problem of survival concerns Leopold Mozart's letters to his son after Wolfgang had moved to Vienna in 1781: although Leopold wrote regularly, someone – presumably Mozart's wife Constanze – later destroyed his letters, possibly because of their inflammatory content (Leopold was happy neither with Mozart's move to the Austrian capital nor with his marriage). And after Leopold's death in the spring of 1787, Mozart lost his primary correspondent.

By including only extracts from Leopold's letters, previous editions of the correspondence render it as overly Mozart-centric and give a false account of the relationship between father and son, to say nothing of the course of Mozart's life; Leopold's letters are here given in full (there are four minor excisions, indicated in the notes). They represent a rich and unexpected source of information concerning eighteenth-century men and manners, music and musicians. During the family's travels in Europe, Leopold wrote frequently, and at length, to his close friend and Salzburg landlord, Johann Lorenz Hagenauer. He boasts of his son's musical successes and comments on everything from his meetings with the great to lightning conductors and the latest Paris fashions. As someone who knew all too well the value of patronage, Leopold would unquestionably have schooled Wolfgang in the political and cultural realities of the day – a world in which German princes held absolute power within the confines of their own sovereign states, but which was beginning to be shaken by the dangerous ideas of the Enlightenment, spreading out from Paris, and in which the old dominance of Habsburg Austria within the German-speaking world was being challenged by the rising military power of Prussia.

Above all, however, the Mozart family correspondence straddles the line between history and the late eighteenth-century individual. And because it is incomplete, it straddles the line between fact and creative narrative – it is the reader who fills in the gaps and draws conclusions about Mozart's motivations and relationships. That the story of his life unfolds in the context of a correspondence ties it conveniently close to late eighteenth- and early nineteenth-century literary traditions, particularly the epistolary novel (see below) – as when, for example, the twenty-one-year-old Mozart, fleeing Salzburg to make his own way in the world, and falling in love with a charming young singer, is pursued across Europe by his father's letters, admonishing, anxious and full of (mostly) unheeded advice.

Mozart's life

Salzburg, where Mozart was born on 27 January 1756, was an independent church-state, ruled by a prince-archbishop. It has been portrayed as something of a cultural and musical backwater, but this was not so – situated between Bavaria, Austria and Italy, the city had strong political and intellectual ties both to Vienna and to Italy, and its mercantile connections extended throughout Germany. Musically it was a distinguished centre of both performance and composition.

Mozart's father, Leopold (b. 1719), originally from Augsburg, was a distinguished musician himself: a violinist, one of the directors of the Salzburg court music, and author of the most influential eighteenth-century violin tutor, the *Versuch einer gründlichen Violinschule*, published at Augsburg in 1756. Leopold and his wife, Maria Anna, née Pertl (b. 1720), had five children that died in infancy and two that survived: Maria Anna Walburga Ignatia (b. 1751), known as 'Nannerl', and Wolfgang Amadeus.[1] Mozart's musical talents were apparent from an early age: trained by his father, he was able to play short, relatively easy keyboard works by the age of four and he composed his first allegros, andantes and minuets by the age of six. His sister, too, was a child prodigy, at least as far as performance was concerned, and in 1762 Leopold – genuinely convinced that his children were miracles and that it was his duty to exhibit them to the world – decided to take them on tour, first to Munich and then to Vienna.

Nannerl and Wolfgang's early successes were unprecedented and in 1763 Leopold conceived a more ambitious plan. He took the entire family on an extended musical tour through Germany, France, England, the Low Countries and Switzerland, showing off the children before the courts of Europe. By the time they returned to Salzburg three and a half years later, Mozart's fame as a musical prodigy had spread. He not only performed, he also composed: his first works, including symphonies, arias and accompanied sonatas, were all written at this time. In 1767 and 1768 the Mozarts visited Vienna, where the children played at court for the Empress Maria Theresa, and Wolfgang was commissioned to write an opera, *La finta semplice* ('The Pretend Simpleton'). And at the very end of 1769, Mozart and his father set out on the first of three trips they made to Italy over the next three years, during which he composed two operas – *Mitridate, re di Ponto* and *Lucio Silla* – and two serenatas – *Ascanio in Alba* and *Il sogno di Scipione*. He became a member of prestigious musical academies at Verona and Bologna, wrote down the score of Allegri's *Miserere* from memory after hearing it in the Sistine Chapel and was made a Knight of the Golden Spur by Pope Clement XIV.

From 1773 to 1777 Mozart was largely based in Salzburg. He visited Vienna in 1773, where he composed the string quartets K168–173, and Munich in 1774, where he completed the *opera buffa*, *La finta giardiniera* ('The Pretend Gardener-girl'), but for the most part he chafed under the demands of his new employer, Hieronymus Colloredo, who in 1772 had succeeded the more congenial Siegmund von Schrattenbach as prince-archbishop of Salzburg. Although Mozart composed prolifically at the time, including masses, smaller church works, symphonies, concertos, dances and chamber music, both he and his father actively sought opportunities elsewhere. His longing for independence came to a head in 1777, and he asked for, and was given, release from court service. In September, Wolfgang and his mother set out for Munich, Mannheim and Paris in search of employment; Leopold, thinking first and foremost of the family's security, remained in Salzburg. The trip was a disaster: Mozart was unable to secure a permanent position; he fell in love with a young singer in Mannheim, Aloysia Weber; and his mother died in Paris in July 1778. Leopold, in the meantime, had arranged for Mozart's return to Salzburg, with increased pay and more responsibilities at court. Rejected by Aloysia en route, Wolfgang arrived back there, unwillingly, in early 1779.

In 1780 Mozart was commissioned to write *Idomeneo* for the court theatre at Munich; the opera was first performed there, under his direction, in January 1781. Archbishop Colloredo – who was making a visit to Vienna – summoned Mozart to join his musical retinue there but he, no doubt encouraged by the success of his opera and his own high opinion of himself, argued furiously with his employer and was dismissed from court service. Leopold was horrified and tried to persuade Mozart to make amends with the archbishop but Wolfgang stood firm, justifying himself to his father both on grounds of his honour and the opportunities that Vienna offered him.

As it happened, Wolfgang was right. Joseph II, sole ruler of Austria since the death of his mother Maria Theresa in 1780, instituted numerous 'enlightened' reforms that directly or indirectly favoured men of talent; these included not only a loosening of censorship and freedom of the press, but also an attempt to foster German culture, both theatrical and operatic. It was thanks to Joseph's German National Theatre (founded in 1776) that Mozart was commissioned to write his first 'international' success, the German opera *Die Entführung aus dem Serail* ('The Abduction from the Seraglio'), a work described in at least one early obituary of him as 'the pedestal upon which his fame was erected.'[2] And Mozart took advantage of that success, as well as his position as Vienna's foremost keyboard player, to promote himself in a series of subscription concerts that were wildly successful: in a letter to his father of 20 March 1784, he named more than 170 subscribers to his concerts. At the same time he was in demand for performances at private salons, he wrote works for the local Tonkünstler-Sozietät (a benevolent society aiding musicians' widows and orphans), he had several piano students from among the nobility and well-to-do middle class, and he joined the Freemasons, which in Vienna was an a-political and a-religious society of intellectuals. By 1786, Mozart was recognized as both the pre-eminent performer in Vienna and, along with Joseph Haydn, the pre-eminent composer. His chief works included fifteen piano concertos (between K413 and K503), the six string quartets dedicated to Haydn (K387, 421, 428, 458, 464 and 465), the piano and wind quintet K452, and several arias and piano sonatas, among other works.

Mozart had had another reason for wanting to stay in Vienna, one he was less forthcoming about with his father. In 1780, Aloysia Weber had moved to Vienna with her family; after a stint as a singer in Munich, she had been appointed to the Habsburg court. Aloysia, now married to the actor Joseph Lange, was beyond reach for Mozart but that hardly mattered (or it mattered only a little): he had, in the meantime, fallen in love with Aloysia's younger sister, Constanze. Leopold was against the match but Mozart went ahead none the less, marrying on 4 August 1782. And in this choice, too, he seems to have been right. Although, like all marriages, theirs had its ups and downs, there is every reason to believe it was a happy one. Wolfgang and Constanze had six children, only two of whom survived to adulthood: Carl Thomas (1784–1858) and Franz Xaver Wolfgang (1791–1844).

For reasons that are not entirely clear, Mozart gave fewer public concerts in Vienna after 1786. Possibly this was a result of his increasing occupation with opera: Le nozze di Figaro ('The Marriage of Figaro') was premiered in 1786 and successfully performed at Prague in early 1787; its success there led to the commission for Don Giovanni, first given in Prague in October 1787 and revised for Vienna in 1788. Così fan tutte ('Women are all the same') was composed in 1789 and premiered in Vienna in January 1790, but its run was interrupted by the death of Emperor Joseph II on 20 February – or possibly it was due to a general decline in Viennese cultural life at the time, usually blamed on the Austrian-Turkish war of 1788–90; with attention and resources diverted elsewhere, both the court and the nobility were less inclined to support public music-making. Whatever the reason, Mozart rarely appeared in concert, he composed fewer significant works in 1788 and 1789 (notable exceptions are the three last symphonies, K543, the G minor K550 and the 'Jupiter' K551), and he ran into financial difficulties; between 1788 and 1790

Mozart wrote several begging letters to his Masonic brother and friend, Michael Puchberg. Perhaps in an attempt to alleviate his financial problems, or perhaps just to get away from Vienna for a while, he undertook a concert tour to Dresden, Leipzig, Potsdam and Berlin in the spring of 1789. But although it was artistically a success, financially it was a failure. Mozart took another journey in the late summer of 1790 to attend the coronation in Frankfurt of Leopold II, Joseph's successor, as Holy Roman Emperor. This, too, brought no financial rewards.

The year 1791 – and a return to political stability in Vienna – saw a remarkable upswing in Mozart's fortunes. In March he performed at a concert by the clarinettist Josef Bähr, he had commissions from patrons in Hungary and in Amsterdam, Viennese publishers produced at least half a dozen editions of his works and he was commissioned (albeit as second choice) to compose the Prague coronation opera *La clemenza di Tito* ('The Clemency of Titus'). And even before he had begun this, he had agreed to compose *Die Zauberflöte* ('The Magic Flute') for his long-time friend, the impresario Emanuel Schikaneder. *La clemenza di Tito* was first given at Prague on 6 September. When *Die Zauberflöte* premiered in Vienna on 30 September it was universally praised, if not for its text then for its music, and quickly established itself as the most popular of all German operas.

During the autumn of 1791, Mozart was engaged with another work, the Requiem, which served ultimately to cement his reputation as a composer of both human and metaphysical importance. The wife of Count Franz Walsegg-Stuppach had died on 14 February 1791, and in July the count approached Mozart to write a Requiem to be performed on the first anniversary of her death. Although numerous stories swirl around the Requiem, Mozart probably knew Walsegg's identity and the occasion for which it was intended. By the same token, there is no compelling evidence that Mozart believed he was writing the Requiem for himself, nor reason to think he was poisoned by the composer Antonio Salieri, jealous of Mozart's superior talent, or by anyone else. Mozart had been ill in Prague in September but seems to have recovered, and his letters of October and November – when he also completed the clarinet concerto K622 – are full of high spirits. If he had not fallen ill again, this time fatally, no mystery would surround the Requiem's composition. His premature death, on 5 December, probably of rheumatic inflammatory fever, was an unfortunate accident, though no less compelling for that. He was not buried – as the stories would have it – in a pauper's grave, but was given a simple funeral according to Viennese customs of the time.

The letters

The texts of the letters given here, newly translated by Stewart Spencer, are based on those of the standard, critical complete edition: Wilhelm A. Bauer, Otto Erich Deutsch and Joseph Heinz Eibl, eds., *Mozart: Briefe und Aufzeichnungen* (eight volumes, Kassel, 1962–2005); this was not the first complete edition of Mozart's letters but it is certainly the best. Among English-language selections from the letters, the edition by Emily Anderson (London, 1935) takes pride of place. What distinguishes Anderson in particular is its inclusion of every single word written by Mozart – indeed, that was explicitly its purpose – but by omitting significant stretches of Leopold's letters, it does not give a balanced picture of the events it recounts – by even a rough accounting, letters by Leopold Mozart account for two-thirds of the family correspondence. There is an implied presumption, not only that Mozart's words speak for themselves but also, perhaps, that they are the only authentic source of information about the composer. By this reckoning, not even Leopold, who is often the villain in many later accounts of Mozart's life, is considered a reliable witness.

In this respect, the most interesting edition of the letters may be one that was never intended as such: Georg Nikolaus Nissen's *Biographie W. A. Mozarts* (Leipzig, 1828). Nissen, a Danish diplomat and Constanze Mozart's second husband (they married in 1809), decided in the 1820s to write Mozart's biography based largely on the family correspondence still in her possession. Although he died before it was finished, Constanze arranged for its completion and it appeared in print two years later. What is remarkable about this work, at least for its time, is its attempt to tell Mozart's story through 'authentic' documents, through the family letters, which are generously extracted and which until then had been otherwise unpublished and unavailable. It is, in effect, an 'epistolary biography', not so far in spirit from the then-popular 'epistolary novel'. The comparison is an apt one, for even a cursory reading of the letters shows that it is not just the record of a life, but also the record of a very specific relationship, that between Mozart and his father. Both show their good sides and their bad sides, both cajole and argue with the other, both strive for the upper hand, for independence or for peace of mind.

It seemed to me important, then, to treat these letters differently here than they have been previously, to allow them to tell their story without editorial intervention, without omitting Leopold's letters and without censoring the material. Accordingly, I have included only complete letters, including long letters from Leopold that go into considerable detail about what they saw and whom they met on their travels, his concerns with contemporary politics and church affairs, his interest in medical remedies and his attention to Wolfgang's welfare. For it is only in the context of complete letters – letters that show both Wolfgang and his father to the fullest, as real human beings rather than historically predetermined constructions – that a story emerges.

By and large the translation preserves the linguistic style and informal character of the originals. (This extends even to the scatological letters: it is important to bear in mind that all four of the Mozarts indulged themselves – Mozart's scatological letters are typical not only of the Mozart family's sense of humour, but of eighteenth-century Salzburg humour generally.) I have not, however, retained the original orthography of places and names, which is variable throughout the letters, sometimes phonetic, sometimes correct and sometimes just wrong; nor have I reproduced the addresses or layout of the letters in every respect: this edition strives for readability rather than literal transcription. However, some things, such as the liberal use of dashes (especially Leopold's), abbreviations of place names and writing of numbers, have been retained to give a flavour of the original. Where appropriate, I have also included selections from contemporary documents describing the events referred to in the letters. My sources for these are Otto Erich Deutsch's *Mozart: A Documentary Biography* (1966) and Cliff Eisen, *New Mozart Documents* (1991); for contemporary pictures of Mozart, his family and acquaintances and the places he visited, the best source is Otto Erich Deutsch, *Mozart und seine Welt in zeitgenössischen Bildern* (1961).

The number of people mentioned in the correspondence is enormous. Wherever possible, they are identified in the footnotes on first mention, or the reader is directed to the List of Important People before the *Life in Letters*; if there is no note, either the person named remains unidentifiable, or what is known of him or her does not contribute to our understanding of the correspondence. For many figures who recur throughout the letters, or whose presence is not always explicit but constantly hovering in the background, readers can always consult this list. I have been greatly helped in the matter of identification by the commentary volumes to the complete German-language edition of the letters, by Heinz Schuler's *Mozarts Salzburger Freunde und Bekannte: Biographien und Kommentare* (Wilhelmshaven, 2004) and by Peter Clive's *Mozart and his Circle* (1993).

A Note on Currencies

Currency conversions – whether among local currencies during the eighteenth century or between eighteenth- and twenty-first century currencies – are problematic at best. The principal unit of currency circulating in Habsburg lands at the time was the florin or gulden, which was divided into 60 kreuzer; the ducat was a gold coin worth about 4½ florins while 2 florins were equivalent to a common thaler. These values were not, however, absolutely consistent between different regions of Austria and thalers could be either Reichsthalers (1½ florins) or Konventionsthalers (2 florins). Currency conventions in Salzburg were slightly different – 1 Viennese florin was worth about 1 florin 12 kreuzer – and international conventions more complex still. The English pound was approximately 8 or 9 Viennese florins, the French louis d'or was about 7½ florins and the Venetian zecchino about 5 florins. Other currencies are mentioned in the Mozart family letters as well, including the Bavarian max d'or (similar to the French louis d'or) and the Salzburg half-batzen, a small silver coin whose value cannot now be exactly determined. It is useful, when dealing with currencies, to bear in mind that during the 1760s Leopold Mozart's basic annual salary in Salzburg was 300 florins and that when Mozart was reappointed to the Salzburg court music in 1779 his and his father's joint salary was 1,000 florins, including a subsistence allowance. When Mozart was appointed imperial chamber musician in 1787 he received 800 florins salary; and the normal fee for composing an opera for the imperial theatres was 450 florins. To put these figures in perspective, Johann Pezzl, writing in Vienna in 1786, calculated that a single person could live 'quite comfortably' on 500 or 550 gulden.[3] It is likely, then, that Mozart and his family could have managed reasonably well, if they were not extravagant and remained healthy, on his income. The cost of living in Salzburg was less.

I am grateful to Penguin Books for their help and advice in preparing this edition and in particular to Susan Kennedy, who copyedited the text and notes and made innumerable good suggestions for their improvement. I am also grateful to Stewart Spencer, who translated the text and pointed out numerous interesting details to me as well as answering all my questions and setting me straight on a number of matters. He also compiled the index. Finally, my wife, Katy, gave me invaluable advice, as always, and for that I am grateful.

NOTES

1. Amadeus was the Latin form of Theophilus (Gottlieb in German), one of his baptismal names. Wolfgang himself usually spelled it Amadè, and occasionally Amadé.
2. See C. Eisen, *New Mozart Documents* (London, 1991), p. 74.
3. H. C. Robbins Landon, *Mozart and Vienna* (London, 1991), p. 74.

Further Reading

Braunbehrens, Volkmar, *Mozart in Vienna* (New York, 1990)

Clive, Peter, *Mozart and his Circle* (New Haven, CT, 1993)

Einstein, Alfred, *Mozart: His Character, His Work* (New York, 1945)

Eisen, Cliff, *New Mozart Documents* (London, 1991)

Eisen, Cliff and Stanley Sadie, eds., *The New Grove Mozart* (London, 2002)

Eisen, Cliff and Simon P. Keefe, eds., *The Cambridge Mozart Encyclopedia* (Cambridge, 2005)

Halliwell, Ruth, *The Mozart Family: Four Lives in a Social Context* (Oxford, 1998)

Keefe, Simon P., ed., *The Cambridge Companion to Mozart* (Cambridge, 2003)

Küster, Konrad, *Mozart: A Musical Biography* (Oxford, 1996)

Landon, H. C. Robbins, *Mozart's Last Year* (London, 1988)

Schroder, David, *Mozart in Revolt* (London, 1999)

List of Important People

ADLGASSER, ANTON CAJETAN (1729–77) Court and cathedral organist in Salzburg from 1750 until his death, and a close friend of the Mozart family; Leopold was a witness at all three of his weddings. He was chiefly a composer of sacred music, and collaborated with Michael Haydn and Mozart on the oratorio *Die Schuldigkeit des ersten Gebots*. Adlgasser died after suffering a stroke while playing the organ; Leopold described the event in a letter of 22 December 1777. Mozart succeeded him as court and cathedral organist in 1779.

ARCO FAMILY Head of one of Salzburg's most illustrious noble families, Georg Anton Felix, Count von Arco (1705–92), chief steward in Salzburg from 1786, and his wife Maria Josepha Viktoria (née von Hardegg, 1710–75) were among the Mozarts' greatest supporters at the archbishop's court. Their son Joseph Adam (1733–1802), bishop of Königgrätz in Bohemia, helped secure Mozart's appointment as organist at Salzburg in 1779. Another son, Karl Joseph Maria Felix (1743–1830), was a member of Archbishop Colloredo's household and figured prominently in Mozart's second departure from Colloredo's service in 1781. Their daughter Maria Anna Felicitas (1741–64) was married to the Bavarian ambassador at Paris, Count Maximilian van Eyck; she died while the Mozarts were staying at her house during their visit to Paris in 1763–4. Another daughter, Antonia Maria, was married to Count Lodron (see below).

AUERNHAMMER, JOSEPHA BARBARA (1758–1820) A student of Mozart's in Vienna in the early 1780s and a fine pianist, judging by contemporary accounts; the Viennese musician Benedikt Schwarz described her as 'a great dilettante on the pianoforte', while Mozart admired her 'enchanting' playing but noted that 'in cantabile playing she has not got the real delicate singing style'. Mozart and Auernhammer are known to have performed together on a number of occasions. He dedicated the accompanied sonatas K296 and K376–380 to her. Auernhammer fell in love with Mozart in 1781, but he did not reciprocate.

BULLINGER, FRANZ JOSEPH JOHANN NEPOMUK (1744–1810) Tutor to the Arco family, he settled in Salzburg between 1774 and 1776 and became the intimate friend and confidant of Leopold Mozart, loaning him a substantial sum of money when Mozart resigned court service in 1777 and set out on his travels with his mother. Wolfgang turned to Bullinger for help when he had to tell Leopold of Maria Anna Mozart's death in Paris in July 1778.

COLLOREDO, HIERONYMUS JOSEPH FRANZ DE PAULA VON (1732–1812) Prince-archbishop of Salzburg from 1772 to 1803. Educated in Vienna and Rome, Colloredo became a canon of Salzburg cathedral in 1747. His election as prince-archbishop on 14 March 1772 was bitterly controversial. Although a reformer who created at Salzburg an intellectual environment attractive to artists and thinkers alike, both Mozarts were unhappy in his service, complaining that travel leave was difficult to obtain, that extra presents of money for compositions were stingy and that Italian musicians were promoted over Germans. Colloredo is generally condemned for his insensitive and mean-spirited attitude towards the Mozarts, but there is blame to be apportioned on both sides. His father, Rudolf Wenzel Joseph, Count Colloredo-Mels und Wallsee (1706–88) was imperial vice-chancellor in Vienna and met the Mozarts there in 1762; his sister, Maria Franziska, Countess Wallis (1746–95), was the most influential woman at the Salzburg court.

DA PONTE, LORENZO (1749–1838) Italian librettist and Mozart's collaborator on *Le nozze di Figaro* (1786), *Don Giovanni* (1787) and *Così fan tutte* (1790). Exiled from Venice (where he had been a friend of Casanova), Da Ponte worked briefly in Dresden before moving to Vienna in late 1781, where he attracted the favour of

Emperor Joseph II. When in 1783 the emperor abandoned his pursuit of German opera and revived the Italian company at the Burgtheater, Da Ponte was appointed chief poet; his subsequent involvement in the remarkable flowering of *opera buffa* in Vienna between 1783 and 1790 made him the most significant librettist of his generation. Mozart was suspicious of his arrogance and penchant for intrigue, while Da Ponte was ambivalent about Mozart in his memoirs, recognizing his genius but doubting his stage skills.

DUSCHEK FAMILY Czech musician Franz Xaver Duschek (1731–99) settled in Prague about 1770 and was influential there as a music teacher and pianist; he was also a successful composer of instrumental music. His wife Josepha (née Hambacher, 1754–1824), a singer, had been his pupil before they married in 1776. Josepha's maternal grandfather was the merchant Ignaz Anton Weiser, mayor of Salzburg from 1772 to 1775 and author of the text of the oratorio *Die Schuldigkeit des ersten Gebots*. The Duscheks first met the Mozarts in Salzburg in August 1777, when Mozart wrote the scena *Ah, lo previdi – Ah, t'invola agl'occhi miei* K272 for Josepha. He stayed at their summer home, the Villa Betramka, when he was in Prague for the premiere of *Don Giovanni* in 1787, on this occasion composing the scena *Bella mia fiamma – Resta, o cara* K528 for her. In March 1786 Mozart accompanied Josepha at the Viennese court and in 1789 she sang at concerts he gave in Dresden and Leipzig.

FIRMIAN FAMILY One of Salzburg's leading noble families; Leopold Anton Eleutherius (1679–1744), prince-archbishop of Salzburg from 1727, was Leopold Mozart's first court employer. His brother, Franz Alphons Georg (1686–1756), had four sons, three of whom are mentioned in the letters. Leopold Ernst (1708–83) was bishop of Passau and later a cardinal; Leopold and Wolfgang Mozart celebrated this promotion in Milan in 1772. Franz Lactanz (1712–86) was chief steward at the Salzburg court from 1736; he represented the archbishop in secular matters and had jurisdiction over the court music. Karl Joseph (1718–82) was governor general of Lombardy and a prominent patron of the arts. He did much to promote Mozart's career during his first visit to Italy in 1769–71.

GILOWSKY VON URAZOWA FAMILY The families of the two barber surgeons Franz Anton (1708–70) and Johann Wenzel Andreas (1716–99) Gilowsky were well known to the Mozarts in Salzburg. Franz Anton's son Johann Joseph Anton Ernst (1739–89) was a court councillor and represented Mozart in the settlement of Leopold Mozart's estate; it seems that his daughter Maria Anna Katharina (1753–1809) was a 'Figaro' chambermaid; Franz Lactanz, Count Firmian is said to have arranged her marriage to his servant Simon Ankner in order to have her sexual services close at hand. Johann Wenzel Andreas's daughter, also Maria Anna Katharina (1750–1802), was a friend of Nannerl Mozart's; she is referred to in the letters as 'Katherl'. Her brother Franz Xaver Wenzel (1757–1816), a doctor, was best man at Mozart's wedding.

GRIMM, FRIEDRICH MELCHIOR, BARON VON (1723–1807) Author and diplomat, Grimm was born in Regensburg, Bavaria, and educated in Leipzig. He settled in Paris in 1749, where he became part of the circle around the *Encyclopédistes* and was for a time secretary to the Duc d'Orléans. In 1757 he began to write a weekly newsletter on cultural affairs that circulated throughout Europe in handwritten copies; they were later published as *Correspondance littéraire* (1812). Grimm was the Mozarts' chief patron during their first visit to Paris in 1763–4, arranging for Wolfgang and Nannerl to appear at Versailles, as well as two public concerts in March and April 1764. On 1 December 1763 he wrote: 'I cannot be sure that this child will not turn my head if I go on hearing him often; he makes me realize that it is difficult to guard against madness on seeing prodigies.' Grimm again helped Mozart and his mother in Paris in 1778, but after Maria Anna Mozart's death, relations between Grimm and Mozart became strained.

HAFFNER FAMILY Prominent Salzburg family of factors, whose business encompassed banking, haulage and the import and export of goods for merchants; the firm reached its zenith under Siegmund Haffner the elder (1699–1772), mayor of Salzburg from 1768 to 1772, who left a great fortune. Mozart wrote the 'Haffner' serenade K250 (plus the march K249), in celebration of the marriage of one of his daughters, Maria Elisabeth (1753–81), to Franz Xaver Anton

Späth on 22 July 1776. It was performed on the eve of the wedding at the Haffners' summer residence. He wrote what became the 'Haffner' symphony K385 to mark the ennoblement of Siegmund the younger (1756–87) on 29 July 1782.

HAGENAUER FAMILY (Johann) Lorenz Hagenauer (1712–92) was Leopold Mozart's closest friend in Salzburg. He inherited the family business, which dealt in medicaments, in Salzburg's Getreidegasse, and married Maria Theresia Schuster (died 1800). The Mozarts rented an apartment from the Hagenauers in the Getreidegasse house from 1747–73, and the eleven Hagenauer children grew up with Mozart and Nannerl. Lorenz and other members of the extended Hagenauer family, as well as his business associates, provided loans, put their mercantile credit network at Leopold's disposal during the family's European travels, and performed numerous extra favours. Their fifth child, Cajetan Rupert (1746–1811), became a Benedictine monk at St Peter's abbey, Salzburg, taking the name Dominicus; Mozart wrote the 'Dominicus' mass K66 to mark the celebration of his first mass on 15 October 1769.

HAYDN, (FRANZ) JOSEPH (1732–1809) Arguably the most famous composer of his day, Haydn was in the employ of the Esterházy family, at their residences at Eisenstadt, Eszterháza and Vienna, from 1761 until his death. It is unlikely that Haydn and Mozart met before Mozart moved to Vienna in 1781; a plausible first meeting has been suggested for 22 and 23 December 1783, when works by them both were played at two charity concerts in the Burgtheater. Certainly they were acquainted by 1784, at which time Mozart was composing the final three of his six quartets dedicated to Haydn (K387, 421, 428, 458, 464, 465). Their last meeting was in 1791, shortly before Haydn's departure for England. It is likely that they saw each other often in the intervening years, and their relationship was characterized by mutual affection and admiration.

HAYDN, (JOHANN) MICHAEL (1737–1806) Younger brother of Joseph Haydn and a prolific and successful composer of sacred and secular music (some of his compositions were mistakenly attributed to Mozart). He joined the Salzburg court music establishment as concert master in 1763 and was appointed court and cathedral organist in 1782, in succession to Mozart. Mozart copied out several of Haydn's church works, presumably for study purposes. In 1783 he asked his father to send some of Haydn's music to him in Vienna, for performance at Gottfried van Swieten's. But despite their admiration of his music, the Mozarts were frequently critical of Haydn's personal behaviour and in particular his excessive drinking. In 1778, Haydn married the soprano Maria Magdalena Lipp (1745–1827), daughter of the third court organist Franz Ignaz Lipp (1718–98); she sang the roles of Göttliche Barmherzigkeit in *Die Schuldigkeit des ersten Gebots* and Rosina in *La finta semplice*.

JACQUIN FAMILY (Emilian) Gottfried von Jacquin (1767–92), who worked at the court chancellery, was one of Mozart's closest friends during his years in Vienna after 1781. Not only did they socialize frequently, but Jacquin was a keen amateur composer and singer, and Mozart composed some works jointly with him, including the five *notturni* K346 and K436–439; in 1791 Gottfried published under his name six songs, two of which were composed by Mozart. Jacquin's sister Franziska (1769–1850) was a keyboard student of Mozart's; it was for her that he wrote the so-called 'Kegelstatt' trio for clarinet, viola and piano K498, and the piano duet sonata K521.

JOSEPH II, EMPEROR (1741–90) The eldest son of Emperor Francis I and Empress Maria Theresa, he succeeded his father as Holy Roman Emperor in 1765 and was co-regent of Austria until his mother's death in 1780. He was married twice: first, happily, to Isabella of Parma (1760–3), and then, miserably, to Josepha of Bavaria (1765–7). An 'enlightened despot', his policies included religious toleration, the suppression of the monasteries and repossession of church property, and the liberalization of censorship. His musical knowledge and attainment were considerable and his preferences for German opera, *opera buffa*, wind music and short and simple church music, together with his dislike of court entertainments, *opera seria* and ballets, set the pattern of Viennese music of the 1780s. He advanced Mozart's career in Vienna by encouraging him to compose *Le nozze di Figaro*, *Don Giovanni* and *Così fan tutte* and created a post for him in 1787 with limited duties and at a salary that many musicians would have considered generous. Nonetheless, history has condemned him for failing to do enough to support Mozart's genius.

KARL THEODOR, ELECTOR PALATINE AND ELECTOR OF BAVARIA (1724–99) On becoming Elector Palatine in 1742, Karl Theodor, a flautist and cellist, transformed his court at Mannheim into one of the outstanding musical centres of eighteenth-century Europe. When, at the end of December 1777, he succeeded his distant cousin Maximilian III Joseph as Elector and Duke of Bavaria, he moved his court to Munich. The Mozart children first played for Karl Theodor at his country home, Schwetzingen, in July 1763, and Mozart visited Mannheim twice in 1777 and 1778. Although he hoped to gain an appointment at court, he was not successful; he was also unsuccessful in Munich in December 1778.

LANGE, (MARIA) ALOYSIA (née Weber, c. 1761–1839) Mozart first met and fell in love with Aloysia, the daughter of Fridolin Weber (see below), during his stay in Mannheim in 1777. He gave her musical instruction and composed the concert arias K294, K316 and probably an early version of K538 for her; their relationship was the cause of considerable anxiety to Leopold. When she moved to Munich in 1778, Mozart followed her there, and may have proposed marriage and been rejected. Shortly after making her Mannheim debut in Schweitzer's *Alceste*, she was engaged at the Nationaltheater in Vienna and married the actor Joseph Lange. From 1782 she was a leading singer of the Italian troupe but seems to have fallen out of favour and in 1785 was transferred to the less prestigious Kärntnertortheater, where among other roles she sang Konstanze in *Die Entführung aus dem Serail*. Mozart married her sister Constanze in 1782.

LODRON FAMILY One of Salzburg's leading noble families. Count Ernst Maria Joseph Nepomuk von Lodron (1716–79) married Antonia Maria (1738–80), the fourth child of Count Georg Anton Felix von Arco, on 4 April 1758. During the reign of Archbishop Colloredo, Antonia Maria enjoyed great influence at court. It became customary to serenade her on her name day (Anthony of Padua, 13 June) with specially composed music: in 1776 Mozart wrote the divertimento K247 (with its march K248) for this occasion, and in 1777 the divertimento K287. He also composed the concerto for three keyboards K242 for the countess and her daughters Aloisia and Giuseppina in 1776. Antonia Maria played a key part in easing Mozart's return to Salzburg as organist in 1778.

MARIA THERESA, EMPRESS (1717–80) The eldest daughter of Emperor Charles VI (1685–1740), her father appointed her heir to his hereditary Habsburg domains by the Pragmatic Sanction – a claim that led to the War of the Austrian Succession (1740–48). She married Francis, Duke of Lorraine (1708–65) in 1736; he became Holy Roman Emperor in 1745; they had ten surviving children. She first encountered Mozart when the six-year-old prodigy performed for her at Schönbrunn in Vienna on 13 October 1762, and saw him again in 1768, but for reasons that remain unknown, she came to disapprove of the family.

MOZART, (MARIA) CONSTANZE (née Weber, 1762–1842) Mozart first met Constanze during his visit to Mannheim in 1777–8, at which time he was infatuated with her older sister, Aloysia (see under LANGE). Their relationship blossomed only in 1781, by which time both Mozart and the Webers (see below) were living in Vienna. Wolfgang and Constanze married on 4 August 1782. It is clear that, on the whole, their marriage was a happy one, although Constanze was in frequent ill health as a result of her repeated pregnancies; his letters to her are affectionate and intimate. Only two of their six children survived: Carl Thomas (1784–1858) and Franz Xaver Wolfgang (1791–1844). Following Mozart's death, Constanze was granted an annual pension of 266 gulden by Emperor Francis II. In 1809 she married a Danish diplomat, Georg Nikolaus Nissen, and lived in Copenhagen from 1810–21; after his retirement they settled in Salzburg, where Nissen began collecting materials for a biography of Mozart. Constanze completed the work after his death in 1826, and it was published in 1828.

MOZART, (JOHANN GEORG) LEOPOLD (1719–87) The son of an Augsburg bookbinder, as a schoolboy Leopold Mozart was a frequent performer in local theatrical productions, and was also an accomplished organist and violinist. In 1737, after his father's death, Leopold left Augsburg to study philosophy and jurisprudence at the Salzburg Benedictine University but was expelled in September 1739 for poor attendance and a failure to show proper deference to his professors and the university establishment. He served as valet and musician to Johann Baptist, Count of Thurn-Valsassina and Taxis, a canon of Salzburg cathedral and president of the consistory, before being appointed fourth violinist in the court orchestra of Archbishop Leopold Anton Eleutherius von Firmian in 1743; in addition to his court duties he taught violin, and later keyboard, to the choirboys of the cathedral oratory. By 1758 he had advanced to the post of second violinist and in 1763 to deputy Kapellmeister. Throughout these years he was a prolific composer of masses, litanies, smaller church works, cantatas, oratorios, symphonies, concertos, dances, divertimentos and other chamber music, and solo keyboard works; references in the family letters show that Leopold Mozart considered himself a 'modern' composer. It is almost certain that he composed new works for the court and for private performance up until c. 1770, but his output decreased dramatically as he became increasingly occupied with Nannerl's, and especially Wolfgang's, musical and general education and the family's tours: he acted as teacher and private secretary to his son, and when necessary as valet, impresario, publicist and travel organizer. His relationship with Wolfgang appears to have become estranged after the death of Maria Anna Mozart in 1778, but the rift between them has probably been exaggerated. His letters, which form a great part of this volume, show him to have been a loving father, albeit querulous and over-anxious when his advice is ignored, and an interested observer of life.

MOZART, MARIA ANNA (née Pertl, 1720–78) The daughter of Wolfgang Nikolaus Pertl, administrator of St Gilgen, a small town near Salzburg, she married Leopold Mozart on 21 November 1747. They had seven children, five of whom died in infancy. Leopold's and Wolfgang's letters to her when they were travelling on their own, and her letters to Leopold from September 1777 to June 1778 (when she and Wolfgang were travelling to Paris on Mozart's quest for an appointment) are full of news, jokes and gossip about Salzburg friends and neighbours, and especially about the target-shooting competitions, for money, that were a regular feature of their social life.

MOZART, MARIA ANNA (NANNERL) (1751–1829) Mozart's elder sister was a promising keyboard player, but even on the early concert tours of 1762–9 she was overshadowed by Wolfgang, who also played the violin and organ, and developed his compositional skills intensively. Surviving exercises and references in the letters show that Nannerl could compose a bass to a melody, accompany at sight and improvise; she also learned to sing and teach, but she never earned a living from music. Mozart and Nannerl remained close until he moved to Vienna: they frequently played duets, performed at private concerts and Wolfgang usually arranged to serenade Nannerl on her name day (it is likely that the so-called 'Nannerl Septet' K251 was written for her in 1776). However, her hopes that Wolfgang would make it possible for her to leave Salzburg dwindled after his marriage in 1782; from this date she appears to have shared with Leopold a degree of disenchantment with Mozart. On 23 August 1784 she married Johann Baptist Franz Berchtold zu Sonnenburg (1736–1801), a magistrate of St Gilgen. He was twice widowed and already had five children; Nannerl bore him three more.

MOZART, MARIA ANNA THEKLA (1758–1841) Usually called Bäsle ('little cousin') by Mozart, she was the daughter of Leopold Mozart's brother, Franz Alois. Mozart became good friends with her during his stay in Augsburg in 1777. Nine of his letters to her survive, unfortunately without her answers. The Bäsle letters are irreverent and scatological (in contrast to those he wrote at about the same time to Aloysia Weber, which are formal, even pompous) and some commentators see in them proof that she and Mozart had sexual relations; others, however, that they merely show him as earthy and playful. After Aloysia rejected him in 1778 on his return from Paris, Maria Anna Thekla softened his homecoming to Salzburg by visiting him there.

ORSINI-ROSENBERG, FRANZ XAVER WOLF, PRINCE (1723–96)

Imperial chamberlain and manager of the Vienna court theatres from 1776 to 1791 and from 1792 to 1794. As chief steward to Grand Duke Leopold of Tuscany (later Emperor Leopold II) in Florence in 1770, Rosenberg helped Mozart and his father gain entry to the grand-ducal court, and after Wolfgang's move to Vienna in 1781 he commissioned *Die Entführung aus dem Serail*. Relations between them cooled later, and Da Ponte, in his memoirs, recorded the details of a controversy that arose when, during rehearsals for *Le nozze di Figaro*, Rosenberg ordered that dancers be omitted from the wedding scene at the end of act three.

PUCHBERG, JOHANN MICHAEL VON (1741–1822) Viennese textile merchant and Masonic brother of Mozart's, who wrote for him either the piano trio K542 (1788) or the string trio K563 (1788). Puchberg loaned Mozart about 1400 gulden during the final years of the composer's life. Between 1788 and 1791, Wolfgang wrote him at least 19 begging letters, some of which are included here.

SALIERI, ANTONIO (1750–1825) Italian composer, active at Vienna from 1766, court Kapellmeister from 1788. He came to personify for Mozart the obstacles he perceived to be blocking the advancement of his own career, and particularly his dismay at the preferential treatment that was commonly given to Italian musicians in the Austrian musical establishments of the day. There is no evidence, however, to support the idea that Salieri conspired against Mozart in a systematic, long-term way.

SCHIKANEDER, EMANUEL (1751–1812) Actor-manager of a touring theatrical company, Schikaneder became friendly with the Mozart family when the troupe played a season in Salzburg in autumn 1780; it was then that Wolfgang composed for him the aria K365a. Schikaneder was active in Vienna on and off between 1783 and 1789, when he became director of the suburban Freihaus-Theater auf der Wieden. His most successful production there was Mozart's German opera *Die Zauberflöte* (1791), for which Schikaneder wrote the text and sang the role of Papageno.

SCHRATTENBACH, SIEGMUND CHRISTOPH VON (1698–1771), Prince-archbishop of Salzburg 1753–71. He was a great supporter of the Mozarts, awarding them with presents for compositions and partly subsidizing their early tours; in 1763 he appointed Leopold Mozart his deputy Kapellmeister, and in November 1769 he gave Mozart his first (unpaid) position at court, as third concertmaster. Schrattenbach is often called Salzburg's 'pious' archbishop: he is reported to have attended up to five church services daily and he kept all the traditional church feast days. He was no intellectual and was said to be not only bigoted, but also incapable of recognizing true virtue. Although there was a small nucleus of would-be reformers in Salzburg during his reign, the Enlightenment did not systematically penetrate institutions there until after his death.

STADLER, ANTON PAUL (1753–1812) Mozart became a good friend of clarinet virtuoso and composer Anton Stadler soon after his arrival in Vienna; it is likely that they first met at the home of Countess Wilhelmine Thun in 1781; four years later Stadler became a Freemason and frequently participated in Mozart's Masonic music. Stadler had created the basset clarinet in collaboration with Theodor Lotz; it included four keys beyond those found on normal clarinets of the time and extended the instrument's range down to include a full four octaves. Mozart probably composed the quintet for clarinet and strings K581 (1789) and his concerto for clarinet K622 (1791) for Stadler on this instrument.

STORACE, STEPHEN (1762–96) and NANCY (1765–1817) Brother and sister from a musical English family of Italian extraction, they became friendly with Mozart in the early 1780s. Stephen was a composer of operas, including *Gli sposi malcontenti* (Vienna, 1785) and *No Song, No Supper* (London, 1790), that often showcased his sister in leading soprano roles. Nancy was a prominent member of the Viennese Italian company from 1783–87 and sang the first Susanna in *Le nozze di Figaro* (1786). The Storaces returned to England in the spring of 1787, and at a farewell concert at the Kärntnertortheater on 23 February Nancy sang the scena *Ch'io mi scordi di te? . . . Non temer, amato bene* K505 for soprano and piano that Mozart had composed for them to perform together specially for the occasion.

SÜSSMAYR, FRANZ XAVER (1766–1803) Studied with Mozart in 1791 and quickly became a trusted friend. He may have composed the recitatives for *La clemenza di Tito* and in December took over the completion of the unfinished Requiem; according to Constanze's sister, Sophie Haibel (née Weber), Mozart issued instructions to Süssmayr the night before he died on how he wanted the work completed. Mozart frequently poked fun at him, describing him as 'that idiotic fellow', 'a full-blown ass' and calling him 'Sauermayr', a pun on *süss* (sweet) and *sauer* (sour). Süssmayr studied with Antonio Salieri soon after Mozart's death, and wrote popular sacred and secular works in Vienna in the 1790s.

SWIETEN, GOTTFRIED (BERNHARD), BARON VAN (1733–1803) A former diplomat and occasional composer, from 1777 van Swieten was director of the court library and president of the education and censorship commission in Vienna. He was an ardent supporter of Mozart and his music, subscribing to his Trattnerhof concerts (1784) and to a series that never materialized in 1789; in the later 1780s he commissioned from him arrangements of some of Handel's works. After Mozart's death, van Swieten organized a Viennese benefit concert for Constanze and contributed to Carl Thomas Mozart's education in Prague.

TEYBER FAMILY Matthäus Teyber (*c.* 1711–85) was a member of the Vienna court orchestra. His son Anton (1756–1822), a keyboard player and composer active in Vienna during the early 1780s, was court organist at Dresden from 1787; in 1793 he succeeded Mozart as court chamber composer in Vienna. Another son, Franz (1758–1810), also a keyboard player and composer, was associated with the actor and impresario Emanuel Schikaneder from *c.* 1786. Their sister Therese (1760–1830) sang the role of Blonde at the first performance of *Die Entführung aus dem Serail* (1782).

WALDSTÄTTEN, MARTHA ELISABETH, BARONESS (1744–1811) An aristocrat and amateur pianist who may have studied with Mozart, Waldstätten accommodated Constanze Mozart three times at her residence in 1781 and 1782, and at Mozart's request housed his student Josepha Auernhammer free of charge in late 1782. She also provided Constanze and Mozart with an extravagant, 'princely' meal on their wedding day, 4 August 1782, and corresponded with Leopold Mozart in an effort to convince him of Constanze's suitability as a wife. A year later she honoured a debt incurred by Mozart, eliciting sincere gratitude in return.

WEBER FAMILY Mozart got to know the Weber family in Mannheim in 1777–8. Fridolin Weber (1733–79) had been a bass singer and music copyist at Mannheim from 1765; he was married to Maria Cäcilia (née Stamm, 1727–93). They later moved to Munich, and then Vienna, and Mozart lodged with Maria Cäcilia, by now a widow, on first quitting his position with the Salzburg court in 1781. The Webers' daughters included the singer Josepha (1758–1819), who later created the role of the Queen of the Night in *Die Zauberflöte* (1791) and in 1788 married the violinist Franz Hofer; Aloysia (see under LANGE); Constanze (see under MOZART); and Sophie (1763–1846), who was present at Mozart's death, and married the choir director Jakob Haibel in 1807.

Map

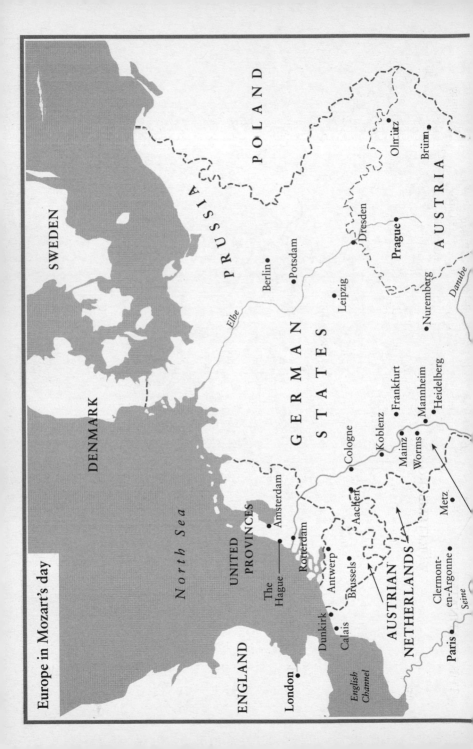

Europe in Mozart's day

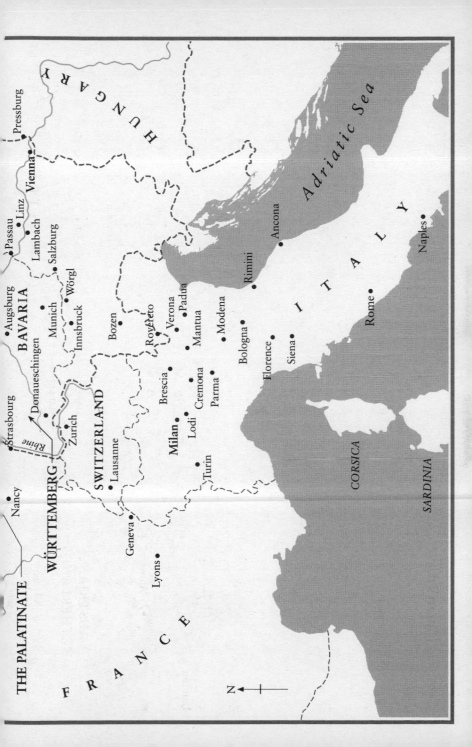

A Life in Letters

A Life in Letters

The works below are cited in the footnotes by the abbreviations:

Briefe: Wilhelm A. Bauer, Otto Erich Deutsch and Joseph Heinz Eibl, eds., *Mozart: Briefe und Aufzeichnungen* (eight volumes, Kassel, 1962–2005)

Deutsch, *Bildern*: Otto Erich Deutsch, *Mozart und seine Welt in zeitgenössischen Bildern* (Kassel, 1961)

Deutsch, *Documentary Biography*: Otto Erich Deutsch, *Mozart: A Documentary Biography* (second edition, London, 1966)

Mozart's works are identified by the numbers assigned to them in the standard catalogue of the composer's works, Ludwig Ritter von Köchel, *Chronologisch-thematisches Verzeichnis sämtlicher Tonwerke Wolfgang Amadé Mozarts* (Leipzig, 1862; sixth edition, ed. Franz Giegling, Alexander Weinmann and Gerd Sievers, Wiesbaden, 1964).

Little is known about Mozart's early childhood in Salzburg. His first documented public performance was in September 1761, when he appeared as a dancer in the Latin school comedy Sigismundus Hungariae Rex. *In December his father Leopold Mozart notated his first compositions, K1c and 1d, in the so-called 'Nannerl Notebook', a collection of short keyboard pieces used for study purposes by Wolfgang and his elder sister, Maria Anna, also known as Nannerl. By January 1762 Leopold was ready to take the children, aged six and eleven, on tour: they spent three weeks in Munich and played for Elector Maximilian III Joseph of Bavaria. Later that spring Wolfgang composed the short piano pieces K2–K5 and in September the family set out for Vienna by way of Passau and Linz (where they gave a public concert on 1 October). They arrived at Vienna on 6 October.*

1. *Leopold Mozart to Lorenz Hagenauer,*[1] *16 October 1762, Vienna*

Monsieur mon très cher ami,
    We left Linz by slow boat at half past 4 in the afternoon on the Feast of St Francis[2] and arrived at Mauthausen in pitch darkness at half past 7 the same day. By noon the next day, Tuesday, we were in

---

1. The merchant Johann Lorenz Hagenauer was the Mozarts' landlord in Salzburg and possibly Leopold's best friend, see List of Important People pp. xxiii–xxxvi.
2. 4 October.

Ybbs, where 2 Minorites and a Benedictine who had been with us on the boat said Mass, in the course of which our Woferl[3] had a whale of a time on the organ, playing so well that the Franciscans, who were just having lunch, left the meal with their visitors and rushed across to the choir, where they were almost struck dumb with amazement. We reached Stein after dark and by 3 o'clock on Wednesday were in Vienna, where we had a combined lunch and supper at 5. It rained throughout the journey and was very windy. Wolfgangl caught a cold in Linz, but in spite of all the upheavals of the last few days, including getting up early, eating and drinking at all hours and contending with the wind and rain, he has remained healthy, thank God. People make more of the rapids than the matter warrants. More on this when we speak in person. On landing we were met by Herr Gilowsky's[4] servant, who came on board and then took me to our rooms. But we soon hurried off to an inn to appease our hunger, having first stowed away our luggage and sorted things out at our lodgings. Herr Gilowsky then came to welcome us. We've now been here for a week and still don't know where the sun rises in Vienna: until now it hasn't stopped raining, and with a constant wind it has snowed a little, too, so that we've even seen snow on the roofs. Moreover, it continues to be, if not very cold, at least very frosty. One thing I must make a point of telling you: we got through customs very quickly – both the customs at the place where we landed, where we were dealt with very swiftly, and the main customs, where we were completely exempted. For this we had to thank our Herr Woferl, for he immediately made friends with the customs official, showing him his keyboard, inviting him to visit us and playing him a minuet on his little violin, and with that we were waved through. The customs official asked very politely if he could visit us and to that end made a note of our address. In spite of the absolutely atrocious weather we have already attended a concert at Count

3. Leopold uses many diminutives of Wolfgang in his letters, including Woferl, Wolfgangl, Wolfgangerl and Wolfgangus.
4. Probably Johann Joseph Anton Ernst Gilowsky von Urazowa (1739–89), a court councillor in Vienna.

Collalto's,[5] also Countess Sinzendorf introduced us to Count Wilczek and on the 11th to His Excellency the imperial vice-chancellor Count Colloredo, where we had the privilege of seeing and speaking to the leading ministers and ladies of the imperial court, namely, the Hungarian chancellor, Count Pálffy, and the Bohemian chancellor, Count Chotek, together with Bishop Esterházy and a whole host of people whose names I was unable to note down.[6] All of them, especially the ladies, were very kind to us. Count Leopold Kuenburg's fiancée spoke to my wife in person and told her she is going to be married in Salzburg.[7] She's a pretty, friendly lady, of medium height. She is expecting her fiancé any day now in Vienna. Countess Sinzendorf is doing all she can for us, and all the ladies have fallen in love with my boy. Everyone is already talking about us, and when I went on my own to the opera on the 10th, I heard Archduke Leopold talking to someone in another box and saying lots of things, including the fact that there was a boy in Vienna who plays the keyboard so well etc. etc.[8] At 11 o'clock that same evening I received orders to go to Schönbrunn[9] on the 12th. But the next day I received fresh instructions to go there on the 13th as the 12th is the Feast of Maximilian and, therefore, a busy gala, and, as I hear, they want to hear the

5. Thomas Vinciguerra, Count Collalto (1720–69). The concert took place on 9 October.
6. Eleonore Elisabeth, Countess Sinzendorf (1713–67) was the widow of Count Sigismund Rudolf Sinzendorf, high chamberlain at the court of Emperor Charles VI (1685–1740); Rudolf Joseph, Count Colloredo-Mels und Wallsee, was imperial vice-chancellor from 1737, was the father of Hieronymus Colloredo, see List of Important People; Leopold Pálffy-Erdöd (1710–73) was Hungarian court chancellor at the Vienna court from 1761; Count Johann Rudolf Chotek von Chotkowa und Wognin (1748–1824) became chancellor of the Bohemian-Austrian court in 1765; Count Karl Anton Esterházy (1725–99) was bishop of Erlau.
7. Leopold Joseph Maria, Count Kuenburg (1739–1812) was chief equerry in Salzburg from 1764; his fiancée was Friederike Maria Anna, Countess Waldstein (1742–1802).
8. Archduke Leopold of Tuscany (1747–92), the future Emperor Leopold II (from 1790), was the third son of Emperor Francis I and Empress Maria Theresa (see list). The opera was *Orfeo ed Euridice* (1762) by Christoph Willibald Gluck (1714–87), one of the most famous opera composers of the day.
9. The imperial summer residence, just outside Vienna.

children at their convenience. The main thing is that everyone is amazed at the boy, and I have yet to hear anyone who is not saying that it's unbelievable. Baron Schell, who used to be known as Loulou, is doing all he can for me and gratefully acknowledges the grace and favour he enjoyed in Salzburg. If you have a chance to do so, please say as much to Herr Chiusole and give him my good wishes. Count Daun also gave me a letter for Baron Schell.[10] I have high hopes that I shall leave Vienna well satisfied. And so it seems, for the court is asking to hear us even before we have announced ourselves. Young Count Pálffy was passing through Linz just as our concert was starting, he was calling on Countess Schlick[11] and she told him about the boy and persuaded him to stop the mail coach in front of the town hall and go to the concert with her. He listened with astonishment, and with a great deal of to-do he told Archduke Joseph, who told the empress.[12] As soon as it was known that we were in Vienna, the command came for us to go to court. That, you see, is the cause.

I wrote the foregoing on the 11th, with the firm intention of telling you on the 12th, when we got back from Schönbrunn, how it had gone. But we had to drive straight from Schönbrunn to Prince Hildburghausen,[13] and 6 ducats were more important than sending you this letter. I have confidence in Frau Hagenauer and trust that she will be kind enough to accept my best wishes on her name day now, rather than later, and in the present brief form of saying merely that we shall pray to God to keep her and all her loved ones well for many years to come and that when the time comes He may invite us all to play cards with Him in Heaven. There is now time only to say in great haste that we were received with such extraordinary kindness

10. Friedrich Alexander, Baron von Schell, imperial Polish and Saxon captain, had lived in Salzburg from 1753–7; Chiusole is probably Dominicus Chiusole de Clusulis (?–1775), who was consistorial councillor in Salzburg; Karl Joseph, Count Daun (1728–?) was a canon of Salzburg cathedral.

11. Maria Antonia, Countess Schlick, wife of Leopold Franz, Count Schlick (1729–70), regional governor in Linz. The Schlicks were related by marriage to the Pálffy-Erdöds.

12. For Archduke Joseph, the future Emperor Joseph II, see List. The empress is Maria Theresa.

13. Prince Joseph Maria Friedrich Wilhelm von Sachsen-Hildburghausen (1702–87).

by their majesties that if ever I tell them about it, people will say I have made it all up. Suffice it to say that Wolferl jumped up into the empress's lap, grabbed her round the neck and kissed her right and proper. In short, we were with her from 3 till 6, and the emperor himself came in from the next room and took me to hear the infanta play the violin.[14] On the 15th the empress sent 2 dresses, one for the boy and one for the girl.[15] They were delivered by the privy paymaster, who drove up to our house in full regalia. As soon as the order arrives, they are to appear at court, and the privy paymaster will collect them. At ½ past 2 today they have to go to the two youngest archdukes,[16] at 4 o'clock to the Hungarian chancellor, Count Pálffy. Yesterday we were with Count Kaunitz[17] and the day before with Countess Kinsky and later with Count Ulfeld.[18] We're already booked up for the next two days. Please tell everyone that we are well and happy, thank God. Every good wish from your old friend

Mozart

Please inform Frau Niderl[19] that we are well. NB: Don't forward any more letters to me, but just open them and read them, otherwise I have to spend a lot of money on postage on needless letters: you'll see what's necessary. Compliments to everyone.

14. Francis I (1708–65), Duke of Lorraine, married Maria Theresa of Austria in 1736 and became Holy Roman Emperor in 1745. The infanta is probably Isabella of Parma, first wife of Archduke Joseph, who died the following year.
15. A portrait of Mozart in the gala dress sent to him by Maria Theresa, possibly by Pietro Antonio Lorenzoni, is reproduced in Deutsch, *Bildern*, 3.
16. Ferdinand (1754–1806) and Maximilian Franz (1756–1801), younger sons of Francis I and Maria Theresa.
17. Count (later Prince) Wenzel Anton von Kaunitz-Rietberg (1711–94), Austrian statesman and diplomat, imperial court chancellor from 1753–92.
18. Maria Theresia, Countess Kinsky (1715–78), wife of privy counsellor Leopold Ferdinand, Count Kinsky (1713–60); Anton Corfiz, Count Ulfeld (1699–1770), chief steward in Vienna.
19. Maria Kunigunde Niderl was the wife of Dr Franz Joseph Niderl von Aichegg (1719–73), of Salzburg.

2. *Leopold Mozart to <u>Lorenz Hagenauer</u>, 29 December 1762, Vienna*

Homo proponit, Deus disponit.[1] I'd planned to leave Pressburg[2] on the 20th and to pass through Vienna on the 26th in order to be back in Salzburg on New Year's Eve. But on the 19th I had unusually bad toothache, I repeat, *for me unusually bad toothache*: it was the whole upper set of front teeth, which are otherwise healthy and in good condition. My whole face swelled up during the night, so that the next day I looked just like the Passau simpleton, so much so that Lieutenant Winckler (the brother of the court timpanist), who'd come to visit us, didn't recognize me when he came into the room and thought he'd got lost. In this unfortunate situation I had to console myself with the thought that we were in any case detained by the unusual cold snap; for the pontoon bridge had been removed, and even ferrying the postbags across the Danube in small boats has been a risky business, leaving the postilion to continue the journey on an old nag. As a result I had to wait for news that the March[3] (not a very wide river) was frozen. And so I left Pressburg at half past 8 in the morning on Christmas Eve and, travelling by a special route, arrived back at our lodgings in Vienna at half past 8 at night. It was not a particularly comfortable journey, because although the ground was frozen, it was indescribably bumpy and full of deep holes and ruts, for the Hungarians don't build roads. If I had not had to buy a carriage with good suspension in Pressburg, we'd undoubtedly have arrived home missing a few ribs. I had to buy the carriage as I wanted to get back safely to Vienna. None of the country coachmen in Pressburg had a 4-seater closed carriage. A town coachman had such a carriage, but town coachmen aren't allowed to travel across country, except for a few hours and with only 2 horses.

We'd only just got back to Vienna when our landlady told me that

1. 'Man proposes, God disposes.'
2. Pressburg, modern Bratislava, was at that time the capital of Hungary.
3. The river March (Morava in Czech) enters the Danube about 5 km west of Bratislava.

Countess Leopold Kinsky had sent someone round every day to ask whether we'd returned. – – I went to see her on Christmas Day, and she said that she had been anxiously awaiting us and had postponed a dinner that she wanted to give for Field Marshal Daun,[4] who would like to meet us. And so she held her dinner on Monday. I shall now definitely be leaving here on Friday morning and with God's help will reach Linz on Sunday; and on the eve of Epiphany, 5th Jan. 1763, I hope to be standing in your front room with you.[5] In the evening, of course! Otherwise you might think I meant *first thing in the morning*, although that wouldn't strike you as all that strange as you're used to getting up for Matins during Advent. You will now add the following to the pile of favours that you've already done for me, namely, wish our Father Confessor[6] the *healthiest* and happiest New Year in my name and ask him to continue to be merciful towards me; I would write to him myself if I were not so hesitant to torment him so often with a succession of my letters. And give my New Year greetings to Madame Robinig[7] and Fräulein Josepha *in optima forma* and to all our excellent friends, including, of course, yourself, your good wife and your whole household. And please give my best wishes to Herr Reifenstuel and ask him if I may leave my carriage at his house for a few days until I've found somewhere to keep it. In the mean time I hope we'll all be well when we see each other on the 5th – I'm burning with desire to tell you a whole host of things and to be able to say to you that I continue to be your true friend

Mozart

---

4. Field Marshal Leopold Josef von Daun (1705–66) was Austria's most successful general in the Seven Years' War (1756–63).

5. In the event, the Mozarts did arrive back in Salzburg on this date.

6. Ferdinand Joseph Mayr (1733–92), Father Confessor to the archbishop of Salzburg.

7. The Robinig family, Salzburg friends of the Mozarts, included Georg Joseph Robinig von Rottenfeld (1710–60) and his wife Maria Viktoria Aniser (1716–83); they had three daughters (one of whom is the Fräulein Josepha referred to here) and a son, Georg Siegmund (1760–1823). Mozart's divertimento K334 (1779 or 1780) may have been written for Siegmund on completion of his legal studies at Salzburg.

Best wishes from my wife and children.

If you could heat the room for a few days, I'd be grateful. It doesn't need to be much in the front stove.

[*On the envelope*]

It has been surprisingly cold here in recent days; and today in particular it's exceptionally cold. Her Majesty the Empress has lost another princess, Princess Johanna, 13 years of age. She took my Wolferl by the hand and led him back and forth in her rooms when we were with her.

The Mozart family arrived back in Salzburg on 5 January 1763. Leopold was promoted to deputy Kapellmeister in the court music establishment on 28 February, receiving a modest increase in salary, and that evening Wolfgang played at court. But they did not stay in Salzburg for long: on 9 June the Mozarts set out on what was to become a three-and-a-half-year tour of the German states, France, England, the Netherlands and Switzerland. Their first stop was Munich, the capital of the prince-electors of Bavaria.

3. Leopold Mozart to Lorenz Hagenauer, 21 June 1763, Munich

We're stuck here in Munich. We got here on Sunday evening, the 12th; Monday was a state occasion on account of the Feast of St Anthony, so we drove to Nymphenburg.[1] The Prince of Zweibrücken,[2] who knew us from Vienna, saw us from the castle as we were walking in the park and, recognizing us, beckoned to us from the window, so we went over to him and after talking to us about various things, he asked us whether the elector[3] knew we were there. We said no; so he

1. The elector of Bavaria's summer residence, to the west of the city.
2. Friedrich Michael von Birkenfeld-Zweibrücken-Rappolstein, Count Palatine (1724–67).
3. Elector Maximilian III Joseph of Bavaria (1727–77).

immediately sent a courtier who was standing next to him to ask the elector if he wanted to hear the children. – – Meanwhile we were to go for a walk in the park and wait for the answer. – – In fact a footman arrived at once and told us to return at 8 for the concert. It was 4 o'clock; and so we continued our walk through the park and saw Babenburg[4] but a sudden downpour and thunderstorm forced us to take shelter. To be brief, Woferl did well. We didn't get home till a ¼ past 11, ate first and as a result got to bed very late. On Tuesday and Wednesday evenings we were with Duke Clemens,[5] on Thursday evening we stayed at home on account of the heavy rain. It's now a matter of some urgency that we work out how to proceed: they have the charming custom here of keeping people waiting for presents for a long time, so you have to be happy to recover your expenses. Herr Tomasini[6] has been here for 3 weeks. Only now has he been paid. Tell Herr Wenzel[7] he can imagine how delighted we were to meet here so unexpectedly. He recognized me before I recognized him as he has now grown tall, strong and handsome. He certainly acknowledged the old friendship that I had shown him in Salzburg, and this touched me and showed me that he has a good heart. He too is going to Stuttgart and Mannheim, but then he's coming back to Vienna. So the bishop of Passau is dead? – – *Requiescat in pace! Judicia Dei* etc. God can thwart so many people's plans [line illegible].

On the 18th the elector dined in town. We too were invited; he and his sister and the Prince of Zweibrücken talked to us throughout the meal; I got my boy to say that we were planning to leave the next day. Twice the elector said that he was sorry not to have heard my little girl, for there wasn't enough time when we were at Nymphenburg, as my boy on his own took up most of the time improvising and then playing a concerto on the violin and at the keyboard; two ladies sang, and then it was over. And so when he said a second time: *I'd like to have heard her*, I could only say that *it wouldn't matter if we*

4. The country seat built for Elector Maximilian II Emanuel (1662–1726) between 1718 and 1721.
5. Clemens Franz de Paula (1722–70) of Bavaria, cousin of the elector.
6. Luigi Tomasini (1741–1808), violinist and pupil of Leopold Mozart.
7. Probably either Wenzel Hebelt or Wenzel Sadlo, both Salzburg court violinists.

stayed a few days longer. And so we've no choice but drive to Augsburg as quickly as possible on Wednesday. For yesterday there was a hunt. Today there is a French play and as a result she can't play until tomorrow. I may thank God if I'm paid on Tuesday. I shan't be detained by the duke, but he's waiting to see what the elector gives me. Herr Tomasini has good reason to be displeased with the elector. He performed on 2 occasions and had to wait a long time before finally receiving 10 max d'or.[8] But the duke gave him a beautiful gold watch. *Basta!* I'll be happy if I recover what I've had to spend here and what I may still need before I get to Augsburg. I can hardly wait to get out of here. I can't complain about the elector. He's extremely kind and said to me only yesterday that we're already old acquaintances; it must be 19 years since we first met. But the apostles[9] think only of themselves and their purses. We dined recently with the Hamburg merchant Monsieur König, who visited us in Salzburg; he too was staying at Stürzer's,[10] but at the front of the building, while we are 2 floors up in the new building. I also met a certain Herr Johann Georg Wahler of Frankfurt, who similarly dined with us and gave me his address. He lives on the Römerberg and is going to find private lodgings for me in Frankfurt. On the same occasion we met two Saxon councillors, Messrs de Bose and Hopfgarten;[11] they are both the most delightful people and, God willing, we shall meet all these gentlemen again, either in Stuttgart or Mannheim, as they are taking the same route as us.

As I'm writing this letter every day, it will eventually be finished. We are leaving tomorrow, the 22nd. Farewell. I am etc.

P.S.: We have now been paid. From the elector we received 100 florins, but from the duke 75. But what our bill will be at the inn we

8. See Note on Currencies, p. xx.
9. Meaning obscure.
10. Engelbert König, a prominent businessman from Hamburg; Johann Heinrich Stürzer (1699–1768) was the owner of the Golden Deer inn in Munich, where the Mozarts were staying.
11. Friedrich Karl, Baron von Bose (1751–?) and Georg Wilhelm von Hopfgarten (1740–after 1806) were both councillors to the court of Saxony at Dresden.

shall have the honour of hearing tomorrow, Herr Stürzer has the reputation of giving good service, but he's also good at writing and doing his sums, patience! Nannerl was most warmly applauded when she played for both the elector and the duke. As we were leaving, both of them invited us to return. The Prince of Zweibrücken will announce our arrival in Mannheim, he's going there soon. Duke Clemens, by contrast, has provided us with a letter of recommendation to the elector of the Palatinate.[12]

Tell our friends that we are well.

From Munich the Mozarts moved on to Augsburg, Leopold's birthplace, where the children gave public concerts on 28 and 30 June and 4 July, and then by way of Ulm to Ludwigsburg, the court of the Duke of Württemberg.

4. Leopold Mozart to Lorenz Hagenauer, 11 July 1763, Ludwigsburg

Monsieur,

I was detained in Augsburg and gained little or nothing from the delay, for what I earned was as quickly spent as everything is extremely expensive, although the landlord of the 3 Moors, Herr Linay, who is the most delightful man in the world, looked after me very well. Herr Weiser is witness to this, and those who came to the concerts were almost all Lutherans.[1] Apart from Herr Provino, who came to all 3 with Madame Perinet, and Herr Calligari, who appeared once for the sake of his reputation, I didn't see a single Catholic

---

12. Karl Theodor (1724–99), Elector of the Palatinate from 1742 (and of Bavaria from 1778), whose court was at Mannheim.
1. Here Leopold refers to the deep-rooted and long-standing social tensions between Lutherans and Catholics in Augsburg, which was a free (i.e. self-governing) city within the Holy Roman Empire; as a native of Augsburg and a Catholic with many Lutheran friends, it was a situation to which he was acutely attuned.

businessman except Monsieur Mayr, the husband of Lisette Muralt; the others were all Lutherans: – – we left Augsb. on the 6th and by the evening were in Ulm, where we stayed only a night and the next morning. We wouldn't even have spent the morning there if we'd not had difficulty obtaining horses. And now a calamity! When we arrived at the post stage at Blochingen we heard that the duke[2] had suddenly decided to go off on the night of the 10th to his hunting lodge at Grafenegg, which is 14 hours away. And so I quickly decided to go straight to Ludwigsburg via Constatt rather than to Stuttgart in order to catch him. I arrived in Ludwigsburg late on the 9th and was in time to see a play at the French theatre. But not until the morning of the 10th was I able to speak to the principal Kapellmeister Jommelli[3] and the Master of the Hounds, Baron Pöllnitz, for both of whom I had letters from Count Wolfegg.[4] But, in a word, it couldn't be done. Herr Tomasini, who had already been there for a fortnight before me, had not managed to gain a hearing, and everyone tells me that the duke has the charming habit of making people wait a long time before hearing them and then making them wait a long time before giving them a present:[5] but I regard the whole business as the work of Herr Jommelli, who is doing all he can to weed out the Germans at this court and replace them with Italians. He has almost succeeded, too, and will be entirely successful because, apart from his annual salary of 4000 florins, his allowances for 4 horses, wood and light, a house in Stuttgart and a house in Ludwigsburg, he enjoys the duke's favour to the highest degree, and his wife has been awarded a pension of 2000 florins on his death. How do you like that as a Kapellmeister's post? – – Moreover, he has unlimited power over his

2. Karl II Eugen, Duke of Württemberg (1728–93).
3. Nicolò Jommelli (1714–74), Italian-born composer, Kapellmeister to the duke of Württemberg 1753–68.
4. Anton Willibald, Count Waldburg zu Wolfegg und Waldersee (1729–1821), canon of Salzburg cathedral from 1762 and president of the exchequer to Archbishop Colloredo.
5. At this time, royalty and noble patrons across Europe normally rewarded visiting musicians to their court with gifts of money or valuable objects such as watches and snuffboxes.

orchestra: and it is this that makes it so good. But you can tell how prejudiced Jommelli is in favour of his country by the fact that he and those of his compatriots who flock to his house to pay him their respects have been heard to say that it is amazing and scarcely credible that a child of German birth could be such a musical genius and have so much spirit and fire. *Ridete amici!*[6]

But I digress. My situation has now become all the more wretched and difficult in that the duke has taken all the horses belonging to the post and the hired coachmen. And so I'm forced to remain here today; even as I'm writing, I'm having to contend with constant interruptions in my attempts to track down some horses and am searching every nook and cranny of Ludwigsburg in order to track them down. So you see that to date I've nothing more to show for my pains than the fact that I have seen countries and towns and people that I wouldn't otherwise have done. Ulm is an appallingly old-fashioned place, so tastelessly built that I often thought of you and wished you could see it. Just imagine houses where you have to see the whole storey and all the timberwork from the outside, just as it's constructed, and if it's a tall building, it's painted, but the brickwork is nice and white or every brick is painted, just as it is, so that the wall and timberwork can be seen all the more clearly. It's exactly the same at Westerstetten, Geissling – where ivory is worked and where *7 females* try to talk every passing stranger into parting with his money – and Goeppingen, Ploching and large parts of Stuttgart. NB. Please keep my letters, so that in due course I can explain things myself that it would take too long to describe here.

Ludwigsburg is a very strange place. It's a town, but the town walls are made not so much of fences and garden railings as soldiers. When you spit, you spit into an officer's pocket or a soldier's cartridge case. In the street you hear nothing but: *Halt! Quick march! About turn!* etc. etc. You see nothing but weapons, drums and the equipment of war. At the entrance to the castle there are 2 grenadiers and 2 mounted dragoons with grenadier caps on their heads and cuirasses on their breasts, but with drawn swords in their hands and over each

6. 'Laugh, friends!'

of them a beautiful large tin roof instead of a sentry box: in a word, it's impossible to see greater precision in sentry drill or a finer body of men. You see absolutely no other men except those of the grenadier type, so that many a sergeant-major is paid 40 florins a month. You will laugh! And it's certainly laughable. When I stood at the window, I thought I could see nothing but soldiers waiting to play their parts in a play or opera. Just think that all these people look the same and every day their hair is done not in ringlets but just like any *petit-maître*,[7] in countless curls combed back and powdered snow-white, but with their beards greased coal-black. I'll write more from Mannheim. I must close now. If you write, write to me at Mannheim and write on it that the letter is to remain at the post until I collect it. I received the music in Augsb. If I were to write everything, I should have much more to say. But I can't help but tell you that Württemberg is the most beautiful country: from Geissling to Ludwigsburg you see nothing to the right or left but water, woods, fields, meadows, gardens and vineyards, and all of these at once, mixed together in the most beautiful way. My regards to everyone in Salzb., especially our Father Confessor, Madame Robinig and her household etc. etc. – etc. etc. *Complimenti sopra Complimenti. Addio!* I am your old

Mozart

My wife is utterly enchanted by the countryside in Württemberg.

[*On the inside of the envelope*]
Tell Herr Wenzel that I have heard a certain Nardini[8] and that one cannot hear a finer player in terms of beauty, purity, evenness of tone and taste in cantabilità. But he plays rather lightly. Herr Wotschitka[9] is still in service in Stuttgart but is hardly to be commended for his childish behaviour: in Augsb. the choirmaster of St Moritz's, Herr Schue, showed me a letter from Herr Meissner[10] in which he signs

7. Fop or dandy.
8. Pietro Nardini (1722–93), Italian composer and accomplished violinist.
9. Ignaz Joseph Heinrich Wotschitka (b. 1732), violoncellist.
10. Joseph Nikolaus Meissner (*c.* 1724–95), bass singer in Salzburg.

himself *Capello Magister*. I explained to him that he was a Magister of singing in order to excuse his childishness.

[*On the outside of the envelope*]
We are now all well, thank God.

From Ludwigsburg the Mozart family travelled to Schwetzingen, the summer residence of Elector Karl Theodor of the Palatinate, and from there to Mannheim, Worms and Mainz.

---

5. Leopold Mozart to Lorenz Hagenauer, 3 August 1763, Mainz

Monsieur,

You'll no doubt have received my letters from *Ludwigsburg* and *Schwetzingen*. In the first I said that you should reply to Mannheim, but in the second I said you should reply to Frankfurt. We'd earlier driven from Schwetzingen to Heidelberg to see the castle and the great cask.[1] Heidelberg is very like Salzburg, that is, in its situation: and the fallen-in doors and walls of the castle, which are an astonishing sight, show the sad fruits of the recent French wars.[2] In the church of the Holy Ghost, which is known to historians for the struggle between the Catholics and the Calvinists and which is the reason why the electors transferred their residence to Mannheim,[3] our Wolfgang played the organ so admirably that on the orders of the town dean

---

1. A giant wine cask, first mentioned in the sixteenth century, still stands inside Heidelberg castle.
2. Louis XIV of France invaded the Palatinate in 1688–9, during the War of the League of Augsburg (1688–97), when his armies caused widespread destruction. Although Leopold describes the wars as 'recent' here, later in this letter he calls them 'the old French wars'.
3. This was in 1709.

his name, with all the particulars, was inscribed on it in perpetual memory of the occasion.

From Schwetzingen, where we received a gift of 15 louis d'or, we travelled via Worms to Mainz. We spent 3 days in Mannheim, where we were freely shown everything worth seeing. We were also paid for at the Prince Frederick by a French colonel who has served all his life in India. If I were to tell you all the strange things that this colonel has brought back with him from these countries, it would fill whole sheets of paper. Amongst other things I've seen a dress made from paper, a dress made from wood and also one in stucco. But you can't tell what it's made from until you tear off a little piece. He gave Nannerl a little ring that may be worth slightly more than a louis d'or and to Wolfgang he presented a delightful toothpick case. The *city of Mannheim* is uncommonly attractive on account of its regularity; but the houses have only one storey and so it looked like a city in miniature. Conversely, the rooms immediately next to the entrance to the houses are uncommonly attractive, and one finds the most elegant lodgings even under the roof. At the end of each street you see 4 main roads intersecting, each completely identical to the other. And on both sides of the streets, between the carriageway in the middle and the gutters at the side, there are painted posts on which lanterns stand at dead of night. As you can well imagine, there is no more beautiful sight than a view lit in this way, especially in the 4 main streets, where you can see, for example, from the castle or residence as far as the Neckar Gate etc.

Worms is an old-fashioned town much blighted by the old French wars. But the cathedral is remarkable for its old associations, and the Lutheran church even more so, for it was here that Luther appeared before the Council.[4] For our evening meal in Worms we dined with Baron Dalberg. This family is so old that it has on display a letter on some rolled-up material, like tree bark, on which a Herr Dalberg reports the news that a carpenter's son who claimed to be the Messiah had been condemned to be crucified. *Credibile est veteres, latro ceu*

---

4. The imperial council known as the Diet of Worms was summoned by the Emperor Charles V to hear charges of heresy against Martin Luther (1483–1546) in 1521.

praesul et hospes,[5] says the Bible of the lowest form at grammar school. If you want to try a really bad road, you should drive from Worms to Oppenheim. In Oppenheim you'll also see the saddest remains of the old French wars. From Oppenheim to Mainz it is utterly delightful: on one side you're right next to the Rhine, and to your left are fields, villages, gardens and vineyards. The centre of *Mainz* is very built-up, the houses close together; it's better in the so-called Bleiche and on the Tiermarkt.

NB: In Mainz I met Count Schönborn, who got married here,[6] also Count Ostein and his major-domo Krell, and Count Bassenheim, too. I was with them all. The Walderdorffs are in Koblenz.

From Mainz the Mozarts travelled to Frankfurt (where the children gave five concerts) and then on to Koblenz (where they gave a concert on 21 October), Cologne, Aachen and Brussels. Here they gave a concert on 7 November, attended by Prince Karl Alexander of Lorraine, governor general of the Netherlands and brother of Emperor Francis I. They arrived in Paris on 18 November and not long afterwards made a visit to the palace of Versailles.

6. *Leopold Mozart to Lorenz Hagenauer, December 1763, Versailles*

You may read the present letter and prepare a summary of it, then seal this summary and hand it with my most humble respects and New Year greetings to our Father Confessor or else get him to seal it himself. Madame de Pompadour is still an attractive woman, she's

5. 'The ancients say all manner of things that are more or less believable.'
6. Hugo Damian, Count Schönborn (1738–1817) had married Maria Anna, Countess Stadion und Thannhausen (1746–1817) earlier that year.

very like the late Frau Stainer née Theresia Freysauff. Also something
of the appearance of the Holy Roman Empress, especially in the
eyes.[1] She is very haughty and still in total command. – – Versailles
is expensive; and we are extremely fortunate *that at present it is almost
as warm as in summer*, otherwise we would be in difficulty as each log
of wood costs 5 sous. Yesterday my boy received a gold snuffbox
from Madame la Comtesse de Tessé,[2] and today my little girl got a
small, transparent snuffbox inlaid with gold from Princess Carignan
and Wolfg. a silver pocket writing case with silver pens to compose,
it is so small and delightfully made that it is impossible to describe it.
Almost everyone here is madly in love with my children: but the
aftermath of the last war[3] can be seen and noticed wherever you look.
It's impossible to commit to paper everything I'd like to. Wish all
my good friends a Happy New Year from us all. I'd like to write to
everyone if only I had time and if every letter didn't cost 20 or 30
sous; if I'd written a longer letter to His Grace[4] I'd certainly have
had to pay 5 livres for it, for they charge according to weight and
size or else according to shape. Did you reply to any of my letters?
Perhaps I'll find your answer when we get back to our hotel in Paris.
Farewell, *à Dieu*!

Together with my wife and children, I send you our kind regards
and wish you, your wife and all your family a happy New Year. We
are all well, thank God. You should see Wolfg. in his black suit and
French hat.

---

1. Jeanne Antoinette Poisson, Marquise de Pompadour (1721–64), mistress of King
Louis XV (1710–74), was famed for her beauty, grace and wit. Maria Theresia
Freysauff von Neudegg (1712–57) was the wife of a Salzburg businessman. The
empress is Maria Theresa.
2. Adrienne-Catherine, Comtesse de Tessé (1741–1814) was lady-in-waiting to the
dauphine.
3. Here Leopold refers to the Seven Years' War (1756–63) between France, Spain
and Britain.
4. Archbishop Siegmund von Schrattenbach of Salzburg, see List.

*7. Leopold Mozart to Maria Theresia Hagenauer, 1 February 1764,
Paris*

Madame!

One shouldn't always write to men but should also remember the
fair and devout sex. Whether the women in Paris are fair, I can't say,
and for good reason; for they are painted so unnaturally, like the
dolls of Berchtesgaden,[1] that thanks to this revolting affectation even
a naturally beautiful woman becomes unbearable in the eyes of an
honest German. As for devotion, I can assure you that it's not difficult
to fathom the miracles wrought by France's female saints; the greatest
miracles are those performed by women who are neither virgins nor
wives nor widows; and these miracles all take place in their lifetime.
We shall speak more fully on this matter in due course. Enough! It's
difficult to work out here who is the lady of the house. Everyone
lives as he or she likes, and if God is not exceptionally merciful, the
French state will suffer the same fate as the former Persian Empire.

Your husband's two letters of 26 Dec. and 19 Jan. have arrived
safely, together with their 3 enclosures.[2] The most important and, to
you, no doubt the most pleasant piece of news that I can give you is
that, thank God, we are all well. By the same token I too always look
forward eagerly to hearing that you are all well. I would assuredly
have written to you since my last letter from Versailles if I had not
kept hesitating while awaiting the outcome of our affair at Versailles
and as a result being able to tell you about it. But here, even more
than at other courts, everything proceeds at a snail's pace, and since
this matter has to be dealt with by the *Menu des plaisirs,*[3] we have to
be patient. If the court's liberality matches the pleasure that my
children have given it, we should do very well. I should add that it
is by no means the custom here to kiss their majesties' hands or to
trouble them with a petition or even to speak to them *au passage,* as

1. Wooden marionettes were a speciality of the town of Berchtesgaden in southern
Bavaria.
2. Both letters, as well as Hagenauer's enclosures, are lost.
3. An independent office in the French court administration.

they call it, namely, when they are going to church through the gallery and royal apartments.

Nor is it usual to do homage to the king or to any other member of the royal family by a nod of the head or by bending the knee. Rather, you remain erect, without the slightest movement, and in such a position you are free to watch the king and his family pass right next to you. You can easily imagine, then, how impressed and amazed were these French people, who are so infatuated with the customs of their court, when the king's daughters stopped stock still not only in their apartments but in the public gallery when they saw my children and approached them and not only let them kiss their hands but kissed them countless times in turn. The same thing happened with Madame Dauphine.[4] But the most extraordinary thing of all in the eyes of these French people was that at the grand *couvert* after nightfall on New Year's Day, not only was it necessary to make room for us all to go up to high table, but my Herr Wolfgangus was privileged to stand next to the queen,[5] speaking to her constantly, entertaining her, repeatedly kissing her hands and consuming the dishes that she handed him from the table. The queen speaks German as well as we do, but as the king knows none, the queen translated everything our heroic Wolfg. said. I stood beside him: my wife and daughter stood on the other side of the king, where M. Dauphin and Mlle Adélaïde[6] were sitting. Now you must know that the king never dines in public, except on Sunday evenings when the whole royal family dines together. But not everyone is allowed in. However, if there's a big festival like New Year's Day, Easter, Whitsuntide, name days etc. it is called the great *couvert*, and all people of distinction are admitted: only there's not much room, and so it soon fills up. We arrived late, so the Swiss Guards had to clear a passage for us, and we were taken through the hall into the room next to the royal table

4. Maria Josepha of Saxony (1731–67), second wife of the dauphin and mother of Louis XVI (1754–93).
5. Maria Leszczynska (1703–68), wife of Louis XV and daughter of the deposed King Stanislas I Leszczynski of Poland (1677–1766).
6. Dauphin Louis Ferdinand (1729–65) and Princesse Adélaïde (1732–1800), eldest son and daughter of Louis XV.

– the room through which their majesties enter the hall. As they passed, they spoke to our Wolfg. and we then followed them to table.

You can't possibly expect me to describe Versailles for you. I'll say only this, that we arrived there on Christmas Eve and attended Matins and 3 Masses in the Chapel Royal. We were in the royal gallery when the king returned from seeing Madame Dauphine, whom he had just informed of the death of her brother, the elector of Saxony.[7] I heard good and bad music there. Everything that was intended to be sung by single voices and to resemble an aria was empty, cold and wretched – in a word, French, but the choruses are all good and even very good. So I have been to Mass in the Chapel Royal every day with my little man to hear the choir in the motet that is always performed there. The king's Mass is at 1 o'clock. But if he goes hunting, his Mass is at 10 o'clock and the queen's Mass at half past 12. More on all this in due course. Our 16 days in Versailles have cost us about 12 louis d'or. Perhaps you think this is too much and hard to understand? – – In Versailles there are no *carosses de remise* or fiacres[8] but only sedan chairs. Every journey costs 12 sous. You'll soon see that some days the chairs cost us a laubthaler and more, as we always need 2, if not 3, chairs: and then the weather was always bad. If you add 4 new black suits,[9] you'll not be surprised if our visit to Versailles comes to 26 or 27 louis d'or. Let's see what we get from the court in return. Apart from what we hope to receive from the court, we've earned no more than 12 louis d'or in Versailles.[10] My Master Wolfgang has received a *gold snuffbox* from *Madame la Comtesse de Tessé*, together with a *gold watch*, which is valuable because it is so small and whose size I'm indicating here,

7. Friedrich Christian, Elector of Saxony (1722–63).
8. Hired carriages.
9. Presumably black suits were needed because the court was in mourning.
10. Leopold seemingly expected his visit to Versailles to cost something over 200 florins, approximately his annual salary in Salzburg. However, for his appearances he eventually received a purse filled with 50 louis d'or, about 400 florins; see Note on Currencies.

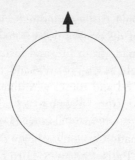

and Nannerl has received an uncommonly beautiful *heavy toothpick case made entirely of gold*. From another lady Wolfg. received a silver writing case and Nannerl an uncommonly fine tortoiseshell snuffbox inlaid with gold. Our collection of snuffboxes has been further increased by a red one with gold bands, by another in some kind of glass material set in gold and by one in *vernis martin*[11] inlaid with the most beautiful flowers in coloured gold and various pastoral instruments. To these may be added a cornelian ring set in gold with an antique head, and a host of trifles that are of no value, such as sword-bands, ribbons and armlets, flowers for bonnets and scarves etc. for Nannerl etc. In a word, I hope that within 4 weeks I shall be able to tell you a better tale of louis d'or for it takes longer to be properly known in Paris than to walk to Maxglan;[12] and I can assure you that it needs no telescope to see the evil aftermath of the last war everywhere you look. For the French are keen to continue their superficial splendour to the highest degree, and as a result no one is rich apart from the *fermiers*,[13] whereas the gentry are deep in debt. The bulk of the country's wealth lies in the hands of some 100 persons, a few big bankers and *fermiers généraux*; and, finally, most of the money is spent on Lucretias who don't stab themselves. All the same, you can well imagine that particularly beautiful and valuable things can be seen here, but one also sees astonishing follies. In winter

11. A type of lacquer, the speciality of the frères Martin.
12. Maxglan was then a village outside the city; today it is a suburb of Salzburg.
13. Tax farmers; private individuals to whom the French crown had contracted out the collection of taxes.

the women wear not only clothes trimmed with fur, but collars and neckties, and instead of decorative flowers to pin in their hair, they wear the same things made from fur, and instead of armlets etc., but the most ridiculous sight is the sword-band that's fashionable here and that's wrapped round and round with fine fur – it's a good way of stopping the sword from freezing. In addition to this idiotic modishness in all things, there is also their great love of comfort, which means that this nation no longer hears the voice of nature, and as a result everyone in Paris sends new-born children to be raised in the country. It is the midwives who take these children to the country, each with a large book in which the names of the father and mother etc. are entered by the local clergyman, followed by the name of the nurse or, rather, the peasant and his wife at the place where the child is taken. This is done by persons of both high and low rank, and they pay a trifle for it. But you can see the most pitiful consequences of this: you'll hardly find any other place where there are so many wretched and maimed individuals. You have only to spend a minute in church or walk along a few streets before you come across someone who's blind or lame or limping, or some half-putrefied beggar or someone lying in the street whose hand was eaten away by pigs when he was a child, or someone else who as a child fell into the hearthfire and had half his arm burnt off while his foster-father and family were working in the fields etc. There are whole crowds of such people that so disgust me that I avoid looking at them when I pass. But I shall now move swiftly from the ugly to the charming and, indeed, to someone who has charmed a king. I'm sure you'd like to know what Madame Marquise Pompadour looks like, wouldn't you? – – She must have been very beautiful indeed, for she's still very comely. She's tall and stately in appearance, fat or, rather, plump, but very well-proportioned, blonde, looks a lot like the late Tresel Freysauff, while her eyes have a certain similarity to those of Her Majesty the Empress.[14] She does herself great credit and is uncommonly intelligent. Her apartments at Versailles are a veritable paradise and look out on to the gardens; in Paris she has a magnificent hôtel, entirely

14. See letter 6 and n. 1.

rebuilt, in the Faubourg St Honoré.[15] In the room that contains the *clavecin*[16] – which is all gilt and most artistically lacquered and painted – there is a life-size portrait of her and beside it a portrait of the king. But now for something different! – – There's a constant war here between Italian and French music. The whole of French music isn't worth a tinker's curse; but terrible changes are afoot: the French are starting to vacillate, and in 10 or 15 years French taste will, I hope, have vanished altogether. The Germans are now showing them a thing or two in publishing their compositions. Among these, the most popular are Monsieur Schobert, Monsieur Eckard and Monsieur Honauer for the keyboard, Monsieur Hochbrucker[17] and Monsieur Mayr for the harp. Monsieur Le Grand, a French keyboard player, has abandoned his own style completely, and his sonatas reflect our own taste. Monsieur Schobert, Monsieur Eckard, Monsieur Le Grand and Monsieur Hochbrucker have all brought us their engraved sonatas and presented them to my children. 4 sonatas by Monsieur Wolfgang Mozart are currently being engraved.[18] Just imagine the stir that these sonatas will make in the world when it says on the title-page that they are the work of a 7-year-old child, and when the sceptics are challenged to test him, as has already happened, and he gets someone to write down a minuet or whatever and then – without even touching the keyboard – adds the bass and, if desired, the 2nd violin as well. You'll hear in due course how good these sonatas are; one of them has an andante in a very unusual style.[19] And I can tell you, dear Frau

15. Today the Elysée palace.

16. Harpsichord.

17. Johann Schobert (*c.* 1735–67), composer resident in Paris from *c.* 1760; in 1767, Mozart adapted the first movement of his sonata op. 17 no. 2 as the second movement of the keyboard concerto K39. Johann Gottfried Eckard (1735–1809) was a German keyboard player and composer active in Paris from 1758; Leontzi Honauer (1737–90), keyboard; Johann Baptist Hochbrucker (1732–1812), harpist.

18. The sonatas K6–7, published in Paris in early 1764, were dedicated to Louise-Marie-Thérèse (1733–99), Madame Victoire, the second daughter of Louis XV; K8–9, published at the same time, were dedicated to the Comtesse de Tessé.

19. Although this movement is identified in *Briefe* v. 103 as the second movement of K7, the tempo marking there is adagio; it is more likely to be the unusual andante of K9.

Hagenauer, that every day God works new wonders through this child. By the time we return home, God willing, he will be in a position to perform court duties. He is always accompanying other performers at public concerts. He even transposes the arias while accompanying them *à prima vista*; and everywhere people place Italian and French works before him that he has no difficulty in sight-reading. – – My little girl plays the hardest pieces by Schobert and Eckard etc., Eckard's being the more difficult, with incredible precision, so that the *contemptible Schobert* cannot conceal *his jealousy* and envy and is making himself a laughing stock in the eyes of Monsieur Eckard, who is an honest man, and of many others. I shall have more to say on several matters that it would take me too long to explain here. Monsieur Schobert isn't at all the man he is said to be. He flatters you to your face but is the falsest of men; yet his religion is the one that's in fashion. May God convert him! – But now *some very sad news*, something extremely upsetting: we are all in a state of great anxiety and confusion. In a word, *Countess Van Eyck*[20] is in a critical condition and without God's special mercy is unlikely to live. We were with her on Sunday before lunch, from 12 till 1, and she was very cheerful. She had been at home for a few days, suffering from a cold, but that day she had been to church. As always, she talked an incredible amount with Wolfgang. That night I heard a carriage during the night and a certain commotion. In the morning I heard that the countess had suddenly been taken ill and brought up a lot of blood. On Monday she was bled 3 times; by Tuesday she seemed to be improving; but that night she again coughed up blood and was again bled. But it remains as before, the bleeding was always extremely bad, she fainted, and, in a word, there's little hope that she will get better. You can imagine our distress, which is all the greater in that I can only look on from a distance and may never speak to her or see her again. My children are praying for her and are in tears as Wolfgang loves the countess and she is exceptionally fond of him, too. *I am writing this on* the evening of *1 Feb*. God grant that I may

20. Countess van Eyck, wife of the Bavarian ambassador in Paris, was a member of the Arco family of Salzburg, see List; the Mozarts were staying at her house.

have more cheerful news before I finish this letter tomorrow morning. *2 Feb.* I heard nothing of any import last night; the countess did not sleep all night, but things are no worse, and there are even grounds to be more hopeful, as her stools are no longer coloured with blood and her temperature has gone down a little. I hear that the count has not left her bedside, and there are 2 nurses in the house and 2 doctors. I hope that the count will already have informed his parents-in-law in Salz.[21] But I don't know if this is so, *and so I would ask you not to say anything to anyone until you have spoken to Mlle Rosalia Joly[22] who – in the unlikely event that their lordships know nothing – will be able to make sensible use of my news.* Enough! We are always wretched individuals, whether we be in Salzburg or in Paris. My wife can think only of the poor dear countess all day long, and indeed we are all deeply concerned.

I'm now running out of space, but I must tell you that the archbishop here has been cast out into the wilderness or, to put it more mildly, has been sent into exile. He had a lampoon printed that was directed against the *parlement* and in favour of the Jesuits, and it was this that brought his punishment down on him.[23] As far as I know, virtually everyone blames him as the king, on hearing that he planned to publish this piece, tried in a friendly manner to dissuade him, but he persisted and as a result forcibly dashed his head against the wall. The king hastened to exile him, otherwise the *parlement* would have arrested him. *The secular arm is a little too powerful here.* On the other hand, the clergy run around the streets on their own here, lowering their cowls below their shoulders and clasping their hats beside them, so that they are indistinguishable from any lay pedestrian. Farewell and thank God that there's no paper left, otherwise you'd have to put on your glasses. With greetings from myself, my children and my wife, I am your most obedient servant

Mozart

21. Count Georg Anton Felix von Arco and his wife, Maria Josepha Viktoria, see List.
22. Maria Anna Rosalia Walburga Joly (1726–88) was a Mozart family friend.
23. Christophe de Beaumont, archbishop of Paris, had published *Apologies des Jésuites*, the work that caused so much offence, in 1763.

[*On the inside of the envelope*]
Could I ask you to pass on our most humble good wishes to all our good friends? They will all be reasonable enough to realize that it is impossible to do more than name a long list of people. What is our honest Delmor doing? Is he still in our neighbourhood? He'll no doubt think of us occasionally when he sees no one at our windows. Please give him my good wishes and especially those of little Wolfgang. He's an honest man. Is it cold in Salzb. too? – It was snowing when we arrived here but hasn't done since then. It's like autumn here, but mostly it's been misty and unsettled. But it's good that it's not been very cold as a *klafter* of wood costs 1 louis d'or. I must write to Herr Spitzeder and Herr Adlgasser.[24]

I'm finishing this at 9 in the morning on 3 Feb. The countess has had another bad night. Things are a little better during the daytime but it doesn't last: her pulse remains feverish: perhaps her lung is affected.

8. *Leopold Mozart to Lorenz Hagenauer, 22 February 1764, Paris*

Monsieur,

The sun can't always shine, clouds often gather, only for the sky to clear again. I delayed reporting the sad death of Countess van Eyck, as I thought it sufficient to prepare the hearts of the people of Salzburg for this sad event and to leave others to report the end. Once I am out of Paris, I shan't fail to report a number of details; and I would have written a few friendly words to Mlle Rosalia, to whom I send my good wishes, but I must beg her indulgence, she will find my reasons more than justified. Enough! No one likes to die anywhere, but here it is doubly sad for an honest German if he falls ill or even dies. Moreover, the death of the late countess left the count feeling unwell, although he is now slowly recovering. Their German

---

24. Anton Cajetan Adlgasser, court and cathedral organist at Salzburg, see List; Franz Anton Spitzeder (1735–96), tenor active at the Salzburg court.

nursemaid, Sophia, who will be returning to Germany in a few days' time, almost paid for her distress with her life. Soon afterwards a sudden and unexpected occurrence placed me in a certain embarrassment. My dear Wolfgang suddenly contracted a sore throat and a cold, so that, having noticed the cold early on the 16th, he developed such an inflammation in his throat during the night that he was in danger of choking: but the mucus that he suddenly produced and that he could not bring up fell back into his stomach; I then got him quickly out of bed and walked him back and forth across the room. He had an astonishingly high fever, but I gradually reduced this with *pulvis antispas*[*modicus*] *Hallen*[*sis*] and, God be praised, he was up again within 4 days and is now fully recovered. As a precaution I wrote by the local post to our friend the German doctor Herrenschwand, the doctor of the Swiss Guards. But he did not think it necessary to come more than twice. I then gave him a little *aqua laxat*[*iva*] *Vien*[*nensis*] [1] as a laxative; God be praised, he is now well. My little girl, too, is suffering from a cold, but is not feverish. And it's no wonder because we arrived in Paris on 18 November, and it snowed heavily for a few days, but this soon disappeared, and since then we've seen no snow in Paris; the weather has always been misty or damp and so mild that autumn in Germany is much colder: indeed, we've had some extraordinarily beautiful warm days that quickly gave way, however, to the most appalling rain, so that people virtually never go out here without taking a silk umbrella with them. This explains why these handy silk umbrellas are so fashionable here, because the weather in Paris is in such total accord with the character of its inhabitants and subject to change. Colds here are worse and more dangerous than in Germany, they are generally feverish colds, and because the local doctors are very fond of bleeding their patients, they despatch many to the next world by bleeding them. Could I ask you to have *4 Masses* said as soon as possible at *Maria Plain* and 1 at the Holy Child at Loreto,[2] which we promised for the sake of our children, and make

1. Leopold seems to have travelled with his own supply of medicaments.
2. The pilgrimage church of Maria Plain, near Salzburg, was built by Giovanni Antonio Dario in 1671–4. In 1774, Mozart played at celebrations for the church's centenary. The Loreto church stands in what is now the Paris-Lodron-Strasse in Salzburg.

a note of this for me? I hope that the Masses will continue to be said at Loreto as long as we are away, just as I asked. As a result of what I've told you about the wet weather, I must add that the Seine was so amazingly high about 2 weeks ago that the people here had to cross the Place de Grève in boats, and many parts of the city, towards the river, were impassable. You'll have read in the newspapers about the damage caused by the water around Frankfurt and in Holland and elsewhere. We shall be driving out to Versailles again in 2 weeks at the latest in order to present the great Herr Wolfgang's opus 1 – his engraved sonatas – to Madame Victoire, the king's second daughter, to whom it is dedicated. His opus 2 will be dedicated, I think, to Madame la Comtesse de Tessé.[3] God willing, important things will have happened within 3 or, at the most, 4 weeks; we have tilled the soil well and may now hope for a good harvest. But one must take things as they come. I should have had at least 12 louis d'or more if my children had not had to stay at home for a number of days. Thank God they are better – – – do you know what the people here want? – – They want to persuade me to have my boy inoculated with smallpox. But now that I have made known my aversion to this proposal, they are leaving me in peace. Here it is the universal fashion and may be done without permission, not in the city, but in the country: but this is only because inoculation has been very successful, with the result that people are having themselves inoculated in droves and all at the same time, children and adults alike, so that there are sometimes 3, 4 or more persons suffering from smallpox under the same roof. But as this could have unfortunate consequences, it has to be done in the country or be notified to the *Intendant*[4] of Paris. For my own part, I leave it to the grace of God. It depends on His divine mercy whether He wishes to keep this prodigy of nature in the world in which He has placed it or to take it to Himself. I shall certainly watch over it, so that it is all one whether we are in Salzburg or anywhere else in the world. But it is this that makes travelling so

3. Opus 1, K6–7; opus 2, K8–9; Mozart's dedication to the Comtesse de Tessé is reproduced in Deutsch, *Documentary Biography*, 29.
4. Administrator.

expensive. No one who has not travelled can imagine what demands it makes. You have to keep your hands constantly in your purse and always have your wits about you and invariably keep in your mind's eye a plan for the next few months, but a plan that can be changed at once if circumstances change. Now for something else. Don't be surprised if I write things down in no particular order, but in cases like these you have to write down your ideas while they strike you, otherwise you forget them. In Germany people believe mistakenly that the French are unable to withstand the cold; but this is a mistake that is revealed as such the moment you see all the shops open all winter. Not just the businessmen etc. but the tailor, shoemaker, saddler, cutler, goldsmith etc., in a word, all kinds of trades work in open shops and before the eyes of the world, so that all the shops are so many rooms where you can see people working, year in, year out, whether it's hot or cold. As soon as evening falls, the shops are all lit, so that in some there may be 6, 7, 8 or as many as 10 lights burning, in others there may be several sconces, and a beautiful chandelier hanging in the middle. Most of the shops are open until 10. The shops that sell victuals are open until 11. Here the women have nothing but *chauffrettes*[5] under their feet: these are small wooden boxes lined with lead and full of holes, with a red-hot brick or hot ashes inside, or little earthenware boxes filled with coal. As soon as it is daylight, you see an incalculable throng of people of both sexes, young and old, walking in the Tuileries, the Palais Royal, the boulevard and other promenades throughout the winter, even in the coldest wind. Tell me now whether the French are afraid of the cold. All the windows are thrown open at the least sign of sunshine. And no matter how cold the wind, the doors are open, and they sit by the fireside.

Before the family left Paris, Wolfgang and Nannerl gave concerts on 10 March and 9 April at the theatre of M. Félix, in the rue St Honoré;

5. Foot-warmers.

both performances were arranged by the German journalist and critic Friedrich Melchior von Grimm (1723–1807), long resident in Paris and acquainted with many important figures in French society. The family set out for London on 10 April 1764, travelling by way of Calais and Dover. They arrived on 23 April.

9. Leopold Mozart to Lorenz Hagenauer, 28 May 1764, London

Monsieur!

You know that the further away a thing is, the smaller it presents itself to the eye. And so it is with my letters. My handwriting becomes smaller and smaller according to the distance I am from Salzburg. If we were to sail to America, it would become completely illegible. It costs a shilling to send to Germany a mere letter without a cover and another shilling for the cover, so that a letter with a cover costs 2 shillings. A guinea is 21 shillings and is equal in value to a louis d'or, for in Dover the banker *Miné*, who had been recommended to me in Paris, gave me 12 guineas for 12 louis d'or: for French money isn't accepted here. You can easily work out, then, what a shilling is worth.[1] In the letter that she was kind enough to write to me in Paris, our dear Frau Hagenauer asked whether we *might even go to England and Holland.* When I left Salzburg, I was only half resolved to go to England: but as everyone, even in Paris, urged us to go to London, I made up my mind to do so; and now, with God's help, we are here: but we'll not be going to Holland, I can assure everyone of that. Although I am assured that I could soon earn 2 to 300 ducats in The Hague, for example, I know that the cost would be exorbitant; the people, especially the Dutch, are rather uncouth. And in general one should visit places only in winter in order to take proper advantage of the situation; and that's simply impossible, unless we were to spend 4, 5 or more years travelling. We could also go to Hamburg if we wanted to: but it's too far away for me, too far north. We could go

1. 24 kreuzer.

to Copenhagen to the greatest advantage in the world; both the Royal
Danish Minister in Paris, Baron de Gleichen, and the Danish envoy
here, Count Bothmer, were prepared to guarantee us a certain sum
in advance, but it would never occur to me to accept. Even less has
Prince Galitzin[2] persuaded me to give him any grounds for hoping
that we might ever resolve to go to Russia. These countries are too
remote, and too cold. The present country is sufficiently remote, even
though it is one of the most beautiful and blessed countries in terms
of the produce of its fields and its cattle, but it is a dangerous country
on account of the constant variations in temperature between hot and
cold. Because England is an island, it suffers a lot from the constant
variations in the winds that blow in off the sea. Some days it is
uncommonly hot; but within a moment a north wind may rise up,
and within a quarter of an hour it is uncommonly cold: that is why
you see only clothes of woollen cloth here. The food is uncommonly
nourishing, substantial and rich; the beef, veal and lamb are better
than you'll find anywhere else in the world. You see the finest cattle
in the fields, and lambs that are almost as big as a calf, with wool
that's thick and long. Hence the excellent manufactured goods. But
this food is too rich, while the beer, which you can get in various
kinds, is quite amazingly strong and good. But because beer is a
product of the country, the wine, by contrast, is indescribably expensive, with an astonishing tax on it. The same is true of coffee, which
costs more than 4 German florins a pound. Moreover, you have to
buy it already roasted and ground, for which a number of shops exist:
anyone who roasts a pound of coffee at home is fined 50 guineas.
You can imagine the face that my wife pulled when she heard about
this arrangement. Enough, the English are trying to sell off their tea
and prevent the money for coffee from leaving the country. The tea
kettle is on the hearth all day, and when you visit people, they serve
you tea with bread and butter, in other words, a thinly sliced loaf of
bread covered in butter. I should add that lunch is generally taken
between 2 and 3 o'clock, and at night most people eat nothing or else
only cheese, butter and bread, which they wash down with a good

2. Prince Dmitri Alekseevich Galitzin, Russian ambassador in Paris 1763–8.

jug of strong beer. No woman goes out into the street without wearing a hat on her head, but these hats are very varied; some are completely round, others are tied together at the back and may be made of satin, straw, taffeta etc. All are decorated with ribbons and trimmed with lace. Even a modest one costs half a guinea. Initially you think you are seeing only maskers. Men never go out bare headed, and a few are powdered. Whenever the street urchins see anyone decked out and dressed in a vaguely French way, they immediately call out: *Bugger French! French bugger!* The best policy is then to say nothing and pretend you haven't heard. Were it to enter your head to object, the rabble would send in reinforcements and you'd be lucky to escape with only a few holes in your head. For our own part, we look entirely English. I just had to get a few clothes made for me and Wolfg. and buy a few women's hats, which cost *12 guineas* in all. The least you'd pay to have a simple suit made up is 14 shillings, and you'd have to pay another pound sterling – 20 shillings – if it were to be lined. – – It doesn't surprise me that you find little or no fine English cloth in Germany or have to pay an astonishing amount for it, superfine cloth, a kind that respectable people most usually buy and which I've taken myself, costs 18 shillings an English yard, which is much shorter than the French yard. But the *finest* cloth costs 21 shillings. You can easily imagine that everything is uncommonly expensive here. The reason is that a guinea causes less stir here than a ducat does with us: but the people who believe that the English throw away their money are wrong; there's no middle way for them. Most are over-punctilious in the way they manage their affairs; a very few are uncommonly generous. We still don't know how things will turn out for us. We should really have been here during the winter. From 6 to 9 o'clock on 27 April we were with the queen and king at the Queen's Palace in St James's Park,[3] in other words, we were already at court within 5 days of arriving. We were given only 24 guineas, which we received immediately on leaving the king's

3. King George III (1728–1820, succeeded 1760) had bought Buckingham House (later Buckingham Palace) on his marriage to Princess Charlotte Sophia of Mecklenburg-Strelitz (1744–1818) in 1761.

apartment, but the kindness with which both their majesties – the king as well as the queen – received us is indescribable. In short, their common touch and friendly manner allowed us to forget that they were the king and queen of England; we have been received at every court with quite extraordinary courtesy, but the welcome that we were given here surpasses all the others: a week later we were walking in St James's Park; the king came driving past with the queen: and although we were wearing different clothes, they still recognized us and not only greeted us but the king opened the window, leant out and, laughing, greeted us and especially our Master Wolfgang as he was driving past, nodding and waving his hand. Talking of driving reminds me that I wish you could come here for a few days and see the beautiful horses and the most frightful carriages. The horses are as beautiful as the carriages are frightful. These latter are low and wide. The coachman's seat is just like a dovecote roof, so that if the coachman falls off his seat, it's like falling from the first floor of a low house. But the horses! the beautiful horses! if I'd a hundred English horses that were mine, standing in Calais, I'd have enough. To see English people in Germany is nothing to write home about; but to see them in their own country and by choice is very different. The sea and especially the ebb and flow of the tide in the harbour at Calais and Dover, then the ships and, in their wake, the fish that are called porpoises rising up and down in the sea, then – as soon as we left Dover – to be driven by the finest English horses that run so fast that the servants on the coach seat could scarcely breathe from the force of the air – all this was something entirely strange and agreeable. However strange it may have been for us in Paris to see a woodcutter, a carpenter etc. with an axe or saw under his arm, a tattered coat on his back and a snow-white powdered court wig on his head, it was no less odd for us to see the common women in the market in London with pipes of tobacco in their mouth. The city is very beautiful, but I have too little space to describe it here; the architecture is completely different from that in France. The pavement in front of the houses is paved with large flat square stones, so that walking is very easy; the roads, by contrast, are calculated to break your neck. All the houses have their main apartments below ground, the 2nd you enter at ground level, and rooms 1 and 2 are up to 3 floors up. The apartment below ground is light, it has the biggest windows, and smiths and locksmiths and all the other artisans generally have their workshops down here. That is why there are grills of iron or wood outside all the houses, so that no one falls down them. My enclosed letter to His Grace, our most gracious prince and master, will have reached you safely, I hope;[4] I sent it off straight after our arrival in London. May I ask you to have the following Masses said as soon as possible, namely: *3 Masses at the Holy Child of Loreto. 3 Masses at Maria Plain. 2 Masses at St Francis of Paula in Bergl and 2 at St John of Nepomuk in the parish church or wherever you want. Also 2 at St Anthony in the parish church.*[5] I should add that we've left most of our luggage with the banker Herr Hummel in Paris. We've also left there, separately, all the snuffboxes and 2 watches and other valuables, together with 2 beautiful new satin dresses, one ruby-coloured with white trimmings belonging to my wife and one blue dress with white trimmings belonging to my little girl, as well as all the accessories that go with them and many other things besides. The expensive dress that I bought my little girl in Paris – it has a pale yellow background, with flowers and broad gold stripes, and is very beautiful – I brought with me to England.

Our sworn friend Monsieur Grimm did everything for us in Paris and, quite apart from all his other kindness, gave Nannerl a gold watch as a parting gift, while to Wolfgang he gave a fruit knife of the kind that people tend to use with sweetmeats in Paris, the handle is made of mother-of-pearl set in gold, and it has 2 blades, one of gold, the other of silver. I also left 7 pieces of double louis d'or in a gold snuffbox there, and I have a letter of credit for 4800 livres for the 200 louis d'or that I entrusted to Herr Tourton & Baur;[6] I'd intended to send off the present letter a week ago; but I was prevented

4. Leopold's letter to Archbishop Schrattenbach is apparently lost.
5. The church of St Francis of Paula on the north slope of the Mönchsberg in Salzburg was abandoned in 1801. St John of Nepomuk and St Anthony are side altars in the Franciscan church in the street of that name, which was the Mozarts' parish church.
6. Tourton & Baur were bankers in the Place des Victoires, Paris.

from doing so, partly because I wanted to wait for some news. But I can report only that on 19 May we were again with the king and queen from 6 to 10 in the evening, when the only other people present were three princes – two of the king's brothers and the brother of the queen. As we were leaving, we were again handed 24 guineas. If this happens every 3 or 4 weeks, it won't be too bad. We are now going to give a so-called benefit or *concerto al nostro profitto* on 5 June. It is really not the time to give such concerts, and little profit can be expected as it's out of season and the cost of putting on a concert like this is 40 guineas: but it's the king's birthday on the 4th, so that many of the nobility will come up to town from the country, and so we must take the risk and seize the moment to make ourselves better known. Each person pays half a guinea, and if it were winter, I'm sure I could count on 600 persons, in other words, 300 guineas: but now they all go to the pleasure gardens and into the country. *Basta!* all will be well as long as we stay healthy with God's help and if He keeps our invincible Wolfgang in good health. The king gave him not only works by Wagenseil to play, but also Bach, Abel and Handel,[7] all of which he rattled off *prima vista*.[8] He played the king's organ so well that everyone rates his organ playing far higher than his harpsichord playing. He then accompanied the queen in an aria that she sang and a flautist in a solo. Finally he took the violin part in some Handel arias that happened to be lying around and played the most beautiful melody over the simple bass, so that everyone was utterly astonished. In a word, what he knew when we left Salzburg is a mere shadow of what he knows now. You can't imagine it. Together with the rest of us, he sends you his best wishes from the clavier, where he is now seated, playing Kapellmeister Bach's trio, and not a day passes without his speaking at least 30 times of Salzburg and his and our friends and patrons. He now has an opera constantly

7. Georg Christoph Wagenseil (1715–77), keyboard instructor to the imperial court at Vienna; Johann Christian Bach (1735–82), youngest son of Johann Sebastian Bach (1685–1750), composer and music master to Queen Charlotte from 1764; Carl Friedrich Abel (1723–87), German composer active in London; George Frideric Handel (1685–1759), German-born composer resident in England from 1710.
8. 'at sight'.

in his head that he wants to perform with just young people in Salzburg. I have already had to count up all the players he's noted down for the orchestra, among whom Herr Kolb and Herr Ränftl[9] are mentioned quite often.

10. Leopold Mozart to Lorenz Hagenauer, 28 June 1764, London

Monsieur!

I have just received the enclosed bill of exchange from Paris and therefore hasten to forward it to you without delay in order that you can make use of it straightaway. I do not really understand how these matters are transacted at a distance and so I spoke with two local bankers, Loubier et Teissier, who are very good friends of mine and who, after seeing the letter I received from Messrs Tourton et Baur and noting the figure of £179½ quoted therein, have agreed that the value of 200 louis d'or is correct, given the difference in the exchange rate. You will not fail, therefore, to send this as soon as possible to Hamburg and, once it has been accepted, credit me with the sum of 2250 f. At the same time I have pleasure in reporting that I have again deposited a small sum of *100 guineas* with the afore-named bankers Loubier and Teissier, which I could pay to someone in the service of Salzburg who is currently in these parts. If you yourself can use this sum in Paris, The Hague, Amsterdam, Hamburg etc. or elsewhere, it would be most agreeable to me, and as I see that I shall probably still have to transfer a certain balance to Salzburg, I would ask you to be mindful of this and lend me a hand. In the event that a larger sum is to be paid, I can transfer an extra 30, 40 or even 50 guineas without depriving myself of money. I must also let you know that from now on you should send your letters to the following address: *Monsieur Mozart chez Mrs Charles Loubier et Teissier Banquiers. Austin-Friars. London.*

9. Joachim Kolb, an amateur violinist, was a member of a prominent Salzburg business family; Franz Anton Mathias Ränftl was also an amateur player.

At the end of this week we are going to Tunbridge Wells, about 30 English miles from here, which the mail coach can cover in 3 or 4 hours as an English mile is no more than a German quarter of an hour. It's a health resort and lies in a corner between east and south, where many of the nobility assemble in July and August, when no one who has time and money remains in London. If you write to me at the above address, I shall be sure to receive your letter as these gentlemen invariably know where I am. Meanwhile, I hope that you will have received 2 letters from me, namely, one dated – I believe – 28 or 29 May and the other 8 or 9 June. But I must now give you a small taste of the price of things in London. The lodgings that I have are too small for us and consist of 3 small rooms, one of which, like the second, is slightly larger, whereas the 3rd is not even as big as the closet in our rooms in Salzburg. For these we are paying 12 shillings a week. Now you know that 21 shillings is a guinea. If we had not known that we were in any case going to the country, we would have changed it straightaway: we must have rooms for at least 18 shillings or a guinea a week because only people of quality come to visit us and because a couple of harpsichords take up a lot of space and at present we can accommodate only one with difficulty; and because the location and size of the lodgings in such a populous city, where there is so much steam, smoke, dust and fog, contribute greatly to the preservation of one's health. For a one-manual harpsichord one pays ½ a guinea a month: with 2 manuals a guinea. The cheapest wine is from Florence at 2 shillings a *buttelia*: these are wicker bottles like the ones from Monte Pulciano: so that, if my wife and I both drink and if we pour some out for the children diluted with water, as water on its own is no good, one can easily get through a bottle a day. That makes 60 shillings a month just on wine. To begin with, we wanted to get used to beer, but both I and my wife soon noticed that it was very harmful to our health, and so we had to abandon it. Lunch, which is at 3 o'clock, costs 4 shillings. We thought we could manage on 3 shillings and tried 4 different caterers, but it wasn't possible. In the evening we can't get a plain soup for less than 8 pence and can't get a little potted veal for under a shilling. A chicken costs 2 shillings. I've already told you that *12 pence equals a shilling*. Not to mention sugar, tea, milk, bread etc., coal — wood isn't used — and candles and night lights: for instead of oil people burn homemade candles that have a wooden wick. Nor shall I speak of the powder, pomade etc. and the many other minor household expenses: still less shall I speak of clothes and the weekly *laundry bill* which, by the time you've added the silk stockings, is no small item. − − If you tot all this up − and I'm sure I've not included everything − you'll find that our expenses are astonishing. And to this you have to add the unavoidable expense of entertaining ourselves, for as soon as the weather is fine, you have to walk or drive out of the city and enjoy the fresh air if you want to remain healthy. You then see many 100s of people walking to and fro in St James's Park or in Green Park or in Hyde Park. If you want to go to Chelsea, Ranelagh, Mary-le-Bone or Vauxhall, that's another guinea; and no matter how thrifty you may be, you can always reckon on 3 guineas a month for such expenses. I'm not including the cabs and *carosses de remise* as I need them less frequently than in Paris, first, because the pavements are good, while the roads are wretched, so that people would rather walk than run the risk of breaking a couple of ribs; and, secondly, I'm living in a part of Westminster; in other words, I'm close to the aristocracy. But we often have to take a coach. A cab costs a shilling or even 15 or 18 pence for a single short journey. A *carosse de remise* or hired coach for just half a day comes to 15 or 16 shillings, including the tip. My dearest Frau Hagenauer, what do you think a servant girl earns in a year in a tavern, a merchant's house or any other house where there's a lot to do? − − *10 guineas, even 12 guineas*. NB: without the tips that are very much in vogue here. The usual wages in an ordinary household are 5 or 6 guineas; a household servant or lackey etc. never earns less than a guinea a week, including his clothing and tips. But he has to provide his own board. All journeymen have to provide their own board and lodging and report for duty on time in the morning. A wigmaker's apprentice, for example, is normally paid 2 shillings a day and has to be at work at 6 o'clock. There are even some who earn 3 shillings. Most good workers get a guinea a week. A goldsmith doesn't start work until 9 and goes home at 6 etc. You'll be able to tell from these few facts what London is like. − − Now let

me say something *about Ranelagh and Vauxhall*.[1] – – These are 2
pleasure gardens unlike anything else in the world: it would be
impossible to describe them adequately. But in due course I shall –
God willing – show you some copper engravings not only of these
places but of many other things both in Paris and London. You can
then have a fuller explanation of them. I've left a number of copper
engravings in Paris that are worth 2 louis d'or. I only regret that
I can't tell you about it all now, but it's simply not possible, for I
haven't come to England for a few thousand florins. If Almighty God
keeps us in good health and doesn't withdraw His divine blessing,
which He has so graciously granted us, I hope to be able to send a
few 100 guineas from here to Salzburg. And it will be no bad thing
if there's someone at the Salzburg court who can speak English: you
never know when it may be useful. Ranelagh Gardens isn't big, but it's
attractive and is illuminated every Monday, Wednesday and Friday.
Within it is an amazingly large rotunda that you enter at ground level
and that's lit by an incredible number of large chandeliers, lamps and
wall-lights. The orchestra is arranged in tiers on one side, with an
organ at the top. The music lasts 3 hours, from 7 till 10: then quartets
are played on hunting horn, clarinets and bassoon for an hour or
more, in other words, until 11 or 12 o'clock. In the middle is a large
stove where a fire is lit if it's cold, as these gardens are open in March
or April; and most of the entertainments take place in this hall.
Around the stove are lots of tables, and along the walls of the whole
hall are nothing but niches or a kind of alcove or small chapel, in
each of which is a table and from them you go up a flight of steps to
a similar number of boxes, just as in a playhouse, with a similar
number of tables. On each table there is everything necessary for a
drink of coffee or tea. On entering the gardens you pay 2½ shillings.
For this, you get coffee, tea, bread and butter – as much as you can
eat and drink. Here there is room to walk in addition to the space in

1. Vauxhall Gardens, on the south bank of the River Thames, became a fashionable
resort for the court of Charles II in the seventeenth century and was remodelled as
a pleasure garden by Jonathan Tyers in 1732. Ranelagh Gardens, on the north bank
in Chelsea, was founded as a rival attraction in 1741 and for a time outdid Vauxhall
in popularity.

the middle, with 2 to 3 or even 4500 people walking round and round and constantly meeting each other. Partly in order to make it easier on the feet and partly to reduce the noise of walking, the floor is entirely covered in a finely woven mat or carpet of straw. There is space for at least 6000 people in the gardens and hall. The hall itself holds 3000 people comfortably. Each servant or attendant has a badge on his breast with the numbers of the box or chapel that he has to serve. Here all men are equal, and no lord will allow anyone to stand before him bare headed: in return for their money, all are equal. *Vauxhall* is every day. Ranelagh will soon stop because as soon as it gets very hot everyone hurries off to Vauxhall. On Friday 29 June – the Feast of St Peter and St Paul – there will be a concert or benefit at Ranelagh for a newly established *Hospital de femmes en couche*,[2] as a result everyone must pay 5 shillings to get in. I have arranged for Wolfgang to play a concerto on the organ and in that way to perform the action of an English patriot who, as far as he can, seeks to further the usefulness of this hospital, which has been built *pro bono publico*.[3] This, you see, is a way of winning the love of this quite exceptional nation.

Vauxhall amazed me and is impossible to describe. I imagined the Elysian Fields. Just picture to yourself an uncommonly large garden with all manner of tree-lined avenues, all of which are lit as in broad daylight by many 1000s of lamps, all enclosed within the most beautiful glass. In the middle is a kind of tall, open summerhouse, in which can be heard an organ and a full orchestra, with trumpets and timpani and all the other instruments. On every side and in every corner there are tables laid for supper, then certain – NB – regularly designed structures like theatre boxes with tables; a large hall that is very beautiful, with an organ and choir; the lighting at the end of the avenues enchantingly arranged like pyramids and arches, so that I did not know which way to look next. Just imagine how astonished my wife was. Of our many good friends, we both wished that Frau von Robinig and Frau Hagenauer could have been with us, something

2. Lying-in hospital.
3. 'for the public good'.

we wish on frequent occasions. Here I must speak of a completely different matter and tell you of lace, ribbons, taffeta, cloaks, neckties, bonnets, tippets, pearls, all manner of jewellery and especially perse,[4] which we see every day worn by English women and in the shops. More on this on another occasion, suffice it for now to say that the ribbons, taffeta and perse surpass their French equivalents and are not even imported to our parts of Germany: it's called East Indian perse. But to return to Vauxhall. Here people pay only *one shilling*: and for this shilling you have the pleasure of seeing many 1000s of people and the most beautifully lit gardens and of hearing beautiful music. When I was there, more than 6000 people were there. *1 shilling* isn't much, but although you know very well that you can get in for a shilling, you don't know how much you'll get out with. Though you may be firmly resolved not to spend any money, you could hardly be more wrong. You wander around; you grow tired; you sit down; finally you order a bottle of wine, perhaps a few biscuits to go with it, that already costs you 4 or 5 shillings, finally you see a couple of chickens carried past, you call them over; they arrive; and so you see your guineas coaxed from your pocket. To anyone who cannot imagine what the light from several 1000 lights is like, I can only say that *in a single glass that represents one light*, there are always 2 lamps, and that in many of them there are 3 or 4 lamps. This is something that you couldn't find anywhere else in the world but here because neither *private individuals alone* nor *the aristocracy alone* are in a position to *incur such expenses on a daily basis*, whereas nowhere are the aristocracy and the common man as united as they are here; as a result, such a costly enterprise can be sustained only in England. My fingers are now tired. I send my regards to the whole of Salzburg: I commend my wife to you, together with Nannerl and Wolfgang, who often thinks of Salzburg. I am your old friend

Is poor Herr Zugseisen[5] no better?

4. *Broderie perse*, or Persian embroidery, an appliqué technique popular in the eighteenth century.
5. Joseph Zugseisen (*c.* 1728–92) was a tenor in the Salzburg court music establishment.

PS: On the 18th – it was noon, i.e., 2 in the afternoon – there was an amazing thunderstorm that, among other things, struck a church tower in the part of the city not far from the Thames, toppling a whole block of stone. It was like the one that stuck the tower and church at Mülln that time.

It also passed along the clock wire. 2 milords told me recently that in China a wire runs down into the earth from each house and that the effect is always that the thunder attaches itself to the wire and travels down into the earth without damaging the houses.[6]

The Mozarts remained in London for fifteen months altogether. The summer of 1764 was spent partly in Chelsea, where Leopold recovered from a serious illness, the family was at court again on 25 October, and toward the end of the year Leopold had Wolfgang's sonatas K10–15 published with a dedication to Queen Charlotte. The children gave public concerts on 21 February 1765 at the Haymarket Theatre and on 13 May 1765 at Hickford's Great Room in Brewer Street. By July the family had moved to the downmarket Swan and Harp Tavern in Cornhill, where the children were available for daily performances between 12 and 3 o'clock. In addition to the sonatas, Wolfgang also composed his first symphonies (K16, 19, and possibly 19a) and the motet God is our Refuge *K20 while in London. The family departed for the Netherlands on 24 July 1765, despite Leopold's earlier resolution not to go there. Their journey took them to Dover, Calais, Dunkirk, Lille, Ghent, Antwerp and Rotterdam before arriving in The Hague on 10 September.*

6. It is odd, perhaps, that Leopold's English acquaintances described the lightning rod as a Chinese invention. Benjamin Franklin had first experimented with lightning rods in 1752 and his discoveries were hotly debated in England during his time there – particularly among theologians. The first church lightning rod erected in London was at St Bride's in 1762, some two years before the Mozart family's arrival; a lightning rod was installed at St Paul's in 1768.

11. Leopold Mozart to Lorenz Hagenauer, 19 September 1765, The Hague

Monsieur!

You are now receiving a letter from the Haag; but not the Haag near Munich, nor the Haag near Lambach in Austria. No! From Den Haag in Holland. You're bound to find this very surprising, not least because you may have hoped, even if you did not believe it, that we were not so far away but already closer. We would in fact have been, if not near you, at least already out of Holland if we had not been held back for 4 weeks by an indisposition that affected first my Wolfgang, then me myself in Lille. But first you must hear all about the chance occurrence that brought us to Holland, as I had never intended to go to Holland, but, rather, to Milan and back home again via Venice. The Dutch envoy in London repeatedly urged us to visit the Prince of Orange[1] in The Hague. But I let this go in at one ear and out at the other. We prepared for our departure, and so little did I think of going to Holland that I sent *all our furs* and other things in a trunk to Paris. In the event we actually left London on 24 July and spent a day in Canterbury, before staying until the end of the month on the estates of an English gentleman[2] in order to see the horse racing. On the very day of our departure the Dutch envoy drove to our lodgings and discovered that we had gone to Canterbury for the races, after which we would be leaving England. He was with us in a trice and begged me to go to The Hague, saying that the Princess of Weilburg[3] – the sister of the Prince of Orange – was extraordinarily anxious to see this child, about whom she had heard and read so much. In a word, he and everyone else had so much to say on the subject, and the proposal was so attractive that I had to decide to

1. Prince Willem V of Orange (1748–1806) succeeded in 1751. He obtained his majority in March 1766 (see next letter).
2. Horace Mann (1744–1814), nephew of Sir Horace Mann (1701–86), British minister at Florence, whom Mozart would later meet during his stay in Florence in 1770.
3. Princess Caroline of Nassau-Weilburg (1743–87).

come, not least because, as you know, one shouldn't refuse a pregnant woman.

NB: It wasn't the envoy who was pregnant but the princess. And so I left England on 1 August and we sailed from Dover at 10 in the morning, we had the most beautiful weather and such a good wind that in 3½ hours we had landed in the port of Calais and partook of our midday meal with a healthy stomach, not having been at all ill during the crossing. Our plan was now to spend the month of August in Holland, to arrive in Paris towards the end of September and then gradually move on until we were finally in sight of the Untersberg. In Calais we made the acquaintance of the Duchesse de Montmorency and the Prince de Croy;[4] and from there I went to Dunkirk, which I wanted to see on account of the port and the endless bickering between England and France over the demolition of the fortifications. The place is very beautiful, the streets mostly wide and the majority of the houses neat and tidy. An attractive Exchange Building, much commerce and, unfortunately, the finest fortifications already torn down. I say 'unfortunately' as it pains me to see such fine fortifications, which cost so much, demolished. In spite of this, the English were still not satisfied and there were constant complaints in England that the fortifications hadn't all been demolished as had been stipulated in the terms of the treaty.[5] As a result a commission was set up under the terms of which the Duc de Choiseul and the Duke of Bedford[6] were to meet and examine the case. We drove to Lille, where we had been persuaded to go by the commandant in Dunkirk, the Chevalier de Mezières. Here too we found a beautiful, well-built town, with a large population and a fair amount of commerce, and we also saw 5 regiments at firing practice and performing the most wonderful

---

4. Louise-Françoise-Pauline, Duchesse de Montmorency-Luxembourg (1734–?); Emanuel, Prince de Croy, Meurs et Solre (1718–84), commander in Picardy, Calais and Boulogne.

5. The recently signed Treaty of Paris between Britain, France and Spain had ended the Seven Years' War (1756–63).

6. The statesmen leading the peace negotiations: Étienne-François, Duc de Choiseul (1719–85) for the French; John Russell, 4th Duke of Bedford (1710–71) for the British.

military exercises on the occasion of a visit by the Duc de Choiseul. In particular I noticed that the French are now better drilled than they used to be: only with 2 German regiments, the Swiss and the Nassau regiments, can they not stand comparison. I should add that the daily parade was one of the finest I've ever seen. Now we have further proof that our human plans count for nothing. In Lille, Wolfgang succumbed to a very bad cold, and when it had got somewhat better after a couple of weeks, it was my turn; I was overcome by dizziness of a most peculiar kind. If I remained in bed, all was well, but as soon as I got up, everything started to swim and I couldn't take 3 steps on my own across the room; it was so bad that if I tried to force myself to remain standing, I was sick. As I didn't know if it originated in my head or my stomach, I took a laxative, then tried a footbath and, in a word, defended myself against 2 enemies at once: but this alone delayed us by 4 weeks, and I left Lille more dead than alive and was not much better when we arrived in Ghent, where we stayed only a day. Ghent is a large but sparsely populated town. In the afternoon Wolfg. played on the big new organ at the Bernardines[7] etc. We remained in Antwerp for 2 days on account of Sunday. Wolfgang played on the big organ in the cathedral. NB: There are some really good organs in Flanders and Brabant. But a great deal could be said about the paintings, which are quite exquisite. Antwerp is the place for these. We went to all the churches. I've never seen more black and white marble and such a surfeit of outstanding paintings, especially Rubens,[8] as I did here and in Brussels. Above all, Rubens's 'Descent from the Cross' in the main church in Antwerp surpasses everything you could imagine: I left my carriage in Antwerp and took one from the postmaster to drive to Moerdijk. There we crossed a small arm of the sea, and on the other side were coaches ready to drive you to Rotterdam, where you get into a small boat and are taken almost as far as the inn. It was a good day's journey from Antwerp to Rotterdam, namely, from half past 6 in the morning to 8 in the evening. We spent only half a day in Rotterdam

7. Today the Sint-Pieterskerk in the Sint-Pietersplein.
8. Peter Paul Rubens (1577–1640), Flemish artist.

as we left in the afternoon on a Trek Schuyt[9] for The Hague and were already there by 7. I must admit that I should have been very sorry not to have seen Holland: for in all the towns in Europe that I've seen, nearly everything looks the same. But both the Dutch villages and the Dutch towns are completely different from all other towns in Europe. It would take too long to describe them, but suffice it to say that I like the fact that they're all so neat, a quality that strikes many of us as excessive, and I shall say only that I enjoyed seeing the statue of the famous Erasmus of Rotterdam[10] in the square. We've now been in The Hague for a week, and have twice been with the princess and once with the Prince of Orange, who had us collected and brought back home in his carriage: only my daughter was not with us; for it was now her turn to develop a very heavy chest cold that is only now beginning to loosen. As soon as she is better,[11] we have to return to the Prince of Orange and the Princess of Weilburg and the Duke of Wolfenbüttel:[12] – – the journey here has been paid for; – – but I'll have to see who will pay for the return journey. For I'd prefer not to touch my money in Amsterdam. – – You'll see from all this that your 2 letters from Monsieur Joseph[13] and yourself arrived in London only after we'd left. I received your third – undated – letter in Lille, where it was forwarded by Monsieur Carpentier. As you mentioned 2 other letters here, I immediately suspected that Monsieur Teissier[14] will have sent them to Amsterdam. As soon as I got to The Hague, I wrote to my banker in Amsterdam and the very next day received both letters, together with another one from

---

9. River barge.

10. Desiderius Erasmus (1466–1536), humanist. The statue is close to the *Leuvehaven*, not far from the Erasmus Bridge in the north of the city.

11. Nannerl's condition worsened and she was given extreme unction on 21 October; she had recovered by 15 November, at which time Wolfgang was taken seriously ill with intestinal typhoid.

12. Ludwig Ernst, Duke of Brunswick-Wolfenbüttel (1718–88), brother of the Prince of Brunswick.

13. Ignaz Joseph Hagenauer (1743–80), son of Lorenz Hagenauer, employed in his father's business.

14. Pierre Bernard Carpentier (1726–1800), royal procurator; Stephen Teissier was a partner in the banking house Loubier & Teissier.

Monsieur Teissier. What was communicated to me in a newspaper is true. I am grateful to Herr Joseph for his kind letter and look forward to his safe return.

A 1000 compliments to all our good friends. – – That my letter reached you after having been opened and resealed surprises me greatly. I posted it in London myself: this never happened in London. – – The most important thing I have to tell you is that I've arranged for Monsieur Teissier to send you via Hamburg a very large *chest or strongbox*. Signed: LM. I don't know when it will arrive, assuming it hasn't already done so. Monsieur Teissier informs me that it left for Hamburg on board the *Wilhelmus* under Captain Adrian Janssen. I'd have preferred it if he'd written to tell me who he's sent it to in Hamburg. There are all manner of things inside it. Leave it unopened until we arrive, and see that it's not left somewhere that's too damp, although the polished steel items that it contains are well wrapped. – – I also need you to buy me a good *stationery box*: I mean one like yours, with good large drawers. In short, a beautiful and good box: even if it's expensive; where else shall I put all my rubbish? – – Could I ask that on receipt of this letter you address your reply to me in *Amsterdam* and add: *Chez Messrs Jean Néel et Fils à Amsterdam*. If I've already left, he'll forward the letter. The word Neel was elided above, which is why I'm repeating it. My best wishes to you and the whole of Salzburg, I am your old friend.

PS: My wife asks you to have 6 Masses said, namely, 3 at St John of Nepomuk in the parish church, 1 at Maria Plain, 1 at Loreto at the Holy Child, and 1 in honour of St Walburgis, which is where you should have it said.

We heard of the emperor's death in Lille on 26 August.[15] Before we left London, I read in the paper that General Plaz[16] had died. But I can't find anything about this in Herr Johannes's[17] list.

In his 2nd chapter, my news reporter Herr Johannes goes on to

15. Francis I.
16. Joseph Anton, Count Plaz (1677–1767), imperial master of the ordnance.
17. Johann Nepomuk Hagenauer (1741–99) was the eldest son of Lorenz Hagenauer.

say that Herr Franz Gschwendtner,[18] Herr Joseph Hagenauer etc. have arrived from Italy. But he says nothing about Madame Fesemayr. Is she still in Venice? – – – *tanto meglio!* – –

Please give our best wishes to Court Councillor Gilowsky[19] and congratulate him for us. It will be a source of infinite pleasure to see him again.

It's very good that we're not yet close to Salzburg as there are so many thieves in the country, make sure it's safe otherwise we'll stay out of the country even longer. – And how's the Neutor[20] coming along? – – I've always assumed that we'd enter by the Neutor.

But why didn't Herr Estlinger[21] wait till we were back so that we could dance at his wedding? – – Congratulations to him. Old love never dies! It's said that he still reveres an old bass fiddle, even though he has a newer one. Oh, how often he's patched it up! – – If my old faithful carriage gets me safely home again, it will have done its duty. It certainly sets me thinking when I think of our journey. *Ma foi*, it's been quite a jaunt.

The Mozarts spent about eight months in the Netherlands: the children gave public concerts at The Hague (22 January 1766), Amsterdam (29 January, 26 February and 16 April 1766) and Utrecht (21 April 1766); additionally, Wolfgang composed two sets of keyboard variations (K24 and K25), six sonatas for keyboard and violin (K26–31) and the Galimathias musicum K32, which was performed as part of the festivities surrounding the installation of Willem V, Prince of Orange, in March. On 8 May 1766 the family arrived in Brussels; from there they travelled to Paris – where they arrived on 10 May – by way of Valenciennes and Cambrai.

18. Joseph Franz Xaver Gschwendtner (1740–1800), was the son of Salzburg iron merchant Johann Markus Gschwendtner (1709–75). He and his brother Vital (1751–1818) frequently travelled abroad on business and were part of the network of Salzburg contacts that Leopold Mozart made use of on his travels.
19. Johann Joseph Anton Ernst Gilowsky von Urazowa, see List.
20. The Neutor (New Gate), a tunnel through the Mönchsberg connecting Salzburg with its northern suburbs, opened on 26 June 1767.
21. Joseph Richard Estlinger (c. 1720–91) was court bassoonist and music copyist.

12. Leopold Mozart to Lorenz Hagenauer, 16 May 1766, Paris

Monsieur!

You'll undoubtedly be exceedingly surprised not to have received a letter from me for so long. I wouldn't have left you without news of our circumstances if I'd not been assured that you'd received news of us on at least two occasions from Herr Kulman of Amsterdam. The only reason why I didn't send you and my friends as detailed a description of Holland as I did of France and England was because my children have been ill. We returned to The Hague from Amsterdam for the celebrations held by the Prince of Orange – they began on 11 March and went on for some time – when our little composer was asked to write 6 keyboard sonatas with violin accompaniment for the prince's sister, namely, the Princess of Nassau-Weilburg, which were engraved straightaway.[1] He also had to write something for the prince's concert[2] and compose arias for the princess etc. All of which will be produced on our arrival. I asked Herr Kulman to send you a small chest in Salzburg. As soon as it arrives, please open it and look for the small wide parcel with the word 'Musica' on it that's not sealed. In it you'll find two copies of the sonatas engraved in The Hague; take one of these copies, together with the violin part that goes with it, and have both the keyboard part and the violin part bound separately, and then present them most humbly to His Grace in our name. In the same parcel there are also two sets of variations that Wolfgang had to write on an aria that was composed for the prince's coming of age and installation; and one that he dashed off hurriedly on another melody that everyone in Holland is singing, playing and whistling.[3] – – These are trifles! If you want to add a copy of each, you may do so as they are unusual. I shall

1. The sonatas K26–31 were dedicated to Princess Caroline of Nassau-Weilburg and published in March.
2. Probably the *Gallimathias musicum* K32.
3. K24, based on the Dutch song 'Laat ons Juichen, Batavieren!' by Christian Ernst Graf (1723–1804); K25, based on the popular Dutch song 'Willem van Nassau'.

have the honour of showing you my violin tutor in Dutch.[4] This has been translated by the Dutch in the same format, with a dedication to the prince, and was presented to him in my presence at the festivities accompanying his installation. The edition is uncommonly fine, even finer than my own. The publisher – *the printer in Haarlem* – came to me with respectful mien and handed me the book in the company of the organist,[5] who invited our Wolfgang to play on the famous large organ in Haarlem, which he did the next morning from 10 to 11.

It's an extremely fine instrument with 68 stops. NB: everything's tin, as wood doesn't last long in this damp country.

It would take too long to describe our journey from Holland through Amsterdam, Utrecht, Rotterdam, across the Maas, and then across an arm of the sea at Moerdijk to Antwerp. Still more impossible would it be to describe the present sorry state of the once very great trading centre of Antwerp and list the reasons for its decline; we shall speak of this anon. We travelled via Mechlin, where we visited our old acquaintance, the local archbishop,[6] to Brussels, where we rested for only a day, leaving by the mail coach at 9 in the morning and arriving in Valenciennes at half past 7 in the evening. In Brussels we bought some lace for our requisites and in Valenciennes some batiste or cambric linen for our own personal use, namely, one bolt of plain and one of a floral pattern. In Valenciennes I saw the intricate clock in the town hall and in Cambrai the tomb and marble bust of the great Fénélon,[7] who achieved immortality with his Télémaque, his book on the education of young girls, his dialogues of the dead, his fables and other sacred and secular writings. Then, without any further stops, we travelled on to Paris, where we moved into the

4. Leopold Mozart's *Versuch einer gründlichen Violinschule* (1756) was the most important violin tutor of the eighteenth century; a Dutch translation was published in 1766.

5. Henrikus Radeker (1708–74).

6. Johann Heinrich, Count Frankenberg und Schellendorf (1726–1804); the Mozarts had previously visited him on 4 November 1763.

7. François de Salignac de la Mothe-Fénélon (1651–1715), French writer who was bishop of Cambrai from 1695; *Les Aventures de Télémaque* was published in 1699.

rooms reserved for us by our friend Monsieur Grimm. I'll tell you when I see you how we are lodged and what it costs. – – –

Could I ask you to reply to this letter as soon as you receive it so that I get your letter before I leave? You may care to add only: *À Monsieur Mozart, chez Monsieur Grimm Secrétaire des commandemens de Msgr le Duc d'Orléans Rue neuve Luxembourg. À Paris.*

Thank God we found our luggage here in good condition; and since we have to dress in black again, one can see how much my children have grown. We are all well, for which we are infinitely grateful to God, and we commend ourselves with all our hearts to you, your wife and all your family and good friends. I doubt if anyone in Salzburg will recognize Wolfgangerl any longer; we've been away a long time, and since then he has seen and got to know many 1000s of people. I'll be sending a large trunk from here, then a somewhat smaller one and, I think, another small chest. On top of all my other preoccupations, it's a real torment having to organize these matters; no one can appreciate this if they've not experienced it for themselves. In addition to all this, we've still got our large trunk with us, as well as a smaller one, also a large valise and 2 seat-chests, together with the boot, which is full of luggage. We arrived here a day after Monsieur de Lally, the former viceroy of Pondicherry, was beheaded; I expect you'll already have read about it in the newspapers.[8] My dearest Herr Hagenauer! in Amsterdam we met someone from Salzburg who because of certain circumstances has become a Calvinist. There was nothing I wanted more than to lead him back to the right path. I did all I could. It was this that persuaded me to return to Amsterdam and kept me longer in Holland than I'd intended. And perhaps I'd have achieved my objective if a single thing had not stood in my way. Don't waste time thinking who it may be; you can't possibly guess, even though you once knew him and still know all his relations. It's too long ago! I shan't say who it is as long as a glimmer of hope remains. Good God! in what a state of confusion he

8. Thomas-Arthur, Comte de Lally, Baron de Tollendal (1702–66) was governor general of Pondicherry (French India) from 1757; after it was taken by the British in 1761, he was imprisoned in the Bastille and eventually beheaded.

left us! The most bitter tears prevented him from speaking. How many troubled and thoughtful hours this man has caused me! This is the result of persuading young people to choose a profession that is against their calling. Sad consequences! – – So many examples that I have experienced for myself in the course of my travels have confirmed me in my firm conviction that it is very wrong, and tantamount to selling souls, to force young people to take a vow before they are 25. If the supreme head of the church and all the prelates of the church – I don't know about the prelates in the monasteries – were to travel through England, Holland and Switzerland and were properly informed about all this, they wouldn't hesitate for a moment but would postpone the taking of monastic vows until the 25th year of life. England, and especially Holland, is teeming with these unhappy individuals, I can give you a whole list of them: and you mustn't think that they're all lascivious youths. Oh, I know many who are single, who have not even changed their religion and who lead thoroughly edifying lives. It's impossible to write about things as they are. I'll have to leave it until we can talk about it in person: my heart bleeds whenever I think about such things. Why not delay it until their 25th year? Perhaps because many a wealthy candidate or worthy individual might in the meantime question his calling and realize – the one with his money, the other with his clever mind – that he might better pursue his calling by serving not a dead body but a living, universal state. Don't take my zealousness amiss: I love my fellow humans and value their peace of mind: but my heart is oppressed whenever I see someone wretched and tormented all his life, with only a miserable eternity to look forward to. Let's change the subject.

Has Herr Otto[9] in Frankfurt not paid anything through Herr Wallner? I must now try gradually to recover all that I'm owed from Frankfurt, Nuremberg, Augsburg, London, Paris etc., so that I can sort everything out. By the way, has Godfather P.[10] not yet handed over the half-dozen silver knives, spoons and forks? No? No! Well,

9. Possibly David Otto, organist at the Barfüsserkirche in Frankfurt.
10. Mozart's godfather, Johann Gottlieb Pergmayr (1709–87), a businessman and city councillor in Salzburg.

I expect he's preparing to present them to us on our return: he cannot help but be deeply moved to have held up for their holy baptism two children who have caused such a stir in the world. I've bought various things for our own use, but in the case of the above, I've relied on our godfather's promise. Give him our good wishes! You're surprised, aren't you, at this request of mine, which is so completely out of character? But, remember, I'm coming straight from Holland! People take something with them from every country: and in Holland you learn to be selfish. Now I expect you'd like to know when we plan to arrive in Salzburg. Had it been left to us, we'd have been home long ago; and now that we're in Paris, it seems to us that, judging by the distance we've covered so far, we're already halfway home. That we're staying here for a short time is correct; and that's why I'd be grateful if you could write to me soon, so that the letter arrives while I'm still here. But if, at all events, I've already left, our friend Monsieur Grimm will send on the letter. But you'll understand that we're not about to mount our horses and drive straight back to Salzburg. It would be too much of a strain on my children and my purse. There are many people who will still contribute to our journey, even though they do not yet know it. Enough! We'll do all in our power to return home soon. In the meantime please commend us to His Grace etc. etc. Give our good wishes to our friends, and rest assured that we await with impatience the moment when I may say to you in person that I remain yours etc.

Let me say in haste that Herr Kulman is a man of means; the rest when we see each other.

Let's see how things will turn out for us in Salzburg.

I'll let you know more once we get closer.

At the beginning of July 1766, the family left Paris for Dijon, at the invitation of Louis-Joseph de Bourbon, Prince de Condé; from there they travelled to Lyons, and then to Switzerland, stopping in Geneva and Lausanne, where Mozart composed the flute solos K33a, now lost, for Ludwig Eugen of Württemberg. They continued to Donaueschingen, the seat of the princes of Fürstenberg, finally arriving at Munich on 8 November.

13. Leopold Mozart to Lorenz Hagenauer, 10 November 1766, Munich

Monsieur!

As far as I recall, my last letter was from Lyons, which we left after a 4-week stay in order to go to Geneva. There we found the civil war[1] still raging, though this did not prevent us from staying 3 weeks there, and after seeing some of the sights and making the acquaintance of persons famed for their skill and special talents, we continued our journey to Berne. You perhaps know that just outside Geneva the famous Monsieur Voltaire has his castle, where he lives and which is called Ferney.[2] If you want to go to Berne, you have to travel through Lausanne; and although we had intended to stay there only until after lunch, the servants of Prince Ludwig of Württemberg,[3] Madame d'Aubonne, Madame d'Hermenches and Monsieur de Sévery etc. came up just as we were alighting from our carriage, and I could not but allow these distinguished people to talk me into staying 5 days in Lausanne. I must wait until I see you in person to tell you the sort of man that His Serene Highness Prince Ludwig is. It will be enough to say that Württemberg could think itself fortunate to have this worthy man as its regent. He was still with us when we got back into the carriage and, even after we'd already taken our seats and I was shaking his hand, I had to promise that I'd write to him often and let him know how we are faring. – – I am saying nothing here about most of our journey. – – I know how differently people judge things, depending on the differences in their often feeble understanding. From Lausanne we went to Berne and thence to Zurich. In the former place we stayed only 8 days, in the latter 14. In both places we had a chance to meet men of learning: in the latter place the two Gessners,

1. Here Leopold refers to a local dispute between Geneva's patricians and towns-people that had gone to mediation during the Mozarts' visit there.
2. The French philosopher Voltaire (pseudonym of François-Marie Arouet, 1694–1778) had settled at Ferney, near to Geneva, in 1758.
3. Ludwig Eugen (1731–95) was the younger brother of Karl II Eugen, reigning duke of Württemberg (1728–93).

both men of learning, made our stay most agreeable and were very sad when we left.[4] We took away with us tokens of their friendship. From there we drove via Winterthur to Schaffhausen, where our 4-day stay was again very pleasant, and when we arrived in Donaueschingen, Herr Meissner came into our carriage to welcome us and helped us and our luggage out! He stayed with us in Donaueschingen for a further 4 days. I was the first person to tell him about his wife's indisposition. I was as astonished at his ignorance as he was by my account. But within days he had received a letter from his wife. I gave him a letter of recommendation to my friends in Switzerland and hope that things will work out for him, especially in Berne. His Serene Highness[5] welcomed us with extraordinary kindness; we didn't have to announce our arrival but were already eagerly awaited, as Herr Meissner can testify, and the director of music, Councillor Martelli, came at once to pay his respects and invite us to call on him. In short, we were there for 12 days. On 9 of them there was music from 5 in the evening till 9; on each occasion we did something special. If the season had not been so advanced, we would still be there. The prince gave me 24 louis d'or and to each of my children a diamond ring; he was in tears when we took our leave, and in fact we all wept on saying goodbye; he asked me to write to him often, and, indeed, our stay was as agreeable as our departure was sad. We then travelled at breakneck speed via Messkirch to Ulm, Günzburg and Dillingen, where we stayed only 2 days, picked up 2 rings from the prince[6] and, after spending a day in Augsburg, arrived in Munich. *Herr Provino will be sending you a small packet or safebox for me.* Haha, you'll say. You're now in Munich. That's good. I promised not to come until I could drive in through the Neutor; but I now hear that no one is yet being allowed to enter by the Siegmund Gate: that would be most unwelcome news. I await your reply, we're staying *at Stürzer's* and I foresee that we shan't get away from here for some time. We arrived the evening before last; yesterday

4. Johannes Gessner (1709–90), physicist; Salomon Gessner (1730–88), poet.
5. Prince Joseph Wenzeslaus of Fürstenberg (1728–83).
6. The prince-bishop of Augsburg.

58

– Sunday – we visited His Highness the Elector at table and were most graciously received. Even while we were still at table, Wolfgangl had to compose a piece while standing beside the elector, who sang the beginning or, rather, a few bars of the theme, and he then had to play it for His Highness after dinner in the music room.[7] You can easily guess how astonished everyone was to see and hear this. During the night, however, I noticed that he was not at all well. He had a very disturbed night. And so I've had to keep him in bed today and may have to keep him at home for a few days. But I hope it will soon be over, as indeed it shows every sign of doing. With this weather, it's no wonder that so delicate a frame should have to suffer a little, especially as we've had to get used to having the room heated by a stove: it's just a nuisance that it has held us up. Every good wish to your wife, your whole family, our good friends. I am your old friend.

[*Enclosed with letter*]
Something just for you!
Could we ask you or, rather, your wife, to see to a good housemaid? Moreover, it's now the time of year when the stove needs stoking with wood. Both are indispensable, a necessary evil. Could I ask you to see to this? Or perhaps you've already done so? – As far as room for a servant is concerned, I think it more important to think of room for ourselves. And I've made up my mind to continue what little is left of our journey – albeit not without difficulty – without a servant, as I got rid of him a short time ago. I'm concerned about the necessary arrangements for our rooms, something that you yourself will understand to some extent and that you will see for yourself on our – may God grant it so! – safe arrival. God – who has been far too good to the wretched sinner that I am – has given my children such talent that, irrespective of all thought of my obligation as a father, this alone would spur me on to sacrifice everything to their decent education. Every moment I lose is lost for ever. And if I ever knew how valuable time is for young people, I know it now. You know that my children

7. This work is apparently lost.

are used to work: if – on the excuse that one thing prevents another – they were to get used to hours of idleness, my entire edifice would collapse; custom is an iron shirt. And you yourself know how much my children, especially Wolfgangerl, have to learn. – – – But who knows what's being planned for us on our return to Salzburg? Perhaps we'll be received in such a way that we'll be only too pleased to shoulder our bundles and go on our way. But, God willing, I shall at least be bringing my children back to their fatherland; if they are not wanted, it won't be my fault: but people won't get them for nothing. – – Enough, I rely entirely on your rational understanding and true friendship; conversation in person will give us more pleasure. Farewell.

NB: If your wife finds a good maid, a few florins more or less don't matter for her wages. She has complete control.

The Mozarts arrived back in Salzburg on 29 November 1766. In less than eight months Wolfgang composed the first part of the oratorio Die Schuldigkeit des ersten Gebots *K35 and a passion cantata, the* Grabmusik *K42. His Latin school drama* Apollo et Hyacinthus *K38 was given on 13 May 1767. On 11 September he left with his sister and parents for Vienna, ostensibly to help celebrate the wedding of Archduchess Josepha to Ferdinand IV of Naples; Leopold may also have hoped for an appointment at court, or at least some significant commissions. His plans were waylaid by a smallpox epidemic.*

14. Leopold Mozart to Lorenz Hagenauer, 10 November 1767, Olmütz

> *Te Deum Laudamus!*
> Wolfgangerl has recovered from smallpox!
> And where? – – – in Olmütz!

And where? – – – At the residence
of His Excellency Count Podstatsky.[1]

You'll have gathered from my previous letters[2] that everything
turned out a mess in Vienna. I must now add a few details that
concern us alone and from which you'll see how divine providence
holds everything together, so that, if we trust in it completely, we
cannot fail to accomplish our destiny. You already know how badly
things went at the Viennese court at the very time that they could
have turned out best for us.[3]

At that very time we were affected by a different occurrence that
caused us no little anxiety. The elder son of the goldsmith with whom
we were staying went down with smallpox immediately after we
arrived, but we discovered this only after he had almost got over it
and the 2 younger children had caught it, too. I tried in vain to find
alternative lodgings for us all. I was obliged to leave my wife and
daughter there and to flee with Wolfgang to my good friend, where
we remained. Our servant remained with my wife: we were as far
from each other as it is *from the Hospital to St Cajetan's*.[4] Throughout
Vienna people were talking about nothing but smallpox. Of 10 children on the death register, 9 had died of smallpox. You can easily
imagine how I felt; whole nights were spent without sleep, and during
the day there was no rest either. I was resolved to leave for Moravia
immediately after the young princess's death and not return until the
initial period of mourning was over; but it was impossible to get away
as His Majesty the Emperor[5] spoke of us so often that we could never
be certain when it might occur to him to send for us; but as soon as

1. Count Leopold Anton Podstatsky (1717–76), formerly president of the consistory
in Salzburg; Leopold begins his letter with the first sentence of the *Te Deum*: 'We
praise thee, O God'.
2. These are lost.
3. Archduchess Josepha (1751–67), fifth daughter of Francis I and Maria Theresa,
had died of smallpox on 15 October, shortly before her marriage was due to take
place to Ferdinand IV of Naples (1751–1825), which threw the Vienna court into
mourning.
4. The distance between these two Salzburg landmarks is about 1 km.
5. Joseph II had succeeded his father in 1765 (see letter 11).

the Archduchess Elisabeth fell ill,[6] I refused to be detained any longer and could scarcely wait for the moment when I got my Wolfgang out of Vienna, which was completely infected with smallpox, and provided him with a change of air.

We were planning to leave on the morning of 23 October, but as it is the delightful custom in Vienna that the post horses generally arrive half a day late, it wasn't until the afternoon that we got away. We were in Brünn by the Saturday. Together with Wolfgang I called on His Excellency Count Schrattenbach and Countess Herberstein.[7] They spoke of a concert that would allow them to hear my children, and, indeed, everything was arranged. But I had a certain inner feeling that I couldn't get out of my head and that persuaded me to continue my journey to Olmütz and delay the concert in Brünn until my return, so that on the Sunday evening I told His Excellency of my plans, which he felt were all the more sensible in that the members of the nobility who were still in the country would have returned to town by then. And so we quickly packed our things together and on Monday the 26th drove to Olmütz, where we arrived slightly later than planned because some work had to be done on our carriage over lunch at Wischkau and the blacksmith held us up for 3 hours. We had the annoyance of having to take a bad, damp room at the Black Eagle where we put up, as all the better ones were already taken. So we were obliged to have a fire lit and – another source of annoyance – the stove gave off so much smoke that we were almost blinded. At ten o'clock Wolfgang complained about his eyes; but I noticed that his head was warm, his cheeks hot and very red, whereas his hands were as cold as ice. His pulse wasn't right either, and so we gave him some black powder and put him to bed. He had a fairly restless night, and his dry fever continued throughout the next morning. We were then given 2 better rooms; we wrapped Wolfgang in furs and took him to the other rooms. His fever increased; we gave him some

6. Maria Elisabeth (1743–1808), third daughter of Francis I and Maria Theresa.
7. Franz Anton, Count Schrattenbach (1712–83) and Maria Augusta, Countess Herberstein, brother and niece of Archbishop Siegmund von Schrattenbach. Brünn is modern Brno; Olmütz is Olomouc.

margrave powder and black powder.[8] By the evening he had started to become delirious, and this continued all night and the morning of the 28th. After church I went to see His Excellency Count Podstatsky, who received me with great kindness; and when I told him that my little boy was ill and thought he might have smallpox, he told me that he would take us in as he was not at all afraid of smallpox. He sent at once for his housekeeper, told him to prepare 2 rooms, and immediately sent instructions for his doctor to call on us at the Black Eagle.

It was now only a question of whether it was still possible to move the boy. The doctor said yes, because there was still no rash and it was not yet certain that it was smallpox.

At 4 in the afternoon Wolfgang was wrapped up in leather sheets and furs and lifted into the carriage, and in this way I drove with him to the cathedral deanery. On the 29th we saw a few small red pocks, but we doubted whether it really was smallpox as he was no longer very ill; and he took nothing but a powder every 6 hours [. . .] and always scabious tea afterwards.

On the 30th and 31st – *his name day* – the smallpox came out completely [. . .].[9]

As soon as the smallpox came out, the fever went away and, thank God, he still felt well. He was very full, and, as he was amazingly swollen and had a thick nose, when he looked at himself in the mirror, he said: *I now look like little Mayr*, he meant the musician Mayr. Since yesterday the pustules have started to fall off; and the swelling went away 2 days ago.

You'll see now that my motto is true: *in te Domine speravi, non confundar in aeternum.*[10]

I leave it to you and the whole of Salzburg, too, to reflect on how strange it was that our fate drew us to Olmütz and how extraordinary it was that, of his own accord, His Excellency Count Podstatsky took us in with a child who was to develop smallpox. I need not tell you

8. Black powder is a cathartic; margrave powder is an antiperspirant.
9. The prescriptions for medicines given by Leopold have been omitted.
10. 'In thee, O Lord, have I put my trust: let me never be put to confusion.' (The last verse of the *Te Deum*.)

with what kindness, graciousness and liberality we were waited on in every way; I should just like to ask how many people there are who would receive into their homes an entire family with a child in such a condition and to do so, moreover, from no other urge than their love of their fellow human beings? - - This deed will do Count Podstatsky no little credit in the life story of our little boy that I shall have printed when the time comes;[11] to a certain extent it is here that a new era in his life begins.

I am sorry that I shall have to return to Salzburg later than I thought. Everyone will easily understand that at this time of the year I cannot set off again so soon and cannot undertake a long journey without further ado. I had barely heard that Herr Meissner was to go to Frankfurt when I resolved to be in Salzburg for the consecration[12] of our most gracious master, His Grace, but now there is no point as we cannot leave here so soon without endangering Wolfgang's health. In the meantime, please have *3 Masses* said for us at the Holy Child of Loreto and *3 Masses* at Maria Plain. Herr Thomas, who visited us nearly every day when the illness was at its height, will tell you all about it.

Wolfgang and the rest of us send our best wishes to Herr Alterdinger. It has taken some time for him to achieve anything: but I hope that His Grace will not leave as useful a man as Herr Alterdinger with the barren subsistence of a valet de chambre *et fruges consumere nati!*[13]

I've received the letter with the enclosure from Monsieur Grimm in Paris. You'll have seen from Monsieur Grimm's letter what he writes about the Russian court and the hereditary prince of Brunswick; also how and in what company Herr Schobert went to meet his maker.[14]

---

11. Leopold later repeated his unfulfilled intention to write a biography of Wolfgang in the second edition of the *Gründlichen Violinschule* (1769–70).

12. That is, the annual celebration, on 21 December, of the anniversary of Schrattenbach's consecration.

13. 'and born to consume the fruits of the earth' (Leopold omits the first phrase of this verse: 'we are mere ciphers'). Rochus Alterdinger (*c.* 1734–94) was an administrator at the archbishop's residence in Salzburg.

14. The composer Johann Schobert, his wife and child had died from eating poisonous mushrooms.

The two letters congratulating Herr Wolfgang have also arrived. Please continue to write to Herr Peisser.[15] Other people in Brünn and Olmütz have already written to me through him. Farewell. I and all of us send our best wishes to Salzburg, and I am your old friend.

Here is the reply to Herr Joseph that Wolfgang wrote in bed.[16]

I am still worried that my little girl might get smallpox, for who knows whether the few pocks that she had were the right ones?

[*On the envelope*]

The 6 symphonies[17] that Herr Estlinger has copied must be rolled up neatly and handed to the mail coach with the address: *À Son Altesse S: S:^{me} Le Prince de Fürstemberg etc: à Donaueschingen.* I'll write a letter to the prince from here. The concerto for two keyboards by Wagenseil should be added to the other printed sonatas[18] and sent to Herr Gessner in Zurich. You'll see how awry everything has gone and how, when we thought that everything had turned out badly, God filled us with His great mercy and allowed our dear Wolfg. to recover from his smallpox. Nothing matters to me except that this is now behind us. I received another 30 ducats from Herr Peisser before leaving Vienna, and before I leave Olmütz I shall no doubt have to take as much from his friend, to whom he has referred me. *Basta!* Who knows who the father gives the white horse to! – – What do you say to Count Podstatsky's behaviour towards us? – Does such a deed not deserve some sort of expression, if not of gratitude, at least of approval, from His Grace, *if not in person*, at least through his brother in Brünn or through Count Herberstein or at the very least by means of a letter from our Father Confessor or the court chancellor? Try and arrange this. I beg you.

15. Franz Xaver Peisser (1724–1807), banker and business associate of the Hagenauers.
16. Wolfgang's message to Joseph Hagenauer is lost.
17. These works remain unidentified; they may have been six symphonies by Wolfgang, six by Leopold or possibly works by both father and son.
18. Wagenseil's concerto remains unidentified. The sonatas presumably included some or all of K6–9, K10–15 and K26–31.

*The Mozarts remained in Olmütz until 23 December, returning to Vienna
on 10 January 1768. On 19 January they had an audience with Empress
Maria Theresa and Emperor Joseph II and at the end of the month, a few
days after his twelfth birthday, Wolfgang began work on the* opera buffa,
La finta semplice *("The Pretend Simpleton") K51.*

15. Leopold Mozart to Lorenz Hagenauer, 30 January 1768, Vienna

Something for you alone!
It's now time to give you a fuller and clearer account of our circumstances – whether fortunate or unfortunate, I do not know – and to
hear your kind opinion. If money is man's sole source of happiness,
we are doubtless to be pitied because, as you know, we have spent
so much that there is little apparent hope of our being able to recover
it. But if health and skill in knowledge are man's greatest possession,
then – God be praised – we are still well off. We have survived the
greatest and most dangerous storm; by God's grace we are all well,
and my children have certainly not forgotten anything but, as you'll
see, have made even greater progress.

Nothing, I know, will be more incomprehensible to you than how
it is that our affairs have made so little progress. I'll explain this to
you as best I can, although I must omit things that cannot be entrusted
to my pen. That the Viennese, generally speaking, have no desire to
see serious and sensible things and have little or no idea about them,
but want to see only foolish stuff, dancing, devils, ghosts, magic,
buffoons, Lipperl, Bernardon,[1] witches and apparitions is well known:
their theatres prove this every day. A gentleman, even if he is
bemedalled, will clap his hands and laugh till he is almost breathless
at some bawdy harlequinade or silly joke, but at the most serious
scene, the most moving and beautiful action, and the wittiest turns of

---

1. Lipperl is a stage character in the tradition of Hanswurst, a popular buffoon figure.
Bernardon was the stage name of the actor Joseph Felix von Kurz (1717–84).

phrase, he will talk so loudly to a lady that honest people cannot understand a word. That is the main reason. The domestic arrangements at court, which I cannot describe here, are such that they have many consequences that it would take too long to explain here or to illustrate by means of examples. And this is the second reason. From these two reasons spring any number of oddities, because everything depends on pure blind chance but more often on some appalling baseness, which is not, however, typical of everyone, or even on some extremely brazen and daring boast. But to come to our own affair, many other adverse incidents have taken place. On our arrival, we had no choice but to obtain an entry to the court. But Her Majesty the Empress no longer maintains her own orchestra and goes neither to the opera nor to see plays: her way of life is so unworldly that it is impossible for me to describe it.[2] She referred us to the emperor, but as this gentleman absolutely loathes anything that might entail any expenditure, it took him a long time to reach a decision; meantime there was the sad event concerning the young princess and all the others incidents that you already know about from my letters. On our return from Moravia, we met their highnesses without really expecting to, for hardly had the empress been told what had happened to us in Olmütz and that we had returned when we were told the day and hour when we should appear. But what was the use of this astonishing kindness, this indescribable affability? What did it produce? Nothing but a medal which, it is true, is beautiful, but so worthless that I do not even care to put a value on it. She is leaving everything else to the emperor, who enters it in his book of things to be forgotten and no doubt thinks that he has paid us off with his most gracious conversation. You will ask me what the rest of the nobility in Vienna is doing. – – – What are they doing? – – They are all cutting back on their expenses, as far as is possible, in order to ingratiate themselves with the emperor. If their master is prodigal, then everyone follows suit; but if, conversely, he is frugal, everyone wants to run the most economical household. – – – –

2. Since the death of her husband, Maria Theresa had more or less retreated from social life.

As long as the carnival lasts, people here are thinking of nothing but dancing. There are balls wherever you turn, but always at public expense; even the *masked ball at court costs next to nothing*. And who benefits from this? – – – *The court!* For all the dances, masked balls, other balls and spectacles are leased. Others take the credit, and the profits are divided between the court and the lessee. And so everyone who attends them is doing the court a service. These, then, are the aristocracy's political expenses. Among our patrons are the foremost members of the aristocracy: Prince *Kaunitz*, the *Duke of Braganza*, Fräulein von *Guttenberg*, who is the empress's right hand, the chief equerry Count *Dietrichstein*, who can do what he wants with the emperor – these are our friends.[3] But, by sheer accident, we have not yet been able to speak to Prince Kaunitz, because he has the weakness to be so afraid of smallpox that he avoids people who still have red spots on their faces: as Wolfgangerl still has lots of red spots on his face which, it is true, are small but which are visible when it's cold, he sent word through our friend *de Laugier*[4] that he would see to our interests during Lent but that during the carnival it was impossible to get all the nobility together.

As I was weighing up this matter as best I could and thinking of all the money I had already spent and how it would be very foolish to go home now, without waiting for anything else to happen, something quite different occurred. I heard that all the keyboard players and composers in Vienna were opposed to our advancement, with the single exception of Wagenseil, but Wagenseil was ill at home and unable to help us or work to our advantage. The chief maxim of these people was to avoid most carefully every occasion of seeing us and admitting to Wolfgangerl's abilities: and why? – – – so that on the many occasions when they were asked whether they'd heard the boy and what they thought of him, they could always say *that they hadn't heard him and that it couldn't possibly be true: it was all a sham, a foolish trick, it was prearranged as he was given music that he already*

3. Prince Kaunitz, imperial chancellor; Juan Carlos de Braganza, Duke of Lafoënt (1719–1806); Josepha von Guttenberg, lady-in-waiting at the Viennese court; Johann Karl, Count (later Prince) Dietrichstein (1728–1808).
4. Alexandre-Louis Laugier (*c.* 1719–74), physician-in-ordinary to Maria Theresa.

knew, that it was absurd to think that he could compose etc. etc. – – – –
That, you see, is why they're avoiding us. For those who have seen
and heard for themselves can no longer talk in this way without
running the risk of losing face.

I managed to trick one of these people. We had arranged with
someone to let us know in secret when he was there. He was to come
and hand this person a really exceptionally difficult concerto that was
then to be put before Wolfgangerl. And so we turned up, and he had
the opportunity of hearing his concerto played by Wolfgangerl as if
he knew it by heart. The astonishment of this composer and clavier
player, the things that he said and the turns of phrase that he used in
expressing his amazement made us realize the truth of what I said to
you earlier. And finally he said: *As an honest man I can say only that
this boy is the greatest man now living in the world. It was impossible to
believe it. – – –* Now, in order to convince the public of what is
involved here, I decided on a completely exceptional course of action,
namely, to get him to write an opera for the theatre. – – – And what
kind of an uproar do you think immediately arose among these
composers? – – What? – Today we are to see a Gluck[5] and tomorrow
a boy of 12 sitting at the harpsichord and conducting his own opera?
– – – Yes, despite all those who envy him! I've even won Gluck over
to our side or at least to the extent that, even though he is not entirely
whole-hearted, he will not show it, for our patrons are also his, and
in order to be sure of the performers, who usually cause the composer
the greatest trouble, I have broached the matter with them, and one
of them has given me all the ideas for the work. But, to tell the truth,
it was the emperor himself who first gave me the idea of getting
Wolfgangerl to write an opera in that he twice asked him if he'd like
to write an opera and conduct it himself. Of course, he said yes, but
the emperor could do nothing more as operas are the concern of
Affligio.[6] The consequences of this undertaking – if God helps us to
bring it off – are so great but also so easy to see that they require no

5. Gluck was attached to the court at Vienna at this time.
6. Giuseppe Affligio (1719–87), impresario at the Burg- and Kärntnertor theatres
from 1767–70.

explanation. But I must not allow myself to regret spending any money, for I shall no doubt recoup it today or tomorrow. Fortune favours the brave. I must present things in the right light. We must succeed or fail! And what is more suitable for this than the theatre? But the opera won't be given until after Easter, of course. I'll shortly be writing for permission to remain here longer. – – – It's not an *opera seria*, however, as no *opere serie* are being given at present and people don't even like them, but an *opera buffa*.[7] Not a short *opera buffa*, however, but one lasting 2½ or 3 hours. There are no singers here for serious operas, even Gluck's tragic opera *Alceste* was performed entirely by *opera buffa* singers. He too is now writing an *opera buffa*, as there are some excellent people here for an *opera buffa*: Sgr *Garibaldi*, Sgr *Caratoli*, Sgr *Poggi*, Sgr *Laschi*, Sgr *Pulini*, Sgra *Bernasconi*, Sgra *Eberardi* and Sgra *Baglioni*.[8] What do you say? Isn't the reputation of having written an opera for the Viennese theatre the best way to gain credit not only in Germany but in Italy too? Farewell.

---

7. Although definitions falsify the diversity and variability of eighteenth-century operatic genres, *opera seria* is generally used to signify Italian opera on a tragic or heroic subject; it consists of arias and recitatives, with relatively few ensembles. *Opera buffa* is the name given to comic opera, which includes a greater variety of musical and theatrical structures, forms and gestures. The terms were relatively new in 1768: '*opera buffa*' was only beginning to appear as a generic designation in librettos while '*opera seria*' was more commonly referred to as '*dramma per musica*'.
8. Giacchino Garibaldi (1743–after 1792), tenor; Francesco Caratoli (*c.* 1705–72), bass singer; Domenico Poggi, actor; Laschi is presumably the father of Luisa Laschi, the first Countess in *Le nozze di Figaro* (1786) and who also sang Zerlina in the first Viennese production of *Don Giovanni* (1788); Pulini, tenor, later sang in a private performance of *Idomeneo* in March 1786; Antonia Bernasconi (1741–1803), soprano and the first Aspasia in *Mitridate, re di Ponto* (1770); Teresa Eberardi, alto; Clementina Baglioni, singer, daughter of Domenico Poggi, married to the tenor Antonio Baglioni, creator of the roles of Ottavio in *Don Giovanni* (Prague, 1787) and Titus in *La clemenza di Tito* (1791).

16. Leopold Mozart to Lorenz Hagenauer, 30 July 1768, Vienna

You've made everything all right again! – – We were afraid only that a member of your household was unwell. From that point of view we're all the more pleased in that we can now see that the reason for your silence was, rather, that you were all well and enjoying the garden. From another point of view, however, namely, our unduly long stay in Vienna, we are extremely displeased. Indeed, only our honour keeps us here, otherwise we'd have been back in Salzburg long ago. For would you want everyone in the whole of Vienna saying that Wolfgang was simply unable to write the opera or that it had turned out to be so wretched that it was impossible to perform it or that it wasn't he who'd written it but his father etc.? Would you want people to look on in cold blood as such calumnies were everywhere put about? Would this redound to our honour? Indeed, would it redound to the honour of our most gracious prince? You will say: *What does His Majesty the Emperor say to all this?* – – Here I must be brief, as I can't go into detail. But you'll understand. If I'd known what I know now and if I could have foreseen all that has happened, Wolfgang would never have written a single note but would have been home long ago. The theatre has been leased or, rather, it has been handed over to a certain Affligio; he has to pay some 1000 florins a year to people whom the court would otherwise have to pay. The emperor and the whole of the imperial family pay nothing but have free admission. And so the court cannot say anything to Affligio as he undertakes everything at his own risk and is now in real danger of being ruined, as you shall hear in a moment.

His Majesty asked our Wolfgang whether he'd like to write an opera, adding how much he'd like to see him conduct it from the keyboard; His Majesty sent word to this effect to Affligio, who came to an arrangement with us in return for a payment of 100 ducats. The opera was initially to be given at Easter; but the poet[1] was the first to

---

1. *La finta semplice*; the poet was Marco Coltellini (1724–77), active at Vienna from 1758.

thwart this plan by repeatedly holding us up, claiming that he wanted to make a handful of necessary changes, so that by Easter we had received only two of the revised arias from him. The production was fixed for Whitsuntide, and then for His Majesty's return from Hungary. But at this point the mask fell. – – – For in the meantime all the local composers, foremost among whom is Gluck, have undermined our plans in their attempts to prevent the opera from making any progress. The singers were incited, the orchestra turned against us, and everything was done to stop the production from going ahead. The singers, who in any case barely know their parts and who include one or two who have to learn everything by ear, were now prevailed upon to say that they were unable to sing their arias, which they had previously heard in our room, approving and applauding them and saying that they were happy with them. The orchestra was to say that it was reluctant to be conducted by a boy etc. and a hundred similar things. Meanwhile some people were putting it about that the music was entirely worthless, while others were claiming that the music did not fit the words and was unmetrical because the boy had insufficient command of Italian. – – – No sooner had I heard this than I demonstrated in the most eminent quarters that Hasse, the father of music, and the great Metastasio[2] had both declared that the slanderers who were spreading this report should go to them and hear out of their own mouths that 30 operas have been performed in Vienna that cannot hold a candle to this boy's opera, which they both admire to the highest degree. It was now said that it was not the boy but the father who had written it. – – But here too the slanderers were discredited, falling *ab uno extremo ad aliud*[3] and ending up looking foolish. I got someone to take down from the shelf a volume of Metastasio's works, open it at random and give Wolfgang the first aria that fell into his hands: he took up his pen and, without giving it

2. Johann Adolf Hasse (1699–1783), composer of Italian opera, Kapellmeister at Dresden 1731–60, now active at Vienna; the poet Pietro Metastasio (1698–1782) was the most important librettist, for *opera seria* in particular, during the eighteenth century; he served as court poet in Vienna from 1730–69, when he was succeeded by Coltellini.
3. 'from one extreme to the other'.

any further thought and with the most amazing speed, wrote the music for it, with several instruments, in the presence of several eminent persons. He did this at the homes of Kapellmeister Bonno,[4] Abbate Metastasio, Hasse, the Duke of Braganza and Prince Kaunitz. Meanwhile another opera has been cast, and since there are no further objections, Wolfgang's will be given immediately afterwards. – – – A hundred times or more I've been on the point of packing up and leaving; and if this opera had been an *opera seria*, I'd have left at once, at the first available opportunity, and laid it at the feet of His Grace: but as it's an *opera buffa* and, indeed, one that demands certain types of *buffo* characters, I must salvage our honour here, no matter what the cost. The honour of our most gracious prince is also at stake. His Grace has no liars, charlatans and swindlers in his service who with his prior knowledge and gracious permission go to other towns and like conjurors throw dust in people's eyes; no, they are honest men who to the honour of their prince and their country announce to the world a miracle that God allowed to see the light of day in Salzburg. I owe it to Almighty God to see this through, otherwise I'd be the most thankless of creatures: *and if it were ever my duty to convince the world of this miracle, it is now, when people are ridiculing all that is called a miracle and denying all such miracles.* And so they have to be convinced: and was it not a great joy and a great triumph for me to hear a Voltairean say to me in amazement: *For once in my life I have seen a miracle; it is the first!* But because this miracle is too visible and therefore undeniable, people want to stamp on it: *they are reluctant to let God take the credit for it*; they think that in a matter of years it will sink back to the level of something quite natural and cease to be a divine miracle. And so they want to remove it from the eyes of the world: for how could it be more visible than at a public spectacle in a large and populous city? – – – But why should we be surprised to find ourselves persecuted away from home when almost the same has happened in the child's home town? – – What a disgrace! What inhumanity! You may wonder why Prince Kaunitz and other great

---

4. Giuseppe Bonno (1710–88), court composer at Vienna from 1739 and Kapell-meister from 1774.

73

men, indeed, why even His Majesty the Emperor himself, do not give orders for the opera to be performed. In the first place, they cannot do so as it is the sole concern of Sgr Affligio (whom some people call Count Affligio); 2nd, they might possibly order him to give it at another time: but as it was Prince Kaunitz who, against His Majesty's will, persuaded Affligio to invite to Vienna some French actors who are costing him more than 70,000 florins a year and who are ruining him as they aren't drawing the crowds that were hoped for, Affligio is now blaming Prince Kaunitz, while the prince, conversely, is hoping to persuade the emperor to take an interest in the French theatre and defray Affligio's expenses; the result is that His Majesty has not appeared at any performance for several weeks. You see the annoying circumstance that had to happen at the same time and that helped persuade Affligio to shove Wolfgang's opera to one side in order to keep his 100 ducats, while on the other hand this same circumstance prevented people from speaking to Affligio in an insistent, commanding and emphatic tone for fear that they'd have to compensate him for the 70,000 florins. Meanwhile all of this was going on behind our backs. Affligio blamed the singers for the postponement, saying that they were both unable and unwilling to sing it, while the singers for their part blamed Affligio, claiming he had said he would not perform it and that he had even told them so himself: but of course they could always have this or that passage changed. And so it is going to be performed. But if some new obstacle is to present itself, as is bound to happen, I shall address my complaint to Their Majesties the Emperor and Empress and demand such satisfaction as shall salvage our honour in the eyes of the whole of Vienna and the rest of the honest world; for it would be no honour for us or, indeed, for the court in Salzburg if we were simply driven away by the envy that has been pursuing us and if, after our departure, we were to allow these villains to tell the ignorant public – as has already happened – that Wolfgang never managed to write the opera at all or that it had turned out to be so bad that it was simply impossible to perform it etc. etc. You see how we have to struggle to make our way in the world. If a man has no talent, he is unhappy enough; but if he has talent, he is pursued by envy in proportion to his ability. On top of all this, one of the singers, Bernasconi, has now gone down with a bad cold, and Baglioni isn't very well either: this is holding us up and will in turn delay the business for at least 3 weeks, so that it is with the most extreme annoyance, such as I have not known at any other time on our travels, that I now have to await the outcome of this hateful affair. All sensible people must note with shame that it is a national disgrace that we Germans are trying to stamp on a fellow German to whom other nations have done justice by their tremendous admiration and even by publicly acknowledging him in writing. But only patience and perseverance will help to convince people that our adversaries are malicious liars, slanderers and envious creatures who would laugh in their sleeves at their victory if we were to allow ourselves to be frightened or worn down or if we were to leave in a huff: and all the more so in that in Vienna such people as those who are invited to instruct a princess, for example, or an imperial prince, indeed, even those who merely breathe the air here and who are already proud enough that the emperor himself lives here, people, finally, who serve foreign princes – all these people must be viewed with contempt and spoken of contemptuously and basely by foreign princes. You now know my circumstances, I think, – – even though I have described them in only the most general terms. I would have told His Grace, our most gracious lord, about this occurrence if I had not hesitated to distract him from more important matters by so lengthy a tale. We all send our good wishes to our Father Confessor and beg him to lay them at the feet of His Grace. Herr Joseph will see from this report that my enemies in Salzburg wish us well as they are putting it about that Wolfgang received 2000 florins for his opera. Herr Peisser's letters will tell you a different story, and we shall no doubt have to ask him for 50, perhaps 100 ducats, before we return to Salzburg. My wife and daughter thank you kindly for your good wishes. They have spent the day outside the city with a good friend, who has invited us back there this evening to celebrate Nannerl's birthday tomorrow. Oh, we've already been thinking of the Nonntal![5]

5. The Hagenauers' summer home.

Who'll become Prince of Berchtesgaden? Baron Kulmer?[6] — — *I was told yesterday that Herr Küffel[7] has arrived here. He owes me 4 ducats, so I don't suppose he'll be asking to see me.* Farewell, we send our best wishes to you and to all our good friends. I am your old friend.

17. Leopold Mozart's petition to Emperor Joseph II, 21 September 1768, Vienna

Species facti[1]

Many members of the local nobility having been convinced of my son's extraordinary talent both by reports from abroad and by examining him for themselves, including setting him tests, it was invariably regarded as one of the most astonishing events of these and earlier times that a boy of 12 might write an opera and conduct it himself. A learned paper from Paris confirmed this opinion by declaring, after a detailed account of my son's genius, that *there is no doubt that at the age of 12 this child will write an opera for one or other of the Italian theatres*; and everyone thought that a German should reserve this distinction for his own country alone.[2] I was unanimously encouraged in this; I heeded the general voice, and the Dutch minister, Count Degenfeld,[3] was the first to put this suggestion to the impresario Sgr Affligio, since he was already well acquainted with the boy's ability from our meeting in Holland. The singer Caratoli was the second person to suggest it to Affligio; and the matter was decided with the impresario at the home of the physician-in-ordinary Laugier in the

6. In the event, Helfried Franz Philipp Kulmer, Baron Rosenbichl und Hohenstein did not become prince of Berchtesgaden.

7. Ignaz Küffel, violoncellist.

1. Phrase denoting the setting out of a petition.

2. Here Leopold refers to an article by Grimm (published in *Correspondance littéraire* and dated 15 July 1766; see Deutsch, *Documentary Biography*, 56–7), which concluded: 'If these children [Wolfgang and Nannerl] live, they will not remain at Salzburg. Before long, monarchs will vie for their possession.'

3. Frederik Christoph von Degenfeld-Schomburg (1722–81), Dutch minister at Vienna from 1767–81.

presence of young Baron van Swieten[4] and two singers Caratoli and Garibaldi, the more so in that all of them, and especially the 2 singers, declared most emphatically that the whole of Vienna would be drawn to the theatre by even very mediocre music composed by so young a boy because of the extraordinarily wondrous nature of the event, not least to see this child in the orchestra, conducting his work from the keyboard. I therefore allowed my son to write it.

As soon as the first act was finished, I asked Caratoli to listen to it and criticize it in order to be sure of my position. He came, and so great was his surprise that he returned the next day, bringing Garibaldi with him. Garibaldi, no less amazed, brought Poggi to see me a few days later. All demonstrated such uncommon acclaim that, on my repeatedly asking: *whether they really thought it was any good? – whether they felt he should continue?* – – they were annoyed at my misgivings and more than once exclaimed with some feeling: *cosa? – – come? questo è un portento! questo opera andera alle stelle! è una meraviglia! – non dubiti, che scrivi avanti!*[5] – &c. and a whole host of other remarks. Caratoli said the same to me afterwards in his own room.

Assured of the desired success by the singers' approval, I left my son to get on with the work; but I also asked the physician-in-ordinary Laugier to sort out in my name the matter of payment with the impresario. This was done; and *Affligio promised 100 ducats*. In order to shorten my stay in Vienna, which was proving expensive, I then suggested that the opera be performed before Your Majesty left for Hungary; but some changes that the poet had to make to the text delayed work on the score; and Affligio declared that he would perform it after Your Majesty's return.

The opera had by now been finished for some weeks. A start was made on copying the parts; and the first act was handed to the singers, followed shortly afterwards by the second: in the meantime my son was on several occasions asked by the nobility to perform this or that aria and even the first-act finale at the keyboard, and this was admired

4. See List.
5. 'What? – – how? he's a prodigy! this opera will storm the gates of heaven! it's a marvel! – don't doubt it, he should go on writing!'

by all, as Affligio saw and heard for himself at Prince Kaunitz's. The rehearsals were now to begin.

But – how could I have suspected this! – this was also where the persecutions of my son began.

It is very rarely that an opera turns out a complete success at its very first rehearsal and that the occasional change does not have to be made. This is why we normally begin with the keyboard alone and why we never rehearse with all the instruments until the singers have rehearsed their parts together, especially the finales.

But here exactly the opposite happened. The roles were still inadequately rehearsed, the singers hadn't had any keyboard rehearsals and the finales hadn't been rehearsed together, and yet the first act was rehearsed with the full orchestra in order to ensure that from the outset the whole affair appeared deficient and confused. No one who was present will be able to call this a rehearsal without blushing; I shall say nothing about the unkind behaviour of those who have this on their consciences. May God forgive them.

After the rehearsal Affligio said to me: *it was good; but as this and that passage was too high, a few changes would have to be made here and there: I'd just like to speak to the singers; and as His Majesty will be here in 12 days, he could present the opera in 4 or, at the most, 6 weeks from now so as to have time to get everything into proper shape. I was not to dwell on this; he was a man of his word and would do as he'd promised; there was nothing new in this; with other operas, too, changes had to be made etc. etc.*

The changes demanded by the singers were duly made and two new arias added to the first act: but in the meantime *La Caschina*[6] was performed at the theatre. By now the agreed term was over, and I heard that Affligio had cast another opera. It was even being said that Affligio would not perform the opera at all and that he had given people to understand *that the singers were unable to sing it*, even though these same singers had previously not just approved of it but praised it to the skies.

6. *La Cecchina, ossia La buona figliuola* by Niccolò Piccinni (1728–1800), then active in Italy, later in Paris.

In order to defend me against such gossip, my son had to play through the whole opera at the clavier at the home of young Baron van Swieten in the presence of Count Spork,[7] the Duke of Braganza and other people knowledgeable about music. They all expressed their surprise at the behaviour of Affligio and the singers; all were much exercised by this turn of events and declared to a man that such un-Christian, untruthful and malicious behaviour was incomprehensible, that they preferred this opera to many an Italian opera and that instead of encouraging such a heaven-sent talent, a cabal was behind it all, a cabal evidently designed to prevent the innocent boy from achieving the honour and fortune he deserved.

I went to see the impresario to learn the truth of the matter. He said to me: *he had never been against performing the opera, but I would surely not hold it against him if he looked to his own interests; some doubts had been expressed to the effect that audiences might not like it; he'd put* La Caschina *into rehearsal and now intended to do the same with* La buona figliuola,[8] but after that he'd perform the boy's opera; if, contrary to his wishes, it failed to please, he would at least be provided with two other operas. I drew his attention to my already lengthy stay and the fact that I had had to extend it. He replied: *Come now! What are 8 days more or less, I'll then take it in hand at once.* And we left it at that. Caratoli's arias were altered; everything was sorted out with Garibaldi; and the same was true of Poggi and Laschi etc. Each of them assured me repeatedly that *they had no objections; everything depended on Affligio.* Meanwhile more than a month had passed. The copyist told me that he had received no further instructions to copy out the revised arias; and on hearing at the dress rehearsal of *La buona figliuola* that Affligio was planning to give another opera, I tackled him myself. In the presence of myself and Coltellini he thereupon ordered the copyist to have everything distributed within two days and gave instructions for the opera to be rehearsed with the orchestra in a fortnight at the latest.

But the poor child's enemies – whoever they may be – have again

7. Johann Wenzel, Count Spork (1724–1804), general director of theatres.
8. i.e. *La buona figliuola maritata* (1761), also by Piccinni.

prevented this. That very same day the copyist received orders to stop work: and a few days later I discovered that Affligio had decided not to give the boy's opera in the theatre after all. Wanting to know what was going on, I went to see him and was told *that he had called the singers together and they had admitted that although the opera was incomparably well written it was untheatrical and as a result they could not perform it.* Such talk was utterly incomprehensible to me. For would the singers really dare, without blushing for shame, to dismiss what they had earlier praised to the skies, a work that they themselves had encouraged the boy to write and that they had commended to Affligio himself? – – I replied to the effect that *he could not expect the boy to have taken the trouble to write an opera for nothing. I reminded him of his agreement; I gave him to understand that he had led us by the nose for four months and that as a result we had incurred expenses of more than 160 ducats. I reminded him of the time I had wasted and assured him that I would hold him responsible not only for the 100 ducats that he had agreed with the physician-in-ordinary Laugier but also for all other expenses.*

To this reasonable demand of mine he gave an incomprehensible answer that betrayed the embarrassment with which he now sought – I know not how – to rid himself of the whole affair, before leaving me with the most scandalously unkind remarks: *if I wanted to see the boy prostituted, he would ensure that the opera was booed and laughed off the stage.* Coltellini heard all this. Was this, then, to be the reward that my son was to be offered for the great labour of writing an opera – the manuscript of which runs to 558 pages – and for the waste of time and the expenses we have incurred? – – And ultimately – and it is this that concerns me most – what of my son's honour and fame now that I no longer dare insist on a performance of the opera, since I have been given to understand plainly enough that no effort will be spared in performing it as wretchedly as possible; and since, further-more, they are claiming now that the work is unsingable, now that it is untheatrical, now that it does not fit the words, now that he is incapable of writing such music – and all manner of foolish and self-contradictory nonsense, all of which would vanish like smoke to the shame of our envious and perfidious slanderers if, as I most urgently and humbly entreat Your Majesty for my honour's sake, the musical powers of my child were to be properly examined, so that everyone would then be convinced that the only aim of these people is to stamp on and destroy the happiness of an innocent creature to whom God has granted an extraordinary talent and whom other nations have admired and encouraged, and to do this, moreover, in the capital of his German fatherland.

As a result of Leopold Mozart's petition, Joseph II ordered an investigation by Spork, but nothing came of it and La finta semplice *was not performed. Presumably as a consolation, Wolfgang composed a trumpet concerto (K47c, lost), offertory (K47b, lost) and mass (K139) that were given on 7 December at the dedication of the orphanage church Mariae Geburt in the Rennweg. He also composed the singspiel* Bastien und Bastienne *K50, but it is not known if it was performed. The family returned to Salzburg on 5 January 1769. The following letter, presumed to have been written at this time, is the first in Wolfgang's own hand.*

18. Mozart to an unknown girl, 1769(?), Salzburg

Dear friend,

Forgive me for taking the liberty of tormenting you with a few lines, but you said yesterday that you can understand everything, no matter what I may jot down in Latin, and so my curiosity has got the better of me and persuaded me to write down sundry Latin words and lines for you: once you've read them, please be so kind as to send your answer by one of Hagenauer's maidservants, as our Nandl[1] can't wait (but you must write me a letter too).

1. The Mozarts' maid. She may be the maid Nandl referred to in later letters, who has been identified as Anna Maria Pietschner (1732–1805), but this is not certain.

Cuperem scire, de qua causa, a quam plurimis adolescentibus otium adeo æstimatur, ut ipsi se nec verbis, nec verberibus, ab hoc sinant abduci[2]

Wolfgang Mozart

Its cancellation in Vienna notwithstanding, La finta semplice *was performed in Salzburg about the beginning of May and during the summer Wolfgang may have composed some or all of the cassations and serenades K62, 63 and 100 – a performance of at least one of these works was given on 8 August as part of the graduation ceremonies at the Salzburg Benedictine University. Later, in October, he composed and performed the 'Dominicus' mass K66 for the celebration of Fr Dominicus Hagenauer's first mass. Archbishop Schrattenbach appointed the thirteen-year-old Wolfgang third concertmaster in the Salzburg court music establishment; although the position was unpaid, it represented the normal first step towards full, paid employment at court. On 13 December father and son set out for Italy with the purpose of giving Wolfgang the opportunity to win fame and commissions through public concerts in the towns they visited and private performances at the homes of influential noblemen; even in the late eighteenth century, Italy remained the first port of call for aspiring composers and performers. But first came the arduous journey across the Alps.*

19. *Leopold Mozart to his wife, 14 December 1769, Wörgl*

We arrived in Kaitl at 1 o'clock and had some potted veal for lunch accompanied by the most fearful smell; we washed it down with a few draughts of good beer as the wine was no better than a laxative. It was after seven by the time we reached Lofer; after I'd ordered

---

2. 'I should like to know for what reason idleness is so popular with many young people that it is impossible to dissuade them from it either by words or by chastisements.'

the meal, we went to visit the prefect, who was very put out that we'd not called on him straightaway. As we'd already ordered our meal at the inn, we had it brought over to the prefect's house and ate it there, gossiping till 10 o'clock, when we were given a fine room and a good bed there, in the morning I had some chocolate to drink and Wolfg. had some excellent soup. By midday we were in St Johann and arrived this evening in Wörgl, where I'd arranged for us to meet the vicar, Herr Hartmann Kellhammer from Chiemsee. He has just arrived. He sends his good wishes. It's now 10 o'clock, we have to go to bed as we've got to be up at 5 in the morning. I'm told that the roads were very bad, but I slept soundly throughout the journey as I saw that we had a very good driver. There's an amazing amount of snow hereabouts, especially between Lofer and St Johann. Keep well and stay cheerful! I'll write again from Innsbruck.

[*Postscripts added by Mozart, to his mother and sister*]
Dearest Mama,

My heart is bursting with sheer pleasure as I'm enjoying this journey so much, it's so warm in the carriage and our coachman is a jolly fine fellow who drives so fast whenever the road lets him. Papa will already have given Mama an account of the journey, my reason for writing to Mama is to show that I know my duty and that I am, with the deepest respect, her devoted son

Wolfgang Mozart

[*Next section entirely in Italian*]
My dearest sister,

We've arrived safely in *Wörgl*, thank God, if I must tell the truth, I have to say that travelling is good fun and that it's not at all cold and that it's as warm in our carriage as in a room. How's your sore throat? Didn't our Signor Seccatore[1] turn up on the day we left? If you see Signor Schiedenhofen,[2] tell him that I'm for ever singing:

1. That is, 'Mr Bore'.
2. Johann Baptist von Schiedenhofen (1747–1823) was a city official of Salzburg and a family friend; his diary, which he kept from 1774–8, has numerous references to performances of Mozart's works and to social events in the archdiocese.

Tralaliera, Tralaliera, and tell him that it's not necessary for me to pour sugar in my soup now that I'm no longer in Salzburg. At Lofer we ate and slept at the home of Signor Helmreichen, who's the prefect there. His wife is a splendid woman, she's the sister of Signor Moll.[3] I'm hungry, I feel a great desire to eat something. Meanwhile, farewell. *Addio*:

Wolfgang Mozart

PS: My best wishes to all my good friends, to Signor Hagenauer (the merchant), to his wife, to his sons and daughters, to Signora Rosa and her husband, and to Signor Adlgasser and Signor Spitzeder. Ask Signor Hornung[4] from me whether he again thought it was me in bed, not you.

From Wörgl, the pair continued on through the mountains to reach Verona on 27 December. On 5 January 1770, Wolfgang gave his first Italian concert, at the Philharmonic Academy of Verona.

20. *Leopold Mozart to his wife, 7 January 1770, Verona*

I'm very sorry not to have received your first letter. It must still be lying at the post office in Bozen.[1] I'll make enquiries: it will have gone there from Innsbruck. Let me say straightaway that *we're all well, thank God*. You'd be doing me a great favour by letting me know how many letters you've received from me: I sent you one

3. Maria Klara Helmreichen zu Brunfeld (1729–1802), sister of Ludwig Gottfried Moll (1727–1804), a civil servant in the archdiocese. Ludwig's wife was related to the Cristani di Rall family who proved helpful to the Mozarts in Italy.
4. Joseph von Arimathaea Hornung, bass and tenor singer at the Salzburg court from 1768.
1. Bolzano.

from *Wörgl*, one by the *hired coachman*, one by post from *Innsbruck* and one *from Bozen*. I must start by asking you to give Herr Ranftl my best wishes and telling him that we were given a warm welcome by Herr Stockhammer and most lavishly entertained. I also met my old acquaintance Herr Stickler there. Please give my best wishes to Herr Kerschbaumer, too, and tell him that Herr Senblrock received us most courteously and also gave us a letter of recommendation to take with us to Bologna. We spent only a day and a half in Bozen. We'd only just arrived in Rovereto when we received a visit from a certain Cristani, who took the woman's part in the play *Cato's Child* at the Collegio Rupertino and who invited us to have lunch with him and his brother the next day. And who was this brother? – – The very same Nicolò Cristani who stayed with the Master of the Pageboys and consistorial councillor Johann Andreas Cristani and whom I taught to play the violin; he's now the most important person in Rovereto and the whole district, namely, the country lieutenant, representing Her Majesty the Empress. I expect you'll still remember him, he stayed with the pageboys. As soon as we arrived, he said how much Wolfg. resembles you, he remembers just what you look like. And who else did we find there? – – Signor Comte Settimo Lodron,[2] consistorial councillor Cristani, a certain Pilati, Festi etc.: the first 2 of them had driven over from Villa Lagarina on Count Lodron's[3] estates, for the news that we were coming had already reached Rovereto from Innsbruck. You can easily imagine how pleased we were to see each other again after 19, 20 and more years and that it was a most enjoyable lunch. While we were at table, Herr Cosmi's valet arrived and invited us to lunch the next day. It was another delightful occasion, all the more so in that as a widower Herr Cosmi was engaged to a respectable young lady whom he married a few days after we'd left. His mother and 3 sisters were also there. If we'd remained in Rovereto any longer, we'd have had to stay with them; and if ever we return, we are to lodge with them. Baron

2. Massimiliano Settimo von Lodron (1727–96), dean of the cathedral at Villa Lagarina near Rovereto, was a distant relation of the Lodron family of Salzburg.
3. Nikolaus Sebastian, Count Lodron (1719–92) was also distantly related to the Salzburg Lodrons.

Pizzini and Count Lodron, to whom we were recommended by His Excellency the Marshal of the Prince's Household, honoured us with all manner of civilities. The nobility organized a concert at the home of Baron Todeschi.[4] And who was this Baron Todeschi? – – The same gentleman whom Herr Giovanni once brought to us in Vienna to hear Wolfg. play. Perhaps you still remember him. I don't need to say what a credit to us all Wolfg. has been. In the afternoon of the following day we went to see the organ in the main church; and although only 6 or 8 leading persons knew we were coming, we found the whole of Rovereto assembled in the church and some strong fellows had to go ahead and make way for us to the choir, where it then took us another five to ten minutes to get to the organ as everyone wanted to get close to us. We spent 4 days in Rovereto. It's not a large town and was once very run-down, but thanks to the hard work of its inhabitants it has become increasingly fashionable for as long as people can remember, with most of the population earning their living by growing wine and trading in silk. There are now many well-to-do houses here, and the people are very polite towards strangers.

In Verona there is an opera every day and so it took the nobility a week to organize a concert or academy, to which we were invited. The *cavalieri* to whom we were given letters of recommendation are *il Marchese Carlotti*, *il Conte Carlo Emilei*, *il Marchese Spolverini*, *il Marchese Donisi dei SS Fermo e Rustico al Ponte*, *Il Sigr. Conte Giusti del Giardino* and *il Sig. Conte Allegri*. We have a standing invitation to visit Marchese Carlotti, also from Herr Locatelli. We've dined twice with Marchese Carlotti, and also with Conte Carlo Emilei. On 2 occasions we were with Conte Giusti, who has a beautiful garden and an art gallery. You'll perhaps find them in Keyssler's accounts of his travels.[5] Then, yesterday, we dined with Herr Locatelli, while today there was utter confusion, which I must tell you about in more detail. We were invited to visit a certain honest individual by the

4. Giovanni Battista Todeschi (1730–99), mayor of Rovereto.
5. Johann Georg Keyssler's *Reisen durch Teutschland, Böhmen, Ungarn, die Schweiz, Italien und Lothringen* ('Travels through Germany, Bohemia, Hungary, Switzerland, Italy and Lorraine'), Hanover, 1751.

name of Herr Ragazzoni.[6] The receiver general of Venice, Signor Lugiati had asked the *cavalieri* to obtain my permission for Wolfg. to have his portrait painted;[7] this took place yesterday morning, and he was to have a second sitting today after church. We were also intended to dine there. Signor Lugiati went in person to see Herr Ragazzoni to ask him to leave us to him, and the latter had to agree to this, albeit most reluctantly, as Lugiati is very powerful in Venice. And so we were to go to Herr Lugiati's house this morning after church and sit for the painter again before lunch. But then an even more powerful or greater man appeared, namely the Bishop of Verona, from the house of Giustiniani, who sent word through Herr Locatelli that he not only wanted us to call on him after church but also to have lunch with him. But when he heard that Wolfg.'s portrait was currently being painted and that we wanted to leave, he agreed to our having lunch with Herr Lugiati but still kept us until after 1 o'clock. The painter then got on with Wolfg.'s portrait and it wasn't until 3 o'clock that we sat down to eat. After lunch we drove to St Thomas's in order to play on the church's 2 organs; and although we decided to do this only over lunch and only a few tickets had been sent to Marchese Carlotti and Count Pindemonte, there was such a crowd inside the church when we arrived that there was hardly enough room for us to get out of the coach. The crush was so great that we were forced to go through the monastery, where so many people rushed up to us that we wouldn't have found any space at all if the fathers who were waiting for us at the monastery gates hadn't taken us into their midst. Once it was over, the noise was even greater as everyone wanted to see the little organist. As soon as we were in the carriage, I asked to be driven home, where I locked the door and began to write this letter: I had to tear myself away, otherwise we wouldn't have been left in peace long enough to write a letter. Tomorrow

6. Michelangelo Locatelli and Francesco Maria Ragazzoni were local businessmen.
7. Pietro Lugiati (1724–88) was a financial administrator in Milan. The portrait, possibly by Saverio dalla Rosa (1745–1821), who was related through his grandmother to Lugiati, contains the only known source for the keyboard piece K72a, which is clearly visible on the music stand of the instrument at which Wolfgang is seated; the portrait is reproduced in Deutsch, *Bildern*, 11.

we're going to see the amphitheatre and other rare sights with Herr Locatelli, we'll then dine with him and afterwards pay our farewell visits, the day after tomorrow we'll pack and on Wednesday evening, with God's help, we'll travel on to Mantua, which, although it's near, is a short winter day's journey away on account of the muddy road. *Have you received no letters from Herr Lotter reporting the safe arrival of the money? – – Has Herr Breitkopf not written from Leipzig to say that he's received the 100 books? – – Have the books been sent to Vienna, and has Herr Gräffer reported their arrival?*[8] – – You must drop me a couple of lines to report on all these matters. – Did you have nice weather – not too cold – in Salzb. during the Christmas holidays? – – It's been very cold here for nearly a week. And just imagine, everywhere we dined, there were neither hearths nor stoves in the dining rooms. Your hands get terribly black and blue and red. I'd rather eat in a cellar. More on this – the greatest cross we have to bear – another time. Perhaps you could write and let me know *how to make the hand paste*, perhaps we'll be needing it. In the meantime, bundle up *12 copies of the Violinschule* and send them to *Joseph Wolff's* bookshop in Innsbruck. Unless I'm much mistaken, the man who runs the shop in Innsbruck is called Felicius or Felicianus Fischer. They'll tell you at Mayr's bookshop.[9] You don't need to enclose anything more than a brief note, perhaps along the lines of: *Here are 12 copies of the* Violinschule *that my husband has instructed me to send you from Verona. As agreed, you may retain them on commission and sell them at 2 f 15 kr (Tirolean currency) each, crediting my husband with 1 f 45 kr (in the same currency) for each copy sold: please would you advertise them in the newspaper and charge the cost to my husband.* I've no more paper. Farewell. I'm your old

Mzt

8. Bernhard Christoph Breitkopf (1695–1777) or his son Johann Gottlob Immanuel Breitkopf (1719–94), publishers in Leipzig; the books are Leopold Mozart's *Gründliche Violinschule*. Rudolf Gräffer (1734–1817), publisher in Vienna, published Mozart's early songs K52 and 53 in 1768.
9. Joseph Wolff was a book dealer in Augsburg; in 1747 he opened a branch of his shop in Innsbruck. Mayr's was Salzburg's leading bookshop.

From Verona, Leopold and Wolfgang travelled to Mantua, where Mozart gave a concert at the Royal Academy of Science, Letters and Arts on 16 January and they attended a performance of Hasse's opera Demetrio *(1732). They also stopped at Cremona, where on 20 January they heard Valentini's opera,* La clemenza di Tito *(1753). They reached Milan on 23 January.*

21. Leopold Mozart to his wife, 26 January 1770, Milan

Herr Troger[1] has safely delivered your letter of the 12th. We arrived in Milan at midday on the 23rd, and your letter arrived on the 24th and with it your first note which, at my request, Herr Anton von Gummer had gone to fetch from the post office in Bozen and sent on to me. You complain that you've not received any letters from me for 3 weeks, but I wrote to you from Verona and Mantua. You ought to have received my first letter from *Verona* by now as I posted it there on *7 January*. The 2nd can't have reached Salzb. yet as it wasn't posted *in Mantua* until the *15th*. We left Verona at noon on the 10th and reached Mantua that evening, but I think I've already told you this. I wish you could have seen the place where the concert was held, namely, what's called the *Teatrino della Accademia Filarmonica*. Never in my whole life have I seen anything more beautiful of its kind; and as I hope *that you are assiduously keeping all my letters*, I shall describe it to you in due course. It's not a theatre but a hall with boxes, built like an opera house; where the stage should be there is a raised section for the orchestra, and behind the orchestra is another gallery, like boxes, for the audience. The crowd of people – – the calling, clapping, shouting and the *bravo* upon *bravo* – in short, the general shouting and the admiration shown by the listeners is something I cannot adequately describe to you.

I don't doubt that in the meantime reports both from Rovereto and from Verona and Mantua will have reached you in Salzb. Give my most humble good wishes to Their Excellencies Count and Countess Arco

1. Court official in Milan.

and tell them that we were received with all manner of kindnesses and courtesies at the home of Count Eugenio Arco[2] in Mantua. Conversely we did not have the good fortune to obtain an audience with Prince von Taxis. I already wrote to you from Mantua to say that his wife had letters to write. We returned there the next morning, but they'd both gone to church: we went to the church in turn and followed them home in their carriage at a distance of some 50 paces, so that the coachman would have no choice but to see us when he turned round in the courtyard. But when we announced our visit, we were told that the prince now had important business to attend to –
– and he was unable to speak to us, we'd have to return on another occasion. The servant's expression, his trembling voice and half-broken words showed me at once that the prince had no wish to see us; God preserve me from ever disturbing anyone from going about his business, especially when it also means walking great distances or having to hire a carriage. Fortunately we both lost nothing by not seeing each other at close hand (for we saw each other in the distance at the opera), in addition to which I saved myself money going there and saved His Excellency from the fear of being in our debt and having to extend to us any small courtesies for the honours shown to him at the Salzb. court and by the Salz. nobility. I'm writing this simply for your information, not because it grieves me, for I wouldn't want anyone in Salzb. to think that I had lacked the good manners to visit the prince.

I am again enclosing a poem, this one by a lady by the name of Sigra Sartoretti, who entertained us in Mantua.[3] Her servant came the next day and brought us an uncommonly beautiful bouquet of flowers on a beautiful plate, with red ribbons beneath it and 4 ducats entwined in the middle of the ribbons; on top was the poem, a copy of which I am appending.

2. A cousin of the Salzburg Arcos.
3. Sartoretti's poem reads, in part: 'See how his fingers move,/Hear with what art/He makes the keys respond/In ev'ry part;/How he to you imparts/All his accomplished arts./Europe has witnessed him,/Where, as a child,/Her ev'ry region/He newly beguiled./Woe! If to them he's near,/Let not the Sirens hear.' It is reproduced in Deutsch, *Documentary Biography*, 108–9.

I can assure you that everywhere I have found the most delightful people and that everywhere we have had our particular favourites who have remained with us until the very last moment of our departure and done everything in their power to make our stay agreeable. Thus it was, for example, with Count Spaur's household in *Innsbruck*, Baron Pizzini, Counts Lodron, Cristani, Cosmi etc in *Rovereto* and Count Carlo Emilei, Marchese Carlotti, Count Giusti, the Lugiati household and especially Herr Locatelli in *Verona*. Then in *Mantua* Count Arco's household and especially a Sigr. Bettinelli[4] who, together with his brother and his brother's wife, was entirely at our service. The wife was really just like a mother to Wolfgangl and we left each other with tears in our eyes. I'm also enclosing the newspaper from Mantua, which we received only when we arrived here in Milan. Among other things you'll find in it the printed programme of the music performed at the concert, but you must know that neither the concert in Mantua nor the one in Verona was given for money, for everyone is admitted free.[5] In Verona only the nobility can attend as it's they who run it, but

4. Gaetano Bettinelli (1729–94), mathematician.
5. The article from the *Gazzetta di Mantova* for 19 January 1770 reads, in part: 'Last Tuesday evening ... the public Philharmonic Academy ... was given before its time, in order opportunely to catch the incomparable boy Sig. Wolfango [*sic*] Amadeo Mozart, who is passing through here, with the express aim of letting this town admire the amazing talent and extraordinary mastery which he already possesses in music at the age of 13. To write at a desk (as the best masters do) in as many parts as you wish, concertato or obbligato, vocal and instrumental, is so easy for him that he can do it just as well at the harpsichord, even extempore. On the evening here mentioned, apart from opening and closing symphonies of his composition, he performed ... concertos and sonatas for harpsichord, extemporized with most judicious variations, and with the repetition of a sonata in another key. He sang a whole aria extempore, on new words never before seen by him, adding the proper accompaniments. He improvised two sonatas on two themes successively given him on the violin by the leader of the orchestra, elegantly linking them both together the second time. He accompanied a whole symphony with all the parts from a single violin part submitted to him on the spot. And what is most to be esteemed, he composed and at the same time extemporaneously performed a fugue on a simple theme given him, which he brought to such a masterly harmonic interweaving of all the parts and so bold a resolution as to leave the hearers astounded; and all these performances were on the harpsichord. Finally he also played marvellously well the violin part in a Trio by a famous composer.' See Deutsch, *Documentary Biography*, 107.

in Mantua it's the nobility, the armed forces and the most prominent members of the community as it's a foundation set up by Her Majesty the Empress.[6] You'll easily conclude from this that we shan't grow rich in Italy and that we'll do well to recover our travelling expenses. These I've always recovered: and you can be assured that although there are only 2 of us, our travelling expenses are not small, as we've already spent about *70 ducats*. But, as I write this, we've already been away from Salzb. for 6 weeks, and even if you live *à pasto*[7] and, moreover, even if you often, nay mostly, don't lunch at home, then supper, rooms, wood etc. are all so expensive that after 9 to 11 days at an inn you rarely get away with paying less than 6 ducats. I often thank God that I left you at home. First, you'd not have been able to stand the cold. Secondly, it would have cost an astonishing amount of money, and we'd not have been free to live as we do, as we're now staying *at the Augustinian monastery of San Marco*; not that it's free here, no! but we can live here comfortably and safely and in close proximity to His Excellency Count Firmian.[8] We have 3 large guest rooms. In the first room we have lit a fire and dine and receive visitors here; in the second I sleep and we've put our trunk there; and in the third Wolfg. sleeps and there we keep the rest of our smaller items of luggage etc.

We each sleep on 4 good mattresses, and every night the bed is warmed, so that Wolfg. always goes to bed happy. We have our own brother, Frater Alphonso, to wait on us and are being very well looked after. How long we'll remain here, I can't say. His Excellency the Count has a cold and was very keen to give a concert in his house and invite the Duke of Modena,[9] so I've not yet been able to hand over the other letters, as this has to take place first. I think the concert will be next Tuesday or Wednesday as His Excellency is already feeling a little better. I told you that Wolfg. has got red hands and a

6. Maria Theresa; Lombardy, which included Milan and Mantua, was ruled by Austria.
7. 'half-board'.
8. Karl Joseph, Count Firmian, governor general of Lombardy and a member of the Firmian family of Salzburg, see List.
9. Either Ercole III Rainaldo d'Este (1727–1803), or his father Francesco III (1698–1780).

red face from the cold and fire, but all is now well again. Madame Sartoretti in Mantua gave him a pomade to rub on his hands every evening and in 3 days he was better: he now looks just as he did before. *Otherwise we've kept well, thank God*, and the change of air gave Wolfg. only a cold which he got over long ago. I very much doubt whether we'll hear Herr Meissner performing in Florence for not only shall we be staying here for some time, but because Turin is so close, we'll undoubtedly be popping over there.[10] We'll also be staying briefly in Parma and Bologna, and so I don't think we'll be in Florence before the start of Lent.

As for the horse, you can sell it or raffle it or give it away, for all I care, I just want it out of His Grace's stables. The old saddle etc. is in the stables, the *court stabler* must know where it is.

If it can be sold with the new saddle and bridle, it may be possible to get a better price for it. You can also sell *my carriage*. It's not getting any better; and we shan't be going on any more long journeys. Sell it as best you can, it's done good service. The harness is still in good condition – when I bought it, it cost only *23 ducats*. Talk to people who understand these things. I don't mind what you do: but before you sell it, it needs cleaning. All the letters that you write in future should be *addressed to Monsieur Troger*, as you did last time.

Every good wish to all our friends at home and abroad. I am your old honest

L Mzt

We kiss you both 100,000 times.

22. Mozart to his sister, 26 January 1770, Milan

I'm heartily glad to hear that you enjoyed yourself so much when you went sledging and hope you find a thousand opportunities to enjoy yourself, so that you may have fun all your life. But one thing

10. In the event, they did not visit Turin until January 1771.

annoys me, that you made Herr von Mölk[1] sigh and suffer so much and didn't go sledging with him, so that he could have knocked you over: how many handkerchiefs will he have got through that day, crying because of you? I expect he'd earlier taken an ounce of tartar to empty his hideously unclean body. I've no news except that the Leipzig poet, Herr Learned,[2] has died and hasn't written any more poems since then. Just before starting this letter I set an aria from *Demetrio* that begins:

Misero Tu non sei:
Tu spieghi il Tuo Dolore;
e se non desti amore;
Ritrovi almen pietà.

Misera ben son io
che nel segretto laccio
amo, non spero e taccio
e l'idol mio nol sà.[3]

The opera at Mantua was nice, they gave *Demetrio*, the *prima donna* sings well, but quietly, and if you don't see her acting but only singing, you'd think she wasn't singing at all as she can't open her mouth but just whines – not that that's anything new to us. The *seconda donna* looks like a grenadier guardsman and has a powerful voice too and she doesn't sing at all badly, considering it's the first time she's acted. *Il primo uomo il musico* sings beautifully, though his

1. Probably Joseph von Mölk (1756–1827), son of the court chancellor Franz Felix Anton von Mölk (1715–76), whose daughter Anna Barbara (1752–1823) was a close friend of Nannerl's. Mozart appears to be teasing his sister about the boy's adolescent crush on her.
2. Christian Fürchtegott Gellert (1715–69) was one of Leopold's favourite poets. Wolfgang's pun on his name – he writes Gellert as Gelehrt, that is, 'learned' – may be good-natured or it may be an adolescent dismissal of parental authority.
3. 'You are not unhappy: you can explain your sadness; and if you do not awaken love, you at least find pity. I am truly sad that I love in secret toils, I have no hope and I say nothing, and my beloved does not know,' from act 1, scene 4 of Hasse's setting of *Demetrio*, which Mozart heard in Mantua. Mozart's setting, K73A, is lost.

voice is uneven, he's called Caselli. *Il secondo uomo* is already old, and I don't like him. He's called [. . .][4] Tenors: the one called Uttini doesn't sing badly but as with all Italian tenors it's a heavy sound, also he's a very good friend of ours. I don't know what the other one's called, he's still young, but nothing special. *Primo ballerino*: good. *Prima ballerina*: good, and people say that she's not bad-looking, but I haven't seen her close up, the rest are very ordinary: there was also a *grottesco*[5] who jumps well but who can't write like me, like sows pissing.

The orchestra wasn't bad. In Cremona the orchestra was good, and the first violin is called Spagnoletto.[6] *Prima donna* not bad, already old, I think, not good-looking, acts better than she sings, and is the wife of a violinist who plays in the opera and who's called Masi. The opera is called *La clemenza di Tito*.[7] Second *donna* not bad-looking on stage, young, but nothing special. *Primo uomo musico* Cicognani.[8] An attractive voice, and a beautiful *cantabile*. The other two castratos, young and passable. Tenor: calls himself *non lo sò*.[9] Has a pleasant manner and looks just like Leroy, who was in Vienna but who's now with Lehmann. *Ballerino primo*: good; *ballerina prima* good but extremely unattractive. There was a female dancer there who didn't dance badly and who – what a *chef-d'œuvre* – isn't bad-looking off stage and on. The others very ordinary. There was a *grottesco* there, too, who farted each time he jumped. I really can't tell you much about Milan as we haven't been to the opera yet, though we've heard that it wasn't a success. Aprile, the *primo uomo*, sings well, he has a beautiful even voice, we heard him in church, where a great festival was taking place: Madame Piccinelli from Paris, who

4. There is a gap in Mozart's letter here.
5. Comic acrobat.
6. Francesco Diana (1717–?), known as Spagnoletto.
7. By the Neapolitan composer Michelangelo Valentini (*c.* 1720–after 1768) to a text by Metastasio (see *Briefe* v. 227–8). Mozart set Metastasio's text, in a version by Caterino Mazzolà, in 1791 (K621).
8. Giuseppe Cicognani later sang the role of Farnace at the first performance of Mozart's *Mitridate, re di Ponto* in Milan in December 1770.
9. 'I don't know'.

sang at our concert, is appearing at the opera: Monsieur de Picq, who used to dance in Vienna, is dancing here in Milan.[10] The opera is called *Didone abbandonata*.[11] This opera will soon be finishing, and Sig. Piccinni, who's writing the next opera, is here in Milan: I've heard that his opera is called *Cesare in Egitto*: there are also *feste di ballo* here: as soon as the opera's over, the *festo di ballo* begins: the wife of Count Firmian's steward is from Vienna, we dined there last Friday, and next Sunday we'll be dining there again. Farewell, and kiss Mama's hands a thousand times for me, I remain, true till death, your brother

Wolfgang de Mozart
Baron Hochenthal
Friend of the Counting-House.[12]

23. *Leopold Mozart to his wife, 13 March 1770, Milan*

It was impossible for me to write last Saturday as Wolfg. had to compose *3 arias* and *1 recit. with violins* for the concert that was held yesterday at Count Firmian's,[1] and I was obliged to copy the violin parts myself and then have them duplicated so that they wouldn't be stolen. There were over 150 members of the leading nobility present, foremost among whom were the duke, princess and

10. Giuseppe Aprile (1731–1813), castrato; Clementine Piccinelli (active in Paris 1761–6 and in Italy thereafter) had performed at Mozart's concert in Paris on 9 April 1764; Carlo de Picq (1749–1806) later danced in the ballet performed with Mozart's *Lucio Silla* at Milan in December 1772.

11. Two new productions of the opera were mounted in Italy in 1770, by Niccolò Piccinni at Rome on 8 January, and by Giacomo Insanguine (1728–95) at Naples, but it is likely that the Milanese *Didone* was a revival of an earlier setting, of which there were many.

12. Mozart has made up this title for himself.

1. The concert was held on 12 March 1770 at the Palazzo Melzi and probably included some or all of *Misero tu non sei* K73A (see letter 22), *Misero me! – Misero pargoletto* K77 and *Fra cento affanni* K88.

cardinal.[2] It has now been decided that, with God's help, we'll leave Milan next Thursday, in other words, the day after tomorrow, but as we're travelling with a coachman and not leaving until midday, we shan't be in Parma until Saturday morning; you can easily imagine that I've an amazing amount of things to do, not least because the whole trunk has been unpacked on account of our long stay here. Another matter also has to be resolved between this evening and tomorrow: they want Wolfg. to write the first opera for next Christmas.[3] If this goes ahead, you can be glad because we shall then certainly be home sooner than would otherwise appear to be the case: we have enough on our hands trying to get to Rome by Holy Week. You know that *Rome* is the one place where you absolutely have to stay. We'll then move on to Naples, a place so important that even if a contract doesn't take us back to Milan to write an opera there, some other occasion may well present itself that will detain us there throughout the coming winter.

If the contract is signed, the libretto will then be sent to us, Wolfg. can think the matter over a little, we can take the Loreto[4] road and be back in Milan by Advent; and inasmuch as the composer isn't obliged to stay on after the opera has been staged, we can then return home via Venice and be back within a year. I leave it all to Providence and God's decree. Could I ask you to offer my apologies to all and sundry and congratulate everyone called Joseph, as this is my most tiring week: you know how difficult, sad and tiring every departure is. In particular I would ask you to give my most humble good wishes and apologies to our Father Confessor.

Please continue as before to address your letters to Herr Troger, who can be relied upon to forward them.

As soon as I'm in Bologna or Florence, I'll write to you, perhaps also from Parma.

Tomorrow, to mark our departure, we're dining with His Excel-

2. Duke of Modena, see letter 21, n. 9; Maria Beatrice Ricciarda d'Este (1750–1829); Archbishop Pozzonbonelli (1696–1783).
3. *Mitridate, re di Ponto*, premiered at the Teatro Regio Ducal, Milan, on 26 December 1770.
4. Loreto, near Ancona in the Marche, was a popular place of pilgrimage.

lency, who is providing us with letters of recommendation for Parma, Florence, Rome and Naples.[5] I can't tell you how kind His Excellency has been to us throughout our stay. I'd already have written to His Excellency the Chief Steward[6] if I'd not had to wait until tomorrow to do so in greater detail. Give my best wishes to all our good friends. Farewell, I kiss you and Nannerl 1000 times and am your old

Mzt

In particular give all conceivable good wishes to Monsieur Selzam from us both.

[*Wolfgang's postscript*]
Best wishes from me too, I kiss Mama and my sister millions of times and am well, thank God, *addio*.

Mozart and his father left Milan on 15 March, travelling by way of Lodi (where Mozart composed his first quartet, K80) to Piacenza, Parma, Modena and Bologna, where they arrived on 24 March.

5. One such letter, written on 14 March 1770 to Count Giovanni Luca Pallavicini at Bologna, stated: 'Your Excellency, seeing that Sig. Leopoldo Mozart, Chapel Master in the service of the Prince-Archbishop of Salzburg, and with him his son, is making his way to your city, I take the liberty of recommending them warmly to Your Excellency, moved by the assurance I have of your well-known generosity and kindness, and by the thought that perhaps you will not be displeased to find in young Mozart one of those musical talents but rarely produced by nature, inasmuch that at his tender age he not only equals the Masters of the art, but even exceeds them, I believe, in readiness of invention. I hope therefore that Your Excellency will be pleased to honour them with your protection during their stay there and to find them means of appearing in public, as I also urgently beg you will help them in the matter of their prudent and most advantageous conduct.' See Deutsch, *Documentary Biography*, 110–11.
6. Franz Lactanz, Count Firmian, see List.

24. *Leopold Mozart to his wife, 27 March 1770, Bologna*

I wrote to His Excellency the Chief Steward from Parma, and from here I wrote to His Grace and to you on the 24th inst. I await your reply as to whether all these letters have arrived safely. There was a concert yesterday at the home of His Excellency Field Marshal Count Pallavicini, to which His Eminence the Cardinal and leading members of the nobility were invited.[1] You know His Excellency Count Karl von Firmian; I'd now like you to get to know Count Pallavicini, too. They are 2 gentlemen who in every respect share the same outlook, the same friendliness, generosity, placidity and particular love and insight into all kinds of knowledge. On Sunday I was privileged to pay my respects to His Excellency Count Pallavicini and to give him His Excellency Count Firmian's letter; and scarcely had he heard that I was planning to be in Rome by Holy Week when he said at once that he would try to arrange to have the pleasure not just of hearing this extraordinary young virtuoso tomorrow but of affording the same pleasure to the city's leading aristocrats. I shall not touch on all the circumstances and tell you how we were collected in His Excellency's carriage and how we were waited upon, but shall say only that about 150 members of the leading aristocracy were present: the famous Padre Martini[2] was also invited, and although he normally never goes to concerts, he did come to this one: it began at around half past seven and went on until half past eleven, because the nobility showed no sign of leaving. Sgr Aprile and Sgr Cicognani sang. We're leaving the day after tomorrow, Thursday the 29th, and shall be in Florence by Friday evening, remaining there until the 5th, before continuing our journey to Rome, so that, if God places no obstacle in our way, we could be there by midday on the 11th. What pleases me most of

1. Giovanni Luca, Count Pallavicini-Centurioni (1697–1773); Mozart performed at the Palazzo Pallavicini on 26 March. The cardinal was Antonio Colonna-Branciforte (1728–86).
2. Giovanni Battista Martini (1706–84), music theorist and historian. Mozart's puzzle canons K73r and canonic studies K73x are based on models taken from volumes 1 and 2 of Martini's *Storia della musica* (Bologna, 1757).

all is that we are uncommonly popular here and Wolfg. is admired here even more than in all the other towns in Italy, because many composers, artists and scholars live and work here. He has also been most comprehensively tested here, and this increases his fame throughout the whole of Italy, because Padre Martini is the idol of the Italians and speaks of Wolfg. with such admiration and has done all the tests with him.

We've visited Padre Martini on 2 occasions: and on each occasion Wolfg. worked out a fugue for which Padre Martini had written only a few notes of the *ducem* or *guida*. We've also visited Cavaliere Don Broschi – also known as Sgr Farinelli – on his estates outside the town.[3] And we also met La Spagnoletta here as she'll be the *prima donna* in the opera that'll be given in May, replacing Gabrielli,[4] who's still in Palermo and who has left the people of Bologna in the lurch. Presumably she'll also leave the people of Milan in the lurch.

We met Sgr Manfredini here – the castrato who called on us in Salzburg while on his way from Russia with Herr Panter of Vienna etc. etc.

A certain *old Sgr Abbate Zanardi* joins me in sending his good wishes to Herr Andrino. A number of people have been asking about Kapellmeister Lolli. Herr Prinsechi and many other people have enquired about the court *statuarius*, all send their good wishes along with mine.[5] We were at the *Instituto* and saw the beautiful statues of our court *statuarius*. What I've seen here surpasses the British Museum, for here there are not only unusual objects from the world of nature *but everything that comes under the name of science*, preserved like a lexicon in beautiful rooms and neatly arranged in an orderly manner: in a word, you'd be amazed etc. I'll say nothing about the

3. Carlo Broschi (1705–82), castrato, who took the name of Farinelli; he was one of the most renowned singers of his day and performed throughout Europe before settling in Bologna in 1759.
4. Clementina Spagnoli (*c.* 1735–after 1788), soprano; Catarina Gabrielli (1730–96), soprano.
5. Giuseppe Francesco Lolli (1701–78) was deputy Kapellmeister at Salzburg 1752–63, Kapellmeister 1763–78; Johann Baptist Hagenauer (1732–1810), a member of the extended Hagenauer family, was court *statuarius* (sculptor) in Salzburg.

churches, paintings, beautiful architecture and the furnishings of the various palazzos as I'm so tired that I can hardly write any more, it's past 1 o'clock, Wolfg. has long been snoring and I'm falling asleep as I write.

You don't need to submit a report on the horse, for anyone who gives away my things without my knowledge and against my wishes will replace them with something better: if he's a gentleman who has only noble thoughts – – – –

It's good that you've arranged for someone to write to Leipzig.[6] Get them also to write to Herr Gräffer or *Heufeld*. Farewell! Farewell, all of you, I kiss you and Nannerl 1000 times. Best wishes to the whole of Salzb. I am your faithful and sleepy husband

Mzt

It wasn't a bad idea to send us the ball minuet[7] in Bologna so that it could be arranged for the keyboard, as there's no one in Salzb. who could have done it. Wolfg, I may add, couldn't have been more pleased and thanks Herr von Schiedenhofen and Nannerl. He'll be writing himself very soon. I wrote this yesterday when he was already in bed and I'm adding this now while he's still asleep, as the post leaves in a moment. He's now sending you the minuet that Monsieur Picq danced in the theatre in Milan. Best wishes to all our good friends. Please ask Herr von Schiedenhofen, Herr von Mölk and others who've written to me not to take it amiss that I've not replied. I hope that on reflection they'll realize what a traveller has to do, especially as I'm on my own. *Kommabit aliquando Zeitus bequemmus schreibendi. nunc Kopfus meus semper vollus est multis gedankibus*.[8]

Wolfg. kisses you and Nannerl 1000 times.

Keep sending your letters to Herr Troger in Milan. They're arriving safely and don't cost me very much. Once we're in Rome, I'll write more on this matter.

6. To the publisher Breitkopf.
7. Probably K122.
8. A macaronic combination of German vocabulary and Latin inflections, meaning, 'There will be a convenient time for writing. Now my head is always full of many thoughts.'

Among the medical prescriptions you'll find one for a coltsfoot electuary[9] – I think it's on a long piece of paper – as you know, it's one I've often had made up for myself. Please copy it out clearly in your next letter. Thank God, there's nothing wrong with me, but I suddenly thought of this coltsfoot electuary as one never knows what might happen. So far, we've opened the medicine bag only once, thank God – it was to give Wolfg. a spoonful of tartar.

[*Postscript, written on one of Mozart's manuscripts*]
Padre Martini has asked me for a copy of the *Violinschule*, so you'll have to speak to the consignee, Herr Haffner.[10] Would he be kind enough to take one with him to Bozen and include one with a bale of linen for Herr Prinsechi? But you'll have to have it bound first. But only in half-calf, very light: but it has to be bound because the Italians wouldn't understand the instructions to the binder.

From Bologna Leopold and Wolfgang travelled to Florence, where they took the chance to hear again the violinist Pietro Nardini, met the famous contrapuntist Eugenio, Marquis de Ligniville (1730–88) and renewed their acquaintance with the castrato Giovanni Manzuoli (c. 1720–82), whom they had first met during their visit to London in 1764–5. Mozart also struck up a friendship with the fourteen-year-old English prodigy, Thomas Linley (1756–78), who was a violin pupil of Nardini's. Almost of the same age and height, they performed together several times, playing 'not like boys, but like men!', according to Leopold. On the last occasion 'Little Tommaso accompanied us home and wept bitter tears, because we were leaving the following day.' Mozart later wrote to Linley (see letter 29), but they did not meet again. The Mozarts set out from Florence on 6 April, arriving at Rome on 11 April.

9. A medicinal syrup made from the coltsfoot plant.
10. For the Salzburg Haffner family and their business contacts, see List.

25. Leopold Mozart to his wife, 14 April 1770, Rome

We arrived here safely at midday on the 11th. It would have been easier to persuade me to go to Salzb. than Rome as we spent 5 days travelling from Florence to Rome in the most appalling rain and cold wind. In Rome itself I heard that it's been raining constantly for the last 4 months, and we certainly got a taste of it when we went to the Sistine Chapel to hear the *Miserere*[1] during Mass on the Wednesday and Thursday, setting off on both occasions in fine weather, only to be surprised by such a terrible downpour on our way home that our coats have never been as wet as they were on that occasion. But I won't bore you with a long description of our appalling journey here. Imagine only a largely uncultivated country and the most appalling inns, filth everywhere, nothing to eat except – if we were lucky – the occasional meal of eggs and broccoli: and sometimes they even made a fuss about giving us eggs on fast days. Fortunately we got a decent supper and slept well in Viterbo. While there we saw St Rosa of Viterbo – like St Catherine of Bologna, she can be seen in a perfectly preserved state. From the former we took away an ague powder and some relics as a souvenir, while from the latter we brought with us a belt. After arriving here on the 11th, we went to St Peter's after lunch and then to mass, on the 12th we attended the foot washing and found ourselves very close to the pope[2] while he was serving the poor at table, as we were standing beside him at the top of the table. This is all the more surprising in that we had to go through two doors guarded by Swiss Guards in armour and force our way through several 100 people – and remember that as yet we'd made no acquaintances. But our fine clothes, the German language, and my usual freedom in telling my servant to speak to the Swiss Guards in German and make way for us soon helped us through everywhere. They thought Wolfg. was a German gentleman, others even took him for

1. The famous *Miserere* by the Italian baroque composer Gregorio Allegri (1582–1652) was traditionally sung in the Sistine Chapel on the Wednesday of Holy Week and Good Friday.
2. Clement XIV (1705–74), elected pope in 1769.

a prince, and our servant let them believe this; I was taken for his tutor. And so we made our way to the cardinals' table. There it chanced that Wolfg. ended up between the chairs of two cardinals, one of whom was Cardinal Pallavicini.[3]

The latter beckoned to Wolfg. and said to him: *Would you be good enough to tell me in confidence who you are?* Wolfg. told him everything. The cardinal replied with the greatest surprise and said: *Oh, so you're the famous boy about whom so many things have been written?*

To this, Wolfg. asked: *Aren't you Cardinal Pallavicini?* – – The cardinal answered: *Yes, I am, why?* – –

Wolfg. then said to him *that we'd got letters for His Eminence and were going to pay him our respects.* The cardinal was very pleased by this and said that Wolfg. spoke very good Italian, saying, among other things: *ik kann auck ein benig deutsch sprecken*[4] etc. etc.

As we were leaving, Wolfg. kissed his hand, and the cardinal removed his biretta and bowed very politely.

You'll often have heard of the famous *Miserere* in Rome, which is held in such high regard that the musicians in the chapel are forbidden on pain of excommunication to remove even a single part, to copy it or to give it to anyone else. But *we already have it.* Wolfg. has already written it down, and we'd have sent it to Salzb. with this letter except that it would require our presence to perform it; the manner of its performance must play a greater role than the work itself, and so we'll bring it home with us, and as it's one of the secrets of Rome, we don't want it to fall into the wrong hands, *ut non incurremus mediate vel immediate in Censuram Ecclesiæ.*[5]

We've already explored St Peter's thoroughly, and I've no doubt that of all the sights here, none will be overlooked. Tomorrow – God willing – we'll see His Holiness preach. You simply can't imagine how arrogant are the local clergy. Any individual who has the slightest contact with a cardinal thinks himself as good as the cardinal. And whenever he's on papal business, every cardinal drives with a cortège

3. Lazaro Opizio Pallavicini (1719–85), a distant relative of Giovanni Luca, Count Pallavicini-Centurioni.
4. 'I too can speak a little German.'
5. 'So that we shall not incur the Church's censure, now or later.'

of 3 or 4 carriages, each of them crammed full of chaplains, secretaries and valets, each taking up as much space as he can, and so I'm looking forward to tomorrow when I shall walk past all these proud gentlemen and leave them guessing who we are, as we've not yet presented ourselves anywhere because of the foot washing. On Monday we'll make a start on delivering our 20 letters of recommendation.

Pleased though I am that the two of you didn't come on this trip with us, I'm sorry that you're not able to see all the towns and cities of Italy, but especially Rome. It's useless, indeed impossible, to describe it in only a few words. Once again I advise you to read *Keyssler's account of his travels*. I wrote to you from Bologna and Florence. 2 hours after our arrival we called in at the German College and found Herr von Mölk in excellent health, as were all our other acquaintances there. Out of regard for Herr von Mölk I intend to get Wolfg. to perform for the whole college as they'd very much like to hear him. Abbate Marcabruni[6] had already sorted out our lodgings in a private house and we were able to move in straightaway: but since there's only one room here and we must have 2 rooms to receive people who call on us, we'll be moving this evening to more spacious accommodation. Today and yesterday I've been something of an invalid, as I took 3 digestive powders, but I now feel well, thank God. Wolfg. also feels well and is sending you a contredanse.[7] He'd like Herr Cyrill Hofmann[8] to compose the steps for it; when the 2 violins play as leaders, he wants only 2 people to lead the dance, but each time that the full orchestra comes in with all the instruments, the whole company should then dance together. It would be best if it were danced by 5 couples. The first couple starts the first solo, the 2nd dances the 2nd and so on, as there are 5 solos and 5 tuttis.

The season is fast approaching that causes me the greatest anxiety, as it will soon be getting hot; but everyone tells me that Naples has incomparably more air and that it's much healthier than Rome. And so I'll need to take all possible precautions to ensure that we can set

6. He was the postmaster at Rome.
7. Probably K123.
8. Dancing master at the Salzburg court.

off on our return journey with no risk to our lives, especially from the bad air and malaria. But since everything depends on the weather and especially on heavy rain and wind, I can neither decide nor write. Herr Meissner is in Naples, we hope to see him there in 3 or 4 weeks. Pray to dear God for our health: we'll be all right, for I can assure you that we are taking every possible care and that Wolfg. pays as much attention to his health as if he were the most grown up of people. May God keep you, too, in good health. Remember us to all our good friends, I am your old

Mzt

Wolfg. and I kiss you and Nannerl 1000 times.

[Mozart's postscript]
Praise and thanks be to God, I and my wretched pen are well, and I kiss Mama and Nannerl a thousand or 1000 times. I only wish my sister were in Rome, she'd certainly like the city, as St Peter's is regular, and many other things in Rome are regular, too. The most beautiful flowers are just being carried past in the street, Papa has just this moment told me. I'm a fool, as everyone knows. Oh, I'm having a hard time, there's only one bed in our lodgings, Mama can easily imagine that I get no sleep with Papa, I'm looking forward to our new lodgings: I've just drawn a picture of St Peter with his keys, St Paul with his sword and St Luke with my sister etc. etc., I had the honour of kissing St Peter's foot in St Peter's, and as I'm unlucky enough to be so small, it was necessary for me, that same old fool

Wolfgang Mozart,
to be lifted up

26. Pietro Lugiati[1] to Maria Anna Mozart, 22 April 1770, Verona

Madame,

Since the beginning of this year, this City of ours has admired in

---

1. Lugiati had commissioned Mozart's portrait in Verona, see letter 20.

the most highly prized Person of Sgr Amadeo Volfango Mozart, Your Son, a prodigy, it may be said, of nature in Music, inasmuch as Art could not yet have performed her Office if she had not taken account of his tender age.

I have certainly been among his admirers, even though, however much pleasure Music may invariably have afforded me and however much I may have heard on my travels, I cannot hope to be an infallible judge of it; but I am certainly not mistaken in the case of so rare and prodigious a Youth, and I have conceived such a regard for him that I have had him painted from life with the inscription copied from the end of the cantata[2] – which he will be pleased to read.

This sweet likeness is a comfort to me, and it also serves as a stimulus to take up his Music from time to time, so far as my public and private preoccupations allow me, although I have not lost track of Sgr Amadeo and Sgr Leopoldo, his most amiable Father, having with pleasure received news of them from Mantua, Milan and most recently from Florence, reporting universal applause, as we shall soon hear from Rome, where I have already directed them to the most illustrious people.

I cannot but recall, Madame, the pleasure you felt on taking him at an even more tender age to the leading Cities in Europe, together with your astonishing Daughter, who was the object of universal admiration, as he himself is at present.

I can only repeat the esteem that I feel for the one as for the other and, in consequence, how much I prize their Parents who with such careful education have cultivated such rare talents, talents which, having given you such lively pleasure, shall yet offer the world cause for universal admiration.

Please accept these sentiments, which are born of good intentions and true esteem, since while expressing them I take this opportunity to fulfil a commitment to let your Son have two pieces of Music which he saw while he was staying with me and which I have had copied in order to please him,[3] so that he may make full use of them. You will

2. Unidentified.
3. Also unidentified.

receive these from the merchant Sgr Soldini, who assures me that he will deliver them safely to you. I shall be grateful if you will acknowledge them at your convenience.

I may conclude by wishing you and your most esteemed Family every happiness, while signing myself, with sincere and devoted esteem, Madame,

Your Most Devoted and Humble Servant
Pietro Lugiati

From Rome, Mozart and his father travelled on to Naples, arriving there on 14 May, after a journey of a week. During their stay in the city, they met the distinguished English ambassador Sir William Hamilton, gave a concert on 28 May, and on 18 and 19 June visited Vesuvius and Pompeii.

27. Leopold Mozart to his wife, 19 May 1770, Naples

You'll have received my last letter from Rome by now – the one dated 2 May. I'm sorry I wasn't able to write for so long – you must have been very anxious in the meantime. We left Rome at 10 in the morning on 8 May in the company of three other *sedias* – 2-seater carriages – and had a light lunch at 1 o'clock at the Augustinian monastery at *Marino*. On the evening of the 11th we were again well looked after at another Augustinian monastery at Sessa, calling in on the Augustinian friars in Capua at midday on the 12th in the belief that we'd be in Naples that same evening. But on the 13th, as fate would have it, a woman was to take the veil at a convent where one of my travelling companions, Padre Segarelli, was Father Confessor some years ago. He was to attend the ceremony and asked us to remain there, too, and so we attended the ceremony, which was a splendid occasion and for which a Kapellmeister with 3 or 4 carriages of virtuosos arrived on the evening of the 12th, opening the proceedings with some symphonies and a *Salve Regina*.

All these virtuosos stayed at the monastery, so you can easily imagine that we got to bed very late that evening. The veiling or, rather, the service did not take place until noon on the Sunday, and the whole affair went on until around 3. Apart from those ladies and gentlemen who were close friends of the woman, nobody apart from us 2 was invited to dine at the convent. It would be impossible to describe it all. On the Monday we slept until 10 and after lunch drove to Naples, where we arrived in good time that same evening. We spent 2 nights in a house belonging to the Augustinian monastery of San Giovanni a Carbonara, but we're now in rooms for which we're having to pay 10 silver ducats a month, or 4 ducats in our own money. We drove out to Portici yesterday to call on the minister, Marchese Tanucci.[1] We'll be driving out there again tomorrow. We had terrible rain yesterday and a very cool breeze. We left our fine cloth suits in Rome and have had to wear our beautifully braided summer suits. Wolfg.'s is made of pink moiré, but the colour is so unusual that in Italy it's called *colore di fuoco*, or flame-coloured: with silver lace and lined with a light sky-blue material. My suit is a kind of cinnamon colour, piquéd Florentine cloth, with silver lace and lined in apple-green. Both suits are very beautiful, but we'll look like a couple of old maids by the time we get home. Yesterday evening we called on the English ambassador, Sir William Hamilton (our acquaintance from London), whose wife plays the keyboard with exceptional feeling and who is a most pleasant person.[2] She trembled at having to play for Wolfg. She has a valuable instrument made in England by Tschudi,[3] with 2 manuals and pedal stops that can be uncoupled by means of the foot. Also present were Mr Beckford and Monsieur Vyse, 2 other acquaintances from England. On the 16th we lunched

1. Bernardo, Marchese Tanucci (1688–1783), Neapolitan prime minister.
2. Sir William Hamilton (1730–1803), diplomat and art collector, was the English ambassador to Naples from 1764–1800; his first wife Catherine (née Barlow) died in 1782, and in 1791 he married Emma Hart, the later mistress of Admiral Horatio Nelson.
3. Burkat Tschudi (1702–73), instrument maker in London. Mozart had played on one of his harpsichords in London in July 1765. He has no apparent connection with the Baron Tschudi mentioned below.

with Baron Tschudi, who had been in Salzb. He asked me to convey his good wishes to His Excellency Count Spaur[4] and all our good friends, especially you and Nannerl. He kissed us countless times, especially when we arrived and as we were leaving, and offered us his services, no matter what the occasion. The day before yesterday we bumped into Monsieur Meuricoffre[5] from Lyons, who had been looking everywhere for us. He'd left a card for us, with his address, at the Augustinian monastery and had finally run into us by chance. He came back with us to our rooms and then took us to his own house. We were supposed to have lunch with him tomorrow, but as we have to go to Portici tomorrow, we can't make it. He sends you his cordial best wishes. He's set up a company here with another person: both of them have offered me their services in all eventualities. I expect you still remember him: a young man with brown hair, who often had to sing the Italian song to Wolfg. with his glasses on his nose. I still can't tell you how long we'll be staying here. It could be 5 weeks or 5 months. I think it'll be 5 weeks, but it all depends on the circumstances.

While I was listening to High Mass on the Feast of St Philip and St James in the Church of the Holy Apostles in Rome, I saw a familiar face. He came over to me; and who do you think it was? – – it was our former servant, Porta. He was neatly dressed, lace cuffs, a gold watch, etc. etc. He'd been with the French troops in Corsica. The next day he came to offer me his services just as Herr Meissner was arriving. I refused even so much as to listen to him. Just ask Herr Meissner, he saw him. The fellow's an adventurer.

I was sincerely sorry to hear about Frau Adlgasser's accidents and hope she'll soon be better.[6] Best wishes to them both. Frau *de Amicis*[7] sends her best wishes to you and Nannerl, together with those of her mother, brother etc.

4. Ignaz Joseph, Count Spaur (1729–79), canon of Salzburg cathedral. He became bishop of Brixen in 1778.
5. Jean-Georges Meuricoffre (1750–1806), banker; he had met the Mozarts in Lyons in summer 1766.
6. Maria Anna (née Fesemayr), wife of the Salzburg organist Anton Cajetan Adlgasser.
7. Anna Lucia de Amicis (*c.* 1733–1816), soprano.

When we read the article on the *Miserere*, we couldn't help laughing out loud.[8] There's not the slightest cause for anxiety. People are making far more of it elsewhere. The whole of Rome knows; even the pope knows that Wolfg. wrote down the *Miserere*. There's absolutely nothing to be afraid of: quite the opposite, it's done him great credit, as you'll shortly be hearing. You must make absolutely certain that everyone reads the letter, so that we can be sure that His Grace gets to hear about it.

If the portraits have turned out to be a good likeness, you may pay whatever you like for them.[9]

I must close now as we're off to see the imperial ambassador, Count Kaunitz.[10] Farewell, we kiss you and Nannerl 1000 times and I am your old

Mzt

I hope you've recovered from your cold.

[*Note enclosed by Mozart to his sister written in a mixture of Italian and German*]
Cara sorella mia,
My dear sister, I really don't know how to reply to your letter as you wrote almost nothing. I'll send you Sgr Haydn's[11] minuets when I have more time. I've already sent you the first one. But I don't understand. You say that they've been stolen, these minuets. Did you steal them? Or what? Please write soon, and write every post-day. Thanks for sending me the maths book, and if ever you want a headache, please send me more of the same. Forgive me for writing so badly, but the reason is that I too have a slight headache. I really like the twelfth minuet by Haydn that you sent me, and you've written a wonderful bass for it, without the slightest mistake. I'd like you to try your hand at such things more often: Mama mustn't forget

8. This article has not been found.
9. These portraits appear not to have survived.
10. Ernst Christoph, Count Kaunitz-Rietberg (1737–97), eldest son of Prince Kaunitz.
11. Michael Haydn, composer, see List; his twelfth minuet (below) is unidentified.

to have both the guns cleaned: write and tell me how Mr Canary is. Is he still singing? Is he still whistling? Do you know why I'm thinking of the canary? Because there's one in our front room that makes a noise just like ours. By the way, I assume that Herr Johannes has received the letter of congratulation that we were going to write to him, but if he hasn't received it, I'll tell him in person what it would have contained when I get back to Salzburg. We wore our new suits for the first time yesterday and were as beautiful as the angels, but I'm afraid that we won't be bringing any other beautiful things back home with us. *Addio*, farewell, best wishes to Nandl, tell her to be a good girl and pray for me. I am

Wolfgang Mozart

The opera[12] that Jommelli is writing will open on the 30th, we saw the king and queen[13] during Mass in the court chapel at Portici, and we also saw Vesuvius: Naples is beautiful, but it's as crowded as Vienna and Paris. Of London and Naples, I'm not sure whether the people in Naples are not more impertinent than those in London, for here the common people, the *lazzeroni*, have their own general or chief who receives 25 silver ducats from the king every month, just to keep the *lazzeroni* in order. De Amicis is singing in the opera, we called on her and she recognized us at once. The second opera is being written by Cafaro, the 3rd by Cìcio de Majo,[14] it's not yet known who's writing the 4th. Be a good girl and go to Mirabell[15] to hear the litanies and the *Regina Coeli* or *Salve Regina*, and sleep well and don't have any bad dreams. Give Herr von Schiedenhofen my barbarous good wishes, tralaliera, tralaliera, and tell him to learn how to play the repeating minuet on the keyboard, so that he *doesn't* forget it, he should *do* so soon so that he may *do* me the pleasure of letting me *do* the honours and accompany him. *Do* give my good wishes to

12. *Armida abbandonata.*
13. Ferdinand IV (1751–1825), king of Naples, and his wife, Maria Carolina (1752–1814), sixth daughter of Maria Theresa; she had married Ferdinand in 1768 instead of her sister Josepha (see letter 14, n. 3).
14. Pasquale Cafaro (1715/16–87), *Antigono*; Francesco de Majo (1732–70), *Eumene*.
15. The summer residence of the archbishop of Salzburg.

all our other good friends, and *do* keep well and *do* not die but *do* me a favour and write me another letter, so that I can *do* the same, and we can then keep on *doing* so until we are *done*, for I'm someone who will keep on *doing* things until finally there's nothing left to *do*, but for now I'll have done.

Wolfgang Mozart

Mozart and his father set out from Naples on 25 June, arriving back at Rome the next day. On 5 July Mozart was awarded the Order of the Golden Spur by Pope Clement XIV, with whom they had an audience on 8 July. They left Rome on 10 July, arriving at Bologna on 20 July. From 10 August until 1 October, Leopold and Wolfgang lodged at the country home of Giovanni Luca, Count Pallavicini-Centurioni just outside Bologna, where Mozart received the libretto to Mitridate, re di Ponto *('Mithridates, King of Pontus'). He started work on the opera on 29 September.*

28. Leopold Mozart to his wife, 11 August 1770, Bologna

You'll have received my letter of the 28th on the 4th, in other words, on the day after you wrote to me, and in the meantime you'll also have received my letter of the 4th inst.

We arrived here on this estate at around midday yesterday after hearing Mass in Bologna, it's about as far from the city as Maria Plain is from Salzb.[1] We were finally able to get a good night's sleep, and I don't need to describe the excellent service here. You can imagine the rooms and the beds, the sheets are of finer linen than many an aristocrat's shirt etc., everything is made of silver, even the chamber utensils and nightlight, etc. etc. In the evening we went for a drive in 2 *sedias* – Wolfg. with Her Excellency the Countess and the young

1. About 3 km.

Count, and I and His Excellency the Field Marshal,[2] we have a footman and a servant to wait on us, in other words, 2 people, and the footman sleeps in our anteroom so that he's always on call, while the servant has to dress Wolfg.'s hair. His Excellency has put us in the first rooms – in Salzb. they'd be on the ground floor – as these are the best rooms in summer, when the upper rooms get very hot, so that we don't feel the slightest heat during the day and especially at night. Apart from our rooms, there's the Sala Terrena where we eat and everything is fresh, cool and pleasant. The young count, who is Wolfg.'s age and the only heir, is very talented, plays the keyboard, speaks German, Italian and French and has 5 or 6 tutors a day for lessons in various branches of knowledge and other exercises. He's already an imperial chamberlain. As you can imagine, this young gentleman and Wolfg. are the best of friends.

We'll be remaining here for a while – how long I don't know. Perhaps for the whole of the month, until the worst of the heat is over. And my foot?[3] – – Thank God, it's better. The wound has healed completely and the skin is gradually falling off. But however much I try to avoid doing so, I have to use it during the daytime, with the result that by evening I have a slight swelling near my ankle, but this always goes away again during the night, and each day it grows less. Their lordships never make me stand but insist on my remaining seated, with my leg resting on a second chair. They even arranged 2 chairs for me for mass in the chapel today. We have Mass every day before noon, when the young count serves; after Mass the *Rosary*, *Litany*, *Salve Regina* and *De Profundis* are said.

You're invited to enjoy the finest figs, melons and peaches! And I'm extremely pleased to be able to tell you that we are well, thank God. If I'd not removed the ointments and plasters, I'd have had a lot more trouble, as these drew all the salts and pus and water to them, and since the body is provided with enough of these liquids through its daily intake of food and drink, I'd have had to wait a

2. Count Pallavicini-Centurioni, his second wife, Maria Caterina Fava, and their son, Giuseppe Maria (1756–73).
3. In a letter of 30 June 1770 Leopold reported to his wife that he had sustained a leg injury while travelling in a coach.

long time for the end. If nature itself had made this opening, it would, of course, have been very bad to prevent such a discharge, but since it resulted from an unforeseen incident, it was enough and more than enough to have an open wound on my foot for 6 whole weeks. It should be a warning to everyone not to apply a plaster but to use nothing but paper and urine, in order to prevent pus from collecting.

Give my good wishes to Kapellmeister Lolli and tell him that I shall, of course, deliver his messages and that I've already spoken to a number of his old acquaintances. We forgot to congratulate Nannerl on her name day.[4] My foot brought back all my old melancholy thoughts. It's very sad to hear that things are getting more and more expensive in Salzb. Is no thought being given to ways of combating this increase? – – Give my very best wishes to Herr von Schiedenhofen and his dear Mama. I'll be replying to Herr von Schiedenhofen's letter shortly. I received all 3 letters at once today. I must close. His Excellency's letters are being sent to town, and this one has to go with them. We kiss you and Nannerl 1000 times. Wolfg. has just gone for a drive with the countess. We send our good wishes to all – to all etc. and I am your old

Mzt

29. *Mozart to Thomas Linley,*[1] *10 September 1770, Bologna*

[*In Italian*]
Dear Friend,

Here at last is my letter! I have only just got round to replying to the one that you most kindly sent to me in Naples but which I did not receive until two months after you'd written it. My father's plan was to take the road from Loreto to Bologna; from there to travel to Florence, Livorno, Genoa and Milan and in consequence give you a surprise by turning up in Florence unexpectedly. But, my father

4. 26 July.
1. After returning to England, Linley died prematurely in a boating accident in 1778.

having had the misfortune to injure his shin quite badly when the shaft horse of our mail coach fell and as this not only forced him to remain in bed for three weeks but kept him in Bologna for 7, this nasty accident meant that we had to change our plans and travel to Milan via Parma.

First, we have missed the opportunity to undertake such a journey and, second, it is no longer a suitable time to do so as everyone is in the country and we'd be unable to recover the cost of our journey. You may be assured that this accident is a source of infinite annoyance to us. I would do everything in my power to have the pleasure of embracing my dear friend and, like me, my father would very much like to see Signor Gavard again, to say nothing of his most dear and kind family, as well as Signora Corilla[2] and Signor Nardini, and then to return to Bologna; we'd do this if we had any hope of recovering the cost of our journey.

As for the lost engravings, my father thought of an expedient and your note arrived just in time to allow him to keep back two. Could I ask you, therefore, to let me know as soon as possible how I should send them to you?

Keep me in your dear friendship and believe me when I say that, with undying affection, I am and shall always remain

Your most devoted servant and loving friend
Amadeo Wolfgango Mozart

[*Leopold's postscript, also in Italian*]
Could I ask you to give our good wishes to all our friends? Leopoldo Mozart

---

On 9 October Mozart was admitted to the Philharmonic Academy of Bologna, and four days later Leopold and Wolfgang left Bologna for

2. Giuseppe Maria Gavard des Pivets, administrator general in Florence; Maddalena Morelli-Fernandez Corilla (1727–1800), poet. Linley and Mozart had performed at their houses in Florence.

Milan, arriving there on 18 October for the rehearsals of Mitridate, re di Ponto, *to be performed at the Teatro Regio Ducal, Milan.*

30. Leopold Mozart to his wife, 20 October 1770, Milan

We arrived in Milan safe and sound, thank God, at 5 in the evening on the 18th. We had to spend a whole day in Parma as the rivers were so swollen by the amazingly heavy rain that no one could cross them. All afternoon on the 14th we drove through an amazing thunderstorm and terribly heavy rain, but my luggage didn't get wet, as I'd protected it in a double thickness of oilcloth. I've had very painful rheumatism in my right arm for 3 weeks now, and I suffered from it on the journey, too. But at least it hasn't got any worse and is in fact noticeably better, even if it's not gone away completely. NB: I don't need anything for it and haven't needed anything. I expect it to leave as it came. The movement of the *sedia* wasn't at all good for me, but I kept thinking: evil must be banished by evil. So it was a somewhat tiresome journey on account of the thunderstorm and heavy rain, and a somewhat painful one on account of my arm.

We left Bologna a few days later than planned because the Philharmonic Academy unanimously elected Wolfg. a member of their society and presented him with the diploma of *accademico philarmonico*. But this happened only after all the necessary preliminaries and after he had been duly examined. He was required to appear at the Hall of the Academy at 4 in the afternoon on 9 Oct.; in the presence of all the members, the director of the academy and the 2 invigilators – who are all old Kapellmeisters – gave him an antiphon taken from an antiphoner, of which he had to write a 4-part setting in an adjoining room, where he was taken by the beadle, who locked the door after him. Once he'd finished it, it was examined by the invigilators and all the Kapellmeisters and composers, and a vote was then taken, which was done by means of black and white balls.

As all the balls were white, he was called in, and everyone clapped their hands at his appearance and congratulated him, after the director had previously told him in the name of the society that he had been accepted as a member. He thanked them, and with that it was over. Herr Prinsechi[1] and I were meanwhile locked in the Academy's library on the other side of the hall. Everyone was amazed that he completed it so quickly, as many people had spent 3 hours on a 3-line antiphon. NB: You must know that it's no easy task, as this type of composition excludes many things that aren't allowed and that he had been told about previously.[2] He completed it in a good half hour. The beadle then brought the certificate to our house. It's in Latin and includes the following words: – – – *testamur Dominum Wolfgangum Amadeum etc:* – – *Sub die 9 Mensis octobris anni 1770 inter Accademiæ nostrae Magistros Compositores adscriptum fuisse* etc.[3] This does him all the more credit in that the academy is already more than 100 years old and apart from Padre Martini and other distinguished Italians, the most distinguished men of other nations are members of this *Accademia Bonnoniensis.*[4]

I was handed your letter of 5 Octob. at the gate as we were driving into Milan, as it was enclosed with Herr Troger's letters, which he had left there. As you'll see from my earlier replies, I've received all your letters. I'm glad that Herr Breitkopf has paid. Make a note of all the books *that you sell* or *for which you're paid* or *that you give away*, in short, everything, so that when I get back I shall know where I stand with all these people. Farewell, both of you, we kiss you 100,000 times, and I am your old

Mozart

All manner of good wishes to all our friends.

1. Giuseppe Prinsechi was a local merchant.
2. The antiphon composed by Mozart on this occasion was K86, *Quaerite primum regnum Dei.* It is possible that Martini helped Mozart with the test piece: Wolfgang's autograph is bound with a version by Martini that is nevertheless attributed to Mozart. A second copy, by Leopold and dated 10 October, also transmits Martini's version.
3. 'We testify that Master Wolfgang Amadeus etc. was enrolled among the Master Composers of our Academy on the 9th day of the month of October 1770.'
4. Academy of Bologna.

[Wolfgang's postscript]

My Dear Mama,

I can't write much as my fingers are hurting a lot from writing so many recitatives:[5] please pray for me, Mama, that the opera goes well and that we can all be happy together again. I kiss Mama's hand a thousand times, and I'd have many things to say to my sister, but what? That's something that only God and I know, if it's God's will I hope I'll soon be able to tell her so in person, but for now I kiss her 1000 times. Best wishes to all our good friends. We've lost good little Martha,[6] but with God's help we'll meet her in a better place.

[Leopold Mozart's postscript]

Wasn't it a good idea about the diary? – I can now receive 2 diaries in 4 or 5 letters, and even if they contain only 2 or 3 months each, I'll still get them soon enough, I've already got the main part. I won't open Herr and Frau Hagenauer's wound by writing a letter of condolence. What can't be changed must be left to God's discretion. What else can be done? –

31. Leopold Mozart to his wife, 10 November 1770, Milan

The miscellany from our good friends has arrived safely, and we're very pleased that you enjoyed yourselves in Triebenbach. Do give our very best wishes to Frau von Schiedenhofen and her worthy son, and thank them once again, just as the two of us thank all our friends *in optima forma* and send them our sincere good wishes for the entertainment that they have given us with the letters they've sent us and for the poetry that far surpasses that of all German poets. We wish Herr Spitzeder every happiness and a whole parlour full of children, as it's now getting more and more expensive in Salzb. What's his new wife called? – – Do I know her? – – I think I do!

5. For *Mitridate, re di Ponto*.
6. Maria Martha Hagenauer (1751–70), daughter of Lorenz Hagenauer and his wife.

I'm only afraid that he'll have worn himself out dancing at his wedding and got over-excited.

If our good friends add the occasional joke to your letters, they'll be doing us a good turn, as Wolfg. is now busy with serious matters and as a result has become very serious, I'm glad if he occasionally gets his hands on something amusing. Please ask my friends to forgive me for not writing to anyone. I'm now less in the mood to do so than ever, and in time to come you'll be surprised to discover what kind of a storm we've had to weather, something that requires presence of mind and constant thought. We've won the first battle, thank God, and defeated an enemy who brought to the *prima donna*'s house all the arias that she has to sing in our opera and tried to persuade her not to sing any of Wolfg.'s.[1] We've seen them all, they're all new arias, but neither she nor the rest of us know who wrote them. But she said no to this evil man and is now beside herself with delight at the arias that Wolfg. has written according to her wishes and desires, as is her maestro, Sgr Lampugnani,[2] who is rehearsing her part with her and who can't praise Wolfg.'s arias enough. When we were with her today, she was just rehearsing her first aria with the maestro. But a second storm[3] is gathering in the theatrical sky and we can already see it in the distance. But I expect that with God's help and if we remain good-natured we shall win through. But you mustn't be surprised, these are unavoidable matters that even the greatest composers have to deal with. As long as we keep well and our bowels remain open, the rest is unimportant, we just mustn't take things too much to heart. You'll hear about it all in due course. It continues to

1. The singer was Antonia Bernasconi. Mozart's 'enemy' may have been the composer Quirino Gasparini (1721–78), Kapellmeister at Turin 1760–70, who had set the same text, based on a translation of a play by the French dramatist Jean Racine (1639–99), in 1767. In the event, the *primo uomo*, Guglielmo d'Ettore (c. 1740–71), sang Gasparini's version of the aria 'Vado incontro al fato estremo' instead of Mozart's.
2. Giovanni Battista Lampugnani (1708–88), harpsichordist at the Teatro Regio Ducal from 1758, rehearsed the singers for the performance of *Mitridate*.
3. Leopold later explained (in a letter of 17 November, not included here) that the second 'storm' involved d'Ettore, who demanded at least four rewrites of the aria 'Se di lauri il crine adorno', two of 'Vado incontro al fato estremo' (neither of which he eventually sang) and two of the recitative 'Respira alfin'.

rain here most of the time and then there are dense mists which, even if we have one good day, return the following day. We kiss you both 1,000,000 times and send our good wishes to our friends inside and outside the house. I remain your old

Leop. Mozart

I don't know if I told you that young Herr Kreusser[4] called on us in Bologna. Young Kreusser from Amsterdam, whose brother is the first violin there – he called on us constantly and wanted to travel with us. He asked after us in Rome and Naples, but on each occasion we'd already left. He's now returning to Holland via Turin and Paris; he sends you both his best wishes.

I've just this minute received your letter of 2 Nov. If you haven't already sent off the 2 violin tutors, *hang on to them and don't send them off*. Dr Bridi of Rovereto is himself a good keyboard player. I know Count Castelbarco very well. I'm writing this in the steward's rooms at Count Firmian's.

32. Leopold Mozart to his wife, 22 December 1770, Milan

A Happy New Year!

Although, with God's help, I shall be writing to you again this year, my letter will arrive a few days too late. The first stage rehearsal was on the 19th, having been preceded by one in the *Sala di Ridotto*[1] on the 17th. It went very well, thank God; yesterday evening there was a rehearsal for the recitatives, and today, after *Ave Maria*, there'll be a second rehearsal on stage, with the dress rehearsal on Monday. Now you know from my previous letters and also from this one that we've had 5 rehearsals in all, namely, one with only a few violins, a full rehearsal in the *Sala di Ridotto* and 3 on stage. I'll tell you at

4. Georg Anton Kreusser (1746–1810), violinist and brother of Johann Adam Kreusser (1732–91), also a violinist in Amsterdam.
1. Ballroom.

once how the performance goes on the 26th. My one consolation is that I can see that the performers and the orchestra are all pleased; and, thank God, I too still have ears. During the rehearsal I went to stand at the very back, beneath the main entrance, in order to be able to hear it properly at a distance. But perhaps my ears were too partial! Meanwhile we see and hear that our good friends are happy and contented and delighted to be able to congratulate my son, those who are ill disposed, by contrast, are now silent. The greatest and most distinguished conductors in the city, namely, Sgr *Fioroni* and Sgr *Sammartini*, have complete trust in us and are our true friends, as are Lampugnani, Piazza, Colombo etc.[2] As a result, the envy or rather disbelief and prejudice that some people previously felt towards our son's composition will do him little harm. At least I hope he won't have the same bad luck as Sgr Jommelli, whose second opera in Naples has been such a flop that there are even plans to replace it. He's such a famous composer, and the Italians make a terrible fuss about him. But it was a little foolish of him to undertake to write 2 operas for the same theatre within the space of a year, not least because he must have noticed that his first opera – which we saw – wasn't a great success.[3] At least you now know that, starting on the 26th, we'll be at the opera every evening from an hour after *Ave Maria* until around 11 or almost 12 o'clock, the only exception being Fridays. In 2 weeks at the most I'll be able to report on my journey to Turin. After that, things will move quickly, so that we can spend the last few days of the Carnival in Venice. Just arrange for Herr Haffner's letters to be sent on to a friend in Venice and let me know who has them. In the meantime I hope to hear something about a secure private apartment, *NB a secure apartment*, as I've no great love of staying at inns unless I absolutely have to. Farewell to you both, we kiss you many 100,000 times and I am, as always, your old

Mozart

2. Giovanni Andrea Fioroni (1715/16–78), Giovanni Battista Sammartini (1701–75), Gaetano Piazza and Giovanni Colombo, all active at various Milanese churches.
3. The first, *Armida abbandonata*, premiered on 30 May 1770 at the Teatro San Carlo (see letter 27), the second, *Demofoonte*, on 4 November 1770.

Best wishes and a Happy New Year to all our friends.

Can you imagine Wolfg. in a scarlet suit with gold braid and sky-blue satin lining? The tailor is starting work on it today. He'll be wearing this suit on the first 3 days, when he sits at the keyboard.[4] The one that was made for him in Salzb. is too short by a standing hand, and certainly too tight and small.

[*Wolfgang's postscript to his sister*]
Sinfonia

Sinfonia

Ask whether or not they've got this symphony by Mysliveček[5] in Salzburg, for if they haven't, we'll bring it with us.

33. *Leopold Mozart to his wife, 29 December 1770, Milan*

Praise be to God, the first performance of the opera passed off to general acclaim on the 26th: and two things that have never before happened in Milan took place; namely, that – contrary to first-night custom – one of the *prima donna*'s arias was encored, although usually at the first performance no one ever calls out *fuora*; and, second, there was extraordinary applause and cries of *Viva il Maestro, viva il Maestrino* after nearly all the arias, except for a few *delle ultime Parti*.[1]

On the 27th 2 of the *prima donna*'s arias were encored: as it was Thursday, with Friday to follow, they had to try to cut back, otherwise

---

4. Mozart was to conduct the performances of his opera from the harpsichord.
5. The overture to *Demofoonte* by Josef Mysliveček (1737–81), Czech opera composer active in Italy.
1. 'Encore' . . . 'Long live the maestro, long live the little maestro' . . . 'at the end'.

the duet,[2] too, would have been encored, as the noise was already starting. But most people still wanted to eat at home, and the opera, plus 3 ballets, lasts a good 6 hours: but they'll now be shortening the ballets, which last a good 2 hours. How we wished that you and Nannerl could have had the pleasure of seeing the opera! – –

Never within living memory has there been such a desire to see the first opera in Milan as there was this time, as there had previously been such a terrible controversy: for every two people who said that the opera would be good, there were 10 who knew in advance that it was foolish nonsense, others that it was a muddle, and yet others that the music was German and barbarous. Here not even patronage helps to ensure that an opera is a success as everyone who attends is determined to talk, shout and criticize it in return for his money. Patronage was useful to us and, indeed, was necessary to ensure that the work was not prevented from going ahead and that a spoke wasn't put in the maestro's wheels while he was writing it and, later, during the rehearsals, so that he wasn't prevented from appearing and so that the handful of spiteful individuals in the orchestra and among the performers were unable to play any tricks on him. I am writing this in haste as today is the 3rd performance. You know that in Italy people are always given other names, so that Hasse, for example, is called *il Sassone*, Galuppi *il Buranello* etc. etc. They are calling our son *il Sgr Cavaliere Filarmonico*.[3]

We kiss you both 100,000 times and send our good wishes to all our friends. I am your old

Mozart

You'll be paid *60 ducats* in the name of Madame d'Asti née Marianne Troger. I'll tell you more next time.

2. 'Se viver non degg'io' for Aspasia and Sifare, in act 2, scene 15.
3. Hasse's name means 'the Saxon'; composer Baldassare Galuppi (1706–85) is called 'the man from Burano' (after his birthplace); Mozart's name means 'Signor Knight of the Philharmonic Academy'.

34. *Leopold Mozart to his wife, 5 January 1771, Milan*

Milan, 5 January in the year that's the same at the back as at the front and double in the middle (1771)

I can hardly find time to write to you as we're at the opera every day and as a result don't get to bed until half past 1 or even 2 o'clock as we also want to have a bite to eat after the opera; and so we get up late in the morning, and the days, which are in any case very short now, become even shorter in consequence. We've so many visits to make that we don't know how we'll manage. On Thursday we had lunch with Madame von Asteburg, formerly Mariandl Troger, who treated us to *liver dumplings and sauerkraut, which Wolfg. had particularly asked for*, as well as other fine dishes, including a splendid capon and a pheasant. Yesterday there was a small concert at His Excellency Count Firmian's, at which Dr Bridi sang a cantata and gave Wolfg. a new, beautiful and difficult concerto to play. He gave us your good wishes, told us all that had happened and had nothing but praise for Nannerl. Today we're again having lunch with His Excellency; and on the 11th or 12th we'll be going to Turin but will be staying there for only about a week, after which we'll return to Milan, pack everything properly together and move on to Venice. But we shan't be staying more than 4 days in Milan – just enough time to see the second opera.[1] Our son's opera continues to enjoy universal acclaim and, as the Italians say, is *alle Stelle!*[2] Since the 3rd performance we've been listeners and spectators, now in the stalls, now in the boxes, or *palchi*, where everyone is eager to speak to the Sgr Maestro and see him at close quarters: throughout the performance we wander around, wherever we like, for the maestro is obliged to conduct the opera from the orchestra on only 3 evenings, when Maestro Lampugnani accompanied at the 2nd keyboard, but as Wolfg. is no longer

1. *Nitteti* by Carlo Monza (*c.* 1735–1801), first given at the Teatro Regio Ducal on 21 January 1771.
2. 'in the stars!', i.e. heavenly.

playing the first one, Maestro Melchiorre Chiesa[3] is now playing the second one. If anyone had told me some 15 or 18 years ago, when Lampugnani had written so much in England and Melchiorre Chiesa so much in Italy and I had seen their operatic arias and symphonies, that these men would be instrumental in performing my son's music and that, when he left the keyboard, they would have to sit down and accompany that music, I'd have said that he was a fool fit only for an asylum. And so we see what Almighty God does with us humans if we do not bury the talents that He has most graciously given us.

Write regularly every Friday and, as before, send all letters to Herr Troger until I instruct you otherwise.

I'd love to know when His Grace, our most gracious lord, will celebrate the 50th anniversary of his entry into the priesthood. If you discover when it is, write and tell me: I need to know for several reasons.

I'm enclosing the local newspapers,[4] which I've just received. You'll find the opera right at the end.

Best wishes to the whole of Salzb. We kiss you 1,000,000 times. I am your old

Mozart

Please send these newspapers to His Grace, you need give them only to His Excellency the Chief Steward.

---

3. Melchiorre Chiesa (*fl.* 1758–99), from 1762 *maestro di cappella* of S. Maria della Scala, Milan.

4. On 2 January 1771 the *Gazzetta di Milano* reported that 'On Wednesday last the Teatro Regio Ducal reopened with the performance of the drama entitled *Mitridate, Re di Ponto*, which has proved to the public's satisfaction as much for the tasteful stage designs as for the excellence of the Music and the ability of the Actors. Some of the arias sung by Signora Antonia Bernasconi vividly express the passions and touch the heart. The young *Maestro di Cappella*, who has not yet reached the age of fifteen, studies the beauty of nature and exhibits it adorned with the rarest Musical graces.' See Deutsch, *Documentary Biography*, 130–1.

Mozart and his father left Milan on 4 February and by the beginning of March were in Venice, where Wolfgang gave a concert on 5 March. From Venice they travelled to Padua, where on 13 March Mozart received a contract for the composition of the oratorio La Betulia liberata. *From here they at last turned north, arriving back at Salzburg on 28 March; at the end of that month Wolfgang was commissioned by Empress Maria Theresa to compose a two-act serenata,* Ascanio in Alba *K111, for the forthcoming marriage of her fourth son Archduke Ferdinand to Beatrice d'Este, the heiress of Ercole III d'Este, Duke of Modena. Father and son set out again on 13 August for Milan, where they arrived on 21 August. By the middle of September Wolfgang had composed the recitatives and choruses for* Ascanio in Alba.

35. Leopold Mozart to his wife, 21 September 1771, Milan

The first orchestral rehearsal of Sgr Hasse's opera[1] will take place today after the *Angelus*. He is well, thank God. The serenata will be put into rehearsal at the end of next week; the first rehearsal of the recitatives is on Monday, and on the other days the choruses will be rehearsed.

Wolfg. will have finished by Monday or Tuesday at the latest. Sgr Manzuoli often calls on us, but we've been to his place only once. Sgr Tibaldi calls on us almost every day at 11 and sits at the table till around 1, while Wolfg. composes.[2] They're all uncommonly kind and have the greatest respect for Wolfg., indeed, we've not had the least trouble as we're dealing only with good and famous singers and with sensible people. The serenata is really a short opera; the actual music in the opera is just as short but is prolonged by the 2 grand ballets that are performed after the 1st and 2nd acts, each of which is likely to last 3 quarters of an hour.

1. *Ruggiero, ovvero L'eroica gratitudine*, also composed to celebrate the wedding of Archduke Ferdinand.
2. Giovanni Manzuoli, who sang the title role in *Ascanio in Alba;* Giuseppe Luigi Tibaldi (1729–c. 1790), tenor.

I don't have enough space to describe all the preparations for these celebrations. The whole of Milan is astir, not least because many, if not most, of the preparations were postponed till the last moment, with the result that everyone is now at work, some at the theatre, others for His Highness's reception – for the apartment and rooms etc. – for fencing off and lighting the cathedral – for clothes – – the servants' liveries – – – carriages – horses etc. balls etc., painting and renovating the whole theatre etc. etc. – – in short, a hundred things that don't occur to me. – – Everyone, everyone is on the move!

Miss Davies arrived here a few days ago; she drove past our lodgings in the mail coach. I recognized her, and she recognized us, just as we were standing on the balcony. A few hours later I went to call on her at the Three Kings, as I imagined that she'd be staying there, because it's the most respectable inn and not far from us. She, her sister, father and mother could hardly express their delight: I showed her servant Herr Hasse's lodgings, and a moment later Herr Hasse's daughter appeared, incapable of expressing her delight, as they've been close friends since Vienna. They all asked after you and send you their best wishes. I expect you remember Miss Davies and her glass harmonica?[3] – – –

Did you see the tightrope walkers when they were in Salzb? – They're now on their way to Milan; people are busy building an extraordinarily large tent for them. The Italian plays finished 2 days ago as the theatre is needed for the rehearsals and to allow the painters to work day and night. These players were exceptionally good, especially in character parts and tragedies.

Anyone coming to Milan for these wedding celebrations is bound to see some wonderful things. A carriage for 4 persons travelling together wouldn't cost much. The biggest problem would be finding a room. But I could help out here and take you in myself. We'd have to live like soldiers for a short time and make savings by having our meals cooked at home.

3. The Mozarts had met the glass harmonica virtuoso Marianne Davies (1744–1819) in London; her sister, the soprano Cecilia Davies (c. 1756–1836), was a pupil of Hasse and sang in *Ruggiero* when it was performed at Naples in January 1772.

I've just received your letter of the 13th. I hope that *the violinist de Hey* isn't that joker who's the brother of the businesswoman in *Amsterdam* – the one who absconded? I'm sure you'll remember who I mean. He too was called de Haie or La Haie. He wasn't very old. Count Castelbarco still hadn't arrived by yesterday. He'll have broken his journey in Innsbruck and then on his estates at Ala and Rovereto.

In your last letter you said that *many people had gone mad*, and now you say that many are dying from *bloody flux*.[4] That's very bad, for if it affects people in the head and the arse, it certainly looks dangerous. I must have brought quite a dose of it with me from Salz. as I still have frequent fits of dizziness. But it's hardly surprising – – where the air is already infected – – you can easily catch something.

That's why I wrote to you about the pills. I want my arse to cure my head.

Best wishes to all our good friends. We kiss you both 10,000,000 times. I am your old

Lp Mozart

[*Wolfgang's postscript to his sister*]
I'm well, all praise and thanks be to God. I can't write much: first, because I don't know what to say: second, my fingers are hurting so much from writing. Farewell. I kiss Mama's hands. I often whistle my tune but not a soul answers. I'm now missing 2 arias from the serenata and then I'll be finished. Best wishes to all our good friends. I no longer feel like returning to Salzburg, I'm frightened that I too could go mad.

Wolfgang

[*Leopold Mozart's postscript on the inside of the envelope*]
You need to be careful when putting together the books. I've brought with me the two half-bound copies that were lying in the cabinet and discovered that in one of them *the whole sheet, or K k* was bound in twice.

This was an act of idiocy on the part of the bookbinder, who

4. Dysentery.

should have noticed. From now on address all your letters to Herr Troger.

The royal wedding took place on 15 October. Hasse's Ruggiero *was performed the next day and Mozart's* Ascanio in Alba *on 17 October.*

36. Leopold Mozart to his wife, 19 October 1771, Milan

Herr Marcabruni sends his best wishes, he's here now, we're just leaving for the theatre, the opera was on the 16th, and on the 17th was the serenata, which went down so amazingly well that it's having to be repeated today. The archduke recently ordered 2 copies. All the courtiers and other people keep stopping us in the street to congratulate Wolfg. In short, *I'm sorry* that Wolfg.'s serenata has knocked Hasse's opera into a cocked hat, so much so that I can't even begin to describe it. I'll answer your last letter and Nannerl's postscript as soon as I can. You'll see Italy in more enjoyable conditions than would have been the case amidst the present terrible din. *Addio.* We kiss you 10,000 times. I am your old

Mzt

Pray! And thank God!
Best wishes to all our friends.
Herr von Troger sends his good wishes, especially to you and Nannerl, who is sighing so much for Milan.

Before leaving Italy, Leopold applied to Archduke Ferdinand for a position at the Milanese court for Wolfgang. However, when the archduke advised Maria Theresa of this, she wrote to him: 'You ask for my permission to take the young Salzburger into your service. I do not know why, not

believing that you have need of a composer or of useless people. If however it would give you pleasure, I have no wish to hinder you. What I say is intended only to prevent your burdening yourself with useless people and giving titles to people of that sort. In addition it lowers the standing of your court when these people go about the world like beggars.' The reasons for her animosity are not clear. Mozart and his father left Milan on 5 December, arriving home on 15 December. The next day, Archbishop Siegmund von Schrattenbach died.

37. Leopold Mozart to Johann Gottlob Immanuel Breitkopf, 7 February 1772, Salzburg

Honourable and Most Respected Sir,

You will, I trust, permit me to have recourse to the expedient of writing to you on a certain matter. I have to order some wind instruments for our court and have come to trust in the work of a certain *Herr Grenser of Dresden*,[1] whom I know only from his name, which I have found on a number of flutes and oboes. It is a matter of some concern to me and my honour that I should obtain a couple of well-tuned oboes and two bassoons as soon as possible, as a new prince will be elected on 9 March[2] and I am concerned that, because of the absence of the necessary address, the enclosed letter may arrive late or may not reach Herr Grenser at all: and so I would ask you as a matter of the utmost urgency to forward this letter to him as quickly as possible and, if it is not inconvenient, to include with the letter a short letter of recommendation of your own, but do let me know the cost of sending the letter.

We returned from Milan on 15 Decemb. and as my son again added to his reputation by writing the serenata for the theatre, he has again been asked to compose the first opera for next year's carnival in

1. The Grenser firm of instrument builders had been founded in 1744 by Carl Augustin Grenser (1720–1807).
2. i.e. the new prince-archbishop of Salzburg.

Milan[3] and, immediately afterwards, the 2nd opera for the same carnival at the Teatro San Benedetto in Venice.[4] And so we'll be staying in Salzburg until the end of this coming September, before setting off for Italy – the third time we'll have been there.

If you wanted to print anything by my son, the best time would be between now and then: you've only got to say what you consider most appropriate. It could be *keyboard pieces* or a *trio* for 2 violins and cello, or *quartets*, that is, with 2 violins, a viola and cello; or *symphonies* for 2 violins, viola, 2 horns, 2 oboes or flutes, and bass. In short, it could be any sort of piece that you think will make a profit, he'll write anything as long as you can let us know soon. In the meantime my wife received the 78 fl. 30 kr. while I was away: I remain in great deference

Your Worship's

Most Obedient Servant
Leopold Mozart

Have you had any more news of our friend Herr Grimm? – Have any of the portraits and sonatas been sold?[5]

On 14 March, Hieronymus Joseph Franz de Paula, Count Colloredo, prince-bishop of Gurk, was elected archbishop of Salzburg, a position he would hold until 1803. Mozart's serenata Il sogno di Scipione *was performed as part of the celebrations celebrating his accession. Originally composed for the 50th anniversary of Siegmund von Schrattenbach's ordination (but never performed due to his death), the serenata was reworked by Mozart to reflect the very different occasion on which it was to be performed. On 21 August,*

3. This was to be *Lucio Silla* K135.
4. On 17 August 1771, Leopold had come an agreement with the impresario Michele dall'Agata for a Venetian opera, but for unknown reasons the work was never composed.
5. The sonatas are probably K6–7, K8–9, K10–15 and K26–31; the portrait may be a copy of the 1764 engraving by Jean-Baptiste Delafosse (1721–75), based on the watercolour by Louis de Carmontelle (1717–1806), of Wolfgang, Nannerl and Leopold Mozart performing.

Colloredo converted Mozart's appointment as third concertmaster in the Salzburg court music to a paid position and on 27 October, Leopold and Wolfgang set out again for Italy, arriving at Milan on 4 November, where preparations for his opera Lucio Silla *were underway.*

38. Mozart to his mother, 7 November 1772, Milan

Don't be alarmed at finding my own handwriting rather than Papa's; the reasons are as follows: 1st, we're at Herr von Asti's, and Baron Cristani is here and they've so much to talk about that he doesn't have time to write. And, 2nd, he's too – – – lazy. We arrived here safely at noon on the 4th; we're well. All our good friends are in the country and at Mantua, except for Herr von Taste[1] and his wife, who have asked me to give you and my sister their best wishes. Herr Mysliveček is still here. There is no absolutely no truth in the reports of an Italian war about which people are talking so much in Germany or about any fortifications to the castles here. Sorry my handwriting is so bad. If you write, just write straight to us, as it's not the custom here, as it is in Germany, for people to carry letters around, but they have to be collected from the post, and so we go and collect them every post day. There's nothing to report from here, we await news from Salzburg. We hope you'll have received the letter from Bozen. I can't think of anything else, so I'll close. Best wishes to all our good friends. We kiss Mama 100,000 times – I didn't bring any more noughts with me – and I kiss Mama's hands, and prefer to embrace my sister in person rather than in my imagination.

[Wolfgang's postscript to his sister; entirely in Italian]
Dearest Sister,
   I hope you've called on the woman you know who I mean. Could I ask you if you see her to give her my best wishes. I hope and do not doubt that you are in good health. I forgot to tell you that we met

1. d'Asti, i.e. Francisco Aste d'Asteburg.

the dancer Sgr Bellardo here, whom we knew from The Hague and Amsterdam and who attacked the dancer Sgr Nieri with his sword because he thought it was because of him that he'd not been allowed to dance in the theatre. *Addio*. Don't forget me. I am always your faithful brother

Amadeo Wolfgango Mozart

[*Leopold Mozart's postscript*]
We spent Wolfg.'s name day most enjoyably with the 2 Pizzini brothers in Ala. We also broke our journey in Verona, which is why we reached Milan later than planned. The weather is always fine here – it rained only once on our journey, during the afternoon of the day after St Simon and St Jude,[2] that was all. Keep well! *Addio!*
     Best wishes to all our friends.
     We've seen comic operas both here and in Verona.[3]

39. Leopold Mozart to his wife, 21 November 1772, Milan

We're hale and healthy, thank God, like fish in water as it's been raining astonishingly heavily, day and night, for the last week, so it's no wonder that we're still waiting for the post that should have arrived today. Apart from the heavy rain and wind, there was a violent thunderstorm during the night of the 19th to the 20th, starting with lightning at 10 at night and lasting without a break until 4 in the morning, with lots of violent thunder. For my own part, I was woken by a violent clap of thunder at 2 and then again after 5 but fell asleep again straightaway, whereas Wolfg., having gone to bed around 12, heard none of the rest of the storm. We've got far better rooms than we've had in the past, more beautiful, more comfortable, even closer to the theatre and as a result some 50 yards from Madame d'Asti,

2. 28 October.
3. These may have included *La locanda* by Giuseppe Gazzaniga (1743–1818) and *La sposa fedele* by Pietro Guglielmi (1728–1804).

who has lent us a few good pillows as these Italian bacon rinds are too hard for us. I should add that whereas our previous bed was 9 spans wide, the present one is 10 spans. I don't doubt that you're well. Today is our wedding anniversary. It must be 25 years since we had the idea of getting married – – although we'd had the idea many years before that. All good things take time! The *primo uomo*, Sgr Rauzzini,[1] has now arrived, so there'll be more for us to do and things will start to get livelier. There'll be no lack of the little dramas that are usual in the theatre, but these are mere trifles! The figs that Joseph[2] gave Wolfg. when he left were as miraculous as the loaves and fishes in the Gospel, as we were still eating them at our evening meal yesterday, a meal that consists of nothing but grapes and bread and a glass of wine. Best wishes to all our friends. The day is short! There's a lot to do, if it's not work, it's just chores. We kiss you – – as often as you want – – and, together with Wolfg., I am your old

Mozart

[Wolfgang's postscript to his sister]
Thanks, you know what for. I hope Herr von Heffner[3] will forgive me for not having got round to replying to him. But it was impossible and is still impossible: for as soon as I get home, there's something to write, there's often already something on the table, and I can't write out of doors, in the street. If you see him, read him the following and ask him to be satisfied with this for the present. I shan't take it amiss that my worthless friend hasn't replied, as soon as he has more time, he will assuredly, doubtlessly, undoubtedly, certainly, unfailingly do so. Best wishes to all our good friends. I kiss Mama's hands. Well fare and news me soon some send. The Germany from post hasn't arrived yet.

Oidda.
always as am I

Milan à 2771 November 12 the   Mozart Wolfgang

1. Venanzio Rauzzini (1746–1810), soprano castrato. Rauzzini was engaged at Munich from 1766 and sang the role of Celio in the first performance of *Lucio Silla*.
2. Ignaz Joseph Hagenauer.
3. Heinrich Wilhelm von Heffner (?–1774), Salzburg court councillor.

On 21, 22 and 23 December, Mozart took part in concerts at the palace of Count Firmian; Lucio Silla was premiered on 26 December in the presence of Archduke Ferdinand and his wife. On 17 January 1773, Rauzzini performed Mozart's newly composed motet 'Exsultate, jubilate' K165 at the Theatine church, and on 30 January Leopold and Wolfgang saw a performance of Sismano nel Mogol *by the Neapolitan composer Giovanni Paisiello (1740–1816), the second carnival opera of the season. Leopold and Wolfgang remained in Milan until the beginning of March.*

40. Leopold Mozart to his wife, 2 January 1773, Milan

A Happy New Year!

Last time I forgot to wish you a Happy New Year as I was writing not just in a hurry but in a state of some confusion, my thoughts were elsewhere as we were just on the point of leaving for the theatre. The opera passed off successfully, even though a number of extremely annoying incidents took place on the first night. The first problem was that the opera was due to start, as usual, *one hour after the Angelus* but in the event began 3 hours after it, in other words not until around 8 o'clock German time, and didn't end until 2 in the morning. The archduke finished his midday meal only shortly before the *Angelus* and then had to write 5 letters or New Year greetings to Their Majesties the Emperor and Empress, and he writes very slowly etc. etc.

Just imagine: the whole theatre was so full by half past 5 that no one else could get in. At every first night the singers are always very nervous at having to appear for the first time before such a distinguished audience. For 3 hours the singers were kept anxiously waiting, while the orchestra and entire audience – many of them standing – had to wait in a state of impatience for the opera to start, growing increasingly hot as they did so.

Secondly, you need to know that the tenor, whom we've had to take *faute de mieux*, is a church singer from Lodi and had never performed in such a prestigious theatre and had appeared as *primo tenore* only about twice before in Lodi, and was signed up only about a week before the opening night.[1] He has to gesture angrily at the *prima donna* in her first aria, but his gesture was so exaggerated that it looked as though he was going to box her ears and knock off her nose with his fist, causing the audience to laugh. Fired by her singing, Sgra de Amicis[2] didn't immediately understand why the audience was laughing and was badly affected by it, not knowing initially who was being laughed at, so that she didn't sing well for the whole of the first night, in addition to which she was jealous because the archduchess clapped as soon as the *primo uomo* came onstage. This was a typical castrato's trick, as he'd ensured that the archduchess had been told that he'd be too afraid to sing so that the court would encourage and applaud him. In order to console Sgra de Amicis she was summoned to court at noon the very next day and for a whole hour had an audience with Their Royal Highnesses, only then did the opera start to go well, and whereas the theatre is normally very empty for the first opera, it has been so full on the first 6 evenings – today is the seventh – that it's hardly been possible to slip in, and generally it's the *prima donna* who has maintained the upper hand and had her arias encored. I'm writing this at Madame d'Asti's. She sends her regards and wishes you a Happy New Year. Best wishes to all our good friends at home and abroad. We kiss you many 1,000,000s of times. I am your old

Mzt

Wolfg. sends his special greetings, we are well, thank God.

Wolfgang and his father spent four months in Salzburg before setting out again, this time for Vienna, where they arrived on 16 July. They had an audience with Empress Maria Theresa on 5 August.

1. Cordoni, who was to sing in the opera, took ill and was replaced by Bassano Morgnoni.
2. Anna Lucia de Amicis sang the role of Giunia in *Lucio Silla*.

41. *Leopold Mozart to his wife, 12 August 1773, Vienna*

All your letters have arrived safely. Although Her Majesty the Empress was very kind to us, that was all – I'll have to save it up and tell you on our return, as it's not something I can set down in writing. As for the enclosure, this too contained nothing to our advantage because this gentleman lives a solitary life, remote from every court, although I have to say that his letter was uncommonly polite, and he certainly suggested something that I have in any case been thinking about for a long time, but as always there are obstacles.[1] His Grace[2] is returning from Laxenburg today and will be spending a few days with his father at Sierndorf before returning to Salzb., which is unlikely to be before next Saturday or Sunday, with the result that he won't be back until next week. You'll hear by the next post when we'll be leaving. Herr Gscheider isn't here but is with his employers in Bohemia. Frau Leutgeb called on me again today, she'll be staying here until Sunday week. We were recently at Herr von Mölk's,[3] the day before yesterday we met him with Herr von Geyer and Herr von Mehofer on the Bastey. Herr von Geyer and Herr von Gilowsky recently called on us at home. If we don't set off next Monday, we shan't be back until early September, I'll know for certain today or tomorrow. Fräulein Franzl[4] was again close to death, and blisters had to be applied to her arms and feet, but she's now so much better that she has knitted a red silk purse for Wolfg. in bed and given it to him as a keepsake. She sends you her best wishes, as do

1. Maria Anna Mozart's letters to her husband are lost, so many references in Leopold's letters to her (such as the 'obstacles' mentioned here) are obscure.
2. Archbishop Hieronymus Colloredo. Laxenburg was the imperial summer residence, south of Vienna.
3. Court chancellor Franz Felix Anton von Mölk.
4. Franziska Oesterling, the daughter of an army captain from Baden. She was a patient of Dr Franz Anton Mesmer (1734–1815) and had lived in his house since 1772. Mesmer, who had known the Mozarts since their visit to Vienna in 1768, was famous for treating his patients with magnets and hypnotism, hence the term 'mesmerism'. He is parodied in Mozart's *Così fan tutte* (1790).

all of them, the whole litany of the Landstrasse, the 2 Frau Fischers and Herr Fischer,[5] the Bonnis etc. etc.

Young Mesmer's boy[6] is really talented, so much so that I wish he were my own son or at least were living with me. As for the girl, she's none other than the daughter of Dr Auenbrugger.[7] In fact both his daughters – but especially the older one – play incomparably well and have a total grasp of music. We've dined with them, but they don't have a pension from the empress. Young Herr Mesmer has a prestigious post, he's in charge of organizing the training college for all the Empire's hereditary regions, with a courtier as its governor. Do you know that Herr von Mesmer can play Miss Davies's musical glasses extremely well? He's the only person in Vienna to have learnt it and has a much finer set of glasses than Miss Davies. Wolfg. has already played on them, and I only wish we had a set of our own. On the Feast of St Cajetan[8] the Fathers invited us to have lunch with them and to attend their service, and as their organ was not good enough for a concerto, Wolfg. borrowed a violin and a concerto from Herr Teyber[9] and was cheeky enough to play a violin concerto. – One of Wolfg.'s masses – the Dominicus mass – was performed in the octave of the Feast of St Ignatius at the Jesuit church *am Hof*.[10] I conducted, and it was amazingly well received. We're pleased that the graduation music[11] passed off successfully, Wolfg. will be writing to thank Herr Meissner, for the present we send our best wishes.

I've told you lots of things, we send our best wishes to all our good friends at home and abroad and kiss you many 100,000 times. I am your old

Mzt

5. Gottlieb Friedrich Fischer was an engraver in Vienna.
6. Joseph Mesmer, son of Joseph Conrad Mesmer (1735–1804) and a second cousin of Dr Franz Anton Mesmer.
7. Joseph Leopold von Auenbrugger (1722–1809) was a doctor at the Holy Trinity Hospital in Vienna. The reference to his daughter is unexplained.
8. 7 August.
9. Matthäus Teyber, see List.
10. K66, written in 1769. St Ignatius' feast day is 8 August.
11. K185, composed for the Mozarts' Salzburg friend Judas Thaddäus von Antretter (1753–?) on the occasion of his graduation.

[*Wolfgang's postscript to his sister*]
hodie nous avons begegnet per strada Dominum Edlbach welcher uns
di voi compliments ausgericht hat, et qui sich tibi et ta mère Empfehlen
lässt. Addio[12] W. M.

42. *Leopold Mozart to his wife, 11 September 1773, Vienna*

†

I hope that on Dr Niderl's departure you will have been prepared for
what is certainly a sad occurrence, so that you will not be as pained
to hear of his death as I was when I called on him and found that he
had already passed away.[1] He was operated on between 10 and 11 on
the morning of Thursday the 9th, in the presence of all the experts
in their field and so successfully, moreover, that it was all over in 1½
minutes or even quicker. I had the stone in my hands shortly afterwards, it was bigger than a large walnut. I left him that same afternoon, when he was as well as such a patient can be, there weren't the
slightest ill omens at that stage. On Friday the 10th we called on him
between 10 and 11 in the morning in order to ask after his condition.
We were full of hope, so you can imagine my shock when we found
him stretched out on the bed and people busy washing him, as he had
just died – 24 hours after the operation.

As far as I could gather in my haste and the most terrible state of
shock, everything changed after midnight, when it became clear that
he was going to die. *Requiescat in pace!* I feel completely devastated,
as I've now had 2 restless and virtually sleepless nights, as I woke at
4 on Thursday, feeling as though it was I who had to undergo the
operation, and on Friday morning at 4 I woke up wondering how he
was, and today I was already awake at half past 3, and his operation,

12. A jumble of Latin, French, German and Italian, meaning 'Today we met Herr
Edlenbach in the street. He gave us your best wishes and asked to be remembered
to you and your mother. Farewell.'
1. Dr Franz Joseph Niderl von Aichegg.

his death and the sudden and unexpected sight of his dead body lay on my mind and stopped me from sleeping and robbed me of a third night's sleep. And the burial is still to come. This too is bound to give me pause for thought, all the more so in that it reminds me of the fact that I now have to accompany a friend to his grave in Vienna, just as I had to accompany another friend in Munich, Herr von Robinig.[2] Herr von Günther will tell you the remaining details. That's all I have to say on this sad tale. –

The Jesuits are starting to move out of their monasteries.[3] The court Fathers, those who preached at St Stephen's etc. and 6 Father Confessors left yesterday and will perform their functions next Sunday as usual, *but in lay preachers' clothes*, as the higher Jesuits have been told that no one may hear confession or preach in Jesuit dress. I am too annoyed and dull-witted to write any more today. We send our best wishes to all our good friends at home and abroad and kiss you many 100,000 times. I am your old

Mzt

I had to send for Madame Rosa[4] yesterday, and she duly came. I'd just met her in the street as she had to paint the poor doctor as there wasn't even a portrait of him in the Niderls' house.

The case with the brother is now over![5]

How upset Madame von Schiedenhofen and Madame von Heffner[6] etc. etc. are bound to be: we send our special wishes to both their houses.

I have good reason to join with the whole of Salzb. in grieving over the loss of a 2nd Salzb. doctor; any successor will send many to

2. Georg Joseph Robinig von Rottenfeld, who had died in 1760.
3. Joseph II had begun the process of confiscating Jesuit property in Vienna following the suppression of the Jesuit Order by Pope Clement XIV in July.
4. The painter Maria Rosa Barducci (*c.* 1744–86) was the wife of Johann Baptist Hagenauer, the court sculptor; she had painted a portrait of Mozart's mother (see letters 105 and 110).
5. Johann Anton Niderl von Aichegg (?–1774) was the regional apothecary in Salzburg, but nothing is known about this case.
6. The wife of Franz Friedrich von Heffner.

meet their maker before he knows the true nature of a nation and its climate.

I half suspect that Frau Niderl will leave her son here. Only a poor education can be expected of a deaf mother.

Perhaps it will work to the boy's advantage.

You don't need to write to me again. In my next letter I'll tell you when we'll be leaving and where we'll be going.

We'll probably come by the most direct route, the alternative via Graz strikes me as too inconvenient.

Frau Niderl has just arrived, distressed beyond belief, he'll be buried this evening at 8.

In addition to the serenade K185, Mozart also composed six string quartets (K168–173) during his stay in Vienna. He and his father left Vienna for Salzburg about 24 September. In December Wolfgang composed the 'little' G minor symphony K183 and his first keyboard concerto, K175. His activities in Salzburg during 1774 are largely unknown, although he was compositionally active: his major works that year included two masses (K192 and 194), two litanies (K193 and 195), the symphonies K201, 202 and possibly 200, the serenade K204, the concertone K190 and the bassoon concerto K191. Possibly in the late spring or summer, he received a commission to compose the opera buffa, La finta giardiniera *('The Pretend Gardener-girl'), for Munich, and Mozart and his father travelled there on 6 December to finish composing the work, oversee the rehearsals and direct the first performances.*

43. Leopold Mozart to his wife, 14 December 1774, Munich

You should have received a letter from me; but I've not yet seen one from you, presumably you thought that you first needed to have an address: but this isn't necessary, the post already knows where we're staying. Although it's superfluous, you can write at the bottom, if you want: *Chez Monsieur de Pernat in Belval's House.*[1] Thank God, we are well! I still haven't been able to find anywhere suitable for Nannerl,[2] as great care is needed in Munich on this point. And there's something else. It's like Salzb. here. An opera for which one pays can't be performed more than twice in succession, otherwise there'd be very few people in the theatre, other operas have to be given for 2 or 3 weeks, and only then can the earlier one be put on again – it's just the same with plays and ballets. As a result they know at least 20 operas by heart, operas that are performed in rotation while a new one is put into rehearsal. And Wolfgang's opera will not be given for the first time before Christmas and, I think, on the 29th, so it's likely that Nannerl won't see it at all, for once the carnival is in full swing, only short, lightweight operettas are given on a small stage run up in the *Redoutensaal,*[3] where masks gather and there are lots of gaming tables and where there's nothing but noise, masks, conversation and gambling at the many tables. Nothing sensible is performed here as no one pays any attention.

I'll write at greater length in my next letter. Could I now ask you to look out the 2 Litanies de Venerabili, or *Holy Sacrament, that are performed at the Hours.* One is *by me* and is *in D* – the score will be with it, the more recent one starts with a violin and bass staccato – you know the one, the 2nd violin has nothing but triplets in the *Agnus Dei.* Then Wolfgang's great Litany.[4] The score is with it, bound in blue paper. NB: make sure that all the parts are there, as these 2 Litanies will be performed here during the Hours on New Year's Day. They must be handed in at the post on Saturday evening as the mail coach leaves on Sunday. The address needs to be written on it: *À Monsieur Jean Nepomuc de Pernat chanoine e grand Custos de Notre Dame à Munic*

1. Johann Nepomuk Sebastian Pernat (1734–94), canon of Munich cathedral; from 1775 he was spiritual councillor to the court of Elector Maximilian III Joseph of Bavaria. Maximilian Klement von Belval (?–1795) was a military official in Munich.
2. Nannerl was to come to Munich for the premiere of *La finta giardiniera*.
3. Dance hall.
4. Leopold's Litany is his last known work in the genre, composed in 1762; Mozart's is K125 of March 1772.

We kiss you many 1000 times and send everyone our best wishes.
I am your old

Mzt

44. Leopold Mozart to his wife, 28 December 1774, Munich

On the evening of Holy Innocents' Day,
as the post leaves tomorrow at noon.

Happy New Year!

On the very day that you were with His Excellency Count Saurau,[1] the first rehearsal of Wolfg.'s opera was held at 10 in the morning. People liked it so much that it has been postponed until 5 January 1775 so that the singers are more familiar with their parts and, having the music more securely in their heads, may act with greater confidence so as not to ruin the opera, which would have been an overhasty affair if we'd had to have it ready by 29 Decemb. In short, the music proved amazingly successful and will be performed, therefore, on 5 January. All now depends on the production, which I hope will go well as the performers are by no means ill disposed towards us. So it was a good time to inform His Excellency Count Saurau of our journey. I'm happy with that. I'm fully prepared to believe that they are all perfectly polite – that, after all, is their policy, but they suspect all manner of things. You or Nannerl must go to Herr Hagenauer and ask him to give her a *letter of credit* for me to one of his agents. For even if we receive a present straightaway, it's often delayed and you can't wait for it, indeed sometimes it's not sent until later, and I can't rely on this as everything here is slow and often confused. You need only inform Herr Joseph and give him my best wishes. I've some Spanish tobacco in a tin. Nannerl can fill a small snuffbox with it and bring it with her, as my Spanish tobacco is running out. There's an oval pinchbeck tin in Wolfg.'s drawers, that'll do. I again urge Nannerl to wear a man's good fur coat and wrap her feet in straw.

1. Joseph Gottfried, Count von Saurau (1720–75), cathedral dean in Salzburg.

Wolfg. has had to stay indoors for 6 days with a swollen face. His cheeks were swollen both inside and outside, as was his right eye, for 2 days he could eat only broth. So you need to protect your face and ears as you'll be driving into the wind and it cuts into your face the whole time in a half-open coach. And if you get into the coach without having warmed your feet first, you'll not be able to get them warm again for the rest of the day. I expect she'll get in at Herr Gschwendtner's,[2] so her fur boots should be taken there the day before and hung by the stove so that they're warmed through and through and not put on until she's ready to leave. I expect Nannerl will take some money with her for emergencies. If anything else occurs to me, you'll hear from me on Monday before she leaves, otherwise I can't think of anything else. Farewell, we kiss you both. Best wishes, I am your old

Mozart

[*Wolfgang's postscript to Nannerl*]
My dearest sister,

Please don't forget to keep your promise before you leave and call on you know who – – – – I have my reasons. Please give them my best wishes – – – but in the most emphatic and most tender way – – – and – – oh, I don't need to worry, I know my sister, tenderness is second nature to her; I know she'll do her utmost to give me this pleasure, and from self-interest too – – – a bit malicious – – – we'll argue over this in Munich. Farewell.

[*Leopold Mozart's postscript*]
Nannerl also needs to know where she's going. She must write out the following on a slip of paper and give it to Herr Gschwendtner or keep it about herself:

When you drive up through the Thal, through the arch, on to the main square, you keep close to the arches on your left, and once you've passed the narrow passageway at the end of which you can see the Rindermarkt,

2. Leopold had arranged for Nannerl to travel to Munich with Joseph Franz Xaver Gschwendtner.

it's the 5th house along from the passageway. In the middle of this house, which is painted white, is a small round painting of St Francis Xavier, and right at the top, on the 4th floor, is a statue of Our Lady. Frau von Durst is on the third floor. We'll be there from just after 2 until half past.

NB: It's the 5th house once you've passed the passageway through which you can see St Peter's on the Rindermarkt, it's called the Spatzenreuther House on the square.[3] I think I've explained it sufficiently clearly.

45. Mozart to his mother, 14 January 1775, Munich

Praise be to God! My opera was staged yesterday, the 13th, and it turned out so well that I can't begin to describe the noise to Mama. First, the whole theatre was so packed that many people had to be turned away. After every aria there was invariably a tremendous din, with clapping and shouts of *viva Maestro*. Her Highness the Electress and the Dowager Electress[1] – who were opposite me – also said bravo to me. Once the opera was over, during the time when people are normally quiet until the ballet begins, there was nothing but clapping and shouts of bravo; as soon as it stopped, it started up again, and so on. Afterwards I went with Papa to a particular room through which the elector and the whole court have to pass and kissed the hands of the elector and electress and their majesties, all of whom were very kind. First thing this morning His Grace the bishop of Chiemsee[2] sent word, congratulating me on the fact that the opera had turned out so well. As for our return home, this won't be happening so soon, and Mama must not wish it otherwise, for she

3. That is, the Marienplatz in Munich.
1. Maria Anna Sophie, wife of Elector Maximilian III Joseph; Maria Antonia Walpurgis (1724–80), sister of Maximilian III Joseph and widow of Elector Friedrich Christian of Saxony (1722–1763).
2. Ferdinand Christoph, Count Waldburg-Zeil (1719–86), bishop of Chiemsee in Bavaria and a member of the Munich court, had formerly been dean of Salzburg cathedral.

knows how good it is to breathe freely[3] – – – – we'll be back soon enough. One good and necessary reason is that the opera will be given again next Friday and I'm very much needed at the performance – – otherwise people won't recognize the piece – for very strange things happen here. I kiss Mama's hands 1000 times. Best wishes to all our good friends. My compliments to Monsieur Antretter, I hope he'll forgive me for not yet having replied to him, but I simply haven't had the time. I'll do so very soon. Adieu. *1000 kisses* to Pimperl.[4]

[Leopold Mozart's postscript]
You must have received 2 letters from me and one from Nannerl. I still don't know how Nannerl will get back and whether she can travel with Frau von Robinig; perhaps she'll return with us. Farewell. We kiss you many 1,000,000 times. I am your old

Mozart

I've received all your letters.
Best wishes to everyone.

46. Leopold Mozart to his wife, 18 January 1775, Munich

That the opera has been an all-round success you'll have gathered from my last letter and from others that have arrived in Salzb. and you'll soon be hearing it from Herr Gschwendtner even if you haven't already done so. Just imagine how embarrassed His Grace was on hearing the opera praised by the whole of the elector's family and the entire aristocracy and on receiving their most solemn congratulations.[1] He was so embarrassed that he could answer only by nodding his head and shrugging his shoulders. We still haven't spoken to him, as

---

3. Here Mozart refers obliquely to the sense of confinement that he felt in Salzburg.
4. The Mozarts' fox terrier.
1. Archbishop Colloredo had arrived in Munich on 13 January 1775.

he's fully occupied receiving the good wishes of the nobility. He arrived at half past 6 in the evening, just as the main opera was starting, and went and sat in the elector's box. It would take too long to describe the remaining ceremonies. The archbishop won't be hearing Wolfg.'s *opera buffa*, as all the other days are taken and so it can be given only on a Friday, except that it can't be this Friday as it's the anniversary of the death of the emperor of Bavaria.[2] And who knows if it can be performed on the following Friday, the 27th, as the second soprano is very ill. I'm sorry that so many people have come from Salzburg more or less in vain, but at least they've seen the main opera. How amazed I was to see Herr von Antretter entering our building, and when I went to Albert's[3] in the evening, he took us upstairs to a room where to my amazement I found Waberl Eberlin,[4] who had arrived only after the archbishop, in other words, only when the main opera was nearly over, as their rear axle had broken outside Munich. Neither you nor Nannerl had mentioned that Herr Gschwendtner was no longer able to bring her up here, but how shall I get her back without incurring considerable expense? – – – I've already read here the printed news about the masked balls in Salzb.

It's not bad, I just hope they make lots of money.

Farewell, be patient, keep the rooms well locked, best wishes to Fräulein Mitzerl[5] and everyone else etc. etc. We still don't know if the archbishop will leave the day after tomorrow or next Tuesday. *Addio*. We kiss you many 1,000,000 times. I am your old

Mozart

2. Charles VII (1697–1745), father of Elector Maximilian III Joseph, was Holy Roman Emperor (1742–5), during the War of the Austrian Succession (1740–48).
3. Franz Joseph Albert (1728–89), landlord of the Black Eagle in Munich.
4. Maria Cäcilia Barbara Eberlin (1728–1806), eldest daughter of the former Salzburg Kapellmeister and composer Johann Ernst Eberlin (1702–62).
5. Maria Anna Raab (?–1788), owner of the Tanzmeisterhaus on the Makartplatz, Salzburg, where the Mozarts' had rented lodgings since the late autumn of 1773. In the Mozart family letters, she is frequently referred to as 'Mitzerl'.

[*Mozart's postscript to Nannerl*]
My dear sister,

How can I help it if it's just struck a quarter past 7? – – – Papa's not to blame either – – Mama will hear more from my sister. This isn't a good time to travel as the archbishop isn't staying here for long – – it's even being said that he'll stay until he leaves. – – I'm only sorry that he won't see the first masked ball. Best wishes to Baron Zemen and all our good friends. I kiss Mama's hands. Farewell. I'll fetch you in a moment. Your faithful

Franz of the Nosebleed
Milan, 5 May 1756

[*Leopold Mozart's postscript*]
Tell Frau Moshammer, who's living with us, that Baron Gienger, about whom she enquired, was dismissed as a pageboy a year ago and is presumably now in Innsbruck. I think there'll be a big concert in the Kaisersaal on Saturday and so the archbishop will presumably be staying on until Monday or Tuesday.

47. Leopold Mozart to his wife, 15 February 1775, Munich

Herr von Antretter[1] has now really bought the cornet post in Prince Taxis's Cuirassier Regiment. His father will have received the news this morning, he'll soon be having his uniform made and presumably will be travelling back to Salzb. with us. All 3 of us are well, thank God. I'll be glad when this carnival is over, I expect we'll be returning home on Ash Wednesday. *Herr von Moser* is here, also Count *Joseph von Überacker*,[2] I knew they'd come. Herr *von Moser* arrived on Monday, *Überacker* at midday on Tuesday. I gathered from a letter from the Guards Lieutenant[3] that you're not going out much, as he

1. Siegmund von Antretter (1761–1800), Bavarian cadet.
2. Wolf Joseph Ludwig, Count Überacker (1743–1819), court councillor.
3. Official title of Leopold, Count Lodron (1719–84).

asked me in his letter to give you his best wishes, evidently in the belief that you're here with us in Munich. But you should at least go to the ball, even if only once, and see how magnificent it is. Herr von Moser, Count Überacker and the 3 of us met yesterday at the masked ball in the Kielmgarten. Last Sunday a short mass[4] by Wolfg. was performed in the court chapel, and I conducted. Another will be performed this Sunday. We had some amazing April weather yesterday, now fine, now rain. And at 1 o'clock there was a fire alarm. Fire was coming out of the chimney and had already spread but was immediately put out by the crowd of people that gathered. We're not going to the masked ball today as we have to rest; it's the first one that we've missed. Yesterday Nannerl went dressed as an Amazon, which really suited her. All this is being written up every day, so it will all be read to you. Farewell, we kiss you all many 100,000 times and send everyone our best wishes. I am your old

Mozart

Frau von Durst, Herr von Belval, Herr Pernat, Herr Dufraisne etc. have been pestering us to send you their best wishes.

Don't tell anyone about the letter from the Guards Lieutenant as he wrote to me about Lene in secret through Überacker. He also told me that Fischietti[5] is putting it about that he'll be taking up an appointment in Naples at the end of March. If he's to go there in style and if we're to believe him, he'll have to compose something first.

The family arrived back in Salzburg on 7 March. On 23 April, Mozart's serenata Il re pastore *was performed to celebrate the visit to Salzburg of Archduke Maximilian Franz and in August the serenade K204 may have been given as part of the annual graduation ceremonies at the Salzburg*

4. Up to this time, Wolfgang had composed four *missae breves:* K49 (1768), K65 (1769), K192 (1774) and K194 (1774); it is likely that the mass performed in Munich was one of the more recent ones, K192 or K194.
5. Domenico Fischietti (?1725–?1810), formerly chief Kapellmeister at Dresden, active in Salzburg from 1772.

Benedictine University. In early 1776 a performance of Tobias Philipp von Gebler's tragedy Thamos, König in Ägypten *by Karl Wahr's company may have included incidental music by Mozart (K345). His litany K243 was performed on Palm Sunday, 31 March, and in June he composed the divertimento K247 to celebrate the name day of Antonia Maria, Countess Lodron. In July he composed the serenade K250 for the wedding festivities of Elisabeth Haffner and Franz Xaver Anton Späth.*

48. Mozart to Padre Giovanni Battista Martini, 4 September 1776, Salzburg[1]

Most Reverend Padre Maestro,
My Most Esteemed Patron,

The veneration, esteem and respect that I bear towards your most distinguished person have impelled me to importune you with the present letter and to send you a feeble Piece of my Music, which I submit to your magisterial Judgement. For last year's carnival in Munich in Bavaria, I wrote an *opera buffa, La finta giardiniera*. A few days before I left, His Excellency the Elector asked to hear some of my contrapuntal music: and so I was obliged to write this motet[2] in some haste in order to leave time to have the score copied for His Highness and the parts to be extracted from it so that it could be performed the following Sunday during the offertory at High Mass. Dearest and most esteemed Sgr Padre Maestro! You are fervently entreated to tell me frankly and without reserve what you think of it. We live in this world in order that we may always learn industriously, and by means of rational discussion enlighten each other and strive to promote the sciences and the fine arts. Oh, how many times I have longed to be nearer you in order to speak to you, Most Reverend Father, and discuss these matters with you. I live in a country where

1. Although signed by Mozart, this letter, entirely in Italian, is in Leopold's hand and was presumably composed by him too.
2. K222.

Music suffers a most wretched fate, even though, apart from those who have left us, we still have some excellent teachers and, in particular, composers of great knowledge, wisdom and taste. As for the theatre, we are in a bad way as a result of the lack of singers. We have no *musici*, and we shall not get them so easily because they want to be well paid: and generosity is not one of our failings. Meanwhile I am amusing myself by writing for the chamber and the church: and we have two of the finest contrapuntalists here, namely, Sgr Haydn and Sgr Adlgasser. My father is in charge of music at the cathedral, which gives me an opportunity to write music for the church whenever I want to. My father has been *in the service of this court for 36 years and, knowing that the present archbishop is neither able nor willing to tolerate people of an advanced age*, he no longer puts his whole heart into it but has taken an interest in literature, which was always his favourite study. Our church music is very different from that in Italy in that a complete mass, including the *Kyrie, Gloria, Credo, Epistle sonata, Offertory or motet, Sanctus and Agnus Dei* – and even the most solemn Mass said by the Prince himself – must not last longer than 3 quarters of an hour.[3] A special study of this kind of composition is necessary. And yet such a mass must have all the instruments – *trombe di guerra, timpani* etc. Oh, if only we were less far apart, my dearest Sgr Padre Maestro! How many things I'd have to tell you! – – Please give my humble good wishes to the Signori Filarmonici: I commend myself to you and never cease to grieve that I am so remote from the one person in the world whom I love, revere and esteem more than any other. I am

My Reverend Father's
Most Humble and Devoted Servant,
Wolfgango Amadeo Mozart

If you would be so kind as to write to me, please send your letter *via Trento to Salzburg*.

3. Shortly after his election as archbishop, Colloredo instituted a number of modernizing reforms, including a shortening of the mass. Mozart's (or his father's) characterization is slightly disingenuous however: for some important feasts and occasions, especially those celebrated by the archbishop himself, the length of masses in Salzburg was not restricted.

Little is known of Mozart's activities in early 1777; his most significant work of the time was the keyboard concerto K271. But it is clear that both Wolfgang and his father found their situation in Salzburg increasingly intolerable, and in the summer Mozart asked to be released from the archbishop's service.

49. Mozart's petition to Archbishop Colloredo, 1 August 1777, Salzburg

Your Grace,
Most Worthy Prince of the Holy Roman Empire,
Most Merciful Prince of the Realm
and
Lord!

I shall not presume to importune Your Grace with a detailed account of our sad circumstances, which my father most meekly set forth in the most humble petition that he submitted on 14 March[1] and which he swears by his honour and his conscience contains nothing but the truth. But the favourable decision that he hoped that Your Grace would reach was not taken, and so my father would have asked Your Grace most humbly in June to allow us most graciously to travel for several months in order for us to make ends meet, had Your Grace not given his most gracious instructions that the orchestra should prepare for the imminent visit by His Majesty the Emperor.[2] My father afterwards asked most humbly for this permission; but Your Grace refused his request, while most graciously allowing me myself, part-time servant as I am, to travel alone. Our situation is pressing, and so my father has decided to send me away on my own. Yet even here Your Grace has been gracious enough to raise a number of

1. This petition does not survive.
2. In April 1777, Joseph II (travelling incognito as Count Falkenstein) had visited Paris on a diplomatic mission to save the marriage of his sister Marie Antoinette (1755–93) and the dauphin; on 31 July, on the return journey to Vienna, he stopped briefly in Salzburg.

objections. Most Gracious Prince of the Realm and Lord! Parents strive to place their children in a position in which they can earn their own livelihood: they owe this to their own interest and to that of the state. The greater the talents that the children have received from God, the more they are obliged to make use of them in order to improve their own and their parents' circumstances, to assist their parents and see to their own advancement and look to the future in general. The Gospel tells us to use our talents in this way. And so I believe in my conscience and in the sight of God that I owe it to my father, who has devoted his time untiringly to my education, to show him my gratitude as best I can, to lighten his burden and look after myself and also my sister, for I should be sorry to think that she has spent so many hours at the harpsichord without being able to put it to any profitable use.

Your Grace will therefore permit me most humbly to ask most submissively for my discharge as I am obliged to take advantage of this before the coming month of September in order not to be exposed to the bad weather during the cold months that will soon follow. Your Grace will not respond ungraciously to this most humble request as you yourself most graciously declared three years ago, when I asked for your permission to travel to Vienna, that I had nothing to hope for and would do better to try my luck elsewhere. I thank Your Grace in the deepest humility for all the favours that I have received, and in the most flattering hope of being able to serve Your Grace with greater success in my years of manhood, I commend myself to your continuing grace and favour,

the most humble and obedient servant

of Your Grace,

My Most Gracious Sovereign Prince

and

Lord,

Wolfgang Amade Mozart

*5o. Court Decree of the Archbishop of Salzburg,
1 September 1777*

To His Grace the Archbishop of Salzburg the most humble and submissive petition of Wolfgang Amade Mozart By His Most Serene Highness's decree, 28 August 1777.

To the Court Exchequer with the request that father and son be given permission to seek their fortune elsewhere, according to the Gospel.
In Cons[ili]o C[ame]rae, 1 September of this year. By Decree

Decree to His Highness of Salzburg's Konzertmeister Wolfgang Amade Mozart.

His Highness having received the most humble petition of the afore-named asking to be released from His Highness's most gracious service, he most graciously decrees that father and son have per-mission to seek their fortune elsewhere, the aforementioned Mozart herewith informed accordingly of His Highness's supreme decision.
                    Decretum in Consilio Camerae Salzburgensi[1]
                                                1 September 1777

Decree to the Court Treasury here.
The Court Treasury hereby informed, so that it may regulate his salary in the event of his leaving the court's service.
Decretum ut supra.[2]

In an act of calculated maliciousness, Archbishop Colloredo had granted both Wolfgang and his father permission to leave his service, but Leopold

1. Decreed in the council chamber of Salzburg.
2. Decreed as above.

himself had no intention of doing so. He remained behind in Salzburg when on 23 September Mozart, accompanied by his mother, set out on a journey to secure a position for himself. It was the first time the twenty-one-year-old had travelled without his father. Their immediate destination was Munich.

51. Mozart to his father, 23 September 1777, Wasserburg

Mon très cher Père,

Praise and thanks be to God, we arrived safely in Waging, Stein, Frabertsham and Wasserburg; now for a brief description of our journey. As soon as we reached the gates, we were held up for almost a quarter of an hour until the gates were fully opened, as some work was being done there. Outside Schign we encountered a number of cows, one of which was remarkable – – it had *only one side*, something we've never seen before. At Schign, finally, we saw a carriage that was stationary, and lo and behold – our postilion called out – – we have to change here – – as you like, I said. As my Mama and I were talking, a fat gentleman came up to our carriage, and I recognized his symphony[1] at once – – he's a businessman from Memmingen. He looked at me for a while, then finally said: you're Herr Mozart, aren't you? At your service. I recognize you, too, but I don't know your name. I saw you at a concert at Mirabell a year ago. He then told me his name, but, praise and thanks be to God, I've forgotten it. But I've remembered someone who's possibly more important. When I saw him in Salzburg, he had a young man with him, and this time he had this young man's brother with him, someone from Memmingen by the name of Unold;[2] this young man urged me to go Memmingen if at all possible. We gave these gentlemen 100,000 good wishes for Papa and my *scoundrel* of a sister; they promised that they would

1. Physiognomy. The businessman was Johann von Grimmel (1738–94).
2. Georg von Unold auf Grünenfurt (1758–1828); his brother was Jakob (1755–1809).

certainly pass them on. This change of mail coaches was most unwelcome as I wanted to give the postilion a letter to take with him from Waging. After we'd had a bite to eat at Waging, we had the honour of being taken to Stein by the same horses as those that we'd had for the last hour and a half. In Stein I was briefly alone with the priest, who was wide-eyed with amazement as he didn't know our story. From Stein we travelled with a postilion who was terribly phlegmatic – *as a driver, I mean.* We thought we'd never reach the post house but finally got there. Mama is already half asleep as I'm writing this. From Frabertsham to Wasserburg everything went very well. *Viviamo come i Principi.*[3] All that's missing is Papa, but, then, that's God's will. Everything will turn out for the best. I hope that Papa is well and that he's as happy as I am. I'm coping well. I'm a second Papa. I'm seeing to everything. I immediately asked to be able to pay the postilions as I can speak to these fellows better than Mama. We're being splendidly well looked after at the Star here in Wasserburg. I'm sitting here like a prince. Half an hour ago – Mama was just in the pr--y – the innkeeper knocked and asked about all manner of things, and I replied with all the seriousness that you know from my portrait;[4] I must stop, Mama has finished undressing. Both of us ask Papa to take good care of his health, not to go out too early; not to get worked up, to have a good laugh and be merry and all the time be pleased to remember, as we do, that Mufti H. C.[5] is a prick, but God is merciful, compassionate and loving. I kiss Papa's hands 1000 times and embrace my scoundrel of a sister as often as I've – – – taken snuff today.

P.S: This pen is as coarse as I am.

Wasserburg, 23 Sept. 1777. *undecima hora nocte tempore.*[6]

I think I left my diplomas[7] at home. – – Could you send them on

3. 'We're living like lords.'
4. Presumably Mozart refers to the anonymous portrait of 1777 showing him aged twenty-one, wearing the Cross of the Golden Spur; see Deutsch, *Bildern*, 13.
5. Hieronymus Colloredo.
6. '11 o'clock at night.'
7. The certificates he received on his election to the musical academies at Bologna and Verona.

as soon as possible? Half past 6 in the morning. 24 Sept. Your most obedient son,

Wolfgang Amadé Mozart

52. Leopold Mozart to his wife and son, 25 September 1777, Salzburg

My Dears,

It was with the greatest pleasure that I received dear Wolfg.'s letter this morning. Herr Bullinger,[1] too, has just read it and laughed uproariously – he sends you his best wishes. I'm very pleased to hear that you're both well: for my own part, I'm now much better, thank God. After you'd left, I came upstairs very wearily and threw myself into an armchair. I made every effort to curb my feelings when we said goodbye, in order not to make our farewell even more painful, and in my daze forgot to give my son a father's blessing. I ran to the window and called after you but couldn't see you driving out through the gates, so we thought you'd already left as I'd been sitting for a long time, not thinking of anything. Nannerl was astonishingly tearful and it required every effort to comfort her. She complained of a headache and terrible stomach pains, finally she started to be sick, vomiting good and proper, after which she covered her head, went to bed and had the shutters closed, with poor Pimpes beside her. I went to my own room, said my morning prayers, went back to bed at half past 8, read a book, felt calmer and fell asleep. The dog came and I woke up. She made it clear that she wanted me to take her for a walk, from which I realized that it must be nearly 12 o'clock and that she wanted to be let out. I got up, found my fur and saw that Nannerl was fast asleep and, looking at the clock, saw that it was half past 12. When I got back with the dog, I woke Nannerl and sent for lunch. Nannerl had no appetite at all; she ate nothing, went back to bed after lunch and, once Herr Bullinger had left, I spent the time

1. Franz Joseph Johann Nepomuk Bullinger was a close family friend, see List.

praying and reading in bed. By the evening Nannerl felt better and was hungry, we played piquet, then ate in my room and played a few more rounds after supper and then, in God's name, went to bed. And so this sad day came to an end, a day I never thought I'd have to endure. On Wednesday, Nannerl went to church early. In the afternoon we had target-practice.[2] Herr Bullinger won for Sallerl,[3] he played for both Mama and Sallerl, and so Mama has won 11 kr., whereas Wolfg. has lost 4 kr. Herr Bullinger and Katherl[4] played with us till 6, and the day ended with the Rosary, which I say for you every day. This morning I sent for Herr Glatz[5] of Augsb., and we agreed that in Augsb. you should stay *at the Lamb in the Heilige Kreuzgasse*, where lunch costs 30 kr. per person, the rooms are attractive and the most respectable people stay – English, French, etc. You'll also be very close to the church of the Holy Cross, and my brother Franz Alois is also nearby in the Jesuitengasse.[6] So you shouldn't say anything to Herr Albert, as it's too expensive at the 3 Moors,[7] he asks an extraordinary amount for the rooms and each meal works out at 45 or even 48 kr. per person. If you go to Augsb., Wolfg. should arrange to be taken at once to the *organ-builder, Herr Stein*,[8] who hasn't seen him since he was 7 and is unlikely, therefore, to recognize him. He can say that he's come from Innsbruck with a commission to inspect his instruments. Herr Glatz tells me that Herr Stein, Herr Bioley and Herr Fingerlin[9] are in a position to organize

2. Target-shooting with airguns was among the Mozart family's favourite pastimes, and is mentioned many times in Leopold's letters to his wife and son.
3. Rosalia Joly; she is often called Sallerl in the letters.
4. Maria Anna Katharina (Katherl) Gilowsky, see List.
5. Johann Christoph Glatz was a merchant in Augsburg. Wolfgang and his mother intended to go on there from Munich.
6. Leopold's brother Franz Alois Mozart (1727–1791) still lived in Augsburg. Leopold had important contacts at the Catholic church of the Holy Cross, dating back to his youth.
7. Landlord of the Black Eagle in Munich; Leopold and Mozart had stayed at the Three Moors in Augsburg in 1763.
8. The instrument builder Johann Andreas Stein (1728–92) was a long-standing friend of the Mozarts. He had last seen Wolfgang on his visit to Augsburg in 1763.
9. Franz Bioley, cloth merchant, and Johann Conrad Fingerlin, manufacturer.

a particularly good concert. You must also call on Herr *Christoph von Zabuesnig*, who wrote that beautiful German poem about you in Salzb.,[10] he's a businessman and a scholar. *In Augsb. this gentleman may be able to arrange for something nice and impressive to be published in the papers.* Herr Gasser is the businessman who packed up my books without charging me a penny, took them to Frankfurt and brought back for me the money that he got for them, so you must call on him and thank him for me, it's a favour that he can always do for me. My brother or his daughter[11] will no doubt take you to see *His Grace*, the magistrate Herr von Langenmantel,[12] to whom you should give my most humble good wishes. Mama knows how well we know each other, we travelled to Salzb. together, when Herr von Heffner's father was also present. You don't have to wear your cross[13] at court, except in Augsburg, where you should wear it every day, for here it will earn you esteem and respect, as indeed it will wherever there is no ruling lord. If you want to visit the monasteries of the Holy Cross and St Ulrich, you can certainly do so and try out their organs. Herr Stein will no doubt show you his organ at the church of the Discalced Friars. *Herr Hilber's son is at St Ulrich's Monastery.*[14] NB: There is a certain organist and composer in Augsb.,

10. The writer and theatre poet Johann Christoph Zabuesnig (1747–1827) had visited Salzburg in 1769 and written a poem in honour of Mozart. It reads, in part: 'Here, where the Salza springs from gloomy rocks/And greets the open land with waters fair,/Cutting in two the happy land's fair town,/Whose castle now with it the name can share,/A child, by Nature formed a work of art,/A wondrous boy one fortunate day was born,/Whose genius turned the fables of the past/To foolish stories, justly laughed to scorn./O child! by noble mind so lofty raised/That all too lowly writes my feeble pen,/If e'er thy merits can be duly praised,/Thy fame itself will be a poem then.' See Deutsch, *Documentary Biography*, 86–7.

11. Maria Anna Thekla Mozart, see List.

12. The imperial councillor Jakob Wilhelm Benedikt Langenmantel von Westheim und Ottmarshausen (1719–90) was a childhood friend of Leopold Mozart. Both had studied at the Jesuit high school in Augsburg and in 1737 they travelled together to Salzburg, where they matriculated at the Benedictine University.

13. Of the Order of the Golden Spur.

14. Fr Anselm Hilber (1755–1827) was the son of Joseph Hilber, a violinist active in Salzburg from 1749.

of whom the locals have been making a great fuss. I've forgotten his name.[15]

Wherever you are, always make sure that the innkeeper puts the boot-trees in your boots. − −

The music can always remain at the front in the trunk, but you should buy a large oilcloth and use both this and the old one to wrap it well, in order to ensure that it's really safe.

I think I also need to remind you that the *Salzb. half-batzen*[16] won't be of any use to you from now on, not even in Munich. I don't suppose you've got any, but if you do, the Salzb. guard will be able to change them. Whether the batzen are any good, I don't know, you need to enquire of Herr Albert about the smaller denominations.

I'd intended to be up by 9 this morning, but Herr Glatz found me still in bed, as did Sergeant Clessin, so I was unable to get up till 11. Everyone admires Wolfg.'s portrait. Herr Clessin thought you were coming straight back, as did Herr von Schiedenhofen, who called on us yesterday evening from 5 till 7; indeed, everyone thinks so.

If you leave Munich without being able to inform me, you must leave a note at the post office in Munich, stating: *If letters arrive with the following address − à Monsieur Wolfgang Amadé Mozart Maître de Musique − please forward them to the landlord of the Lamb in the Heilige Kreuzgasse in Augsburg.*

You left behind the *trousers of your pike-grey suit.* If I can find no other opportunity to send them on, I'll include them with the *Antretter music, a number of contredanses,* the *Adagio and Rondo* that was written for Brunetti[17] and anything else that falls into my hands, and give them to the messenger, who can send them to my brother in Augsburg in the event that he misses you − I don't think he's due to arrive until midday on Monday. There was a row yesterday between Haydn and

---

15. Johann Michael Demmler (1748−85). Mozart later recommended Demmler to succeed Adlgasser as court and cathedral organist in Salzburg; in the event, he gained the post himself.

16. A small silver coin; see Note on Currencies.

17. The 'Antretter' music is the serenade K185; the contredanses cannot be identified. The violinist Antonio Brunetti (c. 1744−86) was concert master in Salzburg; Mozart wrote the adagio K261 and the rondo K269 for him.

the Kapellmeister. The english horn concerto was to be rehearsed again after Vespers, even though it has already been performed once, and Ferlendis and Brunetti weren't there; Haydn became angry and said that the rehearsal was in any case unnecessary and why should they wait for those Italian fools? Rust said that it's he who gives the orders around here etc. – The service lasted till a quarter to 11, and an *Agnus Dei* by Haydn was again given as Rust wasn't ready. The sonata was one of Wolfgang's.[18]

Don't forget to obtain some letters of recommendation in Munich, especially from the bishop of Chiemsee.

Count Seinsheim could give you one to take with you to Würzburg, the bishop is his father's brother. Nannerl and I send our good wishes to Mama and kiss you both a million times, *addio*.

Mozart

53. *Mozart to his father, 26 September 1777, Munich*

Mon très cher Père,

We arrived safely in Munich at half past 4 on the evening of the 24th; the first thing that was new is that we had to drive to the customs, accompanied by a grenadier with a fixed bayonet. The first familiar face that we saw on our way there was Sgr Consoli,[1] who recognized me at once and who was indescribably happy to see me. He called on me the very next day. I can't begin to tell you how delighted Herr Albert was. He really is a thoroughly decent man, and

18. The row was between Michael Haydn and Giacomo Rust (1741–86), Kapell-meister in Salzburg from 12 June 1777; at the end of the year he asked to be relieved of his post because the bad weather in Salzburg affected his health. Giuseppe Ferlendis (1755–1802) was an oboist active in the Salzburg court music establishment from 1775–8. The sonata is one of Wolfgang's so-called epistle sonatas, one-movement instrumental works played between the reading of the Epistle and the Gospel during Mass; to this date, Mozart had written twelve such works: K67–69 (1771–2), 144, 145 (both 1774), 212 (1775), 241, 244, 245, 263 (all four 1776), 274 and 278 (both 1777).
1. The castrato Tommaso Consoli (1753–after 1811) sang the roles of Ramiro in *La finta giardiniera* (Munich, 1775) and Aminta in *Il re pastore* (Salzburg, 1775).

our very good friend. Following my arrival, I remained at the keyboard till it was time to eat. Herr Albert still hadn't returned home, but he finally arrived and we went down to supper together. There I met Monsieur Sfeer and a certain secretary, who is a very good friend of his. Both men send their best wishes. It was late when we got to bed, and we were tired after the journey. We were already up again at 7 on the 25th, but my hair was in such a mess that it wasn't until ½ past 10 that I arrived at Count Seeau's[2] and when I got there, I was told that he'd already gone hunting: patience! I then wanted to go and see the choirmaster, Herr Pernat, but he had gone off with Baron Schmidt to his estates. Herr Belval was very busy when I called on him and had time only to pass on his best wishes. Rossi arrived during lunch. Consoli came at 2, Becke[3] and Herr von Belval at 3. I paid a courtesy call on Frau von Durst, who is lodging near the Franciscans. At 6 I went for a short walk with Herr Becke. There is a certain Professor Huber[4] here – you may remember him better than I do – who says that he saw and heard me at young Herr von Mesmer's the last time I was in Vienna. He's not especially tall, nor is he especially short, but pale, with whitish grey hair and in his appearance he looks a bit like the under riding master. He's also deputy intendant at the theatre; his job is to read the plays that they want to perform and to improve or ruin or lengthen or shorten them. He comes to Albert's every evening. Today, Friday the 26th, I was at Count Seeau's at ½ past 8. I was just entering the building when Madame Nieser, the actress, came out and asked me whether I was going to see the count. Yes. He's still in his garden, and God knows when he'll return. I asked her where his garden is, well, she said, I too want to speak to him, let's go together. We'd scarcely reached the gates when the count came out to meet us, and was still some 12 paces away when he recognized me and called me by name. He was very polite. He already knew what had happened to me. We

2. Joseph Anton, Count Seeau (1713–99), director of opera and drama at the Munich court.
3. Johann Baptist Becke (1743–1817), flautist in the Munich court chapel, who was a family friend.
4. Klemens Huber, actor and dramaturge active in Munich, 1776–9.

went slowly up the steps, just the two of us; I told him briefly why I'd come. He said I should waste no more time but ask for an audience with His Highness the Elector. But if I couldn't arrange this, I should put my case before him in writing. I begged him to say nothing about all this, – he gave me his word. When I told him that a good composer was badly needed here, he said: I know! I then called on the bishop of Chiemsee and was with him for half an hour. I told him everything. He promised to do all he could in this matter. He was going to Nymphenburg at 1 o'clock and gave me his word that he'd speak to Her Highness the Electress[5] about it. The court is returning on Sunday evening. At lunch today we were guests of Herr von Belval at Rasco's; Rasco and the others – Herr von Lori,[6] Belval, Passauer – all send their best wishes. We then called on Frau von Durst. She lives 3 flights up in Bürgermeister Schmädel's house. Herr von Lori has rooms on the 2nd floor. From here we were collected by Herr Sigl[7] – he's been married for 2 months – and all of us went to see Frau von Hofstetten; her husband isn't here but will soon be returning. Franz Dufraisne is a court councillor but so far *sine auro*:[8] Sigl then drove Mama home as she'd promised Becke that she'd go and see a play with him, and I took Frau von Durst home and then went to the theatre, where we all met up again. They were playing *Henriette, Or She's Already Married*.[9] At ½ past 11 this morning I went with Becke to see Fräulein von Seeau, who's as pretty as a picture. Fräulein d'Hosson has made a very good match. He's called Hepp. People say he's very rich. Herr Johann Cröner[10] has been appointed deputy Konzertmeister on the strength of his coarse language. Two of his symphonies – *Dio mene liberi*[11] – have been performed here: the elector asked him: did you really write that? – – Yes, Your Highness. Who

5. Maria Anna Sophie.

6. Johann Georg von Lori (1723–87), court councillor in Munich.

7. Sigl was apparently a local piano teacher.

8. 'without any money'.

9. A comedy by Gustav Grossmann (1744–96) based on *Julie, ou La nouvelle Héloïse* (1761) by Jean-Jacques Rousseau (1712–78).

10. Johann von Cröner (*c.* 1737–85) was a violinist.

11. 'may God spare me them'.

taught you? – A schoolteacher in Switzerland – – people make such a fuss about composition – – but this schoolteacher told me more than all our composers here could tell me. Count Schönborn[12] arrived today with his wife, the archbishop's sister. I happened to be at the theatre at the time: in the course of his conversation with them, Herr Albert told them that I was here and that I'm no longer in service. Both of them expressed their surprise. They simply refused to believe that I earned 12 fl. 30 kr. of blessed memory! They were just changing horses or else they'd have liked to have spoken to me. But I didn't see them again. But how are things with you? How are you feeling? Mama and I hope that you're both well.

I remain in the best of moods. I feel a great weight has been lifted from my mind now that I've left all that chicanery behind me! – – I've also got fatter. Herr von Wallau spoke to me in the theatre today, and I paid a courtesy call on Countess Larosée in her box. I must now leave a bit of space for Mama. Best wishes to the whole worshipful company of marksmen from 3 of its members, namely, me, Mama and Monsieur *Novac*, who comes to Albert's every day. In the meantime, farewell, my dearest Papa; I kiss your hands innumerable times and embrace my scoundrel of a sister.

Wolfg. Amadé Mozart

[*Maria Anna Mozart's postscript*]
Wolfgang has left me with nothing to say, I hope to receive a letter from you soon and look forward to hearing that you're well. We're all keeping well, thank God, and wish only that you were here, something which, with God's help, will happen, meanwhile don't worry and forget all your troubles, everything will turn out for the best in the long run. We're leading charmed lives, getting up early, going to bed late, and with visitors all day long: after living like lords, we shall get our rewards.

Addio ben mio,[13] keep well till we're back, stick your tongue up

12. Eugen Franz Erwein, Count Schönborn (1727–1801), hereditary high steward of Austria; his second wife, Maria Theresia (1744–1828), was the sister of Archbishop Colloredo.
13. 'Farewell, my treasure.'

your crack. And then shit in your bed. It's turned 1 – enough said. We both wish you good luck – you can add your own rhyme.

All manner of good wishes to my dear Sallerl, Katherl, Nannerl, Pimperl.

Maria Anna Mozart

54. Leopold Mozart to his son, 28 September 1777, Salzburg

Today was the first time I've been out – I went to Mirabell for the last Mass and sat up in the side oratory. During the Mass I saw Herr von Gilowsky with Frau von Riedl on his arm and Herr Grenier with Herr von Riedl walking through the Mirabell courtyard. They were looking at the rooms. So, when Mass was over, I walked down the passage to the rooms to pay them my respects. They were very surprised when I told them you were in Munich and had perhaps already left. They promised to visit us on Monday. The marksmen arrived after lunch. The paymaster put up the prize, which Herr Bullinger won. But I came second, and as I was shooting for Mama, I won 7 kr. for her. Wolfg., for whom Herr Bullinger shot, won 13 kr. Afterwards Cassel[1] and Katherl played with us until the dress rehearsal of the French play,[2] which was at 5. All 3 of them went to the theatre, while I took Pimperl for a walk – we went about 100 yards beyond the city gates, after which I brought her home, then went to the rehearsal myself. It was in costume, but no one else was admitted. 500 tickets are being distributed for Tuesday's performance. The archb. has been in Weitwörth for a few days, but Count Gundacker[3] and his wife arrived this morning, so he returned this evening. The days have been extremely fine and warm. I'm feeling very well

1. Joseph Thomas Cassel was a violinist, flautist and double bass player in the Salzburg court music establishment.
2. Voltaire's *Zaïre* (1732), performed in German with incidental music by Michael Haydn.
3. Franz de Paula Gundacker, Count Colloredo (1731–1807) was the archbishop's eldest brother.

today, thank God, and have coughed very little – barely 3 times in 2 hours. I'm still taking humectants and shall discuss this with Dr Barisani,[4] as I've gone very thin. I trust that with God's help things will improve, as I'm now feeling calmer, but I'll have to take great care of myself. I would only ask you, my dear Wolfgang, not to indulge in any excesses, you've been used since your youth to an orderly life. So you should avoid stimulants, as you know that you soon get hot and that you prefer cold to warmth – *clear proof that your blood has a tendency to heat up and start to boil at once*. Strong wines and, indeed, drinking large amounts of any wine are harmful to you. Just imagine the unhappiness and distress that this would cause your dear mother in a far-off country – I shall not even mention myself in this context. I have written to Monsieur Duschek at great length and added that you will find an opportunity in the course of your journey to write to him too. Madame Duschek[5] has answered my letter and told me that she too had heard about our troubles in Salzb., that both he and she take the keenest interest and hope to see our merits rewarded and that Wolfg. – naughtier than ever – should come to Prague either directly or indirectly, where he will always be most warmly welcome. I must now copy out for you the reply to my memorandum; you'll see how they must have toiled to put it together.

Ex Decreto Cels^{mi} Principis[6] 26 Sept. 1777. To signify to the supplicant that as a matter of extreme urgency His Grace desires that his music staff should be on good terms. In the most gracious confidence that the supplicant will behave calmly and peaceably towards the Kapellmeister and other persons employed in the court orchestra, His Grace is willing therefore to retain him in his service and at the same time to enjoin him most graciously to apply himself to serving the Church and his august person.

Did you ever in your life read such nonsense?

4. Silvester Barisani (1719–1810), physician to Archbishop Colloredo.
5. Czech composer and music teacher Franz Xaver Duschek and his singer wife Josepha, see List.
6. 'From the Most Exalted Prince's (i.e. the archbishop's) Decree.' This decree is in reply to Leopold Mozart's petition (now lost) to be reappointed as deputy Kapellmeister.

Anyone reading the petition and then this reply is bound to think that the chancery clerk wrote the reply to the wrong memorandum. Fortunately, no one has read it apart from Herr Bullinger, and I don't expect anyone else will do so either as the paymaster told me today that I should just send for the money, adding that he had no need to read anything and wouldn't in any case have objected to sending me the money as he hadn't received the necessary instructions to strike me off.

Last Friday Herr Kolb[7] gave a big concert for the businessmen from out of town, also present were Ferlendis, Ferrari, Cassel, Stadler, Pinzger etc.[8] He played your *concerto* and *serenade*,[9] and as the music was so highly praised, causing an amazing stir and eliciting considerable applause, he said these were works by a good friend who was no longer here, at which everyone exclaimed: *What a shame that we've lost him!* It was in the hall at Eizenberger's. By the end they were all drunk and carried each other in procession round the room, colliding with the lustre, or chandelier, in the middle and breaking the centre bowl and other pieces, which will have to be replaced, and so a part of it will have to be sent to Venice.

I sent off the parcel with the trousers by the mail coach this morning, I hope you'll receive it, otherwise we'll have to make enquiries, things often find their way to the customs, which is why I wrote on it: *one old pair of trousers and music.*

Monday morning, the 29th. I've just received your first letter from Munich. Perhaps things will turn out well. – I've got to go, *Frau von Riedl* has just arrived. – – – – She stayed till half past 11, she sends you her best wishes and hopes you'll be staying in Munich, she'll be away for 2 months. To get back to the question of Munich, it might help if you can find an opportunity to let the elector know what you can do, especially in regard to fugues, canons and contrapuntal compositions. You really must flatter Count Seeau and tell him about

---

7. Joachim Kolb.
8. Antonio Ferrari, cellist; Franz de Paula Stadler (*c.* 1744–1827), tenor and violinist; Andreas Pinzger (1740–1817), violinist.
9. The works cannot be identified.

all the arias etc. and ballets that you want to write for his theatre, but without demanding any payment. You must be amazingly polite to the courtiers, for they all have a say in the matter. Consoli could sing the new scena[10] for Madame Duschek. You could mention Madame Duschek in passing to Count Seeau. Perhaps you could hold a concert in Count Seeau's garden. If the affair appears at all hopeful, you'll have to extend your stay in Munich; make friends with Herr Wotschitka,[11] he always has an opportunity to speak to the elector and his stock is high; if the elector asks you to write something for the gamba, he can tell you what it should be like and show you the pieces that the elector likes most, so you can see what his taste is like. If you haven't spoken to the elector or if you can't speak to him and are obliged to apply to him in writing, Herr von Bellvall will advise you on who should write the letter. You can inform the elector and Count Seeau both in person and in writing that in regard to your knowledge of counterpoint, His Highness need only consult Padre Maestro Martini of Bologna and Herr Hasse in Venice to find out what these gentlemen think about you, and if you feel that it is necessary, I can send you the 2 diplomas appointing you *maestro di cappella* of the academies in Bologna and Verona when you were still only 14. I have every confidence in you; and I'm very happy that Mama, whom I kiss 1000 times, is well: and I can well believe that you're feeling light-hearted. The whole company of sharpshooters sends you their best wishes. Nannerl went to see Frau von Schiedenhofen this morning, she may be calling on us this afternoon with Anna Kranach. Tomorrow's gala has been abandoned, but there's a big party today instead. The story about Monsieur Albert – do give him our best wishes – and Countess Schönborn is priceless. Give our best wishes to all our friends and acquaintances – – so has Herr Sigl got himself hitched up? – Hearty congratulations! Misses Mitzerl, Sallerl, Pimperl, Tresel,[12] Katherl Gil. etc. all send their best wishes,

---

10. K272, *Ah, lo previdi – Ah, t'invola agl' occhi miei*, composed in August 1777. A scena is an extended dramatic episode, often for solo singer.
11. Franz Xaver Wotschitka (*c.* 1727–96), chamber virtuoso at Munich.
12. Therese Pänkhlin (1738–?), the Mozarts' maidservant.

especially Frau von Riedl and Count Leopold Arco etc. etc. I kiss
you both with all my heart and am your old abandoned hermit with
his housekeeper,

Mozart

I'm sending you the 2 diplomas and Padre Martini's testimonial;
make sure that the elector reads them, Count Seeau must read them
too and see that the elector reads them. They will be a sensation!
That you were made a *maestro di cappella* of these academies 7 years
ago!

[Postscript added by Abbé Joseph Bullinger]
My very dearest friend, I'm delighted to hear that you're well; I knew
very well that you'd be better off abroad. Farewell, and think of me
a little from time to time. My most humble good wishes to your dear
Mama

Your very good friend
Jos. Bullinger

[Postscript added by Nannerl Mozart]
I was pleased to hear that Mama and the clown are both cheerful and
well. But we poor orphans just have to mope and while away our
time. As for Pimperl, please send me a short prelude, but this time
one from C to B flat, so that I can eventually learn it by heart.[13]

Young handsome Herr Fichtl has just been given the last rites and
looks set to sacrifice his life in his 17th year. His Mama is inconsolable.
I've no good news for you. So kiss Mama's hands and to you, you
churl, you rogue, I give a juicy kiss and am Mama's obedient daughter
and your sister, who lives in hope – –

– – Marie Anne Mozart

Miss Pimpes still lives in hope and stands and sits by the door for
half an hour at a time, thinking you'll return at any moment. In spite
of this, she's well, can eat, drink, sleep, s--t and p--s.

13. In the event, Mozart sent Nannerl four preludes, K395, on 11 October 1777.

55. Mozart to his father, 2 October 1777, Munich

I was again at Count Salern's[1] yesterday, 1 October, and today, the 2nd, I even lunched there. These last 3 days I've played quite enough, even though I've really enjoyed myself. Papa shouldn't imagine that I like going to Count Salern's because of – –, no, as she's unfortunately in service and therefore never at home, but I'll see her tomorrow morning at 10 when I go to court in the company of Madame Hepp née Fräulein d'Hosson. The court is leaving on Saturday and not returning until the 20th. Tomorrow I'm having lunch with Frau and Fräulein de Branca,[2] who is now half my pupil, as Sigl rarely appears and Becke, who normally helps her with the flute, isn't here. During the 3 days that I was at Count Salern's I played a lot of things from memory, then the 2 cassations for the countess and finally the graduation music with the rondeau.[3] You can't imagine how pleased Count Salern was: but he understands music, for he was shouting bravo all the time, when other courtiers take a pinch of snuff – – blow their nose, clear their throat – – or strike up a conversation – – I told him that I only wished the elector had been there, so that he could have heard something – – he doesn't know anything about me. He doesn't know what I can do. But these gentlemen believe the first passer-by and are unwilling to find out for themselves. *It's always the same*. I mean to put it to the test. He should summon all the composers in Munich and can even write to a few in Italy and France, Germany, England and Spain, I'm confident that I can [stand comparison] with each and every one of them. I told him all that had happened to me in Italy. I asked him to mention these things whenever conversation turned to me, he said I am the lowest of the low but I'll gladly do so whenever I can. He's also of the opinion that if I could stay here in the meantime, the affair would sort itself out. It wouldn't

1. Joseph Ferdinand Maria, Count Salern (1718–1805) was Count Seeau's predecessor as the director of opera and drama at Munich.
2. Wife and daughter of Johann Georg von Branca (1714–89).
3. The cassations are possibly K247 and K287. The identity of the rondeau is disputed – the serenade K250 has been proposed, but K251 is more likely.

be impossible for me to get by on my own here, as I'd ask for at least 300 florins from Count Seeau; as for food, I wouldn't need to worry as I'd always be invited out, and if I wasn't invited out, Albert would be delighted to have me at his table. I eat little, drink water and just have a small glass of wine with my fruit at the end of the meal. I'd enter into a contract with Count Seeau along the following lines – all on the advice of my good friends: to deliver 4 German operas a year, partly comic, partly serious, and I'd have a *sera*[4] of each, the proceeds going to me, as is the custom here. This alone would bring in at least 500 florins, making 800 florins with my salary – but it would undoubtedly be more. For the actor and singer Felix Reiner earned 200 florins at *his* benefit; and I'm *very popular* here. And how much more popular I'd be if I could help to promote the German national theatre in music? – – – And that would certainly happen with me; for I was already eager to write something when I heard the German singspiel.[5] The leading singer is called Kaiser,[6] she's the daughter of a cook by one of the local counts. A most attractive young woman. Pretty on stage. I've not yet seen her close to. She was born here. When I heard her, it was only the third time she'd appeared on stage. She has a beautiful voice, not powerful, but not weak either. Very pure. Good intonation. Her teacher is Valesi;[7] and you can tell from her singing that her teacher not only understands singing but also knows how to teach it. When she sustains a note over a few bars, I was amazed at the beauty of her crescendo and diminuendo. She still has a slow trill, something I like very much, as it means that it will be all the purer and clearer once she wants to develop a quicker trill – it's certainly easier to do a fast trill. The people here are genuinely pleased with her – – – just as I am with them. Mama sat in the stalls, she was there by half past 4 in order to be sure of a seat, but I didn't

4. Benefit performance.
5. Singspiel is the term for German-language opera, usually comic, with spoken dialogue.
6. Margarethe Kaiser, active at Munich 1776–84.
7. Giovanni Baptist Valesi (Johann Evangelist Wallishauser, 1735–1816), active at the Mannheim court during the 1770s; he sang the role of the High Priest of Neptune in the first performance of *Idomeneo*.

get there until half past 6 as I can go into any of the boxes. After all, I'm well known. I was in the Brancas' box. I watched Mlle Kaiser through my opera glasses, and she often drew a tear from me; I often called out *brava*, *bravissima*, as I kept thinking that it was only her third time on stage. The piece was *The Fishermaiden*, a very good translation of Piccinni. They don't yet have any original works. They'd like to stage a German *opera seria* as soon as they can and want me to write it. Professor Huber, whom I've already mentioned, is one of the people who wants me to do so. Time for bed; there's no alternative. It's just turned 10! – –

Baron Rumlingen[8] recently complimented me by saying how much he enjoys spectacles, good actors and actresses, good singers, and, in addition, a fine composer like me – – – of course, it's all just talk – – and it's easy to talk. – – But he's never talked like that with me before. Good night. Until tomorrow, when, God willing, I'll have the honour of writing to you again, my dearest Papa.

[Maria Anna Mozart's postscript]
Wolfgang is having lunch today with Madame Branca, while I had lunch at home, but as soon as it strikes 3 I'm going to see Frau von d'Hosson, who's sending someone round to collect me. Herr von Grimmel called on us again yesterday with Herr von Unold, he's our good friend and is trying hard to talk us into going to Memmingen and giving a good concert there, he assures us that we'll make more there than at a court, I think that's true, as people rarely go to such places, so that they're glad to have what they can get.

How is your health? I'm still not satisfied with your letters, I don't like that cough, which has been going on for such a long time, there shouldn't be anything the matter with you. Use the sago soon, the sooner the better, so that you finally get your strength back. We received the parcel by the mail coach and the other one by the ordinary post. Best wishes to Nannerl, and tell her not to be cross with you but to make sure that there's nothing to annoy you and to

8. Wilhelm Ernst Sigmund von Rumlingen (?–1825) was later music director of the German court opera in Munich.

help you pass the time, so that you don't get melancholy. Pimperl – I hope – is doing her duty and ingratiating herself with you, she's a good and faithful fox terrier. Best wishes also to Tresel and tell her it's all the same whether

[*Mozart's postscript*]
I shit the dirt or she eats it. But now for something more sensible.

I'm writing this on *3 October*. The court is leaving tomorrow and won't be coming back before the 20th. If they'd stayed, I'd have continued to take the necessary steps and would have remained here for some time longer, but as it is, I hope to continue my journey with Mama next Tuesday; it's like this: the company I recently told you about will be formed in the meantime, so that, when we grow tired of travelling, we shall have a safe place to return to. Herr von Grimmel saw the bishop of Chiemsee today, he often has dealings with him, not least because of the salt. He's a strange individual. Here he's called Your Grace – by his *servants*, that is. He'd like nothing better than for me to remain here and was most enthusiastic when he spoke to the prince about me. He told me, just leave it to me, I'll speak to the prince. I know how best to speak to him, I've often done lots of favours for him. The prince promised that I'd *certainly* be taken on, but things can't move as quickly as that. Once the court returns, he'll speak to the elector with all the necessary seriousness and zeal.

I was at Count Seeau's at 8 this morning; I was very brief and said only 'I'm only here, Your Excellency, to explain myself and my business; it has been objected that I should go to Italy. But I've spent 16 months in Italy and written 3 operas,[9] so I'm already well enough known. Your Excellency will see from these papers what other progress I've made.' I showed him the diplomas: I'm showing Your Excellency all this and telling you this simply so that, whenever people speak of me and do me any injustice, Your Excellency may be justified in taking my part. He asked me if I was now going to go to France, I said I'd be staying in Germany, but he understood me to

9. *Mitridate, re di Ponto, Ascanio in Alba* and *Lucio Silla*.

mean *Munich* and, smiling delightedly, said: So, you're staying on here? I said, no, I'd like to have stayed and, to tell the truth, I'd like to have received something from the elector only so that I could then have served Your Excellency with my music and without any thought of self-interest. It would have been a pleasure for me to do so. He even adjusted his nightcap at this.

By 10 o'clock I was at court, where I saw Countess Salern. She'd already received the arias. Of course, the Robinigs say whatever comes into their heads. I then had lunch at the Brancas. Privy Councillor Branca had been invited to the French ambassador's and so he wasn't at home. People call him their Excellency. His wife is French. She can barely speak a word of German, I spoke French to her all the time. I was quite cheeky. She told me that I didn't speak too badly and had a good habit of speaking slowly, which made me easy to understand; she's a most excellent woman, with a real *savoir vivre*. Her daughter plays well, though she still can't play in time. I thought that she or her ear was the cause, but now I can blame only her teacher. He's too indulgent and instantly satisfied. I practised with her today. I'd be willing to wager that if she studied with me for 2 months she'd be able to play really well and accurately. She asked me to send her best wishes to you both and also to the whole of the Robinig household. She was at the convent at the same time as Fräulein Louise.[10] Later a certain Fräulein Lindner, who is now at Count Salern's as governess to the 2 little countesses, likewise asked me to send all manner of messages to the Robinigs and to Fräulein Aloisia von Schiedenhofen, with whom she was at the same convent. At 4 I went to see Frau von d'Hosson, where I found Mama and Frau von Hepp. I played till 8 o'clock, then we came home. I should add that at half past 9 a small group of 5 players – 2 clarinets, 2 horns and 1 bassoon – turned up. Herr Albert – whose name day it is tomorrow – had arranged for them to play in honour of the two of us. They didn't play at all badly together. They were the same people

10. That is, Maria Aloisia Viktoria Robinig von Rottenfeld (1757–86). Aloisia von Schiedenhofen (1760–1831), below, was the sister of Johann Baptist von Schiedenhofen.

as those who are on duty in Albert's hall, but it's clear that they've been coached by Fiala.[11] They played works by him, and I have to say that they were very attractive pieces. He has some very good ideas. Tomorrow we're holding a little scratch concert – on the wretched keyboard, of course. Ow! Ow! Ow! I hope you have a very restful night and improve a good wish by hearing to hope that Papa is recovered full. I forgive your begging on account of my frightful handwriting, but ink, haste, sleep, dreams and everything else. – – – I Papa you, my very own kissing, 1000 times the dearest, and my embrace, the hearts, sister I with all my scoundrel, and am now and ever shall be, Amen,

> Wolfgang most obedient your
> Amadé Mozart son

Munich, 3 Oct. 1777
To all good friends
bad friends
good friends
bad friends
all manner of messages!

56. Leopold Mozart to his son, 4 October 1777, Salzburg

Mon très cher Fils,

I can't imagine that anything good will come of Munich, the elector is bound to take no one on unless there's a vacancy: and on top of everything, there are always secret enemies who would thwart you *out of fear*. Herr Albert's plan certainly demonstrates the greatest friendship imaginable, yet, however possible it may seem to you that you'll find 10 people, each willing to give you a ducat a month, I see this as an impossibility. And who could these philanthropists or music

---

11. Joseph Fiala (1748–1816), an oboist active at the Palatine court (first at Mannheim, later at Munich) from April 1777.

lovers be? – – And what kind of a commitment or service would they demand from you in return? That Count Seeau may give you something makes much more sense to me: but without the former, the latter would be insignificant. If Herr Albert can arrange this for a year – I won't ask for more – you could agree to a proposal from Count Seeau: but what would he demand? – – Perhaps all the work that Herr Michl[1] has done? – – Running round, training singers? – – It would be the devil's own work; it would be impossible! In short, I don't see where these 10 charming friends would come from. Also, Herr Albert may not be able to speak to them straightaway, as some of them may be out of town. I'd prefer them to be businessmen and other honest people rather than courtiers, for a lot depends on whether they will keep their word and for how long. *If the matter is feasible, well and good! You should accept it.* But if the matter can't be brought to an immediate conclusion, you can't sit around, wasting time and money as you can't expect to earn a penny in Munich, in spite of all the compliments and the demonstrations of friendship. If this affair can't be set going now, Herr Albert and our other good friends can think about setting things in motion while you continue your journey and wait to hear from him. The rage for the Italians no longer goes very far and is virtually restricted to Munich. That's all it is – a fashion that's got out of hand! In *Mannheim*, on the other hand, everyone apart from a few castratos is already German. *In Trier*, at the court of His Royal Highness the Elector Prince Clemens of Saxony, there's only Maestro Sales,[2] the rest are German, in *Mainz* they're all German, in *Würzburg* there's only a violinist, Sgr Fracassini,[3] who I think is now leader or even Kapellmeister – but that's only because of his German wife, a singer and a native of Würzburg. There isn't a single Italian working for any of the minor Protestant princes. I'm writing this in haste, Herr Lotter wants to take it with

1. Joseph Christian Willibald Michl (1745–1816), court composer at Munich.
2. Clemens Wenzel, Prince of Saxony, archbishop-elector of Trier; Pietro Pompeo Sales (1729–97) was music director at Ehrenbreitstein, the palace of the archbishop-electors of Trier, near Koblenz.
3. Aloisio Lodovico Fracassini (1733–98).

him. I'm enclosing the chorales[4] – you may find them useful and even necessary; one has to know everything. – – I've just been to see the *chief steward*[5] who'll be coming here specially during the next few days so that I can tell him about everything – his own house is in a state of constant uproar, with people always being announced or his countess rushing in. He's genuinely fond of you, and before he heard what had happened, he'd already bought 4 horses and was looking forward to the pleasure he'd give you by coming with 4 riding horses. Once he knew what had happened, his annoyance was indescribable. When he was paying a courtesy call on the archbishop, the latter said to him: *At least we've now one less person in the orchestra.* He replied: *You Grace has lost a great virtuoso.* – *Why?* asked the prince. – – His reply: *He is the greatest keyboard player I've heard in my life. On the violin he has served Your Grace well, and he was also a very good composer.* The archbishop fell silent, as there was nothing he could say to this. I must sign off now as there's no more space. You should at least write and *let me know that you've received such and such a letter.* By now you should have received the packet and roll with the diplomas and Padre Martini's testimonial. There was a hanging this morning. This evening there's a play, tomorrow a masked ball that's being given by Prince Breuner.[6] We kiss you millions of times. I am your old

Mozart

Make sure you don't lose Padre Martini's testimonial.

[*Postscript added by Nannerl Mozart*]
Dearest Mama and Brother,

I'm delighted to hear that you're both well and in good spirits. I still haven't told you my daily routine since you left. So I'll start today.[7]

4. Unidentified.
5. Franz Lactanz, Count Firmian.
6. Prince Franz Xaver von Breuner (1723–97), cathedral dean at Salzburg.
7. Nannerl's diary entries, which she included here, have been omitted.

Keep well, and let us know if you've received our 4 letters and the parcel. I kiss Mama's hands and remind you not to forget me.

Maria Anna Mozart

Secretary Strasser has finally decided to marry the apothecary's daughter, Tresel Ruprecht, within a month.

No position was forthcoming in Munich so Mozart and his mother left for Augsburg on 11 October.

57. Mozart to his father, 16 October 1777, Augsburg

Mon très cher Père,

As for the daughter of the secretary of war, Herr Hamm,[1] I can say only that she must necessarily have a gift for music as she has been studying it for only 3 years but can play many pieces very well. But it's not easy for me to explain how she strikes me when she plays; – – – she seems strangely affected – – with her long bony fingers she clambers over the keyboard in such a strange way. Of course, she has never had a decent teacher, and if she stays in Munich she'll never become what her father wants and demands of her. He wants her to excel at the keyboard – – if she were to study with Papa in Salzburg, she would find it doubly useful, both from a musical point of view and in terms of her intelligence, for there's not much sign of the latter. I've already had a good laugh at her expense, you'd certainly be well rewarded for your pains. She can't eat much as she's too simple-minded for that. Should I have tested her? – – I couldn't do so for laughing. If I showed her what to do by playing something a

1. Joseph Konrad von Hamm von Sonnenfels (1728–95), secretary in the war department at Munich; his daughter was Maria Anna Joseph Aloysia (1765–?). It seems that Leopold was considering taking her as a boarding pupil, but this plan did not materialize, see letter 79.

number of times with my right hand, she would immediately say *bravissimo* in a mouse-like voice. I'll now finish off my account of my time in Augsburg as briefly as possible. Herr von Fingerlin, to whom I gave Papa's best wishes, was also at Director Graf's. The people there were all very polite and kept talking about a concert. They also said it would be one of the most brilliant we've had in Augsburg. You've a great advantage in that you're acquainted with our magistrate, Herr Langenmantel; and the name Mozart, too, carries great weight here. We parted in the best of spirits. Now, Papa must know that at Herr *Stein's* young Herr Langenmantel said he'd arrange for a concert to be held at the Stube[2] – as something exceptional that would do me great credit – just for the patricians. You can't imagine how emphatically he spoke and promised to pursue the matter. He agreed that I'd return the next day and hear his response. I went there – it was the 13th – he was very polite but said that for now he had nothing definite to tell me. I again played for about an hour. He invited me to have lunch with him the next day, the 14th. During the morning he sent word, asking me to come at 11 and bring something with me, he'd invited some members of the orchestra and they wanted something to play. I sent him something at once. Arrived at 11. He then offered a whole string of excuses, saying quite calmly: Listen, the concert's off. Oh, I got very angry yesterday because of you. The patricians told me that their coffers are nearly empty and that you're not the sort of virtuoso to whom one could give a souverain d'or. I smiled and said I didn't think so either. *NB: He's intendant of the orchestra at the Stube and his old man is the magistrate.* I didn't make any fuss about it. We sat down at table. His old man was also having lunch up there; he was very polite but didn't say anything about the concert. After lunch I played 2 concertos.[3] Something from memory.

2. The Stube or Bauernstube was an inn across from the Augsburg city hall. In the preceding passage Mozart mentions a number of Leopold's Augsburg contacts, including the instrument builder Johann Stein (see letter 52); Friedrich Hartmann Graf (1727–95) was music director in Augsburg and the brother of the composer Christian Ernst Graf (1723–1804), whom the Mozarts had met in The Hague.
3. Mozart had by this date composed four solo keyboard concertos: K175, 238, 246 and 271.

Then a trio by Hafeneder[4] on the violin. I'd like to have played more on the violin but was so badly accompanied that it gave me the colic. He was very friendly and said we should spend the rest of the day together and go to the theatre and then have supper together. We enjoyed ourselves enormously. When we returned from the theatre, I again played until it was time to eat. We then went in to supper. He'd already asked me about my cross that morning. I explained to him quite clearly what it was and how I'd got it. He and his brother-in-law said more than once: we should get our own crosses so we can become members of Herr Mozart's Corporation. But I paid them no attention. And more than once they called me sir and addressed me as knight of the spur. I said nothing. But during supper it really became too much. How much does it cost? 3 ducats? – – Do you have to have permission to wear it? – – Does this permission cost something too? We really must get our own crosses; a certain officer was there, Baron Bach, who said: Fie, you should be ashamed of yourselves, what would you do with the cross? That young ass Kurzenmantl[5] winked at him. I saw him. He noticed. Everyone went very quiet; he then gave me some snuff and said: Here, take a pinch. I said nothing. Finally he started making fun of me again: I'll send someone round tomorrow and perhaps you'll be good enough to lend me your cross for a moment, I'll send it straight back, it's just so that I can speak to the goldsmith. I'm sure that if I ask him what it's worth – he's quite an odd character – he'll say about a Bavarian thaler. It's certainly not worth any more, as it's not gold but copper, ha ha! No, no, I said, it's tin, ha ha! I was burning with anger and rage. But tell me, he said, I suppose I can leave out the spur? – – Oh yes, I said; you don't need it, you've already got one in your head.[6] I've got one of my own, but it's different from yours. I certainly wouldn't like to swap it with yours. Here, take a pinch of snuff. I gave him some snuff. He turned rather pale. But then he began again: it looked good recently on your expensive waistcoat. I said nothing.

4. Joseph Hafeneder (1746–84) was a court violinist in Salzburg; his trio is lost.
5. A pun on the name Langenmantel (literally 'longcoat'); *kurz* means 'short'.
6. Here, too, Mozart plays with words. *Sporn* ('spur') is also dialect for *Sparren* ('spar' or 'pole'); *einen Sparren zu viel haben* is 'to have a screw loose'.

Finally he called out *to his servant*, Hey, you'll have to show us more respect when the two of us – me and my brother-in-law – wear Herr Mozart's cross. Here, take a pinch of snuff on that; that's odd, I began, as though I'd not heard what he'd said, but I can sooner get all the orders that you can get than you can become what I am, even if you were to die twice and be reborn. Here, take a pinch of snuff on that, and I stood up. They all stood up and were deeply embarrassed. I took my hat and sword and said I'd have the pleasure of seeing them the next day. Oh, I'm not here tomorrow. Then I'll come the day after tomorrow, if I'm still here. Oh, surely you won't – – I won't. It's like an almshouse here. In the meantime, goodbye. *And with that I was gone.* The next day, the 15th, I told Herr Stein, Herr *Gignoux*[7] and Director Graf all that had happened – not about the cross but that I was utterly disgusted at being taken in by their promises about a concert and how it had all come to nothing. This is what's called making a fool of people and taking them in. I sincerely regret having come here. Never in my whole life would I have believed that in Papa's native town of Augsburg his son would be so insulted. Papa can't imagine how sorry and angry the 3 of them were. Oh, you must give a concert here. We don't need the patricians. But my mind was made up; and I said yes, I'll give a small farewell concert at Herr *Stein's* for my few good friends here, who are connoisseurs. The director was utterly dismayed. It's appalling, he exclaimed; it's a disgrace – – who'd have imagined it of Langenmantel – – *Pardieu*, if he'd wanted to, it could have been arranged. We parted. Wearing his dressing gown, the director accompanied me downstairs and as far as the front door. Herr *Stein* and Herr Gignoux – who sends Papa his best wishes – walked home with me. They urged us to stay here a little while longer; but our minds were made up. Now Papa must know that after mumbling his news about the concert as if it were a matter of total indifference, young Herr Langenmantel told me that the patricians are inviting me to their concert next Thursday. I said I'd go along and listen. Oh, won't you give us the pleasure of hearing

---

7. Anton Christoph Gignoux (1720–95), director of the local music society, was a long-standing acquaintance of Leopold Mozart.

you play? — — *Well, who knows? Why not?* But I was so insulted the following evening that I decided not to return there but to let the whole of the town's patricians lick my arse, and then leave. On Thursday, the 16th, while we were eating, I was called out; it was one of Langenmantel's girls wanting to know if I was definitely going with him to the concert. — — And would I call on him immediately after lunch? I sent him my most humble regards, adding that I was not going to the concert and couldn't call on him as I was already spoken for — *as was indeed true.* But I'd go there the next day and say goodbye to him as I was leaving on Saturday at the latest. Meanwhile, Herr *Stein* had run off to the other patricians in the Evangelical camp and harangued them so pitilessly that they were quite terrified. What, they said, are we to allow a man who does us so much honour to leave without hearing him? Herr von Langenmantel must think that it's enough that he's heard him himself. *Enfin,* they got so worked up that our good young Herr von Kurzenmantel had to go and see Herr *Stein* in person and beg him on everyone's behalf to do his utmost to persuade me to go to the concert. I wasn't to expect anything much *et caetera.* And so, after a great deal of hesitation, I went off with him. The leading members of the nobility were perfectly polite, especially a local official, Baron Rehlingen, who's also a director or some such beast. He even unpacked my music. I'd also taken a symphony[8] with me. They played it, I sat with the violins. But the orchestra here is enough to drive you mad. That young fop Langenmantel was perfectly polite, but he still had a contemptuous look. He said to me: I really thought you'd give us the slip. I even thought you might have been annoyed at our recent joke. Oh, not at all, I said, you're still young. But you should be more careful in future. I'm not used to jokes of that kind. And the subject that you were laughing at does you no credit whatsoever, quite apart from the fact that it was pointless as I'm still wearing it. You should have joked about something else. I assure you, he said, it was only my brother-in-law who — — Forget it, I said. We almost didn't have the pleasure of seeing you. Yes, if it hadn't been for Herr *Stein*, I'd

8. Unidentified.

certainly not have come; and to tell you the truth, I've come only so that you, the good people of Augsburg, wouldn't be laughed at in other countries if I were to say that I'd been in my father's home town for a week without anyone taking the trouble to hear me. I played a concerto.⁹ Apart from the accompaniment, it all went well. To end with, I played another sonata. Then Baron Rehlingen thanked me most politely in the name of the whole company and asked me to note only their good will, and with that he gave me 2 ducats. But I'm still not being left in peace, I'm supposed to give a public concert between now and Sunday – – perhaps – – but I'm already so sickened of the whole affair I can't even begin to tell you. I'll be glad to move on to a place where there's a court! I can say quite truthfully that if it weren't for my dear uncle and aunt and my lovely cousin, I'd have as many regrets at coming to Augsburg as I have hairs on my head. I must now say something about my dear mistress cousin,¹⁰ but I'll save this up till tomorrow as one has to be in a very good mood to praise her as much as she deserves.

I'm writing this on the morning of the 17th and assure you that our little cousin is beautiful, intelligent, delightful, clever and good fun; and it's all because she gets around a lot. She also spent some time in Munich. It's true, the two of us are well matched as she too is a bit naughty. We both have a good laugh at people, which is great fun. Please don't forget the address of the bishop of Chiemsee. I think I'll send the letter for Gaetano Santoro to Mysliveček today, as we agreed. He's already given me his address. Please write to poor Mysliveček soon as I know that he'll be very pleased to hear from you. In my next letter I'll tell you about Stein's pianofortes and organs and principally about the *Stube* concert. The nobility was out in force, Duchess Arsespank, Countess Pisslike and Princess Shitsniff with her 2 daughters, who are already married to the 2 Princes Potbelly of Pigtail. Farewell, all of you. I kiss Papa's hands 100,000 times and embrace my scoundrel of a sister with bearlike tenderness and am your most obedient son

Wolfgang Amadé Mozart

9. K175, 238, 246 or 271.
10. Maria Anna Thekla (Bäsle).

[Postscript added by his cousin]

Dearest Uncle,

I can't begin to tell you how pleased I was at the safe arrival of my aunt and such a delightful cousin, and my only regret is that we'll soon be losing such noble friends, who've shown us such kindness, we're only sorry not to have had the good fortune to see you here with my aunt; my parents send their most humble good wishes to my uncle and cousin and hope that you're well, something we shall always hope, please give my best wishes to my cousin and ask her always to remain friends with me, just as I flatter myself that she may always be well disposed towards me, I have the honour of sending you my best wishes and of remaining, most respectfully,

Your devoted servant
and cousin M A Mozart

Father can't remember if he told you that on 31 May 1777 he gave Herr Lotter 4 copies of your violin tutor and another 2 on 13 Aug. 1777.

[Mozart's postscript on the envelope]

Monsieur Novac arrived here today and sends you all his best wishes. Especially to Mlle Katherl. Next time I'll write a more cheerful letter. Next Wednesday I'm giving a concert in Count Fugger's hall. My dear cousin sends you her best wishes. All 3 of us are now going to Herr *Stein's* for lunch. The only thing that worries me is the accompaniment at my concert as the orchestra here is truly awful. I must close as it's already 11 o'clock. I kiss Papa's hands 100,000 times, and I embrace my sister, like it or not, I am, I wot, not cold or hot,

your most obedient son W. A. Mozart

Best wishes *a tutti tutti tutti*

58. Mozart to his father, 17 October 1777, Augsburg

Mon très cher Père,

I must start with Stein's pianofortes. Before I saw any of Stein's work, I'd always preferred Späth's[1] pianos; but now I prefer Stein's, as they damp so much better than the Regensburg instruments. If I strike hard, it doesn't matter whether I keep my finger down or raise it, the sound ceases the moment I produce it. However I attack the keys, the tone is always even. It doesn't produce a clattering sound, it doesn't get louder or softer or fail to sound at all; in a word, it's always even. It's true, he won't part with a pianoforte like this for under 300 florins, but the effort and labour that he expends on it can't be paid for. A particular feature of his instruments is their escape action. Not one maker in a hundred bothers with this. But without escape action it's impossible for a pianoforte not to produce a clattering sound or to go on sounding after the note has been struck; when you strike the keys, his hammers fall back again the moment they hit the strings, whether you hold down the keys or release them. He told me that only when he's finished making a piano like this does he sit down and try out all the passagework, runs and leaps, and, using a shave, works away at the instrument until it can do everything. For he works only to serve the music, not just for his own profit, otherwise he'd be finished at once.

He often says that if he weren't such a great music lover and didn't have some slight skill on the instrument, he'd long since have run out of patience with his work; but he loves an instrument that never lets the player down and that will last. His pianos will really last. He guarantees that the sounding board won't break or crack. Once he's finished making a sounding board for a piano he puts it outside, exposing it to the air, rain, snow, heat of the sun and all the devils in order for it to crack, and then he inserts wedges, which he glues in, so that it's very strong and firm. He's perfectly happy for it to crack as he's then assured that nothing more can happen to it. Indeed, he

1. Franz Jakob Späth (1714–86), instrument builder in Regensburg.

often cuts into it himself and then glues it back together again and makes it really strong. He has completed three such pianofortes. Not until today did I play on one of them again. Today – the 17th – we had lunch with young Herr Gasser, a young and handsome widower who's lost his young and beautiful wife. They'd been married for only 2 years. He's a most excellent and polite young man. We were splendidly entertained. Also there was a colleague of Abbé Henri, Bullinger and Wieshofer, an ex-Jesuit who's now Kapellmeister at the cathedral here. He knows Herr *Schachtner*[2] very well, he was his choirmaster in Ingolstadt. He's called Pater Gerbl.[3] I'm to give his best wishes to Herr Schachtner. After lunch Herr Gasser and I went to Herr *Stein's*, where we were accompanied by one of his sisters-in-law as well as Mama and our cousin. At 4 o'clock we were joined by the Kapellmeister and Herr Schmidbaur, the organist at St Ulrich's, a fine old gentleman who's very well-spoken; and I then sight-read a sonata by Beecke[4] that was quite hard and *miserable al solito*;[5] I can't begin to tell you how the Kapellmeister and organist crossed themselves. Both here and in Munich I've played my 6 sonatas many times from memory. I played the fifth one in G at the aristocrats' concert in the Bauernstube.[6] The last one, in D, sounds amazing on *Stein's* pianoforte. The device that you depress with your knee is also better made on his instrument than on others. I scarcely need to touch it and it works; and as soon as you remove your knee even a little, you no longer hear the slightest reverberation. Tomorrow I may get round to his organs – – I mean, *to write about them*; I'm saving up his little daughter till the end. When I told Herr *Stein* that I'd like to play on his organ as the organ was my passion, he was very surprised and said: What, a man like you, so great a keyboard player wants to play on an instrument that has no douceur, no expression, no piano

2. Johann Andreas Schachtner (1731–95), Salzburg court trumpeter, poet and close friend of the Mozart family.
3. Father Philipp Gerbl (1719–1803), Kapellmeister at Augsburg cathedral.
4. Ignaz Franz von Beecke (1733–1803), pianist and composer, music director to Prince Kraft Ernst of Oettingen-Wallerstein.
5. 'as wretched as usual'.
6. See previous letter; sonatas K279–284.

or forte but always sounds the same? – – None of that matters. In my eyes and ears the organ is the king of instruments. Well, as you like. We went off together. I could already tell from what he said that he didn't think I'd do much on his organ and that – for example – I'd play in a way more suited to a piano. He told me that Schubart[7] had asked to be shown his organ, and I was afraid – he said – as Schubart had told everyone, and the church was quite full; for I thought he'd be all spirit, fire and speed, none of which works on the organ; but as soon as he started I changed my mind. I said only this: What do you think, Herr Stein? Do you think I'll run all over the organ? – – Oh, you, that's quite different. We reached the choir. I began to improvise, by which point he was already laughing, and then a fugue. I can well believe – he said – that you enjoy playing the organ if you play like that – – at first the pedal was a little strange as it wasn't divided. It began with C, then D, E in the same row. But with us D and E are above, as E flat and F sharp are here. But I soon got used to it. I also played on the old organ at St Ulrich's. The steps up to it are a nightmare. I asked if someone could play on it for me as I wanted to go down and listen. From up there the organ is totally ineffectual. But I could make nothing of it, as the young choirmaster, a priest, played only scales, so it was impossible to form any impression. And when he tried to play some chords, he produced only discords as it was out of tune. After that we had to go to a coffee-room as my mother and cousin and Herr Stein were with us. A certain Pater Aemilian,[8] an arrogant ass and a simpleton of his profession, was in an especially hearty mood. He kept wanting to joke with my cousin, but she just made fun of him – – finally, when he was drunk (which didn't take long), he started to talk about music. He sang a

7. Christian Friedrich Daniel Schubart (1739–91), writer and editor of the influential *Deutsche Chronik*; in the 27 April 1775 issue Schubart had written, '. . . I also heard an *opera buffa* by that wonderful genius *Mozart*. It is called *La finta giardiniera*. Flashes of genius appear here and there; but there is not yet that still altar-fire that rises towards Heaven in clouds of incense – a scent beloved of the gods. If *Mozart* is not a plant forced in the hot-house, he is bound to grow into one of the greatest musical composers who ever lived.'
8. Father Aemilian Angermayr (1735–1803), professor of theology.

canon and I said I'd never in my whole life heard a finer one. I said I'm sorry, I can't join in as I've no natural gift for intoning. That doesn't matter, he said. He started. I was the third voice, but I made up some very different words, for example, O you prick, lick my arse. *Sotto voce* to my cousin. We laughed about it for half an hour. He said to me: if only we could have spent longer together. I'd like to discuss the art of composition with you. Then the discussion would soon be over, I said. *Get lost.* To be continued.

W. A. Mozart

59. *Leopold Mozart to his son, 23 October 1777, Salzburg*

Mon très cher Fils,

I must congratulate you on your name day![1] But what can I wish you today that I don't always wish you? — — I wish you the grace of God, that it may accompany you everywhere and never abandon you, as indeed it will never do if you strive to fulfil the obligations of a true Catholic Christian.

You know me. — I'm no pedant, I'm not holier than thou, and I'm certainly no hypocrite: but you surely won't refuse a request from your father? — It is this: that you should be concerned for your soul's welfare and not cause your father any anxiety in his hour of death, so that at that difficult time he won't have to reproach himself for neglecting your soul's salvation. Farewell! Be happy! Lead a sensible life! Honour and esteem your mother, who has much toil in her old age, love me as I love you. Your truly solicitous father

Leop. Mozart

1. 31 October.

Mozart and his mother left Augsburg on 26 October, arriving at Mannheim – electoral seat of the Palatinate since 1720 and widely considered one of the most brilliant courts in Europe – on 30 October.

60. Mozart to his father, 4 November 1777, Mannheim

Monsieur mon très cher Père,

We wrote to you the day before we left Augsburg, but you mustn't have received it yet. I hope it hasn't got lost as I wrote a lot. It contains a description of the whole concert;[1] there's also something in it about *Stein's* daughter, as well as my thanks for your congratulations on my name day. But I hope you'll have received it by now. This is my second letter from Mannheim. I've been to see Cannabich[2] every day so far. Today Mama came with me. He's completely changed, the whole orchestra says so too. He's very taken with me. He has a daughter who plays the keyboard very well, and in order to make a true friend of him, I'm now working on a sonata for his daughter,[3] it's finished except for the rondeau. As soon as I'd completed the opening allegro and the andante, I took them round to their house in person and played them; Papa can't imagine how much they applauded the sonata. Some members of the orchestra were there, young Danner,[4] a *horn player* by the name of Lang, and the oboist, whose name I've forgotten but who plays extremely well, with an attractive and refined tone.[5] I made him a present of my oboe concerto. It's being copied out

1. At his Augsburg concert of 22 October 1777, Mozart played an unidentified symphony, the concerto for three pianos K242, the solo sonata K284, the solo concerto K238, and an improvisation consisting of a fugue and sonata.
2. Christian Cannabich (1731–98), composer, violinist and Kapellmeister at Mannheim and Schwetzingen (the elector's summer residence). When the Palatinate and Bavarian courts merged in 1778 he moved to Munich.
3. Rosina Theresia Petronella (1764–?1808), known as Rosa. The sonata is K309.
4. Christian Franz Danner (1757–1813), violinist in the Mannheim court orchestra.
5. The oboist was Friedrich Ramm (1744–c. 1811); a child prodigy, he had joined the Mannheim court music as a fourteen-year-old. Mozart presented him with K314, composed in Salzburg in 1777.

in a room at Cannabich's. The fellow is beside himself with delight; I played him the concerto on the pianoforte at Cannabich's today; and although everyone knew *it was by me*, they still liked it a lot. No one said that it wasn't *well written* on the grounds that the people here don't understand these things – – they should only ask the archbishop, who'll waste no time in putting them right.

I played all six of my sonatas[6] at Cannabich's today. Herr Kapell-meister Holzbauer himself took me to see the intendant, Count Savioli,[7] today. Cannabich was there too. Herr Holzbauer spoke to the count in Italian, saying that I'd like to have the privilege of being heard by His Excellency the Elector.[8] I was here 15 years ago.[9] I was then 7, but now I'm older and bigger and also more knowledgeable about music. Ah, said the count, that is – – heaven knows who he thought I was, but Cannabich interrupted him, I pretended not to have heard and started talking to some other people. But I noticed that as he was speaking to him he looked very serious. The count then said to me, I hear you play the keyboard very passably. I bowed. I must now tell you about the music here. On Saturday – All Saints' Day – I was at High Mass in the chapel. The orchestra is both large and very good. On each side there are 10 or 11 violins, 4 violas, 2 oboes, 2 flutes and 2 clarinets, 2 horns, 4 cellos, 4 bassoons, 4 double basses and trumpets and timpani. They can perform wonderful music, but I wouldn't care to have one of my masses played here. Why? – – Because of its brevity? – No, everything has to be brief here as well[10] – – because of the church style? – No, not that either. But because, as things stand *at present*, you have to write in the main for the instruments, because you can't imagine anything worse than the voices here. 6 sopranos, 6 altos, 6 tenors and 6 basses against 20 violins and 12 basses is in the exact ratio of 0 to 1. Isn't that true, Herr Bullinger? – – This is because the Italians are now held in

6. K279–284.
7. Ignaz Jakob Holzbauer (1711–83), composer and court music director at Mannheim; Louis Aurel, Count Savioli (?–1788), court music intendant.
8. Karl Theodor (1724–99), Elector Palatine and from 1778 Elector of Bavaria.
9. In July 1763, see letter 5.
10. Mozart refers to Colloredo's reforms of the Mass, see letter 48.

wretchedly low regard here. They've only 2 castratos, and even these are already old. They're simply being left to die out. The soprano would rather sing the alto part. He can no longer get his top notes. The few boys that they have here are pitiful. The tenors and basses are like our funeral singers. The assistant Kapellmeister *Vogler*,[11] who wrote the recent mass, is a musical joker with a very high opinion of himself but few abilities. The whole orchestra dislikes him. But today – Sunday – I heard a mass by Holzbauer that's already 26 years old but which is actually very good. He writes very well. A good church style. Writes well for voices and instruments; and good fugues. They've 2 organists here who alone would be worth making a special visit to Mannheim. I had a chance to hear them properly as it's not usual to include a *Benedictus* here, instead the organist has to keep playing. On the first occasion I heard the second organist and the second time it was the first one. But in my own view I think even more highly of the 2nd than the first. When I heard him, I asked who was playing the organ? – Our 2nd organist. He played wretchedly. When I heard the other one, I again asked who it was. – – Our first one. He played even more wretchedly. I think that if you put them together, something even worse would emerge. Watching these gentlemen is enough to make you die laughing. When he's at the organ, the second one is like a child having a shit; you can see from his face what he's up to. But the first one at least wears glasses. I went and stood by the organ and watched him with the aim of learning something from him; at every note he raises his hands as high as he can. But his great strength is to play in 6 parts – except that mostly he just adds fifths and octaves. He often omits the right hand as a joke and plays with only his left hand, in a word he can do as he likes, he has complete mastery over his organ.

Mama has asked me to tell Nannerl that the lining for the coat is in the large box, on the right-hand side and at the very bottom; there'll be all sorts of patches on top of it. Black, white, yellow, brown, red, green, blue etc. Mama sends her best wishes to you all.

11. Georg Joseph Vogler (1749–1814), composer and writer on music, second Kapellmeister at Mannheim.

She can't write as she still has to say her office. We got back home so late from the rehearsal for the main opera.[12] The cotton thread isn't in skeins but in a ball, wrapped in a blue cloth. Yes, that's exactly how it is. Tomorrow, after High Mass, I have to see the stern electress[13] who absolutely insists on teaching me to knit; I'm really worried about it. Both she and His Excellency the Elector want me to knit in public at the great gala scumcert next Thursday evening. The young princess, who's been passed off as the elector's daughter,[14] also knits very nicely; Duke Zweibrücken and his missus arrived here at 8 o'clock on the dot. By the way, Mama and I ask Papa very nicely to be so kind as to send a souvenir to our dear cousin. We both regretted that we'd nothing with us, but we promised to write to Papa and ask him to send her something. Or, rather, two things. From Mama, something like a double headscarf similar to Mama's and from me a trinket. A box or toothpick case etc or whatever you like, as long as it's beautiful; for she deserves it. She and her father went to a lot of trouble and spent a lot of time with us. My uncle collected the money at the concert. *Addio. Baccio le mani di vostra Paternità, ed abbraccio con leggiertà la mia sorella, e facendo i miei Complimenti da per tutto sono di tutto Cuore*[15]

Wolfgango Amadeo Mozart

[Maria Anna Mozart's postscript on the envelope]
A certain Signor Gervasio and his wife, who knows you from Holland, congratulate you on your virtuoso of a son, he plays the mandolin and she sings, they gave a concert today. Best wishes to the whole of Salzburg, especially our true friends, Herr Bullinger and Mistress Sallerl.

---

12. Ignaz Holzbauer's *Günther von Schwarzburg*, composed to celebrate the elector's name day on 4 November and first performed on 5 November 1777.
13. Elisabeth Maria Aloysia Auguste (1721–94), wife of Elector Karl Theodor; Mozart dedicated the accompanied sonatas K301–306 to her.
14. Carolina Josepha Philippine, Countess Bretzenheim (1768–86) was the eldest daughter of the elector with his mistress, the choreographer Josepha Seyffert.
15. 'I kiss my father's hands and embrace my sister tenderly and, in sending my best wishes to all and sundry, I remain with all my heart'.

[*Mozart's postscript on the envelope*]

Katherl Gilowsky, Frau von Gerlichs, Herr von Heffner, Frau von Heffner, Frau von Schiedenhofen, Herr Gschwendtner, Herr Sandner and all who are dead. The targets,[16] if it's not too late, I should like to be as follows: a small man with fair hair, bending over and showing his bare arse. From his mouth come the words: *Enjoy the spread*. The other should be shown in boots and spurs, a red suit and a fine wig according to the latest fashion; he must be of medium height and positioned in such a way that he appears to be licking the other man's arse. From his mouth come the words: *Ah, there's nothing to beat it*. Just like this, please.

If not this time, then another time.

61. Mozart to Maria Anna Thekla Mozart, 5 November 1777, Mannheim

My dearest little cousin dozen,

I've duly received retrieved your kind letter and see free from it that my uncle furuncle, aunt can't and you stew are very well tell; we too, thank God, are in good health stealth. Today I got spot the letter better from my Papa haha. I hope you'll have received aggrieved the letter wetter I sent you from Mannheim. All the better, better the all. But now for something sensible.

I'm very sorry to hear that the prelate pellet[1] has had another stroke broke, but I hope that with God's sod's help the consequences won't be serious deleterious. You tell me knee that you'll perpetrate the promise that you gave me before I left Augsburg[2] and do so soon moon; well, I certainly look backwards to that. You also write, nay, disclose, reveal, announce, let me know, declare, make it abundantly plain, demand, desire, wish, want, indicate, order, hint, inform me,

16. For the next shooting competition.
1. Bartholomäus Christa (1714–78), abbot of Holy Cross, Augsburg.
2. She had promised to send Mozart her portrait.

tell me that I should also send my portrait to you screw. *Eh bien*, I'll certainly send spend it to you. *Oui, par ma la fois*, I'll shit on your nose so it runs down your chin. By the way, have you got the spuni cuni fait too? – – – What? – – Do you still love me – – I think you do. All the better, better the all. Well, that's the way of the world, or so I'm told; Tom has the purse, and Dick has the gold; which do you prefer? – – It's me, isn't it? – – I think it is. But now it gets worse. By the way, don't you want to go and see Herr *Gold*schmid again soon? – But what'll you do there? – – What? – – Nothing! – – Just ask him about the spuni cuni fait, nothing else. Nothing else? – – – Very well; all right. Long live all those who – who – – who – – – how does it go on? – – Now I wish you good night, may your bed burst with shite; sleep sound as a log with your arse in your gob; now I'm off to fool about, then I'll sleep a bit, no doubt. Tomorrow we'll talk more sensibly defensibly; I've things of lots to tell you, you simply believe it can't, but tomorrow you hear it will. Till then, goodbye, ow, my *arse* is burning like fire! What can it mean? – – Perhaps some *shit* wants to get out? – Yes, yes, *shit, I* know you, see you, taste you – – and – – what's that? – – Is it possible? – – Ye gods! – – Can I believe my *ears*? – – Yes, indeed, it's – – what a long, sad sound! – – Today written I've letter fifth the is this. Yesterday I spoke with the strict electress and tomorrow, the 6th, I'm playing at the great gala concert, and then I'll play again for her in private, or so the tresselec tells me. Now for something sensible!

(1) a letter or letters addressed to me will fall into your hands and I must ask you – – what? – – Well, a fox is no hare – – yes, where was I? – – Yes, indeed, I was just coming; – – yes, yes, they'll come – – yes, who? – who'll come – – yes, now I have it. Letters, letters will arrive – – but what sort of letters? – – well, letters to me, of course; please be sure to forward them, I'll let you know where I'll be going after Mannheim. Now for no. 2! I must ask you – why not? I must ask you, my dearest loon – why not? – – If you write to Mme Tavernier in Munich, please remember me to the two Mlles Freysinger,[3] why not?

3. Juliana and Josepha Freysinger, daughters of court councillor Franziskus Erasmus Freysinger, who had been at school with Leopold Mozart in Augsburg during the 1730s.

– – Strange, why not? – – And please ask the younger of them, Fräulein Josepha, to forgive me, why not? – Why shouldn't I ask her to forgive me? – – Strange! – I don't know why I shouldn't. – – I ask her to forgive me for not yet having sent her the sonata[4] I promised, but I'll forward it as soon as possible. Why not? – – What – – Why not? – – Why shouldn't I send it? – Why shouldn't I forward it? – – Why not? – – Strange, I don't know why I shouldn't. – – Well, will you do this favour for me? – – Why not? – – Why shouldn't you? – – Why not, strange! I'd do it for you if you wanted, why not? – – Why shouldn't I do it for you? – – Strange! Why not? – – I don't know why not. – – Don't forget to give my best wishes to the Papa and Mama of the 2 young ladies, as it's a gross failing to forget bet let wet your father and mother. Once the sonata's finished, I'll send it to you with an accompanying letter and hope you'll be good enough to forward it to Munich. But now I must stop, I'm so mad I could hop. Dear cousin, let's go at once to the Holy Cross and see if anyone's still up. – – We'll not stay long, just ring the bell, nothing more. But now I must tell you a sad little story that has just this minute happened. Just as I was doing my best to write this letter, I heard something in the street outside. I stopped writing – – got up, went over to the window – – and – couldn't hear anything any more – – I sat down again, resumed writing – – I'd hardly written 10 words when I heard another sound – – I got up again – – as I was getting up, I could again hear something, this time quite faint – – but I could smell something burning – – wherever I went, it stank. When I looked out of the window the smell disappeared, but when I looked back into the room, the smell got worse – – finally Mama said to me: I bet you've let one off. – – I don't think so, Mama. Yes, I'm certain. I made a test, put my first finger up my arse and then to my nose, and – – *Ecce Provatum est*; Mama was right. Goodbye now, I kiss you 10,000 times and remain as always your little old Piggy

Wolfgang Amadè Rosary

4. Unidentified.

A thousand good wishes from us two travellers to my uncle and aunt.

> To all my good friends blends
> my best wishes fishes! addio loony moony.
> 333 unto the grave as long as I live.[5]

Miehnnam eht ht5 rebotco 7771.[6]

62. *Mozart's mother to her husband, 8 November 1777, Mannheim*

My Dearest,

We've received your latest letter of the 29th, together with all the others, but we can't possibly answer all your questions as precisely as we should like to because we have to seize what opportunities we can and generally write at night, when we don't get to bed till one o'clock and then get up late the next day, just in time for lunch, after which we go to see Director Cannabich and from there come home for supper at 9. The galas[1] are now over, on the first day there was a service at 11 o'clock and during it there were cannons and rockets, after the service Wolfgang had to go and see the electress, to whom he was introduced by the intendant, Count Savioli, she remembered him from his last visit 14 years ago, even though she no longer recognized him. Afterwards there was a great banquet, followed by a great reception in the evening. On the second day the German grand opera *Günther von Schwarzburg* was given, it's very beautiful, with incomparable music and a wonderful ballet.[2] On the 3rd day[3] there

---

5. Robert Spaethling notes in *Mozart's Letters, Mozart's Life* (London, 2000) that '333' (German *drei drei drei*) could be a phonetic transcription of the Salzburg dialect *treu treu treu*, which also has the meaning 'true, true, true' – that is, 'thrice faithful unto death'.

6. Mozart writes the date in reverse but has it wrong; it should be 5th November 1777.

1. For the elector's name day celebrations.

2. The music for the ballet was by Cannabich and the choreography by Étienne Lauchéry, director of the court balls.

3. 6 November.

was a big concert at which Wolfgang played a concerto, then, before the final symphony, he improvised something and played a sonata.[4] The elector and electress and all who heard him were extremely appreciative. On the 4th day – Friday – there was a gala performance of a play that we saw with Monsieur and Madame Cannabich. We both lunched with Herr Cannabich on the day of the concert, and today my son has had lunch with him on his own, as he's going to see the elector's children[5] immediately after the meal, he was also there yesterday and the elector was present throughout, there are 4, of whom 2 play the keyboard, the elector loves his children above all else and told the intendant to take Wolfgang to see them. Wolfgang will be playing for the electress again, just on his own, as she's promised him that he will, but for the present we must await her instructions. In the meantime, my dear husband, I wish you many 1000 happinesses on your forthcoming name day,[6] all good things for your body and soul, including lasting health, but above all I wish I could be with you to congratulate you in person, but since this is not possible, we'll drink your health with a good Rhine wine – with all our hearts we wish you had one like it – and we'll always think of you in the fondest hope of seeing you again, if that is God's will, and of remaining together. Best wishes to Nannerl, and ask her whether her cousin has already sent her the silks as she promised to do so at once. Baron Schaffmann and Herr Döll were here yesterday morning and called on us, they left for Wetzlar today.

[Mozart's postscript]

This morning at Herr Cannabich's I wrote out the rondeau of the sonata[7] for his daughter and as a result they wouldn't let me go. The elector, together with his wife and the whole court, is very pleased with me. On both the occasions that I played at the concert, the elector and his wife came right up to the instrument. After the concert

4. None of the works performed by Mozart can be identified with certainty. It is likely, though, that the concerto was K175, 238, 246 or 271.
5. They were all his natural (illegitimate) children.
6. 15 November.
7. K309, written for Rosa Cannabich.

Cannabich arranged for me to speak to the court. I kissed the elector's hand. He said I think it's 15 years since you were last here. Yes, Your Highness, 15 years since I had the honour – – You play incomparably well. When I kissed the princess's hand, she said to me: *Monsieur, je vous assure, on ne peut pas jouer mieux.*[8]

Yesterday I went with Cannabich to the place that Mama's already told you about. I spoke to the elector as though to a good friend. He's a most kind and good-natured person. He said to me: I hear that you wrote an opera in Munich.[9] Yes, Your Highness. I commend myself to Your Highness's good graces, my greatest wish would be to write an opera here; please don't forget me altogether. Praise and thanks be to God, I also know German, *and I smiled*. That's easily done. He has a son[10] and three daughters, the eldest and the young count play the keyboard. The elector asked me in all confidence to tell him about his children. I told him what I thought, but without criticizing their teacher. Cannabich agreed with me. As he was leaving, the elector thanked me most politely. At 2 o'clock today, immediately after lunch, I went with Cannabich to see the flautist, Wendling. They were all politeness itself. His daughter,[11] who was once the elector's mistress, plays the keyboard very well. I then played myself. I was in such a good mood today, I can't describe it. I played nothing but improvisations; and three duets with violin that I'd never seen in my life and whose author I'd never heard of. They were all so pleased that I – – simply had to kiss the women. In the daughter's case this wasn't so hard as she's not bad-looking. After that we returned to the elector's natural children. There I again poured my whole heart into my playing. I played 3 times. Each time the elector himself asked me to do so. He sat down beside me each time and didn't move. I also asked a certain professor to give me a subject for a fugue, which I then developed. Now for my congratulations:

8. 'Monsieur, I assure you, it's impossible to play any better.'
9. *La finta giardiniera.*
10. Carl August Friedrich Joseph, Count (later Prince) Bretzenheim (1769–1823).
11. Johann Baptist Wendling (1723–97) and his daughter, the singer Elisabeth Augusta Wendling (1752–94).

Dearest Papa,

I can't write poetry, as I'm no poet. I can't arrange figures of speech with the artistry needed to produce light and shade; I'm no painter. I can't even express my thoughts and ideas by mime and gesture as I'm no dancer. But I can do so through sounds; I'm a musician. Tomorrow at Cannabich's I'll play a whole piece at the keyboard congratulating you on your name day and your birthday. For today I can do no more than wish you, *Mon très cher Père*, from the bottom of my heart all that I wish you every day, morning and night: health, a long life and a cheerful disposition. I also hope that you now have less reason to be annoyed than you did when I was still in Salzburg; for I must admit that I was the sole cause of it. They treated me badly; I didn't deserve it. You naturally took my part – – but too much. So, you see, that was the biggest and most important reason why I left Salzburg in such a hurry. I hope too that my wishes come true. I must end now with a musical congratulation. I hope that you live for as many years as it needs for nothing new to be produced any more in music. Now farewell; I beg you most humbly to go on loving me just a little and to make do with these poor congratulations until I get some new drawers made for my small and narrow brainbox in which I can keep the brains that I still intend to acquire. I kiss my father's hands 1000 times and remain until death

Mon très cher Père
your most obedient son
Wolfgang Amadé Mozart

63. Leopold Mozart to his son, 20 November 1777, Salzburg

Mon très cher Fils,

As much as your letter of the 8th gave us a certain hope and delighted us all, especially Herr Bullinger, so much were we dismayed to read your letter of the 13th, which to our great surprise we received on the evening of the 18th, i.e., on the 5th day, as all the others took 6 days at the very least. It would have been much better, of course, if you'd received 15 louis d'or instead of a watch,[1] even if it has been valued at 20 louis d'or, as money is more useful, not to say vital, when travelling. Where will you be reading this letter? – – Presumably in Mainz. In heaven's name – *you must try to get hold of some money*. You won't have received my letter of the 13th, as I sent it to Mannheim, and you'd presumably already left by then.[2] I'd planned it all – – and as for Frankfurt I told you in some detail what Herr *Leopold Heinrich Pfeil*[3] had written. – – But what was the point of my telling you all this, what's done can't be changed; and I never had the pleasure of hearing why you had to go straight to Mannheim in such a tearing hurry. Presumably on the advice of various people who thought they understood the situation and in order not to miss the beautiful German opera. But your journey wasn't direct, of course, as Herr Beecke sent you off on a wild goose chase with *his malicious itinerary* because, as Herr Bullinger says, everyone knows that the way to Mannheim is by *Cannstatt* and *Bruchsal*, not by the *other road*, even if Herr Beecke claims it is *better*. And has Herr Beecke never been to Mannheim? – The wearisome journey to Ellwangen was a waste of time, and you have Herr Beecke's kindness to thank for this needless expenditure. – – And had Prince Taxis already returned to Regensburg? – – Enough! It's all in the past! – But now you must ensure not only that the *Elector of Mainz*[4] hears you but that you receive some money by way of a present and, if at all possible, you should also give a concert in the town as there are lots of aristocrats there, as well as the whole of the government, which is not the case with Mannheim, where the government and most of the aristocracy are in *Düsseldorf*. The concertmaster Herr *Kreusser*[5] is the best person

1. In a letter of 13 November Mozart reported to Leopold that for his performances at court Count Savioli had not given him money, which he would have preferred, but a watch.
2. He had not.
3. Leopold Heinrich Pfeil (1725/6–92) was a French teacher in Frankfurt; he had formerly been secretary to the father of the writer Johann Wolfgang von Goethe (1749–1832).
4. Friedrich Karl von Erthal (reigned 1774–1802), archbishop-elector of Mainz.
5. Presumably Johann Adam Kreusser, concertmaster at Mainz, though his younger brother, the Kapellmeister Georg Anton Kreusser might be intended.

to help you to achieve all this and to arrange matters for you. As for the first point, he himself knows, as someone who has travelled, that there's nothing one needs more than ready cash, and once you've played for the elector you can tell him the entirely natural cause without any reservations, because in Mannheim you received only a trifle. He can also do a lot for your concert as he's well liked throughout Mainz. If he's not there, then the leading soprano *Franziska Urspringer*, to whom I send my very best wishes, will instruct you and tell you to whom to apply. Perhaps to the cellist, Herr Schwachhofer's son, to whom I send my good wishes and who could also introduce you to the *Prince of Biberach*, who lives nearby and who is his pupil. I'm very much in the dark in talking about Mainz, but I assume that you're there, although you've not given me the slightest indication as to where you're going, but this is the nearest court: it will have cost you some 10 or 11 florins to get there in respect of the mail coach and tip. In Mainz you'll not miss the opportunity to give the choirmaster, Herr *Starck*[6] – *to whom I extend my very best wishes* – some of your keyboard pieces which he can simplify for his pupils by altering the difficult passages. – Why didn't you think of giving some of your compositions to the elector in Mannheim? After all, I advised you to do so for your *own good* and also to make your *works better known*, as there's an excellent orchestra there. – No, you'd no time to think about it. Where are you planning to go now? – – To Paris? – Which route do you plan to take? – Do you intend to go to Paris without any letters of recommendation? – – Which route do you plan to take in order to be able to earn something on the way? – – Even without assuming this, do you realize how much money is necessary for this extraordinary journey? – – And once you're there, to whom do you intend to turn? – Don't you need enough money in your purse to enable you to survive until you've made the necessary contacts in order to be able to earn something? – – In Paris you can achieve a lot by giving lessons! That's certain: but do you think that pupils can be found overnight and that people will dismiss their own teachers and take on the first passing stranger? – One can earn a lot

6. Johann Franz Xaver Starck (?–1799), cathedral organist at Mainz.

from works by having them engraved. Indeed! But doesn't all this need some form of patronage, a friend or two, a subscription, and doesn't it all presuppose that you've already made some acquaintances? – – Leaving aside all this, it remains certain that your journey and the initial period of your stay demand a well-filled purse. You know that we owe Herr Bullinger three hundred florins and Herr Weiser over a hundred florins, I don't know how much we owe Herr Kerschbaumer, but it must come to around forty florins. The tailor's and dressmaker's bills will be arriving in the New Year. Not to mention other trifles *amounting to only a few florins* and our unavoidable day-to-day expenses. Food costs very little: but these expenses still exist, especially now *in winter, what with wood and candles* and so many other trifles that I have enough trouble keeping track of them all.

In spite of all this, I'm prepared to make you *an advance of 20 or 30 louis d'or* in the event of your deciding to go to Paris in the hope that it will be doubled or trebled there: but is our friend *Grimm*[7] there? – – Why ever did ill fate arrange for you to be so close to each other in Augsburg without knowing it? – – Perhaps he's in Paris? Perhaps he was just on the point of leaving for Paris? – – But who knows the answers to these questions? – – How would it be if Wolfgang were to write to Paris and address his letter *à Monsieur Grimm Envoyé de S. A. Sereniss^me Le Duc de Saxe-Gotha à Paris*. In this letter he could announce his visit and express his regret that they were so close to each other in Augsb., where the concert or academy took place on the very evening that Herr Grimm booked into rooms at the 3 Moors etc. etc. The address for his reply should be Koblenz or wherever you're going: and as a note left at the post office on your departure is the safest way of ensuring that you receive letters, you'll certainly get an answer from him if he's in Paris. If he's not in Paris, then it doesn't matter if the letter is lost as it contains nothing compromising, but in such letters you mustn't place your signature too low down on the page and thereby leave a blank space above it, otherwise some rogue – if such a letter were to fall into the wrong

7. Friedrich Melchior von Grimm.

hands – might cut out the name and add some small demand for several louis d'or in the blank space above it. I've twice reminded you that if you leave behind you a note indicating your address, you're most likely to receive letters as the post office is anxious to ensure that *letters that have not been paid for* reach their destination. Good friends who are entrusted with such a commission may forget. On arriving in a place you need to ask repeatedly and insistently at the post office. What I said about a cash advance in Paris *is something that I wouldn't be able to arrange if you were now to draw money in Frankfurt*, which is why you should now *try to obtain a gift of money* or at any rate see to it that a lady undertakes to *cash in* your *watch* with the aristocracy, as Lamotte[8] did in Prague with all the trinkets he received there. Herr von Dalberg's beautiful wife could do that. Herr Kreusser knows best how to do this. – – But this is by no means everything! If I ask Mama about the route to Paris, she will say: How shall we travel? – – *We'll simply take the same old road as before.* Mama will recall that there are 34 post stages: but you must remember that you can't use the *chaise* any longer, they'll give you *4 horses equipped with 2 postilions*; there's no alternative, and in Brabant the posts from Brussels to Valenciennes cost 44 florins for 4 horses. At Valenciennes I had to take 6 horses. So you'll have to sell the *chaise* and take the diligence. *Remember also that I don't think the diligence travels by night on these French roads, you must make enquiries on this point at the post offices on the way*: you can't just sell the *chaise* willy-nilly at the last stage and possibly allow yourselves to be taken advantage of: you must think of all this in advance. You'll see from this that one must be prepared and write to me well in advance to tell me what you plan to do as letters have a long distance to cover if you want a reply. I'll wait till the next post day before describing to you the post stages between Brussels and Paris. But please let me know how you plan to continue your journey.

The Prince of Chiemsee[9] had an attack of gout at Zeil in Swabia, otherwise he'd have been in Munich long ago, they're now waiting

8. Franz Lamotte (?1751–81), violinist.
9. That is, the bishop of Chiemsee.

for him there, and if you write to him now in Munich, he'll undoubtedly already be there. You seem to like Munich more than Mannheim. I too would prefer Munich even though the orchestra in Mannheim is good; but I don't like the fact that there are no singers there and that every year there are changes to the singers and *maestri* at the opera. Why don't you write to Prince Zeil and ask him to suggest that the elector[10] and Count Seeau should take you on for a year or 2, just as he does with castratos? Tell him that you're not asking for a formal appointment – –, that you're a young man who's not looking for such an appointment but who is still young enough to make his way in the world but that you have an irresistible desire to serve the elector for as long as he'd like you to. You could write a *separate* letter to the prince, saying that it would do His Excellency Count Seeau no harm to have you make a commitment to arrange his German singspiels for him. And that you would give an assurance and a written undertaking not to importune or worry the elector to keep you on any longer than the agreed period, unless, that is, His Majesty was so inclined etc. – – My thinking behind all this is that you would be closer to Italy, so that if a *scrittura*[11] arrived and you were in Munich, he would let you go and your salary would continue. If no *scrittura* arrives, being in service is the best way to obtain one, not to mention the hundred other things you already know about. There's an amazing number of castles and monasteries around Munich, with hunting, riding and driving as permanent amusements for those who are well known there; there are opportunities to write for the church and the theatre: and in winter there's more in the way of entertainment than anywhere else that I know. – I must close. We both kiss your dear Mama and you. I am your old husband and father

Mozart

We didn't receive a letter from you today, perhaps one will arrive tomorrow by *Friday's post*. Who wrote the German opera?[12] Who

10. Maximilian III Joseph.
11. Contract.
12. The performance of Holzbauer's *Günther von Schwarzburg*.

were the singers and what were they like? – Not a word! And the concert, who played and sang? Who were the brass and woodwind players? Was the music any good? *Not a word!* You're extraordinary! – Oh yes, Mama wrote: *at the opera the music was good.* There we have it, but for the rest – guess! – Who played the violin concertos there? – – Herr Fränzl? – – Guess! And the philosophical and dried-out Raaff?[13] – Guess!

64. Leopold Mozart to his son, 24 November 1777, Salzburg

Mon très cher Fils,

I really don't know what to say, I was so stunned by your last letter of the 16th. In it you announced with a display of the *greatest nonchalance* that Herr *Schmalz* – presumably the father, brother or relation of Herr Schmalz[1] of the leather factory in Munich or possibly even Herr Schmalz himself – had apologized for the fact that he had no instructions to give you any money. I can well believe that; and he was right: you should have asked Herr Herzog or the firm of Nocker & Schiedl to provide you with a little extra credit, *as I used to do*: for they had no orders from Hagenauer's house to extend this credit elsewhere, and no businessman exceeds his literal orders: but it would have been done if you'd asked them. But this incident was described in such matter-of-fact and indifferent terms as though I'd whole chests full of money and should have been terribly annoyed that you'd not been paid at once. I won't waste time with a long-winded account of our circumstances, you know them yourself, as does Mama, and in my letter *of the 20th* I listed the main items, although I forgot a sizeable *sum* that we owe to Hagenauer *for goods* but with whom we're not *writing up a single farthing more on credit.* But what amazed me most of all on receiving your letter was that

13. The tenor Anton Raaff (1714–97), who sang in this performance, was sixty-three years old.
1. Dietrich Heinrich Schmalz (1720–97), banker.

you suddenly came out with this story without telling me about it in your previous letter, in which you simply said that money would have been more useful and appropriate for your journey than a trinket, as you knew even then that you were low on funds. If Herr Schmalz had been willing, I would have been lumbered with instructions for payment *without having received the slightest advance notice* and at a time *when I suspected nothing*. That's a pretty state of affairs indeed! – – I leave you to think it over, in the light of my present circumstances. You wrote to me from Augsb. that you'd lost only 27 florins. – According to my own calculations, you must still have 170 florins even if you'd lost 30 florins. Even if that stupid trip to Mannheim via Wallerstein[2] cost you 70 florins, you should still be left with 100 florins. Even if it cost you more, *can you really not have enough left* to be able to make the journey to Mainz? You'd then be near Frankfurt and if absolutely necessary would be able to draw a little with your second letter of credit from Herr Bolongaro[3] in Frankfurt. Then you'd only have to ask some businessman in Mainz who's in contact with Herr Bolongaro; he would have undertaken to send the letter of credit to Herr Bolong. and to draw what you require.

Wouldn't this have been more sensible than to settle down in Mannheim and squander your money to no avail, as this money would presumably have enabled you to make the journey, which would have cost perhaps 15 or 16 florins. It's only 1¼ stages to *Worms*, 2 to Oppenheim and 1 to Mainz, so only 3¾ in all. And even if you'd had little or no money on your arrival, we have acquaintances there who would help you, and no gentleman need be ashamed if he hasn't a farthing in his pocket but can produce a letter of credit: this can happen to the wealthiest and most distinguished people, indeed it's a maxim when travelling that, if possible, you should carry only as much money as you need. I'm still in the dark and if I speak of *Mainz* it's pure supposition as you haven't done me the honour in any of your letters of telling me where you are intending to go, only at the

2. The seat of the princes of Oettingen-Wallerstein in western Bavaria.
3. The brothers Joseph Maria Marcus and Jakob Philipp Bolongaro had founded a bank (and a tobacco dealership) in Frankfurt *c.* 1740.

very last moment did you write to me from Augsb. and say you were going to Wallerstein; and Herr Stein wrote to say that you left for Wallerstein and Mannheim at half past 7 on Sunday. But such things should be announced some time in advance, as I can sometimes make useful preparations and send reminders, just as I was at pains to do by writing to Herr Otto and Herr Pfeil in Frankfurt. – – Of course, your journey is no concern of mine! Isn't that so? – – You could, of course, have taken a very different route from Mannheim: namely, Würzburg and from there to the Margrave of Darmstadt, then Frankfurt and Mainz. But how can I guess what you're thinking or make suggestions as I'm never consulted and didn't know how things stood in Mannheim, indeed to judge by your letter in which you had an opportunity to speak so familiarly with the elector I was bound to assume that you had very different plans and were intending to stay there for some time; all of which – whatever your opinions, inclinations, aims etc. may be – you should have reported honestly and in good time as it takes *12 days* to receive and reply to a letter even if all goes smoothly. But you didn't bother to consider this either as in your last letter of the 16th you wrote that *I could continue to write to you in Mannheim*, although it would be 12 days at the quickest before you received this letter, in other words, not until the 28th, by which time Herr Herzog will long since have replied and you will have left. But I did not receive your letter until Friday the 21st, as a present on our *wedding day*, and was unable therefore to reply until the 24th; you'll have read this letter – God knows where – on 1 or 2 December. Neither of you must think that I don't know how many incidental expenses are incurred on a journey and how money vanishes into thin air, especially when one's overgenerous or too kind. My dear wife prided herself on getting up early, on not lingering and on doing everything quickly and economically. *16 days in Munich*, *14 days in Augsburg* and now, according to your letter of *16 Nov.*, *17 days in Mannheim*, which, including the time spent waiting for a reply from Augsb., will turn out to be 3 weeks. That's sorcery indeed; you've been away 8 weeks, in other words, 2 months, and you're already in Mannheim? – – That's incredibly quick! When we travelled to England, we spent *9 days* in Munich, called on the *elector* and Duke *Clemens*, and had to wait for our present. – We were *15 days* in Augsb., but we gave *3 concerts* there, namely, on 28 and 30 June and 4 July. – We left Salzburg on *9 June* and did not arrive in Munich until the 12th as new wheels had to be made in Wasserburg, yet in spite of this we were in Schwetzingen by *13 July*, although we broke our journey in Ulm, Ludwigsburg and Bruchsal. So you see that your long and unnecessary stay has ruined everything, the most beautiful autumn in living memory has come and gone, and so far you've regarded your journey as no more than a pleasure trip and spent the time enjoying yourselves: now the bad weather, shorter days and cold are here, with more of the same to come, while your prospects and goals are now correspondingly expensive and distant.

You can't spend the whole winter travelling; and if you plan to stay anywhere, it should be in a large town with lots of people where there are hopes and opportunities of earning some money: and where is such a place to be found in the whole of this region? – Apart from Paris: – – but life in Paris requires a completely different attitude to life, a different way of thinking, you have to be attentive and every day think of ways of earning money and exercise extreme politeness in order to ingratiate yourself with people of standing: I'll write more on this in my next letter, in which I shall also set out my ideas on a quite different route that may be worth taking and which, I believe, will get you to Paris more quickly, namely, from *Koblenz* to *Trier*, *Luxembourg*, *Sedan*, where Herr *Ziegenhagen*, who visited us with Herr Wahler, has a textile factory. Perhaps he'll be there now. Then Rethel, *Rheims*, Soissons and Paris. Note that from Paris to Rethel there are 22 French post stages. From Rethel it's only a stone's throw to Sedan – Luxembourg, too, isn't far, and Trier is close to Luxembourg. Luxembourg is an imposing fortress and there'll be lots of officers there. *Rheims* and *Soissons* are large towns. In all these places it will be relatively easy to earn some money in order to recover your travelling expenses as virtuosos rarely visit such places. By contrast, it's 34 post stages from Brussels to Paris, and these cost us *20 louis d'or* for 6 horses, without our receiving a farthing in return. And between Koblenz and Brussels there's nothing that can be done, except perhaps with the elector of Cologne.[4] Perhaps? – And what about Brussels? – – – – –

Meanwhile, whichever route you take, make sure that you obtain some letters of recommendation to take with you to Paris, it doesn't matter who writes them – businessmen, courtiers etc. etc. And is there no French ambassador or resident in Mainz or Koblenz? I don't think there is. You haven't got any letters of recommendation, whereas I had a lot; they're vital in providing you with both patronage and contacts. A journey like this is no joke, you've no experience of this sort of thing, you need to have other, more important thoughts on your mind than foolish games, you have to try to anticipate a hundred different things, otherwise you'll suddenly find yourself in the shit without any money, – – and where you've no money you'll have no friends either, even if you give a hundred lessons for nothing, and even if you write sonatas and spend every night fooling around from 10 till 12 instead of devoting yourself to more important matters. Then try asking for credit! – That'll wipe the smile off your face. I'm not blaming you for a moment for placing the Cannabichs under an obligation to you by your acts of kindness, that was well done: but you should have devoted a few of your otherwise idle hours each evening to your father, who is so concerned about you, and sent him not simply a mishmash tossed off in a hurry but a proper, confidential and detailed account of the expenses incurred on your journey, of the money you still have left, of the journey you plan to take in future and of your intentions in Mannheim etc. etc. In short, you should have sought my advice; I hope you'll be sensible enough to see this, for who has to shoulder this whole burden if not your poor old father? As I've already said, I didn't receive your letter until the 21st and was unable to reply until today. Yesterday, the 23rd, I confessed my sins at Holy Trinity and with tears in my eyes commended you both to the protection of Almighty God. In the afternoon we had target practice. The prize was offered by Cajetan Antretter and I won. *Herr Bullinger*, who sends his best wishes, was also somewhat taken

4. The archbishop-elector of Cologne at this time was Max Friedrich von Königsegg-Rothenfels (reigned 1761–84).

aback by your letter and it struck me that, in the present serious situation, he didn't appreciate your joke about a public debt. At half past 5 I then went to see Herr Hagenauer to ask him *that if Messrs Nocker & Schiedl had not informed him by post that they had transferred some money to you, he might care to write to Augsb. by today's post.* I returned to the shop this morning and spoke to Herr Joseph. I discovered that although they'd received letters from *Nocker & Schiedl*, there'd been no word about you. He promised to write today. I've now done all I can and hope that in the meantime you'll have received some money, *Nocker* & Schiedl won't send me a report until they know how much you've been given. NB: It's always better when drawing money to accept not *florins* but the local currency, e.g., 6, 7 etc. *louis d'or, carolins* or whatever. I've now told you what was weighing on my mind, it is God's own truth. You'll have to learn for yourself that it is no joke to undertake a journey like this and to have to live on random income: above all you must pray most earnestly to God for good health, be on your guard against wicked people, earn money by every means that is known and available to you, and then spend it with the greatest care. I prefer to give too little to someone who is travelling with me and whom I may never see again and risk being called a skinflint, rather than have him laugh at me behind my back for giving him too much. I've no more paper, and I'm tired, especially my eyes.

Nannerl and I wish you the best of health and with all our hearts kiss you a million times. I am your old husband and father but NB not your son

Mozart

I hope you'll have received my letter of the 20th in which I told you to write to *Monsieur Grimm* in Paris, also what you should write to the Prince of Chiemsee in Munich. By the next post I'll send you a list of all the stages to Paris and my opinion etc., also a list of all our former acquaintances in Paris. *Addio.*

65. *Mozart to his father, 29 November 1777, Mannheim*

Mon très cher Père,

I received your letter of the 24th this morning and see from it that you're unable to reconcile yourself to fate, be it good or bad, when it takes us by surprise; until now, and as things stand, the four of us have never been happy or unhappy, and for that I thank God. You reproach us both for many things, without our deserving it. We are not incurring any expenses that are not necessary; and what is necessary when travelling you know as well as we do, if not better. That we stayed so long in Munich was the fault of no one but *myself*; and if I'd been alone, I'd certainly have stayed in Munich. Why did we spend 2 weeks in Augsburg? – – I'm tempted to think that you didn't receive my letters from Augsburg. – – I wanted to give a concert – I was let down; meanwhile a whole week went by. I was absolutely determined to leave. They wouldn't let me. They wanted me to give a concert; I wanted them to beg me. And so they did. I gave a concert. There are your 2 weeks. Why did we go straight to Mannheim? – – I answered this question in my last letter. Why are we still here? – – Yes – – can you really think that I'd remain somewhere for no reason? – – But I could have told my father – – all right, you shall know the reason and indeed the whole course of events. But God knows that I had no wish to speak about it because I was unable to go into detail – any more than I can today – and I know you well enough to appreciate that a *vague* account would have caused you worry and distress, something I've always tried to avoid; but if you ascribe the cause to my negligence, thoughtlessness and indolence, I can only thank you for your high opinion of me and sincerely regret that you don't know your own son.

I'm not thoughtless but am prepared for anything and as a result can wait patiently for whatever the future holds in store, and I'll be able to endure it – – as long as my honour and the good name of Mozart don't suffer in consequence. Well, if it must be so, then let it be so. But I must ask you at the outset not to rejoice or grieve prematurely; for whatever happens, all is well as long as we remain

healthy; for happiness consists – – simply in our imagination. Last
Tuesday week, the 18th, the day before St Elisabeth's Day, I saw
Count Savioli in the morning and asked him if there was any chance
that the elector would keep me here this winter? – – I wanted to
teach the young princes. He said yes, I'll suggest it to the elector;
and if it's up to me, it will certainly happen. That afternoon I saw
Cannabich and as it was at his suggestion that I'd been to see the
count, he asked me at once if I'd been there. – I told him all that had
happened, he said to me I'd very much like you to spend the winter
here with us, but I'd like it even more if you had a proper, permanent
appointment. I said that there was nothing I'd like more than to be
always near them but that I really didn't know how it would be
possible for me to stay permanently. You've already got two Kapellmeisters,[1] so I don't know what I could do, as I wouldn't like to be
under *Vogler*! Nor shall you, he said. None of the members of the
orchestra here is under the Kapellmeister or even under the intendant.[2]
The elector could make you his chamber composer. Wait, I'll speak
to the count about it. There was a big concert on Thursday. When
the count saw me, he apologized for not having said anything, but
the galas were still going on; but as soon as the galas were over,
namely, on Monday, he would certainly speak to the elector. I left it
for 3 days, and as I'd heard nothing, I went to see him in order to
make enquiries. He said: My dear Monsieur Mozart (this was Friday,
namely, yesterday), there was a hunt today so I've been unable to
ask the elector; but by this time tomorrow I shall certainly be able to
give you an answer: I begged him not to forget. To tell the truth, I
was rather angry when I left him and decided to take the young
count[3] my six easiest variations on Fischer's minuet[4] – which I'd
already had copied out here for this very purpose – in order to have
an opportunity to speak to the elector in person. When I arrived, you
can't imagine how pleased the governess was to see me. I received a
most courteous welcome. When I took out the variations and said

1. Christian Cannabich and Georg Joseph Vogler.
2. Count Savioli.
3. Carl August.
4. K179.

that they were for the count, she said Oh, that's good of you; but have you also got something for the countess?[5] – – Not yet, I said, but if I were to stay here long enough to write something, I'll – – By the way, she said, I'm glad that you'll be staying here all winter. Me? – – I didn't know that! – – That surprises me. It's curious. The elector himself told me so recently. By the way, he said, Mozart is staying here this winter. Well, if he did indeed say that, then he's the one person who *can* say it, for without the elector I certainly can't remain here. I told her the whole story. We agreed that I'd return the next day – namely, *today* – after 4 o'clock and bring something for the countess. You'll speak to the elector – before I arrive – and he'll still be with you when I get there. I went back there today, but he didn't come. But I'll go again tomorrow. I've written a rondeau[6] for the countess. Don't I have reason enough to remain here and await the outcome? – – Should I leave now that the greatest step has been taken? – – I now have a chance to speak to the elector himself. I think I shall probably remain here all winter as the elector is fond of me, he thinks highly of me and knows what I can do. I hope to be able to give you some good news in my next letter. I beg you once again not to rejoice or worry too soon and to confide this story in no one except Herr Bullinger and my sister. I'm sending my sister the allegro and andante from the sonata for Mlle Cannabich.[7] The rondeau will follow shortly. It would have been too much to send them all together. You'll have to make do with the original; you can have it copied more easily at 6 kreuzers a page than I can at 24 kreuzers.[8] Don't you find that expensive? – – Adieu. I kiss your hands 100,000 times and embrace my sister with all my heart. I am your obedient son

Wolfgang Amadé Mozart

5. Carolina.
6. K284f, which is otherwise unknown.
7. K309.
8. A copy of this sonata, entirely in Leopold Mozart's hand, is in private ownership in Switzerland.

You'll probably already have heard a little of the sonata, as it's sung, banged out, fiddled and whistled at least 3 times a day at Cannabich's. – Only *sotto voce*, of course.

[*Maria Anna Mozart's postscript*]
My dear husband, I kiss you and Nannerl many 1000 times and ask you to give our best wishes to all our acquaintances, I'll write more next time, but it's turned midnight, *addio*, I remain your faithful wife

Maria Anna Mozart

66. Leopold Mozart to his wife and son, 4 December 1777, Salzburg

My Dear Wife and Dear Son,

I've no objection to your having to wait for what you told me about in your last letter, and there's nothing more that can be said about all that has happened on your journey and that has turned out differently from what I'd expected and worked out to our disadvantage and even caused us obvious harm, as it is all over and done with and can no longer be changed. – But the fact that you, my son, write *that all speculation is superfluous and of no avail as we cannot know what is to happen* – this is indeed ill considered and was undoubtedly written unthinkingly. No sensible person – I shall not say no Christian – will deny that *everything will and must happen according to God's will*. But does it follow from this that we should act blindly, live carefree lives, make no provisions for the future and simply wait for things to befall us of their own accord? – – Does God himself and, indeed, do all rational people not demand that in all our actions we consider their consequences and outcome, at least as far as our human powers of reason enable us to, and that we make every effort to see as far ahead as we can? – – If this is necessary in all our actions, how much more so is it in the present circumstances, on a journey? Or have you not already suffered the consequences of this? – – Is it enough for you to have taken the step *with the elector in order to remain there throughout the winter?* – – Should you not – shouldn't you long ago have thought of a plan that can be implemented if things don't work out: and shouldn't you have told me about it long ago and learnt my views on it? – – And now you write – what? If we were after all to leave here we'll go straight to Weilburg to the Princess of Nassau-Weilburg – for whom you wrote the sonatas in Holland[1] – etc. – There we'll stay as long as *the officers' table* is to our liking – what sort of a tale is that? Like everything else you wrote, this is the language of a *desperate man* who is trying to console both himself and me. – – But there's still a *hope* that you'll receive 6 louis d'or, and that will make everything all right. – But my question to you now is whether you're certain that the princess is there: she won't be there without good reason as her husband[2] is based in The Hague on account of his military office. Shouldn't you have told me about this long ago? – Another question: wouldn't you do better to go to Mainz – and from there to Weilburg via Frankfurt? After all, if you go from Mannheim to Weilburg, you'll cross the Frankfurt road: and as you're not staying in Weilburg for ever, the Mainz road will take you back through Frankfurt. If you first go to Mainz and then to Weilburg, you'll have only a short distance from Weilburg to Koblenz, which will presumably take you via *Nassau*. Or do you intend to avoid Mainz, where we've so many good friends and where we earned *200 florins from 3 concerts*, even without playing for the elector,[3] who was ill. Tell me, my dear son, are these useless speculations? – – Your dear good Mama told me she'd keep a careful note of your expenses. Good! I've never asked for a detailed account and never thought of demanding one: but when you arrived in Augsburg you should have written to say: We paid such and such at Albert's in Munich, and such and such was spent on travelling expenses, so that we still have *such and such* a sum. From Augsb. you wrote to say that after taking account of the concert receipts you were about 20 florins out of pocket. In your 2nd letter from Mannheim you should at least have

1. K26–31; see letter 12.
2. Prince Karl Christian of Nassau-Weilburg (1735–88); his principality lay north of the river Main and east of the Rhine.
3. Emmerich Joseph von Breidbach-Bürresheim (reigned 1763–74).

said that the journey cost us such and such an amount and we're *now* left with – –, so that I could have made arrangements in good time – – was my arrangement to send you a letter of credit in Augsburg a useless speculation? – – Do you really think that Herr Herzog – *who's a good old friend of mine* – would have provided you with money in response to all your letters from Mannheim if you'd not already given him a letter of credit? – – Certainly not! The most that he would have done would have been to make enquiries with me first. – – Why did I have to discover that you needed money only when you were in trouble? *You wanted to wait to see what the elector gave you.* Isn't that so? Perhaps in order to spare me the worry – – but it would have caused me less worry if I'd been told everything honestly and in good time, as I know better than either of you how one must be prepared for all eventualities on such a journey in order not to be placed in some terrible predicament at the very moment when one least expects it. – At such times all your *friends* disappear! *One must be cheerful; one must enjoy oneself!* But one must also find time *to give serious thought to these matters*, and this must be your main concern when travelling and when not a single day should be allowed to pass to your disadvantage – – the days slip past – days which are in any case very short at present and which all cost money at an inn. Merciful heavens! You ask me not to speculate now that *I'm 450 florins in debt entirely thanks to you two.* – And you think that you may be able to put me in a good mood by telling me a hundred foolish jokes. I'm pleased that you're in good spirits: but instead of the good wishes set out in the form of the alphabet, I'd have felt happier if you'd told me the reasons for, and the circumstances of, your journey to *Weilburg* and what you planned to do afterwards and, most of all, if you'd listened to my opinion; and this could have been done before a post day, as you can't only just have hit on the idea, nor can you know independently that the princess is there, unless someone had already suggested the idea to you. In a word, it is no idle speculation when one has something in mind and formulates 2 or 3 plans and makes all the necessary arrangements in advance so that if one plan doesn't work out, one can easily turn to another. Anyone who acts otherwise is an unintelligent or thoughtless person who, especially *in today's world*, will always be left behind, no matter how clever he is, and who will even be unhappy as he will always be duped by flatterers, false friends and those who envy him. My son, to find *one man in a 1000* who is your true friend for reasons other than self-interest *is one of the greatest wonders of this world.* Examine all who call themselves your friends or who make a show of friendship and you'll find the reason why this is so. If they're not motivated by self-interest on their own account, then they'll be acting in the interests of some other friend whom they need; or they are your friends so that by singling you out they can annoy some third party. If nothing comes of *Mannheim*, you still have your plan to go to *Mainz, Frankfurt, Weilburg, Koblenz* etc.; one should always look for places as close to each other as possible so that, if you can, the journeys should be kept short and you can soon get to a place where you'll find a source of income. If this letter doesn't reach you in *Mannheim* and you're already in *Weilburg*, I can't help you. But if you're still in Mannheim and have to leave, then Mama will see from the map that your best plan is to go to *Mainz* first, otherwise you'll either have to forgo Mainz or retrace your steps a little. In Weilburg you need to bear in mind that you'll not find a *Catholic church* there as everyone is *Lutheran* or *Calvinist*. So I'd prefer you *not to spend too long* there.

And who told you that you'd have to go through the forest of Spessart to get from *Würzburg to Mannheim* as the *Spessart* is near *Aschaffenburg*, between *Fulda and Frankfurt?* – – This is no doubt some other trick that Herr Beecke has played on you. *Aschaffenburg* and *Würzburg* are 10 miles apart. – It may be that one drives past the forest on the right-hand side for some hours as one approaches Mannheim. But there's nothing near Würzburg, whether you've been there or not.

NB: I've another observation to make about any journey that you may choose to make from *Weilburg* to *Koblenz*, namely, that the road is across country and will be safer than the one from *Mainz* to *Koblenz*, which is too near the Rhine. I now want to know all your other plans, *I'd never have suspected that my own dear wife wouldn't have given me the occasional accurate account of your travelling expenses, as I've twice asked about Albert's bill and should also have been told about the bill from the landlord of the Lamb* etc. etc. But I'm not allowed to know about all your expenses. *And so I must ask Mama to write me a confidential letter on this point – I don't want a wordy explanation but would just like to see from the landlord's bill how people have been treating you and where all the money has gone.* We must now give serious thought to the ways and means of getting you out of the present situation, of travelling as economically as possible and of making sensible arrangements, but at all events you must let me know at once what may be to our detriment or advantage. *On no account* must you *sell* the chaise. May God keep both you and me well. Nannerl and I kiss you many 100,000,000 times. I am your own husband and father

Mzt

Count Czernin[4] has asked me to give you his best wishes. There was a rumour not only that the archbishop will be sending Haydn[5] to Italy but that he had already wanted to send him to Bozen with Triendl.[6] But Herr Triendl excused himself. I beg you, my dear Wolfg., consider everything and don't always write about things when they're already over and done with. Otherwise we'll all be unhappy.

67. Mozart to his father, 10 December 1777, Mannheim

Mon très cher Père,

Nothing's to be hoped for from the elector at present. Two days ago I attended the concert at court in order to get an answer. Count Savioli was clearly avoiding me, but I went over to him: when he saw me, he shrugged his shoulders. What, I said, still no reply? – – I'm sorry, he said, but unfortunately no. – – *Eh bien,* I said, the

4. Johann Rudolf, Count Czernin (1757–1845), nephew of Archbishop Colloredo.
5. Michael Haydn.
6. Anton Triendl (1721–96), Salzburg city councillor and son-in-law of Siegmund Haffner the elder.

elector could have told me so before now. Yes, he said, but he wouldn't have come to a decision even now if I'd not urged him to do so and pointed out that you'd been sitting around here for so long, getting through all your money at the inn. It's that that annoys me too most of all, I retorted. It's not very nice; but I'm most obliged to you, Count – he's not called Your Excellency – for having so actively championed my cause, and I wonder if I could ask you to thank the elector on my behalf for his kind, if belated, reply. And I assured him that he'd never have regretted taking me on. Oh, he said, I'm more certain of that than you think. I then told Herr Wendling of the decision, he turned bright red and said very heatedly: we must find ways and means; you must remain here, for at least 2 months, until we can go to Paris together. As soon as Cannabich gets back from hunting tomorrow, we can discuss the matter further. With that I left the concert and went straight to see Madame Cannabich. While going there, I explained all this to the treasurer, who had left with me and who is a most excellent person and a good friend of mine. You can't imagine how angry he became.

As soon as we set foot in the room, he interrupted me, saying: well, here's someone who's been treated by the court in its usual wonderful way. So nothing has come of it? said Madame. – – I told them everything. They then told me about all manner of similar tricks played on people here. When Mlle Rosa – who was 3 rooms away, just dealing with the laundry – had finished, she came in and said: Is it convenient to you now? – It was time for her lesson. I'm at your command, I said. But, she said, we must have a really sensible lesson today. I agree, I retorted, as we can't go on for much longer. Why's that? – Why is that? – – Why? – She went over to her Mama, who told her. What? she said. It's true – – I don't believe it. Yes, yes, it's true, I said. Then, adopting a very serious expression, she played my sonata.[1] Believe me, I couldn't stop crying. By the end, mother, daughter and treasurer were all in tears as she was playing the very sonata that's the favourite of the whole household. Listen, said the treasurer, if the Herr Kapellmeister – they never call me anything

1. K309.

else here – goes away, he'll make us all cry. I must say that I've got some very good friends here, it's in circumstances like these that you get to know who they are; they're friends not just in words but in deeds.

Just listen to the following.

The next day I went to have lunch at Wendling's as usual. He said to me: our Indian – he's a Dutchman, a man of independent means, a lover of all the sciences and a great friend and admirer of mine – is a really exceptional individual.[2] He'll give you 200 florins if you'll write 3 little, easy and short concertos and a couple of quartets for the flute. Through Cannabich you'll get at least 2 pupils, who'll pay well; you can write duets for keyboard and violin here and have them engraved by subscription. You can dine with us both at midday and in the evening. You can have self-contained quarters at the privy councillor's;[3] it won't cost you anything. And we'll find some inexpensive accommodation for your mother for the 2 months it takes for you to write home and explain all this; Mama will then travel home and we'll go to Paris. Mama is happy with this, all that remains is your own agreement, of which I'm already so certain that if we had to leave straightaway, I'd go to Paris without waiting for an answer; for one can expect nothing more from so sensible a father who has always been so concerned for his children's welfare. Herr Wendling, who sends you his best wishes, is a close friend of our own close friend, Herr *Grimm*. He told him a lot about me when he was here. It was after he'd left us in Salzburg. I'll write to him as soon as I receive a reply to this letter. I was told by a stranger whom I met at table here that he's now in Paris. As we shan't be leaving before 6 March, I'd also ask you, if possible, to contact Herr Mesmer or someone else in Vienna and arrange for me to receive a letter for the queen of France:[4] – but only if it can easily be done! – – otherwise it's not really very important, although it's true that it would be

2. Ferdinand Dejean (1731–97), physician and amateur musician who had been a surgeon with the Dutch East India Company from 1758–67.
3. Anton Joseph Serrarius, privy councillor to the elector.
4. Marie Antoinette had become queen of France on the accession of the dauphin as Louis XVI in 1774.

preferable. This is also something that Herr Wendling advised me to do. I imagine that what I've written will seem strange to you as you're in a town where one's used to having stupid enemies and weak or simple-minded friends who, because they are dependent on their miserable livelihood in Salzburg, continue to fawn on their superiors and as a result live from day to day. You see, that's the reason why I've been writing such childish nonsense and jokes and why I've said nothing sensible, as I was waiting to see how things would turn out here in order to spare you any annoyance and protect my good friends, whom you may now blame for what has happened, even though they are innocent, and whom you may accuse of acting in an underhand way, although this is certainly not the case. I already know who is the cause! But I've been obliged by your letters to tell you the whole story. But I beg you not to upset yourself over this, it is God's will. Consider only this all too certain truth that it is not always possible to do all that one is minded to do. One often thinks that something would be very good and that something else would be very bad and wicked, but when it happens, one often discovers the opposite. I must go to bed now. I've got enough to write during the next 2 months: 3 concertos, 2 quartets, 4 or 6 keyboard duets, and I also plan to write a big new mass[5] and present it to the elector. Adieu. Please reply at once to all these points. I kiss your hands 100,000 times and embrace my sister with all my heart. I am your most obedient son

Wolfgang Amade Mozart

Baron Dürnitz[6] wasn't in Munich when I was there. I'll write to Prince Zeil[7] on the next post day in order to expedite matters in Munich. If you too were to write to him, I should be most grateful. But short and to the point. Just don't grovel, that's something I can't

5. Nothing came of Mozart's plan although the fragmentary K322 apparently belongs to this time and may represent an aborted attempt by him to compose a mass for the elector.
6. Thaddäus, Baron von Dürnitz (1756–1803), for whom Mozart wrote the piano sonata K284.
7. The bishop of Chiemsee.

bear. One thing is certain: if he wants to, he can certainly arrange it, for all Munich told me so.

[*Maria Anna Mozart's postscript*]
My Dear Husband,

You want to know how much we've spent on our journey, we've already told you what Albert's bill came to, in Augsburg it came to 38 florins, Wolfgang told you that we'd made a loss of 24 florins, but he didn't include the expenses incurred on the concert, which came to a further 16 florins, nor did he include our landlord's bill, so that by the time we reached Mannheim we'd no more than 60 florins left, if we'd left again after a fortnight, there'd have been very little left. Travelling expenses have gone up as everything has become so expensive, it's not like it used to be, you'd be surprised. As for Wolfgang's journey to Paris, you must decide soon whether you're in agreement, at this time of the year there's nothing that can be done anywhere except in Paris. Monsieur Wendling is an honest man, whom everyone knows, he's travelled widely and has been to Paris more than 15 times, he knows it like the back of his hand, and our friend Herr von Grimm is his best friend, too, and has done a lot for him. So you can decide, whatever you want is all right by me. Herr Wendling has assured me that he will be a father to him, he loves him like a son and he'll be as well looked after as if he were with me. As you can imagine, I don't like to let him go nor do I want to travel home on my own, it's such a long way: but what's to be done? To undertake such a long journey to Paris is difficult for someone of my age, and also too expensive. It's easier to pay a quarter of the total than to pay for everything as you'd have to if you were on your own.

I'll write more next post day, today I've a headache and think I may be coming down with a cold. It's very cold here, I'm so frozen I can hardly hold the pen. Wolfgang has gone out to look at some rooms, the cheaper ones are very difficult to find here, but there's no shortage of expensive ones.

Tell Nannerl that people don't wear jackets here except indoors. Out of doors, it's mostly cloaks and polonaises, the bonnets are much prettier than in Salzburg and very different, too, their hairstyles incomparable, not raised up at the front, the women dress with great taste. If it weren't so far, I'd have sent her a bonnet and a tippet. *Addio.* Keep well. I kiss you both many 1,000,000 times and remain your faithful wife

Maria Anna Mozart

To all our good friends especially Monsieur Bullinger, Mistress Sallerl, Katherl Gilowsky, the Antretters, Hagenauers, Robinigs, Frau von Gerlichs, the Schiedenhofens, Mölks, Mistress Mitzerl, Herr Gött,[8] Mistress Sandl,[9] and Tresel all conceivable good wishes.

A little kiss to Pimperl.

68. Leopold Mozart to his son, 18 December 1777, Salzburg

Mon très cher Fils,

The news contained in your letter of the 10th concerning the unfavourable outcome of the matter in hand did not find me unprepared as I'd already predicted as much to Herr Bullinger and your sister and never imagined that it would turn out any differently. You too will have gathered this from each and every one of my letters. That I'd have preferred a different outcome is quite true, as you could then still have undertaken other journeys from time to time. You'll also have found that in all my letters I had my eyes fixed firmly on Paris. I must now write more fully. You know that for many years our patience was sorely tested in Salzb.: and you know how often you and I wanted to leave. You'll also recall the objections I raised, objections that made it impossible for us *all* to leave Salzb.; you now have proof of this – the great expense of travelling and the fact that one's income is so little or at least insufficient to defray those costs,

8. Johann Gottlieb Pergmayr, Mozart's godfather.
9. Maria Clara Susanna Auer (b. 1742), daughter of the administrator of the cathedral chapter, Franz Christoph Auer.

especially with an entire family. At that time I couldn't let you travel on your own, you know that you weren't used to sorting things out on your own, not used to doing this and that without the help of others – you were largely unfamiliar with different currencies and knew nothing whatever about foreign ones and you didn't have the least idea about packing and about the many needs that arise when one's travelling. I often pointed out to you that – even if you were to remain in Salzb. until a couple of years after you'd turned twenty – you'd lose nothing because in the meantime you'd have a chance to get a taste of other useful sciences, to develop your intellect by reading good books in various languages and to practise foreign tongues. I also pointed out that even if a young man can look down on all his teachers, he will still not gain the respect that he deserves: this takes a certain number of years; and until he reaches 20, his enemies and persecutors and those who envy him know that the basis of their censure and of the objections they raise to him can be attributed to his youth, his lack of years, his *lack of status* and his inexperience. Do you doubt that such things were not brought to *the elector's* attention with regard to *your teaching his children?* – Moreover, I am no more a lover of *grovelling* than you are, and with regard to Munich you'll remember that I told you not to *demean yourself*: and all these attempts to persuade a group of 10 people to arrange things so that you could stay on there seemed to me to involve *too much grovelling*. You were persuaded to stay by kind-hearted and well-meaning friends; yet these are straw fires that flare up quickly – and end in smoke: it was well meant! It's true that I'd like you to have a post, but only one like Munich or Mannheim or else one in which – importantly – you wouldn't be prevented from making the occasional journey. In my view, not a lifetime appointment *per decretum*. If you had such a post even for only a couple of years, you'd be able to travel to France and Italy. One acquires more prestige and respect etc. by virtue of the *length of time* you spend in a post and by the title that you hold as composer to an elector etc. You already know this. That's also my thinking on Munich. As long as you're looking for a fixed-term post, it's *certainly not grovelling*, as you're merely looking for a chance to show what you can already do and know how to do, as there are people at every court who try to prevent this because time and opportunity are needed to show oneself in the right light. – Let's come now to your journey to Paris. – I wish you were already there: that was very much my concern during your disastrously long stay in Mannheim. It's entirely natural that the gentlemen[1] with whom you're to travel to Paris don't want to let you leave without them: they need a *fourth* person; and where will they find a *fourth* person like you? That Herr Wendling is your friend, that he means well, that he knows Paris and will take the best possible care of you – none of this do I doubt for a moment. Nor do I doubt that he'll try to ensure that you find some means of supporting yourself in Mannheim between now and March – after all, he's keen to have your company: there's a reason for every friendship. If this Dutch gentleman[2] gives you 200 florins, you can survive in Mannheim, especially if you dine with Herr Wendling. Supposing that Mama spends 3 florins a week on food, that makes 12 florins a month, or could Herr Cannabich or – for all I care – Herr Wendling – not feed her for 4 florins a week? That would be 16 florins a month – and what might a room cost for a month? – If you get the 200 florins from the Dutchman and if the two of you spend 50 florins a month, that makes 100 florins in two months: but if you were also to get a couple of pupils, you'd still have more than 100 florins left, and how can the two of you spend 50 florins a month if you have free board? – In short, all this is fine by me: the only thing *I won't have* is for you to live with some anonymous privy councillor and for Mama to live on her own. As long as Mama remains there, you should remain with her. *You should not and must not* leave Mama to mope on her own or to be abandoned to other people as long as she is with you and you are with her: however small the room, there'll still be space for a bed for you. – And why not find a larger room straightaway? It will cost only a few florins more, but that doesn't matter for a couple of months, whatever it costs it will still be barely half of what you had to pay at the inn.

1. Wendling, the oboist Ramm and Georg Wenzel Ritter (1748–1808), bassoonist in the Mannheim court orchestra.
2. Ferdinand Dejean.

If only you'd done what I told you to do in Augsburg and on repeated occasions since then, namely, to *look round for a private apartment in Mannheim*, you'd have saved a lot of money as you could then have eaten whenever you wanted or made more appropriate arrangements for this – especially as both of you or at least one of you often ate out. Yes – who'd have thought that we'd stay there for so long? – Who? – – I not only thought it, I knew it. If only you'd taken Munich as your yardstick and looked at a calendar, you'd have discovered, after only a few words of enquiry, that it's impossible to obtain a hearing in less than a week and that by the time you've received your present – and until you can put forward the proposal that you have in mind – until you receive an answer to it – then pack all your belongings together again – and say goodbye to all your good friends and the acquaintances that you've just made and finally get away another 3 or 4 weeks will have passed without your knowing where they've gone. As a result, you could have taken an apartment on a weekly basis or even for a month, and even if you'd paid for an extra week, you'd still have emerged the winner. Mama should think back to our earlier travels. I never put up at inns when I suspected that we'd be staying for any length of time: Paris, London, Vienna etc., even *Brünn* etc. are all places where we *simply don't* know the inns or, if we do, only as temporary accommodation. You'll no doubt appreciate that Mama can't leave Mannheim at present, now that the coldest weather is setting in; also I have to work out the easiest and most convenient way of getting her back. Meanwhile be sure that you stay with her and look after her, so that she lacks nothing, just as she cares for you in turn. But if the Indian's 200 florins turn out to be no more than another straw fire that has gone up in flames in the first flush of friendship and already turned to smoke, then you should pack up and go: but if I'm wrong, you should get down to work as soon as possible: and you'd also do well to write a large-scale new mass for the elector; and so you'll have to plan your time carefully during these next 2 months: *Best of all would be for you to write to* Prince *Zeil*. Tell him that *you are certainly not demanding that the elector take you on* permanently and *per decretum* but that *he might like to take you on* for a couple of years in order to give you the opportunity and privilege of serving him and affording him proof of your *talent*. I'll write again next post day. You must also write to Herr von Grimm, as I shall too. Herr Bullinger etc. etc. and all our good friends send their best wishes. Nannerl and I kiss you millions of times. I am your solicitous father

Mzt

Please give our good wishes to the whole of the Cannabich and Wendling households.

[*Postscript to Maria Anna Mozart*]
My Dear Wife,

I've replied above to the main matter concerning the journey to Paris with Herr Wendling: if it's true about the 200 florins, then I'd like you and Wolfg. to remain together; but if there's a problem here and insufficient certainty, you should pack everything together and go to Mainz at once. As soon as you arrived in Mannheim, you should have sought the help of young Herr Danner or someone similar and looked round for a private apartment without delay. You should have done this without listening to any of the objections that others may have raised: after all, I wrote and told you this often enough; but, to our detriment, you didn't do so. You say that you wrote to inform me of Albert's bill. I received *not a word*! I saw from your letters that both of you tossed them off in a hurry late at night, when you were both half asleep and that as a result you wrote down only the first thing that came into your heads: in short, you yourself don't know what you wrote; and I bet you rarely read any of Wolfg.'s letters to me. My God! What prize specimens you are! – – I can well believe that your expenses have gone up with the general increase, but postal charges are still the same; and I'd already worked out that you'd spent a lot. In a word, if you'd read my letters properly, you'd have known what needed to be done even if you'd arrived penniless in Mainz. But that's how things are! No one has *worked* more against Wolfg. *than Vogler*. I said so long ago to Herr Bullinger and Nannerl. If it's true that you've received 200 florins from the Dutchman, I must consider how to get you back home, for it can't be now, it would be too cold for you now, as the cold is at its worst around Christmas and Twelfth Night: and how? In our chaise? – – On your own? – – It must be given some thought. If only you were in Augsburg! Do you think Wolfg. will now take charge of his affairs? – I hope he'll have got used to this and that his head won't always be full of music. Keep well. I am your old husband

Mzt

The wretched actors arrived from Vienna 2 days ago. *Peringer* the clockmaker has died suddenly.

69. Leopold Mozart to his wife and son, 29 December 1777, Salzburg

My Dear Wife and Dear Wolfg.,

We wish you both a very happy New Year! I pray to God that 1778 may bring us more contentment than the year that has just ended, we hope for this from God's grace and mercy and from the talent, hard work and skill but especially the good heart of our dear Wolfgang, who will undoubtedly do everything to win glory, honour and money in order to save us and to prevent his father from being exposed to the scornful contempt and ridicule of certain persons whom I may not name but whose ridicule would undoubtedly be the death of me. His good fortune and fame will be our sweetest revenge, and indeed we have already had a foretaste of it. Count Starhemberg called on Count Arco while he was being bled. The conversation turned to Adlgasser's death.[1] *Count Arco*: You're stuck, aren't you? – Young Mozart would have done you good service. *Count Starhemberg*: Yes, it's true, he could have been a bit more patient. *Count Arco*: What, be patient? Don't make me laugh! Who

---

1. The cathedral organist Anton Adlgasser had died on 21 December 1777 while playing at Vespers. Franz Joseph, Count Starhemberg (1748–1819) was a canon at Salzburg cathedral.

could have predicted this sudden death? – – And even if they had done, what would you have given him *in addition to his shitty florins*? He's done well to leave! People treated him abominably for long enough. *Count Starhemberg*: Yes, I must admit that he was very badly treated: everyone must admit that he's the finest keyboard player in Europe. But he could still have been more patient. *Count Arco beside himself with anger*! Shit, yes! He's doing very well in Mannheim, he's found some good companions with whom he's going to Paris, you'll never get him back, it serves you right! The same will happen to Hagenauer![2] *Count Starhemberg*: The latter will now be receiving a salary from the start of the New Year. *Count Arco*: That'll be nice, but even so: you've messed him around for long enough and led him by the nose. The conversation then turned to me, with Count Starhemberg claiming that he thought it *impossible to find a better teacher than me*. You'll notice that Count Arco kept saying 'you' = Count Starhemberg and the rest of the company, in order not to have to name the prince and out of political expediency to shift the burden of guilt to his cronies on the other side of the river. As for Hagenauer, he'll be going to Gurk with Prince Auersperg, the bishop of Gurk,[3] to design a building for him there. If the archbishop's decision turns out badly, he'll not object but he won't be coming back.

I was just about to say myself that in future you should write only once a week; there's not enough to write about at present to justify a letter each post day, and letters are so expensive. If I've anything to say, I'll continue to write each post day, if not, you won't hear from me on some post days, but I'll always indicate this in the following letter.

I now have a lot of letters to write in any case as I've decided to activate a whole host of people in Vienna so that, if it's still possible, I can obtain a letter of recommendation from the Viennese court to the queen of France.

Although you'll have received the fullest account in Mannheim of

2. Johann Georg Hagenauer (1748–1835), court architect.
3. Joseph Franz Anton, Count Auersperg, bishop of Gurk from 1772–83.

the critical state of the elector of Bavaria's health,[4] I'm none the less copying out the report that I received from Munich dated 24 Dec. It reads:

Until now most of the intrigues and confusions at our court have been due to the Italian nation, and now it looks as though we are to lose His Excellency the Elector to them, too. Prince Gonzaga has a niece who has been studying for many years at the convent at Nymphenburg but who has been ill for most of that time; as a result the prince took her to Italy, where, much against her old uncle's wishes and intentions, she fell in love. And so he forced her to return with him to Munich, and the elector was obliged to make her a lady-in-waiting.

She'd been there, entirely against her will, for only a short time when she contracted smallpox of the worst possible kind. The doctors may not have realized what it was at the beginning, but the main point is that the Italians kept it a secret and covered it up for so long that in the end she had to stay at the Residence. – Normally everyone has to leave at the slightest sign of smallpox, and this includes even the courtiers and officers, who have to stay away from the court for 6 to 8 weeks if anyone in their household catches smallpox. Meanwhile they all spoke about this Marchesa Riva in the most painfully sympathetic tone in the elector's presence, until the elector finally expressed a certain apprehension and even spoke about it himself: indeed, they were so thoughtless that on occasion they even took the elector past the staircase where her room was situated and where her staff were preparing her meals. – And so it was on the 9th of Decemb. that the elector suffered his first attack, including a headache. On the 10th the master of hounds took him hunting, and they remained away for 6 hours when the weather was extremely cold. In the evening there was the vigil for the Empress Amalia; once again they took him past the invalid's room to the church of the Theatines, where he spent another hour in the cold. He'd suffered a severe shock while out hunting, when his postilion, who

---

4. Maximilian III Joseph died on 30 December 1777. He was the last of the junior branch of the Wittelsbach dynasty, rulers of Bavaria since the early fourteenth century, and was succeeded by his distant cousin, Elector Karl Theodor of the Palatinate, from the senior branch of the dynasty.

was in charge of his relay horses, almost sank into the bog with all 4 horses before his very eyes. – On the 11th he fainted on the privy, his headache got worse and his face turned all red, like a rash. He had to stay in his room – he was given some mild medication and told he was suffering from measles. He was still well on the 12th, 13th and 14th, but on the 15th things got so bad that his personal physician, Dr Sänffiel, told him to stay in bed. From then on things got progressively worse. They were reluctant to call off the plays in order not to alarm even further the general public, which was in any case already dismayed by events. This also explains why no public prayers were arranged until the Augustinian Fathers finally held a votive service on the 17th, and this was followed by others, with 3, 4 or 5 votive services held in the different churches by all the staff-officers – and every social class – indeed, by all the guilds and craftsmen, so that it's impossible to describe the grief, the packed churches, the sight of people weeping and praying. The night of the 19th to the 20th and 21st was the most critical. On the night of the 20th to the 21st he was already close to death, and if his personal valet and his assistant equerry, Baron Segesser, who were with him all the time, hadn't been present, we'd no longer have an elector. Others thought he was asleep, but these two men didn't wait for the doctor on duty to run and fetch his personal physician, but instead decided to seize the elector and shake him violently, bringing him round and causing him to vomit, producing nothing but matter from his mouth, throat and nose. Since then the situation has improved; but we're not yet out of danger:

God will stand by us! He's covered all over in pustules, but, thank God, they're benign; but he's in indescribable pain and the swelling has made him unrecognizable, while the whole of his back is sore from lying in bed. The electress is constantly at his side, apart from the few hours when she sleeps. Wotschitka was obliged to stay with the elector night and day and has now been struck down in turn, it's thought that he too will get smallpox. It's fortunate that the minister, Count *Berchem*,[5] didn't die before the elector's own eyes. He called

5. Maximilian Franz Joseph, Count Berchem (d. 1777), intendant general of the electoral court.

on the elector at a quarter to 3 on the 18th – then went home. Prince Zeil, Count Nogarola and Father Wigand dined with him, together with his wife and daughter and Lauretta Minuzzi. He tucked into the soup, and during the meat course he seized Prince Zeil's hand and said: God, I feel ill, collapsed in his arms and was dead. Father Wigand from Waldsassen pronounced general absolution as fast as he could: so far the elector knows nothing of his death but has simply been told that he's ill etc. –

My good friend, whom you already know, began his letter: *I'd have written to you long ago but I wanted to wait until our opera[6] had gone into rehearsal: so far, however, we've rehearsed only the first act, which is fairly easy and written in an extremely insipid style; at that point our prima donna, Madame Marggetti* – no doubt he means Marchetti – *fell so ill that she's still at death's door and they've written to Signora Flavis. I should add that in terms of his art and personality Herr Monza is exactly as you described him to me.* Here, then, you have the latest news from Munich. He also sent me his New Year greetings and 1000 good wishes to the two of you and asked me to let him know where you are and how things are going. – The verger at St Michael's and the town chaplain[7] have both suffered strokes, both were saved by prompt help, including bleeding etc.: but one wonders for how long. – It's just a stay of execution. They're both old, and the town chaplain likes his glass of wine. Who do you think has been made organist at Holy Trinity? – – Herr Haydn![8] Everyone finds it funny, he's an expensive appointment. He drinks a quart of wine after every litany and sends Lipp,[9] who's also a heavy drinker, to take the other services. – Herr Spitzeder is to teach keyboard to the choirboys until the matter has been properly decided. The players opened on St Stephen's Day[10] with a beautiful piece, *Sophie, or The*

6. *Attilio Regolo* by Carlo Monza (c. 1735–1801).
7. Leopold Lamprecht (d. 1780), who had baptized Mozart.
8. Michael Haydn.
9. Franz Ignaz Lipp (1718–98), third court organist from 1754; he was Michael Haydn's future father-in-law.
10. 26 December.

Just Prince.[11] The theatre was so full that more than 60 people had to be turned away, but it was so badly performed that yesterday – *Sunday* – there wasn't a living soul in the gallery and even the stalls were half empty. It'll look even worse today. Yesterday Nannerl had supper with Hagenauer as I was in the chapel. I collected her at a quarter to 11. Pimperl is still in the best of health, although she's in heat, although not too badly. She doesn't leave the house, and no dogs are allowed in. Herr Deibl[12] calls in every week to enquire after you and to give you his best wishes. We now kiss you a million times, the sheet is full. I am your old

Mzt

[*Postscript from Nannerl Mozart*]
Happy New Year to Mama and my dearest brother! Happiness and good health! I hope that Mama will soon return to us in good health and I hope that all is well with you, dear brother, wherever you are and that you're in good health. And I hope that for my own part I shall have the pleasure of seeing you again soon, but not in Salzburg. I send my best wishes to Mama as her obedient daughter and to my brother as his honest sister and friend. Katherl Gilowsky wishes you both a Happy New Year. We had our target-practice yesterday, Bullinger provided the prize, which the paymaster won. Mama will be providing the prize on New Year's Day. As cashier for us both, I'm still happy with our kitty. By the time that Mama gets back our losses won't be too bad. Forgive me for not writing more often or at greater length, but as you can see, Papa rarely leaves me even a small amount of space.

In Mannheim, Mozart became acquainted with the Weber family (see list). When, on 23 January 1778, Mozart travelled to Kirchheimbolanden, a day's travel from Mannheim, to play at the court of Princess Caroline

11. Drama by Heinrich Ferdinand Möller (1745–98).
12. Franz de Paula Deibl (?1698–1783), oboist.

of Nassau-Weilburg, he was accompanied by Fridolin Weber and one of his daughters, eighteen-year-old Aloysia. Mozart's mother remained in Mannheim.

70. Mozart to his mother, 31 January 1778, Worms

Dearest Madam, darling Mummy,
Spread the word round: butter's yummy.
Lift your hearts and praise the Lord
For giving us our just reward!
Still, our travels aren't so funny
'Cos we've got so little money.
But we're well: no sound of mucus
Or of head colds to rebuke us
For our lifestyle; though catarrh
Affects some other folk, so far
We both have managed to avoid it.
Gas builds up and others void it
Both before and after meals when they
Let rip with farts whose noise, I'd say,
Would wake the dead. But yesterday
The queen of farts was here to stay,
With farts as sweet as honey but
A voice as hoarse as any chestnut.
We've been away for seven nights
And in that time shat many shites.
Herr Wendling will be cross, his 4
Quartets[1] are not yet in full score.
But once I'm back across the Rhine
I'll knuckle down, step into line
And write his works, for I don't fancy
Being called an idle nancy.

1. Presumably these are the flute quartets commissioned by Ferdinand Dejean.

As for the concerto, this must wait till we
Reach Paris, where I'll toss it off as ea-
Sily as shitting. And yet, if I'm to tell
The truth, I'd rather roam the world than dwell
Upon the past with men I so condemn
That it now makes me sick to think of them.
And yet I have no choice, we've got to stick
Together, even though I'd rather lick
Herr Weber's arse than Herr Ramm's head. I'd say
A slice of it beats Wendling's any day.
Our shitting won't offend the Lord a bit,
Still less if we tuck in and eat our shit.
We're honest folk. Who tries to part us dies!
Between the 4 of us we've got 8 eyes,
Not counting those on which we sit. This verse
Must stop. I hope I shan't make matters worse
By saying that on Monday next I trust
I'll have the honour to embrace you. Just
Let me tell you, though, that by the time
I see you, I'll have shat my breeches. I'm

Worms, the 1778th January   Your loving child
in the year 31.   Both scurvy and wild
                                  Trazom

71. Mozart to his father, 4 February 1778, Mannheim

Monsieur
mon très cher Père,
   I couldn't possibly have waited till Saturday, as usual, as it's already too long since I last had the pleasure of writing to you. The first thing I have to tell you is how my good friends and I got on in Kirchheimbolanden. It was a holiday trip, no more. We left here at 8 o'clock on Friday morning after I'd had breakfast with Herr

Weber; we had an elegant four-seater covered coach: we arrived in Kirchheimbolanden at 4 o'clock and immediately had to send a note of our names to the castle. Early the next morning the concert master Herr Rothfischer[1] came to see us, he'd already been described to me in Mannheim as a thoroughly decent man, and so he turned out to be. In the evening we went to court – this was Saturday; Mlle Weber sang *3 arias*. I shall say nothing about her singing, except that it was excellent! – I told you all about her merits in my recent letter; but I can't end this letter without telling you more about her, now that I've got to know her properly and as a result can appreciate all her strengths. We had to dine afterwards at the officers' table. The next day we had to walk quite a long way to church, as the Catholic church is some distance off. This was Sunday. For lunch we were again placed on the officers' table. There was no concert that evening as it was Sunday. As a result they have *only 300* concerts a year. We could have dined at court in the evening, but we didn't want to, preferring to keep our own company at home. All of us would have been heartily glad to have done without the meals at court, as we never enjoyed ourselves as much as we did on our own, but we thought we should save some money – as it is, we've already had to pay enough.

The next day, Monday, there was another concert, with another on Tuesday and another on Wednesday; in all, Mlle Weber sang 13 times and played the keyboard twice as her playing's not at all bad. What amazes me most of all is that she can read music so well. Just imagine, she played my difficult sonatas[2] at sight, *slowly* but without any wrong notes. By my honour, I'd rather hear my sonatas played by her than by Vogler. In all, I played 12 times, and once by request on the organ in the Lutheran church, I also presented 4 symphonies[3] to the princess, for which I received only seven louis d'or in silver, while my poor dear Mlle Weber received five. I really hadn't expected this. I wasn't hoping for much, but I thought that we'd each receive

1. Paul Rothfischer (1746–85), violinist.
2. From K279–284.
3. Unidentified.

eight. *Basta*! At least we've lost nothing by it; I've still made a profit
of 42 florins and had the inexpressible pleasure of becoming acquainted
with some thoroughly honest, good Catholic, Christian people. I'm
only sorry that I didn't get to know them ages ago. But now
for something important, on which I'd be grateful for an immediate
reply.

Mama and I have discussed the matter and agree that we don't like
the life that the Wendlings lead.

Wendling is a thoroughly decent and very kind man, but unfortunately he has no religion, and the same is true of his whole household.
It's enough to say that his daughter was once someone's mistress. Ramm
is a decent soul but a freethinker. I know myself, I know that I have
enough religious convictions never to do anything that I wouldn't be
able to do openly before the whole world; but the very thought of
spending time – even if only on a journey – with people whose way of
thinking is so very different from my own – and from that of all honest
people – horrifies me. Of course, they can do what they want. But I
don't have the heart to travel with them, I'd be miserable all the time
and wouldn't know what to say. In a word, I've no real faith in them.
Friends who've no religious convictions don't last.

I've already given them advance warning of this. I said that 3
letters had arrived during my absence and that I could say only that
it was unlikely that I'd be going to Paris with them. Perhaps I'll go
there later. But perhaps I'll go somewhere else. They shouldn't rely
on me. My thinking is this:

I'll remain here and complete the music for Dejean at my convenience. I'll get my 200 florins. I can stay here as long as I want.
Neither board nor lodging is costing me anything. During this time
Herr Weber will do what he can to obtain engagements for me. We'll
then travel together. When I travel with him, it's just as if I were
travelling with you. The reason why I like him so much is that, apart
from his physical appearance, he's just like you and has your character
and way of thinking. If, as you know, my mother weren't too *lazy* to
write, she'd say the same. I must admit that I was happy to travel
with them. We were cheerful and had lots of fun. I heard someone
speaking as you do. I didn't have to worry about anything. If anything

was torn, I found that it had been mended; in a word, I was waited on like a prince.

I'm so fond of this put-upon family that I want nothing more than to make them happy; and perhaps I can do so. My advice is that they should go to Italy. And so I wanted to ask you to write to our good friend Lugiati,[4] the sooner the better, and enquire how much – and the maximum – they pay a *prima donna* in Verona. – The more the better, one can always come down – – perhaps one could also get the Ascensa[5] in Venice. As for her singing, I'll stake my life that she'll be a credit to me. She's already benefited from her short time with me and how much more will she benefit between now and then? – Nor am I worried about her acting. If anything comes of this, then we – Monsieur Weber, his 2 daughters[6] and I – shall have the honour of spending 2 weeks with my dear Papa and dear sister on our way there. My sister will find a friend and companion in Mlle Weber, as she is known for her good breeding, just as my sister is in Salzburg, her father's like mine and the whole family is like the Mozarts. Of course, there are people who envy her, as there are with us, but when it comes to the point, we simply have to speak the truth. Honesty is the best policy. I can say that there's nothing I look forward to more than coming to Salzburg with them, merely so that you can hear her. She sings superbly the arias I wrote for de Amicis – both the bravura aria and *Parto, m'affretto* and *Dalla sponda tenebrosa*.[7] Please do your utmost to ensure that we get to Italy. You know my greatest desire is to write operas.

I'd happily write an opera for Verona for 50 zecchini if only for her to make a name for herself; for if I don't write it, I'm afraid that she'll be sacrificed. Between now and then we'll travel together and I'll make so much money that it won't hurt me. I think we'll go to Switzerland, perhaps also to Holland. Just write soon. If we stay

4. Pietro Lugiati, who had befriended the Mozarts in Italy.
5. The theatrical high season around the feast of the Ascension.
6. Here Mozart refers also to Weber's eldest daughter, Josepha. There were four sisters in all.
7. Anna Lucia de Amicis; the arias are all from *Lucio Silla*; the bravura aria is 'Ah, se il crudel'.

anywhere for long, the other daughter, who's the oldest, will come in handy as she can also cook, so we can run our own household. By the way, you mustn't be too surprised that I've only 42 florins left out of 77. This was the result of sheer delight at finding myself once again in the company of honest like-minded people. I paid half, I couldn't do otherwise, but I shan't do so on our other journeys, I've already said that I'll pay only for *myself*. We stayed for 5 days in Worms. Weber has a brother-in-law here, namely, the dean of the monastery.[8] NB: He's afraid of Herr Weber's deadly pen. We had great fun there. We had lunch and supper at the dean's house every day. I must say that this brief journey provided me with regular exercise on the keyboard. The dean is an honest, upstanding and sensible man. It's now time to stop, if I were to write down everything that occurs to me, I'd have no paper left. Please reply soon; don't forget my wish to write operas. I'm envious of everyone who writes one. I could literally weep with frustration whenever I hear or see an aria. But Italian, not German, serious, not *buffa*. You shouldn't have sent me Heufeld's letter,[9] it caused me more annoyance than pleasure. The fool thinks I'll write a comic opera – that I'll just toss it off on the off chance and entirely at my own risk. I don't think he'd have disgraced his title if he referred to me as 'your esteemed son' rather than 'your son'. But he's just a Viennese buffoon; or does he think that people remain 12 years old for ever? I've now told you everything that's been weighing on my mind. My mother is entirely satisfied with my way of thinking. I can't possibly travel with people or with a man who leads a life that a child would be ashamed at; and the thought of helping a poor family without harming myself in the

8. Father Dagobert (Joseph Clemens Benedikt) Stamm (1724–?) was the brother of Maria Cäcilia Weber.

9. Franz von Heufeld, director of German plays in Vienna 1773–5, had written to Leopold from Vienna on 23 January 1778 to say that the emperor was not about to engage a composer in light of the fact that both Antonio Salieri (1750–1825) and Gluck were already in his service and that he did not approve of Leopold's idea to appeal directly to Joseph II; he recommended, instead, that Mozart compose a German opera and submit it to the court for consideration. Heufeld also declined to write a letter of recommendation to the queen of France. See Deutsch, *Documentary Biography*, 169–71.

process fills my whole soul with a warm glow of satisfaction; I kiss your hands 1000 times and remain unto death your most obedient son

Wolfgang Amadé Mozart.

Best wishes to all our good friends, especially to my best friend Herr Bullinger.

[Maria Anna Mozart's postscript]
My dear husband, you'll have seen from this letter that when Wolfgang makes new acquaintances, he immediately wants to sacrifice his life and possessions to such people, it's true that she sings incomparably well but one should never overlook one's own interests, I never liked him mixing with Wendling and Ramm, but I didn't dare to raise any objections and no one ever believed me anyway as soon as he got to know the Webers, he immediately changed his mind, in a word he prefers other people's company to mine, if I raise objections about things I don't like, he doesn't like it, so you'll have to decide for yourself what needs to be done, I really don't think it's advisable that he should go to Paris with Wendling, I'd rather accompany him there myself at some later date, it wouldn't cost much by mail coach, perhaps you'll receive a reply from Herr von Grimm, but in the meantime we're not losing anything by staying here I'm writing this in the greatest secrecy while he's eating and must hurry before he catches me. *Addio* I remain your faithful wife Marianna Mozart

72. Leopold Mozart to his son, 5 February 1778, Salzburg

My Dear Son,
   In all probability this will be the last letter that you can be certain of receiving from me in Mannheim, and so it is addressed to you alone. How hard it is for me to accept that you're moving even further away from me is something you may perhaps be able to imagine, but you cannot feel as acutely as I do the weight that lies

on my mind. If you take the trouble to recall what I did with you two children during your tender youth, you'll not accuse me of timidity but, like everyone else, will concede that I am a man and have always had the courage to risk everything. But I did everything with the greatest caution and consideration that were humanly possible: – one can't prevent accidents, for God alone can foretell the future. Until now, of course, we've been neither happy nor unhappy, but, thanks be to God, we've trodden a middle course. We've tried everything to make you happy and, through you, to make ourselves happier and at least to place your destiny on a firmer footing; but fate was against us. As you know, our last step has left me in very deep waters, and you also know that I'm now around 700 florins *in debt* and don't know how I shall *support myself, your mother and your sister* on my *monthly income*, for as long as I live I cannot *hope to receive another farthing* from *the prince*.[1] So it must be clear as day to you that the future fate of your old parents and of your sister, who undoubtedly loves you with all her heart, lies solely in your hands. Ever since you were born and, indeed, before that – in other words, ever since I was married – there is no doubt that I've had a difficult time *providing a livelihood* for a wife and 7 children,[2] 2 servants and Mama's mother, all on a fixed monthly income of only a little more than 20 florins, and to *pay for* accouchements, deaths and illnesses, expenses which, if you think them over, will convince you not only that I have never spent a farthing on the least pleasure for myself, but that, without God's special mercy, I'd never have managed to *keep out of debt* in spite of all my hopes and bitter efforts: yet this is *the first time I've been in debt*. I gave up every hour of my life to you 2 in the hope of ensuring not only that in due course you'd both be able to count on being able to provide for yourselves but that I too would be able to enjoy a peaceful old age and be accountable to God for my children's education, with no more cares but being able to live solely for my soul's salvation and calmly awaiting my end. But God has willed and ordained that I must once again take on the

1. Archbishop Colloredo.
2. Five died in infancy.

undoubtedly wearisome task of giving lessons and of doing so, more-over, in a town where these strenuous efforts are so badly paid that it is not possible every month *to earn enough to support oneself and one's family*. Yet one must be glad and talk oneself hoarse in order to *earn* at least *something*. Not only do I not distrust you, my dear Wolfgang, no, not in the very least, but I place all my trust and hope in your filial love: all depends on your good sense, which you certainly have – if only you will listen to it – and on fortunate circumstances. This latter cannot be coerced; but you will always consult your good sense – at least I hope so and beg of you to do so.

You're now entering a completely different world: and you mustn't think that it is simply prejudice that makes me see Paris as such a dangerous place, *au contraire* – from my own experience I've no reason at all to regard Paris as so very dangerous. But my situation then could not be more different from yours now. We stayed with an ambassador,[3] and on the second occasion in a self-contained apart-ment; I was a man of mature years and you were children; I avoided all contact with others and in particular *preferred not to become over-familiar with people of our own profession*; remember that I did the same in Italy. I made the acquaintance and sought out the friendship only of people of a higher social class – and among these only mature people, not young lads, not even if they were of the foremost rank. I never invited anyone to visit me regularly in my rooms in order to be able to maintain my freedom, and I always considered it more sensible to visit others at my convenience. If I don't like a person or if I'm working or have business to attend to, I can then stay away. – Conversely, if people come to me and behave badly, I don't know how to get rid of them, and even a person who is otherwise not unwelcome may prevent me from getting on with some important work. You're a young man of 22; and so you don't have that earnestness of old age that could deter a young lad of whatever social class, be he an adventurer, joker or fraud and be he young or old, from seeking out your acquaintance and friendship and drawing you into his company and then gradually into his plans. One is drawn

3. Count Maximilian van Eyck, the Bavarian ambassador in Paris.

imperceptibly into this and cannot then escape. I shan't even mention women, for here one needs the greatest restraint and reason, as nature herself is our enemy, and the man who does not apply his whole reason and show the necessary restraint will later do so in vain in his attempt to escape from the labyrinth, *a misfortune that mostly ends only in death.* You yourself may perhaps already have learnt from your limited experience how blindly we may often be taken in by jests, flatteries and jokes that initially seem unimportant but at which reason, when she awakes later on, is ashamed; I don't want to reproach you. I know that you love me not just as your father but also as your staunchest and surest friend; and that you know and realize that our happiness and misfortune and, indeed, my very life – whether I live to a ripe old age or die suddenly – are in your hands as much as God's. If I know you, I can hope for nothing but contentment, and this alone must console me during your absence, when I am deprived of a father's delight in hearing, seeing and embracing you. Live like a good Catholic, live and fear God, pray most fervently to Him in reverence and trust, and lead so Christian a life that, even if I am never to see you again, the hour of my death may be free from care. With all my heart I give you a father's blessing and remain until death[4] your faithful father and surest friend

Leopold Mozart

Here are our Paris acquaintances, all of whom will be delighted to see you. [. . .][5]

[Leopold's postscript to his wife on the envelope]
My Dear Wife,

As you'll receive this letter on the 11th or 12th and as I doubt whether a further letter will reach Wolfg. in Mannheim, I'll take my

---

4. At this point it had been decided that Mozart's mother would return to Salzburg and that Wolfgang would go on to Paris. Leopold therefore had reasonable expectations that he might not see Wolfgang again.
5. Leopold lists some twenty-five names including the writers Denis Diderot (1713–84), Voltaire and Madame d'Épinay (1726–83), the Duc de Chartres (1747–93) and other luminaries.

leave of him with this enclosure! I'm writing this with tears in my eyes. Nannerl kisses her dear brother Wolfg. a million times. She would have added a note to my letter and said goodbye, but the letter was already full and in any case I didn't let her read it. We ask Wolfg. *to take care of his health and to stick to the diet that he got used to at home*; otherwise he'll have *to be bled* as soon as he arrives in Paris, *everything spicy* is bad for him. I expect he'll take with him the big *Latin prayer book* that contains *all the psalms* for the full office of Our Lady. If he wants to have the *German* text of the office of Our Lady in Mannheim in order to have it in German too, he'll have to try to obtain the very smallest format as the Latin psalms are difficult to understand. It would be better if he also had them in German. Learned contrapuntal settings of the psalms are also performed at the Concert Spirituel;[6] it's possible to gain a great reputation in this way. Perhaps he could also have his *Misericordias*[7] performed there. The opera singers aren't coming but have gone instead to Straubing to entertain the Austrian officers. The prince has again forced the magistrature to hold 9 balls, the first one was yesterday and was attended by 30 persons; it lasted till half past one, but not a soul had arrived by half past 9 and it wasn't till 10 that they started dancing; 1 capon and 6 mugs of wine were consumed. I hope you received the 2 sonatas for 4 hands,[8] the Fischer variations[9] and the rondo,[10] which were all parcelled up in the same letter. – – The late Herr Adlgasser hasn't found a decent bellows blower in the afterlife; the cathedral's old bellows blower, the 80-year-old Thomas, has followed him into the next world. The main news is that Mme Barisani[11] has become incredibly jealous of her old and respectable husband as he and Checco[12] have on a handful of occasions been to perform at the home of handsome Herr

6. Founded in 1725, it was the longest-standing independent concert series in Paris.
7. K222.
8. K358, composed late 1773 or early 1774, and K381, composed in the summer or fall of 1772.
9. K179.
10. Possibly the last movement of the sonata K309.
11. Wife of Archbishop Colloredo's personal physician, Silvester Barisani.
12. Their son, Francesco.

Freysauff, who has a relatively pretty but witless wife. There was an incredible fuss. Farewell. We kiss you millions of times

Mzt

Everyone sends their best wishes, especially Herr Bullinger and the wife of the sergeant of the bodyguards, Herr *Clessin*, Waberl Mölk etc.

73. Leopold Mozart to his son, 12 February 1778, Salzburg

My Dear Son,

I've read through your letter of the 4th with bewilderment and shock. I'm starting to answer it today, the 11th, as I was unable to sleep all night and am now so tired that I can write only slowly, one word at a time, but must complete it by tomorrow. Thank God, I have been well until now: but this letter, in which I recognize my son only by his failing in believing the first thing people say to him, laying bare his unduly kind heart to flattery and smooth words, allowing himself to be swayed this way and that by all the ideas that are put to him, and on the strength of ideas and baseless, impracticable and ill-considered plans letting himself be misled into sacrificing his own reputation and interests and even the interests and assistance owed to his old and honest parents to the interests of strangers; this letter has left me all the more dismayed in that I was hoping, not unreasonably, that a number of the situations that you've already faced and my own reminders, both spoken and written, would have convinced you that both for the sake of your own happiness and in order to be able to advance in the world and finally achieve your desired goal among such different types of people, be they good or bad, happy or unhappy, you should have concealed your kind heart beneath a veil of the greatest reserve, undertaking nothing without the greatest deliberation and never allowing yourself to be carried away by enthusiastic imaginings and vague and blind fancies. I beg you, my dear son, read this letter carefully – take time to read it properly – merciful God, gone are those moments of contentment for me when, as child and boy, you never went to bed without standing on a chair and singing me the *oragna fiagata fà*,[1] often kissing me on the tip of my nose and telling me that when I grew old, you'd put me in a glass-fronted box and protect me from the air so that I'd always be with you and you could honour me. – Listen to me patiently then. You are fully aware of our problems in Salzb. – you know how hard it is for me to make ends meet and ultimately why I kept my promise to let you leave and all my troubles. There were 2 reasons for your journey: either to find a good and permanent post; or, if that were not to succeed, to go to some big city where you could earn lots of money. Both plans were intended to help your parents and your dear sister to survive but above all to bring you fame and honour in the world, something that was partly achieved in your childhood, partly in your years of boyhood, but it now depends on you alone to raise yourself gradually to a position of the greatest eminence that a musician has ever known: you owe this to the exceptional talent that you've received from our most merciful God; and it depends only on your intelligence and way of life whether you die as an ordinary musician forgotten by the whole world or as a famous Kapellmeister whom posterity will read about in books – whether, cowed by a woman, you perish on a bed of straw in a parlour full of starving children or whether, after a Christian life of contentment, honour and posthumous fame, you die respected by all the world, with your family well provided for. Your journey took you to Munich – you know the reason for it – there was nothing that could be done. Well-meaning friends wanted to keep you there – your wish was to remain there: it was suggested that you should form a company, I don't need to repeat all the details. At the time you thought the affair was manageable; – I did not think so – reread what I wrote on that occasion. You're not without honour. – – Would it have done you honour, even if the affair had succeeded, to have depended on 10 people and their monthly charity? You were then extraordinarily

1. Apparently this song was part of the child Mozart's bedtime ritual; it is reproduced in Georg Nikolaus Nissen, *Biographie W. A. Mozarts* (Leipzig, 1828), 35.

taken up with that little singer[2] at the theatre and wanted nothing more than to help the German theatre; now you declare that you don't even want to write a comic opera. No sooner had you left the gates of Munich behind you than, as I foretold, your entire company of friendly subscribers had forgotten you. – And what would have become of you in Munich? – – Ultimately we can see God's providence in all things. In Augsburg, too, you had your little fling and amused yourself with my brother's daughter, who then had to send you her portrait. The rest I wrote in my initial letters to Mannheim. In Wallerstein you amused them endlessly, taking up a violin, dancing around and playing so that you were described to absent colleagues as a merry, high-spirited fool, thereby giving Herr Beecke a chance to disparage your merits, merits which thanks to your compositions and your sister's playing these 2 gentlemen[3] have subsequently come to see in a different light, as she kept saying: *I'm only a pupil of my brother*, so that they now have the highest opinion of your art and have been very disparaging about Herr Beecke's inferior compositions. You did very well to ingratiate yourself with Herr *Cannabich* in Mannheim. But it would have borne no fruit if he himself had not been seeking a twofold advantage. I've already written to you about the rest. But now it was the turn of Herr *Cannabich's* daughter to be heaped with praises, with her character portrayed in the adagio of your sonata,[4] in short, she was now your favourite person. You then became acquainted with Herr *Wendling*, and it was now he who was your most honest friend, and I don't need to repeat what happened next. Suddenly I find you have a new acquaintance in Herr *Weber* and everyone else is forgotten; now it is this family that is the most upright and Christian family, and their daughter[5] is the main character in the tragedy to be played out between her family and yours, and in the giddiness into

2. Margarethe Kaiser, see letter 55.
3. The Wallerstein musicians Anton Janitsch (1753–1812), violinist, and Joseph Reicha (1746–95), violoncellist, had visited Leopold Mozart in Salzburg in January 1778, when they presumably gave Leopold this account of Mozart's visit to Wallerstein the previous autumn.
4. K309.
5. Aloysia.

which your kind and open heart has drawn you, you imagine that all your inadequately thought-through plans are as infallibly practicable as if they were the most natural thing in the world.

You're thinking of taking her to Italy as a *prima donna*. Tell me, do you know a *prima donna* who has trodden the boards in Italy without having first performed many times in Germany? How many operas did Signora *Bernasconi* sing in Vienna — operas filled with the most extreme emotions and performed under the most watchful eye and guidance of Gluck and Calzabigi![6] How many operas did *Mlle Teyber* sing in Vienna under Hasse's guidance — and after lessons from the old singer and exceptionally famous actress *Signora Tesi*,[7] whom you saw at Prince Hildburghausen's and whose blackamoor you kissed as a child![8] How many times did *Mlle Schindler*[9] appear on the Viennese stage after she had started her career in a private production on Baron Fries's[10] country estate under the guidance of Hasse and Tesi and Metastasio! − − Did all these people risk exposing themselves to the Italian public? − − And how much patronage and how many powerful recommendations did they need before they could achieve their goal? − − Princes and counts recommended them; famous composers and poets vouched for their skill. And you want me to write to Lugiati; you want to write an opera for 50 ducats even though you know that the people of Verona have no money and never commission a new opera. I'm now to give thought to the Ascensa, even though Michele dall'Agata hasn't even replied to my last 2 letters.[11] Granted that Mlle Weber sings like a Gabrielli;[12] that

---

6. Antonia Bernasconi, see letter 15, n. 8; the librettist Raniero de' Calzabigi (1714–95) was closely associated with Gluck.

7. Elisabeth Teyber was a member of a well-known family of musicians (see List); the actress Vittoria Tesi (1700–1775).

8. Prince Hildburghausen, see letter 1, n. 13; nothing else is known of this incident.

9. It is unclear which of two singers Leopold refers to here: Anna Maria Elisabeth Schindler (1757–79) or Katharina Schindler (1753–88).

10. Baron Johann von Fries (1719–85), banker active at the Salzburg court.

11. Michele dall'Agata was an impresario in Venice. Leopold had negotiated an opera contract for Wolfgang with him in 1771. For reasons that are unknown, the opera was never composed.

12. See letter 24, n. 4.

she has a *powerful enough voice* for the Italian theatres etc.; and that she looks like a *prima donna* etc. – but it's absurd for you to vouch for her acting. There's more to it than that; and old Hasse's childish efforts, for all that they were well meant and motivated by a friendly love of humanity, ensured that Miss Davies[13] was banished for ever from the Italian stage as she was booed on the first night and her part given to de Amicis. Not just women but even men with stage experi- ence quake at the thought of their first appearance in a foreign country. And do you think that's all? – – By no means – *ci vuole il Posesso del Teatro*[14] even in the case of a woman, and this applies to her dress, hairstyle, make-up etc.: but you know this yourself if only you'll think about it – I know that a moment's serious consideration will convince you that your idea, however well meant, needs *time* and *considerable preparation* and that a completely different course is necessary if this plan is to be carried out in the longer term. What impresario wouldn't laugh if one were to recommend a girl of 16 or 17 who has never appeared on stage? – – Your suggestion – I can hardly write when I think about it – the suggestion that you should travel around with Herr *Weber* and, be it noted, his 2 daughters almost robbed me of my wits. My dearest son! How can you allow yourself even for a moment to be taken in by such an appalling idea? Your letter reads just like a novel. – – Could you really bring yourself to travel the world with strangers? To cast aside your reputation – your old parents, your dear sister? – To expose me to the mockery and ridicule of the prince and of *the whole town that loves you*? – Yes, to expose me to mockery and yourself to contempt as I've been obliged to tell everyone who asked me that you'll be going to Paris; and finally you now want to set out at random with total strangers? No, it surely requires little forethought to put this idea from your mind. – In order that I may convince the two of you that you're being overhasty, let me tell you that the time is now approaching when no one in his right mind could consider such a move. The situation is such that it is impossible to know where war may break

13. Cecilia Davies.
14. 'one must have stage presence'.

out as whole regiments are everywhere on the march or waiting in readiness.[15] – In Switzerland? – In Holland? – – But there's not a soul there all summer; and in winter one can just about make enough in *Berne* and *Zurich* not to die of hunger, but there's nothing anywhere else. And Holland now has other things to think about, apart from music, while Herr *Hummel*[16] and your concert expenses will eat up half your income. And what will become of your reputation? – This is a matter for lesser lights, for second-rate composers, for scribblers, for a *Schwindl*, a *Zappa*, a *Ricci* etc.[17] Just name another great composer who'd deign to take such an abject step? – – *Be off with you to Paris!* And soon! Mix with great people – *aut Caesar aut nihil.*[18] – the mere idea of seeing Paris should have kept you from all these flighty ideas. *From Paris the fame and reputation of a man of great talent spread to the rest of the world, there the nobility treats people of genius with the greatest deference, respect and courtesy – there you'll find an attractive lifestyle in remarkable contrast to the coarseness of our German courtiers and ladies, and you'll become proficient in the French language.* As for the company of *Wendling* etc., you simply have no need of it. You've known them for a very long time, and didn't your mother realize? Were you both blind? – No, I know what must have happened, you were taken in by them and she didn't dare oppose you. I'm angry that you both lack the trust and honesty necessary to tell me these things candidly and in detail; it was exactly the same with the elector, although it was all bound to come out in the end. You wanted to spare me the annoyance, but in the end you've lumbered me with a whole pile of worries that have almost cost me my life. You know – and you have 1000 proofs of it – that God in His goodness has endowed me with sound common sense, that my

15. This presumably refers to the growing crisis over the Bavarian succession, which led to war between Austria and Prussia (July 1778–September 1779).
16. Johann Julius Hummel (1728–98), publisher, had published the first editions of Mozart's keyboard variations K24 and 25 and the accompanied sonatas K26–31 in 1766.
17. Friedrich Schwindl (1737–86), violinist and composer; Francesco Zappa (*fl.* 1763–88), Milanese violoncellist and composer; Francesco Pasquale Ricci (1732–1817). The Mozarts had met Schwindl in Brussels in 1763 and Ricci in The Hague in 1765 or 1766.
18. 'either Caesar or nothing'; i.e. all or nothing.

head is firmly screwed on and that I've often found a way out of the most confused situations, predicting and guessing a whole host of eventualities: what stopped you from asking for my advice and from always acting according to my wishes? My son, you should see me as your most honest friend rather than as a stern father. – Consider whether I have always treated you as a friend and served you as a servant serves his master, providing you with all possible support and helping you to enjoy all manner of honest and respectable pleasures, often at great inconvenience to myself. – – Presumably Herr *Wendling* will already have left! Although half dead, I've already managed to plan and arrange everything relating to your journey to Paris. Herr Arbauer, a well-known businessman from Augsburg and Frankfurt, is now with his German agent in Paris and will be remaining there throughout Lent, a letter will go off to him on the 23rd and on the same day I'll send you detailed instructions on what you must do and approximately how much the journey may cost, and I'll enclose an open letter that you must hand over on your arrival, as Herr Arbauer – who, I believe, was at your concert in Augsburg – will already have received news of your arrival. This beastly business has cost me more than one sleepless night. As soon as you receive this letter, I want you to write and tell me *how much money you have in hand*. I hope you can count for certain on the 200 florins. I was astonished when you wrote to say that you now plan to finish off the music for Monsieur Dejean at your convenience. – Haven't you handed it over yet? And you were thinking of leaving on 15 Feb.? – And yet you went off on that jaunt to Kirchheim – and took Mlle *Weber* with you, so that you received less as the princess had 2 people to reward, a gift you'd otherwise have had just for yourself. It doesn't matter – but, really, what if Herr *Wendling* were now to play a trick on you and Monsieur Dejean *were not to keep his word* as the whole idea was for you to wait and travel with them. Send me news by return so that I know how things stand. I now intend to tell you what you can do for *Mlle Weber*. Tell me, who are the people who give Italian lessons, – aren't some of them old *maestri*, but mostly *old tenors*? Has Sgr Raaff heard *Mlle Weber* sing? Talk to him and ask him to hear her sing your arias; *by way of an excuse you can say that you want him to hear some arias of your own composition*. In this way you can do your best for her, then speak to him alone privately afterwards. No matter how he may sing, he knows what he's talking about – and if she can win him over, she'll have won over all the impresarios in Italy who knew him as a great singer. Meanwhile she should find an opportunity to appear onstage in Mannheim: even if she's not paid, it would be of use to her. That you take pleasure in helping the downtrodden is something you've inherited from your father: but above all you must think single-mindedly of the welfare of your parents, otherwise your soul will go to hell.

Remember me as you saw me when you left us, *standing wretchedly beside your carriage*; remember, too, that, although a sick man, I'd been up till 2 o'clock, doing your packing, and was at your carriage again at 6, seeing to everything for you – afflict me now if you can be so cruel! Win fame and *fortune* in Paris, then, *once you have some money*, you can go to Italy and receive invitations to write operas; it will be hard to achieve this by writing letters to impresarios, although I shall keep trying; then you can recommend Mlle *Weber*: one can do more in person! Write by the next post without fail. We kiss you both millions of times. I am your old and honest father and husband

Mzt

Herr Bullinger sends his best wishes.

Nannerl has wept her full share these last 2 days.

[*On the envelope*]
We're in a state of real confusion here, the whole chapter met at court last Monday. There was amazing criticism of the prince[19] and a terrible row so that he's no longer keeping an open table. But that's the least of it. Vienna has informed the prince and chapter in Passau that on his death everything will move to Austria and a bishop will be appointed in Linz.[20] A start will then be made on improving the

19. Archbishop Colloredo.
20. This was part of Joseph II's ongoing efforts to take over church property in Austria; he put his plan into effect in 1783 on the death of the ruling prince-bishop of Passau, Cardinal Leopold Ernst von Firmian.

fortifications of the castle at *Oberhaus* and securing Passau. The archbishop already has worries of his own, regiments are on their way here from Italy and it's feared that some will remain here. No money can be expected from the salt, so how will people be paid?[21] Perhaps we'll see you sooner than expected, everything's in a state of confusion. We'll then travel to Italy together.

Addio.

Mama will go to Paris with Wolfg. so that you can arrange things properly.

74. Leopold Mozart to his wife and son, 16 February 1778, Salzburg

My Dear Wife and Son,

Your letter of 7 Feb., enclosing the French aria,[1] has arrived safely, just as you will have received my letter of the 12th, which was written in fear and anguish. I began a letter yesterday but I'm unable to finish it today: I'll save it for another post day. The enclosed aria has allowed me to breathe a little more easily as it has again enabled me to see something by my dear Wolfgang, and something so excellent, moreover, that it convinced me that you must have been much put upon to prefer a dissolute existence to the fame that can be won in so famous and, to men of talent, so advantageous a city.

Everyone is right to say that people will like your works in Paris: and you yourself are convinced – as I am – that you're capable of imitating all the different types of composition. That you didn't travel with the company in question was undoubtedly a good thing: you long ago saw *the evil nature of these people* yet all the time that you were pursuing their *acquaintance* you didn't trust your father, who cares so much about you, and didn't write to him to ask him for his

21. The archdiocese of Salzburg received considerable income from local salt mines.
1. K307 ('Oiseaux, si tous les ans') or K308 ('Dans un bois solitaire'); both songs were composed in Mannheim between the end of October 1777 and early March 1778.

advice: and – shockingly – your mother didn't do so either. My son! You're hot-headed and overhasty in everything you do! Your whole character has changed since your childhood and your years of boyhood. As a child and boy you were more serious than childish and whenever you sat at the keyboard or were otherwise occupied with music, no one was allowed to play even the slightest joke on you. Yes, the expression on your face was so serious that on seeing your premature talent and your grave and pensive expression many perceptive people in various countries were concerned that you wouldn't reach a ripe old age. But it seems to me now that you are much too ready to respond to the first challenge by adopting a jocular tone – and this is the first step towards familiarity etc., a quality that no one should seek to acquire in this world if he wants to maintain his self-respect. If one has a kind heart, one is of course used to expressing oneself freely and naturally: but that is misguided. And it is very much your kind heart that blinds you to the failings of a person who praises you valiantly, holds you in high regard and lauds you to the skies, so that you offer that person all your trust and love: as a boy, by contrast, you were exaggeratedly modest and even burst into tears when people praised you too much. The greatest art is *to know oneself* and then, my dear son, do as I do and *apply yourself to getting to know other people properly*. You know that that was always my concern, and there is no doubt that it is a fine, useful and, indeed, necessary concern. As for *giving lessons* in Paris, you don't need to worry about that. *First*, no one will dismiss his teacher at once and call on you instead. *Second*, no one would dare to do so, and you yourself would not take on anyone, except perhaps a lady *who already plays well and who wants to learn how to play with style* – that sort of work would be well paid: after all, wouldn't you have gladly given Countess Lützow and Countess Lodron[2] 2 or 3 lessons a week for 2 or 3 louis d'or a month, not least because these ladies are also making every effort to find subscribers for your works? In Paris, the

2. Two important figures in Salzburg society. Antonie, Countess Lützow (née Czernin, 1750–1801) was a niece of Archbishop Colloredo and the wife of Major General Johann Nepomuk, Count Lützow (1742–1822); Mozart composed the piano concerto K242 for her. For Antonia Maria, Countess Lodron (née Arco), see List.

ladies do everything – they're also great keyboard lovers, and many of them are excellent players. – These are the people for you: and these, too, are the works for them, as you can make your fame and fortune by publishing *keyboard works*, *string quartets* etc., *symphonies*, not to mention a collection of good *French* arias with *keyboard* accompaniment, like the one you sent me, and, finally, operas. – How can you possibly object to that? – – But you want everything to be done at once, even before people have seen you or heard anything of yours. Read the long list of acquaintances we had in Paris – all of them – or at least most of them – are the leading people in the city, all of them will want to see you again: and even if only 6 of them were to champion your cause (and a single one would be enough), you can do whatever you like. I'll arrange for the arias Mlle Weber asked for[3] to be copied and I'll send you whatever I can find, but if they go by *mail coach*, they won't reach you before the 23rd at the earliest. I'm enclosing two open letters of recommendation that you must keep safely and then give *to Herr Joseph Felix Arbauer*, one of the *leading* dealers in fancy goods *in Paris*. Monsieur Mayer is his agent. Count Wolfegg[4] used to live there. I'm sending an official letter today to Paris, it will contain all the details about accommodation etc., these letters are simply to explain that you are the people for whom these arrangements have been made. I must close. Nannerl and I kiss you 1,000,000 times. I am your faithful husband and father

Mzt

Martin Grassl, Prince Breuner's valet, was buried today, Wolfg. will recall writing a *little horn piece*[5] for him. War upon war! No more formal dinners at court! 2 windowsills were stolen from the new building in the archbishop's garden outside the town, and a lot of damage was caused during the night.

3. In Mozart's letter of 7 February 1778; according to *Briefe* v. 488, these were 'Alla selva, al prato', 'Aer tranquillo', 'Barbaro, oh Dio?' and 'L'amerò, sarò costante' from *Il re pastore*.
4. Anton Willibald, Count Waldburg zu Wolfegg und Waldersee.
5. K33h (lost).

[*On the envelope*]

At Hellbrunn[6] a tame stag that used to take bread from people's hands and that the prince was very fond of was killed during the night and its body dragged away. There were 200 people at yesterday's ball, last Wednesday there were only 36. The prince still hasn't attended. We've not the slightest reason to think of a ball. Everyone sends their best wishes: Herr Deibl, who asks after you every Sunday, Cat. Gilowsky, Herr Bullinger, Sallerl etc. etc. I'll tell you everything else about Paris in my next letter.

75. Mozart to his father, 19 February 1778, Mannheim

Monsieur mon très cher Père,

  I hope you'll have received my last 2 letters: in the second I expressed my concerns about my mother's return home, but I now see from your letter of the 12th that this was entirely unnecessary. I always assumed that you'd disapprove of my travelling with the Webers and never had any such thought in mind *in our present situation* – that goes without saying; but I gave them my word that I'd write to you. Herr Weber doesn't know how things stand with us; I'll certainly not tell anyone; wishing only that I was in a position of not having to think of others and that we were all well off, I forgot, in the intoxication of the moment, the present impossibility of the matter and failed, therefore, to tell you what I'd done. The reasons why I've not gone to Paris will be sufficiently clear from my last two letters. If my mother hadn't started on about it, I'd certainly have gone with them; but when I realized that she didn't like the idea, I didn't like it any more either; for as soon as people don't trust me, I don't trust myself any longer. The days when, standing on a chair, I sang the *oragna fiagata fà* and at the end kissed the tip of your nose are past, of course, but does this mean that my respect, love and obedience towards you have decreased? – – I'll say no more. As for your

6. The archbishop's summer residence, south of Salzburg.

reproach about the little singer in Munich, I must confess that I was a fool to tell you such a barefaced lie. After all, she simply doesn't know what *singing* means. It's true that for a person who's been studying music for only 3 months she sang extremely well; and she also had a very pleasing, pure voice. The reason why I praised her so much was no doubt because from morning till night I never stopped hearing other people saying that there was no better singer in the whole of Europe and that until you'd heard her, you'd heard nothing; I didn't dare contradict them, partly because I wanted to be good friends with them, partly because I'd come straight from Salzburg, where we've been taught not to contradict. But as soon as I was on my own, I couldn't help laughing out loud, why didn't I also laugh in my letter to you? – I don't know.

Your caustic comments on the fun that I had with your brother's daughter I find deeply offensive; but since things are not like that, I feel under no obligation to reply. As for Wallerstein, I simply don't know what to say; I was very reserved and serious at Beecke's; and at the officers' table, too, I maintained a true air of authority and spoke to no one. But let's forget all this, you wrote it only in the first flush of anger.

All that you say about Mlle Weber is true; and even while I was writing it, I knew as well as you that she's still too young and needs to learn how to act and must first appear on stage, but with some people one must often proceed by degrees. These good people are as tired of being here as – you know *who* and *where*.[1] At the same time they think that everything is possible. I promised them that I'd tell my father everything, but even while the letter was on its way to Salzburg I kept telling them that she just needs to be a bit more patient, she's still a bit too young etc. They accept whatever I say as they think very highly of me. At my suggestion, her father has invited Madame Toscani – the actress – to give his daughter acting lessons. Everything you say about Mlle Weber is true, except one thing, namely, that she sings like a Gabrielli, as I wouldn't like it at all if she sang like that. Everyone who's heard Gabrielli will say that she's

1. Here Mozart obliquely refers to his own family's situation in Salzburg.

capable only of singing passagework and roulades; and she earned admiration by performing these in a very particular way, but people stopped admiring her after they'd heard it 4 times. In the longer term they got no pleasure from it as one soon grows tired of passagework; and she had the misfortune of not being able to sing. She was unable to sustain a breve *properly*, she had no *messa di voce*, she couldn't hold a note, in a word, she sang with art but no understanding. But this singer goes to the heart, and she enjoys singing cantabile most of all. I introduced her to passagework only through the *great aria*[2] as she'll need to sing bravura arias if she goes to Italy. She'll certainly never forget cantabile singing as this is her natural inclination. When asked his honest opinion, Raaff – who's not given to flattery – said she sang not like a pupil but like a teacher. So now you know everything. I commend her to you with all my heart; and please don't forget the arias, cadenzas etc. Farewell. I kiss your hands 100,000 times and remain your most obedient son

Wolfgang Amadé Mozart

I'm too hungry to write any more.

My mother will open up our large cashbox for you. I embrace my sister with all my heart, she mustn't cry at every shitty misfortune, otherwise I'll never come back as long as I live. Best wishes to all our good friends, especially Herr Bullinger.

[*Maria Anna Mozart's postscript*]
My dear husband, I hope this letter finds you in good health again and we're both sincerely sorry our last letter came as such a shock to you, conversely your last letter of the 12th upset us greatly, I beg you by all that's dear to you not to take everything so much to heart, it's bad for your health. Everything can be put to rights again, and nothing will have been lost but bad company. We'll do the best we can to make arrangements for our journey to Paris, our money amounts in total to 140 florins, we'll try to sell the carriage, but I don't think we'll get much more than 60 or 70 florins for it – only

2. Presumably 'Ah, se il crudel' from *Lucio Silla*.

recently a beautiful four-seater carriage with glass was bought for 9 louis d'or – we'll pack all our things into 2 trunks and travel to Paris by mail coach, which won't be all that expensive, decent folk travel that way, but we should have lodgings, so that we shan't need to stay at an inn for long, if the businessman you mentioned would do us this favour and help us, that would be most kind of him. Meanwhile I await your next letter with impatience, so that we can organize what you think needs to be done. *Addio*, farewell, both of you, I kiss you many 10,000 times and remain your faithful wife

Maria Anna Mozart

All conceivable good wishes to all our good friends. This is a terrible pen, and the ink's no better.

76. Leopold Mozart to his son, 23 February 1778, Salzburg

Mon très cher Fils,

Just so that you can convince me good and proper that you're absent-minded and inattentive in everything, you say at the start of your letter of the *14th* that you see from my letter of the 9th that I've not yet received your last 2 letters, in other words, you're claiming that by the 9th I'd already answered your fanciful and near-fatal letter of the 5th, even though you must know from my extended correspondence with you in Mannheim that a letter takes around 6 days and even though I've already told you that your own letters always arrive on a *Tuesday* or *Friday*, so you can't receive a reply to them in under a fortnight. It wouldn't be worth my while to spell this out if it weren't by way of information, *as such an observation is extremely useful for travellers*. I know very well when you'll receive my letters: and I've also been at pains to ensure that you receive everything in good time. – But what's the use of my meticulousness, care, consideration and a father's efforts applied to so important and necessary an undertaking when – faced by an apparently serious obstacle that your Mama may have seen long ago – you fail to place any real trust in your father and change your mind only when caught between two fires and can go neither forwards nor backwards. Just when I think that things are on a better footing and proceeding smoothly, some new idea, as unpredictable as it is foolish, occurs to you or else it turns out that the situation is different from what you'd reported it was. Have I again guessed aright? – So you've received only 96 florins instead of 200?[1] – – And why? – – Because you completed only 2 concertos and 3 quartets.[2] – How many were you supposed to write for him as he paid you only half? – – Why did you tell me *a lie* and say that you were to write only 3 short and easy concertos and a couple of quartets: why didn't you listen to me when I *explicitly* wrote to say that *you should deal with this gentleman's request as a matter of the utmost priority?* Why? So that you'd be sure of getting these 200 florins, because I know people better than you. – Haven't I already guessed everything? It seems that, even though I'm some distance away, I can still see more and judge things better than you, for all that these people are under your very nose. You shouldn't doubt me when I mistrust people but should proceed with all the caution that I always enjoin on you. Much to our detriment, you've learnt this lesson within a short space of time. Admittedly, you've already come to an agreement with Herr Wendling, you'll still be paid and you'll forward the works in due course. Indeed – if Herr Wendling can persuade lovers of the flute in Paris to buy what you've already supplied, he'll try to get some more. One person has to pay; the other takes advantage of it. You also wrote to me about a few pupils and in particular said that the Dutch officer would pay you 3 or even – you thought – 4 ducats for 12 lessons: but it now turns out that you could have had these pupils but that you've abandoned them simply because they missed the odd lesson. You prefer to give lessons as a favour – yes, that's what you want! And

1. From Ferdinand Dejean.
2. In fact, Mozart completed only two quartets, K285 and K285b (the authenticity of the flute quartet K285a is not certain and K298, usually associated with Dejean's commission, probably dates from 1786 or 1787) and one concerto, K313. The arrangement for flute of the oboe concerto K314 is possibly not by Mozart; if it is, however, it may have been intended for Dejean as well.

you'd rather leave your old father in need. The effort is too much for a young man like you, no matter how good the pay, it's more fitting that your 58-year-old father should run around for a pittance so that by the sweat of his brow he can earn what he needs to support himself and his daughter and, *instead of paying off his debts*, support you with what little is left, while you amuse yourself by giving a young girl lessons for nothing. My son, give it some thought and try to be reasonable! Just think whether you're not treating me more cruelly than our prince. I never expected anything from him. – From you I expect everything – from him I must accept everything as a favour – from you I may hope to receive it on the strength of your duty as a child. He is ultimately a stranger to me – but you are my son – you know what I've put up with for more than 5 years – what a burden of care I've taken on because of you. The prince's behaviour could only humiliate me; but you can annihilate me: he could only make me ill; but you can kill me. If I didn't have your sister and Herr Bullinger, this true friend of ours, I would probably not be able to write this letter, on which I have already been working for 2 days. I have to hide my fear from the whole world, these are the only 2 people who are allowed to know everything and who are a comfort to me. I believed that everything you wrote was true, and since everyone here is sincerely glad when all goes well with you and since they are always asking about you, I was happy to give them a *detailed* account of the money that you were making and of the journey you were taking to Paris; you know that people take pleasure in *annoying the archbishop*, and there were plenty who used this account to that end. Old Herr *Hagenauer* was very upset to hear that you had to draw 150 florins in Mannheim as these people want us to do well and earn some money. But when I told him what you'd written and explained that your board and lodging was costing you nothing and that you'd be receiving 200 florins and that you also had some pupils, he was very pleased. I naturally had to ask him to be patient over payment of the 150 florins, but he replied: It doesn't matter. *I've every confidence in Herr Wolfgang, he'll do his duty to you as a son, just let him go to Paris, while you relax.* Just consider these words and our present circumstances, and tell me whether I shan't suffer a stroke because as an honest man I can't leave you in this situation, no matter what it may cost. You can be assured that not a soul knows that we transferred 150 florins to Mannheim as the Hagenauers would never in a million years give the *archbishop* that pleasure: but how upset these friends will be if I again have to support you in order for you to go to Paris. But let me prove to you that this must remain your only firm decision. It's simply not possible to think in terms of travelling around, especially in the present critical situation: it's often impossible even to recover one's travelling expenses; you invariably have to go cap in hand, looking for patrons, simply to ensure that the concert pays its way; you must always go looking for new letters of recommendation to take from one place to the next; you always have to beg for permission to give a concert and have to deal with a hundred eventualities of an often trivial nature; and ultimately you scarcely earn enough to pay the landlord, so that you have to fall back on your own money – assuming you have any – to pay for the journey or else you have to pawn or sell your clothes, watches and rings. I've already experienced the former for myself. I had to borrow 100 florins from Herr *Olenschlager* in Frankfurt, and as soon as I arrived in Paris I had to borrow another 300 florins *from Tourton & Baur*, although in the event, of course, I didn't need it all as we were soon paying our way: but first we had to become better known and deliver our letters of recommendation etc.: and in a large city that took time as it's not always possible to meet people or speak to them. My dear Wolfg., all your letters convince me that you invariably accept the first wild idea that comes into your head or that someone else puts there, and you do so, moreover, without considering it or analysing it properly. For example, you write: I'm a composer and *mustn't bury* my talent for composition etc. etc. But who says you should do so? – Yet that's precisely what you'd be doing if you roamed around like a gypsy. If you want to become universally known as a composer you need to be in Paris, Vienna or Italy. You're now nearest to Paris. The only question is where do I have a better hope of achieving prominence? *In Italy* – where in *Naples alone* there must be at least 300 *maestri* and where, throughout Italy, the *maestri* often have a *scrittura* 2 years in advance from those theatres that pay well? Or in Paris, where there are 2 or 3 writing for the theatre and other composers can be counted on the fingers of one hand? The keyboard must bring you your first contacts and make you popular with the great, then you can have something engraved by subscription, which brings in a little more than writing 6 quartets for an Italian gentleman,[3] for which you may get a few ducats or even a snuffbox worth 3 ducats. It's even better in Vienna, there at least you can arrange a subscription for music in manuscript form.[4] Both you and others have had experience of this. In short, if I could teach you to be more mature and to adopt a more considered approach to these wild ideas of yours, I'd make you the happiest man in the world. But I can see that these things take time – and yet, where your talent is concerned, everything came before its time. Everything about the sciences you've always grasped with the greatest ease. Why shouldn't it be possible to get to know people? – To guess their intentions? – To close one's heart to the world? – And in every case to think things over and in particular not always alight on the good side of a question or the side that flatters me or my secondary aims? Why shouldn't I apply my reason to examining the bad side and looking into all eventualities and all the consequences – and ultimately think of my own interests and show the world that I am capable of *insight and reason*? Or do you think it does me more honour to regard myself as a fool and let others influence me in ways that are of benefit to them but of harm to me, allowing them to laugh up their sleeves and regard you as young and inexperienced and easily led. My dear son, *God has given you excellent judgement*, which – it seems to me – *only 2 things* are stopping you from properly applying. I've taught you how to use it and how to know your fellow humans. When I used to be able to guess what would happen and could predict much of what came to

3. Possibly this is a reference to the quartets K155–160, composed in Italy in 1772 or 1773; it is not known, however, whether these were written on commission for an Italian patron.
4. There was to all intents and purposes no music publishing in Vienna at this time; the majority of music was distributed in handwritten copies, by music dealers or on private subscription. During the 1780s, Mozart twice tried to sell his works by private subscription; see letters 109, 131, the commentary preceding letter 163 and letter 174.

pass, you'd often say by way of a joke: *Papa is second only to God.* What do you think these two things are? – Examine yourself, learn to know yourself, my dear Wolfg.: – you'll find that you have too much *pride* and *self-love*; and that you immediately become over-*familiar* and open your heart to everyone, in short, in wanting to be unconstrained and natural you become too open. The first of these should of course drive out the second, for those who are motivated by pride and self-love do not easily stoop to familiarity. But your own pride and self-love are wounded only when you're not shown the appreciation that is your due: even people who don't yet know you should be able to see from your face that you're a man of genius. But to sycophants who bend you to their self-interested will and praise you to the skies you open your heart with the greatest ease and believe them as readily as the Gospel. And, *naturally, you're taken in*, as they *don't even need to pretend* as *their praise costs them little*; they don't say anything that's untrue and that they'd have to force themselves to admit; *only their intentions remain hidden from you*, intentions which must – and could – show you their ulterior motives. And in order to ensnare you all the more effectively, *women* become involved – if you don't resist them, you'll be unhappy for the rest of your life. Think of all that has happened to you in your short life – think it over in cold blood, with sound common sense – and you'll see that I'm speaking to you now not just as a father but as your true friend. For however delightful and dear to my heart the name of *son* may be, the name of *father* is often hateful to children. But I don't believe that this is true of you, even though a woman in Vienna once said to you: *If only you didn't have a father.* These words should have filled you with disgust. Please don't think that I mistrust your love as a child; everything I say is intended simply to make a decent man of you. Millions of people have not received the great favour that God has granted you. What a responsibility! And what a lasting shame it would be if so great a genius were to be diverted from his course! – But this can happen in a moment! – You're exposed to more dangers than the million people who have no talent as you're exposed to infinitely more persecutions on the one hand and temptations on the other.

Mama will go with you to Paris, you must confide in her in all things in person and confide in me by writing. I'll explain everything in my next letter, including all the addresses and letters to *Diderot*, *D'Alembert*[5] etc. You'll also receive a breakdown of your travelling expenses and other calculations relating to board and the cost of engraving music. I must close. Nannerl and I kiss you many thousands of times. I am

Mzt

Everyone sends their best wishes, especially Herr Bullinger.

By the next post I expect to hear how much money you have. By then the chaise will have been sold.

77. Mozart to his father, 24 March 1778, Paris

Mon très cher Père,

Praise and thanks be to God, we arrived here safe and sound yesterday, Monday the 23rd, at around 4 in the afternoon; in other words, we were 9½ days on the road. We never thought we'd survive. Never in my whole life have I been so bored. You can easily imagine what it was like for us to leave Mannheim and so many dear, kind friends and then to have to spend nine and a half days not only without these good friends but without human company, without a single soul with whom we could associate or speak. But, all praise and thanks to God, we've now reached our destination. I hope that with God's help all will go well. Today we'll take a cab and call on Grimm and Wendling. Tomorrow morning, however, I'll be calling on the minister of the Palatinate, Herr von Sickingen, a great connoisseur and passionate lover of music, for whom I have 2 letters from Herr von Gemmingen[1] and Monsieur Cannabich. Before leaving

5. Jean d'Alembert (1717–83), mathematician and writer.
1. Karl Heinrich Joseph, Count Sickingen zu Sickingen, Palatine ambassador at Paris 1777–91; Baron Otto von Gemmingen-Hornburg (1755–1836), diplomat and author at Mannheim.

Mannheim I had copies made of the quartet that I wrote that evening at the inn at *Lodi* and of the quintet and Fischer variations and gave them to Herr von Gemmingen.[2] He then wrote me a particularly courteous note, expressing his pleasure at the memento that I'd left him and sending me a letter for his very good friend, Herr von Sickingen, with the words: I am sure that you will be a greater recommendation for this letter than this letter can be for you. And in order to defray the copyist's expenses he sent me 3 louis d'or. He assured me of his friendship and asked me for mine. I must say that all the courtiers who got to know me, as well as the privy councillors, chamberlains, other worthy people and the entire court orchestra were very reluctant and sorry to see me go. There's no doubt about that. We left on Saturday the 14th, and the previous Thursday afternoon there'd been another concert at Cannabich's, when my concerto for 3 keyboards[3] was played. Mlle Rosa Cannabich played the first, Mlle Weber the second and Mlle Pierron Serrarius,[4] our house nymph, the third. We had 3 rehearsals, and it all went very well. Mlle Weber sang 2 of my arias, the Aer tranquillo from *Il re pastore* and the new one, 'Non sò d'onde viene'.[5] With this second one, my dear Fräulein Weber did both herself and me indescribable honour. They all said that they'd never been as moved by an aria as by this one; but she sang it as it's supposed to be sung. As soon as the aria was over, Cannabich exclaimed: *Bravo, bravissimo maestro. Veramente scritta da maestro.*[6] It was the first time I'd heard it with instruments. I wish you too could have heard it, but just as it was performed and sung on this occasion, with such immaculate style, piano and forte. Who knows, perhaps you'll still hear it – I hope so. The orchestra never stopped praising the aria and talking about it. I've lots of very good friends in Mannheim – distinguished –

2. These works are K80 (originally composed in three movements, Mozart added a fourth sometime between 1773 and 1775), K174, K179.
3. K242.
4. Therese Pierron (b. 1761) was the step-daughter of Anton Joseph Serrarius; Mozart composed the accompanied sonata K296 for her.
5. K294.
6. 'Truly written by a master.'

well-to-do friends – who very much wanted to keep me there. Well, wherever people pay well, I'll be found. Who knows, perhaps it'll happen. I hope so; and I still feel – I still hope it will. Cannabich is a decent, honest fellow and my very good friend; he has only one failing, namely that, although he's no longer all that young, he's a bit careless and absent-minded. If you're not always at him, he forgets everything; but if it's a question of finding a *good friend*, he roars like a bull and really takes your part, and that produces results as he has great influence. On the other hand, there's no question of politeness or gratitude and I must admit that, in spite of their poverty and lack of wealth and although I've done less for them, the Webers have shown themselves to be the more grateful; for Madame and Monsieur Cannabich didn't say a word to me, still less did they offer a small memento or even a trifle to show their kind hearts; there was nothing, they didn't even thank me, even though I'd taken so much time and trouble with their daughter; there's no doubt that she could now perform anywhere; for a girl of 14 and an amateur, she plays very well; and they've me to thank for that, as the whole of Mannheim knows. She now has taste and a trill, she can play in time and her fingering is better, previously she'd none of this. In 3 months they'll miss me a lot – for I fear that she'll deteriorate and that she'll have only herself to blame; if she doesn't always have a teacher who knows what he's doing, it will all be in vain, because she's still too childish and careless to practise seriously and to any useful purpose on her own.

Out of the goodness of her heart Fräulein Weber has knitted 2 pairs of string mittens for me, which she has given me as a memento and a small token of her gratitude. He[7] copied out, free of charge, all that I needed and also gave me some music manuscript paper; and he presented me with a copy of Molière's comedies, as he knew that I'd never read them, with the inscription: *Ricevi, Amico, le opere del moliere in segno di gratitudine, e qualche volta ricordati di me.*[8] And

7. Fridolin Weber.
8. 'Accept, my friend, the works of Molière in token of my gratitude and think of me sometimes'; presumably the German translation of Molière's works by Friedrich Samuel Bierling, published at Hamburg in 1752; volumes three and four of this edition were among the books listed in the inventory of Mozart's estate in 1791.

when he was alone with Mama, he said: Our dearest friend, our benefactor, is now leaving us. It's true, if it hadn't been for your son! He did a lot for my daughter and took her under his wing, she can never be grateful enough to him; they wanted me to have supper with them on the eve of my departure, but I had to remain at home so I couldn't accept. Even so, I had to give them 2 hours of my time before supper. They never stopped thanking me and wished only to be in a position to show me their gratitude. They were all in tears when I left. I'm sorry, but my eyes fill with tears whenever I think of it. He came downstairs with me and remained standing in the doorway until I'd turned the corner, calling after me: Adieu.

Our journey, including food, drink, sleep and tips, came to more than 4 louis d'or, for the further we got into France, the more expensive it became. I've just received your letter of the 16th. Don't worry, I'll certainly sort out my affairs. I'd ask only that you remain good-humoured in your letters; and if war[9] gets too close, come and join us. Best wishes to all our good friends. I kiss your hands 1000 times and embrace my sister with all my heart. I am your most obedient son

Wolfgang Amadè Mozart

[*Maria Anna Mozart's postscript on the cover*]
My dear husband, praise and thanks be to God, we've arrived here safe and sound. We're staying at Herr Mayer's, in the house where Herr von Waldburg[10] stayed. We don't yet know what we'll have to pay but we'll find out tomorrow, today we went to see Baron Grimm, but he wasn't at home, we left a note there so that he knows we've arrived, Wolfgang will go back there tomorrow and deliver his other letters. On the journey here we had the most beautiful weather for 8 days, amazingly cold in the morning and warm in the afternoon, but during the last 2 days we were almost suffocated by the wind and drowned by the rain, so that we both got soaking wet inside the carriage and could barely breathe. We got through customs with no

9. The War of the Bavarian Succession.
10. Anton Willibald, Count Waldburg zu Wolfegg und Waldersee.

difficulty, except that Wolfgang had to pay duty on his small-sized manuscript paper, which came to 38 sous; there was no inspection at all in Paris. Wolfgang is bored as he hasn't yet got a keyboard, also the weather's been so bad that he's not been able to look round for one. *Addio*, keep well, I kiss you both many 10,000 times and remain your faithful wife

Frau Mozart

Best wishes to all and sundry. We drank Herr Bullinger's health on St Joseph's Day in Clermont.[11]

78. Maria Anna Mozart to her husband, 5 April 1778, Paris

My Dear Husband,

Praise and thanks be to God, we're both well and hope that you and Nannerl are in good health, with God's help all will be well, Wolfgang has lots to do, for Holy Week he has to write a Miserere[1] for the Concert Spirituel, it has to have 3 choruses, a fugue, a duet and everything else, with lots of instruments, it's supposed to be ready by next Wednesday so that it can be rehearsed, he's writing it at the home of Monsieur Legros,[2] the director of the Concert, where he generally has his meals, he can also have lunch every day at Noverre's[3] and at Madame d'Épinay's.[4] After that he has to write 2 concertos for a duke,[5] one for the flute and one for the harp,[6] for the

11. 19 March; Clermont-en-Argonne, outside Metz.

1. K297a; for further details, see below.

2. Joseph Legros (1730–93), tenor and director of the Concert Spirituel 1777–91.

3. Jean-Georges Noverre (1726–1810), dancing master and choreographer active at Vienna, Milan and Paris.

4. The writer Louise-Florence d'Épinay (née Tardieu d'Esclavelles, 1726–83) was noted for the brilliance of her salon; she had earlier had a liaison with the philosopher Jean-Jacques Rousseau (1712–78), and at this time was living with Baron Grimm.

5. Adrien-Louis Bonnières de Souastre, Duc de Guines (1735–1806), governor of Artois.

6. K299.

French theatre he has to write an act for an opera.[7] He also has a female pupil, who pays him 6 livres a lesson, or 3 louis d'or for 12 lessons, though we shan't be paid till he's finished, and we shan't receive a farthing before Easter. Our funds are already fairly low and won't go very far, we'll also have to take some other rooms as it's too far to walk, we've already spent a lot of money on cabs, I'll be very sorry to leave this house, there are some decent folk here with whom I can speak German. Madame d'Épinay has been looking round for some other rooms for us, so you should address the letters you send us just to Herr Mayer, who'll pass them on to us until I let you have another address. We've not yet called on Herr Gschwendtner but if we need money and ours is no longer sufficient, we'll ask him to advance us some, although it would be preferable and better if we didn't need any. Wolfgang is again so famous and popular here that I can't begin to describe it, Herr Wendling had already talked up his reputation even before he arrived and he's now introduced him to his friends, he really is a true philanthropist. And Monsieur Grimm has also urged Herr Wendling to do his utmost to make Wolfgang better known because, as a musician, he enjoys a higher reputation.

As far as my own way of life is concerned, it's not very pleasant as I spend the whole day sitting around alone in my room as if under arrest, as the room is so dark and looks out on a little courtyard so that I never see the sun and don't even know what the weather is like. With great difficulty I'm able to do a little knitting by daylight, and for this room we have to pay 30 livres a month, the entrance and the stairs are so narrow that it would be impossible to bring up a keyboard instrument. And so Wolfgang has to compose away from home, at Monsieur Legros', as there's a keyboard there, so I don't see him all day and shall forget how to speak. My food from the *traiteur* is *superb*, at midday I get 3 courses for 15 sous, first, some soup with herbs, which I don't like, 2nd a scrap of poor-quality meat, 3rd a piece of calf's foot in a dirty sauce or a piece of liver as hard as stone, but at night we don't have any food delivered, instead Frau Mayer buys us a few pounds of veal and has it roasted at the baker's,

7. See below and n. 10.

so we have it hot for the first meal, then cold for as long as it lasts, as is the custom in England, but we never have soup in the evening, the fast days are impossible to describe and are unbearable, everything here is half as expensive again as it was the last time we were here 12 years ago. Today, the 10th, I've spent the whole day packing as we're moving to some other rooms where we have to pay only one louis d'or a month and where we'll have 2 rooms overlooking the street and we'll be nearer the aristocracy and the theatre, I'd have sent off this letter before now but we wanted to wait for one from you so that we could have replied to it, as we have to pay 17 sous for every letter we post and 24 sous for every one that we receive. Baron Grimm came to see me yesterday, he says you shouldn't worry so much, everything will turn out all right in the end. One just needs to be a little patient, he'll reply to your letter but has a lot to do at present;

[*Mozart's postscript*]
Mama's dark allusions need explaining more clearly. Kapellmeister Holzbauer has sent a Miserere here, but because the choirs in Mannheim are weak and underpowered, whereas here they're good and strong, his choruses would be ineffectual. And so Monsieur Legros, the director of the Concert Spirituel, has asked me to write some new choruses.[8] Holzbauer's opening chorus will remain. The '*Quoniam iniquitatem meam ego cognosco*' is my first one. *Allegro*. The 2nd, an adagio, is '*Ecce enim in iniquitatibus*'. Then an allegro. '*Ecce enim veritatem dilexisti*' as far as '*ossa humiliata*'.

Then an andante for soprano, tenor and bass soloists. '*Cor mundum crea*' and '*Redde mihi laetitiam*', but allegro as far as '*Ad te convertentur*'. I've also written a recitative for a bass. '*Libera me de sanguinibus*'. Because a bass aria by Holzbauer follows. '*Domine, labia mea.*'

'*Sacrificium Deo spiritus*' is an andante aria for Raaff, with oboe and bassoon solo, and so I've added a brief recitative, '*Quoniam si voluisses*', it too with concertante oboe and bassoon, as they now like recitatives here. '*Benigne fac*' to '*Muri Jerusalem*' andante moderato.

8. Mozart's choruses for the Miserere (a setting of Psalm 51) are lost.

Chorus. Then '*Tunc acceptabis*' to '*Super altare tuo vitulos*' allegro, and tenor solo – Legros – and chorus together. *Finis.*

I must say that I'm very pleased to have finished these scribblings, which are a damned nuisance when you can't write at home and are pressed for time. But, praise and thanks be to God, I've now finished it. And I hope it'll be effective. When he saw my first chorus, Monsieur Gossec,[9] whom you must know, told Monsieur Legros – I wasn't there at the time – that it was charming and would undoubtedly be effective, adding that the words were well arranged and in general it was admirably set. He's a very good friend of mine, and a very dry wit. I shan't be writing a single act for an opera but a *whole* opera *en deux actes*. The poet has already finished the first act. Noverre – at whose home I dine as often as I want – has taken charge of the matter and provided the basic idea. I think it'll be called *Alexandre et Roxane*.[10] Mlle Jenamy[11] is here, too. I'm now going to write a *sinfonia concertante*[12] for *flute* (Wendling), *oboe* (Ramm), *Punto* (horn)[13] and *Ritter* (bassoon). Punto is a magnificent player. I've just got back from the *Concert Spirituel*. Baron Grimm and I often give vent to our musical anger at the orchestra here – between ourselves, of course. In public it's *bravo, bravissimo*, and we clap till our hands hurt. Farewell, I kiss your hands 100 times and am

Wolfgang Amadè Mozart

[*Inside the cover*]
Monsieur Raaff is here and staying with Monsieur Legros so we see each other almost every day. My dearest Papa, I must ask you not to

---

9. François-Joseph Gossec (1734–1829), composer and from 1778 chorus director at the Académie Royale.

10. Mozart's plans to write an opera on *Alexandre et Roxane* never materialized.

11. Victoire Jenamy (1749–1812), pianist and daughter of Jean-Georges Noverre; Mozart composed the concerto K271 for her in January 1777. Until recently, Jenamy's identity was unknown; in the literature she is traditionally called 'Jeunehomme', a name invented by the French scholars Théodore de Wyzewa and Georges de Saint-Foix.

12. K297B; although this work is lost, it may survive, at least in part, in the similarly (but not identically) scored KAnh. C14.01.

13. Jan Václav Stich (1746–1803), known as Punto.

worry so much and not to be so anxious, as you've no cause for it. I'm now in a place where one can undoubtedly make money, even if this requires a frightful amount of effort and hard work; but I'm ready to do anything to please you. What annoys me most of all is that these French gentlemen have improved their *goût* only to the extent that they can now listen to good things too. But for them to realize that their own music is bad or at least to notice the difference – God preserve us! – And their singing! – *Oimè* – As long as I don't hear a Frenchwoman singing Italian arias, I'd forgive her her French screechings, but to ruin good music! – It's intolerable. Now for our new address.

Rue Gros Genêt, vis à vis celle du Croissant.
à l'hôtel des 4 fils emont.

You need to include the number 4 as that's how it appears on the building.

79. Leopold Mozart to his wife and son, 12 April 1778, Salzburg

My Dear Wife and Son,

In the hope that with tomorrow's post I shall hear from you with news that you're both well, I'm writing today to say that the late Herr Adlgasser's Litany was performed *today* and that Haydn's will be performed *tomorrow* and Wolfgang's on *Tuesday*.[1] In the last of them Sgr Ceccarelli will be singing all the solos and in the *Golden Salve* he'll also sing the *Regina Coeli* that Wolfg. wrote for Frau Haydn.[2] Except when there's a big concert he comes to our house every evening and always brings an aria and a motet, I play the violin and Nannerl accompanies and plays the solos intended for the violas

1. K243. Neither Adlgasser's nor Michael Haydn's Litany can be identified with certainty.
2. Francesco Ceccarelli (1752–1814) was a castrato at Salzburg cathedral; the Golden *Salve* formed part of the liturgy performed at Salzburg during the afternoon of Easter Sunday, the *Regina Coeli* is K127. Michael Haydn had recently married the soprano Maria Magdalena Lipp (1745–1827).

or winds. We then play a *keyboard concerto* or a *violin trio* in which Ceccarelli plays the second violin; we sometimes have to laugh as it was here that he started to play the violin and he's now been playing for 6 months. His time is up at the end of April. If he returns in the autumn or if he now decides he wants to stay, the archb. will pay him 800 florins a year for 6 years. He has declared that he'll come back for this amount, but for only 2 years, if the archbishop will pay his travelling expenses.[3] He's now awaiting a reply. If he comes back, he'll leave all his arias here in the meantime and take only a few with him, before returning on 1 November. He's sorry not to have got to know you both and regrets that he wasn't introduced to us right at the outset, as we're the only people he sees. He joins us for target practice and on 2 occasions he's won, and as Katherl Gilowsky is *very free* with him, as is her wont, he calls her *La Mattarella*,[4] which she doesn't understand; we painted her on the targets holding a harp, with Ceccarelli, open-mouthed, beating time and holding his music in his other hand – just as he sings. – Count Czernin isn't content with fiddling at court but would like to conduct as well, and so he's set up an amateur orchestra that's supposed to meet at Count Lodron's rooms[5] every Sunday just after 3. Count Sigerl Lodron[6] called on us to invite Nannerl – as an amateur – to play the clavier and to ask me to keep the second violins in order. A week ago today, the 5th, we had our first session. Among those present were Count *Czernin, primo violino*, Baron *Bapius*,[7] *Sigerl* Lodron, young *Weyrother*,[8] *Kolb*, Kolb's *student from Nonnberg*, and a few students whom I don't know. Among the *2nd violins* were *me, Sigerl Robinig, Gussetti, Count Althan*,[9] *Cajetan von Antretter*, a *student* and *Ceccarelli, la coda dei secondi*.[10] The 2 *violas*

3. In the event, Ceccarelli remained at Salzburg for ten years.
4. 'Little fool'.
5. For an engraving of Count Lodron's residence, see Deutsch, *Bildern*, 269.
6. Sigmund, Count Lodron, see List.
7. Georg von Bapius, court councillor and amateur musician.
8. Gottlieb von Weyrother (1713–1816), court official.
9. Giovanni Battista Gussetti (1744–89), Salzburg businessman and amateur musician; Michael, Count Althan, a student at the Salzburg Benedictine University.
10. 'at the back of the seconds'.

are the two ex-Jesuits *Bullinger* and *Wieshofer*. 2 oboes *Weber* the lackey and *Schulz's son* who acted in the play in Linz. Two watchmen's apprentices play the horn, and the *doubles basses* are *Cassel, Count Wolfegg* and occasionally Ränftl. The *cellos* were the new young canons, Count *Zeil* and Count *Spaur*,[11] Privy Councillor *Mölk, Sigerl Antretter* and Ränftl. Nannerl accompanied all the symphonies, and as Ceccarelli sang an aria *per l'appertura della Accademia di dilettanti*,[12] she accompanied him as well. After the symphony Count Czernin played a *beautifully written* concerto by *Sirmen*[13] *à la* Brunetti and *doppo un altra sinfonia*[14] Count Althan played a *terrible trio*, although not a living soul can say whether it was scraped or fiddled – whether it was in 3/4 time or common time or even in some new and hitherto unknown tempo. Nannerl was supposed to play a concerto but the countess wouldn't lend them her good harpsichord – which is *Casus reservatus pro summo Pontifice*,[15] only the Egedacher[16] instrument with gilt legs was there, so she didn't play. Finally the 2 *Lodron girls*[17] had to play. There hadn't been the slightest indication beforehand that they were to do so, but ever since I've had them, they've been in a position to play at short notice, so they were both a credit to me.

Monday the 13th

We still haven't had a letter from you today. Although the postman came, it was only with a letter from *Mysliveček*, who tells me that instead of the 25 or 30 ducats he was expecting to receive for the 6 concertones that he rewrote at the archb.'s behest, he received only

11. Siegmund Christoph, Count Zeil (1754–?), nephew of the bishop of Chiemsee; Friedrich Franz Joseph, Count Spaur (1756–1821) had succeeded his uncle Ignaz Joseph Spaur (see letter 27, n. 4) as canon of Salzburg.
12. 'to open the amateur concert'.
13. Maddalena Laura Sirmen (1745–1818), who had been a pupil of the violinist and composer Giuseppe Tartini (1692–1770).
14. 'after another symphony'.
15. 'a case reserved for trial by the pontiff alone'; i.e., for use only in the archbishop's presence.
16. Rochus Egedacher (1714–85) was the most prominent keyboard builder in Salzburg.
17. Aloisia and Giuseppina Lodron.

12 ducats a titolo per il Viaggio.[18] – He also says he'll be leaving Munich on *Maundy Thursday* etc. and, having written to me many times to ask me to lend him a hand, always adding some ridiculous excuse about the *scrittura* that he claims he's expecting with every post from Naples, he now writes: *Finora da Napoli non ebbi la scrittura; ma spero di finir quest' affare alla mia Venuta, per ove partirò Giovedì Santo; frattanto sono a pregarla d'una grazia*[19]– NB: *otherwise he wouldn't have written at all – cio è di mandarmi gli 6 Concerti di Bach etc. etc. io Sono stato pregato dal Sgr. Hamm per questa finezza etc etc. – Non ardiscono loro stessi di Scriver a V.S. etc.*[20] I can well believe that; *Herr Hamm* didn't have the *courtesy* to reply to my letter of 5 months ago when I asked him for only *200 florins* for his daughter's full *board and lodging, including teaching.* – Now Mysliveček has had to ask for the concertos for him, – they'll be waiting for them for a long time – I'll write and tell Mysliveček the reason. The second amateur concert took place on Palm Sunday, the 12th: symphonies by *Stamitz*[21] were played at both the first and the second and were much liked as both are very noisy. Baron Bapius played a very simple violin concerto, but at least it was in tempo and in tune, he's having lessons from Pinzger. – Herr Kolb then played your cassation[22] to the most amazing applause. Count Czernin, who had never heard Kolb play before and didn't know your piece, stood behind him and sometimes beside him, turning the pages for him and showing the greatest attention: he was amazingly fulsome in his praise and, hearing that it was by you, was all eagerness and asked me 3 or four times – when did he write it? – – I can't have been here – with his familiar

18. 'for his travelling expenses'.
19. 'I've not yet received the contract from Naples; but I hope to resolve the affair on my arrival, I'm leaving on Maundy Thursday; meanwhile I'd like to ask a favour of you.'
20. 'This is to send me Bach's 6 concertos etc etc. Sgr Hamm has asked me to do him this kindness etc etc. – They don't dare to write to you themselves etc.' Presumably this refers to Johann Christian Bach and possibly the keyboard concertos op. 1 of 1763 or op. 7 of 1770; in 1772, Mozart had arranged three of Bach's keyboard sonatas (op. 5, nos. 2, 3 and 4) as concertos, K107.
21. Presumably Carl Stamitz (1745–1801), active chiefly at Paris and London.
22. Probably K287.

bright red face and quivering voice he couldn't help expressing his admiration for the piece and its execution. They all listened in total silence, and after each movement Count Wolfegg, Count Zeil, Count Spaur and the others all cried out *bravo il Maestro e bravo il Sgr Kolb!* Countess Lodron and Countess Lützow etc. all listened attentively and liked what they heard, only when she heard the variations, which you often had to play for her, did the countess realize that they were by you, she ran over to me in her delight and told me so — I was playing the 2nd violin, *Kolb's pupil* the viola, *Cassel* the bass and the two watchmen, who'd often played it at Kolb's, the horn. The concert ended with a wretched performance at the keyboard by the 2 *Kletzl girls*, the eldest was indescribably bad, enough to drive you away; it was simply unbearable, even worse than when they sang in Kuenburg's play. On Easter Sunday the 2 *Lodron girls* are to *sing or croak* — I don't know which, as I haven't heard them for a long time. Nannerl has already been asked to accompany them.

The 16th. Still no letter from you. We hope you're well and are fully aware that you'll initially have a lot to do, calling on everyone, making new contacts and renewing old ones. Herr *Mehofer's* son is here from the mountains, finally — after a great deal of trouble — he's now *managing a foundry* in Lungau, at least he's moved on from lead and sulphur to silver and gold and is earning 230 florins a year in addition to *board and other emoluments*. The architect *Hagenauer* has left and won't be coming back. In our building the *elder* of the carpenter's two daughters has died of dropsy, they used to sew clothes and their brother waxed Wolfgang's boots and those of the pageboys. The *assistant riding master*[23] is getting married on Wednesday the 22nd. Herr *von Mölk* will pronounce them man and wife at Mirabell in the morning, after which they're off to *Altötting*. The bride looks in a very poor way,[24] she's very worried when she thinks of the past, present and future. There's a cellist here with his wife. He plays

23. The court position held by Gottlieb von Weyrother.
24. Maria Anna Constantia Barisani, daughter of the archbishop's physician, Silvester Barisani; she died in December.

extremely well. His name is *Xaverio Pietragrua*. He's played at court for *10 ducats (the fee was agreed in advance)* and is giving a concert on the 21st. He and his wife – she's a singer but I don't know how good she is – send you their best wishes even though they don't know you. They've visited us 3 times and are coming to our target practice tomorrow, as I'm writing this on Sunday the 19th.

Monday the 20th

There was another amateur concert yesterday, but it was very short as it didn't begin until after the *Regina Coeli* – admirably sung by the castrato – in the cathedral. I found your letter of the 5th inst. waiting for me when I got home from the service. I'm amazed that it took so long. It must have been posted later as letters normally take 9 days to get here from Paris. I recommend you to write par *Strasbourg*, *Augsburg* – on them as your first letter also arrived late, having come via Mannheim. There are several Salzburgs. These words must be written alongside the others: par Strasb. etc. Augsb. *à Salzburg*.

My dear Wolfgang, I'm heartily glad that you've already got some work and am only sorry that you had such a rush to complete the choruses, a task that needs time if it's to do you credit. I wish and hope that they're well received. With the *opera* you'll no doubt have to be *guided by the taste of the French*. As long as you *meet with approval* and are *well paid*, the devil may take the rest! If people like your opera, there'll soon be something in the newspapers. I'd like to see this in time, in order to spite the archbishop.

I'd like to hear the *sinfonia concertante* with these fine people. If you were able to track down a decent piano[25] in Paris, similar to the one we've got here, I'm sure that you'd prefer it and that it would suit you better than a harpsichord. I'm sorry to hear that French taste remains largely the same: but, believe me, it's bound to change in time, however hard it may be to remould an entire nation. For the present, it's enough that they can also listen to good music; they'll

25. Leopold uses *Klavier* here, by which he presumably means 'piano' specifically rather than 'keyboard', as he goes on to make an implicit distinction with *Flügl* ('harpsichord').

gradually notice the difference. Before you write for the theatre, you should listen to their operas and find out what they particularly like. You'll now become a real Frenchman and I hope you'll take steps to acquire a correct accent. Nannerl and I are well, thank God, and I'm no longer worried but am very happy to know that our very good friend Baron Grimm has taken you under his wing and that you're now in a place which thanks to your innate industriousness can make you famous throughout the world. As long as I don't have to worry so much about you, I'm well: and you know me, all that matters to me is honour and reputation. You acquired this as a child – this must continue. – This was always my aim, and so it remains; these are now the years that you must put to good use both for yourself and all of us. May God keep you both in good health. Best wishes from Nannerl and myself to Baron Grimm, Monsieur and Mme de Noverre, Mme Jenamy, Mme d'Épinay, Monsieur Wendling, Monsieur Raaff, Monsieur Gossec etc. etc. etc. etc. 100,000 good wishes to you both from the whole house and the whole orchestra etc., also Herr Bullinger (who thanks you for drinking his health in Clermont), Sallerl, Katherl Gilowsky, Herr Hagenauer, Herr Deibl etc. etc. It's target practice today, on the target is Katherl Gilowsky in her cradle as it was her birthday yesterday, with the castrato[26] standing beside her, playing the lullaby on his violin. – The castrato is putting up the prize. My dear wife, I'm very sorry to hear that your food is so bad. Isn't it possible to find someone who can cook in the German way? You really must look round for some better food and pay more. I've always been worried about this. Can't you cook for yourself? – – In the longer term you'll have to think of some alternative as you're not in Paris for just a few months, – – this is now the safest place to be, partly because you can make some money there, partly because you can live without fear of war. I really don't like to think of Russia and Turkey being at lasting peace, still less do I like the idea of total peace being concluded between them. Otherwise I'm afraid that Russia

---

26. Francesco Ceccarelli.

[*On the envelope*]

will side with the king of Prussia and that Austria will then have to deal with 2 very great powers.[27] I expect you'll have received my answer to your first letter, and my two terribly long letters will also have reached Baron Grimm. Wolfg. wants an ABC, but he won't have much time to devote to it. Here's something.

I can't write properly today, this pen is useless, and I have to rush away to Vespers, the Italians will also be there, I won the *prize* for Mama. We kiss you both a million times. I am your old faithful

Mzt

Addio. Keep well.

Pimperl is keeping well, whenever she stands on the table she scratches the rolls very gently with her paws to indicate that she wants to be given one, also the knife, indicating that we should cut her a slice. And if there are 4 or 5 snuffboxes on the table, she'll scratch the one containing Spanish tobacco so someone takes a pinch and then lets her lick their fingers.

80. *Mozart to his father, 1 May 1778, Paris*

Mon très cher Père,

Your letter of 12 April has arrived safely, this was the reason why I've not written for so long, as I wanted to wait for a letter from you; and you mustn't take it amiss if I sometimes keep you waiting a long time for a letter; but letters are very expensive here, and unless one's got something important to say, it's not worth while spending 24 or more sous. I'd always intended to delay writing until I had some news and could tell you more about our circumstances; but now I'm obliged, after all, to provide you with an account of the few matters

---

27. A reference to the Russian-Turkish War of 1768–74. Now that Russia is at peace, Leopold fears it will side with Prussia against Austria in the event of war over the Bavarian succession.

that are still unresolved. The little cellist *Zygmontofscky*[1] and his worthless father are here, perhaps I've already told you that – – I do so only in passing as I've just remembered that I saw him at the place that I now intend to tell you about, namely, the home of Madame la Duchesse de Chabot.[2] Monsieur Grimm gave me a letter for her, and so I went to see her. The letter was mainly to recommend me to the Duchesse de Bourbon[3] – who was in a convent last time – and to reintroduce me to her and remind her of me. A week passed without any news at all; but she'd asked me to return after a week had gone by, so I kept my word and turned up. I had to wait half an hour in a large, ice-cold, unheated room that didn't even have a fireplace. Finally the Duchesse de Chabot arrived, politeness itself, and asked me to make do with the piano that was there as none of her other ones had been seen to; she suggested I should give it a try. I said I'd be only too happy to play something but that it was now impossible as my fingers were numb with cold; and I asked her if she'd at least take me to a room with a hearth and a fire. *O oui Monsieur, vous avez raison.*[4] That was her entire answer. She then sat down and started to draw for a whole hour in the company of some gentlemen, who all sat in a circle round a large table. I had the honour to wait a whole hour. Windows and doors were open. By now not only my hands were cold, so were my feet and my whole body; and my head started to ache. In short, there was *altum silentium*.[5] I didn't know what to do for cold, headache and boredom. I kept thinking that if it weren't for Monsieur Grimm, I'd leave at once. Finally – and to be brief – I played on that miserable, wretched pianoforte. But the most annoying thing of all was that Madame and the gentlemen didn't stop drawing for a moment, but continued as before, so that I had to play for the

1. Zygmontofscky, of whom nothing more is known, gave a concert at the Salzburg town hall on 31 May 1777.
2. Élisabeth-Louise de La Rochefoucauld, Duchesse de Chabot (1740–86).
3. Louise-Marie-Thérèse-Bathilde d'Orléans, Duchesse de Bourbon (1750–1822), was the daughter of the Duc d'Orléans.
4. 'O yes, Monsieur, you're right.'
5. 'a deep silence'.

chairs, table and walls. In such adverse circumstances I lost my patience – I started the Fischer variations, played half of them, then got up. They showered me with praise. I just said the only thing I could say, namely, that I couldn't do myself justice on this piano and that I'd very much like to choose another day when there'd be a better piano. But she wouldn't hear of it, and I had to wait another half an hour for her husband to come. He then sat down beside me and listened with the greatest attention, so that I – I forgot all about the cold and my headache and, regardless of the wretched piano, played as I play when I'm in a good mood. Give me the best piano in Europe but with people who, as an audience, understand nothing or who don't want to understand anything and who feel nothing when I'm playing, and I lose all sense of pleasure. I told Monsieur Grimm about it all afterwards. You write that I should pay lots of calls in order to make new contacts and renew old ones. But this isn't possible. It's too far to go on foot – or too muddy, as the filth in Paris is indescribable. And taking a carriage means that you have the honour of wasting 4 or 5 livres a day – and *all for nothing*. People pay you compliments, but that's it. They summon me to appear on such and such a day; I play for them, they say *O c'est un Prodige, c'est inconcevable, c'est étonnant.*[6] And with that, goodbye. At first I wasted a lot of money driving round – and often in vain as the people weren't there. Anyone who's not here can't believe how disastrous this is. Paris really has changed a lot. The French are not nearly as polite as they were 15 years ago. They now verge on coarseness. And they're terribly arrogant.

I must now describe the Concert Spirituel for you. I must add in passing that my work on the choruses was in vain, so to speak, as Holzbauer's Miserere is already very long and wasn't to people's liking, so they performed only 2 of my 4 choruses. As a result they missed out the best bits. But that didn't really matter as hardly anyone knew that I'd had a hand in it and many knew nothing at all about me. Even so, there was lots of applause at the rehearsal; and I myself am very pleased with my choruses – I set little store by the praise of

6. 'Oh, he's a true prodigy, it's unbelievable, it's amazing.'

the Parisians. There's again a snag with the sinfonia concertante, though I think that there's another problem and that I again have my enemies here. Where haven't I had them? – But it's a good sign. I had to write the sinfonia in the greatest haste but I worked very hard, and the 4 soloists were and still are head over heels in love with it. Legros kept it for 4 days in order to have it copied, but I always found it lying in the same place. Finally – the day before yesterday – I couldn't find it but had a good look among the music and found it hidden away. I feigned ignorance and asked Legros: By the way, have you already given the sinf. concertante to the copyist? – No – I forgot. I can't, of course, order him to have it copied and performed, so I said nothing. I went to the Concert on the 2 days when it should have been played. Ramm and Punto came over to me, snorting with rage, and asked why my sinfonia concert. wasn't being given. – I don't know. That's the first I've heard about it. No one ever tells me anything. Ramm flew into a rage and cursed Legros in the green room in French, saying that it wasn't nice of him *etc*. What annoys me most of all about the whole affair is that Legros never said a word to me about it, I wasn't allowed to know what was going on – if he'd offered me some excuse, saying that there wasn't enough time or something similar, but to say nothing at all – but I think that *Cambini*,[7] one of the Italian *maestri* here, is the cause because in all innocence I made him look foolish in Legros' eyes at our first meeting. He's written some quartets, one of which I heard in Mannheim; they're really quite attractive; and I praised them to him and played the opening; but Ritter, Ramm and Punto were there, too, and they wouldn't leave me in peace but told me to continue and make up what I couldn't remember. So I did as they asked. And Cambini was beside himself and couldn't stop saying *questa è una gran Testa!*[8] But I don't think he can have liked it. If this were a place where people had ears to hear and hearts to feel and if they understood even a little about music and taste, I'd laugh heartily at all these things but – as far as music is concerned – I'm among beasts and brutes. But how

7. Giuseppe Maria Cambini (1746–1825), violinist and composer.
8. 'what a great mind!'

could it be otherwise, they're exactly the same in all their actions, emotions and passions – there's nowhere in the world like Paris. You mustn't think I'm exaggerating when I speak like this about the music here. Consult anyone you like – as long as it's not a native Frenchman – and – if it's someone you can consult – he'll say the same. I'm here now. I have to put up with it for your sake. I shall thank Almighty God if I leave here with my taste intact. I pray to God every day to give me grace to hold out steadfastly and to be a credit to myself and the whole of the German nation inasmuch as it is all to His greater honour and glory; and I pray that He will allow me to prosper and make lots of money, so that I may help you out of your present predicament and take steps to ensure that we're soon back together again and can live together happily and contentedly. For the rest, may His will be done on earth as it is in heaven. In the meantime, my dearest Papa, please do all you can to ensure that I get to see Italy soon, so that I may find a new lease of life. Please give me this pleasure, I beg you.

But now I ask you to be cheerful – I'll hack my way out of here as best I can. As long as I can get away unscathed. Adieu. I kiss your hands 1000 times and embrace my sister with all my heart. I am your most obedient son

Wolfgang Amadè Mozart

[*Maria Anna Mozart's postscript on the envelope*]
My dear husband, I hope that you and Nannerl are keeping well. For 3 weeks now I've been plagued by toothache and my head, throat and ears have been hurting, but, thank God, I'm now better, I don't get out much and the rooms are cold even when there's a fire, you just have to get used to it. If Count Wolfegg ever comes to Paris and could bring a black powder and a digestive powder, that would be very kind of him as I've nearly run out. Best wishes to all our acquaintances. Monsieur Heina[9] and his wife send their best wishes,

9. Franz Joseph Heina (1729–90), horn player. He established a publishing house with his wife, Gertrude, in 1773; between 1778 and c. 1783 he published the first editions of Mozart's piano variations K179, 180 and 354, the divertimento K254 and the piano sonatas K309–311.

he often calls on me, *addio* keep well I kiss you many 100,000 times
and remain your faithful wife

Maria Anna Mozart

81. *Maria Anna Mozart to her husband, 14 May 1778, Paris*

My Dear Husband,

Praise and thanks be to God, we're both well and hope that you
too are equally well. Our only pleasure is to hear that this is so. As
for our own circumstances, we can be well satisfied, considering the
time of year, Wolfgang has found himself a good family. He has to
teach composition for 2 hours a day to the daughter of the Duc de
Guines, he pays well and is the queen's[1] favourite, the duke loves
Wolfgang more than anything, at the moment he has 3 pupils, he
could have more but can't take them on because everything's so far
away and he doesn't have time until we've sorted ourselves out, by
winter he'll have so much to do that he won't know whether he's
coming or going, or so everyone's telling him, we also intend – and
all our good friends advise us to do so – to take rooms of our own
at the end of the summer, furnish them ourselves (something that can
easily be done here) and prepare our own meals, in this way we can
live for half the cost, we'll do so as soon as we've got some more
money. Above all I'd like to know more about the war,[2] people here
are saying that peace has been concluded between the emperor and
Prussia, war hasn't been declared between here and England,[3] but
plenty of preparations are being made. The queen is pregnant again,
it's not yet been made public, but there's no question about it, the
French are delighted. Please give our best wishes to Herr Ceccarelli

1. Marie Antoinette.
2. The build-up to the War of the Bavarian Succession; hostilities did not actually
break out until July, when Prussia invaded Bohemia (see letter 88).
3. It was widely believed that England and France would go to war as a result of
France's support for the North American colonies during the War of Independence
(1775–83).

– if he's still in Salzburg –, we're sorry not to have had the pleasure of meeting him. How's Frau Adlgasser, is little Viktoria still with her, and what are Waberl Eberlin and Berhandsky up to, do they still call on us? Is Nannerl still going to Antretter's every week, is young Antretter still at Neu-Ötting[4] now that everything has changed in Bavaria? Are Fräulein von Schiedenhofen and Nannerl Kranach still coming to the target practice, Herr von Schiedenhofen will no doubt be very proud at having such a wealthy wife and will no longer deign to come to our house, not that it matters, otherwise I hope that Salzburg is much the same as ever.

Here in Paris a lot has changed since last time, it's much bigger and has expanded so much I can't describe it, the Chaussée d'Antin where Monsieur Grimm lives is a completely new suburb and there are lots of beautiful broad streets like it, it's true that I haven't seen many of them but I've got a new map of the town, which is very different from our old one. Something for Nannerl: the fashion here is to wear neither earrings nor a necklace nor any jewelled pins in your hair, in fact no sparkling jewels at all, whether real or artificial, their hair is worn extraordinarily high, no heart-shaped toupée, but equally high all over, making more than a third of an ell in all, then come the caps, which are even higher than the toupée, and at the back is the plait or chignon, which goes right down the neck, with lots of curls at the sides, the toupée is made entirely of crêpe, not smooth hair, they've been wearing them even higher so that the carriages had to be made higher as women couldn't sit upright in them, but they've now come down again. Polonaises[5] are very fashionable and exceptionally well made. The corselets worn by unmarried women are smooth round the stomach at the front and have no folds. Nannerl now knows enough about Paris fashions and I must leave room for Wolfgang, so keep well, both of you, I kiss you many 100,000 times, best wishes to all our good friends, Monsieur Bullinger, Sallerl, Deibl, Mistress Mitzerl and all the others. I remain your faithful wife

Marianna Mozart

4. A garrison town near Salzburg.
5. A tight-bodiced dress with a looped-up skirt to reveal a decorative underskirt.

Best wishes to Tresel and a big kiss for Pimperl, is the warbler still alive? − −

[*Mozart's postscript*]
I now have so much to do, what will it be like in winter? − I think I told you in my last letter that the Duc de Guines, whose daughter is my composition pupil, plays the flute exceptionally well and that she herself is a magnificent harpist; she has plenty of talent and genius and, in particular, an exceptional memory as she plays all her pieces − 200 in fact − by heart. But she doubts very much whether she has any gifts as a composer, especially as regards thoughts − ideas; − but her father − who, between the two of us, is far too much in love with her − says that she certainly has ideas, adding that it's simply timidity and that she has too little faith in her own abilities. We'll see. If she has no ideas or thoughts − and at present she doesn't have any at all − it'll all be in vain, for − God knows − I can't give her any. Her father's aim isn't to make a great composer of her − she's not, *he says*, to write operas, arias, concertos or symphonies, but only grand sonatas for her instrument and mine. I gave her her 4th lesson today, and as far as the rules of composition and harmony are concerned, I'm quite pleased with her − she added quite a good bass to the first minuet that I set her. She's now starting to write in 3 parts. It starts off very well, but she soon gets bored, and I can't help her; I can't go on to the next stage yet. It's too soon, even if there really were genius here, but unfortunately there isn't − everything will have to be done with art. She simply doesn't have any ideas. Nothing comes. I've tried everything possible with her; I even had the idea of writing out a very simple minuet and seeing if she could write a variation on it. − But it was a waste of time − all right, I thought, she simply doesn't know how to begin − so I started to write a variation on the first bar and told her to continue in the same vein and keep to the idea − in the end it went fairly well. When she'd finished, I told her to start something of her own − only the leading voice, the melody − well, she thought about it for a whole quarter of an hour − but nothing came. So I wrote down 4 bars of a minuet and said to her: Look what a fool I am; I've started a minuet but can't even complete the first

section; would you mind finishing it off for me; she thought it would be impossible; but finally, after a great deal of effort, something emerged; I was pleased that she'd produced something for once. She then had to complete the minuet – I mean just the leading voice. But for her *homework* I told her just to change my 4 bars and write something of her own – invent a different beginning – the harmony could be the same, only the melody should be different. Well, I'll see tomorrow what's come of it. – I think I'll soon be receiving the libretto for my opera *en deux actes*. I'll first have to show it to the director, Monsieur de Vismes, to see if he'll accept it. But there's no doubt that he will, as Noverre suggested it, and de Vismes owes his position to Noverre. Noverre will also be presenting a new ballet, for which I'll write the music.[6] Rodolphe – the horn player – is in the king's service and a very good friend of mine. He has a thorough understanding of composition and writes very well. He has offered me the post of organist at Versailles, if I'll accept it. It pays 2000 livres a year, but I'd have to spend 6 months at Versailles and the other 6 in Paris or wherever I like. But I don't think I'll accept it. I must be advised by my good friends here. 2000 livres isn't such a vast sum. In German money, of course, but not here. It amounts to 83 louis d'or and 8 livres a year, of course, or, in our own money, 915 florins and 45 kr. – that would be a lot, of course, but here it amounts to only 333 thalers and 2 livres – and that's not much. It's frightening how quickly a thaler disappears here. It doesn't surprise me that people think so little of a louis d'or here as it's worth very little. 4 such thalers, or 1 louis, which is the same thing, are spent in no time. Adieu for now. Keep well. I kiss your hands 1000 times and embrace my sister with all my heart. I am your most obedient son

Wolfgang Amadè Mozart

Best wishes to all our friends, especially to Herr Bullinger.

6. In the event, Mozart wrote parts of the ballet, *Les petits riens* K299b, see letter 87.

82. Maria Anna Mozart to her husband, 29 May 1778, Paris

My Dear Husband,

Your letter of 29 April has reached us safely, and we're delighted to see from it that you and Nannerl are both well, your news amused us greatly. I'm heartily sorry, of course, to hear about Sandl Auer but hope that by now she'll have recovered her wits. As for Sigerl Haffner,[1] I burst out laughing as I know the girl, she was a good friend of our Nandl, who proved such a disappointment, and often came to see her, they're still friends, she's a brewer's daughter from Uttendorf, but she can't be more than 26, she just looks older as she was worn out working for the colonel. If he's married her, he's made a charming match, God bless him he's no reason to be jealous as no one could possibly fall for her. We hear very little about the war here, but I can well believe what you say about the king of Prussia trying to form alliances, but it'll be hard as Russia can't easily commit itself because of the Turks, and the Turks are bent on war. The Swedes certainly can't do so as the king of France has 30,000 Swedish auxiliaries and pays them 12 million livres a year. And Denmark, too, is out of the question as its whole army consists of some 30,000 men, which would empty the country, and do you think they're not afraid of France, which is fully occupied leading the king of Prussia by the nose for the edification of all the other powers? That's why he doesn't attack, otherwise he'd never wait so long as he's always been the aggressor and not thought things over for so long. Here the whole city is behind the emperor, except perhaps for the Lutherans, and not even all of them, some are behind him as he made himself very popular during his stay here.[2] Something for Nannerl: tell her she should get hold of a smart walking stick, it's the height of fashion here for all women – except maids – to take their sticks with them not only when they go to church but also when visiting, walking, wherever they go, but only in the street, of course, not when driving,

1. Siegmund Haffner the younger.
2. When he visited Paris as Count Falkenstein in April 1777 (see letter 49, n. 2).

no one goes out on foot without a stick because it's so slippery here, especially when it's been raining, some time ago a woman twisted her ankle and when a doctor said it would be better if women used sticks, it immediately became the fashion. Otherwise it's indescribably expensive here a lb of good butter costs 30 or 40 sous, and even the poorer quality, which you can't eat, is 24 sous. A lb of beef is 10 sous, veal 12 to 14 sous, a shoulder of lamb 3 livres, a young chicken 3 livres, the wine is expensive and of poor quality, having all been watered down by the landlords here, it's even more expensive than it was when we were in England. You can't buy more with a louis d'or than you can with a Bavarian thaler in Germany, and with a thaler you can't buy more than you can with 24 kr. back home, everything is as expensive again as it was last time. For the rest, we're well, praise and thanks be to God, and only wish you were both here. I shan't forget to be bled, but I must first find a good barber. It's no longer as common as it used to be, just as all fashions change. Best wishes to Herr Cornet Antretter,[3] we were sorry to hear that Herr Bullinger was ill but we're pleased that he's now better, best wishes to him and to my dear Sallerl, what's she doing, does she still think of me, Wolfgang and I often speak of her, how often we talk about our acquaintances in Salzburg when we're sitting together over our supper in the evening.

Addio, keep well, both of you, I kiss you many 10,000 times and remain your faithful wife

Marianna Mozart

All conceivable good wishes from us to all our good friends, greetings to Tresel.

[Mozart's postscript]
I'm bearing up, praise and thanks be to God, though often enough there's neither rhyme nor reason for what I do – I feel neither hot nor cold – I take little pleasure in things; what cheers me up most of all and keeps me in a good mood is the thought that you, dearest

3. Siegmund von Antretter.

Papa, and my dear sister are well – that I am an honest German – and that even if I may not always say what I want, I may at least think it. But that's all. Yesterday was my 2nd visit to see the envoy of the Palatine Electorate, Count von Sickingen – I'd already had lunch there with Herr Wendling and Herr Raaff – I don't know if I've already told you, but he's a charming gentleman and a true connoisseur of music, of which he's inordinately fond.

I spent 8 hours completely alone with him. We were at the keyboard morning and afternoon until 10 in the evening, playing through all kinds of music, praising, admiring, analysing, discussing and criticizing it. He has around 30 opera scores.

I must tell you that I had the honour of seeing a French translation of your violin method. I think it must have been translated at least 8 years ago. I was in a music shop, buying a set of sonatas by Schobert for a pupil of mine. But I'll return there soon and have a closer look in order to be able to send you a more detailed description. I didn't have enough time the other day. Farewell. I kiss your hands 1000 times and embrace my sister with all my heart. *Mes compliments à tous mes amis, particulièrement à Monsieur Bullinger.*

WoAMozart

83. Leopold Mozart to his wife and son, 11 June 1778, Salzburg

My dear wife and son,

I'll start with a wedding as I don't know if I've already told you that *Nicoladoni*, who's in partnership with Herr Spängler and who used to be married to Spängler's daughter, has just married *Nannerl Gschwendtner*.[1] It took place at the Eizenberger-Hof.[2] *Huber*, the *currier*, suffered a fall last winter and was almost fully recovered when

1. Nannerl Gschwendtner (1746–82) was the sister of Joseph Franz Xaver and Vital Gschwendtner; Franz Anton Spängler (1705–84) was a Salzburg merchant.
2. An all-purpose venue used for balls, wedding feasts and parties located outside the town.

he fell again as he was still too weak to walk. He now has to use
2 crutches and can't take a bath as one of his legs is withered. But
otherwise he's hale and hearty and walks past our gate on his
2 crutches. The *statuarius's mother*,[3] old peasant woman, has died.
Haffner's[4] heirs and in-laws have agreed neither to the wedding nor
to the sale of the property at Seeburg. Herr Triendl[5] wouldn't be
opposed to the latter, but he only wants to buy it because of Lucretia
in order to stay in Seeburg and be close to his cook, who's with her
sister in *Trum*. So Haffner intends to wait another 3 years until he's
no longer a ward of court:[6] and he'll then bang his foolish head
against the wall. – Meanwhile a lot can change. The amateur concerts
are still taking place every Sunday in Lodron's hall. The 2 Lodron
girls have already played 3 times each, on each occasion it was music
that I gave them as they couldn't have managed a single one of the
pieces that they'd studied during 5 years with the late Herr Adlgasser.
Little Leopold Arco[7] has also played 3 times. They were all a credit
both to me and to themselves, Fräulein von Mölk played once after
Nannerl had had several lessons with her. Mlle Villersi[8] was also
invited to play, Countess Lützow had Wolfg.'s concerto[9] copied out
for her some time ago, and Spitzeder worked through it with her.
Thinking she could play it, she rehearsed it with the violins in her
room; Herr Bullinger was also there; and they all said – and she
herself agreed – that she played it appallingly badly. She then came
to our house in tears and asked us to show her how it should be
played, postponing her appearance for a fortnight and in the end
learning to play it so well that she was the greatest possible credit to
herself. She's now having lessons with Nannerl and comes here so that
the parlourmaids at the Langenhof don't know about it as Spitzeder is

3. Maria Hagenauer.
4. Siegmund Haffner the elder, who had died in 1772.
5. Siegmund Haffner the elder's son-in-law.
6. Siegmund Haffner the younger would cease to be a ward of court when he was
twenty-five.
7. Count Arco's nephew (1764–1832).
8. Daughter of Casimir Villersi (?–1776), former tutor to Archbishop Colloredo.
9. K246.

still seeing her. The count and countess[10] know. The countess now regrets her whim and doesn't know what to do with the girl, who in 5 whole years has learnt absolutely nothing. The Lodron girls played again on 7 June, the *elder* gave a superb performance of the concerto by Lucchesi.[11] Sigerl Robinig has already played twice, the first time Wolfg.'s piece in B flat (I think) from the graduation music, the second time another easy little concerto – he played it more than passably, only the cadenzas were terribly Pinzgerish.[12] – Did I tell you that last carnival little *Perchtl* opened a coffee-shop in the Linzergasse near Rosenwirth and that it's doing a roaring trade as he makes good coffee? – *The evening of the 7th. Your letter of 29 May reached us on the 7th* and we were delighted to read that both of you are well, praise be to God, we too are well, thank God: only occasionally am I overcome by a sense of melancholy when I think how far away we are from each other and wonder when – or if – I shall ever see you again. – – I must seek to banish these sad thoughts through work – – and through manly fortitude and leave it to God's will. I never doubted that everything would be very expensive and, indeed, more expensive than it was last time in Paris as the same is happening everywhere, year in, year out. It's an infallible rule that *where there's lots of money, everything is expensive; but where everything is cheap, there's less money.* Nannerl intends to start *a fashion for women's walking sticks* next winter as it's slippery to walk here, – fans are unsuitable in winter and yet women are used to having something in their hands. – The war? – Yes, what about it? – It's still the same: nothing but the most terrifying preparations! – And meanwhile one courier after another reporting negotiations. – Today we get reliable

10. Possibly Count Kuenburg and his wife, Friederike Maria Anna. Their daughter was Theresia (1769–1805). The Langenhof was the palace of the Kuenburg family, now Siegmund-Haffner-Gasse 16.

11. Andrea Lucchesi (1741–1801), music director at Bonn from 1774; the concerto may be Lucchesi's keyboard concerto in F major, published at Bonn in 1773.

12. Although *Briefe* v. 526 suggests Mozart's 'graduation music' may be K287, it is more likely to have been either the andante second movement or the allegro fourth movement of the serenade K203 of August 1774; the concerto is unidentified. Andreas Pinzger (c. 1742–1817) was a court violinist in Salzburg.

news of an agreement – and tomorrow equally reliable news that no agreement is possible. Among the many reasons for this delay may be the no slight wish to delay the affair – as far as is possible – until the *harvest is over and the crops have been brought in*, because both armies and the whole nation would be exposed to a terrible famine, and Prussia in particular has a far less adequate supply of foodstuffs than Austria, with all its hereditary dominions, especially Hungary.[13] Moreover, Prussia has sown a certain amount of discord between the house of Austria and the elector of the Palatinate,[14] so that the elector wants to make an exception of some of the places included in the agreement and is most displeased, as a result negotiations have started between the ministers in Munich, with Count Seinsheim at their head, and the imperial ambassador Baron Lehrbach,[15] and all these matters will be laid before the imperial diet at Regensburg. The fortress at Eger[16] is being constantly reinforced, and in general the best possible arrangements are being made not only to ensure the availability of all that the Austrian troops need but to obtain everything as cheaply as possible. The Austrian monasteries have even been selling their wine at a fixed and *very cheap price*, and this is then passed on to the army. – So we must await the outcome with patience – may God grant us peace! I also told you some time ago that the elector won't be leaving Munich in the foreseeable future. – God knows when the Mannheimers will see him again: if things pass off peacefully, there's no doubt that he'll spend most, if not all, his time in Bavaria.

My dear Wolfgang, your *I'm bearing up, praise and thanks be to God, though often enough there's neither rhyme nor reason for what I do – I feel neither hot nor cold – I take little pleasure in things* shows me

13. The war came to be known as the *Kartoffelkrieg* (Potato War) because of the lengthy manoeuvres by both armies to obtain food supplies and deny them to the enemy.
14. Karl Theodor had made an agreement, on becoming elector of Bavaria, to cede Lower Bavaria to Joseph II in exchange for the Austrian Netherlands; this was fiercely opposed by Prussia.
15. Franz Siegmund Adalbert, Count Lehrbach, hunting master for the Austrian Innviertel region and a court official in Salzburg.
16. The town of Eger, now Cheb, is about 150 km west of Prague, on the border with Germany.

that you're *dissatisfied*, that something has annoyed you and that you wrote this in a bad mood. – I don't like this. I can't say anything as I don't know the cause of this ill humour. Having to earn one's own living is very different, of course, from living a life free from such concerns and leaving someone else to see to it. *Experience alone makes us wiser!* You can now appreciate all the work, the effort and the daily cares that I've had to endure in the *30 years* that I've been married in order to support a family, *worries* that will continue to plague me until my dying day. You've no reason to be unhappy. God has given you great talents. – You could scarcely wait to leave Salzb. – you've now discovered that much is as I predicted; otherwise you seem to think that I should long ago have left Salzb., taking my handful of belongings with me. – But you've finally reached a place where, even though things are exceptionally expensive, a lot of money can be made. Yes! It needs toil and hard work! – Nothing can be done without toil! You're young! – Whereas I have to torment myself with *5 pupils* in my *59th year* for a *mere pittance!* If some things don't turn out as you want, hope or imagine – if you have enemies – if you're persecuted – in a word, if things don't work out as you supposed in your thoughts that they would, remember that it has always been like this in the world and will always be so, a circumstance to which everyone, from king to beggar, must submit. – So, wasn't your *sinfonia concertante* performed *at all?* Were you paid for it? – – And didn't you get your score back? – – You didn't say a word about the French opera – no word about your *composition pupil*[17] etc. In short, you only ever tell me about the latest things that are happening at the time you're writing the letter, and on this occasion you must have been particularly absent-minded as you even wrote par *Augsburg, Strasbourg* at the top, as though the letter had to go to *Augsb* first and then to *Strasb.* etc. etc. You can see that I always tell you both a whole series of things and never forget anything: but I'd no doubt not remember many things if I didn't have a sheet of paper in front of me on which I note everything down in a few words as soon as it occurs to me and then quickly cross it off as I'm writing to you. As

17. The daughter of the Duc de Guines.

for the post of organist at Versailles, I replied to this recently, namely, in my letter of *28 May*. I consider the whole affair to be a *pious wish* on the part of Herr Rodolphe. But it has given rise to the following incident here: a few days ago I happened to be passing the countess[18] on the stairs when, as she often does, she asked me how you both were and whether I had any news. I told her very drily and rather hastily (I was hurrying back for lunch) that you were both very well and that, if you'd wanted, you could have had one of the 2 posts of royal organist and so on – in short, exactly what you told me in your letter. So yesterday Herr Bullinger comes to see us at his usual hour, bursting with the news that Abbé Henri[19] had gone specially to see him and told him what I'd told her. She told him that she was very sorry that she had been away when this business blew up; she wanted to know whether I'd like to have you back here; she could assure me *that in time to come you'd definitely be appointed Kapellmeister* but that for the sake of the prince's reputation this was at present impossible as you'd resigned from his service; and for the present you'd be returning as concert master and organist (which would only mean performing on the big organ and accompanying at court) for 50 florins a month. She asked Abbé Henri to speak to Herr Bullinger and find out if he could give him any information (concerning my opinion and intentions). Bullinger replied that I would of course be delighted to have my wife and son living with me again but that he could assure him that when I told them the story about the organist's post at Versailles I had no such intention and that Monsieur Henri should just discuss the matter very frankly with me and that as an honest man I'd speak quite openly to him and the countess. I've been keeping an eye on this bit of nonsense for some time, but I didn't want people to notice, and although we need another organist, I said nothing but let them get on with it in order not to give the impression that I had any ulterior motive. You can imagine how bad things have become as Lipp has been accompanying at court since Adlgasser's death. And

18. Maria Franziska, Countess Wallis, who was the sister of Archbishop Colloredo, see List.
19. Unidentified.

whenever Ceccarelli has sung, he's cursed loudly and publicly. I'm in no hurry to speak to Abbé Henri, as that would show them that I'm not particularly keen on their proposal: but as soon as I've spoken to him, I'll write and let you know what's going on. The archbishop has been firing off letters all over Italy but still can't find a Kapell-meister, – he's written to Vienna and Prague and Königgrätz[20] but can't find a decent organist and keyboard player. – Among the Kapell-meisters nothing can be done with Bertoni – and – you'll laugh at this! – *Luigi Gatti from Mantua*,[21] whom the archb. of Olmütz[22] has recommended as a distinguished keyboard player and whom you'll remember as having written out your mass[23] in Mantua and to whom the prince of Olmütz had to write, refuses to leave Mantua for more than 2 or 3 months. Ceccarelli, too, has been commissioned to find a Kapellmeister and a tenor. I should add that Meissner hasn't sung for the last 3 months – he's finished! – Among keyboard players Hasse won't leave Königgrätz, not that anyone would ask him any longer, now that our canoness Theresia Arco has been telling everyone that he's one of the most infamous drunkards and jokers.[24] – Haydn's promotion is no longer up for discussion, the whole business has taken on a quite sordid aspect since little Judith[25] gave birth to Brunetti's child on the eve of St Joseph's Day and the child was baptized in the cathedral at half past 6 in the evening and christened Josepha Antonia. The wench was always at Haydn's, with the result

20. Königgrätz, modern-day Hradec Králové in the Czech Republic; its bishop was Joseph Adam, Count Arco.

21. Ferdinando Giuseppe Bertoni (1725–1813), a student of Padre Martini, later served as music director at St Mark's, Venice; Luigi Gatti (1740–1817), second music director at the Reale Accademia, Mantua, was appointed music director at Salzburg in 1783.

22. Anton Theodor, Count Colloredo-Mels und Waldsee, archbishop of Olmütz 1777–1811, was the cousin of Archbishop Hieronymus Colloredo.

23. Mozart's mass cannot be identified with certainty; prior to his visit to Mantua in January 1770 he had written four such works: K49 (1768), K139 (1768), K65 (1769) and K66 (1769).

24. Theresia Maria Josepha von Arco (1740–?), daughter of Count Arco; Hasse is unidentified.

25. Maria Judith Lipp, Michael Haydn's sister-in-law. Apparently he had been considered as a possible successor to Adlgasser as court and cathedral organist.

that before her confinement he had to send her home to her father's, otherwise the abbot at St Peter's would have given Haydn notice to quit. Everyone has gone very quiet – why? Because this is Brunetti's 2nd lapse, and people are now waiting for the 3rd in order to report him to the privy council and have his contract annulled, as happened with *Marini*.[26] If Count Czernin leaves, Brunetti will go too! Now for my *violin tutor*. – *If my name's on it, try to buy a copy and send it to me by mail coach*, I already have the Dutch translation, so I'd like to have the French one too;[27] I told you recently that if you can find *some decent keyboard pieces suitable for students*, you might send them to me when you have an opportunity. – You could do so when you send me the French translation: but there's no great hurry, we can easily wait till Wolfg. sends us something of his own, even if it's only keyboard *caprices*[28] for his sister – and only if he has time.   *Vogler* in Mannheim is said to have brought out a book that the government of the Palatinate has prescribed for the use of *all the country's teachers of the keyboard, singing* and *composition*.[29] I shall have to see this book and have already given instructions to be sent a copy. It's bound to contain some good things as he was able to copy the *keyboard method* from *Bach's* book, while instructions for a *method of singing* come from *Tosi* and *Agricola* and the instructions for composition and harmony from Fux, Riepel, Marpurg, Mattheson, Spiess, Scheibe, D'Alembert, Rameau and a whole host of others;[30] these have been reduced to a shorter system of a kind that I've long had in mind; I'm

---

26. Joseph Marini, court confectioner 1772–6.
27. The Dutch translation of Leopold Mozart's *Gründliche Violinschule* was published in Haarlem in 1766 (see letter 12) and an unauthorized French translation, *Méthode raisonée pour apprendre à jouer du violon*, by Valentin Roeser, in Paris in 1770. Roeser is presumed to be the composer of twelve duos and a caprice published with the treatise.
28. Unidentified; *Briefe* v. 527 suggests the caprices may be K395 but these are almost certainly earlier works, described by Mozart as 'preambele' and sent by him from Munich to Salzburg in October 1777.
29. Georg Joseph Vogler, *Gründe der kurpfälzischen Tonschule* (Mannheim, 1778).
30. Here Leopold refers to Carl Philipp Emanuel Bach, *Versuch über die wahre Art das Clavier zu spielen* (Berlin, 1757); Pier Francesco Tosi, *Opinioni de' cantori antichi, e moderni o sieno osservazioni sopra il canto figurato* (Bologna, 1723); Johann Friedrich

curious to know whether his ideas agree with mine. You should get hold of this book – these things are a great help when you're *giving lessons*, it's only through experience that you're alerted to certain benefits when giving lessons and learn how to tackle this or that problem, and these benefits don't always occur to you at once. You know very well – *but that reminds me*! It's *St Anthony's Day* the day after tomorrow, and you're not here! Who'll do the serenade for the countess?[31] – Who? – *La Compagnie des Amateurs*, Count *Czernin* and *Kolb* are the *2 principal violins* with amazing solos, the work is made up of the *allegro* and *adagio* by Hafeneder and the *menuetto* with 3 trios by *Czernin*, all of them – mark you – *newly written*. The march is by Hafeneder, but it's all inferior produce, stolen from others, an absolute *ragbag*! And as false as the world in general! I should add that Gussetti is playing the horn, the courtiers and privy councillors will all accompany the march (*the only exception is me*), as I've *unfortunately lost the ability to learn things by heart*. We had the most pitiful rehearsal *here* yesterday. The first piece will be played at Countess Lützow's, the second one – an old cassation by Hafeneder – not until they reach Countess Lodron's, ouch, ouch, that'll do! – *Something important!* In her next letter Mama should tell me *what I should pay Tresel*. She's received nothing since you left: and we don't

Agricola, *Anleitung zur Singkunst* (Berlin, 1757); Johann Joseph Fux, *Gradus ad Parnassum* (Vienna, 1725); Joseph Riepel, *Anfangsgründe zur musicalischen Setzkunst* (Regensburg and Vienna, 1752); Meinrad Spiess, *Tractatus musicus compositorio-practicus* (Augsburg, 1745); Johann Adolph Scheibe, *Der critische Musikus* (Hamburg, 1738–40); Jean d'Alembert, *Elémens de musique théorique et pratique* (Paris, 1752, but presumably the German translation published Leipzig, 1757); and Jean-Philippe Rameau, *Traité de l'harmonie réduite à ses principes naturels* (Paris, 1722). Friedrich Wilhelm Marpurg and Johann Mattheson both published several important works; Marpurg's include *Der critische Musicus an der Spree* (Berlin, 1749–50), *Abhandlung von der Fuge* (Berlin, 1753–4), *Anleitung zum Clavierspielen* (Berlin, 1755), *Handbuch bey dem Generalbasse* (Berlin, 1755–8) and *Critische Briefe über die Tonkunst* (Berlin, 1760–64); Mattheson's are *Grosse General-Bass-Schule* (Hamburg, 1731), *Kern melodischer Wissenschafft* (Hamburg, 1737) and *Der vollkommene Capellmeister* (Hamburg, 1739).
31. It was the custom to serenade Antonia Maria, Countess Lodron, on her name day.

even know when we last paid her. Mama will no doubt remember, all we can find is a note dating from February 1777, according to which she was paid 15 florins and 20 kreuzers for 5 quarters. There are some actors at the tavern, as the theatre is being renovated, but there are only 9 or 10 of them. I hear they're not very good; they're giving some short plays and singspiels. Today is Grétry's *Das Milchmädchen*.[32] Everyone asks to be remembered to you, especially Bullinger and Sallerl, who are always thinking of you and talking about you, Mitzerl, Tresel, dear Pimperl, – Antretter, Hagenauer etc. etc. and we kiss you millions of times. I am your old

Mzt

Nannerl gets up at half past 5 every day and attends Mass at half past 6, and then her work proceeds smoothly for the whole of the rest of the day.

84. *Maria Anna Mozart to her husband, 12 June 1778, Paris*

My Dear Husband,

Your letter of 28 May arrived safely on 9 June and we were pleased to see from it that you're both well, Wolfgang and I are well, thank God, I was bled yesterday, so I shan't be able to write much today, Wolfgang isn't at home, he's lunching with Monsieur Raaff at Count Sickingen's, where they meet at least once a week as he's immensely fond of Wolfgang and is himself a great connoisseur of music and a composer in his own right, Herr Raaff comes here nearly every day, he calls me 'Mother' and is very fond of us, often staying for 2 or 3 hours, he's come to see me specially to sing for me and sang me 3 arias that I enjoyed a lot, every time he comes he always sings me something, I'm completely bowled over by his singing, he's a decent,

32. The music for the German translation of *Les deux chasseurs et la laitière* (1763), to which this presumably refers, is by Egidio Duni (1708–75) not André-Ernest-Modeste Grétry (1741–1813).

honest man and sincerity itself, if you knew him you'd really like him. You want to know where we're staying, first find the Rue Montmartre and then the Rue Cléry, it's the first street on the left as you enter the Rue Cléry from the Rue Montmartre, it's a beautiful street, almost entirely inhabited by the gentry, very clean, not far from the Boulevard Montmartre, and the air is good, the owners of the house are very kind and honest, not self-interested, which is rare in Paris. The day before yesterday I had lunch with Herr Heina and afterwards went for a walk in the Luxembourg Gardens, then to the palace to see the beautiful picture gallery and was astonishingly tired when I got home, I was alone as Wolfgang was having lunch with Raaff at Monsieur Grimm's, Herr Heina saw me home, he often comes to see us, and his wife has also visited us on 2 occasions, together with their daughter, who is already married. You don't say how the serenata[1] went, whether it was beautiful and whether the archbishop liked it. Which Colloredo is the bishop of Olmütz? Is he a brother or a cousin of our prince?[2]

By the way, what's Lenerl Martinelli up to? Where's she gone? To her cousins or to the Guards Lieutenant, as for the lightning conductor, I can't discuss it here as I don't know the language, but I've not seen any, but in Mannheim there was once talk of one, they don't think it's a good thing there, they say they attract storms where there'd otherwise be none and that if there are lots of rods the storm remains where it is until everything's broken and all the crops in the fields destroyed, it's better to let nature take its course rather than force it, for God can find people out and no lightning conductor will help them.[3] When the Kapuzinerberg collapsed, I'm sure many people were lucky, it could have been a disaster, it's really not good to build houses so close to mountains, the Neutor[4] may also collapse one day. We're having the most glorious summer here, very pleasant, thank God, and no storms yet. When Wolfgang eats at home, he and I pay

1. *Il Parnasso confuso* by Giacomo Rust, performed at Salzburg on 17 May 1778.
2. See previous letter, n. 22.
3. Leopold had shown an earlier interest in lightning conductors when he was in England, see letter 10.
4. The tunnel through the Mönchsberg in Salzburg.

15 sous for our lunch. For our evening meal we get 4 wafer cakes for 4 sous, so that you know what these are in German, they're *Hohlhippen*, in French they're called *plaisirs*. Please give our best wishes to all our good friends, we talk about our friends in Salzburg almost every day and wish they were here, many of them would stare and gape in astonishment if they saw the things that are to be seen here. *Addio*, keep well, I kiss you both many 1000 times and remain your faithful wife Frau Mozart I must stop now as my arm and eyes are hurting.

[*Mozart's postscript*]

I must now tell you something about our Raaff. You'll no doubt remember that what I wrote to you about him from Mannheim was none too good and that I wasn't satisfied with his singing, in a word, I simply didn't like him. But the reason for this was that I really didn't hear him properly in Mannheim. I first heard him at the rehearsal for Holzbauer's *Günther*.[5] He was then in his ordinary clothes, with his hat on and a stick in his hand. Whenever he wasn't singing, he stood there like a child having a shit. When he started to sing the first *recit.*, it went quite well, but every so often he would let out a shout, which I didn't like; he sang the arias in such a lazy way – and often put too much spirit into individual notes – it wasn't at all to my liking. It's a habit that he's always had – perhaps it's all part of the Bernacchi school, as he was a pupil of Bernacchi.[6] At court he always sang arias which in my own opinion didn't suit him at all, so I didn't like him at all. But, finally, when he made his début here at the Concert Spirituel, he sang Bach's scena 'Non so d'onde viene',[7] which is in any case a favourite of mine, and this was the first time I really heard him sing – I liked it – in other words, his way of singing – although the style itself – the Bernacchi school – isn't to my taste.

5. *Günther von Schwarzburg.*
6. The tenor Anton Raaff had been taught by the Bolognese castrato Antonio Bernacchi (1685–1756), known in particular for his performance of ornaments and cadenzas.
7. From Johann Christian Bach's *Alessandro nell'Indie* (1762). The aria was included in the pasticcio *Ezio*, which Mozart heard in London in 1764.

For me, he indulges in too much cantabile. I admit that when he was younger and in his prime, it must have been effective and will have surprised people – I like it, too, but it's taken to excess and often strikes me as ridiculous. What I like about him is when he sings short pieces – andantinos, for example – just as he also has certain arias in which he has his own style. Each to his own kind. I imagine that his forte was bravura singing – which you can still tell, at least as far as his age permits; a well-developed chest and long breath, and then – these andantinos. His voice is beautiful and very pleasing. If I close my eyes when listening to him – he reminds me very much of Meissner, except that Raaff's voice strikes me as being even more pleasing – I'm talking about now, as I've heard neither of them in their prime – so I can speak only of their style or method of singing, which singers always retain. As you know, Meissner has the bad habit of deliberately using vibrato, singing whole crotchets or even quavers on a sustained note – and I've never been able to bear this. It's really appalling. It's entirely unnatural. The human voice is naturally tremulous – but in its own way – and only to the extent that it is beautiful – this is in the nature of the voice. People imitate it not only on wind instruments but on string instruments too and even on the keyboard – but as soon as you overstep the limits, it's no longer beautiful – because it's contrary to nature. It then strikes me as being just like the organ when the bellows are blowing. – Well, Raaff isn't like that, he can't abide it either. But so far as a real cantabile is concerned, I prefer Meissner to Raaff (although I'm not entirely happy with Meissner, as he too can tend to excess). But as for bravura singing and passagework and roulades, there's no one to touch Raaff – and then there's his good, clear diction – that's beautiful. And then, as I said earlier, there are his andantinos, or little canzonettas – he's written four German songs[8] that are quite charming. He likes me a lot. We're very good friends. He comes to see us nearly every day. I must have lunched at least 6 times with Count Sickingen, the Palatine ambassador, where we always stay from 1 till 10. But time passes so quickly with him that you simply don't notice. He likes me a lot. But

8. These songs are lost.

I too enjoy spending time with him – he's such a friendly and sensible person, with such sound common sense – and such a true insight into music; I was there again today with Raaff; I took him some of my own things as he'd asked me to do so a long time ago. Today I took with me the new symphony[9] that I've just finished and that will open the Concert Spirituel on Corpus Christi.[10] They both liked it very much. I too am very pleased with it. But I don't know if others will like it – and to tell the truth, I don't really care. For who won't like it? – I can guarantee that the *few* intelligent French people who'll be there will like it – and as for the stupid ones, I don't consider it a great misfortune if they don't like it – but I hope that even the asses will find something in it that they'll like; and I didn't omit the *premier coup d'archet!*[11] – And that's enough. The idiots here make a great fuss about this! – The devil take me if I can see any difference – they all begin together, just like everywhere else. It's laughable. Raaff told me a story of Abaco's[12] about this – in Munich or somewhere else he was asked by a Frenchman – *Monsieur, vous avez été à Paris? – oui; est-ce que vous étiez au Concert spirituel? – oui; que dites vous du premier coup d'archet? – avez-vous entendu le premier coup d'archet? – oui? j'ai entendu le premier et le dernier – comment le dernier? – que veut dire cela? – mais oui, le premier et le dernier – et le dernier même m'a donné plus de plaisir.*[13]– I must close now. Best wishes to all our good friends, especially Herr Bullinger. I kiss your hands a thousand times and embrace my dear sister with all my heart. I am your most obedient son

Wolfgang Amadè Mozart

9. K297, 'Paris'.

10. 18 June.

11. A common orchestral gesture in which all the instruments started together with a unison or chord.

12. Evaristo Felice dall'Abaco (1657–1742), violoncellist.

13. 'Monsieur, were you in Paris? – Yes. – Were you at the Concert Spirituel? – Yes. – What do you say about the *premier coup d'archet?* Did you hear the *premier coup d'archet?* – Yes. I heard the first and the last. – What do you mean, "the last"? What does that mean? – Yes, the first and the last – and I liked the last even more than the first.'

85. *Mozart to his father, 3 July 1778, Paris*

Monsieur
mon très cher Père!

I have some very disagreeable and sad news for you, which is also the reason why I have been unable until now to reply to your last letter of the 11th. –

My dear mother is very ill – she was bled, as usual, and very necessary it was, too; she felt very well afterwards – but a few days later she complained of shivering and feverishness – she had diarrhoea and a headache – at first we just used our home remedies, antispasmodic powder, we'd like to have used the black one too, but we didn't have any and couldn't get any here, it's not known here even under the name of *Pulvis epilepticus*. – But when things started to get worse – she could hardly speak and lost her hearing so we had to shout – Baron *Grimm* sent his doctor – she's very weak and is still feverish and delirious – I'm told to be hopeful, but I'm not – for long days and nights I've been hovering between fear and hope – but I've resigned myself to God's will – and I hope that you and my dear sister will do the same; what other means is there to remain calm? – or, rather, calmer, as we can't be entirely calm; – come what may, I feel comforted – because I know that God, who orders everything for the best, however contrary it may seem to us, wills it so; for I believe – and I won't be persuaded otherwise – that no doctor, no individual, no misfortune and no accident can give a man his life or take it away, God alone can do that – these are only the instruments that He generally uses, although not always – after all, we can see people fainting, collapsing and dying – once our time comes, all remedies are useless, they hasten death rather than prevent it – we saw this in the case of our late friend Herr Heffner![1] – I'm not saying by this that my mother will and must die and that all hope is lost – she may yet be hale and hearty again, but only if God so wills it – after praying to my God with all my strength for health and life for

1. Heinrich Wilhelm von Heffner had died in 1774.

my dear mother, I like to think this and derive comfort from such thoughts, as I then feel heartened, calmer and consoled – and you'll easily imagine that I need this! – Now for something different; let's banish these sad thoughts. Let us hope, but not too much; let us put our trust in God and console ourselves with the thought that all is well if it accords with the will of the Almighty as He knows best what is most advantageous and beneficial to our temporal and eternal happiness and salvation –

I've had to write a symphony[2] to open the Concert Spirituel. It was performed to general acclaim on Corpus Christi; I also hear that there was a report on it in the *Courrier de l'Europe*.[3] – Without exception, people liked it. I was very afraid at the rehearsal as I've never in all my life heard anything worse; you can't imagine how twice in succession they bungled and scraped their way through it. – I was really very afraid – I'd have liked to rehearse it again, but there are always so many things to rehearse and so there was no more time; and so I had to go to bed with a fearful heart and in a discontented and angry frame of mind. The next day I decided not to go to the concert at all; but in the evening the weather was fine and so I decided to go, determined that if it went as badly as it had done during the rehearsal, I'd go into the orchestra, take the fiddle from the hands of the first violin, Herr Lahoussaye,[4] and conduct myself. I prayed to *God* that it would go well because everything is to His greater glory and honour; and behold, the symphony started, Raaff was standing next to me, and in the middle of the opening allegro there was a passage that I knew very well people were bound to like, the whole audience was carried away by it – and there was loud applause – but as I knew when I wrote it what effect it would produce, I introduced it again at the end – now people wanted to have it encored. They liked the andante, too, but especially the final allegro – I'd heard that

2. K297, 'Paris'.
3. For 26 June 1778: 'The Concert Spirituel on the feast of Corpus Christi began with a symphony by M. Mozart. This artist, who from the tenderest age made a name for himself among harpsichord players, may today be ranked among the most able composers.' See Deutsch, *Documentary Biography*, 176.
4. Pierre La Houssaye (1735–1818), violinist.

all the final allegros and opening ones too begin here with all the instruments playing together and generally in unison, and so I began mine with 2 violins only, playing piano for 8 whole bars, followed at once by a forte – the audience, as I expected, went 'shush' at the piano – then came the forte – and as soon as they heard it, they started to clap – I was so happy that as soon as the symphony was over I went to the Palais Royal – had a large ice – said the rosary, as I'd promised – and went home – just as I'm always happiest at home and always will be – or with some good, true, honest German who, if he's single, lives on his own as a good Christian or, if married, loves his wife and brings up his children well –

You probably already know that that godless arch-rogue Voltaire has died like a dog, like a beast – that's his reward![5] – As you say, we owe Tresel her wages for 5 quarters – you'll have realized long ago that I don't like it here – there are many reasons for this, but as I'm here, it would serve no useful purpose to go into them. It's not my fault and never will be, I'll do my very best – well, God will make all things right! – I've something in mind for which I pray to God every day – if it's His divine will, it will happen, if not, then I'm also content – at least I'll have done my part – when all is sorted out and if things work out as I want, you too must do your part or the whole business will be incomplete – I trust in your kindness to do so – but for the present you mustn't waste time thinking about it, the only favour I wanted to beg of you now is not to ask me to reveal my thoughts until it's time to do so.

As for the opera, it's now like this. It's very difficult to find a good libretto. The old ones are the best but they're not suited to the modern style, and the new ones are all useless; poetry was the one thing of which the French could be proud but this is now getting worse by the day – and yet poetry is the one thing that must be good here as they don't understand music – there are now 2 aria-based operas that I could write, one *en deux actes*, the other *en trois*. The one *en deux* is *Alexandre et Roxane* – but the poet who's writing it is still out of town – the one *en trois* is a translation of *Demofoonte* by

5. On 31 May, in Paris.

Metastasio,[6] combined with choruses and dances and in general arranged for the French theatre. Of this I've not yet been able to see anything –

Let me know if you've got Schroeter's concertos[7] in Salzburg. And Hüllmandel's sonatas.[8] – I was thinking of buying them and sending them to you. Both sets of pieces are very fine – I never thought of going to Versailles – I asked Baron Grimm and some other good friends for their advice – they all thought like me.

It's not much money, you have to spend 6 months languishing in a place where you can't earn anything else and your talent lies buried. Anyone in the king's service is forgotten in Paris. And then, to be an organist! – I'd like a decent appointment, but only as a Kapellmeister, and well paid.

Farewell for now – take care of your health, put your trust in God – it's there that you must find consolation; my dear mother is in the hands of the Almighty – if He returns her to us, as I hope, we shall thank Him for this mercy, but if it is His will to take her to Him, our fears and cares and despair will be of no avail – let us rather resign ourselves steadfastly to His divine will, fully convinced that it will be for our own good, for He does nothing without good cause – farewell, dearest Papa, keep well for my sake; I kiss your hands 1000 times and embrace my sister with all my heart. I am your most obedient son

Wolfgang Amadè Mozart

6. Mozart had already set four arias from *Demofoonte*: K71 (*Ah, più tremar non voglio*), 77 (*Misero me – Misero pargoletto*), 82 (*Se ardire, e speranza*) and 83 (*Se tutti i mali miei*).

7. Johann Samuel Schroeter (1752–88), music master to Queen Charlotte of Great Britain. Mozart refers here to Schroeter's concertos for keyboard, two violins and bass, op. 3, for several of which he composed cadenzas (for op. 3 no. 1, K626a/II, H and N; for op. 3 no. 2, K626a/II/O; for op. 3 no. 6, K626a/II, F and G).

8. Nicolas-Joseph Hüllmandel (1756–1823); his published sonatas include six for keyboard and violin, op. 1 (1774); three for keyboard and violin, op. 3 (1777); and three for keyboard solo, op. 4 (1778).

86. Mozart to Abbé Joseph Bullinger, 3 July 1778, Paris

Best of friends!
For you alone.

Grieve with me, my friend! – This has been the saddest day of my life – I'm writing this at 2 in the morning – but I have to tell you that my mother, my dear mother has just passed away! – God has called her to Him – He wished to take her, I could see that clearly – and so I resigned myself to His will – He gave her to me, so He was able to take her away from me. But just imagine all my anxiety and the fears and cares that I've endured this last fortnight – she was unconscious when she died, her life snuffed out like a candle. She made her confession 3 days previously, partook of the sacrament and received extreme unction – – but for the last 3 days she was constantly delirious, her death pangs began today at 5.21, but she immediately lost all sensation and consciousness – I pressed her hand and spoke to her – but she couldn't see me, couldn't hear me and felt nothing – and so she lay there until she passed away 5 hours later at 10.21 in the evening – there was no one present except for me, a good friend of ours whom my father knows, Herr Heina and the nurse – I can't possibly describe her whole illness to you today – but I'm convinced that she had to die – God willed it so. All I ask of you now is that as an act of friendship you prepare my poor father very gently for this sad news – I've written to him by this same post – but only to say that she's gravely ill – I'm now waiting for a reply so that I can then decide what to do. May God give him strength and courage! – My friend! – I feel comforted, not just now but for some time past! – By God's special mercy I have borne it all with fortitude and composure. When things became critical, I prayed to God for only 2 things, namely, that my mother should die happy and that I myself would find strength and courage – and God in His goodness has answered my prayer and granted me these 2 blessings in abundance.

I would ask you, therefore, as my best of friends, to stand by my father for me and give him courage so that when he hears the worst, he may not take it too badly. I also commend my sister to you with all my heart – please go and see them at once – but don't tell them that she's dead, just prepare them for it – do what you think best – use every means in your power, but just try to ensure my own peace of mind – so that I don't have to dread some other misfortune. – Stand by my dear father and my dear sister. Please reply without delay. – Adieu, I am your most obedient and grateful servant

Wolfgang Amadè Mozart

87. Mozart to his father, 9 July 1778, Paris

Monsieur
mon très cher Père!

I hope that you are prepared to hear with fortitude a piece of news that could not be sadder or more painful – my last letter of the 3rd will have placed you in the position of knowing that the news, when it came, would not be good – that same day, the 3rd, at 10.21 in the evening, my mother passed away peacefully; – when I wrote to you, she was already enjoying the delights of heaven – by then it was all over – I wrote to you during the night – I hope that you and my dear sister will forgive me this slight but very necessary deception – concluding from my own grief and sadness what yours must be, I couldn't possibly bring myself to spring such a terrible piece of news on you – but I hope that you're both now ready to hear the worst and that, after giving way to natural and only too justified grief and tears, you will eventually resign yourselves to God's will and worship His inscrutable, unfathomable and all-wise providence – you'll easily be able to imagine what I have had to bear – what courage and fortitude I needed to endure it all calmly as things grew progressively worse – and yet God in His goodness granted me this mercy – I have suffered enough anguish and wept enough tears – but what use was it all? – and so I had to console myself; you, my dear father and sister, must do the same! – Weep, weep your fill – but ultimately you must take comfort, – remember that Almighty God willed it so – and what can we do against Him? – We should rather pray and thank Him that it all turned out for the best – for she died a very happy death; – in these sad circumstances, I consoled myself with three things, namely, my entire trust and submission in God's will – then the fact that I was present at so easy and beautiful a death, as I imagined how happy she had become in a single moment – how much happier she is now than we are – so much so that at that moment I wanted to take the same journey as she had just done – in turn this wish and desire gave rise to my third source of consolation, namely, that she is not lost to us for ever – we shall see her again – we shall be happier and more contented to be with her than we have been in this world; we do not know when our time may come – but this is no cause for anxiety – when God wills it, then I too shall will it – well, God's most hallowed will has been done – let us therefore say a devout prayer for her soul and proceed to other matters, there is a time for everything – I'm writing this at the home of Madame d'Épinay and Monsieur Grimm, where I'm now lodging, a pretty little room with a very pleasant view and, so far as my state allows, I'm happy here – it will help me to regain my contentment to hear that my dear father and sister have accepted God's will with composure and fortitude and that they trust in Him with all their hearts in the firm conviction that He orders all things for the best – dearest father! Look after yourself! – Dearest sister – look after yourself – you've not yet enjoyed your brother's kind heart as he's not yet been able to demonstrate it – dearest father and sister – look after your health – remember that you have a son and a brother who is doing everything in his power to make you happy – knowing full well that one day you'll not refuse to grant him his desire and his happiness – which certainly does him honour – and that you'll do everything possible to make him happy – Oh, then we'll live together as peacefully, honourably and contentedly as is possible in this world – and finally, when God wills it, we shall meet again there – for this we are destined and created –

Your last letter of 29 June[1] has arrived safely and I'm pleased to

1. Not included here.

learn that you are both well, all praise and thanks be to God, I couldn't help laughing at your account of Haydn's drunkenness, – if I'd been there, I'd certainly have whispered in his ear: *Adlgasser*.[2] – But it's a disgrace that such an able man should be rendered incapable of performing his duties and have only himself to blame for it – in a post that's in God's honour – when the archbishop and the whole court are there – and the whole church is full of people – it's appalling – this is also one of the main reasons why I detest Salzburg – the coarse, ill-mannered and dissolute court musicians – no honest man of good breeding could live with them; – instead of taking an interest in them, he should be ashamed of them! – also – and this is probably the reason – the musicians aren't very popular with us and are simply not respected – if only the orchestra were organized as it is in Mannheim! – the discipline that obtains in that orchestra! – the authority that Cannabich wields – there everything is taken seriously; Cannabich, who's the best music director I've ever seen, is loved and feared by his subordinates. – He's also respected by the whole town, as are his troops – but they certainly behave very differently – they're well-mannered, dress well, don't frequent taverns and don't get drunk – but this can never be the case with you, unless, that is, the prince trusts you or me and gives us full authority, *at least as far as the orchestra is concerned* – otherwise it's no good; in *Salzburg* everyone – or rather no one – bothers about the orchestra – if I were to take it on, I'd have to have a completely free hand – the chief steward should have nothing to say to me on orchestral matters and, indeed, on anything bound up with the orchestra. A courtier can't stand in for a Kapellmeister, though a Kapellmeister could no doubt stand in for a courtier – by the way, the elector is now back in Mannheim – Madame Cannabich and her husband are in correspondence with me. I'm afraid that the orchestra will be much reduced in size, which would be an eternal shame, but if this doesn't happen, I may still remain hopeful – you know that there's nothing I want more than a

2. Leopold had reported that Michael Haydn played the organ so badly on Holy Trinity Sunday that he was worried that Haydn was about to die as Adlgasser had, during a service the previous December (see letter 69); it turned out, however, that Haydn was merely tipsy.

good position, good in character and good in terms of the money –
it doesn't matter where it is – as long as it's in a Catholic area. – You
acted in a masterly way, just like Ulysses, throughout the whole affair
with Count Starhemberg[3] – only continue as before and don't allow
yourself to be taken in – and in particular you should be on your
guard if conversation turns to that arrogant goose[4] – I know her, and
you can be assured that she has sugar and honey on her lips but
pepper in her head and heart – it's entirely natural that the whole
business is still open to discussion and that many points must be
conceded before I could make up my mind and that even if everything
were all right I'd still prefer to be anywhere else but Salzburg – but
I don't need to worry, as it's unlikely that everything will be granted
to me as I'm asking for so much –. But it's not impossible – I'd not
hesitate for a moment if everything were properly organized – if only
to have the pleasure of being with you – but if the Salzburgers want
me, they must satisfy me and all my wishes – otherwise they'll
certainly not get me. – So the abbot of Baumberg has died the usual
abbot's death! – I didn't know that the abbot of the Holy Cross had
died too – I'm very sorry – he was a good, honest, decent man; so
you didn't think that Dean Zöschinger would be made abbot? – Upon
my honour, I never imagined it otherwise; I really don't know who
else it could have been! – Of course, he's a good abbot for the
orchestra! – So the *young lady's*[5] daily walk with her faithful lackey
bore fruit after all! – They were certainly busy and haven't been idle
– the devil makes work for idle hands: – so the amateur theatricals
have finally started up? – But how long will they last? – I don't
suppose Countess Lodron will be wanting any more concerts like
the last one – Czernin is a young whippersnapper and Brunetti a
foul-mouthed oaf.

My friend Raaff is leaving tomorrow; but he's going via Brussels
to Aix-la-Chapelle and Spa – and from there to Mannheim; he'll let

3. In the same letter Leopold had also reported the gist of an oblique conversation
he had had with Starhemberg concerning Wolfgang's possible return to Salzburg as
court organist.
4. Countess Wallis.
5. Unidentified.

me know as soon as he gets there, for we intend to stay in touch –
he sends you and my sister his good wishes, even though he doesn't
know you. You say in your letter that you've heard no more about
my composition pupil for a long time – that's true, but what shall I
tell you about her? – She's not the sort of person who will ever
become a composer – all my efforts are in vain – in the first place,
she's thoroughly stupid and also thoroughly lazy – I told you about
the opera[6] in my last letter – as for Noverre's ballet, all I've ever said
is that he may write a new one – he needed just half a ballet and so
I wrote the music for it – in other words, 6 numbers are by others
and consist entirely of dreadful old French airs, whereas I've written
the symphony and contredanses, making 12 pieces in all – the ballet
has already been given 4 times[7] to great acclaim – but I'm now
absolutely determined not to write anything else unless I know in
advance what I'm going to get for it – I did this just as a favour for
Noverre. – Monsieur Wendling left on the last day of May – if I
wanted to see Baron Bagge,[8] I'd have to have very good eyes as he's
not here but in London – is it possible that I've not already told you
this? – You'll see that in future I'll answer all your letters accurately
– it's said that Baron Bagge will be returning soon, which I should
like very much – for many reasons – but especially because there's
always an opportunity at his house to hold proper rehearsals –
Kapellmeister Bach will also be here soon – I think he'll be writing
an opera[9] – the French are asses and will always remain so, they can
do nothing themselves – they have to rely on foreigners. I spoke to
Piccinni[10] at the Concert Spirituel – he's very polite to me and I to
him – whenever we happen to meet – otherwise I've not made any
new acquaintances – either with him or with other composers – I
know what I'm doing – and so do they – and that's enough: – I've

6. *Alexandre et Roxane.*
7. In fact, the ballet had been given six times, on 11, 20 and 25 June and 2, 5 and
7 July.
8. Karl Ernst, Baron Bagge (1722–91), a well-known amateur musician.
9. Johann Christian Bach; the opera was *Amadis des Gaules*, first performed on
14 December 1779.
10. The Italian composer Niccolò Piccinni was active in Paris from 1777.

already told you that my symphony was a great success at the Concert Spirituel. – If I'm asked to write an opera, it'll no doubt be a source of considerable annoyance, but I don't mind too much as I'm used to it – if only the confounded French language weren't such a dastardly enemy of music! – It's pitiful – German is divine in comparison. – And then there are the singers – – they simply don't deserve the name as they don't sing but scream and howl at the tops of their voices, a nasal, throaty sound – I'll have to write a French oratorio for the Concert Spirituel next Lent[11] – the director Legros is amazingly taken with me; I should add that although I used to see him every day, I've not seen him since Easter, I was so annoyed that he'd not performed my sinfonia concertante; I often visited his house in order to see Monsieur Raaff and each time had to pass his rooms – on each occasion the servants and maids saw me and on each occasion I asked them to give him my best wishes. – I think it's a shame that he didn't perform it, people would have liked it – but he no longer has any opportunity to do so. Where could he find 4 such people for it? One day, when I was planning to visit Raaff, he wasn't at home but I was assured that he'd soon be back. And so I waited – Monsieur Legros came into the room – it's a miracle that I've finally had the pleasure of seeing you again – yes, I've got so much to do – are you staying for lunch? – I'm sorry, but I've a prior engagement. – Monsieur Mozart, we must spend more time together; – it'll be a pleasure. – Long silence – finally: by the way, won't you write a grand symphony for me for Corpus Christi? – Why not? – But can I rely on it? – Oh yes, as long as I can rely on its being performed – and that it doesn't suffer the same fate as the sinfonia concertante – then the dance began – he apologized as best he could – but there wasn't much he could say – in a word, the symphony was universally liked – and Legros is so pleased that he says it's his best symphony – only the andante hasn't had the good fortune to win his approval – he says it contains too many modulations and that it's too long – but this is because the audience forgot to clap as loudly and make as much noise as they did for the first and final movements – but the

11. This project never materialized.

andante won the greatest approval *from me* and from all the connoisseurs and music lovers and most other listeners – it's exactly the
opposite of what Legros says – it's entirely natural – and short.[12] –
But in order to satisfy him – and, as he claims, several others – I've
written another one – each is fitting in its own way – for each has a
different character – but I like the last one even more – when I have
a moment, I'll send you the symphony, together with the violin
tutor,[13] some keyboard pieces and Vogler's *Tonwissenschaft und Tonsezkunst*[14] – and I shall then want to know what you think about them
– the symphony will be performed for the second time – with the
new andante – on 15 August – the Feast of the Assumption – the
symphony is in re and the andante in sol – you're not supposed to
say D or G here. – Well, Legros is now right behind me. – It's time
to start thinking about ending this letter – if you write to me, I think
it would be better if you were to do so *chez Monsieur Le Baron de
Grimm, Chaussée d'Antin près le Boulevard* – Monsieur Grimm will be
writing to you himself very shortly. He and Madame d'Épinay both
ask to be remembered to you and send you their heartfelt condolences
– but they hope that you will be able to remain composed in the face
of a matter that can't be changed – take comfort – and pray fervently,
this is the only expedient that is left to us – I was going to ask you
to have Holy Masses said at Maria Plain and Loreto – I've also done
so here. As for the letter of recommendation for Herr Beer,[15] I don't
think it'll be necessary to send it to me – I still haven't met him; I
know only that he's a good clarinettist but a dissolute companion – I
don't like associating with such people – it does one no credit; and
I've no wish to give him a letter of recommendation – I'd be truly

12. Of the two surviving slow movements for the 'Paris' symphony, it is likely that
the andante in 6/8 is the original, and the andante in 3/4 the replacement movement
composed by Mozart. The first edition of the work, published in Paris in 1788,
includes only the 3/4 andante.
13. The French translation of Leopold's *Gründliche Violinschule* referred to earlier.
14. Georg Joseph Vogler's *Tonwissenschaft und Tonsezkunst* (Mannheim, 1776) was
a method for determining chord roots and chord functions.
15. Joseph Beer (1744–1812), court trumpeter in Paris from 1777–82 and clarinettist
to the Duc d'Orléans. In his letter of 29 June, Leopold reported that he had received
a letter of recommendation for Beer (possibly from Josepha Duschek).

ashamed to do so – even if he could do something for me! – But he's
by no means respected – many people haven't even heard of him –
Of the 2 Stamitzes,[16] only the younger one is here – the older (the
real composer *à la* Hafeneder) is in London – they're 2 wretched
scribblers – and gamblers – drunkards – and whoremongers – not
the kind of people for me – the one who's here has scarcely a decent
coat to his back – by the way, if things don't work out with Brunetti,
I'd very much like to recommend a good friend of mine to the
archbishop as first violin, a decent, honest, upstanding man – a stolid
individual; – I'd put him at around 40 – a widower – he's called
Rothfischer[17] – he's concert master to the princess of Nassau-Weilburg
at Kirchheimbolanden – between ourselves, he's dissatisfied as the
prince doesn't like him – or rather he doesn't like *his music* – he's
commended himself to me and it would give me real pleasure to help
him – he's the best of men. – Adieu. I kiss your hands 100,000 times
and embrace my sister with all my heart. I am your most obedient
son

Wolfgang Amadè Mozart

88. Leopold Mozart to his wife and son, 13 July 1778, Salzburg

My Dear Wife and Son,
    In order not to miss your name day,[1] my dear wife, I'm writing to
you today, even though the letter will no doubt arrive a few days
early. I wish you a million joys in being able to celebrate it once
more and ask Almighty God to keep you well on this day and for
many years to come and allow you to live as contented a life as is
possible in this inconstant world theatre. I'm absolutely convinced
that for you to be truly happy you need your husband and daughter.
God in His unfathomable decree and most holy providence will do

16. Carl Stamitz and his brother Anton Thaddäus Stamitz (1754–before 1809).
17. Mozart had met the violinist Paul Rothfischer on his visit to Kirchheimbolanden
in February (see letter 71).
1. 26 July.

what is best for us. Would you have thought a year ago that you'd be spending your next name day in Paris? – – However incredible this would have seemed to many people then, although not to ourselves, it is possible that with God's help we may be reunited even before we expect it: for my one concern is that I am separated from you and *living so far away, so very far away from you*; otherwise we're well, God be praised! We both kiss you and Wolfgang a million times and beg you above all to take great care of your health. – *The theatre of war has finally opened!* In Paris you'll already know that on the 5th of this month the king of Prussia[2] entered Bohemia from Glatz and that he's passed through Nachod and penetrated as far as Königgrätz. War was bound to break out as neither power could withdraw its armies without losing face. For several weeks Austria, with its marches and countermarches, has provided the king with occasional opportunities to make an incursion and launch an attack: but the king didn't think it advisable to undertake such an attack; now the emperor[3] has established a very powerful *false arsenal* at Nachod, and this persuaded the king to attack. But the arsenal was a *feint* and contained only a semblance of the real thing. They had to take this risk, whatever the outcome, as Austria was neither able nor willing to be the aggressor, while the Croats were merely an advance guard (the only position in which they can really be used) and could barely be restrained any longer, as these people always hope to win booty, which is why they're so keen to go to war. The Saxon troops have formed an alliance with Prussia, and it's presumably true that they've joined forces with Prince Heinrich[4] and will no doubt attack *Eger* and the *Upper* Palatinate. More news will no doubt arrive with the next post: this came with the Austrian post on the 11th. This war will be one of the bloodiest, the king wants to die a glorious death, and the emperor wants to start his army life on an equally glorious note.[5]

I wrote the foregoing yesterday, the 12th. This morning, the 13th, shortly before 10 o'clock, I received your distressing letter of 3 July.

2. King Frederick II (the Great) (1712–86).
3. Joseph II.
4. Of Prussia (1726–1802), brother of Frederick II.
5. In fact the war was largely bloodless.

You can well imagine how we are both feeling. We wept so much that we could scarcely read your letter. – And your sister! – Great God in your mercy! May your most hallowed will be done! My dear son! For all that I am resigned as far as possible to God's will, you'll none the less find it entirely human and natural that I'm almost unable to write for weeping. What am I to conclude from all this –? Only that even as I write these lines, she is presumably already dead – or that she has recovered, for you wrote on the 3rd and today is already the 13th. You say that after being bled she felt well, but that a few days later she complained of shivering and feverishness. The last letter from the two of you was dated 12 June, and in it she wrote – *I was bled yesterday*: so that was the 11th – and why was it done on a Saturday – a fast day? – – I expect she ate some meat. She waited too long to be bled. Knowing her very well, I remember that she likes to put things off, especially in a foreign place, where she'd first have to enquire after a surgeon. Well, so the matter stands – it can't be helped any longer – I have complete confidence in your filial love and know that you have taken all possible care of your mother, who is undoubtedly *good*, and that if God restores her to us, you will always continue to do so – your *good* mother, who always saw you as *the apple of her eye* and whose love for you was exceptional, who was exceedingly proud of you and who – I know this better than you – lived for you alone. But if all our hopes are in vain! Could we really have lost her! – Good God! *You need friends, honest friends!* Otherwise you'll lose everything, what with the funeral expenses etc. My God! There are many expenses about which you know nothing and where strangers are cheated – taken for a ride – tricked – put to unnecessary expense and exploited if they don't have honest friends: you can have no conception of this. If this misfortune has befallen you, ask Baron Grimm if you can store your mother's effects at his house, so that you don't have to keep an eye on so many things: or lock everything up, because if you're often away for whole days at a time, people could break into your room and rob you. God grant that all my precautions are unnecessary: but you will recognize your father in this. My dear wife! My dear son! – as she fell ill a few days after being bled, she must have been ill since 16 or 17 June. But you waited too long – she thought she'd get better through bed rest – by dieting – by her own devices, I know how it is, one hopes for the best and puts things off: but, my dear Wolfgang, diarrhoea when one has a fever requires a doctor to know if the fever should be reduced or allowed to run its course as medicines designed to reduce the temperature cause an increase in diarrhoea: and if the diarrhoea is stopped at the wrong time, the *materia peccans* leads to gangrene. – God! We are in your hands.

Congratulations on the success of your symphony at the Concert Spirituel. I can imagine how anxious you must have been. – Your determination to rush out into the orchestra if things hadn't gone well was presumably just a wild idea. God forbid! You must put this and all such notions out of your head; they're ill considered, such a step would cost you your life, which no man in his right senses risks for a symphony. – Such an affront – and a public affront to boot – would inevitably be avenged by the sword not just by *a Frenchman* but by all who value their honour. An Italian would say nothing but would lie in wait at a street corner and shoot you dead. – From Munich I've received reliable reports that Count Seeau has been confirmed as intendant of music for Munich and Mannheim; that a list of all the orchestral players has been sent to Mannheim; that the two orchestras will be combined and the worst players weeded out; Herr *Wotschitka* and the other *valets de chambre* have been pensioned off on a pension of 400 florins, *which surprises me*; Dr *Sänfftel* had the effrontery to demand 3000 florins for his treatment, whereupon he was stripped of his title and salary; finally, it is hoped in Munich that the elector and his wife, the electress, will be back in Munich with their entire court by 10 August.   I began this letter with my congratulations, – and Nannerl was planning to end it with her own. But, as you can imagine, she's incapable of writing a single word, now that she has to write – each letter that she's supposed to write down brings a flood of tears to her eyes. You, her dear brother, must take her place, if – as we hope and desire – you can still do so.

But no! You can no longer do so – she has passed away – you are trying too hard to console me, no one is as eager as that unless driven to it quite naturally by the loss of all human hope or by the event itself. I'm now going to have some lunch, though I don't suppose I'll have much of an appetite.

I'm writing this at half past 3 in the afternoon. I now know that my dear wife is in heaven. I'm writing this with tears in my eyes but in total submission to God's will! Yesterday was the annual celebration of the dedication of the Holy Trinity, so our usual target practice was postponed till today. I was unable to cancel it at such a late hour and didn't want to either, in spite of your sad letter. We ate little, but Nannerl, who had cried a lot before lunch, was violently sick and had a terrible headache, so she went to lie down on her bed. Herr Bullinger and the rest of them found us in this deeply distressing situation. Without saying a word, I gave him your letter to read, and he acted his part very well and asked me what I thought of it. I told him that I was firmly convinced that my dear wife was already dead: he said that he was indeed inclined to suspect as much himself; and he then comforted me and as a true friend told me all that I had *already* told *myself*. I made an effort to cheer up and to remain so, while submitting to God's most holy will, we finished our target practice and everyone left, feeling very saddened, Herr Bullinger remained with me and, without appearing to do so, asked me if I thought that there was any hope in the condition that had been described to us. I replied that I thought that not only was she now dead but that she was already dead on the day you wrote your letter; that I had submitted to the will of God and had to remember *that I still had 2 children who I hoped would continue to love me inasmuch as I lived only for them*; that I was so firmly convinced that she was dead that I'd even written to you, reminding you to take care of her succession etc. To this he said, *yes, she's dead*. At that moment the scales fell from my eyes, scales that had been put in place by this sudden and unexpected turn of events, preventing me from seeing what had happened, for otherwise I'd have quickly suspected that you'd secretly written the truth to Herr Bullinger as soon as I'd read your letter. But your letter had really stunned me – at first I was too dumbfounded to be able to think properly. Even now I still don't know what to write! You don't need to worry about me; I shall play the man. But just think of your mother's tender love for you and you'll realize how much she cared for you – just as when you reach maturity you'll love me more and more after my death – if you love me – *as I do not doubt* – you should take care of your health, – *my life depends on yours*, as does the future support of your sister, who honestly loves you with all her heart. It is unbelievably difficult when death severs a good and happy marriage, but you have to experience that for yourself to know it. – *Write and tell me all the details*; perhaps she wasn't bled enough? – – The only thing that's certain is that she trusted too much in herself and called in the doctor too late; meanwhile the inflammation of her intestines gained the upper hand. *Take good care of your health!* Don't make us all unhappy! Nannerl doesn't yet know about Bullinger's letter, but I've already prepared her to believe that her dear mother is dead. – Write to me soon – tell me everything – when she was buried – and where.[6] – – Good God! To think that I'll have to go to Paris in search of my dear wife's grave! – We kiss you both with all our heart. I must close as the post is leaving. Your honest and utterly distraught father

Mozart

Make sure that none of your things are lost.

89. *Mozart to Fridolin Weber, 29 July 1778, Paris*

Monsieur mon très cher et plus cher ami!

I've just received your letter of 15 July – I'd been longing for it so much and thought so much about it! – *Basta!* – Your esteemed letter reassures me – apart from its main contents, which made my blood boil – so that – but I'll say no more – you know me, my friend – you'll doubtless know what I felt when reading through your letter – I can't avoid it – I must reply at once as I consider it very necessary – but I must ask you whether you've also received my letter of

6. Mozart's mother was buried on 4 July at one of the burial grounds associated with the parish church of St Eustache, Paris.

29 June? – I sent you 3 letters in quick succession[1] – one dated the
27th and addressed to you direct – one on the *29th* to Herr Heckmann,
and one on *3* July to the same address; now to the matter in hand: –
have I not always said that the elector would choose to live in Munich?
– I've already heard here that Count Seeau has been confirmed as
intendant for both Munich and Mannheim! – I must now tell you
something you need to know but which I can't possibly entrust to
any known language – you'll soon find out what I mean; – in the
meantime I hope that, whether the court moves to Munich or remains
in Mannheim, your salary will be increased and that your daughter
will receive a decent salary – so that your debts may all be paid and
you can breathe a little more freely – things must get better in time
– if not, our present situation is so good that we can afford to be
patient – and wait for the right time – and as a result improve our
situation by moving *elsewhere*; – my friend, if I had the sort of money
that many people squander so disgracefully without having earned it;
if I had it – oh, how happy I'd be to help you! – But unfortunately,
he who can doesn't want to, and he who wants to can't! – Listen
now; I wanted to use my influence – and perhaps not in vain – to
bring you and your daughter to Paris this winter – but the position
is this: Monsieur Legros, the director of the Concert Spirituel, to
whom I've already spoken about my friend, can't have her here this
winter – because he's already engaged Madame Lebrun[2] for this
period – and *for the present* he's not in the fortunate position of being
able to pay 2 such persons according to their merit – *I'd not agree to
anything else* – so there's no money to be earned here – but it can
certainly be arranged for the winter after next – I just wanted to tell
you that if you can't hold out any longer – really can't – you could
come to Paris – the journey, board and lodging, wood and light
would cost you nothing – but that's not enough, of course. You'd be
able to get through the winter – there are private concerts – and I may
be able to arrange something for you at the Concert des Amateurs; –

1. All three are lost, as is the letter from Fridolin Weber mentioned by Mozart.
2. The singer Franziska Dorothea Lebrun née Danzi (1756–91) was the wife of the
oboist Ludwig August Lebrun (1752–90); both were engaged at Mannheim.

but what about the summer? – on the other hand, I'm not worried about the winter after next – you'd certainly be engaged by the Concert Spirituel – – *basta*, write and let me know what you think; – I'll then do all I can; – my dearest friend! I'm almost ashamed to make you an offer which – even if you agree to it – is still uncertain – and not as advantageous as you deserve and as I desire! But – don't ignore the fact that my intentions are good – the will is there; – I'd really like to help, but – I'm looking around to see if I can find anything – if the matter can be arranged; – wait; – I'll see; – if it works – what I have in mind right now – – but you must be patient – – one should never force an issue, otherwise it goes wrong or else it doesn't work out at all; – in the meantime press *as hard as you can* to get your salary increased and to get a good one for your daughter – keep writing to them – and, note well, if our heroine is to sing at court – and if *you've* received no reply – or at least not a favourable one to your application, don't let her sing – pretend that she's indisposed – do it often – I beg you; – and when you've done this on several occasions, then all of a sudden let her sing again – you'll see how effective this is; – but it needs to be done with great subtlety and cunning; – you must seem to be very sorry that Aloysia is indisposed just when she has to perform – but note that if you do this 3 or 4 times *in a row*, people will realize that they're being fooled! – but this is just what I want – and if she does then sing again, it must be made clear that she is just doing it to oblige! – She must not be fully recovered – she's just doing her best to please the elector – you understand; – but at the same time she must make every effort to sing with all her heart and soul; – and at the same time it goes without saying that you must continue to make your entirely justifiable grievances known, both verbally and in writing – and if the intendant[3] or *anyone else* who you know *gossips about it* enquires after your daughter's health – tell them as a great secret that it's no wonder – the poor girl is suffering from a disorder of the mind that can scarcely be cured here – she has devoted herself to singing with great industry, has shown great application and has made real progress – which no

3. Count Savioli.

one can deny – but unfortunately she now realizes that all her trouble and hard work have been in vain and that her desire and eagerness to serve His Highness the Elector have come to nothing – and that she would have lost all her pleasure in music, have neglected herself and actually abandoned singing, had I not said to her: My daughter, your effort and your hard work have not been in vain; if people won't reward you here, they'll reward you elsewhere; – and that is what I intend; I can't stand it any longer – I can't have my child criticizing me any longer, however justified her reproaches may be; – and then – if he asks where you're planning to go – *I don't yet know* – put that in your pipe and smoke it! – But this is only if you think that all hope is lost – which I simply cannot believe; it's impossible for the elector to keep her waiting any longer – if he sees that he can't use your daughter without offering her a salary, he'll be obliged to pay her as he really must have her – he positively needs her. – After all, who has he got in Mannheim? – Danzi?[4] – As sure as I'm writing this, she won't stay. – And in Munich? – He won't find anyone there so soon. – I know Munich like the back of my hand, I've been there 5 times – and so he has no choice – he can't let her go there – and as for you, your chief grievance must always be your *debts*; – but now, so that you're not made to look *foolish*, – in the event that nothing can be done (which I hope is not the case), you would do well to cast around in secret for a more secure appointment – but at a court, of course – and I too, rest assured, will do all I can. – As for yourself, my idea is that you should apply in secret to Mainz – you were there quite recently – there must be *someone* there who can do something and who's in a position to do so – only don't mention Seyler's company[5] to me! – I couldn't bear to think of your daughter – and even if she weren't your daughter – even if she were a foundling – I'd be very sorry if anyone as *talented* as *she* is should fall among actors, as if she were good enough only as a stopgap – for the main thing about the Seyler company and, indeed, about all troupes is

---

4. Lebrun, see n. 2.
5. Abel Seyler (1730–1800) managed a successful travelling theatrical troupe that during the 1770s played at Mainz, Mannheim, Gotha and Weimar.

always the plays – the singspiel is there only to give occasional relief to the actors – often only to give them time and room to *change* – and in general serves only as a distraction – you always have to think of your reputation – at least, I always think of mine – well, there you have my candid opinion – you may not like it, but with my friends I'm used to *speaking my mind* – in any case, you can do as you like – I'll never take the liberty of telling you what to do – I'll just advise you as a true friend – you see that I'm not obstinately resolved that you should remain in Mannheim – I'd love you to come to Mainz – but only with honour and reputation – my God, my delight at going to Mainz would be much reduced if I had to seek out your daughter among the actors – which could easily happen – it's by no means impossible that I may go to Mainz – under contract, of course – this *just between ourselves*, of course – you, my friend, are the only person in whom I've confided my affairs, just as you've confided yours in me – something else: could you, my friend, bear to see your daughter acting with players in the very place where Mlle Hellmuth (who simply can't be compared with her) is engaged at court? and where she has therefore been preferred to her?⁶ – My dearest friend – let this be my ultimate and most extreme argument – I'm now going to repeat everything I've just said – it seems to me (you mustn't take this amiss) that you easily get depressed – you soon lose heart – you abandon hope too quickly – you can't deny this, as I know your circumstances – – they're depressing, it's true – but by no means as depressing as you imagine; I know how it pains and hurts an honest man to run up debts – I know this from experience – but if we examine things more closely, who is it who is running up these debts? – You? – No, the elector; if you were to leave today and not come back – and not pay your debts – you'd be entirely justified – and no one, not even the elector, could object – but – you don't need to do this – you're bound to find yourself in the position of being able to pay off these debts – and so I advise you to be patient until the winter after next – but meanwhile do your utmost to improve your situation

6. Josepha Hellmuth, formerly a member of Seyler's troupe, was engaged as court chamber singer in Mainz from 1778.

in Mannheim – and try to find another post elsewhere – if either of these alternatives comes off, so much the better – if not, then come to Paris the winter after next – by then I guarantee that you'll be able to earn at least 60 louis d'or – meanwhile Aloysia will have made progress in both *singing* and, more especially, *acting* – during this time I'll see if I can find an opera for her in Italy – once she has sung in an opera there, she'll be made – if in the meantime Mme Lebrun comes to Mannheim – you should both make friends with her – she might be useful to you in London – she's going there this winter – I'll approach her at once; – although, as I'm sure you do not doubt, I'd prefer to see you here today rather than tomorrow, as a true friend I must dissuade you from coming here *this winter* in the way I've described (the only possible way at present) – first, it would be rather risky – and not exactly good for your reputation if you came here without an engagement – and, secondly, it's very sad to have to be supported by someone else – yes, my God, if I were in the fortunate position of being able to support you free of charge, you could certainly come without having to fear for your reputation – as I swear to you on my honour that not a soul would know about it, apart from you and me – and they'd never discover it, – well, there you have my thoughts, opinion and advice; do as you think best – I would only ask you not to think that I'm trying to prevent you from setting out on your travels and attempting to persuade you to remain in Mannheim or to find an engagement in Mainz, simply because I myself have hopes of obtaining an engagement in one or other of these places – I mean, in order to have the pleasure of embracing you very soon – no, it's because I'm convinced for many reasons that you should wait a little longer; yes, my dearest friend, if I could arrange for us to live together in the same place, happily and contentedly – I would, of course, prefer this above all else – this would suit me best of all – but rest assured that I value your happiness more than my own peace of mind and pleasure – and that I would sacrifice all my happiness to know that you were happy and contented – with full confidence in God that He will one day grant me the pleasure of seeing again the people whom I love so dearly with all my heart and soul – and perhaps – even of being able to live with them – and so you must be patient, dearest, most beloved friend! – And in the meantime keep on looking out for something – now let me say just a little about myself – I simply can't tell you what a dreadful time I'm having here – everything moves so slowly, and until you're well known, nothing can be done in the matter of composition – in my previous letters I told you how hard it is to find a good libretto – from my account of the music here, you can easily imagine that I'm not particularly happy here – and that (between ourselves) I'm trying to get away from here as soon as possible; unfortunately Herr Raaff won't arrive in Mannheim until the end of August – but he'll then do what he can for me – so there's perhaps some cause for hope – if this doesn't work out, it's more than likely that I'll go to Mainz – Count Sickingen (whom I saw yesterday and to whom I spoke very positively about you) has a brother there – he himself made the suggestion – so I think it's feasible – now you know my prospects, which have been kept a secret from everyone except the count, you yourself and me – but, however sad my present circumstances, there is nothing that grieves me more than my inability to be of help to you – as I should like to be – I swear this on my honour – adieu, my dearest friend, farewell; write soon – reply to everything – including my earlier letters, I beg you; give my best wishes to your dear wife and to all your dependants, and rest assured that I shall do everything in my power to improve your situation – if I hadn't a father and sister for whom I must *live* more than for myself and whose livelihood I have to ensure – nothing would give me greater pleasure than to neglect my own interests – and to concern myself with your fate alone – because your well-being – your contentment – your happiness are synonymous with mine (if I may think of myself alone) – farewell –

your constant Mozart

90. Mozart to his father, 31 July 1778, Paris

Monsieur mon très cher Père,

I hope my last two letters have arrived safely – they were written, I think, on the 11th and 18th – in the meantime, I've received your 2 letters of 13th and 20th – the first brought tears of anguish to my eyes – as I was again reminded of the sad demise of my dear departed mother – and it all came flooding back to me; I'm sure that I'll never forget it as long as I live – you know that at no time in my life had I seen anyone die before, however much I may have wished it – and it had to be my own mother who was the first person I saw die – I dreaded that moment most of all – and I prayed fervently to God for strength – my prayers were answered – I found the strength; – sad as your letter made me, I was beside myself with joy when I heard that you'd taken it all as it should be taken – and that as a result I don't need to worry about my beloved father and my dearest sister. As soon as I'd finished reading your letter, the first thing I did was fall to my knees and thank our dear Lord with all my heart for this blessing; – I'm now quite calm – because I know that I don't need to fear for the two people who are dearest to me in the world – this would have been the greatest misfortune for me – and it would undoubtedly have crushed me; – so you must both take care of your health, which is so precious to me – I beg you – and grant to him who flatters himself that he is now the dearest thing in the world to you that happiness and contentment and joy of soon being able to embrace you; – your last letter drew tears of joy from me as it convinced me once and for all of your true fatherly love and concern – I shall strive with all my might to deserve your fatherly love now and evermore – I kiss your hand in the most tender gratitude for sending me the powder – and I'm sure that you'll be glad to hear that I haven't needed to use it; – I almost needed to do so once during my late mother's illness – but now, praise and thanks be to God, I'm hale and hearty again – only occasionally am I overcome by bouts of melancholy – but I can most easily avoid them by writing or receiving letters; this immediately cheers me up again. But, believe

me, there's always a reason for this. Do you want to know how much
I had to pay for your last letter, which included the powder? – 45
sous; – do you want a brief account of her illness and everything
else? – and so you shall, but I hope you won't mind if it's rather brief
and if I describe only the principal events, as the affair is now over
and unfortunately can't be altered – and I need space to write about
things that concern our present situation; first, I have to tell you that
my late mother *had* to die – no doctor in the world could have saved
her this time – for it was manifestly God's will; her time had come –
and God wanted to take her to Him; you think she was bled too late
– perhaps; she delayed it a little; but I rather agree with the people
here who advised against her being bled and who tried to persuade
her to have an enema – but she refused – and I didn't dare say
anything as I don't understand these things with the result that it
would have been my fault if she'd reacted badly to it – if it had been
me, I'd have given my consent at once – as it's very much in vogue
here – if someone is feeling at all flushed, they have an enema –
and the cause of my mother's illness was nothing but an internal
inflammation, or at least that's what people thought; I can't say
precisely how much blood was let as it's measured here not by the
ounce but by the plate – they took a little less than 2 platefuls; the
surgeon said it was extremely necessary – but it was so terribly hot
that day that he didn't dare take any more; for a few days all went
well; but then the diarrhoea started – but no one gave it any further
thought as it's quite common here for strangers who drink a lot of
water to get diarrhoea; and it's true; I had it myself the first few days
I was here, but since then I've stopped drinking plain water and
always mix some wine with it, so that I don't suffer from it any more;
as I can't manage without drinking plain water, I purify it with ice
and drink it *en glace*; I always drink 2 whole glassfuls before going
to bed –

But, to continue: on the 19th she complained of a headache – and
for the first time she had to spend the whole day in bed – she was up
for the last time the previous day, the 18th. On the 20th she complained that she was shivering – and then fever; and so I gave her an
antispasmodic powder; all this time I kept wanting to send for a

doctor – but she refused; and when I insisted, she said she'd no confidence in French physicians – and so I looked round for a German doctor – I couldn't go out of course – meanwhile I waited anxiously for Monsieur Heina, who called on us unfailingly every day – except that on this occasion he had to remain away for 2 days – he finally came, but the doctor was prevented from coming the next day and so we couldn't get him. As a result he finally came on the 24th – on the previous day, when I'd wished he'd been there, I'd had a great fright as she'd suddenly lost her hearing – the doctor, a German already turned 70, gave her powdered rhubarb mixed with wine – I don't understand this – it's usually said that wine makes you hot – but when I said this, they all screamed at me – for heaven's sake; what's that you're saying? Wine doesn't make you hot – it's just a restorative; it's water that makes you hot – and meanwhile the poor patient was longing for a drink of cold water – how gladly I'd have given it to her – dearest father, you can't imagine what I endured – there was nothing for it, in heaven's name I had to hand her over to the doctor – all that I could do with a good conscience was to pray to God without ceasing that He would arrange everything for her own good – I felt I was going out of my mind – it would have been an ideal time for composing, but I wouldn't have been able to write a note; the doctor didn't come on the 25th – he called again on the 26th; imagine how I felt when he said to me wholly unexpectedly – – 'I'm afraid that she won't last the night – if she feels sick on the night-stool she could die at any moment – see to it that she confesses.' So I ran to the end of the Chaussée d'Antin, well beyond the Barrière, to find Heina, who I knew was at a concert with a certain count – he told me he'd bring a German priest the next day. On my way back I called in for a moment on Grimm and Madame d'Épinay – they were put out that I'd not told them sooner, they'd have sent their own doctor at once – but I'd said nothing to them as my mother didn't want a French doctor – now, however, I was at my wits' end – they said they'd send their own doctor that very evening. When I got home, I told my mother that I'd met Monsieur Heina with a German priest who'd heard a lot about me and was eager to hear me play – and they were coming tomorrow to pay me a visit; she was entirely happy with that; and because I thought she seemed better (although I'm no doctor), I said nothing more – I see that I can't possibly keep this account short – I like to describe things in detail, and I think you'll prefer it too – so, as I have more urgent matters to write about, I'll continue my narrative in my next letter. Meanwhile you know from my recent letters where I am and that all my own and my late mother's affairs are in order. When I return to this point, I'll explain how it was all arranged – Heina and I did everything. Clothes, linen, trinkets and all her other belongings I'll pack up properly and send to Salzburg at the first opportunity; I'll arrange it all with Herr Gschwendtner.[1] Now for our own affairs; – but first I must ask you not to worry any further about all that I told you in my letter of the 3rd, in which I begged you not to insist on my revealing my thoughts until the time was right – I ask you again now; I still can't tell you about it as the time is not yet right and I'd do more harm than good – but let me reassure you that it concerns only *me*; your own circumstances won't be affected, either for better or worse – and I shall give it no further thought until things have improved for you – but once we're living together somewhere, happy and contented (and this is my only ambition) – once this happy time comes – and may God grant that it comes soon! – then it will be time and it will depend on you alone; so don't worry about it for now – and rest assured that in all matters where I know your happiness and contentment are concerned, I shall always place all my trust in you, my dearest father and truest friend; – and I'll explain everything to you in detail – if I haven't done so before – I'm not entirely to blame. Monsieur Grimm asked me recently what he should write to my father? – What course did I intend to pursue? – Was I remaining here or going to Mannheim? – I couldn't stop myself laughing. – What am I supposed to do in Mannheim now? – If only I'd never come to Paris – but seeing that I'm here, I must do everything possible to make my way here – well, he said, I really don't think that things will work out for you here – why? – I see here a crowd of miserable bunglers, all of whom are able to get on, so why shouldn't someone as talented as I am be able

1. Vital Gschwendtner, who was presumably in Paris on business.

to do so? – I assure you that I enjoyed being in Mannheim – and should very much like to be in service there – but only if it brings honour and reputation – I must be certain how I stand before I take a step like that; yes, he said, I'm afraid that you're not sufficiently active here – you don't get about enough – yes, I said, that's been my biggest problem – in any case I've not been able to get out recently because of my mother's long illness – and 2 of my pupils are out in the country – and the third (the daughter of the Duc de Guines) is getting married – and won't be continuing, although this is no great loss to my honour. I shan't lose anything as he pays no more than everyone else. Just imagine, the Duc de Guines, where I had to go every day and remain for 2 hours, let me give 24 lessons (although everyone else pays after 12), then went off into the country and came back after 10 days without letting me know – if I'd not enquired out of sheer curiosity, I'd not have known they were here – finally the housekeeper pulled out a purse and said: Forgive me for paying you for only 12 lessons this time, but I don't have enough money – that's generosity for you! And she paid me 3 louis d'or, adding: I hope you'll be satisfied with that – if not, please let me know – so Monsieur le Duc didn't have a spark of honour and thought: He's a young man, and a stupid German into the bargain – all Frenchmen say this about the Germans – so he'll be happy with that – but the stupid German wasn't happy and didn't take it – he was trying to get 2 lessons for the price of one – and that from *égard*, because for the past 4 months he's already had a concerto of mine for flute and harp[2] for which he's not yet paid – so I'm just waiting till the wedding is over, then I'll go and see the housekeeper and demand my money. What annoys me most of all here is that these stupid Frenchmen think I'm still seven years old because that's how old I was when they first saw me – there's no doubt about it. Madame d'Épinay told me as much in all seriousness – people treat me here as a beginner – except the people from the orchestra – they think differently; but it's the majority that counts. After this conversation with Grimm I went the next day to see Count Sickingen – he agreed with me entirely –

2. K299.

namely, that I should be patient and wait for Raaff, who'll do everything he can to help me – if this is no good, Count Sickingen himself
has offered to find a post for me in Mainz – this, then, is my prospect
at present; – I shall now do everything in my power to get along
here by teaching and earn as much money as I can – I'm doing this
in the fond hope that my circumstances change very soon, for I can't
deny and, indeed, must admit that I shall be glad to be released from
here; giving lessons here is no joke – you really have to wear yourself
out; and if you don't take on a *lot* of pupils, you don't make much
money; you mustn't think that it's laziness – no! – it's because it goes
against my genius, against my way of life – you know that I'm
completely immersed in music – that I spend all day with it – that
I'm fond of thinking about it – studying – contemplating it – well,
I'm prevented from doing this by the life that I'm leading here – I
shall, of course, keep some hours free, but – I shall need these few
hours more for rest than for work – I told you about the opera in my
last letter. I can't help it, I have to write a grand opera or none at all;
if I write a short one, I'll get little for it; everything here is taxed;
if it has the misfortune not to please these stupid Frenchmen, that
would be it – I'd never get another one to write, – I'd have gained
little from it – and my reputation would have suffered – but if I
write a grand opera, the pay is better – I'll be in my element, which
I enjoy – I'll have greater hopes of success, for with a big work you
have more chance of doing yourself credit – I assure you that if I'm
asked to write an opera, I shan't be in the least afraid – true, French
is the devil's own language – and I'm fully aware of all the difficulties that all other composers have encountered – but in spite of
this I feel as capable as the next person of overcoming this difficulty
– *au contraire*, each time I imagine that things have worked out with
my opera, my whole body seems to be on fire, and I tremble from
head to foot with the desire to teach the French to know, appreciate
and fear the Germans; why is a grand opera never entrusted to a
Frenchman? – Why does it always have to be foreigners? – For me,
the most intolerable part of the affair would be the singers – well,
I'm ready – I'm not going to get involved in any arguments – but if
I'm challenged, I shall know how to defend myself – but if a duel

can be avoided, it would be preferable – I don't like wrestling with dwarfs. May God grant that a change comes soon! – Meanwhile, I shall not lack industry, effort and hard work; I'm pinning my hopes on next winter, when everyone returns from the country – meanwhile farewell – and continue to love me – my heart leaps at the thought of the happy day when I shall have the pleasure of seeing you and embracing you with all my heart; adieu. I kiss your hands 100,000 times and I embrace my sister as her brother; I am your most obedient son,

Wolfgang Amadè Mozart

Some more random thoughts!

You told me that Count Seeau has been confirmed as intendant in both Munich and Mannheim – this seemed to me so incredible that I still wouldn't have believed it if a letter from Mannheim hadn't convinced me that it's true –

Two days ago my dear friend Weber wrote to report, among other things, that the day after the elector's arrival it was announced that he'd be moving to Munich, an announcement that came as a thunderbolt to Mannheim, completely extinguishing the joy that its inhabitants had shown the previous day when the whole town had been lit up. – The court musicians were likewise informed of this development and additionally told that each was at liberty to follow the court to Munich or to remain behind in Mannheim on the same salary – each was to hand the intendant his written decision in a sealed envelope within 4 days. Weber, who, as you know, is undoubtedly in the worst possible situation, sent in the following: 'However much I desire to do so, my circumstances are in such disarray that I am not in a position to follow my gracious lord to Munich.' Before all this took place, there was a big concert at court, and poor Fräulein Weber was made to feel the long arm of her enemies; – on this occasion she didn't sing – no one knows who was the cause of this – but immediately afterwards there was a concert at Herr von Gemmingen's – Count Seeau was also there: she sang 2 of my arias[3] – and she was

3. The arias cannot be identified with certainty.

fortunate enough to find favour in spite of those Italian curs. These infamous *cuioni* are still putting it about that she's going downhill with her singing – but when the arias were over, Cannabich said to her: 'Mademoiselle, I hope you'll continue to go downhill in this way; I shall be writing to Herr Mozart tomorrow in order to praise you.' Well, the main thing is that if war had not already broken out, the court would have moved to Munich by now – Count Seeau, who's absolutely determined to have Fräulein Weber, would have done everything in his power to take her with him – and so there would have been some hope that the whole family's situation might have improved – but everything's now gone very quiet again about the journey to Munich – and these poor people may have to wait a long time, while their debts grow worse by the day. – If only I could help them! – My dearest father! – I commend them to you with all my heart – if only they could enjoy 1000 florins for even a few years! –

As for the war, well, what's new? – Since I wrote to you in my last letter, I've heard only that the king of Prussia had to retreat for 7 hours – it's even said that General Wunsch has been taken prisoner with 15,000 of his men – but I don't believe it – although I wish it with all my heart if only the Prussians get a sound beating! – I daren't say this here where I'm staying; *Adieu.*

Best wishes to the whole of Salzburg, especially Herr Bullinger, and to the whole distinguished company of marksmen –

[*Mozart's postscript to Nannerl*]
Ma très chère sœur,

I hope you'll be pleased with the little prelude[4] – true, it's not what you wanted, I mean, it doesn't go from one key to the next and you can't stop when you like – but I didn't have time to write a prelude like that – something like that takes longer to write out – as soon as I have time, I'll present you with one – when I send things home, I'll use the opportunity to include this new prelude with Schroeter's concertos, Hüllmandel's sonatas, the violin method and a few other

4. K395, sent by Mozart to Nannerl in a letter of 20 July 1778.

sonatas of my own.[5] Adieu, farewell – I don't want to start reminiscing – submit to God's will, trust in Him – remember that you have a brother who loves you with all his heart and who will always see to your welfare and happiness – adieu, love me, I kiss you most tenderly and am ever your faithful and true brother

Wolfgang Mozart

Best wishes to all and sundry – especially Cornet Antretter if he's still in Salzburg – Salzburg is better than Bohemia, at least your head's safe there –

91. Mozart to Abbé Joseph Bullinger, 7 August 1778, Paris

Dearest Friend,

Allow me above all to thank you most emphatically for this new token of your friendship, which you've given me by taking such care of my dearest father, preparing him and consoling him in so friendly a manner; – you played your part admirably – these are my father's own words; best of friends! – How can I thank you enough! – You've saved my dearest father for me! – It's you I have to thank for the fact that I still have him; – allow me, therefore, to say no more about this and not even begin to thank you, as I feel too weak, too inadequate – too indolent – best of friends! – I shall always be in your debt; – but patience! – On my honour I'm not yet in a position to repay you – but do not doubt me; God will be merciful and allow me to show you by my deeds what I cannot express in words – indeed, I hope so! – But until that happy time comes, allow me to ask you to continue your precious and most invaluable friendship towards me – and at the same time to accept mine anew, now and hereafter; and I pledge

5. For these works by Schroeter and Hüllmandel see letter 85, nn. 7 and 8; according to *Briefe* v. 540, the sonatas may be K330–332, traditionally dated 1778, but recent research shows that Mozart did not compose them until the early Vienna years; here he probably refers to some of his recently composed accompanied sonatas K296 and K301–306, or perhaps even the solo sonatas K309–311.

this to you with a wholly sincere and good heart; – it will, of course, be of little use to you! – But it will be all the more sincere and lasting – you know very well that the best and truest of friends are the poor – the well-to-do know nothing about friendship! – especially those who are born to riches; – but even those whom fate makes wealthy often become absorbed in their own good fortune! – But when a man is placed in advantageous circumstances not by blind fate but by equitable good fortune and merit and if he did not lose heart at an earlier date, when his circumstances were less fortunate, but remained devout and continued to trust in God and was a good Christian and an honest individual and knew how to value his true friends – in a word, if he really deserved better luck, – no evil should be feared from such a man! – I'll now answer your letter; I don't suppose that you'll need to worry about my health any more as you must in the meantime have received 3 letters from me – the first of them, containing the sad news of my late mother's death, was addressed to you, my dearest friend;[1] – I know that you too will forgive me for saying no more about this whole affair, even though I can't stop thinking about it. – In your letter you say that I should now think only of my father and that I should be quite frank in telling him what I think and place my trust in him – how unhappy I should be if I needed that reminder! – It is very useful for me to be reminded of this; – but I am pleased to say – and you, too, will be glad to hear it – that I do not need it; – in my last letter to my dear father I told him as much as I know at present – and I assured him that I'd always report everything in detail and tell him quite candidly what I thought because I trust in him completely and have total confidence in his fatherly care and love and in his true goodness, knowing very well that *one day* he will not deny me a request on which the entire happiness and contentment of the whole of the rest of my life depend, a request which – as he cannot expect otherwise – is most certainly fair and reasonable.[2] Dearest friend – don't let my dear father read this; –

1. Bullinger's letter is lost; of Mozart's three letters, only that of 3 July survives.
2. Presumably Mozart was thinking of proposing marriage to Aloysia Weber and sought Leopold's approval.

you know him; it would only give him pause for thought, – and *needlessly*; – now for our Salzburg story! You know, my dearest friend, how much I loathe Salzburg! – not just because of the injustices that my dear father and I endured there, although this in itself would be enough to make us want to forget such a place and erase it from our thoughts for ever! – But let's forget all this and ensure that we can lead *respectable* lives; – to lead respectable lives and to lead contented lives are two very different things – and I couldn't do the latter without recourse to witchcraft; it really wouldn't be in the natural course of things! – And in any case it's not possible as there are no longer any witches; – but I have an idea; there are certain people in Salzburg – people who were born there, indeed the town swarms with them – you have only to change the first letter of their true name[3] and they might then be of use to me; – well, whatever happens, it will always give me the greatest pleasure to embrace my dearest father and dearest sister, and the sooner the better; but I can't deny that my joy and contentment would be doubled if I could do so elsewhere – – for I have *more* hope of being able to lead a happy and contented life anywhere but there! – You may perhaps not understand me correctly but think that Salzburg is too small for me? – If so, you'd be greatly mistaken; – I've already told my father some of the reasons; for the present you may content yourself with this, namely, that Salzburg is no place for a man of my talent! – In the first place, the people associated with the orchestra are not respected, and secondly one hears nothing – there's no theatre there, no opera! – And even if they wanted to perform an opera, who'd sing in it? – For 5 or 6 years the Salzburg orchestra has been rich in all that is useless and unnecessary but very poor when it comes to what's necessary and entirely lacking in what's most indispensable of all; and such is the case at present! – The ruthless French are the reason why the orchestra has no Kapellmeister! – The orchestra, I'm sure, will now be leading a peaceful, orderly existence! – Well, that's what happens if you don't take precautionary measures! – You must always have half a dozen Kapellmeisters ready and waiting so that, if one

3. A wordplay on *Hexen* ('witches') and *Fexen* ('fools').

falls by the wayside, he can immediately be replaced – where can they find one now? – – Yet the danger is pressing! – Order, calm and harmonious understanding can't be allowed to gain the upper hand in the orchestra! – – Otherwise the evil will spread and in the end be impossible to deal with; are there really no more periwigs with asses' ears, no scurvy knaves capable of restoring things to their former halting progress? – I'll certainly do my best to help; – tomorrow I'll hire a cab for the day and drive round to all the hospitals and infirmaries and see if I can find someone for them; why were they so incautious as to let Mysliveček escape? – And he was so near; he'd have been a real catch; it won't be so easy to find anyone else like him – and he was fresh from the Duke Clemens' *Conservatorio*![4] – He would have been the very person to terrify the whole of the court orchestra with his presence; well, I don't need to worry; where there's money, you'll always find plenty of people! – I just think that they shouldn't delay for too long – not because of any foolish fear on my part that they won't find anyone, as I know only too well that all these gentlemen are waiting for a Kapellmeister as eagerly and optimistically as the Jews are awaiting their Messiah – but simply because the present situation is intolerable – and so it would be more important and useful to look round for a Kapellmeister, as they really don't have one at present, rather than writing to all and sundry (as I've been told is the case) in the hope of finding a good female singer; I really can't believe it! – A singer! – When we have so many already! – And all of them outstanding; a tenor would be more understandable, though we don't need one of these either; but a female singer, a *prima donna*! – When we now have a castrato; – it's true that Frau Haydn isn't well; – she has overdone her austere lifestyle; but there are few like her! – I'm amazed that with her perpetual scourgings and flagellations, her wearing of a hair shirt and her unnatural fastings and night-time prayers she didn't lose her voice long ago! – – But she'll keep it for a long time to come – and instead

4. This passage is ironic, a reference to the ducal hospital in Munich where the Czech composer Joseph Mysliveček was being treated for venereal disease. What follows is meant ironically as well.

of getting worse, it'll keep getting better; – but when God finally numbers her among His saints, we'll still have 5 left, each of whom can contest the others' claims to pre-eminence! – So you see how unnecessary this is! – But let me posit an extreme case! – Let's assume that, apart from our weeping Magdalene,[5] we had no other singer, although this isn't, of course, the case; but suppose that one suddenly went into labour, another was thrown into prison, the 3rd was whipped to death, the 4th beheaded and the fifth was perhaps carried off by the devil – what would happen? – Nothing! – After all, we've got a castrato: – do you know what sort of a beast that is? – He can sing high parts and can thus play women's parts quite admirably; – the chapter would interfere, of course; but interference is always better than doing nothing – and he wouldn't have much to do; meanwhile let's leave Herr Ceccarelli to be sometimes a woman, sometimes a man; finally, because I know that, with us, people like change, variety and novelty, I see before me a wide field of epoch-making potential; even as children, my sister and I tilled this field a little, what couldn't grown-ups achieve? – Oh, if one's generous, one can have everything; – I have no doubt (and I'll undertake to arrange it myself) that Metastasio could be persuaded to come from Vienna or at the very least he could be invited to write a few dozen operas in which the *primo uomo* and *prima donna* never meet. In this way the castrato could play the parts of both the lover and his mistress, and the piece would be all the more interesting for the fact that audiences could admire the virtue of the two lovers, a virtue that goes so far that they do everything in their power to avoid speaking to each other in public; – there you have the opinion of a true patriot! – Do your utmost to find an arsehole for the orchestra – that's what's needed most of all; it now has a head – and that is its misfortune! – Until a change has been made in this department, I'll not come back to Salzburg; but I'll then come and turn over the page each time I see V.S.;[6] – now for the war; from what I hear, we'll soon have peace in

5. A play on Haydn's wife's name, Maria Magdalena.
6. That is, *volti subito*, an instruction to turn the page quickly, frequently found in music manuscripts of the time.

Germany; the king of Prussia is somewhat afraid. I read in the papers that the Prussians attacked an imperial detachment but that the Croats and 2 regiments of cuirassiers were nearby and heard the noise, coming to their rescue, attacking the Prussians, placing them between 2 fires and capturing 5 cannon; the route that the Prussians took to Bohemia is now completely cut up and hacked to pieces so that they can't return along it; the Bohemian peasants are also causing the Prussians tremendous harm; and the Prussians are plagued by constant desertions – but these are matters that you've known about for a long time and about which you're better informed than we are here; but I now want to let you know what's been happening here. The French have forced the English to retreat;[7] but it wasn't a particularly lively encounter – the most remarkable thing about it is that, of friend and foe alike, only 100 men were killed; in spite of this, there's tremendous jubilation here, and people are talking about nothing else; it's even being said that we'll soon be at peace again; – it's all the same to me as far as the situation here is concerned; but for various reasons I'd be very pleased if peace were to come soon to Germany; – farewell now, my dearest friend! I'm sorry my writing's so bad, but this pen is useless; best wishes to the whole of Salzburg, especially to your count,[8] regards to Count Leopold[9] and a long, long compliment in verse to dear Sallerl – and to my dear father and dear sister say all that a son and brother would say if he were fortunate enough to be able to speak to them himself; adieu; I beg you to continue your invaluable friendship and I assure you that I shall always be your true friend and most grateful servant

Wolfgang *Romatz*

---

7. Mozart refers here to the American Revolution.
8. Sigmund, Count Lodron, who was Bullinger's pupil.
9. Arco.

92. Leopold Mozart to his son, 27 August 1778, Salzburg

My Dear Son,

You'll have received my letter of the 13th. In it I promised that I'd reply very soon to your last two letters, both of which arrived at the same time. The first, which was written on the 18th and 20th, told me a host of things about the start and growth of your invaluable friendship with Herr Raaff. I hope that his efforts on your behalf, of which you expect so much, may prove effective; but I recall that you once wrote to me from Mannheim to say that Monsieur Raaff was a very honest, decent and sincere old man but that *he was unable to achieve results*: to tell the truth, I found that hard to believe, for a man like that must have a certain standing, even if he may no longer be such a good singer because he's old. I've already written to Padre Martini. Let's wait and see what happens. What you said about the papers there was nothing but lies from start to finish. Monsieur Hopfgarten, whom we know, wasn't a soldier but a councillor in the civil service. And as for your comments at the end about the valet and the *25 blows* that he received for not marrying Katherl,[1] I don't know if he'd not have received a million if he'd actually married her. My son, *one has to get to know people gradually*. You can't imagine a worse housekeeper or a more frivolous individual than this Katherl, she spends the whole day calling on others and sponging off them, while avoiding work like the plague. She puts on a new dress or a cap or a pair of shoes etc. and wears them until they're in tatters or dirty. Rain or shine, she always dresses the same and turned up *at the cathedral* for the *Feast of the Assumption* wearing the same filthy cap and the same ordinary clothes that she'd been walking around in the previous day. She's an honest girl, but a total fool and no better than a poodle when it comes to shop assistants and students etc., her husband will never be able to give her enough money as she can't keep control of it etc. And why should he marry her? The Cardinal

1. Presumably Gilowsky; the valet is unidentified.

of Passau will soon be 80,[2] if he dies, his office will die with him: and how long can things go on with the chief steward?[3] What will become of him then? What other job could he do? – – *Adam*,[4] who used to be a *valet de chambre* but who's now steward, has been trying to get better acquainted with your sister. On one occasion he caught us off our guard, but since then we've never been at home, and finally – after he'd repeatedly told our servant Tresel about his love – I told her to inform him that once he was married it would be an honour to welcome him and his wife to our house but that as long as he was a widow, I had to ask him not to visit us as I didn't want my daughter being gossiped about in town. He then turned his attentions to Katherl, informing both her and her father of his love for her. She's proud of it and finds it amusing, he's always round at her place. Is that wise? She's also conceived a fancy for *Siegmund Haffner*, I hope she's successful as she needs a match with plenty of money. At least it's true that Herr Haffner has now thought more seriously about his affair and, after having given the matter some thought, has seen reason, so that the acquaintance has now started to cool off. *Your second letter* of 31 July[5] included *details of the illness* of your dearly departed mother. The fact that your mother was the first person you saw die was an example of divine ordinance, indeed I remarked as much to everyone the moment I received your news. My dear son! Fate gave rise to a second and very different remark. Your dear mother was happy to leave Salzb. with you and raised no objections. She was to have returned home once you'd left Mannheim. It was only after you'd got to know the Webers and started to travel around with them that you began to have serious thoughts and decided not to travel with Wendling. – You wrote your letter so late that Wendling had already left before my reply could reach you. I'd seen it all coming, otherwise you wouldn't have remained behind. And so I had

2. Cardinal von Firmian, born in 1708, was in fact approaching his seventieth birthday. Leopold seems to have been attached to him; earlier, in Milan in December 1772, he and Wolfgang had participated in the festivities marking his elevation to cardinal.
3. Franz Lactanz von Firmian.
4. Johann Baptist Adam, whose wife had died the previous year.
5. Letter 90.

to write and tell you to be off to Paris as soon as you could as the season was coming to an end. Your dear mother realized what was happening but wanted to spare you every annoyance and at the end of her letter[6] she wrote: *My dear husband, you'll have seen from this letter that when Wolfgang makes new acquaintances, he immediately wants to sacrifice his life and possessions to such people, it's true that she sings incomparably well but one should never overlook one's own interests, I never liked him mixing with Wendling and Ramm, but I didn't dare to raise any objections and no one ever believed me anyway, as soon as he got to know the Webers, he immediately changed his mind: in a word he prefers other people's company to mine, if I raise objections about things I don't like, he doesn't like it. I really don't think it's advisable for him to go to Paris with Wendling, I'd rather accompany him there myself at some later date, perhaps you'll receive a reply from Herr Grimm.* This, my dear son, is the only thing that your late mother wrote to me in confidence about you during the whole time that you were away. And although she could have expressed herself more clearly and called a spade a spade, she loved us both too much to explain things more plainly. If your mother had returned from Mannheim to Salzburg, she wouldn't have died, but since divine providence had fixed the hour of your mother's death for 3 July, she had to leave Salzburg with you and was prevented by your new acquaintance from returning here. Her death, the whole course taken by this affair and the context as a whole shows me that the links in the chain of human destiny and divine providence can't be broken, otherwise you'd have told me sooner about your decision not to go with Wendling and your reservations about him, and I, *trusting in your intelligence and virtue*, would have talked you out of them, so that you would have left and arrived in Paris at the right time, you'd have furthered your interests and made more friends, and my poor wife would now be in Salzburg. Man's senses must be clouded, just as the cleverest doctor becomes blind, his remedy fails and he longer recognizes the illness when providence wills it so. May God grant that all that has happened so far does not have far worse consequences for us all. There is still

6. Postscript to Mozart's letter of 4 February 1778 (letter 71).

time to take preventative measures. But if you continue to build castles in the air and fill your head with empty speculations on future prospects that are still very remote, then all that it is particularly important for you to do at present if these prospects are to be realized will be neglected, your head is full of things that render you incapable of dealing with the present; you'll make no progress like this as you now need some form of livelihood, and *to judge from the thoughts that you plan to reveal to me only when it is time*, you need a good and remunerative job, – but this is not as easy to find as you think, given all the things you want with it, and since you know my circumstances and the *debts that still have to be paid*, I hope that sound common sense will finally prevail and you'll see that, now that you're in Paris and the season when you can earn something is approaching, you should think only of making your mark there, ensuring that you become better known and earning a reputation and, with it, some money. As for *Mannheim*, you've already done all that can be done – you must await the outcome, and no amount of speculation will help you here. Whether anything happens or not, you can't leave Paris at present, whereas if nothing happens, you must remain in Paris in order to survive – for where else could you go? – At all events it's good that Count Sickingen has offered to find you a post in Mainz – but you mustn't imagine that it's certain, you must understand that it means only that he'll try to find you a post. Whether he succeeds is another matter. There's an old Kapellmeister in Mainz, Herr *Schmid*, who no longer does anything. *Kreusser* couldn't have gone to Mainz at a better time, as the concertmaster, *Jacobi*, had just died.[7] People liked his symphonies, which are easy to listen to, and so he was made concertmaster straightaway. He's now studying for the post of Kapellmeister; he's universally popular and in time will apply for this position.

I can't forgive you for not having gone *to Mainz* during such a lengthy stay in Mannheim. If you examine the matter impartially, you'll have to admit that you've rarely heeded my advice and acted as I prescribed. A visit to Mainz would have been of more use to you

7. Kreusser, see letter 63 n. 5; Gottfried Dominikus Jacobi (?–1773).

than that disastrous trip to Kirchheimbolanden, Mainz is a court, after all, with certain prospects, where we've many acquaintances among the nobility, as well as other friends. So you see that at present *all your thoughts must be directed solely at supporting yourself in Paris*. As for *Mannheim, Mainz* and *Salzburg*, you must wait and not depend on mere empty dreams that serve no useful purpose except to render you incapable of dealing with the most pressing concerns of the moment, at all events nothing happens except that which eternal providence has decreed for us as long as we seize the necessary means and do not harm our present situation by constantly thinking about things that are necessarily still very far off. In *Mannheim* or, rather, in *Munich*, where the court will be moving at the end of this month, there's unlikely to be much to do, unless they decide to cast round for a composer for the German opera and if *Raaff* and *Cannabich* recommend you. *Wendling* is your friend, but I don't know if your acquaintance with the Webers has robbed you of the goodwill of the Wendling household. *Singers invariably hate each other*. *Mainz* doesn't pay very well, but *Mainz* has the same advantage as *Salzburg*, namely, that it *won't die* with the death of the prince. – *Mannheim* is on a less secure footing. *Salzburg* – assuming one's properly paid – has the advantage over *Mainz* that church music in particular is more magnificent – and the town is closer to *Italy*. I've already told you that people would like to see you back here again, and that, although I refused to be drawn, they went on at me until finally, following Lolli's[8] death, I was obliged to tell the countess[9] that I'd handed in a petition to the archbishop in which I said only *that I commended myself to His Grace after so many years of uncomplaining service* etc. The conversation finally turned to you – I told her quite plainly what was needed, just as I'd told Count Starhemberg. Finally she asked me if you'd come back on condition that the archb. paid me Lolli's salary and gave you Adlgasser's,[10] which – as I'd already worked this out

8. Kapellmeister Lolli had died earlier on 11 August.
9. Countess Wallis.
10. Leopold is suggesting that Mozart should have the position of organist, unfilled since Adlgasser's death.

in advance – would come to 1000 florins a year in total, I could say
only that I was in no doubt that, if this came about, you'd accept out
of your love of me, especially when she added that there was no
doubt whatsoever that the archbishop would allow you to go to Italy
every other year, as he himself has always insisted that from time to
time one needs to hear different things and that he'd provide you
with some good letters of recommendation. If this comes about, I can
reckon with some certainty on our having an assured income of at
least *115 florins a month* and, as things stand at present, more than *120
florins a month. Not to mention what I make from the sales of my violin
method*, which *at a conservative estimate* brings in *50 florins* a year, and
without taking account of what your sister earns, which is at present
10 florins a month, which is enough to clothe her, as she is teaching
the countess's[11] 2 little daughters, whom she sees every day, while I
teach the 2 bigger ones. This doesn't include any additional fees that
you could earn for yourself, because although you can't count on it
here, you know that you've earned the occasional extra fee, and in
that way we'd be better off than anywhere else, where it's twice as
expensive, and if you don't have to keep such a close eye on your
money, *you can start to enjoy yourself*. But the main point is that I'm
not counting on all this as I know how difficult it is for the prince to
reach such a decision. That the countess is entirely serious, however,
and that there's nothing she wants more is beyond doubt. And it's
also true that old Arco, Count Starhemberg and the bishop of
Königgrätz also want to bring this about in a dignified manner – and,
as with all things, they have their reasons: as I've told you a thousand
times, the countess is afraid, no less than old Arco, *that I too may
leave*. They've no one to teach keyboard; I have the *reputation* of
being a good teacher, and the proof of this is at hand. They don't
know *if* and *when* they'll get anyone else: and if someone were to
come from Vienna, will he give 12 lessons for 4 florins or 1 ducat,
when one pays 2 or 3 ducats elsewhere? – – This has placed them all
in a predicament. But, as I've said, *I'm not counting on it* as I know

11. Lodron.

the archbishop even though it's clear that deep in his heart he would like to have you, he's incapable of reaching a decision, especially when it involves *giving*. The plan that you've always had in mind would certainly be furthered by this means, as a visit to Italy or the favourable circumstances here could do a lot. You continue to harp on the difficulties faced by the Webers. But tell me, how could it ever enter the head of any sensible person to think that it had to be you who's uniquely capable of helping these people to find fame and fortune? You must gradually have come to realize – or at least I hope so – *how much money a single person needs to live a reputable life*. This is the case with you now, – since 23 Sept. of last year, there were 2 of you – your late mother and you – whom, in order to equip for your journey and provide with travelling expenses, I had to support with 300 florins, followed by a further 200 florins in Mannheim. That makes 500 florins, which I owe *for this reason* alone. You're now on your own – don't you have to struggle to survive from one day to the next? And is that enough? – – Shouldn't you try to save some money in case of emergencies? Suppose – God forbid – that you fell ill and had no savings – what would you do then? – – Wouldn't you be abandoned to your misery? – Wouldn't you be obliged to rely on the mercy and compassion of kind-hearted people? – – And where are these kind-hearted people? If, *in health of body*, you already have enough to do to provide for yourself as a single person, while *making friends* and prosecuting your plans, what sort of pitiful plight can someone expect who is prevented by illness or some other indisposition, however slight, from earning any money and dealing with his affairs? If he doesn't have a ready supply of money in his purse, he'll be abandoned there and then by the world – his few friends will gradually withdraw – and the one friend who may remain will find himself in the situation of being able to demonstrate his friendship only in words but of not being able to do anything practical as he himself is poor. – And are we poor people safe from being struck down by some indisposition? – – Don't you have before you the sad example of your own dearly departed mother and of the hundreds of people around you who are healthy today but sick tomorrow? Just think whether, in all the time you've been away, you have a single friend who had the strength to do anything for you? – You yourself told me on one occasion *that you had very many good friends who were not, however, in a position to do anything for you.* There are plenty such friends, who can express only pious wishes and make empty suggestions. If one accepts each such wish and suggestion as though it were uniquely true, one will only be disappointed. *I beg you to take pity on yourself and your poor father, see to your present needs and don't expose me to the risk of becoming an object of mockery and ridicule here.* As far as possible, an effort may be made to help Mlle Weber and in due course to achieve everything else you want, but are our resources really sufficient to assist a family with 6 children? Who can do this? – I? – You? – When we can't even help ourselves! How can you help others before you've helped yourself? You write – *dearest father! I commend them to you with all my heart. If only they could enjoy 1000 florins for even a few years.* My dearest son! When I read that, am I not bound to fear for your sanity? – In God's name, you expect me to help them out with 1000 florins for a number of years? – Even if I could do so, I'd first help *you* and *me* and your *dear sister*, who's *already 27 years old and isn't provided for, while I'm already old.* Where are the courts, where is there a single court at present that will give a singer 1000 florins? – In Munich they get 5–6 or at most 700 florins, and do you really imagine that someone's going to give 1000 florins straightaway to a young person who's regarded as a beginner? – – You'll never find this even if you think about it day and night and imagine it already half done or very easy to arrange, especially since, *as you're always hearing and seeing for yourself,* one must first make a name for oneself or become famous before one can take bigger steps and find fame and fortune in the world. Even if you spend the whole day thinking about it and imagine that a hundred thousand things are possible, not only will the thing itself not come to pass but, unless you turn your present situation to your own profit and advantage, you'll spend your time being wholly ineffectual, remaining unknown and poor, ruining the pair of us and helping no one. All that you should do is to write to Cannabich and Raaff and ask them to propose you to the elector and Seeau as a composer for the German opera. *Count Sickingen* should write a similar letter to Baron Gemmingen and other correspondents, you should also write a letter in French to the *imperial ambassador, Baron Lehrbach. Baron Grimm could draft it for you.* In short! You must write to all the people who may have any influence on the elector, for German operas will always be performed in Munich in future. The opera by Wieland and Schweitzer[12] will be given on 4 November, St Charles's Day, and will presumably continue throughout the carnival. I'll also make my approaches to Count Seeau from here. Even if you were to get only 600 florins. One has to make a name for oneself. When did Gluck – and Piccinni – and all the others first come to prominence? – Gluck must now be 60, and it's only 26 or 27 years since people first started to talk about him, and you expect the French public, or even just the theatre managers, to be convinced of your skills as a composer even before they've heard a note of your music and know of you only from your childhood as an outstanding keyboard player and a genius of the front rank? In the meantime you must make every effort to get on and be able to prove your abilities as a composer in all the different genres – and for this you must seek out opportunities to do so and be tireless in looking for friends, spurring them on, leaving them no peace and, if they show signs of tiring, encouraging them to redouble their efforts, while never believing that they have already done what they said they would do; I'd have written to Monsieur de Noverre long ago if I'd known his *title* and *address.* Meanwhile I and your friends will do what we can about Munich. Like my own, your thoughts and worries about Herr Weber are futile until your own situation has improved, and to this you must now turn your attention: only when you're in credit or have a good position will your concern and help have any more force and prove effective, for the present you'll only dissipate your energies, while harming yourself and not being able to help them.

Your sister and I kiss you a million times with all our hearts, she was unable to write as I've written too much. So until next time. In

12. *Rosamunde*; Christoph Martin Wieland (1733–1813), poet, dramatist, journalist and tutor to the dukes of Weimar, was considered one of the most prominent writers in Germany; Anton Schweitzer (1735–87), composer, was attached to Abel Seyler's travelling troupe from 1769.

God's name, look after your health, otherwise we'll both perish. I'm your true friend and honest father

Mzt

A note on the war! As *Prince Heinrich* failed to advance at *Komotau* in Bohemia, he retreated to *Pirnau* near *Dresden* and attacked from above near *Rumburg*, *Tollenstein*, *Zwickau* and *Leipa*. Laudon[13] had to cover the entire Saxon frontier from *Eger* as far as the *Lausitz*. He was in the middle at *Leitmeritz*, then hurriedly withdrew to *Turnau*, so that Prince Heinrich had to retreat to *Niemes* and was unable to advance on *Turnau* via *Arnau* and join the king, the emperor then faced the king at Nachod, while Laudon faced Heinrich, with his battle line facing Niemes, so that the emperor and Laudon formed a single line and were able to help one another. *Heinrich* couldn't hold his ground but retreated to *Leitmeritz*, the *king* abandoned *Nachod*, where he'd been encamped since 5 July, and withdrew into the mountains beyond *Trautenau* in order to force the armies of the emperor and Laudon to split up as well. We're now waiting to see how they'll continue to cut off the road from each other. *Addio*.

93. Leopold Mozart to his son, 3 September 1778, Salzburg

My Dear Son,

I hope that all my letters have arrived safely. I wrote to you on *3 Aug.* – *13 Aug.* and *27 Aug.* and finally enclosed a brief note for you with my letter to Herr Grimm. – Conversely, I've not received so much as a single word from you since *31 July*, making my already anxious heart even more agitated. Time was too short to explain everything clearly in my last brief letter, but if you read carefully all my previous letters, you'll have seen that I've been trying to bring you closer to your goal in keeping with your own instructions and

13. Field Marshal Gideon, Baron Laudon (1717–90), famous for his capture of Belgrade during the Austrian-Turkish War of 1788–90.

attempting to set all our minds at rest in this way. *You don't like Paris.* – If it were impossible to find some means of getting you away from there, you'd have to endure the situation, of course, *laboriously troubling yourself with pupils – running round* till you find some – *running round* when you've got them, and then, *tired* and *annoyed* by this disagreeable work, *sitting down* at home *to compose*, placing your health at risk, having to worry every day not only about *the money for your necessary upkeep* but also for *unforeseen eventualities*, money that you need to buy *linen, clothes* and a *hundred necessities* that one never thinks about until one needs them and which you've never been used to having to *think about in advance*: and *doesn't one need a contingency fund in order to be able to look after oneself in case of illness*, without having to depend like a beggar on the alms of kind-hearted friends? Or, even if God in His mercy grants you good health, do you intend to live from hand to mouth, day in, day out, in Paris? In a place that you don't like? I suspect that nothing could be further from your thoughts. But if you want to set off and leave Paris, – who would give you the money for the journey? Me, perhaps? – Who'll then pay off your current debts? Do you want to risk ignoring what you're assured of here and neglect what you could enjoy in peace and quiet here, well looked after, while *pursuing your interests at close quarters* in order to run around in Paris, which you hate, slaving away and consumed by care day and night? – *Bach*[1] promised to write to you from England and maybe find something for you. But it would be the same old story there, with the additional danger that people are arrested there for debts of 3 or 4 guineas. There can be absolutely no thought of this. I can still help you now – I want to help you and, indeed, must. But if things go on like this, you'll destroy me with your vain hopes, which have led you away from the path of virtue, and you'll turn me and your sister into beggars, *I'd no longer be in a position to help you*, and at the very moment that you were entertaining the most ambitious thoughts, you'd sink unnoticed into utter poverty and only realize this when neither *I* nor *you yourself* can help you any longer. As your father, who loves you with all his heart, I've had to

1. Johann Christian Bach.

reflect on the fact that if you remain in Paris this winter or if you're obliged to remain there, this would only be out of necessity if no other expedient is found. You must await the outcome of your business with the elector. In Paris you're too remote to pursue the matter. Here people kept approaching me without my giving them an answer. Finally Lolli died. Things then became more serious. People led me to hope that my situation might improve, and I thought that the time had come when I could bring you closer to your goal. As the elector's whole court is expected in Munich on 15 September, you may be able, while travelling through the city, to speak to *your friends*, *Count Seeau* and *perhaps the elector himself* – you can say that your father in Salzburg wants to see you back home as the prince has offered you a salary of 7 or 800 florins as his concertmaster (you should knowingly add 2 or 300 florins) and that you've accepted this out of filial respect for your father, *although he'd like to have seen you in the elector's service*, but, *mark me well*, don't say anything more than this! You can then *express the wish to write an opera for Munich*. – This latter goal can and must be pursued from here, and it's bound to work *as there's a shortage of composers able to write German operas*. *Schweitzer* and *Holzbauer* won't produce something every year, and even if *Michl* were to write one, he'll soon be played out. If people sought to prevent it by expressing doubts or by other such tricks, you have professors among your friends, and they will vouch for you: and this court also occasionally mounts performances during the year. – In short, you'd not be far away: our income would be as I described it; – the life that you lead here wouldn't prevent you from studying and making plans; *you wouldn't have to play the violin at court but could conduct from the keyboard*, just as I've now been entrusted with *the whole orchestra, all the prince's scores and inspection of the Chapel House*. Although our debts are considerable, they're all owed to local people, who are very decent and who aren't pressing for payment, and, as you'll have seen from my last letter, our joint income will soon be enough to allow us to pay off *a few hundred florins or so* every year and yet still *be able to amuse ourselves*; and you'll always be able to remind Munich of your existence. And there's something else that you mustn't forget. *You must take with you the names and addresses of the best music dealers, who may buy something from you and have it engraved*, so that you can then correspond with them. This applies especially to the dealer who bought your keyboard sonatas.[2] In this way it'll be just as though you were still in Paris, one can negotiate with them, then send the work to a businessman or friend who'll deliver it to the music publisher in return for a cash payment, and in this way you can earn 15 or 20 louis d'or a year from Paris and in part make yourself better known and in part retain your existing reputation. – Ask Baron Grimm if I'm right. Here you'll certainly find plenty to entertain you, if you're not obliged to count every penny, then all will be well. During the carnival we can now attend all the balls in the town hall. The actors from Munich are coming at the end of Sept. and will be remaining here all winter until Lent, giving plays and operettas: we've got target practice every Sunday, and if we want to have company, it depends on us alone, it changes everything when you've got a better salary.

As for Mlle Weber, you mustn't think that I've anything against this acquaintanceship. All young people have to make fools of themselves. You can continue to write to each other, I'll not ask you about it, still less will I demand to read any of it. Moreover, I'll give you some advice, you know enough people here, you can address your Weber letters to someone else and keep them to yourself if you don't feel safe from my curiosity.

But it seems to me that, without the help of others, you'll not be of much use to Herr Weber, nor will he be of much use to himself. Do you know why I wrote that I didn't think Herr Weber had much of a head on his shoulders? It certainly gives one pause for thought. – As for the question asked by the court: *who'll follow it to Munich* etc? he replied in writing: *However much I desire to do so, my circumstances are in such disarray that I am not in a position to follow my gracious lord to Munich.* Now, it may be that I'm jumping to conclusions, as I don't know how far this man is in debt, but in his place, having

2. K301–306. In the eighteenth century, works for keyboard with violin were not considered violin sonatas but accompanied keyboard sonatas, hence Leopold's description. They had been bought for publication by Jean-Georges Sieber.

4 days in which to act, I'd have gone to my creditors and said: *It's now a question of whether I can follow the court to Munich or not, if I can follow the court, I am confident that through my daughter I'll be able to improve my own fortune, too, I'll be at the court, where one can hope to earn some extra income and as a result am more justified in hoping that I'll be able to satisfy my creditors: but if the burden of my debts means that I have to remain in Mannheim, my daughter will be out of sight of the court, Mannheim will become a desert, and I'll have fewer opportunities for earning any extra income, so that on my death you'll find a room full of children, rather than any money: if I move to Munich, I'll still be serving the same master, and you'll be able to find me just as easily as if I were in Mannheim.* – I really can't judge the matter properly as this would need a detailed knowledge of all the circumstances, but I'll advise you and help you as best I can. You won't be able to help them in Paris. Here you'll soon hear people talk about Mlle Weber; I've praised her far too often, I'll think of all the different ways of ensuring that she's heard here. – I must now say something about the Duc de Guines's debt. I hope that you'll have demanded payment or that you'll be doing so? – You won't leave something like this behind? – – *Baron Grimm will advise you.* Has the concerto[3] not been paid for either? – It's quite appalling. I had a similar experience in Vienna,[4] on that occasion I wrote to Princess Ulfeld's maid, saying *that we'd received no token of the princess's gratitude and were forced to assume that, although she had no doubt made the necessary arrangements, the person who had received her orders had forgotten to carry them out and I was sure that the princess would be very upset if I left Vienna without reporting back to her and using the occasion to praise the house of Ulfeld's innate generosity.* The princess sent me 20 ducats and thanked me for having written, while apologizing for the oversight. Ask Baron Grimm whether – if the prince won't admit you – the present affair may be dealt with in the same way. I must repeat – and I swear it to you as your father and friend – that you won't have

3. K299, for flute and harp.
4. Here Leopold refers to a performance in Vienna on 14 October 1762 at the home of Count Ulfeld, the court chief steward.

to play the violin at court but that, like the late Herr Adlgasser, you'll only have to accompany singers. And you'll have to play the cathedral organ only on the principal feast days, all the other duties will be taken by Paris.[5] The last thing I want is to tie you down here, but if you and your friends want to try your luck at the court in Munich, it would be far easier to do so from here, as you can send 2 letters and receive 2 replies all within the space of a week and can discover and take advantage of every favourable opportunity. I'd far rather you commended yourself to the imperial ambassador, Baron Lehrbach, who'll now be in Munich, and told him that you're only wanting to write an opera in order to be able to show what you can do. How, in heaven's name, is the elector supposed to make up his mind to take you on as his court composer as he's not heard any of your works? – The matter must be sorted out from here, it'll now be easier to obtain a commission to write an opera as the Italians can no longer interfere; the matter will then proceed of its own accord. And finally I solemnly swear to you that, as you yourself know, I bound myself to Salzburg only because of your dearly departed mother, in order to ensure that she would at least have a pension. This is all over now, I don't need it any longer, from now on let's not allow ourselves to be annoyed, otherwise we'll leave. In your last letter you wrote: *my heart leaps at the thought of the happy day when I shall have the pleasure of seeing you and embracing you with all my heart.* That day is now coming, my dear son, I hope that God will let me live to see it, you'll scarcely recognize your poor father, on the 2 occasions when I was summoned to see the archbishop, he was so shocked at my appearance that he told everyone about it. I was ill when you left me, it's now just a year ago, and what haven't I had to endure during that time? – I've an iron constitution, otherwise I'd already be dead, but if you don't lift this heavy burden from my heart with your presence, it will crush me, all the restoratives in the world are powerless to heal a sick mind. No one can save me from death except you – and no one will help you more loyally than your father, who blesses, loves and kisses

5. Anton Ferdinand Paris (1744–1809), court organist.

you and who desires with all his heart to embrace you and will do everything humanly possible to ensure your happiness

Mozart

My most humble good wishes to Baron Grimm.

I told you that the archbishop is in Laufen and that you shouldn't leave until I have in my hands the signed decree. Because of the heavy rain no one has driven down there, – but some people went down there today, I'll write one last time on the 7th inst. and at the same time make contact with *Strasbourg*, I'll *report back to you* in the same letter.

I beg you, my dear son, to look after your health and, with it, my life, believe me when I say that I've thought through everything sensibly, with your own best interests at heart. You will see and discover for yourself that I'm taking you the quickest way to your own happiness, if God wills it so. Your sister kisses you a million times. Once again, my dearest Wolfgang, take pity on your old father and look after yourself.

94. Mozart to his father, 11 September 1778, Paris

Mon très cher Père,

Your 3 letters of 13, 27 and 31 August have all arrived safely; but for now I'll reply only to the last, as this is the most important one;[1] when I read it through – Monsieur Heina, who sends you both his best wishes, was here – I trembled with joy, already seeing myself in your arms; it's true, as you'll admit, that no great fortune awaits me there, but when I imagine kissing you, my dearest father, and you, my dear sister, with all my heart, no other happiness matters; and this is really the only thing that can serve as an excuse with the people

1. In a letter of 31 August, Leopold reported to Wolfgang that he had finalized arrangements with Colloredo for Mozart's return to Salzburg, with greater responsibilities and a pay rise – in short, everything Leopold had demanded of the archbishop.

here who are always going on at me to remain here: I always say to them at once: what do you want? – I'm content, and that's all there is to it; I've somewhere that I can call my home – where I can live in peace and quiet with my beloved father and dearest sister – I can do as I like because, apart from the duties associated with my appointment, I'm my own master – I have a permanent livelihood – can leave when I like – can undertake a longer journey every other year – what more do I want? – If you want to know what I really feel, the only thing that disgusts me about Salzburg is that you can't really mix with the people there – and that the orchestra isn't held in higher esteem – and that the archbishop has no faith in intelligent people who have travelled the world – for I can assure you that people who don't travel – at least people in the arts and sciences – are pitiful creatures! – and I assure you that if the archbishop doesn't allow me to travel every other year, I can't possibly accept the engagement; a man of mediocre talent remains mediocre, whether he travels or not – but a man of superior talent – which, without being Godless, I cannot deny is true in my own case – will go to seed if he stays in the same place all the time; if the archbishop were to trust me, I'd soon make his orchestra famous; this is undoubtedly true; – I assure you that this journey wasn't a waste of time – from the standpoint of my work as a composer, I mean – for I already play the keyboard as well as I can; there's only one thing I would ask for in Salzburg and that's that I don't have to play the violin as I used to – I want to give up being a violinist; I'll conduct from the keyboard – and accompany the arias; it would have been good if I could have had a written assurance about the post of Kapellmeister; for otherwise I may have the honour of doing two jobs and being paid for only one – and in the end he may again appoint some stranger over my head; my dearest father! I have to admit that if it weren't for the pleasure of seeing you both again, I really couldn't agree to this – – and also to get away from Paris, which I can't abide – even though my situation is starting to improve, and I've no doubt that if I could make up my mind to hold out here for a few years, I'd certainly be able to make a go of things; I'm now fairly well known – at least people know *me*, even if I don't know them. My 2 sym-

phonies[2] – the 2nd of them was performed on the 8th – have helped
my reputation no end; now that I've said I'm leaving, I should really
have written an opera – but I told Noverre: if you'll guarantee that
it'll be *produced* as soon as it's finished – and if I'm told exactly what
I'll get for it, I'll remain here for another 3 months and write it – I
couldn't reject the idea out of hand, otherwise people would have
thought that I'd no faith in my own abilities; but they wouldn't agree
to this – I knew in advance that they wouldn't as it's not the custom
here; as you probably already know, the situation here is that when
the opera's finished, it's put into rehearsal and if these stupid Frenchmen don't like it, it's not performed – and the composer has written
it in vain; if they like it, it's staged, and the more successful it is, the
more the composer is paid; but there's no certainty; in general, I'm
saving up these matters to discuss with you in person; but I can tell
you in all honesty that things were starting to look up for me; nothing
can be hurried; *chi va piano, va sano*;[3] my willingness to please has
won me friends and patrons; if I were to write and tell you everything,
my fingers would hurt; I'll tell you all about it in person and explain
to you in detail that Monsieur Grimm may be able to help *children*
but not grown-ups and – but no, I don't want to write about it – and
yet I must; please don't imagine that's he's the same person he was
before; if it weren't for Madame d'Épinay, I wouldn't be in his house
at all; and he needn't be so proud about this fact as there are 4 houses
where I could have had board and lodging; the good man didn't
know that if I'd *remained here*, I'd have moved out next month and
gone to a less stupid and dull-witted household where people can do
you a favour without constantly flaunting it in your face – in this
way I could all too easily *forget* a favour done to me – but I mean to
be more generous than he is – I'm only sorry that I'll not be remaining
here in order to show him that I don't need him – and that I'm just
as good as his Piccinni – even though I'm only a German; the greatest

2. The first of these is K297, 'Paris'; the second was for some time thought to be
K311A, but this work is unlikely to be by Mozart. Although he gives his father the
impression that he has composed two new symphonies in Paris, it is probable that
an earlier work was performed on 8 September.
3. 'slow and steady wins the race'.

kindness he's shown me consists of 15 louis d'or, which he lent me bit by bit while my dearly departed mother was still alive and then at the time of her death – do you think he's afraid of losing them? – If he has doubts about this, he really deserves a kick up the backside – as he's distrusting my honesty – which is the only thing capable of making me angry – and also my talent – but I already know this, as he once told me himself that he didn't think I was capable of writing a French opera; I shall return the 15 louis d'or when I leave, accompanying my thanks with a few well-chosen words; my dearly departed mother often used to say: I don't know, but he strikes me as completely changed; but I always took his part, even though I was secretly convinced that it was so; he spoke about me to no one – or if he did, it was always stupid and clumsy; – mean-spirited; he wanted me to keep running off to see Piccinni and Garibaldi – – there's a wretched *opera buffa* on at present – but I always said: No, I shan't take a single step in that direction *etc*. In a word, he's in the Italian faction[4] – he's false – and he's trying to hold me back; it's incredible, isn't it? – But it's true; here's the proof: I opened up my whole heart to him as a true friend – and he certainly made good use of it; he invariably gave me bad advice because he knew that I'd follow it – but he succeeded only 2 or 3 times as I didn't ask him any more after that, or if he gave me his advice, I didn't act on it; but I always said yes, so that I wouldn't suffer any more of his rudeness;

But enough of this – we'll talk about it more in person; Madame d'Épinay is certainly more kind-hearted; the room where I'm staying belongs to her, not to him; it's the sickroom – when anyone in the house is ill, they're taken there; there's nothing attractive about it apart from the view; just bare walls; no cupboard or anything else – you can see now that I couldn't have put up with it any longer; I'd have told you this long ago but was afraid you wouldn't believe me – but, whether you care to believe me or not, I can't stay silent any longer – but I'm certain that you'll believe me – I still have enough

---

4. Here Mozart refers to the ongoing dispute between the partisans of Italian and French opera in Paris, waged on stage and through pamphlets. Piccinni was the leader of the Italian faction, Gluck of the French.

credit with you to convince you that I'm telling the truth; I also take my meals with Madame d'Épinay; you mustn't think he pays her anything as I cost her next to nothing – they have the same meals whether I'm there or not; – they never know when I'll be eating with them so they don't count on me; and at night I eat only fruit and drink a glass of wine; throughout the time I've been in the house – which is now more than 2 months – I've not lunched with them more than 14 times at most; and so, apart from the 15 louis d'or, which I'll be returning with thanks, he's incurred no expenses with the exception of the candles; and I'd be more ashamed of myself than of him if I were to offer to supply my own; – I really couldn't bring myself to say such a thing – on my honour; that's the sort of person I am; recently, when he spoke to me in a quite gruff, silly and stupid way, I couldn't bring myself to say that he needn't worry about his 15 louis d'or – because I was afraid of offending *him*; I just put up with it – and asked him if he'd finished – and then said only that I was his most obedient servant; he claims that I should leave in 8 days' time; *he's in such a hurry* – I told him I couldn't – and gave him the reasons; well, that makes no difference, it's what your father wants – I'm sorry, but he wrote to say that only when I received his next letter would I see when I should leave – just be ready to leave – I'm telling you that I can't possibly leave before the beginning of next month – or by the end of this month at the earliest, as I still have to write 6 trios[5] – for which I'll be well paid – I still have to be paid by Legros and the Duc de Guines – and as the court is going to Munich at the end of this month, I'd like to be there to present my sonatas[6] to the electress in person, which may perhaps lead to a present; I'll pack my things together and talk to Herr Gschwendtner – and I'll send them off at once or at least as soon as possible; it's not advisable to leave things with him; in return for cash I'll send 3 concertos – the ones for Jenamy and Lützow and the one in B flat[7] – to the engraver who engraved my sonatas – and, if possible, I'll do the same with my

5. These works do not survive and were probably never written.
6. K301–306.
7. K271, K246 and K238.

6 difficult sonatas;[8] even if it's not very much – it's still better than nothing. One needs money for the journey. As for the symphonies, most are not to the taste of the people here; if I've time, I'll rearrange some of my violin concertos[9] and make them shorter as the taste with us in Germany is for long works – but it's better that they should be short and sweet – in your next letter I shall no doubt find some instructions for my journey – I only hope that you've written just to me as I don't want anything more to do with him; I hope so – and it would also be better – in general, a Gschwendtner and a Heina can arrange things better than such an upstart baron[10] – certainly I owe Heina more than I owe him if you examine the matter aright by the light of even the shortest piece of candle – well, I await an early reply to this letter and shan't leave till I receive it; I've already worked it all out; you'll receive this letter on 22 September and will reply straightaway; the post leaves on Friday the 25th, and I'll receive your answer on 3 October; I can then leave on the 6th, as I don't need to hurry, and my stay here isn't futile or fruitless as I can shut myself away and work in order to earn as much money as possible; but there's something I want to ask you – I still don't know how you want me to travel; as I shan't have much extra luggage with me – when I have a moment, I'll send on in advance what I don't need – I could perhaps get someone to give me a nice cabriolet of the kind that's now very fashionable here – that's what Wendling did; I can then continue the journey as I like and take the mail coach or a *vetturino*; the cabriolets here aren't as they used to be, namely, open, but are closed – with glass – it's just that they have 2 wheels and can seat 2 not very fat people; well, I can arrange all this when I receive your reply to this letter. I've something else to ask you and hope that you won't refuse, namely, that if it's the case that the Webers have not gone to Munich but have remained in Mannheim (although I

8. K279–284. However, the sonatas were first published posthumously, by Breitkopf & Härtel in Leipzig in 1799.

9. Mozart's five violin concertos date from 1773 (K207) and 1775 (K211, 216, 218 and 219); there is no evidence that he arranged them to suit Parisian taste.

10. Grimm had been made a baron on his appointment as minister plenipotentiary at the French court in 1776.

hope and believe that this isn't so), I'd like to have the pleasure of passing through and visiting them. – It's a detour, of course, but only a small one – or at least it wouldn't seem very much to me – but I don't think that it'll be necessary – I'll meet them in Munich – I hope to be assured of this by a letter in the morning; but if this proves not to be the case, I'm already convinced in advance by your kindness that you won't refuse me this pleasure. Dearest father! If the archbishop wants a new singer, by heaven I know of none better;[11] he won't get a Teyber or a de Amicis; and the rest are undoubtedly worse; I'm only sorry that when people go there from Salzburg for the coming carnival and *Rosamunde* is performed, it's quite possible that they won't like poor Fräulein Weber, or at least that people won't judge her as she deserves to be judged as she has a wretched part, almost a *persona muta*[12] – she has only a few verses to sing between the choruses, together with an aria in which you might expect the ritornello to be good, but the vocal line is *à la* Schweitzer, suggesting nothing so much as yelping dogs; she has only one number – a kind of rondeau in the 2nd act – where she has any sustained singing and can show what she can do; yes, unhappy the singer who falls into Schweitzer's hands, for as long as he lives he'll never learn how to write for the voice! Once I'm in Salzburg, I shall certainly not fail to show great enthusiasm in speaking out in favour of my dear friend – in the meantime I would ask you not to fail to do all you can for her, you can give your son no greater pleasure than that; I can think of nothing now except the pleasure of soon embracing you again – please make sure that everything that the archbishop has promised is fully assured – and the same applies to what I asked you about, that my place is at the keyboard; every good wish to all our good friends, especially Herr Bullinger; oh, what fun we'll have together! – I can think of nothing else and can already see it all in my mind's eye; adieu. I kiss your hands 100,000 times and embrace my sister with all my heart; hoping to receive a reply at once, so that I can leave straightaway, I am your most obedient son

Wolfgang Amadè Mozart

11. than Aloysia Weber.
12. 'silent role'.

[*On the inside of the cover*]

By the way: you'll know from my last letter that I was at St Germain, where I was asked to run an errand. Madame de Folard, the wife of the former French ambassador in Munich[13] and a close friend of the bishop of Chiemsee, would like to know if he's received the letters she wrote to him as she's had no reply. Could I ask you to look into this, as she was very insistent about it – *adieu*;

I await your answer and shan't leave till it arrives – don't let on that you know what I've told you about this gentleman – I prefer to repay people like this with courtesy – this hurts them more as there's nothing they can say to it. *Adieu.*

95. Leopold Mozart to his son, 24 September 1778, Salzburg

My Dear Son,

It was with immense pleasure that I read your letter of the 11st inst. *I'm not really surprised by what you write about a particular person*[1] *as his letters always struck me as suspect*: you'd have done well to have told me all this before now. *I'm not writing to him today as I wrote to him on the last post day but one.* You'll also have received my letter *of the 17th.* I should tell you that Baron Grimm wrote to say that he'd see to your journey to Strasbourg for you. I realized from his letter that he must have advanced you some money – and so I told him that I intended to repay it all and asked him only to send instructions to Augsburg. In the name of God! I had to write it, how could I have left you in the lurch? But he replied: – *je ne veux pas entendre parler de remboursement dans ce moment ci, quand vouz serez plus à votre aise, nous solderons nos comptes. Je vous l'ai dit, je voudrais être en état de faire une pension à votre fils etc.*[2] My dear son, this is really most civil

13. Hubert, Chevalier de Folard, French ambassador at Munich 1756–76.
1. Baron Grimm.
2. 'I don't want to hear any talk of reimbursement at present, when you're better off, we'll settle our accounts. I've already said that I'd like to be in a position to provide your son with an allowance.'

of him, and you can see that he has complete faith in us. He goes on
– *ne vous inquiétez pas de m'envoyer de l'argent, mais tracez à votre fils
tout ce qu'il doit faire pendant sa route. Je vous le livrerai jusqu'à
Strasbourg; si vous lui faites trouver là de l'argent pour continuer sa route
par Augsb. et Salzbourg etc.*[3] This shows that, far from having no faith
in me, he has complete confidence in me. I found this very reassuring
as he's travelled a great deal and must know better than us the safest
and most convenient way from Paris to Strasbourg, without incurring
any great expense, as he knows the way, whereas I don't, and he'll
pay your travelling expenses. Doesn't that suggest a lot of confidence?
– Think it over! Isn't this the greatest weight off my mind that I
could wish for? – Where else would I find the money? – – He wants
to help me, especially because we're so far apart and in addition he
knows how many debts I already have to pay off as I wrote to tell
him this a long time ago – and yet he's still willing to advance me
this amount of credit? He ends his letter with the words: *Employez
donc l'argent, que vous voulez m'envoyer, à son Voyage depuis Strasbourg
à Salzburg etc.*,[4] so you may judge from this whether you were not
over-suspicious on this point. This was also the reason why I felt
confident in making arrangements through *Herr Haffner* and was able
to enclose a note to Herr *Johann Scherz*[5] in Strasbourg, who'll give
you the money you need to get to Augsburg and help you in every
way in word and deed. Why only as far as Augsburg? – *Because one
has to pay an agio*[6] *to the businessmen involved*, and in Augsburg I can
obtain money for you without paying an *agio*: I'll send instructions
to my brother to this effect. As for your journey to Strasbourg, *you
must of course rely on the sensible advice of those who have more experience
than yourself.* There are often hired carriages from Strasbourg there,

3. 'Don't worry about sending me any money, but explain to your son everything
he has to do on his journey. I'll deliver him as far as Strasbourg if you can arrange
for him to receive some money there so that he can continue his journey to Augsburg
and Salzburg etc.'
4. 'Use the money that you were going to send me to pay for his journey from
Strasbourg to Salzburg etc.'
5. Johann Georg Scherz, Haffner's corresponding agent in Strasbourg.
6. 'premium'.

ritorni, that stop at certain inns, allowing you to get to Strasbourg conveniently and for relatively little money. You just need to ask. That's how Dr Prex[7] travelled from Paris to Strasbourg. And Baron Grimm must already have had some idea how he plans to get you there. One mustn't reject everything out of hand on the strength of a mere preconception. You say that you could get someone to give you a nice cabriolet. My dear Wolfgang, this will remain a wish; it also seems to me to *run counter to the need to save money*; for no one readily gives away something that's still in good condition. And if the cabriolet is *dilapidated* or if its *wheels* and *axle*, for example, are in a poor condition, then it could break down at any moment and you'll be left *sitting in the road, wasting time and money*, you'll have to *have it repaired* and the delay and repairs will cost more than the whole pile of junk is worth, quite apart from which there's probably no one in Paris or very few people who operate as hired coachmen. If you've got your own carriage and if they only have to provide the horses, you have to pay them a lot as they're not allowed *to bring people back* and can't earn anything for the return journey but have to come back with just the horses and no carriage. Also, such a driver would have to be someone you could trust as you'd be entirely alone with him. The mail coach would cost an astonishing amount of money as there are *55 and a half stages* from Paris to Strasbourg: it's *25 sous* for each horse, so *50 sous* for 2 horses, which makes 2 livres and 10 sous – *without the tip*. In short, I can't advise you on this, I'm too far away, and it depends on circumstances and calculations and above all on the good advice of people with knowledge and experience. I think that Herr Gschwendtner travelled from Strasbourg to Paris.

You shouldn't leave anything behind, that's not my opinion and never has been, but, if you can, you should sell some music straightaway. It's better if works that do you no credit are not made known, which is why I've not released any of your symphonies, as I knew in advance that, with maturity and greater insight, you'd be pleased that no one's got hold of them, even though you were pleased with them

---

7. He seems to have been a Salzburg doctor whom the Mozarts had met in Paris in 1766.

when you wrote them. One becomes increasingly discriminating. There's no point in thinking of going to Mannheim because at the end of this month everyone who's not already in Munich will be going there. Your wish that the Weber family should have 1000 florins a year has been realized, as I received news from Munich on 15 September that Seeau has engaged Mlle Weber for the German theatre on a salary of 600 florins. With her father's 400 florins, that makes 1000 florins. However kind your concerns for our Salzburg orchestra, I must ask you to set them aside as they are too high-flown for us. You think I should have demanded a written assurance that you'd be offered the post of Kapellmeister? – – Do you think that I attach such importance to this post? – By no means! – Isn't one always perfectly free to leave such a small court? – – You also say: *I don't mean to play the violin any more.* – Previously you were nothing but a *violinist*, namely, as *concertmaster*; you're now concertmaster and court organist, and your main task is to *accompany at the keyboard*. *As a music lover* you'll not consider it shaming to play the violin in the first symphony, for example, just as the archbishop himself does, as do all the courtiers who perform with us. Herr Haydn, after all, is not someone whose musical achievements you'd deny. Has he, as concertmaster, become a *court viola player* because he plays the viola at chamber concerts? – – People do this for their own entertainment; and I can assure you that as the concerts are now so short and consist of only 4 pieces, they serve as an entertainment, as people otherwise don't know what to do with their evenings. If something else turns up, *eh bien*, one stays away – just as others have done. And I bet that you'll join in rather than let your own works be bungled. But it doesn't follow from this that you'd be officiating as a violinist, while leaving the others to enjoy a night off and performing their trios and quartets. Far from it! My chief source of satisfaction consists in the fact that thanks to your own salary and my improved one *our situation will be more secure* and we shall definitely be able to pay off our *debts* and live comfortably. You're returning with your reputation unimpaired *because* everyone knows *that you've been asked back*, and the whole town praises your resolve in coming back to help your father following the loss of his wife and to provide him with the support that he needs in his old age. May God keep you well and grant you a safe journey! It is a long one! Look after yourself! Don't make any close friends on the journey, trust no one! Keep your medicines in your night bag, in case you need them. Keep an eye on your luggage when getting in and out of the coach. Don't show anyone your money. And *give some thought* to whether you stay with the Prince of Fürstenberg in Donaueschingen[8] or go on ahead from Strasbourg and wait for the diligence there. – Or whether you give the place a miss. In Augsburg go straight to the Holy Cross, the abbot has already written to me 3 times to say that you can stay there. Give my best wishes to Baron Grimm *and don't play any impudent tricks on him*. I'll write to him once I've heard that you've left. We're counting the days until we can embrace you. That fool of a wench, Tresel, has bought another 6 capons, and Nannerl bought a beautiful pair of *lace cuffs* for you yesterday. Madame de Folard will soon be receiving a reply from the prince of Chiemsee and will see from it that I've run the errand that was asked of me. Herr Bullinger, Herr Deibl, Mistress Mitzerl and a thousand others send their best wishes, Nannerl and I kiss you a million times. Hoping to see you again soon,

Mzt

Mozart left Paris on 26 September, ostensibly to return to Salzburg. Although it is often claimed that he composed little in the French capital, his output during the spring and summer of 1778 was considerable, including the 'Paris' symphony K297, ballet movements for Les petits riens *K299b, the concerto for flute and harp K299, the accompanied sonatas K304 and 306 as well as part of K305, the solo keyboard sonata K310 and the variations on 'Je suis Lindor' K354. He also probably wrote several lost works, among them the sinfonia concertante for winds K297B and a scena K315b.*

8. Prince Johann Wenzeslaus of Fürstenberg; the Mozarts had played at the Fürstenberg court at Donaueschingen in late October 1766.

96. Mozart to his father, 15 October 1778, Strasbourg

Monsieur
mon très cher Père,

Your 3 letters of 17 *September*, 24 *September* and 1 *October* have all arrived safely, but it was impossible for me to reply to them before now; – I hope you'll have received my last letter from Nancy; – I can't tell you how happy I am that you're both well, all thanks and praise be to God; I too am well, thank God, and, indeed, very well; – as far as possible, I'll now reply to the most important points in your 3 letters –

What you wrote about Monsieur Grimm I know better than you, of course; – he's always very polite and good-natured – I know that very well – if he'd not been, I'd certainly not have stood on such ceremony with him; – I owe Monsieur Grimm no more than 15 louis d'or, and it's his own fault that he's not been repaid – I told him so myself; – but what's the point of all this tittle-tattle? – We'll speak about it in Salzburg – I'm very grateful to you for having recommended me so warmly to Padre Martini – and also for writing to Monsieur Raaff in a similar vein – nor did I ever doubt that you would – for I know how much you like to see your son happy and contented – and that you know that there is nowhere I'd rather be than Munich – it's so close to Salzburg that I can visit you often; – that Mlle Weber or, rather, my dear Fräulein Weber is now being paid a salary and that justice has finally been done to her gave me great pleasure, as may be expected from someone who takes such an interest in her; – I continue to commend her to you most warmly; – but unfortunately I may no longer hope for what I'd wanted so much, namely, to get her a post in Salzburg, for the archbishop won't give her what she's getting there – the only possibility is that she may come for a while to Salzburg to sing in an opera; I've received a letter from her father, written in great haste on the eve of his departure for Munich and informing me about this particular piece of news – these poor people had all been immensely worried about me – they thought I was dead as they'd not heard from me for a whole month, my last letter but one having gone missing – and they were further confirmed in their belief by the fact that they were told in Mannheim that my dearly departed mother had died of an hereditary illness; they'd already prayed for my soul; – the poor girl went every day to the Capuchin church; – do you find this funny? – I don't; I'm touched by it, I can't help it; – but, to proceed; –

I think I'll definitely go to Augsburg by way of Stuttgart as I can see from your letters that there's nothing, or, at most, very little, to do in Donaueschingen – but you'll discover all this from a letter that I'll send you before I leave Strasbourg; –

Dearest father! – I assure you that if it weren't for the pleasure of embracing you soon, I'd certainly not be returning to Salzburg! – Apart from this praiseworthy and genuinely beautiful urge, I am in fact committing the greatest folly in the world; – believe me when I say that these are my own private thoughts and are not borrowed from other people; – when they knew of my decision to leave, people opposed it, of course, with truths that I was incapable of resisting and defeating with any other weapons save my true and tender love for my beloved father, for which people could naturally do nothing but praise me, while adding that if my father knew of my present circumstances and excellent prospects – and if he hadn't been differently and, indeed, falsely informed by a certain good friend – he would most certainly not have written to me in such terms that I was utterly incapable of resisting; – and I thought to myself that if I'd not had to put up with so much annoyance at the house where I was lodging and if one thing hadn't led to another like a series of thunderclaps, with the result that I'd no time to consider the matter in cold blood, I'd definitely have asked you to be patient for a little while longer and let me stay in Paris, where, I assure you, I'd have gained honour, reputation and money – and would certainly have got you out of debt; – but now the thing is done; don't for a minute think that I regret it; – for only you, dearest father, only you can sweeten for me the bitter pill that is Salzburg; and you'll do so; I'm convinced of that; but I freely admit that I'd arrive in Salzburg with a lighter heart if I didn't know that I'll be in the service of the court; – this thought alone is intolerable to me! – Consider it yourself – put yourself in my position; – in Salzburg I don't know who I am – I'm everything – and sometimes nothing at all – I'm not asking for *a lot* – but nor am I asking for *very little* – I just want something – as long as I'm *something* – everywhere else I know what I am – everyone else, if he's placed with the violins, sticks to it; – it's the same with the keyboard *etc*. – But we'll sort something out, – I just hope it all works out to my own good fortune and contentment; – I rely on you entirely; –

Things are in a poor way here – but the day after tomorrow, Saturday the 17th, I'm giving a subscription concert *all by myself* – so that I have no expenses – in order to please a few kind friends – music lovers and connoisseurs; – if I had an orchestra, it would cost me more than 3 louis d'or, including lighting, and who knows if we'll bring in as much as that; – I'm indebted to you for such excellent arrangements to cover the cost of my journey, I don't think I'll need it even if I don't give a concert; – but just to be on the safe side I'll withdraw a few louis d'or here or in Augsburg as you never know what may happen – meanwhile farewell; I'll write more next time – my sonatas can't have been engraved yet, although they were promised for the end of *September*[1] – that's what happens if you're not there in person – and again it's Grimm's obstinacy that's to blame – they're quite likely to turn out full of mistakes as I wasn't able to look through them myself but had to entrust the task to someone else – so I may find myself in Munich without these sonatas; – something that seems so slight can often bring us happiness, honour and money, but it can also bring us disgrace; – well, adieu; – I embrace my dearest sister with all my heart and you, my dearest, most beloved father, I kiss in the flattering hope of soon being able to embrace you and kiss your hands myself. I am your most obedient son

Wolfgang Amadè Mozart

Best wishes to the whole of Salzburg, but especially to our dear and true friend Herr Bullinger.

1. K301–306; they were not published until late November 1778.

97. *Leopold Mozart to his son, 19 November 1778, Salzburg*[1]

Mon très cher Fils,

I really don't know what to say – I shall lose my senses or succumb to some wasting disease. It's simply impossible for me to remember all the projects that you've thought up and communicated to me since leaving Salzburg, without losing my reason. They all boiled down to suggestions, empty words and ultimately *nothing whatever*. Since 26 Sept. I'd been consoling myself with the hope that I'd have the pleasure of seeing you in Salzburg on *your name day*,[2] but then had to *endure my first taste of mortal anguish* when you wrote from Nancy on the 3rd, saying that you were going to Strasbourg the next day, the 4th, only for the Frank brothers to write to me on the 9th to announce that you'd not yet arrived there. You finally wrote to me from Strasbourg on the 14th.[3] During your stay in Nancy you'd therefore been throwing your money down the drain when, instead of frittering it away needlessly, you could have spent it on a conveyance of your own and made your way more quickly to Strasbourg. You then hunkered down in Strasbourg until the rains set in, even though I'd already written to tell you that, if nothing was to be achieved there, you should leave again right away and not spend your money needlessly, and although you yourself told me that things were in a poor way there and that you'd leave immediately after giving a small concert on the 17th, *people praised you* – and *for you that's already enough!* You remained there – without writing a single word to me, but *giving me my second taste of mortal anguish* as we had floods and rain here too, and only on 10 November were we wrenched from our state of anxiety by your letter of the 2nd. If, following your concert on 17 Oct., you'd left on the 19th or 20th, you'd have arrived in Augsburg before the great floods and we'd not have feared for your life and the money that was needlessly squandered in Strasbourg would still be in your pocket. We were then told that you were

1. This letter is addressed to Mozart in Mannheim.
2. 31 October.
3. In fact, the 15th.

leaving on the 5th, or so Herr Scherz wrote to inform us. With each post day I hoped to receive news that you'd arrived in Augsburg: but I kept being told that you were not yet there – indeed, a letter of 13 Nov.[4] even claimed that you wouldn't be going there at all; and so, not having seen a letter from you until today, the 19th, I was inevitably reduced to *a state of anxiety for the 3rd time* as it would never for a moment have occurred to me that you'd hit on the mad idea of staying on in Mannheim, where there's no court, but assumed that you'd been in Augsburg since the 10th at the latest – indeed, I was all the more convinced of this in that I thought you'd lose no time in going to *Munich* where, as I assumed when you left Nancy, you'd apply for work in connection with the Feast of St Charles.[5] Was it only as a precaution that you withdrew 8 louis d'or in Strasbourg, so that you could then sit around in Mannheim? You hoped to obtain a post in Mannheim? An appointment? – – Whatever are you thinking of? – – You mustn't accept an appointment in Mannheim or anywhere else in the world at present –, I won't hear the word *appointment*. If the elector were to die today, a whole battalion of musicians who are now in Munich and Mannheim would have to set off into the world in search of a livelihood as the Duke of Zweibrücken[6] himself has an orchestra of 36, and the orchestra of the elector of Bavaria and Mannheim currently costs 80,000 florins a year.

The inhabitants of Mannheim are fools if they think that the elector will leave Munich; they are flattering themselves with the hope because that's what they want. My own information is better and more reliable – for political reasons of state alone it will never happen: – but what's the point of all this idle gossip! The main thing is *that you return to Salzburg now*. I don't want to know about the 40 louis d'or that you may *perhaps* be able to earn.[7] Your whole plan seems to be to drive me to ruin, simply in order to build your castles

4. This letter is lost.

5. 4 November.

6. Karl II August, Duke of Zweibrücken (reigned 1775–93) was Elector Karl Theodor's heir.

7. In a letter of 12 November 1778 Mozart wrote to his father that he intended to offer to write a melodrama for Baron von Dalberg (1749–1806), director of the Mannheim theatre, and Abel Seyler for 40 louis d'or.

in the air. You'd more than 15 louis d'or in the pocket when you left Paris.

That makes – –	165 florins

You told me that you'd made at least	
7 louis d'or in Strasbourg	77 florins
8 louis d'or from Herr Scherz	88 florins
	330 florins

The carriage from Paris was paid for. So that's a fine sum for a single person, seeing that the cost of a diligence is small, proportionately speaking, of course.

In short, I have absolutely no intention of dying a shameful death, deep in debt, on your account; still less do I intend to leave your poor sister destitute; – you know as little as I do how long God will allow you to live. If I were to write to Madame Cannabich and tell her that

on your departure I borrowed	300 florins
that in Mannheim I arranged for you to draw	200
that in Paris I paid *the money that you received from*	
Gschwendtner	110
that I owe Baron Grimm 15 louis d'or	165
that you received 8 louis d'or in Strasbourg	88
so that in 14 months you've *plunged me into debt to the*	
tune of	
	863 florins

if I tell her *to give this information to all those people who are advising you to stay in Mannheim and tell them that I want you back in service in Salzburg for a few years because I'll then have the prospect of paying off these debts*, they'd not say a single word in an attempt to detain you but would wear completely different expressions on their faces. In short! – Until now I've written to you not only as a father but as a friend; I hope that on receiving this letter you will immediately expedite your journey home and conduct yourself in such a way that

I can receive you with joy and not have to greet you with reproaches: indeed, I hope that, after your mother died so inopportunely in Paris, you'll not have it on your conscience that you contributed to your father's death, too. God be praised, I've not yet lost my reason – it's incumbent on me to do what is best and see to the temporal and spiritual welfare of my children – I must answer to God for this and be strictly accountable to Him – I must pay careful heed to my own and my children's honour. The 863 florins have to be repaid. I'm better at *making plans* than someone like you, who believes every flattering word. I know that I can pay off this sum in 2 years. But I can't pay it off on my own. And you're incapable *at present* of considering anything calmly: you care little for the reputation of your father who until today has not even known where to write to you for the last 2 months. In short! *My debts have to be repaid*, and *you'll leave on receipt of this letter*. I refuse to be an object of ridicule in the town that wishes to see you, while we flattered ourselves into thinking that, as you'd not written to me for so long, you were planning to surprise me on my name day. But that would have been too great a display of affection! How could I have deserved such a thing? – – Herr Fiala has resigned his Munich appointment, although he hasn't lost a penny of his salary – he foresees the confusion that will arise on the death of the elector. His luggage is here in my hall. A cello, 2 violins, a viola, a small crate containing music and a box.[8] He and his wife will be arriving this evening by diligence. I hope to receive a letter from you very shortly, announcing that you've left. May God grant you a safe journey. I kiss you a million times. Expecting to see you soon, I am your father

Mzt

Your sister embraces you – and hopes to embrace you soon. Signor Ceccarelli sends his best wishes and can scarcely wait to see you again. If I had time, I'd tell you the whole story of the punishment meted out to the son for his disobedience towards his parents. *Count Sigerl Lodron has had to be operated on with 3 long incisions in his side*

---

8. Joseph Fiala was a composer, cellist and viol player as well as an oboist.

as far as the ribs, his life hangs in the balance; pitifully painful! It would take too long to describe it. It was an extraordinary operation. All the surgeons and doctors were summoned, as well as Dr Quella from Passau.[9]

Finding that Aloysia Weber was not in Mannheim, Mozart followed her to Munich, pursued by letters from Leopold. It is likely that he declared his love for her but was rejected.

98. Leopold Mozart to his son, 31 December 1778, Salzburg

My Dear Son,

I was very upset to read the letters from you and Monsieur Becke.[1] If your tears, sadness and heartfelt anxiety have no other reason but that you doubt my love and affection for you, you may sleep peacefully – eat and drink peacefully and return home even more peacefully.

I see that you don't really know your father. It seems from our friend's letter that this is the main reason for your sadness: oh, I hope there is no other! For you really have no cause to fear that your welcome will not be affectionate and that the days that you spend with me and your sister will not be agreeable. Haven't we kept postponing our autumn entertainment, which is paid for from the proceeds of our shooting competitions? And we're still waiting for you. Don't you realize that I myself can see the sort of life that you're exchanging for the one you'll be leading here – and have I not always allowed you to pursue all manner of amusements here and even arranged them for you? – And do you think I'll do so less in the future? – And don't I, too, need to seek entertainment and the greatest possible enjoyment in order to prolong my life and make it agreeable?

9. He was the personal physician to the bishop of Passau.
1. The flautist, Johann Baptist Becke.

But what worries me most and is bound to concern me is your lengthy absence. It's 4 months since I received your provisional certificate of appointment – as people know that you left Paris on 26 Sept. – as they know that I've kept writing to say that you should come; – – as they thought that you'd be here for my name day – then for Christmas – and finally for the New Year, tell me if people aren't saying to my face that you're treating the prince – and, what's worse, your own father – as a fool; and that I'd simply have to accept it if the prince took back his certificate as I know that he's impatient about it and is bound to end up believing that I've been deliberately trying to make him look foolish – yet I've done all this only because I know for certain that, until you're a few years older, we can hope for no better prospects, i.e., with regard to our general situation at present. You're not helping matters by staying away any longer *but are making things worse*. People are being led by the nose by means of promises and the hope of things to come, until finally nothing comes of them or at best a proposition that's impossible to accept: meanwhile one loses the real morsel while trying to catch shadows. If you were the only person involved here, you could be content to be treated like a *horse* that allows itself to be ridden and dutifully draws a carriage each time it is harnessed to it as long as it has a stable and some food – *all the people who think they're contented as long as they have food and a room and who work hard* or, even worse, idle their time away *are like horses*. Very well! I'll let you get on with it! And will your father take precedence? – – You've been in Munich since the evening of the 25th – you wrote to me on the 29th and told me you hadn't yet handed over the sonatas:[2] but you won't have been able to get them bound because of the holidays. Meanwhile all this will have been done. You say that *I should comfort you* – and I write that *you should come here and comfort me*, how joyfully I shall embrace you. – I'm almost going mad writing this letter, it's New Year's Eve, and although the door is closed, the bell keeps ringing, Pimperl is barking, Ceccarelli is shouting and gossiping and people are deafening me with their good wishes even though they can see that I'm writing and hurrying to get

2. K301–306.

this off to the post and I've already lit the candles as it's 5 o'clock. – The bellows blower has just this minute come to say that Gussetti has received a letter announcing *that you're coming next week*, tomorrow the whole town will be telling me this as he'll tell everyone he sees. As for the mass that you mention,[3] I thought you'd been working on it little by little during your stays in Strasbourg, Mannheim and Kaisheim[4] – I assumed you'd had the idea so that you'd be fully prepared when you got to Munich. But it's now too late – – composing – copying etc. God forbid! And in the end it's a present, of which Count Seeau *will keep half.* In short! I return to the point that I'm being belittled, as things have now gone too far. – No certain or good or sensible prospect – still less the prospect of anything permanent in Munich. Here you have certainty and permanence – as long as you want it – just get Monsieur Becke to read the letter that I enclosed with the one I sent you on the 28th or read it to him yourself, I hope he'll find my opinion well justified. Mlle Moulin left for Munich this morning in her own carriage, a two-seater coach with glass windows, the coachman is bringing you a letter from me. He can wait a couple of days if you prefer to travel with him in so comfortable a coach, rather than the bone-rattling diligence, it's all the same whether you leave on the 5th or 6th as you'd also have to travel all night with the diligence. We'll be well entertained as there are plays on at present and then there'll be the balls: and I pray and hope that in a year we'll be able to go to Italy as Ceccarelli intends to go there as well. I must close now, otherwise the post will leave without me! If you love your father and sister, you must also believe *that they'll do all they can to accord you every pleasure.* With all our hearts we wish you a Happy New Year – oh, if only you were already here, how peacefully I'd sleep: may God grant you a safe journey, we kiss you a million times in the hope that I may soon tell you that I am your father who loves you with all his heart

Mzt

3. In a letter of 29 December, Mozart had told Leopold of his intention to compose a mass for the Munich court. This plan remained unrealized although it is usually thought that the fragmentary Kyrie K322 may be what Mozart had in mind.

4. Mozart had stayed in the abbey of Kaisheim from 13 to 24 December.

99. Mozart to his father, 8 January 1779, Munich

Mon très cher Père,

I hope you'll have received my last letter, which I intended to give to the hired coachman but which, having missed him, I sent by post; I've received all your letters, including your last one of *31 December*, which Herr Becke passed on to me; – I let him read my letter and he let me read his; –

I assure you, my dearest father, that I'm very much looking forward to returning to *you*, if not to Salzburg, because your last letter convinces me that you know me better than before! – This doubt was the only reason for my long delay in returning home – for the sadness that in the end I could no longer conceal, with the result that I opened up my whole heart to my friend Becke; – what other reason could there have been? – I'm not aware that I've done anything that would make me fear any reproaches; – I've committed no fault – by fault I mean something that ill becomes a Christian and a man of honour; – in a word, I am looking forward to and already anticipating the happiest and most agreeable days together – but only in the company of yourself and my dearest sister; –

I swear to you on my honour that I cannot abide Salzburg and its inhabitants – I mean the people who were born there; – their language – their whole way of life are intolerable; – you won't believe what I suffered during Madame Robinig's visit here; – it's a long time since I've spoken to such a fool; – and to make matters worse, the simple-minded and deeply stupid Mosmayer was with her – but let's move on; – yesterday I went with my dear friend Cannabich to see the electress and present her with my sonatas;[1] she's in lodgings here just as I too shall undoubtedly be one day – just as any private individual can be lodged, nice and cosy, apart from the view, which is wretched – we were with her for a good half hour and she was really very kind; – I've ensured that she's told that I'll be leaving here in a few days so that I'm paid promptly – you don't need to

1. K301–306.

worry about Count Seeau as I don't think the matter will pass through his hands, and even if it does, he wouldn't dare say a word against me; – well, to be brief, believe me when I say that I'm burning with desire to embrace you and my dear sister again – if only it weren't in Salzburg; – but since it's impossible to see you without going to Salzburg, I shall be happy to go there –

I must hurry as the post is leaving; – my little cousin[2] is here – why? – to please her cousin? – That, of course, is the obvious reason! – But – we'll talk about this in Salzburg; – and this is why I'd very much like her to come back to Salzburg with me! – You'll find something in her own hand appended to the fourth page of this letter; – she'd like to come; – so, if you'd enjoy having her in your house, I wonder if you'd be good enough to write at once to your brother, saying that it's all right – when you see her and get to know her, you'll certainly be pleased with her – everyone likes her; – now farewell, dearest, most beloved father; – I kiss your hands 1000 times and embrace my dear sister with all my heart and ever remain

Your most obedient son
W A Mozart

Madame Hepp *née* d'Hosson died yesterday in childbirth; – she too was killed by her doctors; –

[*His cousin's postscript*]
Monsieur mon très cher oncle

I hope that you and my mistress cousin are well; I have had the honour of finding your son[3] in very good health in Munich, he wants me to come to Salzburg, but I don't know if I'll have the honour of seeing you:

[*inkblot, beneath it two lines in Mozart's hand*]
a portrait of my cousin;
she's writing in her shirtsleeves! –

2. Maria Anna Thekla Mozart.
3. Mozart added the word 'cousin' above 'son'.

[In his cousin's hand]
but my cousin is a real fool, as you can see. I wish you well, *mon cher oncle*, 1000 good wishes to Mademoiselle Cousine *je suis de tout mon cœur*[4]

[In Mozart's hand]
Monsieur
votre invariable Cochon[5]

[In his cousin's hand]
Munich the 8 January

1779   Fräulein Mozart

[In Mozart's hand]
where the last person has not yet shat –

Mozart arrived back in Salzburg during the third week of January 1779, at which time he formally petitioned Archbishop Colloredo for his appointment as court and cathedral organist: 'Your Serene Highness was most graciously pleased after the decease of Cajetan Adlgasser most graciously to take me into your service: I therefore most submissively beg that I may be graciously assigned the post of Court Organist in your exalted service; to which end, as for all other high favours and graces, I subscribe myself in the most profound submission.' On 17 January Colloredo decreed: 'Whereas We by these presents have graciously admitted and accepted the suppliant as Our Court Organist, that he shall, like Adlgasser, carry out his appointed duties with diligent assiduity and irreproachably, in the Cathedral as well as at Court and in the Chapel, and shall as far as possible serve the court and the church with new compositions made by him; We decree him therefor, like his predecessor, an annual salary of four hundred and fifty gulden, and command Our Court Pay Office to

4. 'I am with all my heart'.
5. 'Sir, your invariable pig'.

discharge this by monthly instalments, and to render account for each outlay in the appropriate place.' (Deutsch, Documentary Biography, 181–2).

Mozart composed several substantial works during this period, including the masses K275, 317 and 337, the vespers K321 and 339, the symphonies K318, 319 and 338, the 'Posthorn' serenade K320, the sinfonia concertante for violin and viola K364, the concerto for two pianos K365, and the accompanied sonata K378. The diary that Nannerl Mozart kept at this time provides a fascinating insight into the everyday life of the Mozart family. The following extract is typical; the entries were read at the time by Mozart, who added a few comments of his own.

100. Nannerl Mozart's diary, 15–28 September 1779

15th. To church at 8 o'clock, at Lodron's and the Mayrs':[1] afternoon Katherl and Feigele and Herr Finck[2] called on us:

[*In Mozart's hand*]
Rained all day.

16th. To church at 8 o'clock. Afternoon with Lodron. At 4 o'clock visit from Feigele. Played tarot. Changeable weather, just like April. And very cool.

17th. To church at half past 7. At Lodron's and the Mayrs'. At half past 2 Fräulein Nannerl, Therese and Luise Barisani called. From 5 to 6 the 2 Mlles Hartensteiner called. At 6 Fräulein Josepha[3] came. Feigele was also there. We played cards. At half past 7 Mölk[4] came,

1. The Salzburg high steward Joachim Rupert Mayr von Mayrn (1732–96), his wife Anna (1744–96) and their three daughters.
2. Karl Bernhard von Feigele, Joseph Finck (c. 1762–84).
3. Maria Josepha Johanna Gilowsky von Urazowa.
4. Albert von Mölk.

but left straightaway. At 9 my brother took the girls home. Weather changeable like yesterday.

18th. To cathedral at 9. Hours.
Katherl and Paris[5] had lunch with me, as Papa and my brother were lunching at Holy Trinity. Feigele provided the prizes. Wirtenstätter won. Played tarot. At 6 Papa, I, Feigele, Wirtenstätter and Pimperl went for a walk. Back home by half 7. Fine weather.

19th. Mass at the University Church at half past 9. Then to the Mayrs' and assistant riding master.[6] At 2 to Lodron's. Visit from Feigele. Played tarot. At 6 Papa, Feigele, my brother, I and Pimperl to the Robinigs'. Back at half 8. Very beautiful weather.

20th. To church at half past 7. At Lodron's and the Mayrs'. Visit from Feigele during the afternoon. Played tarot.
Weather changeable; rained heavily. A fine evening.

21st. To church at half past 7, then called in at the Barisanis to congratulate Frau Barisani. Afternoon at Lodron's. Visit from Katherl and Feigele.
Played tarot. Heavy showers alternating with sunny spells all day.

22nd. At Lodron's; then Mass at Holy Trinity at half past 10. Then to the Mayrs. At 2 my brother and I called on Frau von Antretter. Papa joined us there. Returned home at 4 with Feigele. Played tarot. Then went for a walk. At half past 8 Herr Heydecker, the ropemaker from Ischl, called. The valet Angerbauer[7] returned from court with my brother. Rain. Stopped. Beautiful evening later on.

23rd. To Mass at 7 o'clock. Called on Mayr and assistant riding master. Bite to eat at Lodron's. Katherl and Schachtner called. Played

5. Possibly Anton Ferdinand Paris.
6. Gottlieb von Weyrother.
7. Johann Ulrich Angerbauer, chamber valet to Archbishop Colloredo.

tarot. At half past 4 the couple from Ischl. Rained and didn't rain. In the evening a thunderstorm and not a thunderstorm.

[*In Nannerl's hand*]
24th. To Mass at Holy Trinity at 10 and half past 10. In the afternoon Messrs Ferrari,[8] Fiala, Schachtner and Brindl[9] called, rehearsed for a concert, afterwards at Katherl's the
[*In Mozart's hand*]
Mezgers[10] there. Half past 11 played. At 4 my father and brother joined us. At 5 we all went bowling in the Mezgers' courtyard. At 9 a serenade in the street outside Herr Döll's on the Kollegienplatz. The march from the last graduation music.[11] 'Lustig sind die Schwobemedle'.[12] And the Haffner music.[13] Rained during the morning. Cleared up during the afternoon.

25th. Mass at half past 9. Target practice in the afternoon. Feiner[14] provided the prizes. Katherl and Wirtenstätter won as a team. Played tarot. Fine weather in the morning. Rained during the afternoon.

26th. Massed at 7 o'clock. Later lost patience with Regine, the assistant riding master's daughter, and at the Mayrs. Lodronned on in the afternoon and Lodronned off at 3. At 4 we were Feigeled and then demoneyed at tarot. The sky dewatered itself nearly all day and we were badly winded.

27th. At Lodron's. Mass at half past 10. Then home. My brother

8. Antonio Ferrari, court violoncellist.
9. Joseph Anton Brindl, court tenor.
10. Johann Peter Mezger (1723–95), mayor of Salzburg from 1775–95.
11. Presumably one of the two marches K335, written about August 1779 to accompany the serenade K320 (3 August 1779), composed for the annual graduation ceremonies at Salzburg University.
12. Swabian folksong, 'Merry are the Swabian maids'.
13. K250, composed in 1776 for the wedding of Maria Elisabeth Haffner.
14. Joseph Feiner, court oboist.

went to Lodron's instead of Papa, who has rheumatism. Schachtner afternoon till 5 Feigele and Katherl called. Played tarot. Weather same as yesterday.

28th. Mass at 7. At the Mayrs and assistant riding master's. Afternoon Mlle Braunhofer[15] called. Katherl, Feigele — played tarot. Weather changeable. But the evening delightful.[16]

In the late spring or summer of 1780, Mozart was commissioned to compose the opera Idomeneo, re di Creta *('Idomeneo, king of Crete') for Munich. He left for the Bavarian capital on 5 November, arriving the next day. An extended correspondence between Leopold and Wolfgang survives from this time, detailing Mozart's compositional decisions and Leopold's involvement in them. The following letters, though by no means complete, are representative.*

101. Mozart to his father, 8 November 1780, Munich

Mon très cher Père,

I arrived here happy and contented! — Happy, because nothing untoward happened to us on the journey, and contented, because we could hardly wait for the moment when we reached our destination on account of the journey which, although short, was very uncomfortable; — I assure you that it was impossible for any of us to get even a minute's sleep all night — this type of carriage jolts the very soul out of your body! — And the seats! — As hard as stone! — After we'd left Wasserburg I began to think I'd never get my backside to Munich in one piece! — It was really sore — and presumably bright red — for

15. Maria Anna Braunhofer (1748–1819), daughter of the organist and singer Franz Joseph Braunhofer.
16. The last five sentences of this entry are written in Salzburg dialect.

two whole stages I sat supporting myself on my hands on the upholstery, holding my backside in the air – – – but enough of this, it's all behind me now! – But as a rule I'd prefer to walk in future – anything rather than travelling by mail coach. Now for Munich. – We didn't arrive till 1 in the afternoon but by the evening I'd already been to see Count Seeau and left a note as he wasn't at home – the next morning I went back there with Becke, who sends his best wishes to everyone, including the Fialas and all his other acquaintances in Salzburg; – Seeau is like putty in the hands of the Mannheimers – as for the libretto, the count says it's not necessary for Abbate Varesco[1] to copy it out again before sending it here – it's being printed here – but *I* think he should write it out straightaway and not forget the *stage directions* and send it here as soon as possible, together with the synopsis – as for the names of the singers, this is the least of our worries, as these can easily be added here.

Some small changes will have to be made here and there – the recitatives need shortening a little – but it will *all be printed*;

I've a request to make of the Abbate; – Ilia's aria in the second scene of act two[2] I'd like to change a little to bring it into line with what I need – *se il padre perdei in te lo ritrovo*: this line couldn't be better – but then comes something that has always struck me as unnatural – I mean in an aria – namely, *an aside*. In a dialogue these things are entirely natural – a few words are hurriedly spoken as an aside – but in an aria, where the words have to be repeated, it creates a bad impression – and even if this weren't the case, I'd still prefer an aria here – if he's happy with it, the opening can stay as it is, as it's delightful – an aria that flows along in an entirely natural way – where I'm not so tied to the words but can just continue to let the music flow, as we've agreed to include an andantino aria here with 4 concertante wind instruments, namely, flute, oboe, horn and bassoon. – Please make sure I receive it as soon as possible. –

Now for something disagreeable: – although I've not had the

---

1. Giambattista Varesco (1735–1805), court chaplain in Salzburg, had written the libretto to *Idomeneo*.
2. 'Se il padre perdei'.

honour of meeting the hero dal Prato, it seems from the description I've been given of him that Ceccarelli is almost to be preferred: – he often runs out of breath in the middle of an aria and – would you believe it? – he's never appeared on stage – also, Raaff is like a statue – – so you can imagine their scene in the opening act.[3] –

But now for something good. Madame Dorothea Wendling is *arcicontentissima* with her *scena* – she wanted to hear it 3 times in succession.[4] The Grand Master of the Teutonic Order[5] arrived yesterday – *Essex*[6] was given at the electoral court theatre – with a magnificent ballet. The theatre was all lit up; – they began with an overture by Cannabich, which I didn't know as it's one of his latest. – – – I assure you that if you'd heard it, you'd have liked it and been as moved by it as I was! – And if you'd not previously known it, you'd certainly never have thought it was by Cannabich – come soon and hear and admire the orchestra. I don't think there's anything else to report. There's a big concert this evening. Mara[7] will be singing 3 arias – is it snowing in Salzburg as much as here? –

Best wishes to Herr Schikaneder, I'm sorry I can't yet send him the aria,[8] as I haven't quite finished it –

I kiss your hands a thousand times and embrace my sister with all my heart. I am, *Mon très cher Père*,

Your most obedient son,
Wolf. Amadè Mozart

3. Vincenzo dal Prato (1756–1828), castrato, sang the role of Idamante, Anton Raaff that of Idomeneo.
4. Dorothea Wendling (1736–1811), wife of Johann Baptist Wendling, sang the role of Ilia; the scena is probably 'Solitudini amiche – Zeffiretti lusinghieri'.
5. Archduke Maximilian Franz.
6. *Essex oder Die Gunst des Fürsten* by Christian Heinrich Schmid (1746–1800), a translation of John Banks's play *The Unhappy Favourite or the Earl of Essex* (1682).
7. Gertrud Elisabeth Mara (1749–1833), singer.
8. Emanuel Schikaneder, see List; the aria, which survives only as an incomplete fragment, is K365a, 'Die neugeborne Ros' entzückt', performed on 1 December 1780 as a musical number in Schikaneder's production of J. G. Dyk's *Wie man sich die Sache denkt! oder Die zwey schlaflosen Nächte*.

A thousand good wishes from Cannabich and Wendl., they hope they'll soon have the pleasure of getting to know you both. *Adieu.*

[*On the envelope*]
Il vostro Figlio Giovane Beckio fa i suoi Comp. con suo sigillo[9]

102. *Mozart to his father, 15 November 1780, Munich*

Mon très cher Père,

Your letter or, rather, the whole packet, has arrived safely. Many thanks for the bill of exchange — so far I've not had lunch at home — and so I've no expenses except for the hairdresser, barber and laundress — and breakfast. —

The aria[1] is excellent as it is; — but there's now a further change, for which Raaff is to blame — but he's right; — and even if he weren't, one would still have to do something to acknowledge his grey hairs. — He was here yesterday — I ran through his first aria[2] with him and he was very pleased with it; — well — the man is old; in an aria like the one in the second act, '*fuor del mar ho un mare in seno*' etc., he can no longer show off his abilities — and so, because he has no aria in the third act and because his aria in the first act can't be cantabile enough for him as a result of the expression of the words, he wanted to replace the quartet with a nice aria following his final speech: '*O Creta fortunata! o me felice*'. In this way another useless number will be cut here — and the third act will now be far more effective. — Now — in the final scene of act two — Idomeneo has an aria or, rather, a kind of cavatina between the choruses — it'll be better to have just a recitative here,[3] with the instruments working hard beneath it — for in this scene, which — because of the action and the grouping, which

9. 'Your young son Becke sends his best wishes with his seal.'
1. 'Se il padre perdei'.
2. 'Vedrommi intorno', from the first act.
3. 'Eccoti in me, barbaro nume! il reo.'

we've recently agreed on with Le Grand[4]– will be the finest in the whole opera, there'll be so much noise and confusion on stage that an aria would cut a poor figure – also, there's the thunderstorm, which I don't suppose will stop for Herr Raaff's aria, will it? – And the effect of a recitative between the choruses is incomparably better. – Lisel Wendling has already sung through her two arias[5] half a dozen times – she's very pleased. I have it from a third party that the 2 Wendlings have praised their arias very highly. Raaff is in any case my best and dearest friend! –

But I have to go through the whole opera with my *molto amato* castrato dal Prato. He's incapable of singing a meaningful cadenza in an aria, and his voice is uneven! – He's been engaged for only a year, and as soon as this period is over, which will be next September, Count Seeau will take on someone else. Ceccarelli could then try his luck. *Sérieusement* –

I almost forgot the best piece of news of all, last Sunday after the service Count Seeau introduced me *en passant* to His Highness the Elector, who was very gracious to me. He said: *I'm delighted to see you here again.* And when I said that I'd strive to retain His Highness's approval, he clapped me on the shoulder and said: *Oh, I've no doubt at all that all will go well. – à piano piano, si va lontano.*[6]

Please don't forget to answer all the points relating to the opera, including, for example, what I said about the translator in my last letter. – – I'm supposed to sign a contract. –

What the devil! – I've again been prevented from writing what I'd like to write. Raaff has just this minute been to see me. He sends his best wishes, as does the whole of the Cannabich household and both the Wendling households.

Ramm, too. Now farewell, I kiss your hands a thousand times, the driver is just leaving – adieu, I embrace my sister.

I remain ever your most obedient son

Wolf Am. Mozart

4. A dancer involved with the production of *Idomeneo*.
5. 'Tutte nel cor vi sento' and 'Idol mio, se ritroso'. Elisabeth Augusta 'Lisel' Wendling (1746–86), who sang Elettra, was Wendling's sister-in-law.
6. 'Slow and steady wins the race.'

My sister mustn't be lazy but should practise hard. – People are already looking forward to hearing her play. –

My lodgings are with Monsieur Fiat in the Burggasse – but you don't need to include the address as they know me at the post office – and they also know where I'm staying. *Adieu.*

Eck and his son[7] and Becke send their best wishes.

103. Mozart to his father, 19 December 1780, Munich

Mon très cher Père,

I've received the final aria[1] for Raaff (who sends you his best wishes), together with the 2 trumpet mutes, your last letter of the 15th and the pair of socks. – The last rehearsal, like the first, turned out very well – the orchestra and the whole audience discovered to their delight that they'd been wrong in thinking that the 2nd act couldn't possibly be more powerful than the first in terms of its expression and originality – both acts will be rehearsed again next Saturday. But in a large hall at court, which I've long been wanting, as it's far too small at Count Seeau's – the elector will listen – incognito – from an adjoining room – we'll have to rehearse for all we're worth, Cannabich said to me – at the last rehearsal he was dripping with sweat – by the way, talking of sweat reminds me that I think that in the play both remedies must have worked at the same time – has my sister passed on my good wishes? – –

Herr Esser,[2] too, attended the rehearsal – he should've lunched at Cannabich's on Sunday but had found a way of getting to Augsburg, so he'd left. *Bon voyage!* – He came to say goodbye, or so the other

---

7. Georg Eck was a horn player in Munich; his son, Friedrich Johannes (1767–1838), was a violinist.

1. 'Sazio è destino al fine'.

2. Karl Michael Esser (1737–*c.* 1795), violinist. Wolfgang had first met him in Mainz in August 1763.

people in the house tell me, but I wasn't at home, I was with Countess Paumgarten.[3]

Herr Director Cannabich, whose name day it is today and who has just this minute left and who sends you his most friendly greetings, told me off for not wanting to finish my letter – which is why he left again straightaway. –

As for Madame Duschek, it is of course impossible at present[4] – but once the opera is finished, I'll do so with pleasure – meanwhile please write and give her my best wishes; – as for the debt, we agreed to settle it when she next came to Salzburg. – What would give me pleasure would be to have a couple of courtiers like old Czernin[5] – it would be a little help each year – but not less than 100 florins a year. – It could then be any type of music they liked. –

I hope that, praise and thanks be to God, you're now well again? – Yes, if you have yourself rubbed down by someone like Theresia Barisani, it can hardly be otherwise. – That I'm well – and contented – you'll have noticed from my letters. – After all, who wouldn't be happy to be finally rid of such a great and laborious task – and to be rid, moreover, with honour and fame – for I've nearly finished; – all that's still missing are 3 arias and the final chorus from act three – the overture – and the ballet – and then *adieu partie*! –

As for the arias for Heckmann that have no words, there are only 2 that you don't know. – The rest are by me – one, or rather two, from *Ascanio in Alba* – and the one for Frau Duschek[6] – you can send this one to me without the words as I already have them here and can write them in myself – there's also one by Anfossi[7] and another by Salieri[8] with oboe solo – both of these belong to Frau

3. Josepha, Countess Paumgarten (1762–1817).
4. In a letter of 15 December 1780 Leopold reported having received an aria text from Josepha Duschek that she hoped Mozart would set for her.
5. In December 1776 Prokop Adalbert, Count Czernin (1726–77), the father of Johann Rudolf, Count Czernin, had arranged to pay Mozart 20 ducats a year for newly composed works. He is known to have visited Salzburg in summer 1775.
6. K272, *Ah, lo previdi! – Deh, non varcar.*
7. Pasquale Anfossi (1727–97), composer of more than 60 operas.
8. Antonio Salieri, see List.

Haydn – I forgot to copy out the text as I didn't think I'd be leaving in such a hurry. I don't know the words by heart –

By the way – the most important thing of all, as I'm in a hurry – I hope that by the next mail coach I'll receive at least the first act, including the translation. – The scene between father and son in act one – and the first scene in act two between Idomeneo and Arbace – are both too long – they're bound to bore the audience – especially because in the first scene both singers are poor actors – and in the 2nd scene one of them is – and their entire content consists of retelling what the spectators have already seen with their own eyes – these scenes are being printed as they are –

I'd now like the Abbate[9] to indicate how they can be shortened – and, indeed, made as short as possible – otherwise I'll have to do it myself – for these 2 scenes can't be left as they are – when set to music, that is. –

I've just received your letter which, as my sister began it, is undated – 1000 good wishes to Tresel, my future under- and senior nursemaid. I can well believe that Katherl would like to come to Munich – if (apart from the journey) you were to let her take my place at table – *eh bien*, I'll see what I can do – she can share a room with my sister. By the way, please let me know at least eight days in advance when you'll be arriving, so that I can have a stove installed in the other room. Adieu.

What beautiful handwriting! I kiss your hands 100 times and embrace my sister with all my heart. I remain ever your most obedient son

Wolf. Amde. Mzt

Mes compliments à tous nos amis et amies.
My next letter will be longer and less messy.

9. Varesco.

104. Leopold Mozart to his son, 22 December 1780, Salzburg

Mon très cher Fils,

Forgive my haste, but the mail coach leaves early tomorrow morning, that is, a day earlier than usual. Here are the *pills*.[1] Take 5 in the morning *a day after the moon begins to wane*, then, if you like, you can have breakfast *an hour and a half later*. Another 5 in the evening before going to bed. Continue in this way until the moon has finished waning. It's extremely inconvenient, of course, that for women *there are times* when they have to postpone this treatment or break it off completely.

Here are the 3 acts copied out for the printer. Space has been left for the *names of the performers* – – *details* of the ballet – the *ballet music* etc.

What has been added before each major *scene change* can easily be altered in the libretto if Herr Quaglio[2] has changed it. – – In *Atto primo scena VIII*, for ex., it says: *Nettuno esce* etc. and then *Nel fondo della prospettiva se vede Idomeneo, che si forza arrampicarsi sopra quei dirupi* etc.[3] I think that the *description* and *explanation of these scenes* should reflect the way you intend to stage it, in other words, according to whether Idomeneo remains on his ship or whether, although not actually shipwrecked, he leaves the ship with his crew in the face of the apparent danger and seeks shelter on the rocks. In short, it depends on how it's staged. It should be left to Herr Quaglio, who's a man of skill and experience. But there must be shipwrecked vessels as *Idamante* says in his recitative in *scene 10 'vedo frà quel' avanzi di fracassate navi su quel Lido sconosciuto guerrier'*.[4] But, to continue! You're absolutely insistent on shortening 2 recits. I sent for Varesco at once as I

1. In a letter of 16 December, Mozart asked his father to send pills for Cannabich, who had put on weight and whom Mozart feared might develop gout.
2. Lorenzo Quaglio (1730–1805), scenery designer.
3. 'Neptune appears etc. . . . At the back of the stage Idomeneo is seen, struggling to clamber over some rocks etc.'
4. 'I see amid the remnants of wrecked ships an unknown warrior on that beach.'

didn't receive your letter till 5 o'clock this evening, and the mail coach leaves early tomorrow morning. We've examined it from every point of view and can find no reason to shorten it. It's translated from the French, as the draft envisaged. Indeed, if you look at the draft, you'll see that it was demanded that this recit. should be lengthened a little so they don't recognize each other too quickly and now there's the risk that it'll be made to seem ridiculous if they recognize each other after only a few words. Let me explain:

Idamante has to say why he's there, he sees the stranger and offers him his services. *Idomeneo* goes so far as to speak of his anguish and yet he must also return his greetings. At that point *Idamante* will tell him that he sympathizes with the unfortunate man as he too has known misfortune, *Idomeneo's* answer must necessarily be a question. *Idamante* now describes the king's misfortune and Idomeneo, with his *puzzling* words *non più di questo*,[5] gives *Idamante* a glimmer of hope and he asks in his eagerness *dimmi amico, dimmi dov'è?*[6] This eagerness makes Idomeneo ask *ma d'onde*[7] etc – surely Idamante must now explain things in such a way as to depict himself as a son worthy of his father and to excite in Idomeneo feelings of surprise, respect and the desire to discover who this young man is, so that, when he realizes that he's his son, the whole affair becomes more interesting? − − But if something really has to be left out, I've thought the matter over and think that it should be after Idamante's recit. *che favella? vive egli ancor'*[8] etc., which ends: *dove quel dolce aspetto vita mi renderà? Idomeneo, ma d'onde nasce questa, che per lui nutri tenerezza d'amor?*[9] You can then go straight to *perchè qual tuo parlar si mi conturba? Idamante. e qual mi senti anch'io*[10] and go on from there etc. In this way you'll lose 1½ pages on page 32 of the copy of Varesco's libretto enclosed with this letter, namely, the beautiful account of Idamante's

5. 'no more of this'.
6. 'tell me, friend, tell me where he is?'
7. 'but whence?'
8. 'what are you saying? Is he still alive?'
9. 'where is that sweet face that will restore me to life? *Idomeneo*: But whence comes it that you nurture such loving tenderness for him?'
10. 'why do your words so confuse me? *Idamante*: And I too feel'.

heroic feat, beginning with Idam.'s *Potessi almeno etc.*[11] This may shorten it by a *minute*, yes, *in puncto* a whole minute. A great gain! Or do you want father and son to run into each other and recognize one another in the way that the disguised Harlequin and Brighella meet as servants in a foreign country and quickly recognize and embrace each other?[12] Remember that this is one *of the most beautiful scenes in the opera*, indeed, it's the main scene and the one on which the whole of the rest of the story depends. In any case, this scene can't weary the audience *as it's in the first act*.

Nothing more can be cut in the 2nd act, except in Idomeneo's 2nd speech. *Idomeneo un Sol Consiglio or mi fà d'uopo. ascolta: Tu sai quanto a Trojani fù il mio brando fatal. Arbace tutto m'è noto etc.*[13] It then continues, and no sane person could leave out another word, quite apart from which this whole recit. can't last long as it contains lots of things that must be declaimed eagerly and rapidly, and you'd gain only *half a minute*! A great gain! Nor can this recit. weary a single soul as it's *the first one* in the 2nd act. At best you could omit the passage after *Arbace's recit. male s'usurpa un Rè*[14] etc so that *Idomeneo* says immediately: *Il voto è ingiusto.*[15]

You could then omit Idomen: *Intendo Arbace* etc and Arbace *Medica man*[16] etc. etc. Whether it's worth making a change for such a trifle that would save 2½ minutes at most, I don't know, especially as these recits. come at points where they can't be at all wearisome. In the first act everyone is patient, and the opening recit. in the 2nd act can't possibly be wearisome. It strikes me as risible: at a rehearsal, where there's nothing for the eye to see, it is, of course, boring, but in the theatre, where between stage and spectators there are so many objects to distract one, such a recit. passes almost unnoticed. You can tell

11. 'Would that I might at least etc.'
12. Here Leopold pokes fun at recognition scenes in popular *commedia dell'arte* theatre.
13. '*Idomeneo*: I need only one piece of advice. Listen. You know how fatal my sword was to the Trojans. *Arbace*: All is known to me etc.'
14. 'a king is an unworthy ruler'.
15. 'Your decision is unjust.'
16. 'I hear you, Arbace' . . . 'Medical help'.

everyone I said that. If, in spite of this, something still has to be omitted, I would ask that the text is still printed in full. Herr Varesco doesn't know that I've written all this. – If Herr Schachtner[17] hasn't done everything to the greatest perfection, you must remember that time was very short. Here are all the arias written out by Aesopus. Also a letter from Schachtner, who sends his best wishes, as does Varesco. We wish you luck and hope that the opera turns out a success. More next time. *Addio.* I wrote all this by candlelight, wearing my spectacles. Best wishes to *everyone.* We kiss you a million times. Your faithful old father

L. Mozart

On 26 January 1781, Leopold and Nannerl travelled to Munich for the premiere of Idomeneo *on 29 January. They remained in Munich throughout February, and in early March visited Augsburg before returning to Salzburg on 12 March. Mozart meanwhile had been summoned to Vienna by Archbishop Colloredo, who was visiting his father, the imperial vicechancellor. Although Mozart and his father continued to write regularly to one another, especially during Wolfgang's first years in Vienna, none of Leopold's letters have survived for this period – it is presumed that Constanze Mozart destroyed them after Mozart's death. As a result, the correspondence between Mozart and his father from March 1781 until Leopold's death in 1787 is entirely one-sided.*

105. Mozart to his father, 24 March 1781, Vienna

Mon très cher Père,

Your letter of the 20th inst. has arrived safely, and I'm delighted to see from it that you both got back safely and are well. – You have

17. Johann Andreas Schachtner had provided a German translation of the text of *Idomeneo*, for publication with the libretto.

my wretched ink and pen to blame if you have to spell out this letter rather than read it. – *Basta*; it has to be written – and the gentleman who cuts my nibs for me, Herr von Lierzer, has let me down on this occasion. You presumably know him better than I do – I can describe him only by saying that I think he's a native of Salzburg and I've only ever seen him on the odd occasion at the Robinigs' so-called 11 o'clock concerts. – But he called on me at once and seems to me to be a well-mannered and – because he cuts my pens for me – polite person – I think he must be a secretary. But the person who really surprised me with a visit was Katherl Gilowsky's brother – why was I surprised? – because I'd completely forgotten that he's in Vienna – how quickly a strange city can change a man! – He'll undoubtedly become an honest, respectable person, both professionally and in his outward demeanour. –

You will in the meantime have received the letters from the emperor[1] and Prince Kaunitz – What you say about the archbishop – the way in which I flatter his ambition – is to a certain extent true – but what use is it all to me? – – You can't live on it; – believe me only when I say that he acts as a kind of *screen* for me – what distinction does he confer on me? – Herr von Kleinmayr and Bönike have a separate table with the illustrious Count Arco;[2] – it would be a mark of distinction if I sat at that table – but not with the valets who, *apart from occupying the best seats at table*, have to light the chandeliers, open the doors and remain in the anteroom, *when I'm there* – and with the cooks. – And then, whenever we're summoned to a house where there's a concert, Herr Angerbauer has to remain on watch outside till the Salzburgers arrive, at which point he sends a lackey to say that they can come in – when Brunetti said this in the course of a conversation, I thought: Just wait till I get there! – So, recently, when we had to go to Prince Galitzin's,[3] Brunetti said to

1. Joseph II was now sole ruler of Austria following the death of Empress Maria Theresa the previous year.
2. Franz Thaddäus von Kleinmayr (1733–1805), high court councillor in Salzburg; Johann Michael Bönike, secretary of the Salzburg consistory; Karl Joseph, Count Arco, see List. All three had accompanied Archbishop Colloredo to Vienna.
3. Prince Dmitri Michailovich Galitzin (1721–93), Russian ambassador in Vienna.

me in his usual polite manner: *tu, bisogna che sei qui sta sera alle sette, per andare insieme dal Principe Galitzin. L'Angerbauer ci condurrà. – ho risposto: va bene – ma – se in caso mai non fossi qui alle sette in punto: ci andate pure; non serve aspettarmi – so ben dov'è sta, e ci verrò sicuro;*[4] – and so I made a point of going on my own as I feel ashamed of going anywhere with them; – when I got upstairs, Herr Angerbauer was standing there, waiting to tell the servant to show me in – but I paid no attention either to the valet or to the servant but went straight through the other rooms to the music room as the doors were all open. – And I went straight over to the prince and paid him my respects, remaining where I was and continuing to talk to him; – I'd completely forgotten Ceccarelli and Brunetti as they were nowhere to be seen – they were hidden away, leaning against the wall behind the orchestra, not daring to come out. – If a courtier or a lady talks to Ceccarelli, he just laughs. – And if anyone talks to Brunetti, he turns red and gives the driest answers. – Oh, it would take for ever to describe all the scenes that have taken place between the archbishop and Ceccarelli and Brunetti since I've been here and before I arrived. – I'm only surprised that he's not ashamed of Brunetti; I'd be ashamed in his position. – And how the fellow hates being here – everything's far too grand for him – I think he's at his happiest when he's at table – Today Prince Galitzin expressed a desire to hear Ceccarelli sing – next time I expect it'll be my turn – this evening I'm going with Herr Kleinmayr to see a good friend of his, Court Councillor Braun,[5] who everyone says is the greatest lover of the keyboard – I've lunched twice with Countess Thun[6] and go there virtually every day – she really is the kindest and most charming lady I've ever met; and she

4. 'Hey, you must be here at seven o'clock this evening so we can go to Prince Galitzin's together. Angerbauer will take us there. I replied: All right. But if I'm not there at seven on the dot, go ahead without me; there's no point in waiting for me – I know where he lives and will be sure to be there.' Brunetti and several other members of the Salzburg court music establishment had accompanied the archbishop to Vienna.

5. Johann Gottlieb von Braun (?–1788).

6. Maria Wilhelmine, Countess Thun-Hohenstein (1744–1800) was among Mozart's earliest patrons in Vienna.

thinks very highly of me, too – her husband is still the same strange but well-meaning and honest courtier. – I've also had lunch with Count Cobenzl, an invitation I owe to his cousin, Countess Rumbeke, the sister of the Cobenzl in the Pagerie, who was in Salzburg with her husband.[7] –

My chief object is now to introduce myself to the emperor in a suitably well-mannered way as I'm absolutely determined that he *shall get to know me*. – I'd very much like to whip through my opera[8] with him and then play some fugues, as that's his thing. – Oh, if only I'd known that I'd be in Vienna for Lent, I'd have written a short oratorio and performed it for my benefit at the theatre, as everyone here does – I could easily have written it beforehand as I know all the voices; – and how much I'd like to give a public concert, as is the custom here, but I wouldn't be allowed to, I know that for certain, because – just imagine – there is, as you know, a society here that gives concerts for the benefit of the widows of musicians[9] – everyone who is anyone in music performs there for nothing – the orchestra is 180 strong – no virtuoso with even an iota of love of his neighbour refuses to play here if the society asks him to do so for in this way he can make himself popular with both the emperor and the general public. –

Starzer[10] was commissioned to ask me and I agreed at once, but he said that I first had to get my prince's approval – for my own part, I had no doubt at all that he'd give it as it's a charitable concern and unpaid, but just involves doing good work; – *he wouldn't allow me*; – the nobility were all much aggrieved at this. – I'm sorry about this, but only because I wouldn't have played a concerto. Instead – because the emperor sits in the proscenium box – Countess Thun would have

---

7. Marie Karoline, Countess Rumbeke (1755–1812) was Mozart's first piano student in Vienna. Her cousin, Johann Philipp, Count Cobenzl (1741–1800), was deputy state chancellor.
8. *Idomeneo.*
9. The Tonkünstler-Sozietät, founded in 1771, gave concerts at Easter and Christmas.
10. Joseph Starzer (1728–87), composer and one of the founders of the Tonkünstler-Sozietät.

lent me her beautiful Stein pianoforte[11] and I've have extemporized on my own and then played a fugue and finally the variations on 'Je suis Lindor'.[12] – Whenever I've played all this in public, I've always received the greatest applause as the pieces set each other off and everyone has something to savour; but pa*ʒ*ien*ʒ*a; –

Fiala has risen 1000 times in my estimation for refusing to play for less than a ducat. – Hasn't my sister been asked to play yet? – I hope she'll *demand* 2. – We've differed from the other court musicians *in every other respect*, so I wouldn't like it if we didn't differ on this point too – if they don't want to pay her, they should forget it – but if they want to have her, in God's name they should pay her. –

I'll be going to see Madame Rosa[13] one of these days and you'll certainly be pleased with your clever go-between – I'll handle the affair as delicately as *Weiser* when the death knell tolled for his wife's mother; –

Herr von Zetti offered right away to take charge of my letters, he'll send them off with the parcel. –

I don't need the 2 quartets or the Paumgarten aria.[14]

By the way, what's happening about the elector's present?[15] – Has anything been sent yet? – Did you call on Countess Paumgarten before you left?

Please give my good wishes to all our good friends, especially Katherl – Schachtner and Fiala. – Herr von Kleinmayr, Zetti, Ceccarelli, Brunetti, the *contrôleur*, 2 valets, Leutgeb[16] and Ramm, who's leaving on Sunday, send their best wishes to you all;

By the way, Peter Vogt is here. – Farewell now I kiss your hands

---

11. She later lent Mozart this instrument for his piano duel with Clementi, see letter 122.

12. K354.

13. The painter Rosa Hagenauer-Barducci. Leopold was anxious to obtain the portrait she had painted of his wife.

14. The aria, commissioned by Countess Paumgarten, was *Misera, dove son! – Ah! Non son io che parlo* K369; the quartets are unidentified.

15. For the composition of *Idomeneo*.

16. Joseph Leutgeb (1732–1811), horn player at the Salzburg court.

1000 times and embrace my sister with all my heart. Ever your most obedient son

Wolfg. Amadè Mozart

The *buffo* Rossi is here too.

28 March. I didn't manage to finish this letter as Herr von Kleinmayr arrived to fetch me in his carriage to go to the concert at Baron Braun's – so I can now tell you that the archbishop has allowed me to play at the widows' concert. – *Starzer* went to the concert at Galitzin's and he and the whole of the nobility nagged him until he gave his permission. – *I'm so happy*; – since I've been here, I've lunched at home on only 4 occasions; – it's too early for me – and the food is really bad. – Only if the weather's very bad do I stay at home – like today, for example –

Write and let me know what's going on in Salzburg, as I'm being asked a frightful amount of questions about it, – the people here are far more eager for news of Salzburg than I am –

Frau Mara is here; – she gave a concert at the theatre last Tuesday. – Her husband didn't dare show himself, otherwise the orchestra wouldn't have accompanied her as he'd published a piece in the newspapers, claiming that there was no one in the whole of Vienna capable of accompanying her. – *Adieu*.

Herr von Moll[17] called on me today – I'll be having breakfast with him tomorrow or the day after and shall take my opera along with me. – He sends his best wishes to you both – I'll visit Herr von Auernhammer and his fat daughter[18] as soon as the weather improves. You'll see from this that I've received your last letter of the 24th. Old Prince Colloredo[19] – at whose house we gave a concert – gave each of us 5 ducats – Countess Rumbeke is now my *pupil* – Herr von Mesmer – the schools' inspector – and his dear wife send their regards.

17. Ludwig Gottfried von Moll.
18. Johann Michael von Auernhammer and his daughter Josepha Barbara, Mozart's pupil, see List.
19. Archbishop Colloredo's father, the imperial vice-chancellor.

– His son plays *magnifique* – except that, fancying he always knows enough, he's lazy – he's also a gifted composer – but is too indolent to devote himself to it – his father doesn't like that. Adieu.

106. Mozart to his father, 8 April 1781, Vienna

Mon très cher Père,

    I'd already started a longer and more sensible letter – but I wrote too much about Brunetti in it; and was afraid that he might open it, perhaps out of curiosity as Ceccarelli is here –

    I'll send you this letter by the next post and also be able to write more than I can now – in the meantime you'll have received my other letter. – I told you about the applause at the theatre, but I should add that what delighted and surprised me most of all was – the amazing silence – and the cries of bravo while I was still playing. – For Vienna, where there are so many keyboard players and such good ones, too, this was an honour indeed. –

    Today – I'm writing this at 11 o'clock at night – we had a concert.[1] 3 of my pieces were played – new ones, of course; – a concerto rondeau for Brunetti – a sonata with violin accompaniment for me – I wrote it yesterday evening between 11 and 12 – but, in order to finish it, I wrote out only the accompanying part for Brunetti and retained my own part in my head – and then a rondeau for Ceccarelli[2] – which he had to repeat. – I must now ask you to write as soon as possible and give me your fatherly and most friendly advice on the following. It's said that we're to return to Salzburg in two weeks' time – I can stay here not just without detriment to myself but to my *advantage* – And so I intend to ask the archbishop to allow me to remain here – dearest father, I love you very much, you can see this from the fact that for your sake I am renouncing all my wishes and

1. At Prince Colloredo's.
2. The concerto rondeau for Brunetti, K373; sonata K379; the rondeau for Ceccarelli, K374 *A questo seno deh vieni – Or che il cielo a me ti rende.*

desires – if it weren't for you, I swear to you on my honour that I wouldn't hesitate for a moment but would *resign* my position at once – I'd give a big concert, – take four pupils and get on so well that I'd make at least a thousand thalers a year. – I assure you that it's often hard enough to set aside my own happiness – As you say, I'm still young, that's true, but to idle away one's youth in inactivity in such a beggarly place is sad enough and such a loss – I'd value your fatherly and considered advice on this – but soon – – as I have to explain what I mean to do – but you must have every confidence in me – I'm now more sensible – farewell I kiss your hands 1000 times, and I embrace my sister with all my heart. I am ever your most obedient

W. A. Mozart

107. Mozart to his father, 28 April 1781, Vienna

Mon très cher Père,

You're looking forward to seeing me again, my dearest father! – That's the only thing that can decide me to leave Vienna – I'm writing all this in plain German *as the whole world must know that it's you alone, my most beloved father, whom the archbishop of Salzburg must thank for the fact that he didn't lose me yesterday for ever – I mean, as far as he personally is concerned* – we had a big concert here yesterday[1] – probably the last one; – it turned out very well, and in spite of all the obstacles put in my way by His Archiepiscopal Grace, I had a better orchestra than Brunetti, as Ceccarelli will tell you; – I had so much trouble arranging all this – it's better if I tell you about it in person, rather than in writing; if anything like it were to happen again, which I hope it won't, I can assure you that I shall lose all patience, and you'll surely forgive me for doing so – and I would ask you, dearest father, to allow me to return to Vienna next Lent, towards the end of carnival – this depends only on you, not on the

1. Also at Prince Colloredo's.

archbishop – for if he won't allow me, I'll still go, it won't be to my disadvantage, it certainly won't! – Oh, if only he could read this, how happy I'd be; – but in your next letter you must promise me this, for it's only on this condition that I'll come to Salzburg; – *a definite promise,* so that I can give my word to the ladies here – Stephanie will be giving me a German opera to write[2] – and so I await your reply. –

To date, Gilowsky still hasn't brought me an apron – if he does bring one, I'll not fail to lay it flat among the linen in the trunk, so that it's not creased or ruined. I shan't forget the ribbons either –

I still can't tell you when and how I'll be leaving – it's sad that these gentlemen never tell you anything – and then suddenly we're told *allons,* we're off! – One moment we're told that a carriage is being prepared so that the *contrôleur,* Ceccarelli and I can return home, and the next moment it's by diligence, only for us then to be told that each of us will be given our fare for the diligence and can travel in whatever way we like – which is in fact my preferred solution. One moment we're told we'll be leaving in a week, then in 2 weeks, then in 3 – and then even sooner – God! – We really don't know where we are, and there's nothing we can do about it; – but I hope to be able to let you know by next post day – *à peu près* –

I must stop now as I'm off to see Countess Schönborn[3] – after yesterday's concert the ladies kept me at the keyboard for a whole hour – I think I'd still be sitting there if I'd not stolen away – I thought I'd played enough *for nothing* –

Adieu – I kiss your hands 1000 times and embrace my sister with all my heart. I remain ever your obedient son

W. A. Mozart

P. S. Best wishes to all our friends – I embrace young Marchand[4] with all my heart. –

2. Gottlieb Stephanie the younger (1741–1800), actor and playwright; the opera was *Die Entführung aus dem Serail* ('The Abduction from the Seraglio').
3. Archbishop Colloredo's sister.
4. Heinrich Wilhelm Marchand (1769–c. 1812), son of Theobald Marchand (1746–1800), theatre director in Munich, was lodging in Salzburg as Leopold Mozart's pupil.

Please ask my sister to do me a favour: if she happens to write to Mlle Hepp, could she give her 1000 good wishes and explain that the reason why I've not written to her for so long is that I'd have to write and tell her not to reply to me until she's received another letter from me – as I couldn't say anything else to her in my second letter, I should never – as I'm in such a state of uncertainty – never receive another letter from her in Vienna – and that would be intolerable to me – but as things now stand, I've no right to expect one – I'll write to her before I leave. *Adieu.*

108. *Mozart to his father, 9 May 1781, Vienna*

Mon très cher Père,

I'm still seething with rage! – And you, my most beloved, dearest father, will undoubtedly be as well. – My patience has been tried for so long that it's finally given out. I'm no longer so unfortunate as to be in the service of the Salzburg court – today has been a happy day for me; listen; –

Twice that – I really don't know what to call him[1] – has said to my face the silliest and most impertinent things, which I've not told you about in my letters as I wanted to spare your feelings, and it was only because I kept thinking of you, my dearest father, that I didn't avenge them there and then. – He called me a knave and a dissolute fellow – and told me I should leave – and I – I put up with it all – although I felt that not only my own honour but yours as well was under attack – but – you wanted it so – so I said nothing; – now listen; – a week ago the footman arrived unexpectedly and told me to leave that instant; – the others had all been given their date of departure, but not me; – so I quickly shoved everything into my trunk and – old Madame Weber[2] was kind enough to offer me her

1. Archbishop Colloredo.
2. Maria Cäcilia Weber. The Weber family had moved to Vienna in 1779. After Fridolin's death on 23 September 1779 she took in lodgers to supplement her income.

house, where I now have a nice room and where I'm with obliging people who've provided me with all the things that you often need in a hurry and that you can't have when you're on your own. –

I arranged to return home by the *ordinaire* on Wednesday the 9th, in other words, today – but I didn't have time to collect the money still due to me, so I delayed my journey till Saturday – when I turned up today, the valets told me that the archbishop wanted me to take a parcel for him – I asked if it was urgent; they said yes, it was of great importance. – Then I'm sorry that I can't have the privilege of serving His Grace as I can't leave before Saturday – for the reason given above; – I'm no longer staying here but have to live at my own expense – so I naturally can't leave until I'm in a position to do so – no one will expect me to ruin myself. – Kleinmayr, Moll, Bönike and the 2 valets agreed with me. – When I went in to see him – by the way, I should have said that Schlauka[3] advised me to make the excuse that the *ordinaire* was already full – he said this would carry more weight; – well, when I went in to see him, the first thing he said was: *arch*: Well, my *lad*, when are you leaving? – *I*: I wanted to leave tonight but there's no room. He didn't stop to draw breath. – I was the most dissolute lad that he knew – no one served him as badly as I did – he advised me to leave today, otherwise he'd write home and have my pay stopped – it was impossible to get a word in edgeways, it was like a fire out of control – I listened to it all calmly – he lied to my face that I was on 500 florins[4] – he called me a scoundrel, a scurvy rogue and a cretin – oh, I'd prefer not to tell you all he said – finally, my blood began to boil, so I said – so Your Grace isn't satisfied with me? – What, are you threatening me, you cretin, O you cretin! – Look, there's the door, I want nothing more to do with such a miserable knave – finally I said – Nor I with you – Well, go then – *and I*, as I was leaving – so be it; you'll have it in writing tomorrow. – Tell me, dearest father, didn't I say this too late rather than too soon? – – Listen; – my honour means more to me than anything else, and I know that it's the same with you. –

3. Franz Schlauka (1743–1829), personal valet to the archbishop.
4. Mozart at the time earned 450 florins.

Don't worry about me; – I'm so sure of my position here that I'd have resigned for no reason at all – but now that I have a reason – and, indeed, thrice over – I can gain nothing by waiting; *au contraire*, I twice behaved shabbily and couldn't do so for a third time; –

As long as the archbishop is here, I shan't give a concert. But you're completely wrong if you think that I'll get a bad name with the nobility and the emperor himself – the archbishop is hated here, and by the emperor most of all – he's angry that the emperor didn't invite him to Laxenburg – by the next mail coach I'll send you some money to prove that I'm not starving.

For the rest, I would ask you to be cheerful – my good luck is now beginning, and I hope that my good luck will be yours too. – Write to me in secret and let me know that you're pleased, which you've good reason to be – but publicly rebuke me so that people don't blame you – but if, in spite of this, the archbishop is in any way rude to you, you must come at once with my sister to Vienna – all 3 of us can live here, I give you my word of honour on this point – but I'd prefer it if you can hold out for another year – don't send any more letters to the Deutsches Haus[5] or with the archbishop's parcel service – I don't want to hear another word about Salzburg – I hate the archbishop so much it drives me mad just to think about it. Adieu – I kiss your hands 1000 times and I embrace my dear sister with all my heart. I am ever your obedient son

W. A. Mozart

Just write 'To be delivered Auf dem Peter im Auge Gottes 2nd floor'.[6]

Let me know soon that you're pleased, as this is the only thing missing from my present happiness. *Adieu.*

5. When he was in Vienna, Archbishop Colloredo lodged at the house of the Deutscher Ritter-Orden, now Singerstrasse 865.
6. The Webers' address.

109. Mozart to his father, 19 May 1781, Vienna

Mon très cher Père,

I really don't know what to say, my dearest father, as I can't get over my astonishment and shall never be able to do so as long as you continue to think and write as you do; – I must confess that there isn't a single line in your letter by which I recognize my father! – I see a father, of course, but not that most beloved and most loving father who cares for his own honour and that of his children – in a word, not *my* father; but it was all just a dream – you've now woken up and have no need of any reply from me to your points in order to convince yourself that – *now more than ever* – I cannot give up my resolve. – But I must reply to some of your points as your letter contains a number of passages in which my honour and character have been most grievously impugned. – You can never approve of the fact that I resigned in Vienna; – I think that if one wants to do a thing – although at the time I had no desire to do so, otherwise I'd have done so at the first available opportunity – it would be most sensible to do so in a place where one has a good standing and the best prospects in the world. – That you can't approve of this in the presence of the archbishop is entirely possible, but to me you must surely approve of it; I can salvage my honour only by abandoning my resolve? – How can you be so self-contradictory? – When you wrote this, you evidently didn't think that for me to go back on my word in this way would make me the most contemptible creature in the world. – The whole of Vienna knows that I've left the archbishop – and knows why! – knows that it was because my honour was impugned – and, moreover, that it was impugned three times – and you expect me publicly to prove the opposite? – Am I to make myself out to be a coward and the archbishop a fine upstanding prince? – No one can do the former, I myself least of all, and the latter is something that God alone can do if He elects to enlighten him. –

So I've never shown you any love? – So I have to show it now for the first time? – Can you really say that? –

I won't sacrifice any of my pleasures for your sake? – – –

What sort of pleasures do I have here? – That I have to think of ways of filling my purse, with all the effort and worry that that involves? – You seem to think I'm living a life of pleasure and amusement. – Oh, how you deceive yourself! – That is, at present! – At present I've only as much as I need – the subscription for my 6 sonatas is now under way and I'll be receiving some money from this – things are working out with the opera, too – and during Advent I'm giving a concert, after which things will continue to get better and better[1] – in winter it's possible to earn quite a lot here. – If you can call it pleasure to be rid of a prince who doesn't pay you and who bullies you to death, then it's true, I'm pleased; – if I had to do nothing but think and work from early morning till late at night, I'd gladly do so in order not to depend on the grace and favour of a I prefer not to call him by his rightful name. – I was forced to take this step – and so I can no longer stray from this course by so much as a hair's breadth – it's impossible – all I can say to you is this, that because of you – and solely because of you, my father, – I'm very sorry that I was driven to such lengths and I wish the archbishop had acted more prudently, if only to have enabled me to devote my whole life to you. – To please you, dearest father, I'd sacrifice my happiness, health and life – but my honour – that means more to me than anything else, just as it should to you. – Let Count Arco and the whole of Salzburg read this. – After this insult – after this threefold insult – I wouldn't accept the archbishop's money even if he offered me 1200 florins in person – I'm not a lad or a knave – and if it weren't for you, I wouldn't have waited for him to say *clear off* three times before taking him at his word; what am I saying: waited!? – I, I should have said it, and not he! – I'm only surprised that the archbishop could have acted so thoughtlessly in a place like Vienna, that he could have been so thoughtless! – Well, he'll see that he's been deluding himself; – Prince Breuner and Count Arco need the archbishop, whereas I don't. – And if it comes to the worst and he

---

1. Here Mozart refers to the accompanied sonatas K296+376–380 and *Die Entführung aus dem Serail*. Apparently his plan to give a concert never materialized.

forgets all the obligations of a prince – a *spiritual prince* – then come and join me in Vienna; you'll have 400 florins wherever you are – if he were to do that, how do you think he'd disgrace himself in the eyes of the emperor, who already hates him! –

My sister, too, would be much better off here than in Salzburg – there are many houses where the gentry have misgivings about engaging a man but who would pay a woman very well. –

All this may still happen. –

As soon as I have a chance – perhaps if Herr Kleinmayr, Bönike or Zetti travels to Salzburg – I'll send you something towards the you know what – the *contrôleur* is leaving today and will be bringing the fine woollen fabric for my sister. –

Dearest, most beloved father, demand of me what you will, but not that, anything but that – the mere thought of it makes me shake with anger – adieu – I kiss your hands 1000 times and embrace my sister with all my heart. I am ever your most obedient son

Wolfgang Amadè Mozart

110. *Mozart to his father,* [26] *May 1781, Vienna*

Mon très cher Père,

You're quite right, just as I am quite right, my dearest father![1] – I know and acknowledge all my faults; but – can't a man change for the better? – May he not already have changed for the better? – In whatever way I examine the matter, I still think that I can best be of help to myself and to you, my beloved father and dear sister, by remaining in Vienna. It looks as if good fortune is about to welcome me here with open arms. – I feel as though I *have* to stay here. – I already felt this when I left Munich. – I was really looking forward to Vienna – I don't know why. – You must be patient for a little while longer, for I shall soon be able to show you in fact just how useful Vienna will be to us all. – You really must believe me when I

1. Mozart writes here in response to a lost letter of Leopold's.

say that I've changed completely – apart from my health, I now recognize that nothing matters more than money; of course, I'm no miser – and it would be hard for me to become one, but people here think I'm more inclined to be stingy than a spendthrift – and that's enough to be going on with. – As for pupils, I can have as many as I want; but I don't want too many – I want to be paid more than the others – and so I prefer to have fewer. – You have to get on your high horse a little right from the outset, otherwise you're permanently lost – you then have to stick to the common highway like the rest. As for the subscription, things are going well – and as for the opera,[2] I don't know why I should hold back. – Count Rosenberg received me most politely on the 2 occasions I called on him and, together with van Swieten and Herr von Sonnenfels,[3] he heard my opera[4] at Countess Thun's. – And as *Stephanie*[5] is a good friend of mine, everything's going well. – Believe me, I don't like idleness but prefer work. – In Salzburg, it's true, it required an effort and I could hardly ever find the resolve. Why? Because my mind was not content; even you yourself must admit that in Salzburg – at least for me – there's not a ha'penny's worth of entertainment; and there are lots of people there with whom *I refuse to associate*. – And for most of the others I'm too unworthy. No encouragement for my talent! – Whenever I play or if any of my works are performed, it's just as if the audience was made up entirely of tables and chairs. – If only there were a theatre there that was any good. – This is my sole entertainment here. – In Munich, it's true, I involuntarily placed myself in a false light with you by enjoying myself too much – but I can swear to you on my honour that I never set foot in a theatre until my opera had been staged and that I never went anywhere except to the Cannabichs. – That I had to write most of the opera – and the most difficult part – at the last minute is true; but it wasn't out of idleness or negligence, it was because for 2 weeks it *was impossible* for me to write a single

2. *Die Entführung aus dem Serail.*
3. See List for Count (later Prince) Orsini-Rosenberg and Baron van Swieten; Joseph von Sonnenfels (1733–1817), writer and academic.
4. Here Mozart refers to *Idomeneo*.
5. The librettist.

note – of course I wrote it down, but not as a fair copy. – And in this way I lost a lot of time, of course. But I don't regret it; – that I had too much fun afterwards was the result of youthful folly; I thought to myself, where are you off to next? – To Salzburg! – And so you must enjoy yourself! – It's true that in Salzburg I pine for 100 entertainments, but not for a single one here. – Just being in Vienna is already entertainment enough. You really must have faith in me, I'm no longer a fool. – And still less can you believe that I'm a godless, ungrateful son. – So you should trust entirely in my brains and good heart – you'll certainly not regret it. –

Where could I have learnt to value money? – I've had too little in my hands until now. – All I know is that once, when I had 20 ducats, I thought myself rich indeed. – Only necessity teaches one to value money. –

Farewell, beloved, dearest father! – My duty now is to make good and replace through my care and hard work what you think you have lost by this occurrence. – I shall certainly do this, and shall be infinitely happy to do so! – *Adieu*. I kiss your hands 1000 times and embrace my sister with all my heart. I am ever your most obedient son

Wolfgang Amadè Mozart

P. S. As soon as any of the archbishop's people go to Salzburg, the portrait[6] will follow. – *Ho fatto fare la sopra scritta d'un altro espressamente, perchè non si può sapere*[7]– You can't trust anyone.

Best wishes to all my acquaintances.

6. Rosa Hagenauer-Barducci's portrait of his mother. It is reproduced in Deutsch, *Bildern*, 33 (no. 39).
7. 'I expressly got someone else to write the address on it as you never can tell.'

111. Mozart to his father, between 26 May and 2 June 1781, Vienna

Mon très cher Père,

Two days ago Count Arco[1] sent word to say that I should call on him at 12 and that he'd be expecting me – he's often sent this kind of message, as has Schlauka, but as I hate conversations in which virtually every word I have to listen to is a lie, I've not attended them; – and I'd have done the same on this occasion, too, except that he'd sent word to say that he'd received a letter from you. – So I went; – it would be impossible to rehearse the whole conversation, which passed off very calmly and dispassionately, as this was the first thing I asked for. – In short, he placed everything before me in the friendliest manner; one could have sworn that it came from the heart. – But I don't think he'd have cared to swear that it came from *my* heart; – with all possible calmness, politeness and the most civil manner in the world I told him the absolute truth in reply to his set speeches, which merely *seemed* true. – And he – he couldn't say a word against it; the outcome was that I tried to make him take the memorandum and my travelling expenses, both of which I had with me. – But he assured me that it would be too upsetting for him to interfere in this matter and that I should give it to one of the valets. – And he'd take the money only when everything was sorted out. – The archbishop has been rude about me to everyone here and doesn't have the sense to see that this does him no credit; people here think more highly of me than they do of him. – He's known as an arrogant, self-opinionated divine who despises everyone here – while I'm known for my amiability. It's true; I grow proud when I see someone trying to treat me with contempt and *en bagatelle*.[2] – And that's how the archbishop behaves towards me. – But – with kind words – he could have made me do as he wanted. – I said this to the count. I also said that the archbishop doesn't deserve the high opinion you

1. Karl Joseph, Count Arco.
2. i.e. as someone of no importance.

have of him. – And finally – what good would it do if I were to go home now? – In a few months' time – even without a further insult – I'd still demand my discharge for I cannot and will not remain in service any longer on such a salary – But why not? – Because – I said – because I could never live happily and contentedly in a place where I'm paid so little that I'm always bound to be thinking, oh, if only I were somewhere else! – But if the pay were such that it wouldn't be necessary for me to think of other places, I'd be content. And if the archbishop pays me that, I'm ready to set off today. –

How happy I am that the archb. doesn't take me at my word. For there's no doubt that it's to your own advantage as it is to mine that I'm here. You'll see. Farewell now, dearest, most beloved father! Everything will work out for the best. – I'm not writing this in a dream – my own wellbeing depends on it. *Adieu.*

I kiss your hands 1000 times and embrace my dear sister with all my heart. I am ever your most obedient son

Wolfgang Amdè Mozart

P. S. Best wishes to all our good *friends.*

112. *Mozart to his father, 2 June 1781, Vienna*

Mon très cher Père,

You'll have gathered from my last letter that I've spoken to Count Arco in person; praise and thanks be to God that everything passed off so well. – Don't worry, you've nothing whatever to fear from the archbishop – Count Arco didn't say a single word to make me think *that you might be adversely affected* – and when he told me that you'd written and complained about me, I immediately interrupted him and said: *But not to me? – He wrote such things that I often thought I'd lose my wits – but, no matter how much thought I give to the matter, I simply cannot* etc. – He then said: Believe me, you're allowing yourself to be too easily dazzled here;[1] – here a man's fame is very short-lived – he's universally praised at the outset and earns a lot, too, that's true – but for how long? – within a few months the Viennese want something new; – you're right, Count, I said; – but do you think I'm staying in Vienna? – – By no means; I already know where I'm going. – The fact that this incident took place in Vienna is the archbishop's fault, not mine; – if he knew how to treat people who have talent, it would never have happened. – Count, I'm the nicest person in the world – as long as people treat me the same; – well, he said, the archbishop thinks you an extraordinarily insolent person; I'm sure he does, I said; and so I am towards him; I treat people as they treat me; – if I see that someone despises me and holds me in low esteem, I can be as proud as a peacock. –

Among other things, he also asked if I thought that he too often had to swallow insults? – I shrugged my shoulders and said: You'll have your reasons for enduring it, and I – I have my reasons for not enduring it. – You know the rest from my last letter. – Do not doubt it for a moment, dearest, most beloved father, this will all turn out for the best, both for me and – consequently – for you too. – The Viennese are no doubt people who like to shoot one down – *but only in the theatre*. – And my speciality[2] is too popular here for me not to be able to support myself. This is without doubt the land of the piano! – And even if it's true, they won't tire of me for a number of years, certainly not before then. – Meanwhile I'll have gained honour and money – after all, there are other places – and who knows what opportunities may arise in the meantime? – I've spoken to Herr von Zetti and shall be sending you *something* with him – for the present you'll have to make do with only a little – I can't send you more than 30 ducats. If I'd foreseen all this, I'd have taken on the pupils who approached me earlier – but I thought I'd be leaving in a week; and now they're in the country. – The portrait will follow; if he can't take it, it will go by post. Farewell now, dearest, most beloved father.

1. In Vienna.
2. Keyboard performance.

I kiss your hands 1000 times and embrace my dear sister with all my heart. I am ever your most obedient son

Wolfgang Amadè Mozart

Best wishes to all our good friends. *I'll be replying to Ceccarelli*[3] *shortly*.

113. Mozart to his father, 13 June 1781, Vienna

Mon très cher Père,

Most beloved of all fathers! How gladly I'd continue to sacrifice the best years of my life to you in a place where one's badly paid if this were the only evil. But to be badly paid and to be mocked, despised and bullied into the bargain – that really is too much. – I wrote a sonata for myself for the archbishop's concert[1] here, together with a rondeau for Brunetti and Ceccarelli,[2] I played twice at each concert and after the last one went on playing variations for a whole hour – it was the archbishop who gave me the theme – and there was such universal applause that if the archbishop were at all human, he must surely have felt pleased; but instead of showing me at least his contentment and pleasure – or, for all I care, not showing me them – he makes me out to be a street urchin – tells me to my face to go to the devil and adds that he can get a hundred people to serve him better than I do. – And why? – Because I couldn't leave Vienna *on the day* he'd got it into his head I should do so; he expects me to leave his house, live at my own expense and then not have the freedom to leave when my purse allows me, quite apart from which I wasn't needed in Salzburg and it made a difference of only 2 days. – Twice the archbishop said the rudest things to me and I never said a word, indeed I even played with the same enthusiasm and commit-

3. Ceccarelli's letter to Mozart is lost.
1. K379; the concert was on 8 April 1781.
2. See letter 106, n. 2.

ment as if nothing had happened; and instead of acknowledging my eagerness to serve him and my desire to please him, he behaves on the third occasion in the most abominable way in the world – at the very time that I might have expected something different. – And in order that I should not be in the wrong but utterly in the right, it's as if they want to get rid of me by force, well – if they don't want me – that's fine by me; – instead of Count Arco accepting my petition or obtaining an audience for me or advising me to send it in later or persuading me to let the matter rest and think it over, *enfin*, whatever he wanted – no, he throws me out of the room and gives me a kick up the backside. – Well, in plain language this means that as far as I'm concerned, Salzburg no longer exists, except to give me a chance to give the count a kick up the arse in return, even if it's in a public street. – I'm not demanding any restitution from the archbishop as he can't provide what I want; but I shall shortly be writing to the count to tell him what he can confidently expect from me as soon as I have the good fortune to meet him, wherever it may be, as long as it's not a place where I'm obliged to show him any respect; –

Don't worry about the good of my soul, most beloved father! – I'm just as likely to err as any other young man and by way of consolation wish only that others were as little likely to err as I am. – You may perhaps believe things about me that aren't true; – my main failing is that I don't always *appear* to act as I should. – It's not true that I boasted that I eat meat on all fast days; but I did say that I set little store by it and don't consider it a sin; for me, fasting means abstaining and eating less than usual. – I attend Mass every Sunday and feast day and, if I can make it, on weekdays too, but you already know that, father. – My only dealings with that person of ill repute were at the ball, and only until I knew she was a woman of ill repute – and then only because I wanted to be sure of having a partner for the contredanse.[3] – But I couldn't then stop without telling her the reason – and who would say something like that to a person's face? – But in the end didn't I stand her up more than once and dance with others? – On this occasion I was perfectly happy when the carnival

<hr>

3. No details are known of this episode.

was over. – In any case, no one can say that I saw her anywhere else or that I ever went to her house – they'd be a liar if they claimed otherwise. – For the rest, you can be assured that I believe in God – and if I should ever have the misfortune (which God forbid) to stray, I hereby absolve you, my most beloved father, of all blame. – I alone would be the villain – it is you whom I must thank for all the good things that have contributed to my temporal and spiritual welfare and salvation.

I must close now, otherwise I'll miss the post. I kiss your hands 1000 times and embrace my dear sister with all my heart. I am ever your most obedient son

Wolfgang Amadè Mozart

P. S. Best wishes to young Marchand, also to Katherl and all our good friends.

114. Mozart to his father, 16 June 1781, Vienna

Mon très cher Père,

The portrait and ribbons for my sister will set sail tomorrow. I don't know if the ribbons will be to her liking. – But I can assure her that they're the latest fashion. If she wants any more or some that aren't painted, she should let me know; and if there's anything else that she'd like and that she thinks will be more attractive in Vienna, she should just write. I hope she didn't have to pay for the apron, as it was already paid for; I kept forgetting to say this as I always had to tell you about that other wretched affair.[1] – I'll send the money as you indicated. –

But I can now tell you more about Vienna; until now I've had to fill all my letters with an account of that other blasted business. – Thank God it's all over. – The present season is the worst for anyone wanting to earn any money; but you know this already; the foremost

---

1. His confrontation with Archbishop Colloredo.

families are in the country, and so there's nothing else to do but prepare for the winter, when one has less time. — As soon as the sonatas[2] are finished, I'll see if I can find a short Italian cantata[3] to set to music; it will then be given at the theatre during Advent — for my benefit, of course; — I'm being slightly devious here, because in this way I can perform the piece twice and make the same profit each time as I'll play something on the pianoforte when I give it the second time. — At present I've only one pupil, Countess Rumbeke, Cobenzl's cousin; I could have more, of course, if I lowered my price. — But as soon as you do that, you lose your reputation — I charge 6 ducats for 12 lessons, while letting people know that I'm doing them a favour. — I'd rather have 3 pupils who pay well than 6 who pay badly. — I can just about manage to *get by* with this one pupil, and for the present that's enough; — I'm telling you this only so that you don't think I'm being selfish in sending you only 30 ducats — rest assured that I'd leave myself entirely destitute if I could! — But it'll come. One must never let people see how things stand.

As for the theatre, I think I told you recently that when he left, Count Rosenberg commissioned Schröder[4] to hunt down a libretto for me. It's now been found, and Stephanie — the younger — has it in his capacity as manager of the opera; Bergopzoomer,[5] who's a very good friend of Schröder and me, tipped me off about it. — So I went to see him at once, *en forme de visite*. — We thought that he might play me false because of his support for *Umlauf*;[6] but our suspicions were unfounded, for I later heard that he'd commissioned someone to tell me to come and see him as there was something he wanted to talk to me about; and as soon as I came in, he said: Oh, you're right

---

2. K296+376–380. The unfinished sonatas included some or all of K376, 377 and 380; K296 had been composed at Mannheim on 11 March 1778, K378 at Salzburg in 1779 or 1780; and K379 at Vienna by 7 April 1781 (see letter 106, n. 2).
3. Nothing came of this plan.
4. Friedrich Ludwig Schröder (1744–1816), actor.
5. The actor Johann Baptist Bergopzoomer (1742–1804) was engaged at the Burg-theater from 1774 to 1782 and from 1791 to 1804.
6. Ignaz Umlauf (1746–96), composer. His *Die Bergknappen* had been the first opera staged by Joseph II's German National Theatre in 1778.

on cue. – The opera is in 4 acts, the first of which he says is unbeatable; but it gets a lot worse after that. If Schröder agrees to our changing it as we like, we could end up with a good libretto. – He doesn't want to give it to the management in its present state but first wants to discuss it with him,[7] as he knows in advance that it would otherwise be rejected. So these two can sort it out between them. – After what Stephanie had told me about it, I saw no point in asking to read it, because if I don't like it, I'd have to say as much and would look foolish. And I don't want to lose Schröder's favour as he has the greatest respect for me. – In this way I can always excuse myself by saying that I've not read it.

I must explain why we had our suspicions about Stephanie. It grieves me to say that this person has the worst possible reputation in Vienna; he's said to be rude, false and much given to slandering others as well as treating them with the greatest unfairness. – But I don't want to get involved. It may be true, as everyone says rude things about him – but at the same time he's highly regarded by the emperor; and he was very friendly to me when we first met and said: we're already old friends and I very much hope that I shall be in a position to be able to help you. – I believe and hope that he will write an opera for me. Whether he's written his plays by himself or with the help of others, and whether he's stolen their ideas or created them himself, he understands the theatre and his plays are always popular. – I've seen only 2 new pieces by him and there's no doubt that they're both very good; one, *Das Loch in der Thüre*; and the second, *Der Oberamtmann und die Soldaten*. – Meanwhile I plan to write the cantata, because even if I did already have a libretto, I'd still not put pen to paper as Count Rosenberg isn't here – if, in the end, he didn't like the libretto, I'd have had the honour of writing it all for nothing. And I can do without that. – I'm not at all worried about the work's reception, as long as it's a good libretto. – Do you really think I'd write an *opéra comique* as though it were an *opera seria*? In an *opera seria* there should be as little frivolity and as much as that is learned and rational as there should be little

7. In this sentence, 'He' refers to Bergopzoomer, 'him' to Schröder.

that's learned in an *opera buffa* and all the more that is frivolous and funny.

I can't help it if people want comic music in an *opera seria*; – but here people make a proper distinction between them.

I find that the Viennese buffoon[8] hasn't yet been eradicated from music; and in this case the French are right. –

I hope that my clothes arrive safely with the next mail coach. I don't know when the coach leaves, but I think you'll receive this letter first, so I would ask you to keep my stick for me. – People carry sticks here, but what's the point? If you want one only for walking, then any stick will do; so you may as well use the stick instead of me, and always take it with you if you can – who knows whether it may avenge its former master on Arco. – I mean, of course, *accidentaliter* or by chance; – that greedy ass will certainly get a taste of it, even if we have to wait twenty years. – For me to see him and give him a kick up the arse will undoubtedly be one and the same, unless I have the misfortune to meet him first on hallowed ground. – Well, adieu; farewell; I kiss your hands 1000 times and embrace my sister with all my heart. I am ever your most obedient son

W. A. Mzt

Best wishes to everyone.

115. Mozart to his father, 4 July 1781, Vienna

Mon très cher Père,

I haven't written to Count Arco and shan't be doing so, as you ask me not to for the sake of your own peace of mind; – it's just as I thought; you're too afraid; and yet there's nothing to be afraid of, as you yourself have been insulted as much as I have. – I'm not asking you to cause a scene or to make even the slightest complaint! – But

8. Hanswurst character (see letter 15, n. 1).

the archbishop and the rest of his rabble must be afraid of discussing the matter with you as you, my father, need have no fear at all of saying quite openly – if you are put to it – that you'd be ashamed to have brought up a son who allowed himself to be called names by as infamous a scoundrel as Arco – and you can assure them all that if I had the good fortune to meet him today, he'd get his just deserts and would certainly remember me as long as he lived; – all I ask for, and nothing more, is that everyone can see that you're not afraid. – Remain silent, but speak if necessary – and speak in such a way that you actually say something; the archbishop has secretly offered *Koželuch*[1] 1000 florins – – but the latter has declined, adding that he's better off where he is and that unless he could improve his position, he'll never leave. But to his friends he said: it's the affair with Mozart that puts me off most of all – if he lets a man like that leave, what might he not do to me? – So you see how well he knows me and values my talents! – The chest with the clothes has arrived safely.

If Monsieur Marchal or the syndic of the chapter comes to Vienna, you'd be doing me a great favour if you could send me my favourite watch; I'll return yours if you'll send me the small one, too; that would be very kind of you. – I wrote to you recently about the masses.[2] – I need the 3 cassations as a matter of urgency – it would be enough for the present for me to have the ones in F and B flat – the one in D[3] you might arrange to have copied and sent on to me later, as copying costs a lot here; and their work is appalling.

I must say a few words about Marchand,[4] at least as far as I can; – when his father corrected the younger boy at table, he took up a knife and said: look here, papa; if you say another word, I'll cut off my finger at the root and I'll then be a cripple and you'll have to feed

---

1. Leopold Anton Koželuch (1747–1818), composer, keyboard virtuoso and teacher to the nobility and court; he later became a music publisher.
2. In a letter of 27 June 1781, Mozart had asked his father to send copies of his (unidentified) masses to Vienna.
3. K247, K287, K334.
4. Daniel Marchand (1770–?), younger brother of Heinrich Marchand, Leopold's pupil.

me. – Both of them have often spoken ill of their father to others. You'll no doubt remember Mlle Boudet,[5] who lives in their house. – Well, the old man is very fond of her. – And the 2 lads have been making the most infamous comments about them. – When Hennerle[6] was 8 he said to a certain girl – I'd far rather sleep in your arms than wake up with a pillow. – He even made her a formal declaration of love and an offer of marriage, adding: I can't marry you now, of course, but when my father's dead, I'll come into some money as he's by no means destitute, and we can then live together very comfortably. In the meantime we can be lovers and enjoy our love to the full; what you allow me to do now you won't be able to allow me to do later. – I also know that in Mannheim no one ever allowed their boys to go near Marchand's – they were caught – – – indulging in a spot of mutual relief. It's a great shame about the boy but I'm sure that you, my father, will bring about a complete transformation in him. As his father and mother are actors, they hear nothing all day but tales of love, despair, murder and death, and that's all they ever read; also, their father is rather feeble for his age – so they're not being set a good example.

I must close now, otherwise Peisser[7] won't get my letter in time. Farewell, I kiss your hands 1000 times and am ever your most obedient son

Wolfgang Amadè Mozart

P.S.: Best wishes to all our good friends. Do let me know the story about my sister's mob cap. You mentioned it once in one of your letters. *Adieu.*

---

5. Marianne Boudet (1764–1835), actress at the Munich court.
6. Diminutive of Heinrich.
7. Mozart and his father apparently sent their letters through Peisser.

116. Mozart to his father, 25 July 1781, Vienna

Mon très cher Père,

   May I say once again that I've long been thinking of finding some other rooms – and all because people have been gossiping; – I'm only sorry that I'm forced to do this on account of some stupid tittle-tattle, not one word of which is true. I'd just like to know what sort of pleasure certain people can take in spreading entirely groundless rumours. – Because I'm living with them, it's said that I'm marrying the daughter;[1] there was never any talk of our being in love, they've omitted that stage; no, I'm in lodgings in the house and so I'm getting *married*. – If there was ever a time in my life when I've thought less of marriage, it's now! – for – although the last thing I want is a wealthy wife – even if I could now make my fortune by getting married, I couldn't possibly go courting, as I've other things on my mind. – God hasn't given me my talent simply for me to get hitched to a wife and fritter away my young life in inactivity. – I'm only now beginning to live, and people expect me to ruin it all? – I've nothing against marriage, of course, but at present it would be a disaster for me. – Well, there's nothing else for it; even though it's untrue, I must avoid giving the appearance that it is – and even though this appearance rests solely on the fact that I'm living here – unless people come to the house, they can't even say whether I have as much contact with her as with all God's other creatures; for the children rarely go out – they never go anywhere except to the theatre, but I never go with them as I'm generally not at home at curtain-up. – We went to the Prater[2] a couple of times, but her mother came too; and as I was in the house at the time, I could hardly refuse to go with them. – And at that time I'd not yet heard any of these foolish remarks. I should add that I was allowed to pay only *for myself*. – And when her mother heard these remarks herself and also heard about them from me, I have to say

---

1. Constanze Weber, Aloysia's younger sister.
2. Pleasure garden in Vienna recently opened up to the public by Joseph II.

that from then on she wouldn't countenance the idea of our going anywhere together and advised me to move in order to avoid any further unpleasantness; she says that she wouldn't like to be responsible for my misfortune through no fault of her own. – This, then, is the only reason why I have for some time – since people started to gossip – been thinking of moving – the truth of the matter is that I've no reason to move, but these rumours are reason enough. – If it weren't for these remarks, I'd certainly not move because, although I could easily get a more attractive room, I wouldn't find such comfort or such friendly and obliging people; – I don't mean that, living in the same house as the mademoiselle to whom I've already been married off, I'm sullen and don't speak to her – but nor am I in love with her; – I fool around and joke with her when I have time – which is only in the evening when I dine at home – during the morning I write in my room and during the afternoon I'm rarely at home – and that's all; if I had to marry everyone with whom I've shared a joke, I'd have at least 200 wives. – But now for the money.

My pupil[3] was out of town for 3 weeks – as a result I had no income, although my outgoings continued as before. – This meant that I couldn't send you 30 ducats, but only 20 – but as I was hopeful about the subscriptions,[4] I wanted to wait until I could send you the sum I'd promised. – But Countess Thun has now told me that a subscription is out of the question before the autumn – because everyone who has any money is out of town – so far she has found only 10 people and my pupil only seven – meanwhile I'm having 6 sonatas engraved, Artaria,[5] the music engraver, has already discussed the matter with me; as soon as they are sold and I get some money, I'll send it to you.

I must ask my dear sister to forgive me for not having written

---

3. Countess Rumbeke.
4. For the sonatas K296+376–380.
5. The Artaria family, originally from the area around Lake Como, established an art dealership at Mainz in 1765 and Vienna in 1766; the firm began publishing music in Vienna in 1778.

to congratulate her on her name day.[6] – The letter that I began is still lying in my drawer. – I'd just started it last Saturday when Countess Rumbeke's servant called and said that they were all going off to the country and would I like to go too – because I don't like to say no to Cobenzl,[7] I left the letter where it was, threw my things together and went with them. – I thought my sister wouldn't take it amiss. – So, in the octave of her name day, I now wish her all the best and all that an honest brother who loves his sister with his whole heart could ever wish for her; and I kiss her most tenderly.

I returned with the count today and am driving out with him again tomorrow. – Farewell now, dearest, most beloved father! – Believe your son and trust in him, for he thinks only the best of all decent people; – and why shouldn't he also cherish such feelings towards his dear father and sister? – – Believe in him and trust him more than you do certain people who have nothing better to do than to slander honest people – adieu now – I kiss your hands 1000 times and am ever you most obedient son

Wolfgang Amadè Mozart

On 30 July Mozart received from Stephanie the libretto of the Turkish-themed singspiel Die Entführung aus dem Serail *('The Abduction from the Seraglio'), the plot of which revolves around the attempts of the hero, Belmonte (assisted by his servant Pedrillo), to rescue his beloved, Konstanze (and her maidservant, Blonde, Pedrillo's beloved), from the Bassa Selim.*

6. 26 July.
7. See letter 105, n. 7.

117. Mozart to his father, 8 August 1781, Vienna

Mon très cher Père,

I must be brief as I've just this minute finished the Janissary chorus[1] and it's already turned 12, and at 2 o'clock on the dot I've promised to drive out with the Auernhammers and Mlle Cavalieri[2] to München-dorf near Laxenburg, where the camp now is. –

Adamberger,[3] Cavalieri and Fischer[4] are extremely pleased with their arias. – I had lunch yesterday with Countess Thun, and tomorrow I'll be having lunch with her again. – I played her some of what I've written. – At the end she told me that she'd venture her life that people are bound to like what I've written so far. – On this point I pay no heed to anyone's *praise or censure* at least until people have seen and heard the work *as a whole*; I simply follow *my own feelings* – but you can see from this how pleased she must have been to have said something like this. –

As I've nothing of any importance to tell you, I'll pass on a terrible story that I heard – you may already know it; it's known here as the Tyrolean tale. – I'm all the more interested in it as I know the unfortunate person concerned. I got to know him in Munich, where he even called on us every day. – His name is Herr von *Wibmer* and he's a nobleman. I don't know whether it was from misfortune or because of a natural propensity for the theatre, but some months ago he formed a troupe that he took with him to Innsbruck. –

One Sunday lunchtime, at 12 o'clock, this good man was walking quietly along the street, when some courtiers started to follow him; one of them   Baron Bulla by name – kept saying rude things about

1. 'Singt dem grossen Bassa Lieder' from act 1, scene 6.
2. Catarina Cavalieri (1755–1801), soprano and pupil (later mistress) of Antonio Salieri, sang the role of Konstanze.
3. The tenor Valentin Adamberger (1740/43–1804) sang the role of Belmonte (Mozart also wrote the arias *Per pietà, non ricercate* K420 and *Misero! o sogno – Aura che intorno spiri* K431, the part of Herr Vogelsang in *Der Schauspieldirektor* K486 (1786) and the cantata *Die Maurerfreude* K471 for him).
4. The bass Johann Ignaz Ludwig Fischer (1745–1825) sang the comic role of Osmin.

him: the fool should teach his dancer to walk before he put her on the stage – and he called him all manner of names – Herr von Wibmer listened for a while, then naturally turned round. Bulla asks him why he's looking at him. – The latter replies very good-naturedly.

Well, you're looking at me; *it's a free country, a person can look round if he wants to.* – And he goes on his way. – But Baron Bulla continues to call him names; finally it gets too much for the good man and he asks him who he's referring to. – You, you cur, was the answer, accompanied by a regular cuff round the ear; Herr von Wibmer immediately gave as good as he got. – Neither man was wearing a sword, otherwise he'd most certainly not have replied in kind. – He returned home, very calmly, in order to tidy his hair – Baron Bulla had also seized him by the hair – and fully intending to put the case before the governor, Count Wolkenstein.[5] – But his house was already full of soldiers, and he was taken off to the main guardhouse; – no matter what he said, it made no difference and he was sentenced to 25 lashes on his backside. Finally he said: I'm a nobleman, I refuse to be beaten when I'm innocent, I'd rather become a soldier in order to have my revenge. – In Innsbruck there must be some stupid Tyrolean custom that no one can strike a gentleman, however much he may be in the right. – At this, he was taken to the local prison, where he was given not 25 but 50 lashes. – Before he lay on the bench, he said publicly: I'm innocent. And I appeal publicly to the emperor. But the corporal answered contemptuously: The gentleman can first have his 50 lashes, and then he can appeal. It was all over in 2 hours – by 2 o'clock. By the 5th lash, his breeches were already torn. – I'm surprised he was able to bear it. – In fact he was taken away unconscious. – He was laid up for 3 weeks. As soon as he'd recovered, he came straight to Vienna, where he's anxiously awaiting the arrival of the emperor, who has already been informed about the whole affair, not only by people here but by his sister, the Archduchess Elisabeth,[6] who is in Innsbruck. – *Wibmer* himself has

5. Paris Ignaz, Count Wolkenstein und Trostburg, governor of Upper Austria.
6. Archduchess Maria Elisabeth (1743–1808), sister of Joseph II, was abbess of the imperial and royal convent at Innsbruck.

a letter from her to the emperor. – The day before this happened, the president had received orders to punish no one, whoever it may be, without first informing people here. This makes the matter even worse. – The president really must be a very stupid and malicious oaf. – But – how can this man ever obtain adequate restitution? – The lashes will remain with him – if I were *Wibmer*, I'd demand the following restitution from the emperor. – He[7] must receive 50 lashes in the same place and in my presence – and he'd also have to give me 6000 ducats. – And if I couldn't obtain this, I'd ask for no other but would run my sword through his heart at the first opportunity. I should add that he's already been offered 3000 ducats not to go to Vienna and to hush up the affair. – The people of Innsbruck call Herr von Wibmer the man who was scourged for us and who will also redeem us. – Not a soul can stand him.[8] – The president's house has been under guard all this time. – There's a regular gospel about him here. – People are talking about nothing else. – I'm very sorry for the poor man, for he's never really well. He's always got a headache and a bad chest complaint.

Farewell now, I kiss your hands 1000 times and embrace my dear sister with all my heart. I am ever your most obedient son

W. A. Mzt

Best wishes to the Duscheks, whom I hope to see here. *Adieu*.

118. Mozart to his father, 22 August 1781, Vienna

Mon très cher Père,

I still can't give you the address of my new apartment, as I haven't got one yet; but I'm arguing over the price of two, one of which I shall certainly take as I can no longer stay here next month and must,

7. i.e. Count Wolkenstein und Trostburg.
8. As above. It has been impossible to confirm the details of this anecdote.

therefore, move out. – It seems that Herr von Auernhammer has written to you – and told you that I've already found an apartment![1] – I did indeed have one; but what a place! – It was fit for rats and mice, but not for human beings. – Even at midday you needed a lantern to find the stairs. And the room could best be described as a small closet and could be reached only through the kitchen. There was a little window in the door of my room, and although they assured me that they'd put up a curtain in front of it, they also asked me to draw it back as soon as I was dressed, as otherwise they wouldn't be able to see anything either in the kitchen or in the adjacent rooms. – The lady of the house called it a rats' nest; in a word, it was terrible. – It would have been a splendid place to receive the various distinguished people who come to see me. – The good man was thinking only of himself and his daughter, who's the biggest *seccatrice*[2] I know. As your last letter included a eulogy of this household worthy of Count Daun, I must tell you a little more about them; I would have passed over in silence all that you're about to read and regarded it as a matter of indifference and as only a private and personal *seccatura*,[3] but as I discover from your letter that you have some confidence in this household, I see myself obliged to tell you quite candidly about their good and bad points. – He is the finest man you could ever hope to meet – too much so, in fact, for his wife, the stupidest and silliest gossip in the world, wears the trousers, so that whenever she speaks, he does not dare to say a word; whenever we've gone out walking together, he has asked me not to say anything in his wife's presence to indicate that we'd taken a cab or drunk a glass of beer. – Well, I really can't trust a man like that; he's too insignificant in the eyes of his own family. – He's a decent enough person and a good friend of mine; I've often been able to have lunch with him, but I'm not in the habit of allowing people to pay for *my favours*, not that a lunchtime bowl of soup would be adequate payment, of course, – but people like that think that it is. – It is not for my

1. With the Auernhammers.
2. 'bore'.
3. 'annoyance'.

own benefit that I set foot in their house but *for theirs*. Indeed, I see no profit whatsoever for myself; – and I've yet to meet a single person there whose name would be worth setting down on this sheet of paper. – They're good people, but nothing more – people sensible enough to realize how useful to them is my acquaintance with their daughter, who, as everyone says who heard her play before, has changed completely since I've been seeing her. – I won't attempt to describe her mother. Suffice it to say that at table it's all one can do not to burst out laughing; *basta*; you know Frau Adlgasser; well, this *meuble* is even worse, as she's also *médisante*,[4] in other words, stupid and malicious. On to the daughter, then: if a painter wanted to paint the devil to the life, he'd have to have recourse to her face. – She's as fat as a farmgirl, sweats so much it makes you want to puke and goes around so scantily dressed that she might as well be carrying a sign: *Please look here.* True, there's enough to see or, rather, enough to make you wish you were blind – you're punished for the whole of the rest of the day if you're unfortunate enough to look in her direction – you then need some tartar! – so disgusting, filthy and horrible! – Ugh! Well, I've already told you how she plays the piano and told you why she asked me to help her. – I'm more than happy to do favours for people, but not if they annoy me. – She's not content for me to spend 2 hours a day with her; I'm expected to sit there all day long. – And she tries to give herself airs! – But, even worse, she's *sérieusement* in love with me – I thought it was a joke, but now I know it for certain; – when I noticed it – because she was taking liberties with me – for example – she reproached me affectionately when I arrived later than usual or couldn't stay any longer and other such things – and so I saw myself obliged, in order not to make her look foolish, to tell her the truth as politely as I could. – But it made no difference. She became even more infatuated; in the end I was always very polite to her except when she got up to her tricks and then I was rude – but she then took me by the hand and said: *dear Mozart; don't be so cross – no matter what you say, I really do like you.* – Throughout the whole town people are saying

4. 'stick of furniture' . . . 'a scandalmonger'.

that we're getting married and they're only surprised that I can choose someone with a face like that. She told me that whenever people said anything like that to her, she always laughed at it; but I know from a certain person that she confirmed that it was true, adding that we'd then travel together. – That infuriated me. – So the other day I told her what I thought of her and that she shouldn't abuse my kindness. – I'm no longer seeing her every day, but only every other day, and shall gradually stop seeing her altogether. She's nothing but an infatuated fool; – before she got to know me, she heard me in the theatre and said: He's coming to see me tomorrow and I'll play him his variations in the same style. – For that very reason I didn't go as it was a conceited thing to say and also because it was a lie. I'd never said a word about calling on her the next day. – Adieu for now, there's no paper left. The first act of the opera is finished. I kiss your hands 1000 times and embrace my dear sister with all my heart. I am ever your ob. son

W. A. Mozart

At the end of August, Mozart took lodgings on the third floor of Innere Stadt 1175 (now 17), not far from the Webers.

119. Mozart to his father, 26 September 1781, Vienna

Mon très cher Père,

I'm sorry you've had to pay more postage on my recent letters! – But I'd nothing important to tell you – and I thought you'd like to have some idea of my opera. – The opera started with a monologue and so I asked Herr Stephanie to turn it into a little arietta[1] and, instead of having the two of them chatter away together after Osmin's

1. 'Hier soll ich dich denn sehen.'

little song[2] to turn it into a duet.[3] – As we've written the part of Osmin for Herr Fischer, who certainly has an outstanding bass voice – in spite of this the archbishop told me that he sings too low for a bass, so I assured him that next time he'd sing higher – we must take advantage of him, especially because he has the whole of the local audience on his side. – But in the original libretto this Osmin has only this one little song to sing and nothing else, except for the trio and finale.[4] And so he's now got an aria in the first act and will have another one in the 2nd.[5] – I've told Herr Stephanie exactly what I want for this aria; – the bulk of the music was already written before Stephanie knew a word of it. – You have only the beginning and the end, which is bound to be highly effective – Osmin's rage is made to seem funny by the Turkish music that I've used here. – In developing the aria, I've allowed his beautiful low notes to gleam – in spite of our Salzburg Midas.[6] – '*Drum beym Barte des Propheten*'[7] etc. is still at the same speed, but with quick notes – and as his rage continues to grow, just when you think the aria is over, the allegro assai – in a completely different metre and different key – is bound to be tremendously effective; just as a person in such a violent rage oversteps all the bounds of order and moderation and overshoots the mark, completely forgetting himself, so the music must forget itself – but because the passions, whether violent or not, must never be expressed to the point of causing disgust, and because music, even in the most terrible situation, must never offend the ear but must give pleasure and, hence, always remain music, I've not chosen a key foreign to F – the key of the aria – but one related to it, not, however, the one closest to it, D minor, but the more remote A minor. – Now for Belmonte's aria in A major, '*O wie ängstlich, o wie feurig*',[8] do you

2. 'Wer ein Liebchen hat gefunden.'
3. At the words 'Verwünscht seist du samt deinem Liede'.
4. Trio: 'Marsch, marsch, marsch!'; finale: 'Nie werd ich deine Huld verkennen.'
5. First-act aria: 'Solche hergelauf'ne Laffen'. In the end, Osmin was not given an aria in the second act.
6. Archbishop Colloredo.
7. From the aria 'Solche hergelauf'ne Laffen'.
8. 'O how eagerly, o how ardently [my lovesick heart is beating]'.

know how it's expressed? – Even his beating, loving heart is indicated – by the 2 violins in octaves. – This is the favourite aria of all who've heard it – and of me too. – It's written entirely to suit Adamberger's voice. You see the trembling vacillation – you see his breast begin to swell – which I've expressed with a crescendo – you hear the whispering and sighing – which is expressed by the first violins with mutes and a flute playing in unison with them.

The Janissary chorus is all that anyone could demand of a Janissary chorus. – Short and comic; – and written entirely for the Viennese. – I've sacrificed Konstanze's aria[9] a little to Mlle Cavalieri's flexible throat. – '*Trennung war mein banges Loos. Und nun schwimmt mein Aug in Thränen*'[10] – I've tried to express her feelings as far as an Italian bravura aria allows. – The *hui* I've changed to *schnell* so it becomes *doch wie schnell schwand meine Freude* etc.[11] I really don't know what our German poets are thinking of; – even if they don't understand the theatre, as far as operas are concerned, they should at least not make people talk as if addressing pigs. – Get a move on, porker! –

Now for the trio, namely, the end of the first act.[12] – Pedrillo has passed off his master as an architect so that he has a chance to meet his Konstanze in the garden. The pasha has taken him into his service; – Osmin, the overseer, knows nothing of this and, being a foul-mouthed boor and the sworn enemy of all strangers, is insolent and refuses to let them into the garden. – The first thing that's indicated is very brief – and because the text gave me an opportunity to do so, I've produced some quite good 3-part writing. But then the major key enters pianissimo – it must go very quickly – and the ending will make a lot of noise – which is exactly what's needed at the end of an act – the more noise the better; – and the shorter the better, so the audience's enthusiasm doesn't have time to cool off and they don't stint on their applause. –

You've got only 14 bars of the overture. – It's very short – it

9. 'Ach ich liebte, war so glücklich.'
10. 'Separation was my unhappy lot. And now my eyes swim in tears.'
11. 'in a jiffy' . . . 'quickly' . . . 'but how quickly my joy disappeared'.
12. 'Marsch, marsch, marsch!'

keeps alternating between forte and piano, with the Turkish music always entering on the forte. – In this way it modulates through various keys – I don't think anyone will be able to sleep through it even if they didn't sleep a wink the whole of the previous night. – But I'm now in a pickle – the first act has been finished for more than 3 weeks – also finished are an aria from the 2nd act and the duet – *per li Sigri viennesi*[13]– which consists entirely of *my* Turkish tattoo; – but I can't do any more work on the opera as the whole story is being changed – and at my own request. – At the start of the third act there's a charming quintet[14] or, rather, a finale, which I'd prefer to have at the end of the 2nd act. In order to be able to achieve this, a big change needs to be made and, indeed, a whole new plot introduced – and Stephanie is up to his eyes in work, so we have to be a little patient. – Everyone is calling Stephanie names – perhaps with me, too, he's only being friendly to my face – but, after all, he's arranging the libretto for me – and, what's more, doing it just as I want – and in God's name I can't expect anything more of him! – Well, I've certainly been chattering on about the opera; but I can't help it. – Please send me the march I mentioned the other day. – Gilowsky says that Daubrawaick[15] is expected soon. – Fräulein von Auernhammer and I await the 2 double concertos[16] with impatience – I hope we'll not wait for it as vainly as the Jews for their Messiah. – Adieu for now – farewell, I kiss your hands 1000 times and embrace my dear sister – whose health, I hope, is improving – with all my heart. I am ever your most obedient son

W. A. Mozart

13. 'for the gentlemen of Vienna'.
14. In its final form, the third act of the opera begins with Belmonte's aria 'Ich baue ganz auf deine Stärke'; perhaps Mozart refers here to what was to become the quartet at the end of the second act, 'Ach, Belmonte, ach mein Leben'.
15. Johann Baptist Anton Daubrawa von Daubrawaick (1731–1810) was a Salzburg court councillor.
16. K242 (originally for three keyboards but arranged by Mozart for two keyboards as well) and K365.

120. Mozart to his father, 17 November 1781, Vienna

Mon très cher Père,

Your letter of the 6th has arrived safely. – As for Ceccarelli, it's impossible, even for a single night;[1] I've only one room, which isn't large and which is already completely filled by my wardrobe, table and piano, so that I really don't know where I'd put another bed. – And sleeping in one bed is something I won't do with anyone except for my future wife. – But I'll have a look round for as cheap a room as possible as soon as I know exactly when he's coming. – I've not seen Countess Schönborn all this time; I didn't have the heart to go there and still don't – *I know her* – she's bound to say something that I might not be able to swallow without answering back – and it's always better to avoid such things – it's enough that she knows I'm here – and if she wants to, she can see me. Czernin couldn't work out what's been going on in the Mölk affair and at a public dinner asked him if he'd had any news of his brother, the privy councillor. – Mölk was so stunned he couldn't reply. – I'd certainly have given him a piece of my mind. He was corrupted in a house that you yourself have often frequented –

I'll call on the Kletzls as soon as I can. – I've finally got some more of my opera to work on. If we were always to believe gossips and place our trust in them! – How often it would be to our detriment! – I really can't tell you how much people tried to incite me against young Stephanie – it really made me very uneasy – and if I'd done what people were telling me to do, I'd have made an enemy of a good friend, an enemy, moreover, who could have done me a great deal of harm; and all for no reason; –

Archduke Maximilian invited me to call on him at 3 o'clock yesterday afternoon – when I went in, he was standing next to the stove in the first room, waiting for me; he came straight over to me and asked me if I was doing anything for the rest of the day. – *Nothing at all, your Royal Highness; – and even if I were, it would*

1. Apparently Ceccarelli intended to visit Vienna.

always be a privilege for me to wait on your Royal Highness. – No, I don't want to inconvenience anyone. – He then told me that he was thinking of giving a concert that evening for his distinguished visitors from Württemberg and would I like to play something and accompany the arias. – I was to return at 6 o'clock, when everyone would be assembled. – So I played there yesterday. – When God gives someone a public office, He also gives them understanding – and so it is with the archduke. – But he was much wittier and more intelligent before he became a priest, and he spoke less but more sensibly. – You should see him now! – Stupidity stares from his eyes. – He goes on and on, never stopping, and always in a falsetto. – He's got a swelling on his neck. – In a word, he seems to have changed completely. – But the duke of Württemberg[2] is a charming gentleman – as are the duchess and the princess. But the prince is a veritable blockhead and a dry old stick, although he's still only 18. –

I must stop now. – Farewell, and be as cheerful as possible! – I kiss your hands 1000 times and embrace my dear sister with all my heart. I am ever your most obedient son,

W. A. Mozart

121. Mozart to his father, 15 December 1781, Vienna

Mon très cher Père,

I've just this moment received your letter of the 12th. – Herr von Daubrawaick will be delivering this letter, together with the watch, the Munich opera, the 6 engraved sonatas, the sonata for 2 keyboards and the cadenzas.[1] – As for the Princess of Württemberg and me, it's

---

2. Friedrich Eugen of Württemberg (1732–97), youngest brother of Karl II Eugen, the reigning duke. His son was Ferdinand August (1763–1834).
1. *Idomeneo,* K296+376–80, probably K448, and cadenzas for the two-piano concerto K365, which Leopold had recently had copied for Wolfgang. Mozart and Josepha Auernhammer had performed K365 at a private concert on 23 November; they performed it again at a public concert in the Augarten on 26 May 1782.

all over;[2] the emperor has ruined everything, only Salieri matters in his eyes. – The Archduke Maximilian recommended *me* to her; – she told him that if it had been up to her, she wouldn't have accepted anyone else but that the emperor had recommended Salieri to her; because of her singing. She was very sorry. What you wrote about the house of Württemberg and yourself may possibly be of use to me. –

Dearest father! You demand an explanation of the words that I wrote at the end of my last letter![3] – Oh, how gladly I'd have opened my heart to you long ago; but the reproach that you might have made me *for thinking of such a thing at so inopportune a moment* dissuaded me from doing so – although thinking about something can never be inopportune. – My aim for the present is to ensure that I have something *secure* here – this, with the help of less secure forms of income, will allow me to live very comfortably here; – and then – to get married! – You're shocked at the idea? – I beg you, dearest, most beloved father, listen to what I have to say! – I have been forced to reveal my most pressing concerns to you, you must now permit me to disclose my reasons, reasons that are very well founded. The voice of nature speaks as loudly in me as in anyone else, perhaps even louder than in many a big strong oaf. I can't possibly live as most young people do nowadays. – In the first place, my religious feelings are too strong, secondly, I have too great a love of my neighbour and my feelings are too honourable for me to seduce an innocent girl; and thirdly, I have too much horror and loathing, too much dread and fear of diseases and am too fond of my own health to fool around with whores; and so I can swear that I've never had anything to do with women of this kind. – If I had done, I'd not have concealed it from you, for it is natural enough for a man to err, and to err *once* would be mere weakness – although I wouldn't trust myself to promise that, having erred once on this point, I would leave it at that.

2. Mozart had hoped to be appointed music teacher to princess Elisabeth Wilhelmine Louise of Württemberg (1767–90).
3. In a letter of 5 December Mozart had answered Leopold's criticisms by noting that he knew perfectly well that he had an immortal soul but this did not mean he could carry out all his father's wishes in the way Leopold might expect.

– But I can stake my life on this. I know very well that this reason – however powerful it may be – is not in itself enough – but it is rather a question of my temperament, which is more inclined to a calm and domesticated existence than to noise and bluster – even in youth I was never accustomed to worrying about my own things, be they linen, clothes etc. I can now think of nothing more necessary to me that a wife. – I assure you that I often spend money unnecessarily because I'm so negligent. – I'm convinced that I'd manage better with a wife – on the same income that I have now – than I do at present. – And how many unnecessary expenses would be avoided? – Of course, some of these would be replaced by others, but one knows what they are, can plan for them and, in a word, can lead an orderly existence. –

A single person, in my view, is only half alive. – That's my view of the matter, I can't help it. – I've given it sufficient thought and reflected on it at length – and I shan't change my mind.

But who is the object of my love? – Don't be alarmed, I beg you; – surely not one of the Webers? – Yes, one of the Webers – but not Josepha – not Sophie – but Constanze, the middle one. – In no other family have I encountered such inequality of temperament as I have in this one. – The eldest is a lazy, foul-mouthed, mendacious person, who's as cunning as they come. – Frau Lange[4] is a snake-in-the-grass and a coquette, who always thinks ill of people. – The youngest – is still too young to be anything. – She's just a good-natured but excessively frivolous creature! May God protect her from being seduced! – But the middle one – I mean my good, kind Constanze – is the martyr among them and precisely for that reason she's perhaps the most kind-hearted, the cleverest and, in a word, the best of all. – She looks after everything in the house – but can do nothing right. O my most beloved father, I could fill whole sheets if I were to describe to you all the scenes that the two of us have witnessed in that house. If you insist, I shall do so in my next letter. – But before I release you from this chatter, I must make you better acquainted

4. Aloysia Weber had married the actor Johann Joseph Lange (1751–1831) on 31 October 1780.

with the character of my dearest Constanze. – She's not ugly, but at the same time she's not exactly beautiful. – Her whole beauty consists in two dark little eyes and a beautiful figure. She has no wit but enough sound common sense to be able to fulfil her duties as a wife and mother. She's not inclined to extravagance – it's completely wrong to claim otherwise. – Quite the opposite: she's used to being poorly dressed. – The little that her mother has been able to do for her children has been done for the two others, never for her. – It's true that she'd like to dress neatly and cleanly, but not nattily. – And most of the things that a woman needs she can make herself. And she also does her own hair every day. – She understands all about housekeeping and has the kindest heart in the world – I love her, and she loves me with all her heart. – Tell me if I could wish for a better wife? –

I must add that at the time I handed in my notice[5] we were not yet in love – it was born of her tender care and attentions – when I was living in their house. –

And so I want only a small secure income – and, praise be to God, I have genuine hopes of this – and shall then never stop begging you to let me save this poor creature and make both her and me – and, I may say, all of us – happy – surely you are happy when I am? – And you, my dearest father, shall enjoy half the money that I'm *assured* of receiving! – I've now opened my heart to you and explained what I said. – I would now ask you to explain what you meant in your last letter, when you said that I can't believe that I knew nothing of *a proposal that had been made to me and to which*, when you heard of it, *I hadn't replied*. – I don't understand a word of this; I know of no proposal. – Take pity on your son! I kiss your hands 1000 times and am ever your most obedient son

W. A. Mozart

[*Postscript to Nannerl on the inside of the envelope*]
Ma très chère sœur,

Here are the 6 engraved sonatas and the sonata for 2 keyboards, I hope you like them. – Only four of them are new to you, the

---

5. That is, when Mozart left Salzburg service.

copyist wasn't able to complete the variations, I'll send them to you with my next letter.

Dear sister! – I have here a letter that I began to write to you, but because I've written so much to papa, I wasn't able to write any more to you; and so I must ask you to make do with this cover for the time being, and I'll write to you by the next post. *Addio*, farewell, I kiss you 1000 times and am ever your honest brother

W. A. Mozart

122. *Mozart to his father, 16 January 1782, Vienna*

Mon très cher Père,

Thank you for your kind and affectionate letter! – If I were to reply in detail to everything, I'd fill a whole quire of paper. – But as this is impossible, I'll answer only the essential points. Her guardian is called Herr von Thorwart[1] – he's inspector of the theatre wardrobe – in a word, everything that affects the theatre has to pass through his hands. – It was also through him that the emperor sent me the 50 ducats. – I also discussed my concert[2] at the theatre with him, because most of the work devolves on him – and he's held in high regard by Count Rosenberg and Baron Kienmayr.[3] – I must admit that I thought he'd disclose the whole affair to you without saying a word about it; – that he hasn't done so but – in spite of his word of honour – has instead told the whole city of Vienna has caused him to sink considerably in my eyes. – I readily concede that Mme Weber and Herr von Thorwart may have erred in being too concerned for their own interests, although Mme Weber is no longer her own mistress but has to leave everything to the guardian, especially in matters of this kind; and the latter – who has never met

1. Johann Franz Joseph Thorwart (1737–1813), from 1783 an administrator in the Viennese court music establishment in Vienna, was guardian to Constanze, then nineteen years old, and her younger sister Sophie.
2. Planned for 3 March 1782.
3. Johann Michael, Baron von Kienmayr (1727–92), deputy director of the court theatre.

me – certainly owes me no trust – but – there's no doubt that he was overhasty in demanding a written undertaking,[4] especially as I'd told him that you didn't yet know about it and that I couldn't possibly tell you about it now; – I asked him to be patient for a little while longer, until my circumstances had changed, when I'd write and tell you everything, and the whole affair would then be sorted out. – Well, this is all in the past; – and love must be my excuse; – but Herr von Thorwart was wrong to act as he did, though not so badly that he and Mme Weber should be thrown into chains, made to sweep the streets and forced to carry a board round their necks with the words: *seducers of youth.* That would be excessive. – And even if what you wrote were true, namely, that they kept open house for my sake, allowing me the run of it and giving me every opportunity etc. etc., the punishment would still be excessive. – But I don't need to tell you that it's not true; – indeed, it pains me to think that you could believe your son capable of frequenting such a house where such things went on. – I shall say only that you should believe the exact opposite of what you've been told. – Enough of this; –

Now for Clementi.[5] – He's a fine cembalo player. – And that's about it. – He has great dexterity with his right hand. – The passages he plays best are those written in thirds. – For the rest, he doesn't have a farthing's worth of taste or feeling. – A mere machine.

After we'd paid each other enough compliments, the emperor decided that *he* should begin. *La santa chiesa Catholica,* he said – because Clementi is from Rome. – He improvised and played a sonata – the emperor then said to me *allons* off you go. – I too improvised and played some variations. – The grand duchess[6] then produced

4. Thorwart had demanded that Mozart sign a document agreeing to marry Constanze within three years; if he failed to do so, he was to pay her 100 gulden per year compensation.

5. Muzio Clementi (1752–1832), composer and piano virtuoso. Here Mozart describes the piano duel that had taken place on 24 December 1781 between himself and Clementi at the instigation of Joseph II.

6. Maria Feodorovna (1759–1828), second wife of Grand Duke Paul of Russia (1754–1801, Czar Paul I from 1796), was the daughter of Friedrich Eugen, duke of Württemberg.

some sonatas by Paisiello[7] – wretchedly written out in his own hand – and I had to play the allegros, he the andantes and rondos. – We then took a theme from them and developed it on 2 pianos. – The odd thing is that I'd borrowed Countess Thun's pianoforte but played on it only when I played on my own – that's what the emperor wanted – also, I should add, the other instrument was out of tune and 3 keys were stuck. *It doesn't matter*, said the emperor; – I assume that what he meant – placing the best possible construction on it – was that the emperor already knew my skill and knowledge of music and just wanted to get a proper idea of the stranger. –

But I know from a very good source that he was extremely pleased. The emperor was very kind to me and said a great deal to me in private. – He also talked to me about my marriage. – Who knows – perhaps – what do you think? – One can but try.

More next time. – Farewell. I kiss your hands 1000 times and embrace my dear sister with all my heart. I am ever your most obedient son

W. A. Mozart

123. Mozart to his sister, 13 February 1782, Vienna

Ma très chère sœur,

Many thanks for sending me the libretto,[1] which I'd been eagerly awaiting! – I hope that by the time you receive this letter you'll have our dear, most beloved father with you again.[2] – You mustn't think that because I never reply to your letters I find them a nuisance! – Nothing will ever give me greater pleasure than the honour of receiving a letter from you, dear sister; – if the necessary business of earning my living allowed me to do so, God knows that I'd answer your letters! – Have I never replied to you? – Really? – It can't be

7. Giovanni Paisiello was Kapellmeister to Catherine the Great of Russia from 1776.
1. For *Idomeneo*.
2. Leopold Mozart had been in Munich in early February.

forgetfulness – or negligence. – So it must be due entirely to immediate obstacles – genuine impossibility! – Don't I write little enough to my father too? – That's bad enough, you'll say! – But in God's name – you both know Vienna! – Doesn't a man who hasn't a farthing's assured income have enough to think about, what with having to work day and night in such a place? – – When our father has finished his duties in church and you've dismissed your few students, you can both spend the whole day doing what you like, including writing letters that contain whole litanies. – But I can't do that. – I recently told my father how I spend my life, and I'll repeat it for you now. – My hair is always done by 6 in the morning. – By 7 I'm fully dressed. – I then write till 9. From 9 till 1 I teach. – I then eat, unless I'm invited out to a place where people lunch at 2 or even 3, as is the case today and tomorrow, for example, at Countess Zichy's[3] and Countess Thun's. – I can't work before 5 or 6 in the evening, and often I'm prevented from doing so by a concert; if not, I compose till 9. – I then go to see my dear Constanze – where the pleasure of seeing each other is, however, generally spoilt by her mother's embittered remarks – I'll explain all this in my next letter to my father – hence my wish to free her and rescue her as soon as possible. – I return home at half past 10 or 11 – this depends on her mother's barbed remarks and my resilience in enduring them. – As I can't rely on being able to compose in the evening because of the concerts that often take place and also because of the uncertainty of being summoned hither and thither, I tend to write some more before going to bed – especially if I get home early. – I then often go on writing until 1 – and then I'm up again at 6. –

Dearest sister! – If you think that I could ever forget my dearest, most beloved father and you, then – – but enough of that! God knows the truth, and that is reassurance enough for me; – He may punish me if ever I forget you! – Adieu – I am ever your honest brother

W. A. Mozart

3. Anna Maria, Countess Zichy von Vásonykö, wife of Karl, Count Zichy von Vásonykö (1753–1826), court councillor.

P. S.: If my dearest father is already back in Salzburg, I kiss his *hands* 1000 times.

124. Mozart to his father, 10 April 1782, Vienna

Mon très cher Père,

I see from your letter of the 2nd inst. that you've received everything safely; I'm delighted you're pleased with the watch ribbons and snuffbox and that my sister is pleased with the 2 mob caps. – I bought neither the watch ribbons nor the snuffbox – they were both presents from Count Szápáry. – I've passed on your best wishes to my dear Constanze she kisses your hands, father, and embraces my sister with all her heart and hopes she may be her friend. – She couldn't have been more delighted when I told her you were so pleased with the 2 mob caps, as that is exactly what she'd hoped. – Your postscript regarding her mother is justified only to the extent that she likes a drink and, indeed, more than a woman should. But – I've never seen her drunk, it would be a lie if I claimed otherwise. – The children drink only water – and even though their mother almost forces wine on them, she can't bring them to drink it. This often results in the most violent arguments – can you imagine a mother arguing in this way? –

As for the rumour that I'm to be taken into the emperor's service, I've nothing to say on the matter as I know absolutely nothing about it. – It's true that the whole town is talking about it and a whole crowd of people have already congratulated me on it. – And I'm more than happy to think that it has already been discussed with the emperor and that he may even be thinking about it; – but so far I know not a word myself. – The situation at present is that the emperor is thinking about it and doing so, moreover, without my having taken a single step. – I've been a few times to see Herr von Strack[1] – who's certainly a very good friend of mine – in order to ensure that I'm

1. Johann Kilian Strack (1724–93), imperial valet.

seen and because I enjoy his company, but not so often as to become a nuisance or to give him cause to think that I've ulterior motives. – If he's honest with himself, he is bound to say that he's never heard me utter a single word that could have given him cause to think that I'd like to stay here, still less that I want to enter the emperor's service. We've spoken only about music. – It's on his own initiative, therefore, and entirely without self-interest that he has spoken so favourably about me to the emperor. – Since we've reached this point without any intervention on my part, I think we can leave things to reach a conclusion in the same way. – If one bestirs oneself, one immediately receives a smaller salary as the emperor is in any case very tight-fisted. – If the emperor wants me, he shall pay for me – the mere honour of serving him isn't enough. – If the emperor gives me 1000 florins while some count gives me 2000, I'll give the emperor my best wishes and go and work for the count. – Assuming, of course, that it were a secure appointment. –

By the way, I meant to ask you to send me the 6 fugues by Handel and the toccatas and fugues by Eberlin when you return the rondo.[2] – At noon every Sunday I visit Baron van Swieten – here nothing is played but Handel and Bach. –

I'm currently collecting Bach fugues. – Not only Sebastian but also Emanuel and Friedemann Bach.[3] – And also Handel's. So I'm missing only these. – And I'd also like the baron to hear Eberlin's. – I expect you already know that the English Bach[4] has died? – What a loss to the world of music! – Farewell for now; I kiss your hands 1000 times and embrace my dear sister with all my heart. I am ever your most obedient son

W. A. Mozart

2. George Frideric Handel, *Six Fugues or Voluntarys* (London, 1735); Johann Ernst Eberlin, presumably the *IX Toccate e fughe per l'Organo* (Augsburg: Lotter, 1747); K382.

3. Johann Sebastian Bach, his sons Carl Philipp Emanuel Bach (1714–88) and Wilhelm Friedemann Bach (1710–84).

4. Johann Christian Bach died in London on 1 January 1782.

P. S.: Could I ask you, when you've a moment – but the sooner the better –, to send me my concerto for Countess Lützow? In C.[5]

125. Mozart to Constanze Weber, 29 April 1782, Vienna

Dearest, most beloved Friend,

Surely you'll allow me to continue using this name? – Surely you don't hate me so much that I may no longer be your friend and you – no longer mine? – And – even if you don't want to be my friend any longer, you can't stop me thinking well of you, my friend, as I've now got used to doing so. – Think about what you said to me today. – In spite of all my entreaties, you snubbed me 3 times today and told me to my face that you wanted nothing more to do with me. – It's by no means a matter of such indifference to me as it is to you to lose the object of my love, and I'm not so hot-tempered, rash and foolish as to accept such a snub. – I love you too much to take this step. – And so I would ask you once again to consider and reflect on the cause of this annoyance, which is that I was angry that you'd been so shamelessly inconsiderate as to tell your sisters – in my presence, be it added – that you had got a young beau to measure your calves. – No woman who cares for her honour does such a thing. – It is a good *maxim* to do only what you would do in company. – But there are many secondary considerations to be taken into account. – Are the people present all good friends and acquaintances? – Am I a child or already a young woman *of marriageable age* – but especially if I'm engaged to be married? – But, above all, whether only people of my own class or of a lower class are present – but especially if there are people there who are my social superiors. – Even if it's true that the baroness herself did so, it's still very different, because she's already past her prime[1] and can't possibly attract men any longer – and in any case she loves – I need say no

5. K246.
1. Martha Elisabeth, Baroness Waldstätten, see List; she was then thirty-eight.

more. – I hope, my dearest friend, that even if you refuse to be my wife, you'll never lead a life like that. – Even if you couldn't resist the urge to join in – although it's not always appropriate for a man to *join in,* still less a woman – then, for heaven's sake, you should have taken the ribbon and measured your calves *yourself* – just as *all women of honour* would have done in such cases in my presence – and not let a beau do it – I – I'd never have done it to you in the *presence of others* – I'd have handed you the ribbon myself. – Still less should you have let it be done by a stranger – someone about whom I care nothing. – But it's over now. – And some slight acknowledgement of your somewhat ill-considered behaviour on that occasion would have put everything to rights again. – And – if you won't take it amiss – could still put everything to rights, dearest friend. – You can see from this how much I love you. – – *I don't get as worked up as you do;* – I think – I consider – and I feel. – *If you feel – if you have feelings* – I know for certain that this very day I shall be able to say very calmly that Constanze is the virtuous, honourable – sensible and faithful sweetheart of one who is honest and who thinks only well of her,

Mozart

126. Mozart to his father, 20 July 1782, Vienna

Mon très cher Père,

I hope you received my last letter, in which I told you that my opera[1] had been well received. – There was another performance yesterday; – can you imagine that there was an even more powerful cabal yesterday than at the first night? – The whole of the first act was hissed. – But they couldn't prevent the loud shouts of *bravo* during the arias. – I'd pinned my hopes on the closing trio[2] – but as

---

1. *Die Entführung aus dem Serail* was premiered on 16 July. Mozart received 100 ducats for its composition.
2. 'Marsch, marsch, marsch!'

ill luck would have it, Fischer went wrong and as a result Dauer[3] – Pedrillo – went wrong too – and Adamberger on his own couldn't sing all three lines so that the whole effect was lost and as a result *it wasn't repeated*. – I was so angry that I was beside myself – as was Adamberger – and said straightaway that I wouldn't allow the opera to be given again without a short rehearsal for the singers. – In the 2nd act both the duets[4] were repeated, as they had been the first time, and so was Belmonte's rondeau *'Wenn der Freude Thränen fliessen'*. – The theatre was almost fuller than on the first night. – By the previous day there'd been no more reserved seats left either in the stalls or in the 3rd tier, and no boxes either. The opera has made 1200 florins in 2 days. –

I'm enclosing the original and 2 copies of the libretto. –

You'll see that I cut a great deal; that's because I knew that the full score is copied at once here – but I'd allowed my ideas free rein – and before I gave it to be copied I made a number of changes and cuts at various points. – It was given just as you see it. – Here and there the trumpets and timpani, flutes, clarinets and Turkish music are missing because I couldn't get hold of any paper with enough lines. – They're written out on extra sheets – the copyist has presumably lost them as he couldn't find them. – The first act unfortunately fell in the mud when I was having it sent somewhere or other – I no longer remember where – which is why it's so dirty. –

I've lots of work at the moment. – By Sunday week I have to arrange my opera for wind band – otherwise someone else will get in first – and they'll be the one to profit from it, not me;[5] and I'm also supposed to be writing a new symphony![6] – How shall I ever manage? – You can't imagine how difficult it is to arrange such a thing for wind band – so that it suits the wind instruments and yet loses none of its effectiveness. – Oh well, I'll just have to sit up all night working on it, there's no other way – and to you, my dearest

3. Johann Ernst Dauer (1746–1812) sang the role of Pedrillo.
4. Blonde and Osmin's 'Ich gehe, doch rate ich dir' and Pedrillo and Osmin's 'Vivat Bacchus, Bacchus lebe'.
5. In the event, Mozart did not complete a wind arrangement of *Die Entführung*.
6. For the ennoblement on 29 July of Siegmund Haffner (K385, 'Haffner').

father, may it be sacrificed. – You'll certainly receive something every post day, and I'll work as quickly as possible – and as far as haste allows, I'll make a good job of it. –

Count Zichy has just this minute sent a message, asking if I'll drive out to Laxenburg with him, so that he can introduce me to Prince Kaunitz. – So I must stop now and get dressed – if I'm not planning to go out, I don't bother to dress.

The copyist has just this minute sent the remaining parts.

Adieu. I kiss your hands 1000 times and embrace my dear sister with all my heart. I am ever your most obedient son

W. A. Mozart

P. S.: My dear Constanze sends you both her best wishes.

127. Mozart to his father, 27 July 1782, Vienna

Mon très cher Père,

You'll no doubt be surprised to receive only the first allegro;[1] but – I'd no choice – I've had to write a Nacht Musique[2] in a hurry, but only for wind band – otherwise I could have used it for *you* too – on Wednesday the 31st I'll send you the 2 minuets, the andante and the final movement – if I can, I'll also send a march – if not you'll have to make do with the one from the Haffner music[3] – which is *very* little known:

– I've written it in D as I know you prefer it. – My opera was given

1. Of the 'Haffner' symphony.
2. Almost certainly the wind serenade K388; in 1782 Mozart also revised the wind serenade K375, a work that is similarly described as a 'Nacht Musique'.
3. The 'Haffner' serenade K250 and its associated march K249.

for the third time yesterday in honour of all Nannerls and was loudly applauded – and the theatre was again packed to the rafters in spite of the appalling heat. – It's to be given again next Friday – but I've protested at this as I don't want it to be flogged to death in this way. – I can truthfully say that people have gone quite mad over this opera. – But it does one good to receive such acclaim. – I hope you'll have received the original. Dearest, most beloved father! – I must ask you – ask you by all you hold dear in the world – to give your consent to my marriage to my dear Constanze. – Don't think that it's just to get married – if that were all, I'd gladly wait. – But I see that it's now unavoidably necessary for my own honour and the honour of my girl as well as for my health and state of mind. – My heart is restless, my head confused – how, then, can I think straight and work? – What's the reason for this? – Most people think we're already married – her mother is very worked up about it – and the poor girl and I are both tormented to death. – And this can so easily be put right. – Believe me that it's just as easy to live in an expensive city like Vienna as it is elsewhere, it's just a question of economy and of being properly organized. – And this is something you never find with a young man, especially one who's in love. – Anyone who gets a wife like the one I'm getting will certainly be happy. – We'll live very quiet, uneventful lives – and yet be happy. – And don't worry – for if – God forbid – I were to fall ill today, especially when married, I'll wager that the leading members of the nobility would offer me their protection. – I can say that with confidence. – I know what Prince Kaunitz has said about me to the emperor and Archduke Maximilian. – I eagerly await your consent, my most beloved father – I feel sure I can count on it – my honour and peace of mind are bound up with it. – Don't put off for too long the pleasure of embracing your son and his wife. I kiss your hands 1000 times and am ever your most obed. son

W. A. Mozart

P. S.: I embrace my dear sister with all my heart. My Constanze sends her best wishes to you both. – *Adieu.*

128. Mozart to his father, 7 August 1782, Vienna

Mon très cher Père,
   You're very much mistaken if you think your son capable of acting wrongly; –

My dear Constanze – now, praise God, my actual wife[1] – has long known my circumstances and all that I can expect to receive from you. – But her friendship and love for me were so great that she willingly – and with the greatest pleasure – sacrificed her entire future to me and my destiny. – I kiss your hands and thank you with all the tenderness that a son has ever felt for his father and for your most kind consent and father's blessing. – But I knew I could rely on them! – After all, you knew that I myself could see everything only too clearly – yes, everything that could be said against such a step – but also that I couldn't have acted otherwise without offending my conscience and my honour – and so I was able to rely entirely on this, too! – And so it was that, having waiting 2 post days in vain for a reply and having arranged the ceremony for the day by which I would most certainly have known the answer, I – already assured of your consent and feeling suitably consoled – was married in God's name to the woman I love. The very next day your 2 letters arrived together; – it's all over now! – I only ask you to forgive me for trusting prematurely in your paternal love; – in this sincere confession of mine you have further proof of my love of the truth and my loathing of lies. – My dear wife will be writing by the next post to ask her dearest, most beloved father-in-law for his paternal blessing and her dear sister-in-law for the continuation of her most valued friendship. – The only people present at the wedding were her mother and youngest sister, Herr von Thorwart as guardian and witness for both of us; – Herr von Cetto (the district councillor), who gave away the bride; and Gilowsky as my best man. – As soon as we were pronounced man and wife, both my wife and I began to cry; –

1. Mozart and Constanze had signed their marriage contract on 3 August. The wedding itself was on 4 August at St Stephen's, Vienna.

everyone, even the priest, was moved by this. – And all of them wept on witnessing how much our hearts were moved. – Our wedding feast consisted of a supper given for us by Baroness Waldstätten that was in fact more princely than baronial – my dear Constanze is now looking forward a hundred times more to travelling to Salzburg! – And I wager – I wager – that you'll delight in my own good fortune when you get to know her! – I'm sure that in your eyes as in mine a right-thinking, honest, virtuous and obliging woman is a source of happiness for her husband! –

Enclosed is a short march![2] – I only hope that everything arrives in good time – and that it's to your liking. – The first allegro[3] must be very fiery. – The last – as fast as possible. – My opera was given again yesterday – at Gluck's insistence; – he's been very complimentary about it. I'm having lunch with him tomorrow. – As you can see, I'm in a hurry. *Adieu.* My dear wife and I kiss your hands 1000 times and we both embrace our dear sister with all our hearts. I am ever your most obed. son

W. A. Mozart

129. Leopold Mozart to Martha Elisabeth, Baroness von Waldstätten, 23 August 1782, Salzburg

My Lady,

I am most obliged to your Ladyship for the particular interest that you have taken in my circumstances and above all I should like to say how obliged and grateful I am for the extraordinary kindness that your Ladyship showed in celebrating my son's wedding day in so lavish a manner. When I was a young lad, I always thought that philosophers were people who said little, seldom laughed and adopted a sullen attitude to the world in general. My own experiences have now convinced me that without knowing it I too am one: I have done

2. Probably K408/2.
3. Here Mozart describes his preferred tempos for the 'Haffner' symphony.

my duty as a true father, making the clearest and most intelligible
representations to him in so many letters and convincing myself that
he knows my tiresome circumstances, which are highly distressing to
a man of my age, and is also aware of the way in which I have been
passed over in Salzburg, since he knows that both morally and
physically I am the victim of his behaviour, – and yet there is nothing
I can now do except leave him to his own devices – which is what
he wanted – and pray to God that He grants him my paternal blessing
and does not take away His divine grace. But I shall not abandon my
innate cheerfulness, which I still retain in spite of my years, and shall
continue to hope for the best. – Indeed, I would be wholly reassured
were it not that I have detected in my son a serious failing, which is
that he is far too *patient* or *sleepy*, too *easy-going*, perhaps sometimes
too *proud* and whatever else you want to call all those qualities that
render a person *inactive*: or else he is too *impatient*, too *hot-headed*,
and can't wait. Two opposing principles rule in him – too much or
too little, and no golden mean. If he's not short of something, he's
immediately satisfied and becomes *lazy* and *inactive*. If he has to act,
he feels his own worth and *immediately wants to make his fortune*.
Nothing is then allowed to stand in his way: and yet it is unfortunately
the cleverest people and those who possess real genius who find the
greatest obstacles placed in their way. Who will prevent him from
making his way in Vienna if only he shows a little patience? – –
Kapellmeister Bonno is extremely old,[1] – on his death, Salieri will be
promoted and make room for someone else, and isn't Gluck an old
man too!? – My Lady! Persuade him to be patient, and permit me to
ask you to be so kind as to give me your Ladyship's opinion on this
point. – My daughter commends herself to your Ladyship and like
me wishes that she had the good fortune to be able to kiss your
Ladyship's hands. She is very moved at being honoured, quite un-
deservedly, with a remembrance from your Ladyship. Oh, if only we
were not so far away! I have a whole host of things that I'd like to
talk to your Ladyship about – and if only we could immerse ourselves
in music! – May my mind be calmed by hope, the unique consolation

1. He was then seventy-two years old.

of our wishes! – Perhaps I may yet be fortunate enough to be able to assure your Ladyship in person not only of my friendship, which is of little worth but none the less genuine, but also of my most heartfelt esteem and reverence as I am indeed

Your Ladyship's
most humble and obed. servant
Leopold Mozart

My son once wrote to say that as soon as he was married he would not wish to live with his wife's mother. I hope that he has indeed left the house. If not, it is his own and his wife's misfortune.

130. Mozart to Baroness von Waldstätten, 28 September 1782, Vienna

Dearest Baroness,

When your Grace was so gracious yesterday as to invite me to lunch tomorrow, Sunday, it did not occur to me that a week ago I had already agreed to have lunch that same day in the Augarten.[1] –

Martin,[2] the little angel, thinks he's under an obligation to me for several things and absolutely insists on treating me to a collation; – I thought yesterday that it might still be possible to bring about an accommodation and that by dint of some reorganization I might still be able to rearrange the matter in accordance with my own wishes; but this wasn't possible as the little angel had already ordered and arranged everything and would therefore have been put to great expense for nothing; – as a result and in consequence of this, I beg your Ladyship's dispensation on this occasion, and with your Ladyship's approbation we shall both have the honour of offering you our salutations and congratulations next Tuesday and giving

1. A park in the second district in Vienna, formerly for the exclusive use of the imperial family but opened to the public by Joseph II in 1775; it contained a billiard room, a dance hall and a restaurant where concerts were also given.
2. The impresario Philipp Jakob Martin.

Fräulein von Auernhammer an enema if she insists on one of her presentations.[3] – But, joking apart, I don't want the concerto that I played at the theatre[4] to go for less than 6 ducats, conversely I don't mind paying for the copying. – As for the beautiful red coat that tickles my fancy so dreadfully, I'd be grateful if you could let me know *where I can get it* and *how much it costs*, as I've forgotten – I was so taken by its beauty that I didn't notice the price. – I really have to have a coat like that, as it's worth it just for the buttons that I've been hankering after for some time; – I saw them once, when I was choosing some buttons for a suit at Brandau's button factory opposite the Café Milani on the Kohlmarkt. – They're mother-of-pearl with some white stones round the edge and a beautiful yellow stone in the centre. – I'd like to have everything that's good, genuine and beautiful! – But why is it that those who are not in a position to do so want to spend all their money on such things, whereas those who *are* in a position to do so do not do so? – Well, I think it's long past the time when I should have put an end to this scribbling, – I kiss your hands, and hoping to see you in good health the Tuesday I am your most humble servant[5]

Mozart

Constanze, my other half, kisses your Ladyship's hands 1000 times and gives Fräulein Auernhammer a kiss, but I'm not supposed to know about this, otherwise it'll give me the creeps.

For the next six months, Mozart worked hard to establish himself as a composer and performer in Vienna. Die Entführung aus dem Serail *was performed on 8 October in the presence of Grand Duke Paul of Russia*

3. Josepha von Auernhammer had lodged with Baroness Waldstätten since the death of her father in March 1782.
4. This presumably refers to a concert Mozart had given at the Burgtheater on 3 March 1782, when he had probably performed his concerto K175 with the newly composed rondo finale K382.
5. The last twenty words of this letter are written in English.

and on 3 November Mozart played at a concert given by Josepha von Auernhammer. In December Wolfgang and Constanze moved from her mother's house to the Hohen Brücke 412 (now Wipplingerstrasse 14) and that same month he played twice for Countess Thun. At the end of the year he completed the first of the quartets eventually dedicated to Joseph Haydn, K387.

131. Mozart to Baroness von Waldstätten, 15 February 1783, Vienna

Most Esteemed Baroness,

I find myself in a pretty pickle!

Herr von Trattner[1] and I recently agreed that we needed a 2-week extension; – as every businessman does this, assuming he's not the most disobliging man in the world, I was completely relaxed about the matter and hoped that by then, even if I wasn't in a position to repay the sum myself, I'd have been able to borrow it! – – Well, Herr von Trattner now tells me that the man in question absolutely refuses to wait and that if I don't pay him between today and tomorrow, he'll institute *legal proceedings* against me; – your Ladyship can well imagine what an unpleasant blow this would be for me! – I can't pay at present – not even half! – If I could have foreseen that I'd make such slow progress with the subscription of my concertos,[2]

1. Johann Thomas von Trattner (1717–98), court printer, music publisher and book dealer; Mozart dedicated his fantasy and sonata in C minor, K457+475, to Trattner's wife Therese, who had been his pupil. No details are known of the financial transaction described here.

2. K413–415. An advertisement for the works in the *Wiener Zeitung* for 15 January 1783 reads: 'Herr Kapellmeister Mozart herewith apprises the highly honoured public of the publication of three new, recently finished keyboard concertos. These 3 concertos, which may be performed either with a large orchestra with wind instruments or merely *a quattro*, viz. with 2 violins, 1 viola and violoncello, will not appear until the beginning of April of this year, and will be issued (finely copied and supervised by himself) only to those who have subscribed thereto. The present serves to give the further news that subscription tickets may be had of him for four

I'd have borrowed the money for a longer period! – I beg your Ladyship in heaven's name to help me so I don't lose my honour and good name! – My poor little wife is slightly unwell and so I can't leave her, otherwise I'd come in person to ask for your Ladyship's help. We kiss your Ladyship's hands 1000 times and are both

your Ladyship's
most obedient children
W. A. & C. Mozart

132. Mozart to his father, 12 March 1783, Vienna

Mon très cher Père,

I hope you haven't been worried but that you guessed the reason for my silence, which is that I couldn't be sure how long you'd remain in Munich, with the result that I didn't know where to write to and therefore waited until now, when I could be certain that my letter would find you in Salzburg. – My sister-in-law, Fräulein Lange, gave a concert yesterday at the theatre and I played a concerto.[1] – The theatre was very full; and I was again received by the local public in so gratifying a manner that I have every reason to feel pleased. – I'd already left but they wouldn't stop clapping – so I had to repeat the rondo; – there was a veritable torrent of applause. – This is a good advertisement for my own concert, which I'm giving on Sunday 23 March.[2] – I've also included my symphony from the Concert Spirituel.[3] – My sister-in-law sang the aria *'Non so d'onde viene'*[4] – Gluck had the box next to the Langes, where my wife was sitting. – He couldn't find words enough to praise both the symphony and the aria and has

---

ducats, counting from the 20th of this month until the end of March.' See Deutsch, *Documentary Biography*, 212.
1. Probably K175 with the new rondo finale K382, see letter 130, n. 4.
2. This was the grand academy, a public concert at the Burgtheater given in the presence of the emperor.
3. K297 'Paris'.
4. K294.

invited all four of us to lunch next Sunday. – It may well be that the German opera will continue, but no one knows about it:[5] –

What's certain is that Fischer[6] is going to Paris in 8 days' time. As for Ramm's oboe concerto,[7] I'd very much like to have it, and very soon; – at the same time you could send me some other things, such as my masses in full score – my 2 Vespers[8] in full score – this is just so that Baron van Swieten can hear them. – He sings treble, I sing alto – and play at the same time – Starzer tenor – and young Teyber[9] from Italy bass. – In the meantime, I'd like *Haydn's Tres sunt* until such time as you can send me something else of his; – I'd very much like them to hear his 'Lauda Sion'. – The *Tres sunt* must exist in full score in a copy in *my own hand*. – The fugue 'In te Domine speravi' has been universally applauded, as have the *Ave Maria* and *Tenebrae*[10] etc. – Please enliven our Sunday music practices with something soon.[11] – On Carnival Monday our company of masqueraders performed at the ball – It consisted of a pantomime that filled the half hour when there was no dancing. – My sister-in-law was Columbine, I was Harlequin, my brother-in-law Pierrot, an old dancing master – *Merk* – Pantaloon. A painter (Grassi)[12] the Dottore. –

5. In 1776 Joseph II had installed a theatrical company (the National Theatre) at the Burgtheater to present plays in German (instead of the French drama favoured by the aristocracy). A singspiel company was established in 1778 but was disbanded in 1783 and replaced by an Italian opera troupe; it was briefly reconstituted from 1785 to 1788, with performances held at the Kärntnertortheater.

6. The bass Johann Ignaz Ludwig Fischer.

7. K314.

8. K321 and K339; the masses are unidentified.

9. Anton Teyber, see List.

10. Mozart is asking Leopold to send copies of Salzburg church music: Michael Haydn's offertory *Tres sunt* (composed 7 June 1773), for which there is a copy by Mozart, KAnh. A13, from the mid-1770s; the sequence *Lauda Sion* (1775); the fugue from the *Te Deum* (1770), for which there is a copy by Leopold Mozart, KAnh. 71; and the offertory *Ave Maria* (from before 1765). The *Tenebrae* (undated) is by Johann Ernst Eberlin; there is a copy by Leopold Mozart, KAnh. A76.

11. A request that Leopold send some of his own church music.

12. The portrait painter Joseph Grassi (*c.* 1758–1838) lived and worked in Vienna during the 1780s; his *Portrait of a Man* (1785), for many years considered lost but rediscovered in Moscow in 1998, is sometimes said to portray Mozart.

The plot of the pantomime and the music were both mine.[13] – The dancing master Merk was kind enough to direct us, and although I say it myself, we gave a really fine performance. – Enclosed is a copy of the programme, which a masquerader, dressed as a local postman, handed out to the other masqueraders. – The verses, though only doggerel, could have been better; they weren't by me. – Müller the actor[14] cobbled them together. – I must close now as I have to go to a concert at Count Esterházy's.[15] Farewell for now – please don't forget the music. – My wife and I kiss your hands 1000 times and embrace our dear sister with all our hearts. I am ever your most obedient son

W. A. and C. Mozart

Mozart's grand academy at the Burgtheater on 23 March consisted entirely of his own compositions: he performed the concertante movements from the serenade K320, a revised version of the 'Haffner' symphony K385, the piano concerto K175 with the newly composed finale K382, the piano concerto K415, and an improvisation on themes by Paisiello and Gluck (K398 and 455) as well as a fugue; Anton Teyber's sister Therese sang Giunia's aria 'Parto, m'affretto' from Lucio Silla, *Aloysia Lange sang Ilia's aria 'Se il padre perdei' from* Idomeneo *as well as the recitative and rondo* Mia speranza adorata – Ah, non sai qual pena *K416, and Valentin Adamberger sang the scena* Misera, dove son! – Ah! Non son io che parlo *K369. In April, Mozart and Constanze, who was pregnant with their first child, took rooms on the Judenplatz 244.*

13. K446. Mozart's pantomime, a silent play with musical accompaniment (in this case based on *commedia dell'arte* characters), survives only incompletely as a fragmentary first violin part.
14. Johann Heinrich Friedrich Müller (1738–1815), actor at the Vienna Court Theatre from 1763 to 1801.
15. Possibly Johann Nepomuk, Count Esterházy (1754–1840); Mozart is known to have performed regularly at his house (see letter 140).

133. Mozart to his father, 12 April 1783, Vienna

Mon très cher Père,

I received your latest letter of the 8th inst. this morning and see you've received everything from Herr von Daubrawaick. – I'm sorry to say that the mail coach doesn't leave again for another week so I can't send you the 2 copies of my sonatas[1] until then. –

At the same time I'll send you the ornamented voice part for the aria *'Non sò d'onde viene'* etc. – If you're planning to send me anything, please include the rondeau for alto voice that I wrote for the castrato with the Italian troupe in Salzburg and the rondeau that I wrote for Ceccarelli in *Vienna*;[2] – when it gets warmer, please look in the attic and send us some of your church music; – you really have no need to be ashamed of it. – Baron van Swieten and Starzer know as well as you and I that taste is continually changing and that this unfortunately extends even to church music, although it shouldn't do – but that's why true church music is now found in attics and virtually eaten by worms. – If, as I hope, I come to Salzburg in July with my wife, I'd like to discuss this point with you in greater detail. – When Herr von Daubrawaick left, my wife could hardly be held back, so insistent was she on following me. – She thought we could get to Salzburg before Daubrawaick; – and if it hadn't been for the very short time that we could have stayed – what am I saying? – she might even have had to be confined in Salzburg! – And so – because it was impossible, our most ardent wish to embrace you, my beloved father, and my sister would already have come true; – as far as my wife is concerned, I'd have had no misgivings about such a short trip. – She's in such good health and has put on so much weight that all women should thank God if they are so fortunate during their pregnancy. And so, as soon as my wife is able to travel after her confinement, there'll be no keeping us from coming to Salzburg at once. –

1. Presumably the accompanied sonatas K296+376–380.
2. K255, *Ombra felice – Io ti lascio*, composed in 1776 for the castrato Francesco Fortini; K374, *A questo seno deh vieni – Or che il cielo a me ti rende*.

You'll have seen from my last letter that I had to play at another concert, namely, that of Mlle Teyber.[3] – The emperor was there too. – I played the first concerto from my concert[4] – they wanted me to repeat the rondo – so I sat down again – but instead of repeating the rondo, I had the desk removed and played on my own. – You should have heard how delighted the audience was at this little surprise – they didn't just clap but they also shouted *bravo* and *bravissimo*. – The emperor too stayed till the end – and as soon as I left the piano, he left his box. – So he was interested only in hearing me. –

If possible, could I also ask you to send me a *report* on my concert.[5] – I'm genuinely pleased that the little I was able to send you came in handy. – There's so much I could still tell you but I'm afraid the post will ride off without me, it's already a quarter to 8. – In the meantime farewell. My dear little wife and I kiss your hands 1000 times and embrace our dear sister with all our hearts. We are ever your most obedient children

W. C. Mozart

Best wishes to the whole of Salzburg. *Adieu.*

3. Therese Teyber's concert was at the Burgtheater on 30 March.
4. The grand academy; the concerto was K415.
5. Carl Friedrich Cramer, *Magazin der Musik*, Hamburg, 9 May 1783: 'Vienna, 22 March 1783 . . . Tonight the famous Herr Chevalier *Mozart* held a musical concert in the National Theatre, at which pieces of his already highly admired composition were performed. The concert was honoured with an exceptionally large concourse, and the two new concertos and other fantasies which Herr M. played on the fortepiano were received with the loudest applause. Our Monarch, who against his habit attended the whole of the concert, as well as the entire audience, accorded him such unanimous applause as has never been heard of here. The receipts of the concert are estimated to amount to 1,600 gulden in all' (Deutsch, *Documentary Biography*, 215). The report gives the wrong date for the concert; it should have been 23 March.

134. Mozart to Jean-Georges Sieber,[1] 26 April 1783, Vienna

Monsieur,

It's 2 years now since I've been living in Vienna; – you'll presumably know of my pianoforte sonatas[2] with violin accompaniment which I've had engraved here by Artaria & Co.; – but I'm not entirely happy with local engraving methods and even if I were, I'd still like my fellow countrymen in Paris to have something of mine, and so I'm now writing to inform you that I have completed 3 keyboard concertos[3] that can be performed with full orchestra or with oboes and horns – and also merely *à quatro*; – Artaria wants to engrave them. But I'd like you, my good friend, to have first refusal; – and in order to avoid any unnecessary delays, I'll tell you the lowest price that I'll accept; – if you'll give me 30 louis d'or for them, I'll consider the matter settled. – I'm also working on 6 quartets for 2 violins, viola and bass[4] – if you want to engrave these, too, I'll give them to you as well. – But I can't let these go as cheaply – I can't let you have these 6 quartets for under 50 louis d'or; – and so, if you're able and willing to do business with me, I would ask you only to reply and I shall send you an address in Paris where you will receive my works in return for your payment.[5] – Meanwhile I remain your most obedient servant

Wolfgang Amadè Mozart

1. Jean-Georges Sieber (1734–1822), publisher in Paris, had published Mozart's accompanied sonatas K301–306 in 1778.
2. K296+376–380.
3. K413–415.
4. These were eventually to be the six quartets dedicated to Joseph Haydn, K387, 421, 428, 458, 464 and 465. By this time Mozart may have completed only the first of the quartets, although K421 and 428 were also written about the time of this letter. K458 was completed in November 1784 and K464 and 465 in January 1785.
5. Although Sieber's reply is lost, he apparently rejected Mozart's offer. Artaria eventually published both the concertos and quartets in 1785.

135. *Mozart to his father, 7 June 1783, Vienna*

Mon très cher Père,

Praise and thanks be to God, I'm fully recovered! – But my illness has left me with a cold as a souvenir, which was very nice of it, I'm sure! – I've received my dear sister's letter. My wife's name day is neither in May nor March but on 16 February and is not to be found in any diary. – But my wife thanks both of you most cordially for your kind good wishes which are appropriate even without her name day. – She wanted to write to my sister herself, but in her present condition one should not hold it against her if she's a little *commode* or if – in German – she's taking it easy. – According to the midwife's examination, she should have been brought to bed on the 4th of this month – but I don't think anything will happen before the 15th or 16th. – She'd like it to be sooner rather than later, especially as she would then have the pleasure of embracing you and my dear sister all the sooner in Salzburg. – As I didn't think that the matter would take so serious a turn so quickly, I've kept delaying going down on my knees, clasping my hands together and begging you most humbly, my dearest father, to be godfather! – But as there is still time, I am doing so now. – Meanwhile – in the confident hope that you'll not refuse me my request and now that the midwife has undertaken the *visum repertum*– I've already seen to it that someone presents the child in your name, whether it be *generis masculini* or *faeminini*![1] – It will be called Leopold or Leopoldine. – I must now say a few words to my sister about Clementi's sonatas;[2] – that they have no value as compositions will be felt by everyone who plays or hears them; – they contain no remarkable or striking passages except those in 6ths and octaves – and I would ask my sister not to waste *too much* time on these otherwise she'll spoil her relaxed and even touch and her hand will lose its natural lightness, flexibility and fluency at speed. –

1. 'examination' . . . 'male or female'.
2. Presumably the sonatas op. 7, published by Artaria in 1782. In 1783 Artaria also published Clementi's sonatas opp. 9 and 10.

For what do you end up with? – Even if she plays the 6th and octaves with the utmost velocity – something that no one can do, not even Clementi himself – all she'll produce is a frightful chopping sound and nothing more! – Clementi is a *ciarlatano*[3] like all Italians. – He writes presto or even prestissimo and alla breve over a sonata – and still plays it as an allegro in 4/4 time; – I know, because I've heard him. – What he does really well are his passages in 3rds; – but he sweated over them day and night in London; – but apart from this, there's nothing he can do – absolutely nothing – he doesn't have the least idea how to perform a piece, he's no taste, still less does he have feeling. –

Now for Herr von Aman; – Herr von Fichtl told me that Privy Councillor Aman is completely mad and has been locked up. – This came as no surprise as he always used to go around looking thoroughly morose. – I told Herr von Fichtl that *study was probably not the cause*, whereupon he laughed not a little. But I'm sorry for Basilius Aman; – and I'd certainly never have thought it of him; – I'd sooner have conceded that he'd become more sensible. – Well, perhaps he'll take me into his service when I come to Salzburg?[4] – I'll certainly call on him. – If you were able to get hold of a German song of his own composition, I wonder if you'd be kind enough to send it to me so that I've something to laugh at. I'll set it to music. – But no! – I know a fool here who'll do it just as well. –

Have you still not heard from Varesco?[5] – Please don't forget; – while I'm in Salzburg[6] we should be able to work together very well if we've come up with a plan by then. –

Farewell for now; my wife and I kiss your hands 1000 times and

3. 'charlatan'.
4. Johann von Fichtl was a Salzburg court agent in Vienna; privy councillor Optat Basilius Aman (1747–85) had bought property near Salzburg, but Mozart's comment is ironic.
5. In a letter of 7 May 1783 Mozart had asked Leopold to approach Giambattista Varesco, the librettist of *Idomeneo*, for a new libretto to set.
6. Mozart and Constanze planned a visit that summer to Salzburg.

embrace our dear sister with all our hearts. We are ever your most obedient children

W. and C. Mozart

P.S.: I hope you've received the ornamented voice part for the aria '*Non sò d'onde viene*'?—

136. *Mozart to his father, 18 June 1783, Vienna*

Mon très cher Père,

Congratulations, you're a grandfather! – Yesterday morning, the 17th, at half past 6 my dear wife was safely delivered of a big strong boy who's as round as a ball; – she went into labour at half past 1 in the morning so that neither of us got any rest or sleep. – At 4 o'clock I sent for my mother-in-law – and then for the midwife; – at 6 she was placed in the delivery chair – and by half past 6 it was all over. – My mother-in-law has now made up for all the harm that she caused her daughter while she was *single*. – She remains with her all day. –

My dear wife, who kisses your hands and embraces my dear sister with all her heart, is as well as can be expected in the circumstances; – I hope to God that by taking good care of herself she'll make a full recovery. –

I'm worried about milk-fever! – Her breasts are quite swollen! – Against my will but with my agreement, the child has now got a foster-nurse! – It was always my firm resolve that, whether she was able to or not, my wife should never feed her child herself! – But nor would my child drink the milk of a stranger! – No, I meant to bring it up on water, like my sister and me. – But the midwife, my mother-in-law and most other people here have literally pleaded with me not to do so, simply because most of the children here don't survive on water as the people here don't know how to do it properly – it was this that made me relent as I don't want to have to reproach myself. –

Now for your godfathership! – Let me tell you what's happened. –

I immediately sent word to Baron Wetzlar[1] – a good and true friend of mine – to let him know about my wife's safe delivery; – he immediately came in person – and offered himself as godfather – I couldn't refuse him – and I thought to myself, I can still call him Leopold – and as I was saying this – he said, beside himself with delight, Ah, now you have a little Raimund – and kissed the child – so what could I do? – I had the boy christened Raimund Leopold. – I can honestly say that if you'd not told me your views on this matter in one of your letters, I'd have been deeply embarrassed – and I can't guarantee that I wouldn't have refused him outright! – But your letter consoles me and makes me think that you won't be unhappy with what I've done! – After all, he's also called Leopold.

– I must close now, – I and my newly confined wife kiss your hands 1000 times and we embrace our dear sister 1000 times. We are ever your most obedient children

W. A. C. Mozart

137. Mozart to his father, 12 July 1783, Vienna

Mon très cher Père,

Your letter of the 8th inst. has arrived safely, and I'm delighted to hear that, all praise and thanks be to God, you're both well.

If you insist on regarding genuine obstacles as a ploy designed to pull the wool over your eyes, there's nothing I can do to stop you; – anyone can give something the wrong name if it pleases him to do so – but whether it's right to do so is another question. – Have I ever suggested that I've no wish or desire to see you? – Certainly not! – But you've no doubt noticed that I've no wish to see Salzburg or the archbishop; – if we were to meet on neutral ground, who then would have the wool pulled over his eyes? *The archbishop and not you.* –

1. Raimund, Baron Wetzlar von Plankenstern (1752–1810) had been Wolfgang and Constanze's landlord when they lived at Wipplingerstrasse 14 from December 1782 to April 1783.

I hope I don't need to say that I care very little for Salzburg and nothing whatsoever for the archb., and that I shit on both of them – and that it would never in my life enter my head to go there specially, if you and my sister weren't there – So the whole affair was due simply to the well-meaning care of my good friends, who do after all have a certain amount of sound common sense; – and I didn't think I was acting unreasonably when I made enquiries with you in the matter with a view to following your advice; – my friends' concern was due entirely to the fact that, as I haven't been discharged, he might have me arrested. – – But they've now entirely reassured me – and we're definitely coming in August – or September at the latest; – Herr von Bapius met me in the street and walked home with me; – he left today. – And if he'd not had a prior engagement yesterday, he'd have lunched with me; – dearest father! – You mustn't think that because it's summer, I've nothing to do. – – Not everyone is out of town. – I still have a few pupils to attend to; – I've now got one in composition – he'll no doubt pull a curious face when I tell him about my journey. – I must close now as I still have lots to do. – In the meantime set up the bowling alley in the garden, as my wife is a very great lover of the game; – my wife is still a little concerned that you may not like her as she's not pretty – but I console her as best I can by telling her that my dearest father thinks less of outward than of inner beauty. – Farewell for now. My wife and I kiss your hands 1000 times and embrace our dear sister with all our hearts. We are ever your most obedient children

W. A C. Mozart

In late July 1783, Mozart and Constanze finally set out to visit Leopold and Nannerl in Salzburg, leaving their son in the care of his foster-nurse. Little is known of their time there: Mozart apparently composed the violin and viola duos K423 and 424 for Michael Haydn, who was ill and unable to complete a commission for six such works, and on 26 October the unfinished C minor mass K427 was performed at St Peter's, Constanze singing one of the soprano parts. On 19 August, Raimund Leopold, just two months old, died of 'intestinal cramp'. Wolfgang and Constanze left Salzburg on 27 October; on the way to Vienna they stopped at Linz, where Mozart composed the symphony K425, which was performed on 4 November. They arrived home about mid-November.

138. Mozart to his father, 6 December 1783, Vienna

Mon très cher Père, –

I'd never expected you to write to me in Vienna until I'd told you about my arrival here, and so it was only today that I went to Peisser to ask about letters and found your letter of 21 November, which had already been lying there for 12 days. – I hope you'll have received my letter from here. – There's something I have to ask you. – You'll remember that when you came to Munich and I was writing my grand opera,[1] you complained about the debt of 12 louis d'or that I'd run up with Herr Scherz in Strasbourg, saying: *What really annoys me is your lack of trust in me – but enough of this – I now have the honour of paying 12 louis d'or.* – I travelled to Vienna; – you returned to Salzburg. – From what you said I was bound to think that I no longer needed to worry about this. – Moreover, I assumed that you'd have written to tell me if nothing had been done – or that you would have told me in person when I was with you. – So you can imagine my embarrassment and surprise when two days ago a clerk from the office of the banker Herr Öchser came to see me and brought with him a letter; – the letter was from Herr Haffner in Salzburg and contained an enclosure from Herr Scherz. – As it's now 5 years ago, he's also demanding interest, but I told him at once that there was nothing doing and added that legally I did not owe him a farthing as the bill was payable 6 weeks after the date and had therefore expired. – But in view of Herr Scherz's friendship I agreed that I would pay the capital. – No interest was included, and so I'm not liable for any. – All I ask of you, dearest father, is that you will be kind enough to

1. *Idomeneo.*

stand surety for me with Herr Haffner or rather Herr Triendl for just a month. – With your experience, you can easily imagine how inconvenient it would be for me to be short of cash right now. Herr Öchsei's clerk had to admit that I was right but said only that they'd inform Herr Haffner. – For me, the most disagreeable part of the whole affair is that Herr Scherz won't have a very high opinion of me – proof that chance, coincidence, circumstances, misunderstanding and heaven knows what else can often – and quite innocently – deprive a man of his honour! – Why did Herr Scherz make no attempt to contact me all this time? – Surely my name isn't all that obscure! – My opera – which was performed in Strasbourg – must at least have allowed him to surmise that I was in Vienna. – And then there was his correspondence with Haffner in Salzburg! – If he'd contacted me during the first year, I'd happily have paid him there and then; – I would also do so now – but I'm not in a position to do so at present; – or perhaps he thought he was dealing with a fool who'd pay what he didn't owe. – In that case he can keep the title for himself. – Now for something else. – Only 3 arias are still missing, and then I'll have finished the first act of my opera. – I can really say that I'm entirely satisfied with the *buffa* aria – the quartet – and the finale and that I'm really looking forward to them.[2] – And so I'd be sorry if I'd written this music to no avail, in other words if what is indispensably necessary doesn't happen. – Neither you nor Abbate Varesco nor I have given proper consideration to the thought that it's very bad and may even cause the opera to fail if neither of the 2 main female characters appear on stage until the very last minute but have to keep pacing around in the fortress, either on the bastion or on the ramparts. – I'm confident that I can rely on audiences to remain patient for one act – but they can't possibly hold out for the 2nd act, it's out of the question. – This thought occurred to me only in Linz. – And so there's nothing for it but to have some of the scenes in the 2nd act take place *in the fortress. – Camera della fortezza.* – The scene can be

2. The opera *L'oca del Cairo* ('The Goose of Cairo') K422, to a text by Varesco, was left incomplete by Mozart; the *buffa* aria was 'Siano pronte alle gran nozze', the quartet 'S'oggi, oh Dei, sperar mi fate' and the finale 'Su via, putti, presto, presto!'

arranged in such a way that when Don Pippo orders the goose to be brought into the fortress, we see the room in the fortress where we discover Celidora and Lavina. – Pantea comes in with the goose. – Biondello *slips out*. – They hear Don Pippo coming. Biondello *again becomes the goose*. – At this point we could have a good quintet that would be all the funnier in that the goose could join in. – But I have to say that I raised no objections to this whole story about the goose only because it never occurred to 2 men of greater insight and understanding than I to complain about it. And these 2 men are you and Varesco. – But there's still time to think of some alternative – Biondello once swore that he'd enter the tower; – how he sets about this; whether he enters in the form of a goose or by some other stratagem is all the same. – I'd have thought that it would be far funnier and more natural if Biondello remained in human form. – For example, we could be told right at the start of the 2nd act that Biondello has thrown himself into the sea in his despair at not being able to enter the fortress. – He could then disguise himself as a Turk or whatever and introduce Pantea as a slave girl – a Mooress, of course. – Don Pippo is willing to buy the slave girl as a bride. – As a result the slave dealer and the Moorish girl can enter the fortress in order to be examined. – In this way Pantea has a chance to bully her husband and to be insolent to him in a thousand different ways. And she'd also have a better role, for the more comic an Italian opera the better. – Please make my views known to Abbate Varesco and tell him to get on with it. – I've already worked fast enough in this short space of time. – Indeed, I could have finished the whole of the first act if I didn't need to have some of the words changed in a number of the arias; – *but please don't tell him this at present*. – – My German opera *Die Entführung aus dem Serail* has been given in Prague and Leipzig – very well – and to great applause. – I know this from people who saw them there – I'll make an effort to go and see Herr von Deglmann[3] and give him the cadenzas together with the concerto and the 4 ducats. – But please send me *my Idomeneo* as soon as

---

3. Bernhard, Baron Deglmann, councillor in the Bohemian-Austrian chancellery.

possible – also the 2 violin duets – and Seb. Bach's fugues[4] – I need Idomeneo as I'll be giving 6 subscription concerts this Lent in addition to my concert[5] at the theatre. And I'd like to perform this opera then; – could you also ask Tomaselli to let us have the prescription for the ointment for rashes, which has done us sterling service: – you never know when you may need it again – or at least be able to help someone else with it. – It's always better for me to have it than to wish I had it. – Adieu for now – my wife and I kiss your hands 1000 times and embrace our dear sister with all our hearts. We are ever your most obedient children

W. and C. Mozart

P. S.: Please give Varesco a good talking to and tell him to hurry up. – Please also send the music soon. – We kiss Gretl, Heinrich and Hanni.[6] – I'll shortly be writing to Gretl. Tell Heinrich that both here and in Linz I've already been singing his praises; – he should move on to *staccato*. – Only on this point can the Viennese not forget Lamotte.[7] – *Adieu*.

On 22 and 23 December, Mozart performed an unidentified piano concerto at the concert mounted by the Vienna Tonkünstler-Sozietät; in addition, Adamberger sang a newly composed scena, probably Misero! o sogno – Aura che intorno spiri *K431. In January, Mozart and Constanze moved to the Trattnerhof, Am Graben 591–596. Shortly afterwards, on 9 February, Mozart began to keep a catalogue of his newly composed works; the first*

4. K423 and 424; Bach's fugues cannot be identified with certainty. About 1782 Mozart had arranged five fugues from Book II of *The Well-Tempered Keyboard* for string quartet (nos. 1–5, K405).
5. For the Vienna Tonkünstler-Sozietät.
6. Maria Margarethe (Gretl) was the sister of Heinrich Marchand, Leopold's pupil; Maria Johanna (Hanni) Brochard (1775–?), daughter of the Munich dancer Georg Paul Brochard, was another pupil.
7. The violinist Franz Lamotte.

entry in the catalogue is the piano concerto K449, composed for his pupil Barbara von Ployer (1765–c. 1811).

139. Mozart to his father, 20 February 1784, Vienna

Mon très cher Père, –

Your last letter has arrived safely; – yesterday I was lucky enough to hear Herr Freyhold[1] play a concerto of his own decomposition. – I found very little in his playing and missed a great deal; – double-tonguing is his only claim to virtuosity – otherwise there's absolutely nothing to hear – I was glad that the adagio was at least short – he played it at your house to start off with, the musicians accompanying him couldn't make head nor tail of it because it's written in four-four time but he played it alla breve – and when I added alla breve in my own hand, he admitted that Papa had also complained about it in Salzburg. – The rondo was supposed to be lively but was the stupidest thing in the world, – during the opening allegro I thought that if Herr Freyhold were to learn how to compose properly, he'd not be a bad composer. – I was very sorry to hear that Herr Hafeneder had died so suddenly, especially because you'll now be burdened with all the *seccatura*:[2] but I can't say that the prince was in the wrong; in his place I'd have done exactly the same; – but I'd have accompanied my instructions with an increase in salary and arranged for the boys to go to you – or I'd have given you free board and lodging in the chapel-house. – 2 gentlemen are coming to Salzburg in a day or so, a vice-*contrôleur* and a cook; – I'll probably ask them to take with them a sonata, a symphony and a new concerto.[3] – The symphony is in full score, and I'd be grateful if you could have it copied some time and sent back to me; but you could also give it away or have it

1. Johann Philipp Freyhold, flautist in service to the Margrave of Baden-Durlach.
2. 'annoyance', meaning that Leopold would be burdened with additional teaching duties to the boys at the Chapel House.
3. Possibly K448, K425 'Linz', K449.

performed wherever you like. – The concerto is also in full score and should be copied and returned to me, but as quickly as possible – please ensure that you don't show it *to a single soul* as I've written it for Fräulein Ployer, who has paid a lot for it – As for the sonata, you can hang on to it. – There's something I must ask and that I know absolutely nothing about and don't understand either. – If you have something printed or engraved at your own expense, how can you be sure that you're not cheated by the engraver? – After all, he can run off as many copies as he wants to and in that way swindle you. – You'd have to keep these people under constant supervision – which wasn't possible when you had your book printed because you were in Salzburg and the book was printed in Augsburg. – I'm inclined not to sell any more of my things to any of the engravers here but to have them printed or engraved by subscription at my own expense, as most people do and have a good profit to show for it; I'm not worried about finding subscribers – I've already received offers from Paris and Warsaw. – Could you let me have some information on this? – And I've another favour to ask of you. Would it be possible for me to have at least a copy of my certificate of baptism? – They're all claiming here that I must have been at least 10 years old when I first came here. – The emperor himself contradicted me to my face last year in the Augarten. – Herr von Strack now believes me *at my word*. – If I could show them my certificate of baptism, I could shut them all up once and for all. – Farewell for now. – My wife and I kiss your hands 1000 times and embrace our dear sister with all our hearts. We are ever your most obedient children

W. and C. Mozart

140. Mozart to his father, 3 March 1784, Vienna

Mon très cher Père, –

Your letter of 24 Feb. has arrived safely; – it's better if you always use the post – I received this letter on Monday, whereas I wouldn't have received it till Tuesday or even Wednesday if you'd sent it via

Peisser. – I haven't received the concertos[1] but shall go at once and make enquiries at Artaria's. – You must forgive me for writing so little but I simply don't have time as I'm giving 3 subscription concerts in Trattner's Room[2] on the last 3 Wednesdays in Lent, starting on the 17th of this month,[3] for which I already have 100 subscribers and expect to get another 30 by then. – I'm charging 6 florins for all 3 concerts. – I'll probably give 2 concerts in the theatre this year[4] – well, you can easily imagine that I'll have to play some new works – so I'll have to write some. – The whole morning is taken up with pupils. – And I have to play nearly every evening. – Below you'll see a list of all the concerts at which I *definitely* have to play. – But I must tell you very quickly how it's come about that I'm suddenly giving private concerts. – The piano virtuoso Herr *Richter*[5] is giving 6 Saturday concerts in the above-mentioned hall. – The nobility subscribed but said that they'd no great wish to attend if I didn't play. Herr Richter asked me to do so – I promised to play for him 3 times – and arranged a subscription for 3 concerts of my own, to which everyone signed up. –

Thursday the 26th of Feb. at Galitzin's.
Monday the 1st of March at Johann Esterházy's.
Thursday the 4th at Galitzin's.
Friday the 5th at Esterházy's.
Monday the 8th Esterházy.
Thursday the 11th Galitzin.
Friday the 12th Esterházy.
Monday the 15th Esterházy.
Wednesday the 17th my first *private* concert.
Thursday the 18th Galitzin.
Friday the 19th Esterházy.
Saturday the 20th at Richter's.

1. Presumably K413–415.
2. The Trattnerhof, the property owned by Johann Thomas von Trattner and his wife where Mozart and Constanze were renting rooms, included a concert hall.
3. The two subsequent concerts took place on 24 and 31 March.
4. In the event, Mozart gave only one concert, on 1 April.
5. Georg Friedrich Richter (*c.* 1759–89).

Sunday the 21st my first concert in the *theatre*[6]
Monday the 22nd Esterházy.
Wednesday the 24th my 2nd private concert
Thursday the 25th Galitzin.
Friday the 26th Esterházy
Saturday the 27th Richter
Monday the 29th Esterházy
Wednesday the 31st my 3rd *private* concert.
Thursday the 1st of April. My 2nd concert in the theatre.
Saturday the 3rd Richter.
Don't I have enough to do? – I don't think I'll get out of practice at this rate. –
Adieu. – We kiss both your hands and embrace our dear sister with all our hearts. We are ever your most obedient children

W. A. Mozart

141. Mozart to his father, 10 April 1784, Vienna

Mon très cher Père,

Please don't be angry with me for not having written to you for so long; – but you know how much I've had to do during that time! – With my 3 subscription concerts I've covered myself in glory. – My concert at the theatre also turned out very well. – I wrote 2 grand concertos and also a quintet[1] that was extraordinarily well received; – I myself think it's the best thing I've ever written. – It's scored for *1 oboe, 1 clarinet, 1 horn, 1 bassoon* and *pianoforte*; – I wish you could have heard it! – And how well it was performed! – To tell the truth, I was quite tired by the end – from all that playing – and it does me no little credit that my listeners were *never* tired.[2] – I now have an errand for you; old Baron du Beyne de Malechamp – who has all

6. This concert did not take place.
1. K450 and 451, K452.
2. The other works on the programme included the 'Linz' symphony K425, arias sung by Adamberger, Cavalieri and Luigi Marchesi (1755–1829), a famous castrato.

kinds of music, good and bad – would very much like to have *Gatti's* rondò and duetto. – *Recit. 'Ah! Non sdegnarti o cara'.* – *Rondò. 'Nel lasciarti in questo istante'.* – *Duetto. 'Ne' giorni tuoi felici'* etc.[3] I'd be most obliged to you if you could procure these 2 pieces for me as soon as possible. – I'll transfer the money for copying them via Herr Peisser. Today I finished another new concerto for Fräulein Ployer;[4] – and I'm now half dressed in readiness for a visit to Prince Kaunitz. – Yesterday I played at Leopold Pálffy's.[5] – Tomorrow at the concert that Mlle Bayer is giving.[6] – Something else – as Hafeneder has died, Herr von Ployer[7] has been commissioned to look for a violinist. – I secretly recommended a certain *Menzel*[8] – a handsome and clever young man. – But I told him not to mention my name, otherwise it may not work out. – He's now awaiting the decision. – I think he'll be getting 400 florins – and a suit I told him off about the suit it's like begging. – If anything comes of it, I'll give Menzel a letter for you, together with the music; – and you'll find that he's a delightful violin player who's also good at sight-reading; – in *Vienna* no one has sight-read my quartets[9] as well as he has. – And he's the nicest person in the world, someone who will be only too pleased to make music with you whenever you like. – I also included him in the orchestra at my concerts. – I must close now; my wife and I kiss your hands 1000 times and embrace our dear sister with all our hearts. We are ever your obed. children

Mozart

3. The texts are from Metastasio's *L'Olimpiade*; Gatti's settings date from 1775.
4. K453.
5. Leopold III, Count Pálffy.
6. There is no record that this concert took place.
7. The civil servant Gottfried Ignaz von Ployer (*c.* 1743–97), a cousin of Barbara von Ployer's father, the tax collector and timber merchant Franz Kajetan von Ployer (1734–1803); Barbara lived at Gottfried's house.
8. Zeno Franz Menzel (1756–1823) did not get the post but later became violinist in the Vienna court chapel.
9. Although these quartets cannot be identified with certainty, they probably included the first three of the quartets dedicated to Haydn, K387, 421 and 428; see also letter 148.

142. Mozart to his father, 24 April 1784, Vienna

We now have the famous Strinasacchi[1] from Mantua here, a very good violinist; she brings a lot of taste and feeling to her playing. – I'm currently working on a sonata that we'll be playing together at her concert at the theatre on Thursday.[2] Also, some quartets have just appeared by a certain Pleyel; he's a pupil of Joseph Haydn.[3] If you don't know them, try to get hold of them; they're worth it. They're very well written, and very enjoyable; you'll also recognize his teacher in them. It'll be good – and fortunate for music if in due course Pleyel is able to replace Haydn for us!

143. Mozart to his father, 26 May 1784, Vienna

Mon très cher Père, –

I see from your last letter that my letter and the music have arrived safely. – Many thanks to my sister for her letter, I'll certainly be writing to her as soon as time permits: – meanwhile please tell her that Herr Richter is wrong about the key of the concerto, or else I've misread her letter. – The concerto that Herr Richter praised to her so highly is the one in *B flat*[1] – this is the first one that I wrote and that he also praised to me at the time. – I can't choose between them – they're both concertos that make you sweat. – But the one in B flat is more difficult than the one in D.[2] – I should add that I'm very curious to know which of the 3 in B flat, D and G[3] you and my sister like best; – the one in E flat[4] doesn't belong in this group. – This is

1. Regina Strinasacchi (1764–1839), a twenty-year-old violin virtuosa.
2. K454; the concert, attended by the emperor, was on 29 April 1784 at the Kärntnertortheater.
3. Ignaz Joseph Pleyel (1757–1831) studied with Haydn from 1772 to 1777.
1. K450.
2. K451.
3. K453.
4. K449.

a concerto of a very special kind and written more for a small orchestra than a large one – so we're really only talking about the 3 grand concertos. – I'm curious to know whether your opinion coincides with the *general* opinion here and also with my *own* opinion – of course, you need to hear all 3 of them well performed and with all the parts. – I don't mind waiting for their return – as long as no one else gets hold of them. – Only today I could have got 24 ducats for one of them; – but I think it'll be more useful if I hold on to them for a couple of years and only then have them engraved.[5] – I must tell you something about Liserl Schwemmer.[6] She wrote to her mother, but she addressed it in such a way that the post office was most unlikely to have accepted it, as it read:

> This letter to be deli
> vered to my very dear
> mother in Salzburg
> Barbarüschbemer[7]
> to be handed in at the
> Jüdengasse in mer
> chant Eberl's house
> on the third floor.

So I told her that I'd readdress it for her. – Out of curiosity and in order to read more of this prize document rather than to discover any secrets, I broke open the letter. – In it she complains that she gets to bed too late and has to get up too early, though I'd have thought one can get enough sleep from 11 till 6. That's 7 hours, after all. – We don't go to bed till around 12 and get up at half past 5 or even 5 as we go to the Augarten nearly every morning. She goes on to complain about the food, which she does in the most insolent language: – she herself has to go hungry, she says, and the four of us – my wife and I, the cook and she herself – don't have as much to eat as she and

---

5. Apparently Mozart did not wait: at least some of the concertos were available in manuscript copies from the Viennese music dealer Lorenz Lausch (?1737–94) as early as 10 July 1784. Only the concerto K453 was published in an engraved edition during Mozart's lifetime (Speyer: Bossler, 1787).

6. The Mozarts' maid.

7. Barbara Schwemmer.

her mother used to have between them . . . you know that I took on this girl purely out of pity, so that as a stranger in Vienna she'd have some kind of support. – We agreed to give her 12 florins a year, and she was entirely satisfied with this, though she now complains about it in her letter. – And what does she have to do? – To clear the table, carry the food in and out and help my wife to dress and undress. – And, apart from her sewing, she's the clumsiest and stupidest person in the world. – She can't even light a fire, let alone make coffee. – These are things that anyone claiming to be a parlourmaid should be able to do. – We gave her a florin; by the next day she was demanding more money. – I got her to give me an account of how she'd spent the money, and it turned out that most of it had gone on beer. – It was a certain Herr Johannes who travelled here with her, but who'd better not show his face here again. – *Twice* when we were out, he came here, ordered *wine*, and the girl, who's not used to drinking wine, drank so much that she couldn't walk but had to be supported and on the last occasion was sick all over her bed. – What sort of people would keep on a person who carries on in this way? – I'd have been content with the lecture I gave her and wouldn't have mentioned it to you, but the impertinence of her letter to her mother has persuaded me to write to you. – Could I ask you, therefore, to send for her mother and tell her that I'll put up with her a little while longer but that she should try and find a job elsewhere – if I wanted to make people unhappy, I'd get rid of her on the spot. – There's something in her letter about a certain Herr Antoni – perhaps he's a future husband. –

I must close now. – My wife thanks you both for your good wishes on her pregnancy and coming confinement, which will probably be in early October. – We both kiss your hands and embrace our dear sister with all our hearts and are ever your most obedient children

W. and C. Mozart

P. S.: We've not been able to do anything about the apron, whether in fine linen, crêpe or muslin as my wife doesn't know whether you want one *untrimmed*. – These cost about a ducat but aren't worn. –

Those with a trimming that's at all attractive cost at least 7 florins in local currency. – And so we await your next letter, and her needs will then be attended to at once. *Addio*.

Could I ask you to send the *buckles* by the next mail coach – I'm dying to see them. –

144. Mozart to his sister, 18 August 1784, Vienna

Ma très chère sœur, –

Good grief! – It's high time that I wrote if I want my letter to find you still a vestal virgin! – A few days more and – it'll be gone![1] –

My wife and I wish you every joy and happiness in your change of state and are only sorry that we shan't have the pleasure of attending your wedding; but we hope to embrace you as Frau von Sonnenburg and your husband next spring both in Salzburg and St Gilgen; – there's no one we feel more sorry for than our dear father, who's now to be left entirely on his own! – Of course, you're not far away and he can often drive out to see you[2] – but he's now tied to that damned Chapel House again! – If I were in my father's place, I'd do as follows: – as someone who's already served him for so long, I'd ask the archbishop to allow me to retire – and on receipt of my pension, I'd go and live quietly with my daughter in St Gilgen; – if the archbishop turned down my request, I'd demand my dismissal and go and live with my son in Vienna; – and it's this that I'd most like to ask you to do, namely, that you try to persuade him to do this; – I've said the same in my letter to him today. – And now I send you 1000 good wishes from Vienna to Salzburg and in particular hope that the two of you may live together as well as we do; – so please accept a small piece of advice from my poetical brainbox; listen:

1. On 23 August 1784, Nannerl, at the age of thirty-three, married Johann Baptist Franz von Berchtold zu Sonnenburg of St Gilgen.
2. St Gilgen was about a six-hour coach ride from Salzburg.

In wedlock you'll learn things, by God,
That once seemed really rather odd;
You'll soon discover – yes, you too –
What Eve herself was forced to do
Before she could give birth to Cain.
But wedlock's duties are so light
That you'll perform them with delight
And easily ignore the pain.
But wedlock's joys are also mixed.
So if your husband's scowl is fixed
And if he acts in ways that you,
Dear sister, feel you don't deserve
And if he proves bad-tempered too,
Remember he's a man and say
'Thy will be done, O Lord, by day,
But then by night my own I'll do!'

Your honest brother
W. A. Mozart

Although Leopold Mozart's letters to Wolfgang are lost, Leopold corresponded regularly with Nannerl between 1784 and early 1787. This rich correspondence includes numerous details of Mozart's life in Vienna, including information from some otherwise lost letters from Wolfgang to his father.

145. Leopold Mozart to his daughter, 9 September 1784, Salzburg

I've not had a moment to myself till now as I was fully occupied arranging for the piano to be sent to Munich: and I'll be heartily glad when I've sorted out the business with the maidservants. I hope to receive a reply from you tomorrow. In the meantime I'll tell you about the *seccatura* I've had. Lieutenant *Hofler's* wife came to see me, hoping that I'd recommend their daughter as a parlourmaid – presumably part chambermaid, part parlourmaid. She can do everything! She's learnt to *make mob caps* and *trim clothes* etc. etc. from Herberstein's chambermaid, and Countess Lützow's valet has taught her how to *dress hair*; – – all according to the latest fashion. If need be, she can also cook. She'd even be willing to lay aside her white cap, if it were found displeasing, and wear the black cap of a parlourmaid etc. etc. – I told her that I'd already written to tell you about 2 other parlourmaids and that it may now be too late as a decision would probably come with the next postman, but that I couldn't pass on the information as the postman comes only once a week. She even had the idea of taking her daughter out to see you and presenting her to you, but I talked her out of that. She told me that her daughter had been with Countess *Sinzendorf*: but of course no one could survive for long there. She then worked as a chambermaid in *Fribourg*, where she ate with her employers, – but both she and the baroness were under the thumb of the parlourmaid, who ruled the roost and ran the whole household in Fribourg as she was the master of the house's mistress – and it's even said that a couple of parlourmaids or chambermaids had already been brought to bed before her. She also told me that she'd heard with some surprise that a certain soldier's daughter was to come out to you as 3rd maid. She asks me not to burden my daughter with this cross because the wench is not used to working, is lazy, can only knit and would be useful only for running errands. – I fobbed Madame off as best I could by promising to tell you all this at the first opportunity. I then made enquiries about the soldier's daughter and discovered that she's called Franziska Hapfinger. I thought of going up to see Frau von Hermes[1] on the Kapuzinerberg in order to find out more, but fortunately she herself came down to see me in her negligee at 8 in the evening, just as I was having supper: and I discovered that this wench is the daughter of that Mönchsberg Babette who was held in such ill repute;

1. Anna Helena née Wohlhaupt (1723–97), wife of the grenadier captain Johann Joseph Hermann Hermes von Fürstenhof (1723–1809).

and that was enough for me! – I also – and unnecessarily – went in secret to see the grenadier captain and demanded that he and his wife be honest with me and tell me the truth. They confirmed everything and said this woman was quite incapable of working. She'd been in Austria – or perhaps in Vienna – for a very short time, but her mother had soon sent a hired coachman to look for her: but she asked me to keep this to myself and not admit that I'd made enquiries with them as these people were the devil himself, but they owed it to me to tell me the truth. My dear daughter has not, of course, got to know the girl's mother and has not been taken in by her daughter's eloquence and powerful appearance: if I'd seen the mother, none of this would have happened, for I know her. The *florin* that I gave her is therefore a form of alms, and we need to turn our thoughts to another maid. On the other hand, I've saved my son[2] 4 florins in another context. His *brother, the head clerk*, told the postmaster that my son would pay the money for the 4 days on his arrival. I wanted to pay him, but he refused to accept it as he wanted to be paid 3 florins a day – *in other words, 12 florins in all*. But he had to make do with 2 florins a day: so I paid him *8 florins*. – My son can now console himself for the florin that the wench received, as he's saved 3 florins and been spared a lot of bother.

10 Sept.

I've just received your letter and see that you're already provided with a parlourmaid. – On the one hand, I'm glad as the *seccatura* I've had with these wenches is now over; and I'll tell the soldier's daughter that you've found someone else as this one is really no good, – but if we still need to look round for another one, I'll need to know very soon: but I don't think you'll have any difficulty finding one.

But I'm surprised that the days are now getting almost too short for you to write a letter every week, the last of which was *undated*, or for you to read the newspapers. I've no objections to the way you arrange your day, except the 3 hours spent playing the piano from 2 till 5 and then only 1 hour for walking.

2. i.e. his son-in-law.

The weather here has been uninterruptedly fine and I'd have come and paid you a surprise visit if I hadn't received instructions from the archbishop to prepare a list of the entire court music staff and their salaries etc. and now have to wait and see what happens next. Hearty congratulations to my son on being bled. It was high time that you visited Strobl: how could you keep postponing it in such fine weather? – And St Wolfgang?[3] – – I'm almost prepared to wager that I'll get to St Wolfgang before my daughter: – O you stay-at-homes, you'll soon be nestling up against the stove! – I'm always out and about by 5 and never return before the Angelus, and on the Nativity of the Blessed Virgin Mary I set off for Mülln at 2, from there I went to see the administrator, then to Maxglan and returned at 7 via the Neutor. Meanwhile we've had target practice on the 5th and there'll be another one on the 12th, the day after tomorrow. We'll be continuing till Michaelmas. – But I don't know what will happen after that. For now, I'm being well looked after: but Veronica[4] is definitely going to Lofer, though she'll remain to do the cooking until you leave, and only then will she return home as she's in no hurry to do so. – I'm sending by post *the machine and all that goes with it*. Also *an apron* that Thresel, the town clerk's daughter, brought. And the old *burnt bodice*. There's still an old green one here.

Mme Zezi[5] has returned the jewels: everyone likes them – only the bride wanted something *jingly-jangly* to hang down more at the front instead of the drops. She's now taken it to the fair at Bozen and hopes to find some *jingly-jangly* jewels there. The wedding should already have taken place, but she asked for it to be held in Salzburg in October or November or even postponed until the new year; she doesn't seem to be impressed by her bridegroom's *jingle-jangle*. Meanwhile I've taken custody of the trinkets, as Mme Zezi says she may have changed her mind by the time she returns. Keep well and be happy, I am ever my dear son's and dear daughter's honest father

Mozart

3. Strobl and St Wolfgang are villages not far from St Gilgen.
4. Leopold's cook.
5. Maria Anna Zezi, wife of the merchant Johann Bernhard Zezi (1742–1813).

The Schiedenhofens are still in Triebenbach. The Hagenauers, Sallerl Joly, Monsieur d'Ippold,[6] the company of marksmen, Captain Hermes of the Grenadiers from the Kapuzinerberg etc etc. all send their best wishes, especially Herr Marchand in his last letter. Bologna[7] in particular would come out to see you if I could come with him, – but he's afraid of travelling and in any case doesn't really have time as he can travel to Munich with the empty coaches that will then be bringing back the merchants, and they're coming at the end of next week.

On my way back here I lost the key to the little trunk that was in my room in St Gilgen – unless I left it behind in my room, perhaps on *the small wardrobe*.

I kiss the children and hope that Fräulein Nannerl will study hard, just like Wolfg.[8] *Addio!*

146. Leopold Mozart to his daughter, 19 November 1784, Salzburg

To mark his name day, my son[1] gave a small concert, at which some of his *pupils* performed and, in addition, Baron Bagge[2] from Paris amused the company with a violin concerto: *There was so much laughter!* he writes, and goes on: *I've received my sister's letter and hope that in the meantime she'll have received mine too.* Presumably he means the letter to me. I expect you already know that we've 2 new stewards. We'd got only 4 left to carry the canopy during Hours, as the others had either gone to meet their maker or were invalids and cripples, so

6. Franz Armand d'Ippold (*c.* 1730–91), court military councillor in Salzburg; Nannerl Mozart had been disappointed in her hopes of marrying him.
7. Michelangelo Bologna, castrato active in Salzburg 1782–4.
8. Two of Nannerl's step-children, Anna Margarete (Nannerl) and Wolfgang. Johann Berchtold zu Sonnenburg, a widower twice over, had five children by his previous marriages.
1. Leopold usually means his son-in-law when he writes 'my son' in his letters to Nannerl, but here he refers to Wolfgang, whose name day was 31 October.
2. The amateur musician; see letter 87.

the prince was forced to look for a couple of young lads to bear the heavy burden of the canopy.[3] *Cajetan Antretter* has already been a trainee at the court council for some time and it was high time he was given something. And so he received *motu proprio* his certificate as steward, together with 15 florins and the salutary reminder to make himself worthy of further high favours by assiduously attending council meetings. Young Anton *Mehofer*, who married Joseph Capeller's daughter and who's long held some other post that I can't remember, received a similar certificate, but I don't know if he also got any extra; meanwhile they both had to pay 25 florins tax on their character references. – Thurner, the army paymaster, was buried some time ago. *Die Entführung aus dem Serail* was fairly well staged on the 17th. It received the greatest applause and 3 numbers were repeated: by 5 o'clock it was impossible to get into the lower part of the theatre, and it was completely full at the top by a quarter past. The Plaz children and their governess, Katherl, had to sit right at the front of the stalls. It'll be performed again on Sunday the 21st: after that they'll probably take it off for 5 weeks. The whole town is pleased with it. Even the archbishop was kind enough to say: *it's really not bad*. I hear they took in 181 florins. The aria with obbligato instruments[4] was played by *Stadler* on the violin (which is easy), *Feiner* on the oboe, *Reiner* on the flute and *Fiala* on the cello, and it went very well. Herr Cassel had been asked to play the flute: he came to the first rehearsal but told Stadler the next day that he'd not be coming any more and that they should find someone else as rehearsing was too boring for him; everyone, even the nobility, took this very amiss. Conversely, Herr Fiala not only played but even refused to accept a fee, saying that he'd done it as a favour for Herr Schmidt[5] and more especially as a favour for Herr Mozart.[6]

3. The stewards were required to carry a canopy over the archbishop's head during services in the cathedral.
4. 'Martern aller Arten'. Of the court musicians mentioned here, nothing for certain is known of Reiner: for the others, see letters 54 and 100.
5. Ludwig Schmidt (*c.* 1740–1814), director of the Ansbach-Bayreuth comedy troupe that was putting on *Die Entführung*.
6. Meaning Leopold.

The postman has just arrived. The seat prices for the opera weren't raised, only the subscription was suspended.

Gretl sang admirably and was much applauded by the elector, who spoke to her afterwards, and also by Maestro Prati etc.[7] You know that people had been waiting to see who'd be the *seconda donna* as *Lisel Wendling* refused to play the *seconda donna* to Madame *Lebrun*, especially because on this occasion she'd such an insignificant part with *2 very short and worthless ariettas*. But since *Lisel Wendling* saw no hope for her daughter,[8] she herself took on this worthless part so that Gretl couldn't steal a march on her and in that way prevented Gretl from appearing at the electoral opera and enhancing her own reputation. Meanwhile she's[9] sent her daughter and husband to Paris. I've not heard a word about Bologna, except that when Pacchierotti[10] was there, I'm told he was again ill and had to be bled. I have to reply to a *long letter* or, rather, *2 letters* from Marchand, but since I can write only a little at each sitting, I'll have to devote a whole week to it in order to deal with everything properly. I'm supposed to go *to Munich* – I'm supposed to go *to Vienna* and God knows where else. Oh! If only I were my own master! I'd soon pack up and leave. As soon as I know *about the post*, I'll ensure that the *glass carrier* has something to take with her.[11]

The boxes that I sent you must of course be returned as I always need boxes when sending things. The one containing the pears belongs in any case to Herr d'Ippold. Now that the weather's turned colder, I've bought 6 lbs of good-quality beef and am having it boiled at home. Of the chickens that I've been fattening up, I occasionally get one roasted at the local inn; and this works very well; I'll have the

---

7. Margarethe (Gretl) Marchand had sung at a 'Concert des Amateurs', a private undertaking, in Munich attended by Elector Karl Theodor; Alessio Prati (1750–88) was a composer.
8. Dorothea Wendling (1767–1839) became virtuosa da camera in Munich in 1788.
9. Lisel Wendling.
10. Gasparo Pacchierotti (1744–1821), castrato.
11. Leopold and Nannerl used the glass carrier, who seems to have made a regular round trip between Salzburg and St Gilgen, as a postal service. It is not known what sort of glass she carried, or why.

last one the day after tomorrow. And so half my food comes from the inn, the other half I provide myself: if I've got something in the house, I get it prepared there. What I usually send for is some soup and a sausage at midday, or cabbage, sometimes with a liver sausage, maybe lights or tripe or calves' feet or preserved meat – most of this I usually keep back for the evening, when Tresel boils up some of the soup or else boils a piece of my beef or gets something from the landlord or cooks some rice or barley that I've bought myself, as everything that comes from the inn has without exception had vinegar added. In short, I live a soldier's life – *if I have something, I eat it, day in day out*. Patience! – –

If I can't find the Haydn variations,[12] I can always get a copy of them from Count Leopold Arco. – Baron Rechberg[13] is no longer coming but is going to Strasbourg instead. – *There was no tempo marking* on the score of the concerto in G,[14] so I didn't add one. –

Baron Bagge is, of course, a very old fool. At his concerts in Paris he always scraped away at the first violin, occasionally playing the flute in the most wretched manner imaginable: only in old age has he hit on the mad idea of wanting to play concertos and making himself look foolish. – As for the war that's currently being waged in the theatre, there's nothing in the least edifying about it, it involved only that *troublemaker Herr Reinike*, who then stirred up Mattausch and Litter.[15] Everything's now calm again.

It's a few weeks now since Frau Schörkhofer sent me this cook. – As far as I know, she's from Kammer, is neatly dressed, with a golden Linz mob cap; she limps – one of her legs must be shorter than the other – but she certainly walks down the street quickly enough. She's not old, – but nor is she very young. At least she's *not at all pretty*: but not exactly ugly either: in her dress she's neat and tidy. I'll speak to Frau Schörkhofer and tell her everything. That she should be

---

12. Unidentified.
13. Alois, Count Rechberg (1766–1849). He and his brother Anton, Count Rechberg (1776–1837) were friends of Mozart's in Vienna.
14. K453.
15. Players in Ludwig Schmidt's troupe.

corrupted is hardly a danger: no one will be placed in temptation's way by this woman.

I feel exactly the same about the war as my son:[16] I read the newspapers every day and always look at the map of Holland; but I'm not making any plans. Count Weissenwolf has been enlisted and has already left for his regiment, which is one of those that's supposed to be going to the Netherlands. *Buon viaggio!* – I must close now and get to bed. I kiss you and the children with all my heart and am ever your honest father

L. Mozart

Hanchen[17] has written both to *me* and *Herr Hagenauer*. The Schiedenhofens didn't return from Triebenbach until last Saturday evening. I'll drop round tomorrow, they weren't at home when I called yesterday.

147. Leopold Mozart to his daughter, [after 21] November 1784, Salzburg

I'm writing this in advance of a possible visit from the woman who transports the glass. The opera[1] was performed again on Sunday to the greatest possible acclaim, it's now becoming so popular that the whole town is praising it and describing it as the most wonderful work. Herr Haydn sat behind the keyboard in the orchestra; of course everyone kept asking him his opinion, and he said: *this opera needed only to have an orchestra of 60–70 persons and the necessary intermediary instruments, namely, clarinets and english horn, whose parts had to be played on violas here – only then would you hear what an admirable work it is. He couldn't have been more pleased.* – The opera will not be taken

16. Leopold agrees with his son-in-law about the current political unrest in the Austrian Netherlands.
17. Maria Johanna Brochard, Leopold's former pupil. In 1790 she obtained a post with the Munich court theatre.
1. *Die Entführung aus dem Serail.*

off *till Christmas*, when there'll be 2 more performances. Countess Gundacker[2] said that the more she's seen the opera, the more she's liked it. Blonde's duet with Pedrillo and her own aria were again repeated: the drinking song *Vivat Bacchus* even had to be repeated *3 times*. – All who've seen it in Vienna are unanimous in saying that the acting at the theatre here is better – it's livelier and more natural and the whole performance is more committed than in Vienna. Much the same has been said by Count *von Eltz* and the 2 Barons Fechenbach, who've seen it in Berlin, Mainz and Mannheim.[3] The latter are the brothers of Baron Fechenbach, who's now dean of Mainz cathedral and who was with us in Lyons[4] with Baron Wayer and Canon Schultheiss. – At his Excellency's supreme command, Herr Haydn was supposed to write an opera for these people: and on the prince's orders Herr Schmidt had to submit all the German opera texts he could find in order for them to be examined, but unfortunately nothing suitable could be found. Both Haydn and Schmidt were extremely pleased at this. Herr Schmidt said: if I'm to do myself credit, I can't rehearse a new work in under *4 weeks*, as we always have 3 other works to rehearse every week. And Herr Haydn said he couldn't toss anything off that would be a credit to him; he said that at some later date he'd prefer to write an Italian opera for the archbish. – – But he knows that this is a long way off as there's no one here to sing it: – at least one foreign female will first have to be begged to come here. So these plans are all currently in the air! And nothing has been decided.

I sent for Frau Schörkhofer and discussed the matter in detail with her, examining it in its entirety. I can honestly say that I'm sorry that I'm saddled with old Tresel, she'd have made an excellent servant as I need one who's good at sewing in order to repair my cuffs and other things and I've often no one or have to pay through the nose. I've thought about it a lot and think that my son may know her

2. The archbishop's sister-in-law.
3. *Die Entführung* was given at Mainz on 24 January 1784 and at Mannheim on 18 April 1784. The earliest documented performance in Berlin is 16 October 1788, some four years after the date of this letter.
4. In late July 1766.

foster-parents and may even have dined with them. He's the *manager of the brewery at Schörfling near Kammer*: because he and his wife have no children, they agreed to foster this child, as her own father, a dissolute man, had run off and abandoned her and her brother, who was taken in by his godfather, a potter. Her foster-mother would now like her to find a job somewhere else and thinks that it would help her to make her way in the world if she didn't stay in Schörfling. Since she's been here, *Countess Engl* has been sending her mob caps to stitch as she used to make them for her previously; she also had to sew mob caps for Baroness Rehlingen here. Frau Schörkhofer says she's not very quick at stitching mob caps but that they couldn't be neater or prettier etc. and that she's a methodical, tidy, God-fearing person, I've noticed her in church at Holy Trinity. The prison governor's wife wants to employ her as a cook, but she doesn't want to work there – and she's quite right – to work as a prison cook doesn't sound very nice. Nor does she want to cook for a member of the clergy – because of the malicious gossip – and once again she's right. – She's not worried about the pay, because, as far as I can see, her foster-parents are providing her clothes: there's only one difficulty – namely, the fact that the work is very hard; for although – according to Frau Schörkhofer – she thinks that she can do everything, Frau Schörkhofer feels, as I do, that she won't be able to carry wood and water, not least because she *limps a little*, having been crippled as a child, with the result that one leg is slightly withered and shorter than the other. To tell the truth, I've spoken only once to this person – and then only briefly: but she struck me as a quiet, rather shy but a very clean and capable person. –

For the present I must protest *in optima forma* that I have no wish to get involved: – but I wish to express an opinion and, indeed, must do so and say what I, as an honest man, think and what everyone is bound to think given the state of the world at present: namely, that servants are one of the biggest problems of domestic life and that it's now more difficult than ever to find good servants. That they're often less intelligent, that they cheat their employers more than they used to over articles of luxury and that, into the bargain, they demand better pay is indubitably clear from our everyday experience. And so

I can no longer say: *it was always like this; that's how my parents did it.* Times have changed. – Also, my son must bear in mind that *he has young children.* If Nannerl[5] learns how to *sew* and *stitch mob caps* and do other *linenwork*, if she sees *good home cooking* and mixes with servants who have a little more style and who don't set her a bad example, and if she doesn't always hear stupid and silly things, it'll be of more use to her than if she's surrounded by *coarse and clumsy peasants* and *infatuated and foolish mares*, all too easily acquiring peasant customs and expressions that she'll never entirely get rid of. *Well, everything will sort itself out*: I know the saying. But no, my dearest son, it doesn't always sort itself out with all children. *Not all children are equally intelligent.* You, dear son, had a different kind of mother! – The mother of your children was a *Polis*,[6] *e questo basta!* One can't be careful enough when bringing up children. On this occasion you won't get a good and capable cook who can also do delicate tasks if she also has to do all the heavy work: – moreover, the more delicate tasks would be neglected, as every peasant girl – of which you have a whole village full – can help to carry wood. The little that you spend you'll save by virtue of the fact that your daughter will become more skilful: my whole attention was invariably directed at my children's education and training. First and foremost are good manners and knowledge, enlightened and sound common sense and skill; money and fortune are secondary to these in the eyes of every sensible person. – *The first* of these remains and cannot be taken away, whereas one can squander or lose or be cheated of *the second* etc.

Frau Schörkhofer has just told me that she was mistaken. My son hasn't dined with this woman's foster-parents in Schörfling, but the manager of the brewery and his wife, together with their foster-daughter, dined with my son at the abbot's house in Mondsee on the occasion of some Mass or other, so it was then that she had the

5. Nannerl's step-daughter, Maria Anna Margarethe.
6. Maria Margarethe Polis von Moulin (1746–79), Berchtold zu Sonnenburg's first wife, was the mother of four of his five children.

honour of meeting my son, whom she found to be such an honest man. Frau Schörkhofer, who'd misunderstood, had to come specially to tell me as the girl doesn't want the slightest untruth to be told about her. – My son may perhaps be surprised that I've gone into such detail in all these matters and filled whole sheets with my scribblings. But, as my daughter knows, that's the way I am; with me, everything must be clear. – – What I wrote above was not aimed exclusively at this woman, but these are my honest thoughts that are *based on experience*: and with that – amen!

Pauernfeind, the postmaster at Stein, is ill; Joseph Barisani[7] has been out there since Friday, the 19th, and hasn't returned yet. – It's said that there's not much hope. –

Have I already told you that Baron Rechberg is going to Strasbourg? But I won't have told you that Countess Wallis wants me to give keyboard lessons to her little son. It won't be news to you that I'd now like to be in St Gilgen, *shooting wild duck*. – The cantor will no doubt have expressed his pleasure at having attended the theatre, seen a comedy, heard some beautiful symphonies and seen 2 plays – a *tragedy* and a *comedy*. The new counsellor of the exchequer, Herr Hartmann, should, as I understand it, be preparing to be appointed attorney to the exchequer. He went to Ulm, presumably to collect his wife and children, although I thought I saw him yesterday. Frau von Gerlichs is still in bed; you have to speak to her very loudly, as she can no longer hear very well: little sleep; – little appetite; – many years on her back; – still suffering from a cold – – it will be quite something if she recovers; today she told me that she was feeling somewhat better. I should add that Herr von Kleinmayr visits her regularly. –

I'm quite willing to believe that it looks like Siberia where you are; but that won't stop me going out in boots whenever possible and at least keeping an eye open for wild duck by the lake. Not a word has been said here about any change at Strasswalchen.[8] – Here's

---

7. Joseph Barisani (1756–1826), eldest son of the archbishop's physician, Silvester Barisani.

8. Strasswalchen is a town northeast of Salzburg, but it is unclear what this refers to.

a list of the promotions at court, promotions miraculously passed *del petto nel culo* and evacuated *del culo*.[9] – As for my travel plans, there's been talk of going *to Munich* for the Carnival and then going on *to Vienna* during the first week of Lent or even sooner: but there are still difficulties about the latter; the former, however, is *certain*, exceptional adverse circumstances notwithstanding. – The administrator of St John's Hospital will not be thinking of marriage at present: he's always sickly; who knows how long he'll live. – The Kletzls are unlikely to begin before the new year or Christmas, they're in Sieghartstein. Nannerl the parlourmaid has gone into service with the administrator of the Langenhof. Mitzerl is well. While I was at the opera, a whole host of people asked me to send their best wishes to St Gilgen; the Schiedenhofens, both the Hermes families etc., the chapter syndic, the Mölks, – Racher etc. were all sitting near me. I now kiss my dear son and my dear daughter and all your children with all my heart. Half blind from writing, your old father

Mozart

Mozart and Constanze's second child, Carl Thomas, had been born on 21 September 1784. On 14 December Mozart became a Freemason, joining the lodge 'Zur Wohltätigkeit' ('Beneficence'). His fame as a composer and performer was mounting, as Leopold found out when he visited Vienna early in 1785. Travelling via Munich, and accompanied by his pupil Heinrich Marchand, he arrived on 11 February to stay with Mozart and Constanze, now living in the Grosse Schulerstrasse 846.

9. 'from the breast to the arse' . . . 'from the arse'. A promotion *in petto* ('within the breast') is one made in secret.

148. Leopold Mozart to his daughter, 16 February 1785, Vienna

We left Munich at 8 o'clock on the morning of the 7th and drove as far as Altötting and left there between 5 and half past on the morning of the 8th, our luggage was inspected in Braunau, although in the event only the trunk was opened and closed again as the customs officials knew my name, we had lunch at midday and then drove to Ried, by which time it was still only half past 4, so we took a third horse as I'd been told that we'd have difficulty getting through the snow with even 3 horses. It would take far too long to describe the *journey at night* from Ried to Haag, but, to cut a long story short, we really thought that the carriage would get stuck in the snow and that we'd have to sleep inside it, which would not have been so unpleasant as we were really very warm, but the postilion would have had to have gone off with the horses in search of a remote farmhouse. But, in short, because Heinrich and I had had to get out when the carriage got stuck in a ditch and found ourselves up to our waists in snow, so that the postilion had to pull us out, and because we'd had to drive across fields in search of another route and the horses had been half worked to death, we continued on our journey to Haag, which we reached 4 hours later. We couldn't leave till 9 the next morning as the peasants first had to clear a part of the road from Haag to Lambach. Shortly after leaving Haag we met 2 gentlemen coming towards us on foot and covered in sweat, they'd had to abandon their carriage and horses and leave them to dig their own way out of the snow. As soon as we came across the first group of peasants clearing snow from the road, we took 2 of them with us to walk alongside the carriage and stop it from running out of control – until we came to another gang of workmen and took another 2, and in this way and after a great deal of effort we finally reached Lambach at half past 1, and at 2 went on, without lunch, *to Enns*. The next day we travelled on to *Perschling* and at 1 o'clock on the Friday arrived at no. 846 Schulerstrasse, first floor. It was an appalling journey, what with the snow and ice and potholes, and everywhere there were workmen clearing away the snow.

That your brother *has beautiful, fully furnished rooms* you'll gather from the fact that he's paying 460 florins in rent. At 6 o'clock that same Friday[1] evening we drove to his first subscription concert, which was attended by a great gathering of persons of rank. Everyone pays a gold sovereign or 3 ducats for these Lenten concerts. They're at the Mehlgrube,[2] he pays only *half a gold sovereign* each time he uses the hall. The concert was incomparable, the orchestra admirable, apart from the symphonies a soprano from the Italian theatre sang 2 arias.[3] There was then an *admirable new piano concerto*[4] *by Wolfgang* on which the copyist was still working when we arrived, your brother didn't even have time to play through the rondeau as he had to oversee the copying. As you can imagine, I met many acquaintances there, all of whom came over to speak to me: but I was also introduced to some other people. On Saturday evening Herr *Joseph Haydn* and the 2 Barons Tinti[5] came round and the new quartets were played, but only *the 3 new ones* that he's written to go with the 3 we already knew,[6] they're a bit easier but admirably composed. Herr Haydn said to me: *I say to you before God and as an honest man, your son is the greatest composer known to me in person or by name: he has taste and, what's more, the greatest knowledge of composition.* On Sunday evening the Italian soprano, Signora Laschi, who's now leaving for Italy, gave a concert at the theatre.[7] She sang 2 arias, there was a cello concerto, a tenor and a bass each sang an aria *and your brother played a wonderful*

---

1. 11 February.
2. The city casino on the Neuer Markt and a venue for concerts.
3. Unidentified.
4. K466.
5. Anton and Bartholomäus Tinti were both members of the Masonic lodge 'Zur wahren Eintracht' ('True Concord'). Soon after this Anton Tinti became resident Salzburg minister in Vienna.
6. K458, 464 and 465, the final three of the six quartets dedicated to the composer Joseph Haydn (1732–1809) and first performed privately on 15 January; Leopold already knew the quartets K387, 421 and 428.
7. Luisa Laschi (*c.* 1760–*c.* 1790) was engaged at the Italian opera in Vienna from 1784 to 1790; she sang the roles of the Countess at the premiere of *Le nozze di Figaro* (1786) and Zerlina at the first Viennese performance of *Don Giovanni* in 1788. The concert was at the Burgtheater.

concerto that he'd written for Mlle Paradies[8] *in Paris.* I was sitting at the back only 2 boxes away from the very beautiful Princess of Württemberg[9] and had the pleasure of hearing the interplay between the instruments so clearly that it brought tears of pleasure to my eyes.

As your brother was leaving, the emperor waved down to him with his hat and shouted *bravo Mozart.* – He'd already been much applauded when he came out to play. – We weren't at the theatre yesterday as there's a concert every day. It's only now that I've started to feel the effects of the cold from the journey. Prior to the concert on Sunday evening I drank some elderflower tea, wrapped myself up very warm and on Monday drank some more tea in bed, remaining there till 10 o'clock, more tea in the afternoon and again this morning: – I was still in bed when I received a visit from the doctor, whom your sister-in-law had secretly summoned, he took my pulse and said it was regular and told me to continue the treatment I'd already started. There's another concert at the theatre this evening, – your brother will again be playing a concerto. I now feel much better and shall again drink plenty of elderflower tea. I'll be bringing back various new works by your brother. *Little Carl* looks just like your brother. He looked very well – but children sometimes have trouble with their teeth, so that he wasn't very well yesterday – but he's better again today. I should add that he's a delightful child, uncommonly friendly, and he laughs as soon as you talk to him: I've seen him cry only once, but the very next moment he was laughing again. – He's now in a lot of pain again with his teeth. – Yesterday, the 15th, there was another concert at the theatre for a young woman[10] who sings charmingly, your brother played the new grand concerto in D [minor].[11] *Magnifique* etc. Today we're going to a concert at the

8. K456; the blind piano virtuosa Maria Theresia Paradies (1759–1824).
9. See letter 121, n. 2; she was the intended wife of Archduke Franz (1768–1835), eldest son of Leopold, Archduke of Tuscany.
10. Elisabeth Distler (1769–89), singer, sister of the violinist and composer Johann Georg Distler (1760–99).
11. K466.

home of the Salzburg agent, Herr *von Ployer*[12] – how would it be if the emperor swapped countries with the elector of Bavaria and if Bavaria were exchanged for the Netherlands?[13] The Dutch would keep *the Scheldt* closed, the *Netherlands* and the *Palatinate* would be closer together, just as *Bavaria* is better annexed to *Austria*. *France* wouldn't then have such a dangerous neighbour in the Netherlands: *Holland* would remain in between and would be a good neighbour if *France* needed money etc.: your brother, sister-in-law, Marchand and I kiss you millions of times. I am ever your honest father

Mozart

149. Leopold Mozart to his daughter, 12 March 1785, Vienna

Your letter of 25 Feb. has arrived safely: I hope you'll be able to get the clavichord out to you as soon as the road allows it. I'm suffering from a slight chill and haven't yet been able to shake it off. Heinrich's concert[1] was both *bad* and *good*: bad because there were so few people there and after taking account of his expenses of more than 115 florins, he was left with only 18 *ducats*, but *good* because he played so well that we can hope for something better at a second concert the day after tomorrow, *the 14th*.[2] My son's sister-in-law, Frau Lange – née Weber – is now back in Munich but left there for Salzburg last night in order to ensure that she becomes better known. She and her husband – both of whom have performed in Munich – are being accompanied on their journey by Fräulein Boudet and her husband[3] and will be here during Holy Week, Fräulein Boudet has been engaged

12. Gottfried Ployer lived in Döbling, a Viennese suburb.
13. Leopold refers to Elector Karl Theodor's proposal to give Lower Bavaria to Austria in exchange for the Austrian Netherlands (roughly equivalent to modern Belgium); this would give him a stronger power base in northern Europe and the hope of a royal crown. It made him very unpopular in Bavaria.
1. Heinrich Marchand gave a concert on 2 March at the Burgtheater.
2. Nothing is known of this concert.
3. The actress Marianne Boudet was married to the horn player Martin Lang.

at the theatre for a short season, she's receiving *50 ducats* travelling expenses and *25 ducats* each time she appears. Herr Lebrun and his wife[4] have given 3 amazing concerts: they made 1100 florins at the first, 900 at the 2nd and 500 at the 3rd. Your brother made 559 florins at his concert, which we'd not expected, as he's got a subscription for 6 concerts at the Mehlgrube for more than 150 people, each of whom is paying *1 sovereign* for the 6 concerts: in addition he has, as a favour, often played at other concerts at the theatre. As for the keyboard arrangement of *Die Entführung aus dem Serail*, all I can say is that a certain *Torricella*[5] is engraving it. But when it says *chez Torricella*, it actually means your brother: but he's not quite finished it yet – perhaps only the *first* act: I'll make enquiries. 3 sonatas[6] have also been published by Torricella, only one of which includes a violin. Enough! I'll buy everything that's appeared. – I'll find out something more definite about the silk, I've been told that you can get 16 ells of gros de Tours for 5 lbs of silk ravelling. But I'll obtain some more reliable information. Quite by chance I stumbled upon old Frau Fischer and her daughter, they were so surprised that they started back in their delight and leapt into the air; I can't begin to describe their delight, especially when they heard that you were married. – They never thought they'd see me again: so you can imagine the delight of these honest people – they now want to see you, too, before they die as they haven't seen you since you were little: I spent 2 hours with them etc. etc. It was the same with Kapellmeister Bonno: but Nannerl is married. We never get to bed before 1 and never get up before 9, we eat at 2 or half past. Terrible weather! Every day a concert, always teaching, music, writing etc. Where should I betake

4. See letter 89, n. 2; the concerts were on 23 and 28 February and 7 March. Mozart may have played at some or all of them.
5. Christoph Torricella (*c.* 1715–98), music publisher. He published the first editions of Mozart's variations on 'Ah, vous dirai-je Maman' K265, 'Salve tu, Domine' K398 and 'Unser dummer Pöbel meint' K455, as well as the keyboard sonatas K284 and 333 and the accompanied sonata K454.
6. In the event, Mozart never completed a keyboard arrangement of *Die Entführung aus dem Serail*; the earliest surviving complete arrangement was published at Mainz in 1785 or 1786. The three sonatas are K284, 333 and 454 (the last with violin accompaniment).

myself off to? – – If only the concerts were over! It's impossible to describe the trouble and the commotion: since I've been here, your brother's fortepiano has been taken to the theatre or some other house at least 12 times. He's had a large *fortepiano pedal* made that fits under the instrument and is about 3 spans longer and astonishingly heavy, it's taken to the Mehlgrube every Friday and has also been taken to Count Zichy's and Prince Kaunitz's.[7] – Joseph, the youngest son of the younger Prince Kaunitz, has died in Spain, where he was imperial envoy. I must close now as it's dark and I'm shortly leaving for a concert at the theatre. We *all* kiss you *all* a million times with all our hearts. I am ever your honest father

Mozart

Tomorrow is the concert for the widows.[8] And on Tuesday is the 2nd concert at which Heinrich has been asked to play a concerto. The sonata for 2 pianos[9] must be there, in the chest in the hall. The scores must have got out of order.

On 4 April, Leopold joined the Masonic lodge 'Zur Wohltätigkeit'; to celebrate the occasion, Mozart composed the Masonic song 'Die ihr einem neuen Grade' K468. Father and son went to a meeting of the lodge 'Zur wahren Eintracht' on 24 April, at which Mozart's cantata Die Maurerfreude *K471 was performed; the next day, Leopold and Heinrich Marchand left to return to Salzburg. Earlier in the year, Anton Klein*

7. Mozart had performed on his pedal piano at his Burgtheater concert of 10 March 1785; the announcement of the concert makes it clear that the instrument was a novelty: 'On Thursday, 10th March 1785 Herr Kapellmeister *Mozart* will have the honour of giving at the I. & R. National Court Theatre a Grand Musical Concert for his benefit, at which not only a *new*, just *finished Forte piano Concerto* will be played by him, but also an especially *large Forte piano pedale* will be used by him in *improvising*.' See Deutsch, *Documentary Biography*, 239.
8. The Tonkünstler-Sozietät concert on 13 March included the first performance of Mozart's cantata *Davidde penitente* K469, adapted from his unfinished mass in C minor K427.
9. Presumably K448.

(1748–1810), professor of poetry and philosophy at the University of Mannheim, had sent Mozart a copy of his play Kaiser Rudolf von Habsburg *in the hope that he might compose an opera based on it.*

150. Mozart to Anton Klein, 21 March 1785, Vienna

Most Worthy Privy Councillor, –

It was very wrong of me, I must admit, not to have written to you at once and acknowledged the safe receipt of your letter and the parcel you sent with it; but it's not true that I have in the meantime received 2 more letters from you; I'd have been instantly woken from my slumbers by the first of them and replied at once, as I'm doing now. – In the event, your 2 letters arrived together last post-day. – I've already admitted that it was wrong of me not to have replied straightaway; – but as far as the opera is concerned, I'd have been able to tell you as little about it then as I can now. – Dear Privy Councillor –! – My hands are so full that I can scarcely ever find a minute to call my own. – As a man of such great insight and experience, you yourself know better than I that something like this must be read through not once but many times – and read through, moreover, with all possible care and attention. – Until now I've not yet had time to read it even once without interruptions. – All I can say at present is that I'd like to hold on to it; I'd be grateful, therefore, if you'd allow me to keep it for a little while longer. – In the event of my deciding that I should like to set it to music, I wonder if I could ask you at this point whether you have a particular place in mind where it could be performed? – In terms of both poetry and music, a work of this kind deserves better than to have been written in vain. – I hope to receive some clarification on this point. – At present, I can give you no more news about the German operatic stage of the future, as things have gone very quiet in this department – apart from the building work on the Kärntnertortheater that has been set aside for this purpose. – It's supposed to be opened in early October. For my own part, I don't expect it'll be very successful. –

To judge by the arrangements that have been made so far, I'd say that they were trying to undermine German opera at a time when it may have gone into only temporary decline, rather than help it to its feet again and provide it with proper support.[1] – Only my sister-in-law, Frau Lange, has been allowed to join the German singspiel. – Cavalieri, Adamberger and Teyber – all Germans of whom Germany may be proud – have to remain at the Italian theatre – and have to compete with their own fellow-countrymen and women! – – – At present German singers, male and female, can be counted on the fingers of one hand! – And even if there really are any other singers as good as or even better than the ones I've mentioned, which I very much doubt, the directors of the local theatre seem to me to be too concerned with balancing their books and too unpatriotic in their thinking to offer large amounts of money to strangers, when they have better – or at least equally good – singers here on the spot who cost them nothing; – the Italian company doesn't need them – at least as far as numbers are concerned; it's entirely self-sufficient. – At the German opera the idea at present is to use actors and actresses who can also sing if necessary; – it is supremely unfortunate that the directors of both the theatre and the orchestra have been kept in their posts, as it is they who, through their ignorance and indolence, have done the most to undermine their own work. If there were only a single patriot in charge, it would all take on a different complexion! – But the *National Theatre* that is just beginning to burst into bud would then perhaps begin to flower, and it would, of course, be to Germany's everlasting shame if we Germans seriously started to think like Germans – to act like Germans – to speak German – and even to sing in German!!![2] –

Don't take it amiss, my dearest Herr Klein, if I've perhaps gone too far in my enthusiasm! – Fully convinced that I'm speaking to a *German*, I've allowed my tongue free rein, something that one is nowadays so seldom allowed to do that after such an unbosoming one could easily drink oneself into a stupor without running the risk

1. The reconstituted German opera company survived until 1788; see letter 132, n. 5.
2. Here Mozart writes ironically.

of endangering one's health. – I remain, with the deepest respect, most worthy Privy Councillor, your most obedient servant

W. A. Mozart

In June 1785 Nannerl Mozart, who was expecting her first child, came to Salzburg for the last stages of her pregnancy. A son, Leopold Alois Pantaleon, was born on 27 July and when she returned to St Gilgen in early September, the child remained in Salzburg with his grandfather.

151. Leopold Mozart to his daughter and son-in-law, 2 September 1785, Salzburg

I hope you reached Hof by 1 o'clock and that by 5 you'd been reunited, safe and sound, with your husband and children. Sad though your departure was, I none the less spent a very happy day – except between 12 and 1 – in the company of little Leopold. I kiss my son with all my heart and would ask him not to worry about the Prince of Asturia,[1] just as I hope that you too will have confidence in my care and attention, as you know how much I love the child. He was again much friendlier and livelier than yesterday – yesterday, as you know, he endeared himself neither to me nor to the rest of us. But this afternoon his eyes are bright and clear again, and he's sleeping gently and calmly: in a word, I'm completely reassured and hope to be able to keep him until I can bring him by hand to St Gilgen, but for that I'd have to live another 10 years or so and as a result it would be little Leopold who would be leading me, not the other way round. The postman didn't call, and when I sent one of the servants round to his rooms, he wasn't in. I'll send him the *box for the mob caps* tomorrow, together with a Sauerbrunn bottle of *mead*, the children

1. i.e. his grandson.

should drink to little Leopold's health. *The Sauerbrunn bottle should be returned, it belongs to Nandl.*[2] – Here's the first playbill. *It's a clumsy adaptation of Count Essex.*[3] Nandl sends her best wishes to you both, as do Monica and Tresel.

[*Postscript to his son-in-law*]
Dearest Son,

I'd like to ask you once again not to worry about the child, – we mustn't be overhasty: you have 5 children under your roof – and the 6th will be well looked after here until you come to a decision, Lena is in any case out there with you and would like to be fed in return for her foolish gossip. – Monica can't start till Michaelmas. – I can keep Nandl, – so why the hurry? Perhaps because of the weather? – Certainly not! – This is the time of year when, if it's fine in the morning, you can be sure that there'll be no rain or storms during the afternoon. During the last 14 days of this month you can travel in confidence if you see a fine day ahead of you, as it's really very warm from 9 in the morning till 4 in the afternoon. So that's how things stand if you think that little Leopold should be brought out to you and if that's what you want; leave it to me, I'll find a day when I can see to it and can do it without the least risk to the child from either the weather or his condition at the time. In a word, it shouldn't be a cause for the slightest concern to you, as I myself will be there. But if my son will allow me to keep little Leopold here, it will be a pleasure for me to look after him and – if God preserves him – the child will have '*got over the worst*', as the servants say, when you get him back, as he'll then be 9 months old. Nandl will stay with me, and I must say that she's looking after the child wonderfully well. It goes without saying that I shall do all this with pleasure, at my own expense. Now you may do as you like, according to your own insights, depending on what you find best, while bearing in mind that the child will be looked after on his own here, whereas with you your nursemaid will be dealing with 4 or at least 3 other children, and

2. Anna Maria Pietschner, see letter 18, n. 1.
3. The play by Christian Heinrich Schmid, see letter 101, n. 6.

Karl[4] certainly needs an eye keeping on him at present. Meanwhile you can keep *Lena* for whatever purpose, so that she has something to eat and isn't deprived of the joys of marriage. Monica can then come out to you at Michaelmas or, in the event of the child rejoining you, she can come out with us 8 or 10 days earlier. – You see, my dearest son, everything can be arranged to your liking, without undue haste: – it's all been thought through! – I must only ask that, if you want little Leopold to be brought out to you, you must leave it all to me and let me work out a suitable time. The postman is waiting! I must close. We *all* kiss you *all*.

Mozart

Following the birth of Nannerl's son, much of the correspondence between father and daughter concerns domestic matters and Wolfgang is mentioned only infrequently. On 3 November 1785 Leopold wrote:

I've not heard a word from your brother, his last letter was dated 14 Sept. and since then the quartets were supposed to have come by mail coach. If he'd been ill, Herr Artaria would have told me in his letter of 28 Oct. I met the journalist a few days ago and he said: It really is amazing to see what a lot of things your son is bringing out just now: in all the musical announcements I see nothing but Mozart. When advertising the quartets, the Berlin advertisements said only: It is unnecessary to recommend these works to the public; suffice it to say that they are by Herr Mozart. There was nothing I could say, as I knew nothing, not having received a letter for 6 weeks now. He also said something about a new opera. *Basta!* We'll no doubt hear about it!

The new opera was Le nozze di Figaro *('The Marriage of Figaro'). On 11 November Leopold wrote again to Nannerl:*

4. Berchtold zu Sonnenburg's son by his second wife.

I've finally received a letter from your brother, dated 2 Novemb. and running to 12 lines in length. He apologizes for not writing as he's up to his eyes in his opera *Le nozze di Figaro*. He thanks both me and you for our good wishes and asks me to apologize on his behalf to you in particular. I'm to give you his best wishes and say that he doesn't have time to reply to your letter at once: in order to keep his mornings free for composition he's had to move all his pupils to the afternoon etc. etc. I know the play, it's a most wearisome piece, and the translation from the French will most certainly have had to be changed if it's to be effective as an opera. God grant that it turns out well in terms of the action; I've no doubt that the music will be good. It'll mean a lot of running round and arguing before the libretto is adapted to suit his purpose: – and in keeping with his delightful habit, he'll no doubt have kept postponing things and taken his time, but he'll now have to make a serious effort as Count Rosenberg is driving him on.

Mozart composed two Masonic choruses, K483 and 484, for the amalgamation on 14 January 1786 of three Viennese lodges, 'Gekrönte Hoffnung', 'Wohltätigkeit' and 'Drei Feuer' as 'Zur neugekrönten Hoffnung' ('The new crowned hope'). On 18 January he began composing the one-act opera buffa, Der Schauspieldirektor *('The Impresario'), which was performed at Schönbrunn on 7 February together with Salieri's* Prima la musica e poi le parole. *And on 13 March Mozart privately performed* Idomeneo *with the newly composed numbers K489 and 490 in the private theatre of the palace of Johann Adam, Prince Auersperg (1721–95).*

152. Leopold Mozart to his daughter, 23 March 1786, Salzburg

Little Leopold is well!

We had another of our usual concerts yesterday. *Marchand* played the concerto in *D minor* that I recently sent out to you; since you have the keyboard part, he played from the full score and Haydn turned the pages for him and had the pleasure of seeing how skilfully and intricately it's written and how difficult it is as a concerto.[1] I chose this concerto because you have the keyboard parts of all the others, whereas I still have the full score of this one and was able, therefore, to perform it; it was rehearsed in the morning, the orchestra having to play through the *rondo* 3 times before they got it right as he took it fairly briskly. There were again lots of people there. All the ecclesiastical councillors and university professors. Madame Schlauka made a good profit on it as there was an interval halfway through and all the members of the orchestra went downstairs, with the result that everyone else squeezed in after them and took some refreshments, which were beautifully, neatly and liberally served. In a word, the emperor himself could have been there. *The archb. didn't leave till after 9 o'clock.*

On Friday – *tomorrow* – the two abbots are being confirmed, those of *St Peter's* and of *Baumburg*. And on Monday, *St Rupert's Day*, there's the *benediction at St Peter's Church. The abbot of Baumburg is from Franconia.*[2]

Tresel sent everything out to you *yesterday morning* with the servant of the wife of the owner of the iron depot. *The other fellow then arrived completely unexpectedly in the afternoon.*

The Hagenauers and even the *old man*[3] were at the concert – the Haslbergers have been to them all. They all send their best wishes.

The postman has just brought your letter and its enclosure of 1 florin 30 kreuzers. – I couldn't say whether the chocolate was good or bad as I didn't try it. But I suppose that, as everything is getting more

1. The concerto played by Heinrich Marchand was K466; Haydn is of course Michael Haydn.
2. Fr Dominicus Hagenauer was abbot of St Peter's in Salzburg; the abbot of Baumburg, an Augustinian monastery in Upper Bavaria, was Albert Knol; the region of Franconia was in southern Germany.
3. Johann Lorenz Hagenauer.

expensive and the *price* of this particular item has remained the same, the item itself is of an inferior quality, I've noticed this for some time with the chocolate at 1 florin 15 kreuzers.

You can rest assured that I'd have come out to see you with the organ builder[4] long ago if we'd not been prevented from doing so by various untoward events; initially we were also prevented by the weather and the bad roads. I'd applied for leave from 30 March, but this is now impossible as *Gluck's* opera *Orfeo* is to be performed at the *Accademia* on 5 April, for which the wordbooks need to be printed and at least 4 rehearsals held with the orchestra, when my presence and that of the organ builder are indispensable. In addition, Herr Altmann has to copy out the Italian text from the score and as he doesn't understand how to put it into verse in the recitatives, I'll have to lend him a helping hand and then read the proofs when it's been set. As a result, I'll have to delay my visit until 6 April in order to be back here by the evening of the 8th at the latest, unless I'm prevented by the weather and unless work on sorting out the main organ – work that the late Herr Egedacher so neglected – isn't so extensive that the organ builder can't come down with me. So you can see that even if I could come myself, it's possible that the organ builder won't be able to come down with me.

The weather here has been permanently fine and warm for some time. To begin with, though, it was very muddy inside and outside the town: but now it's mainly dry. I went walking both when it was muddy and when the roads were dry; but not as long as I used to, I've had so much to do since my return from Vienna or else the house has been overrun and I've been prevented from going out.

I've seen neither the shadowplays nor the marionettes: no one had a good word to say for them. I'd only have gone there for *Pimperl*.[5]

---

4. Johann Evangelist Schmid (1757–1804) was court organ builder in Salzburg; his predecessor (see below) was Johann Rochus Egedacher (1714–85).
5. Probably a Hanswurst character.

I was asked yesterday by Herr Haslberger if it's true that Herr Sonnenburg,[6] the head clerk, has been elected administrative commissioner for Lofer? – I could only say *that I'd not heard a word to that effect. Not a word!* – I hope it's true.

I'm very sorry to hear that Lenerl[7] is ill and wish her a speedy recovery. I too have a patient. Old Tresel has erysipelas all over her face so that her mouth is swollen and she can't really eat even a bowl of soup. And you know how hard it is to get her to take anything.

I assume that the 2 black hats that you want are 2 straw hats. Is that so? – –

As for a housemaid, I've already made enquiries and have spoken to the forest warden's wife, among others, she sends you both her best wishes and thinks of you constantly.

Dr Joseph Barisani keeps asking me how you are: – and Frau Gualbert Daubrawa came up to me at the Casino and told me you were pregnant. The family of Privy Councillor Hermes, the Schiedenhofens, Hagenauers, Barisanis, Mölks and God knows who else keep on asking me time and time again, as does Countess Lützow, the Kletzls, Baroness Schaffmann etc, the bishop of Chiemsee, the dean of the cathedral, Count Daun, the prince's equerry, and even Bishop Schrattenbach of Lavant asked about you yesterday at the Casino as you've not been seen for so long; Herr d'Ippold sends you his best wishes for all eventualities.

Your brother sent me the printed enclosure that you'll find herewith.[8] – Please let me have the cutting back.

6. Franz Anton von Berchtold zu Sonnenburg (1749–1809), Nannerl's brother-in-law.
7. Nannerl's maid.
8. Leopold refers to a cutting with acrostics and riddles; it has not been reproduced here. Some lines in this paragraph referring to riddles have also been omitted.

Please also send me the *sonatas by Clementi* that belong to Bull-inger.

Little Leopold sometimes eats from my table. He kisses you: and I kiss him for you. Heinrich often carries him in his arms and showers him in kisses. Heinrich sends his best wishes and hopes to see you here soon. Each time the Marchands have written, they've asked for their best wishes to be passed on to you in St Gilgen. I'm sending 4 lemons at *10 kreuzers* each. I kiss you with all my heart, say hello to the children. I am ever your honest father

Mozart

The bell was tolled for Louise Robinig at 7 o'clock this morning, *the 24th*, announcing that she was close to death.

Little Leopold is well, he's just having some soup, Heinrich is off to the consistory for the service, and I have to attend Vespers at half past 8 in the cathedral.

An *assessor consistorii* from Augsburg, a young cleric who's the son of *Dr Baader* of Munich, is here to practise at the local consistory – the elector of Trier is paying for him. He preached in the cathedral last Saturday. The sermon lasted a *good half hour* and as people were leaving, they were laughing to themselves as no one had understood a word. His voice wouldn't even fill my dining room, and the *common people* who were standing, open-mouthed, beneath the pulpit and who might have heard him, didn't understand what he was saying. *I*, *Berhandsky*, and *Eyweck* were standing together beneath the pulpit and understood everything of course: but, I said, it's an excellent speech for learned listeners, but not a sermon, more of a rough *sketch* or *outline*, allowing you to make two wonderfully executed sermons out of two parts made up of nothing but the ends of his sentences: that's just how it was. Tomorrow, God willing, I'll hear Herr Rieger, who gave such a good sermon last year, and, in heaven's name, what a crowd there'll be on the 24th, when Herr Hübner[9] preaches. But he has a good voice.

9. Lorenz Hübner (1753–1807), editor of the *Salzburger Staatszeitung*.

It's not at all surprising that so many people were at the Casino as it's possible to take out a subscription *for your whole family* for only a ducat, so that there are often 4, 5 or more people from a single household there for this sum. Prof. Steinhauser is always there with 4 people. Private tickets at 36 kreuzers are available only for amateurs who pay on the door and who sometimes come and sometimes don't. – I should add that this music at the Casino is very popular. The university professors are all assiduous attenders. Most of the town's businessmen and councillors are also subscribers. Privy Councillor Hermes invariably comes with 5 or 6 other people, and so on etc.

On 20 April, Mozart completed Le nozze di Figaro, *his first operatic collaboration with the poet Lorenzo Da Ponte, based on Beaumarchais' subversive comedy* Le mariage de Figaro *(completed in 1781 but not staged in Paris until 1784). Both Da Ponte and the Irish tenor Michael Kelly, who sang the roles of Don Curzio and Don Basilio, say in their memoirs that the idea for the opera was Mozart's, although Joseph II had forbidden the play to be performed in Vienna. It was a sequel to Beaumarchais'* Le barbier de Séville *('The Barber of Seville', 1775), which Paisiello had already turned into a successful opera,* Il barbiere di Siviglia *(premiered at St Petersburg in November 1782 and first given at Vienna in 1783). Mozart and Da Ponte's* Le nozze di Figaro *opened on 1 May and received nine performances; Mozart was paid 450 florins for its composition. Shortly before he completed* Figaro, *Mozart also composed the A major and C minor piano concertos K488 and 491.*

153. Mozart to Sebastian Winter, 30 September 1786, Vienna

Dearest Friend, –
    The music you asked for will be going off tomorrow by the mail

coach,[1] – you'll find at the end of this letter the amount due for copying. – It's entirely natural that some of my pieces should be sent abroad – but these are pieces that I'm deliberately sending out into the world – I sent you only the themes as it was possible that they hadn't reached you yet. But the works that I'm keeping back for myself or for a small circle of music lovers and connoisseurs – with the promise *not* to let them out of their hands – can't possibly be made known abroad as they're not even known here; – this is the case with the 3 concertos that I have the honour of sending to His Highness; in this case I was obliged to add to the cost of copying a small honorarium of 6 ducats for each concerto, with the request that His Highness does not let these concertos out of his hands. – The concerto in A[2] includes 2 clarinets. – If you don't have these at your court, a skilful copyist should transpose them to a suitable key; the first can then be played by a violin, the second by a viola. – As for the proposal that I took the liberty of making to your worthy prince,[3] I first need to know what kind of works His Highness would prefer or find most useful and how many of each genre he would like to have each year, which I'd like to know in order to be able to make my calculations. – Please lay my request at His Highness's feet and inform him of my wishes. – And now, my dearest friend! – Companion of my youth! – As I have naturally often been in Ricken[4] these many years and yet never had the pleasure of meeting

1. Sebastian Winter, the Mozarts' former valet, was now in service to Prince Joseph Maria Benedikt of Fürstenberg (1758–96). In August 1786 Mozart had offered the Fürstenberg court, through Winter, copies of his latest compositions. Fürstenberg purchased copies of the symphonies K319, 338 and 425 (which survive in the Fürstenberg collection at Karlsruhe), and the concertos K451, 459 and 488 (these copies are lost).

2. K488.

3. He had proposed that he should compose exclusive works for the prince, on a regular basis, for a fee.

4. As a boy, Mozart invented a fantasy world called the 'Kingdom of Rücken' with which Winter, as Mozart's childhood valet, would have been familiar. It is possible that Mozart refers to it here; Rücken, which means 'backs', and Ricken are pronounced similarly.

you there, my greatest wish would be that you should visit me in Vienna or that I may visit you in Donaueschingen. – The latter, forgive me, would almost be preferable as I should then not only have the pleasure of embracing you but also have the privilege of paying my respects to your most gracious prince and recalling even more vividly the many favours that I received at your court during my younger years,[5] favours that I shall never forget as long as I live. – Awaiting an early reply and in the flattering hope of perhaps seeing you once again in this world, I remain ever your most obedient friend and servant

Wolfgang Amadè Mozart

Invoice

	fl.	kr.
The 3 concertos, without keyboard parts.		
109 sheets @ 8 kr.	14	32
The 3 keyboard parts.		
33½ sheets @ 10 kr.	5	35
Fee for the 3 concertos.		
18 ducats @ 4 fl. 30 kr.	81	–
The 3 symphonies		
116½ sheets at 8 kr.	15	32
Customs and carriage	3	–
Total:	119 fl. 39 kr.	

Mozart and Constanze's third child, Johann Thomas Leopold, was born on 17 August 1786. He lived only three months, and died on 15 November. When Leopold wrote the following letter to Nannerl, he was still unaware of his grandson's death.

5. The Mozarts had visited Donaueschingen in October 1766, see letter 13.

154. Leopold Mozart to his daughter, 17 November 1786, Salzburg

Little Leopold is well!

And I? – Somewhat better since I shat out the 67th year of my life after drinking a laxative on my birthday;[1] and I was so tempted to drive out to St Gilgen on the 15th, who knows what sometimes cures a man. I have to joke about it so that I don't get depressed. I had to reply to one of your brother's letters today,[2] *it took me a lot of time to write it* and so I can write only very little to you, – it's late, I also want to go to the theatre today, as I can now get in *free*, and I've just finished my letter to Vienna. That I had to express myself *very forcefully* you can well imagine as he suggested nothing less than that I should take charge of *his 2 children*[3] while he goes off on a tour of Germany and England in the middle of next carnival etc. – I've given him a piece of my mind and promised him the next instalment of my letter with the next post. Herr Müller, that good and honest maker of silhouettes, praised *little Leopold* to your brother, which is how he found out that the child is staying here, something I'd never told him: that's how he or his wife hit on the idea. Of course it would suit them down to the ground – they could go off and travel at their convenience – they could die – – they could even remain in England – – and I'd have to go running after them with the children or chase up the payment for the children that he's offering me for them and for the maids to look after them etc. – *Basta!* My excuse is forceful and instructive if he cares to make use of it. –

After the play at around 10 o'clock

Do give my thanks to *Nannerl*[4] for her kind wishes, she wrote very nicely.

1. 14 November.
2. Mozart's letter is lost.
3. Carl Thomas and Johann Thomas Leopold.
4. Nannerl's stepdaughter.

Heinrich sends his best wishes: – has he not asked my son to send him *Ariadne auf Naxos?*[5] – – –

Frau Feyerl, the baker's wife, has died.

I'm sending you herewith a bit of childish nonsense to make you laugh, on one side it's in the original Swabian – and on the other it's written out in an intelligible form. Please send it back soon, it's not mine. Also a book *by Wieland*,[6] which you should read if you have a chance.

Wolfgang[7] came to congratulate me and was so pleased that he couldn't stop telling me about it. They also had an amazing Martinmas banquet with cakes, pastries, game, capons and wine etc. etc. –
    The postman didn't bring me the box, he'll have taken it to Wolfgang. I've already had a new one made.

The 18th, at half past 7 in the morning.
    Tresel has gradually managed to beg several lbs of candles that I'll send with the glass carrier, assuming the woman doesn't call too late, generally she says that she's leaving within the hour. What can one do then? Often I wasn't even at home. – And can one then write anything? If I've got time today or tomorrow, I'll write in advance just in case the woman comes on Monday.
    I'm sending you herewith the measurements of *little Leopold's bed. The whole piece of thread* gives the *length*, whereas the *width* is from one knot to the other. This is the inside measurement of the bedstead. The mattress shouldn't be any smaller but should in fact be somewhat larger because it will inflate when it's full and will then be too narrow and too short. I hope to receive it soon as the cradle is very dangerous.

5. Melodrama by Georg Benda (1722–95), first performed at Gotha on 27 January 1775, which Mozart had heard during his visit to Mannheim. In November 1778 he wrote of his plans to compose a similar work; nothing came of it, however. Leopold of course means von Berchtold zu Sonnenburg by 'my son' in this sentence.
6. Christoph Martin Wieland, poet and dramatist.
7. Nannerl's step-son.

I hope you're keeping well! I kiss you both with all my heart, give my best wishes to the children. I am ever your honest father

Mozart

Herr Bullinger is here, he sends you his kind regards and wishes he could have seen you, but he can't get away, he's staying with the dean of the cathedral and will be leaving for Munich next week to take up his new post as tutor. There was a great to-do in Munich, the elector travelled to Mannheim *at 4 in the morning of the 11th* as a courier had brought news that the electress was close to death. – But she's now better.[8] Vogler's opera, *Castor and Pollux*,[9] will be performed after all as all the music has now arrived.

Leopold sends you a kiss. Nandl and Thresel kiss your hands, my best wishes to Lenerl.

Early in 1787 Mozart and Constanze made a visit to Prague, where Mozart had been invited to direct a performance of Le nozze di Figaro. *He also gave a concert that included a new symphony ('Prague' K504), and received a commission from the impresario Pasquale Bondini for a new opera for the following autumn. The Mozarts returned to Vienna about 12 February, and on 24 March they moved to Landstrasse 224 (now 75 and 77).*

155. Mozart to Gottfried von Jacquin, 15 January 1787, Prague

Dearest Friend,[1] –

I've finally found a moment to write to you; – I'd planned to write

8. She lived until 1794.
9. *Castore e Polluce* by Georg Joseph Vogler was first performed at Munich on 12 January 1787.
1. The amateur composer and singer Gottfried von Jacquin (see List) was one of Mozart's closest friends in Vienna.

four letters to Vienna as soon as I arrived, but in vain! – I was able to manage only one – to my mother-in-law – and even this was only half written. – My wife and Hofer[2] had to finish it.

No sooner had we arrived – at 12 o'clock midday on Thursday the 11th – than we were rushed off our feet in order to be ready for lunch at 1. After the meal old Count Thun[3] regaled us with some music that was performed by his own people and that lasted around 1½ hours. – This was *real entertainment* of a kind that I could enjoy every day. – At 6 I drove with Count Canal[4] to what's known as the Bretfeld Ball, where the most beautiful women of Prague habitually gather, – that would have been something for you, my friend! – I can just see you running – no, hobbling – after all these beautiful girls and women! – I didn't dance or spoon with them. – First, because I was too tired, and the latter because of my ingrained diffidence; – but I was happy to watch all these people leaping around in sheer delight at the music of my Figaro which has been turned into nothing but contredanses and German dances; – here they talk of nothing but – Figaro; nothing is played, sung or whistled except – Figaro: no opera is as well attended as – Figaro and nothing but Figaro; a great honour for me, no doubt. – But to come back to my order of the day. As I got home late from the ball and was in any case tired and sleepy from my journey, it was entirely natural that I should have a long lie-in the next morning; and so it was. – As a result the whole of the next morning was again *sine linea*;[5] – after lunch the count's music must never be forgotten, and as a very good pianoforte had been put in my room that very day, you can easily imagine that I wouldn't leave it unused and untouched that evening and that it would go without saying that we'd play a little quartet *in*

2. Franz de Paula Hofer (1755–96), imperial court violinist, had travelled to Prague with Mozart. In 1788, he would marry Constanze's sister Josepha.
3. Johann Joseph Anton, Count Thun-Hohenstein (1711–88); Mozart had composed the symphony K425 for him in Linz in 1783. He was the father-in-law of Maria Wilhelmine, Countess Thun-Hohenstein.
4. Joseph Emanuel, Count Canal of Malabayla (1745–1827), Freemason and builder of the Canalgarten in Prague, a famous botanical garden.
5. That is, without composing even a single line of music.

caritatis camera[6] – 'and the beautiful ribbon we have too'[7] and that in this way the whole evening would again be spent *sine linea*; and so it was. – Well, for all I care, you can complain to Morpheus, but this god has been very propitious to us both in Prague; – what the cause may have been I don't know; but suffice it to say that we both slept very well. – Even so, we were able to get to Father Ungar's[8] by 11 o'clock for a worm's-eye view of the Imperial and Royal Library and General Seminary; – by the end our eyes were nearly popping out of our heads and we thought we could hear a little stomach aria in our insides, so it was good that we were able to drive to Count Canal's for lunch; – the evening came as a surprise to us sooner than you perhaps imagine; – enough, it was time to go to the opera. – We heard *Le gare generose*.[9] – As far as the performance is concerned, I can't tell you anything definite as I chattered a lot; quite why I chattered contrary to my usual custom is no doubt because of that. – *Basta*; this evening was again wasted *al solito*[10] – not until today was I lucky enough to find a moment to be able to enquire after the wellbeing of your dear parents and the whole of the Jacquin household. – I hope and pray with all my heart that you are all as well as we are. – I must frankly admit that – although I'm enjoying all possible courtesies and honours here and although Prague is indeed a very beautiful and pleasant place – I'm really longing to be back in Vienna again; and, believe me, the main reason for this is undoubtedly *your* house. – When I think that on my return I shall enjoy only briefly the pleasure of your valued company and shall then have to forgo this pleasure for such a long time – perhaps for ever – only then do I really feel the friendship and respect that I cherish for your entire house; – farewell now, dearest friend, dearest HinkitiHonky! – That's your name, just so that you know. On our journey here we

6. 'in the room of charity', i.e. placed at his disposal.
7. Mozart writes '*das schöne Bandel Hammera*', which rhymes with '*camera*' and is Viennese dialect for '*und das schöne Bandl haben wir auch*' – presumably a reference to the trio K441, the so-called Bandel-Terzett, of which only a fragment survives.
8. Karl Raphael Ungar (1743–1807), director of the Clementium Library in Prague.
9. Opera (1786) by Giovanni Paisiello.
10. 'as usual'.

devised names for all of us, here they are: *I*: Pùnkitititi. – *My wife*: SchablaPumfa. *Hofer*: Rozka-Pumpa. *Stadler*: Nàtschibinìtschibi. *Joseph my servant*: Sagadaratà. *My dog Gauckerl*: Schamanuzky. – *Madame Quallenberg*: Runzifunzi. – *Mlle Crux: PS. Ramlo*: Schurimuri. *Freystädtler*: Gaulimauli.[11] Please be so kind as to inform the latter of his name. – Adieu for now. My concert is at the theatre next Friday, the 19th; I'll probably have to give a second one, which will *unfortunately* prolong my stay here.[12] Please give my regards to your worthy parents and embrace your brother – who could be called Blatteririzi – 1000 times for me. – I kiss your sister[13] – Signora Dinimininimi – 100,000 times and ask her to practise hard on her new pianoforte – but this reminder is unnecessary – as I must admit that I've never had a pupil who was as hard-working and as enthusiastic as she is – and I'm certainly looking forward to continuing my lessons with her according to my modest abilities. – By the way, if she wants to come tomorrow, I'll certainly be at home at around 11 o'clock. –

But it's now time to close, isn't it? – You must have been thinking that for some time. – Farewell, best of men! – How I value our friendship – long may it last! – Write to me soon – but soon – and if you're too idle to do so, send for Satmann and dictate the letter to him; – but it never comes from the heart as much as when one writes oneself; – well, I'll see whether you're as much my friend as I am yours. Ever your

Mozart

---

11. The clarinettist Anton Paul Stadler, see List; Elisabeth Barbara Quallenberg, wife of the clarinettist Johann Michael Quallenberg (*c.* 1726–86); Maria Anna Antonia Crux (1772–?), singer, instrumentalist and niece of Johann Michael Quallenberg; Kaspar Ramlo, violinist; Franz Jakob Freystädtler (1761–1841), composer and pupil of Mozart's.

12. It was at the concert on 19 January that Mozart performed the symphony K504 ('Prague') and three piano improvisations, including one on 'Non più andrai' from *Le nozze di Figaro*. The second concert apparently never took place.

13. His brother was the botanist Baron Joseph Franz von Jacquin (1766–1839); for his sister Franziska von Jacquin, see List.

P.S.: In the event of your writing to me, address your letters to *Count Thun's Palace.*

My wife sends her very best wishes to the whole of the Jacquin household, as does Herr Hofer.

N. B.: On Wednesday[14] I'll see and hear Figaro here – if I've not gone deaf and blind by then. – Maybe I'll do so only after the opera – – –

156. Leopold Mozart to his daughter, 1 March 1787, Salzburg

That little Leopold is well you'll have been told by the bailiff and his wife, who safely delivered the letter with the 5 florins 40 kreutzers and the music. I gave them 2 books by Muratori[1] and threw in the programme for the concert at the Casino. I hope they don't get the books dirty. – This *Vanschenz*[2] played with so much expression both at the rehearsal at my own house and later in the quartets at court that we all thought we'd hear him give an outstanding concert yesterday, not least because it was the first time he'd played in public and the concerto was by a composer none of us had heard of: but we were all very disappointed. He played horribly badly and proved hopelessly inept. In short, not a single person applauded, quite the opposite, they all turned up their noses in their displeasure. And the hall was packed! –

On the Wednesday before Carnival Sunday the ball here was absolutely full as there were more than 470 people there. On Carnival Sunday there were some 320 and on Monday, too, around 315 etc.

14. 17 January; Mozart conducted a performance on 22 January.
1. Ludovico Antonio Muratori (1672–1750), philosopher and writer who advocated an enlightened Catholic tolerance.
2. Apparently a violinist; no details are known.

The faro[3] bank lost so much that they no longer felt like holding another one in the Casino as they did last year. I hope to God this nonsense will end of its own accord and that young people won't be tempted to gamble.

On Tuesday evening two days ago His Grace was left *5o ducats* lighter. At half past 6 on Monday evening I received a note from *Mme Storace*, the Viennese theatre singer, announcing that she'd arrived at the *Trinkstube*. I found her with her mother, who's English (the daughter was born in England), and also the Viennese theatre tenor O'Kelly, who's also English, another Englishman whom I didn't know but who's probably the *cicisbeo*[4] of mother or daughter, her brother Maestro Storace and a little Englishman called *Attwood*, who was sent to Vienna 2 years ago specially to have lessons with your brother.[5] Madame Storace had a letter of introduction from Countess Gundacker Colloredo, and so she had to be *heard* and *well treated*, as she's returning to the theatre in Vienna after a year-long stay in London. From 10 till 2 on Tuesday morning I galloped round the town to show them this and that. We didn't get our midday meal till 2. In the evening she sang 3 arias and they left for Munich at *12 o'clock at night*. They had 2 carriages, each with 4 post-horses, a servant rode on ahead as courier to order the 8 horses. And their luggage! Their journey must have cost a fortune! They all spoke English rather than Italian. The silliest thing is that my son had sent a letter for me to the house where his pupil Attwood was staying – he'd gone out and Madame Storace's mother took delivery of it – and was then stupid enough to put it in one of the trunks or possibly even to lose it. *Basta!* The letter couldn't be found. – I'll have to write to your brother about it in the morning.

3. A gambling card game.
4. In this context probably 'lover'.
5. In this passage Leopold mentions a number of Mozart's 'English' friends to whom he was very close at this time. For the Storace family, see List; O'Kelly is the Irish tenor Michael Kelly (1762–1826); the composer Thomas Attwood (1765–1838) was a student of Mozart's.

2 March.

As for your brother, I hear he's back in Vienna, I'd not heard from him since I wrote to him in Prague; I'm told that he made 1000 florins in Prague; that his last boy, Leopold, has died; and that, as I noted, he wants to travel to England but that his pupil[6] is first going to make some definite plans for him in London, in other words, he'll arrange a contract to write an opera or give a subscription concert etc. Madame Storace and the rest of the party will no doubt have been on at him about this, indeed I expect it was these people and his pupil who first gave him the idea of going to England with them. But after I'd written to him in a fatherly way, telling him that he'd earn nothing if he made the journey in summer as he'd arrive in England at the wrong time and that he should have *at least 2000 florins* in his pocket before undertaking such a journey and, finally, that unless he already had a firm engagement in London he'd have to take the risk of suffering hardship at least to begin with, no matter how clever he was – I expect he'll have lost courage, particularly because it will, of course, be the soprano's brother[7] who'll be writing an opera this time.

Now a delightful anecdote! Heinrich,[8] who's still running round Munich visiting people, came home on one occasion and said to me in the presence of everyone: *Bologna gave me some news: he asked me if I knew that Frau Aman was pregnant by Petraȥani; he'd been told this in a letter.* I replied: *It's not to Bologna's credit if he's spreading such lies about a close friend.* Everyone went very quiet! – How do you like that? – – –

I'm sending you herewith 1 lb. of chocolate no. 8 @ *2 florins 30 kreuȥers*, I paid 10 kreuzers for the almond paste. The rest is all ready and waiting and I'll make a note of it and hand it over if you send someone for it.

6. Attwood.
7. Stephen Storace.
8. Heinrich Marchand.

I kiss you with all my heart. Give my good wishes to the children. I am ever your honest father

Mozart

Today was the first time that the weather was warm enough for me to go for a walk.

Vanschenz has been taken on for only *a year* on 300 florins.

Heinrich sends his best wishes.

Tresel and Nandl kiss your hands. Best wishes to Lenerl.

157. Mozart to his father, 4 April 1787, Vienna[1]

Mon très cher Père, –

It's most unfortunate that thanks to Madame Storace's stupidity my letter failed to reach you; – among other things I said that I hoped you'd received my last letter – but as you don't mention this letter – it was my 2nd one from Prague – I don't know what to think; it's entirely possible that one of Count Thun's servants took it into his head to pocket the postage – but I'd rather pay twice the postage than know that my letters had fallen into the wrong hands, – Ramm and the 2 *Fischers*[2] – the bass and the oboist from London – came here for Lent. – If the latter played no better when we knew him in Holland than he does now, he certainly doesn't deserve the reputation that he has. – *But this just between ourselves*. – I was then of an age when I wasn't capable of forming an opinion – I remember only that I liked him enormously, as did the whole world; – but this is hardly surprising when you think that taste has changed enormously. –

1. This may have been Mozart's last letter to his father.
2. The singer Ludwig Fischer and the apparently unrelated oboist Johann Christian Fischer (1733–1800). Ludwig gave a concert at the Burgtheater on 21 March 1787 that included a Mozart symphony and the scena *Alcandro, lo confesso – Non sò d'onde viene* K512. Mozart's keyboard variations (K179) of late 1774 were composed on a minuet from Johann Christian Fischer's first oboe concerto (1768).

Perhaps he plays according to some older method. – But no! – Not to put too fine a point on it, he plays like a wretched pupil – young *André*,[3] who was taught by Fiala, *plays* a thousand times better – and then there are his[4] concertos – of his own composition – every ritornello lasts a quarter of an hour – then the hero enters, lifting one leaden foot after another and then banging on the floor with each in turn – his tone is entirely nasal – and his held notes are like a tremulant on an organ. Could you ever have imagined this scene? – Yet it's nothing but the truth – but a truth that I'm telling no one but *you*. – I've just this minute received news that has come as a great blow – not least because I'd assumed from your last letter that, praise be to God, you were feeling well; – but now I hear that you're very ill! I don't need to tell you how much I long to receive some reassuring news from you; and I'm sure that I shall – even though I've made a habit of always imagining the worst in all things – when looked at closely, death is the true goal of our lives, and so for a number of years I've familiarized myself with this true friend of man to such an extent that his image is not only no longer a source of terror to me but is comforting and consoling! And I give thanks to my God that He has given me the good fortune of finding an opportunity – you understand what I mean – of realizing that death is the *key* to our true happiness. – I never go to bed without thinking that – young as I am – I may no longer be alive the next morning – and yet no one who knows me can say that I'm sullen or sad in my dealings with them – and for this blessing I give daily thanks to my creator and with all my heart wish that all my fellow creatures may feel the same.[5] – I'd already expressed my views on this point in the letter that Madame Storace packed away with her luggage, views occasioned by the sad death of my dearest and best friend, Count von

3. Unidentified.
4. Johann Christian Fischer.
5. The sentiments expressed here echo those of the German Jewish philosopher Moses Mendelssohn (1729–86) in *Phädon oder über die Unsterblichkeit der Seele* (*Phaedo or On the Immortality of the Soul*, 1767), a copy of which, probably inherited from Leopold, was found among Mozart's effects.

Hatzfeld[6] – he was just 31 – like me – I don't feel sorry for *him* – but only for myself and all who knew him as well as I did. – I hope and pray that, even as I write these lines, you're feeling better; but if, contrary to all expectation, you're not better, I would ask you by . . . . . . not to conceal it from me but to tell me the plain truth or get someone else to write to me, so that I may hold you in my arms as fast as is humanly possible; I entreat you by all that is sacred to us. – But I hope that I shall soon receive a comforting word from you, and in this pleasant hope I and my wife and Carl kiss your hands 1000 times. I am ever your most obedient son

W. A. Mozart

Leopold Mozart died on 28 May.

158. Mozart to his sister, 2 June 1787, Vienna

Dearest Sister,

You can well imagine how distressed I was by the sad news of our dearest father's sudden death, as the loss affects us both equally. – – As it's impossible for me to leave Vienna at present – which I'd do if only to have the pleasure of embracing you – and as it would hardly be worth coming simply to sort out our late father's effects, I must confess that I'm entirely of your opinion with regard to a public auction; but I shall first wait to see an inventory in order to be able to choose one or two items from it; – but if, as Herr von d'Ippold[1]

---

6. August Clemens Ludwig Maria, Count Hatzfeld (1754–87). Mozart had met him in 1786 and composed the violin part of K490, the scena 'Non più, tutto ascoltai – Non temer, amato bene', for him.

1. Franz d'Ippold had informed Mozart of Leopold's death in a letter of 28 May 1787, now lost.

tells me, there's a *dispositio paterna inter liberos*,[2] I first need to know about this before I can make any further arrangements; – – I'm now awaiting an exact copy of it and after a brief perusal of its contents I'll inform you of my opinion at once. – Please ensure that the enclosed letter is handed to our good and true friend Herr von d'Ippold; – as he has already proved to be a friend of our family on so many other occasions, I hope that he will again demonstrate his friendship and represent me in any way that's necessary. – – Farewell, dearest sister! I am ever your faithful brother

W. A. Mozart

P.S.: My wife sends her best wishes to you and your husband, as do I. – –

159. Mozart's poem to his dead starling, 4 June 1787, Vienna[1]

> Here lies my foolish darling who
> In life was my pet starling. You
> Were taken from me in your prime
> And snatched away before your time
> And made to feel death's bitter blow.
> The merest thought of it, I know,
> Will cause my heart to bleed. So shed
> A little tear for him. No shred
> Of malice, gentle reader, lay
> Within his heart. I'll only say
> He was a rather lively bird,
> A dear and playful rogue. No word
> Shall I hear said against a friend
> Whom none could ever reprehend.

2. 'testamentary disposition'. Wolfgang wanted d'Ippold to serve as executor of Leopold's will, but because of a possible conflict of interest with Nannerl he declined.
1. Mozart had purchased a pet starling on 27 May 1784 and noted at the time that it was almost able to sing the theme of the third movement of his piano concerto K453.

I'll wager he's already there
At God's right hand and that he'll swear
He's never known a friend as kind
And selfless as the undersigned.
For when he unexpectedly
Fell off his perch and jilted me,
He didn't think about the man
Who rhymes as well as any can.
4 June 1787.   Mozart.

160. Mozart to his sister, 16 June 1787, Vienna

Dearest, most beloved Sister,

It didn't surprise me at all that you didn't inform me yourself about our very dear father's sad and, to me, entirely unexpected, death, as I could easily guess the reason. – May God take him to His bosom! – Rest assured, my dear, that if you want a kind-hearted brother to love and protect you, you'll undoubtedly find one in me, whatever the occasion. – My dearest, most beloved sister, if you were still unprovided for, I'd need none of this. As I've thought and said a thousand times, I'd leave it all to you with genuine pleasure; but as it is of no use to you but, conversely, would be of considerable help to me, I consider it my duty to think of my wife and child.

161. Mozart to his sister, 1 August 1787, Vienna

Dearest, most beloved Sister, –

I'm writing at present only in order to reply to your letter – not much, and even this is in a hurry, as I have too much to do. – As both your husband, my dear brother-in-law, whom I ask you to kiss 1000 times for me, and I are keen to conclude this whole matter as soon as possible, I accept his offer, but on one condition, namely, that he pays me the 1000 florins not in imperial currency but in Viennese currency and, moreover, as a bill of exchange. – I'll send your husband the draft of an agreement or, rather, of a contract between us next post day, to be followed by 2 original copies, one signed by me, the other to be signed by him. – I'll send you some new pieces of mine for the piano as soon as I can. Please don't forget my *scores*.[1] – Farewell a thousand times. I must close. – My wife and Carl send a 1000 good wishes to you and your husband. I am ever your honest brother who loves you,

W. A. Mozart

On 1 October Mozart and Constanze set out for Prague for the preparations for the first performance of his opera Don Giovanni, *his second collaboration with Da Ponte, commissioned earlier that year in the wake of* Figaro's *Prague success. On 14 October Mozart conducted* Le nozze di Figaro *as part of the festivities celebrating the wedding of Archduchess Maria Theresa, niece of Joseph II, and Prince Anton Clemens of Saxony;* Don Giovanni *was premiered on 29 October.*

162. Mozart to Gottfried von Jacquin, 4 November 1787, Prague

Dearest, most beloved Friend,

I hope you received my letter; – my opera *Don Giovanni* was staged on 29 Oct. and met with the most tremendous acclaim. – It was given yesterday for the 4th time – for my benefit; – I'm planning to leave here on the 12th or 13th; as soon as I'm back, you'll have the aria[1] straightaway; *N. B. between ourselves;* – I wish that my good

1. After Leopold's death, Mozart's autograph scores still in Salzburg were sent to him in Vienna; copies of some works were sent to the monastery of the Holy Cross in Augsburg and others sold on the open market. The inventory of Leopold Mozart's estate does not give specific details of the music that he owned.
1. Unidentified.

friends – especially you and Bridi[2] – could have been here for just one evening to share in my pleasure! – But perhaps it'll be performed in Vienna? – I hope so. – People here are doing everything possible to persuade me to remain here for another couple of months and write another opera. – But, however flattering their offer, I can't accept it. – Now, my dearest friend, how are you? – I hope that you're *all* as well and as healthy as we are; – you can't fail to be happy, dearest friend, as you possess everything you could wish for *at your age* and *in your situation*! – especially since you appear to have entirely abandoned your former somewhat *unsettled lifestyle*; – I guess that with each passing day you're becoming more and more convinced of the truth of the little lectures I gave you. – Surely the pleasures of a fickle and flighty passion are worlds apart from the happiness afforded by a true and sensible love. – In your heart I expect that you often thank me for my teachings! – You'll make me quite conceited. – But, joking apart, I deserve at least some thanks if you're now more worthy of Fräulein N[3] . . . . as I played a by no means insignificant part in reforming or converting you; – my great-grandfather used to say to his wife, my great-grandmother, who then told her daughter, my grandmother, who in turn told her daughter, my mother, who in turn told her daughter, my own sister, that to speak well and to talk a flowery language is a very great art but perhaps a no less great art is knowing when to stop; – and so I'll heed the advice of my sister, which she owed to our mother, grandmother and great-grandmother, and put a stop not only to my moral excursus but also to this letter as a whole.

The 9th. – I've received your 2nd letter with a mixture of surprise and pleasure; – if you needed the song[4] in question to be assured of

---

2. Possibly Giuseppe Antonio Bridi (1763–1836), who sang at the private perform-ance of *Idomeneo* at Prince Auersperg's in March 1786.
3. Marianne (Nanette) Natorp; Mozart dedicated the four-hand sonata K521 to Marianne and her sister Barbara (Babette).
4. Possibly the song *Das Traumbild* ('Wo bist du, Bild, das vor mir stand') K530, based on a text by the poet L. H. C. Hölty. Mozart dated the work Prague, 6 November 1787.

my friendship for you, you've no further cause to doubt it – for here it is: – but I hope that you're convinced of my true friendship even *without this song*, and in this hope I remain ever your most sincere friend

W. A. Mozart

P. S.: I *really* can't believe that neither your dear parents nor your sister nor your brother remembered me! – I ascribe that entirely to *your* forgetfulness, my friend. And I flatter myself that I'm not mistaken. – As for the double seal, it's like this: the red wax was useless – so I sealed it on top in black; – and I left my usual seal in Vienna. – Adieu, – I hope to embrace you soon.

We both send our best wishes to your whole family and also to the Natorps. –

Mozart and Constanze returned to Vienna about 16 November. The composer Christoph Willibald Gluck had died in Vienna on 15 November, and on 7 December Joseph II appointed Mozart imperial and royal chamber composer with an annual salary of 800 florins. Mozart and Constanze's fourth child, Theresia Constanzia Adelheid, was born on 27 December. Other details of Mozart's life at this time are scarce. On 10 February 1788 he played at a concert given by the Venetian ambassador Andrea Dolfin, and in February and March he performed his arrangement of C. P. E. Bach's cantata Auferstehung und Himmelfart Jesu *at Count Esterházy's. In March he composed the aria* Ah se in ciel, benigne stelle *K588 for Aloysia Lange and on 2 April he began a subscription for three string quintets (K406, 515 and 516) that failed to fill. A revised version of* Don Giovanni *was premiered at the court theatre in Vienna on 7 May. On 17 June, Mozart and Constanze moved to the Alsergrund suburb, in the Währingerstrasse.*

163. Mozart to Michael Puchberg, 27 June 1788, Vienna

Most honourable B. O.,[1]
Dearest and most beloved Friend,
    I kept thinking that I'd get into town one of these days in order to thank you in person for the kindness that you've shown me – but now I don't even have the heart to appear before you as I'm obliged to admit quite candidly that I can't possibly pay you back the money you lent me as soon as I'd intended and I must ask you to be patient with me! – It worries me greatly that the situation is what it is and that you can't help me as much as I'd like! – My position is such that I'm absolutely forced to raise some money. – But, in God's name, in whom can I confide? No one but you, my dearest of friends! – If you would at least be kind enough to obtain the money for me by some other means! – I'll gladly pay the interest, and whoever lends it to me is, I think, sufficiently indemnified by my character & my income – I'm only sorry to be in this position, but that's why I'd like to have a fairly *substantial sum* for a somewhat *longer period of time* in order to be able to obviate the situation. – If you, my most worthy brother, don't help me in my present situation, I shall lose my honour and my credit, which is the one thing I'd like to keep. – I rely entirely on your genuine friendship and brotherly love and confidently expect that you'll help me in word and deed. If I obtain what I want, I'll be able to breathe freely again as I'll then be in a position to put my affairs in order and *keep* them like that; – do come and see me; I'm always at home; – in the 10 days that I've been here I've done more work than in 2 months in my other lodgings, and if I weren't so often plagued by black thoughts that I can banish only with great effort, things would be even better, as my rooms are pleasant – comfortable – and *cheap!* – I don't want to detain you any longer with my nonsense and shall *say no more* – and *hope.*
                    Ever your obedient servant and true friend and B. O.
                                                        W. A. Mozart

1. Abbreviation standing for Brother of the Order; Johann Michael Puchberg, see List, belonged to the same lodge as Mozart.

164. Mozart to his sister, 2 August 1788, Vienna

Dearest Sister,

You'd have every reason to be angry with me![1] – But will you still be cross when you receive my latest piano pieces by this mail coach? – Oh no! – This, I hope, will put us back on course. –

As you'll be convinced that not a day goes by without my wishing you every possible happiness, you'll not mind if I'm a little late in sending you my best wishes on your name day; – dearest sister; – with all my heart and soul I wish you all that you believe is most beneficial to yourself, and that's that. –

Dear sister! – You can't doubt that I've a lot to do – you also know that I'm rather lazy when it comes to writing letters; – so don't take it amiss if I write to you only *rarely*; – but this shouldn't prevent you from often writing *to me*; – however much I dislike writing letters, I like receiving them. – Also, you've got more to write about than I have as there are more things that interest me in Salzburg than is the case with you and Vienna. –

I now have something to ask of you: – I wonder if Haydn would lend me *his 2 tutti masses* and the *graduals* that he's written?[2] I'd like to borrow them for a time in full score and will return them with many thanks. – It's now a year since I wrote to him and invited him to visit me, but he hasn't replied; – in terms of answering letters he seems to have a lot in common *with me*, doesn't he? – So I would ask you to arrange these matters as follows: – invite him out to your house and play him some of my new works; – the trio and the quartet will surely not displease him.[3] – Adieu, dearest sister! – As soon

1. Presumably because Mozart rarely wrote to her. This is his last surviving letter to Nannerl, possibly the last he wrote her.
2. These works cannot be identified with certainty; Michael Haydn wrote more than 30 masses and 170 graduals.
3. Mozart's most recent piano trios, both for keyboard, violin and violoncello, were K542 (22 June 1788) and K548 (14 July 1788); the piano quartet is possibly K493, composed in June 1786 but not published until 1787. Mozart's earlier quartet, K478, was composed and published in 1785 and had presumably already been sent to Salzburg.

as I've collected together some more new music, I'll send it to you;
– I am ever your sincere brother

W. A. Mozart

P. S.: My wife sends her very best wishes. And we send ours to our dear brother-in-law.

P. S.: In reply to your point about my terms of service, the emperor has taken me into his household and as a result has made a formal *appointment*; *for the present*, however, I'm on only *800* florins – but no one else in the household is getting *so much*. – Although the playbill for my Prague opera *Don Giovanni* – which is being given again today – could hardly be accused of including *too much* information as the management of the Imperial and Royal Theatres was responsible for it, it did say that the music was by Herr Mozart, *Kapellmeister in the actual service of His Imperial and Royal Majesty.*

Between June and August 1788 Mozart composed his last three symphonies, K543, 550 and 551 ('Jupiter'). His daughter Theresia died on 29 June. In November he arranged Handel's masque Acis and Galatea *(1718/32) for Gottfried van Swieten; his arrangement of Handel's* Messiah *(1742) was performed at Count Esterházy's on 6 March 1789. In January he and Constanze had moved back into the city, to Judenplatz 245, and later that spring Mozart decided to undertake a concert tour to Dresden, Leipzig and Berlin. He left Vienna on 8 April in the company of Prince Karl Lichnowsky (1761–1814), a prominent Viennese patron of music (he was later a patron of Beethoven's, who dedicated several works to him).*

165. Mozart to his wife, 10 April (Good Friday) 1789, Prague

Dearest and most beloved little wife,
    We arrived here safely at half past 1 today; meanwhile I hope

you've received my note from Budwitz. – Now for my report on Prague. – We put up at the Unicorn; – after I'd been shaved, had my hair done and got dressed, I drove out to Canal's, intending to dine with him; but as I had to drive past the Duscheks, I made enquiries there and discovered that Madame had yesterday left for Dresden!!! – – – So I'll meet her there. He was dining at Leliborn's, where I too often used to dine; – so I drove straight there. – I sent in a message to the effect that someone was wanting to speak to Duschek and that he should come out. You can imagine his delight. – So I dined at Leliborn's. – After we'd eaten, I drove off to see Canal and Pachta,[1] but they weren't at home; – and so I went to Guardasoni's – who has virtually arranged for me to be given 200 ducats for the opera next autumn[2] and 50 ducats as travelling expenses. – I then returned home in order to write all this to my dear little wife – something else; – Ramm left here only a week ago to return home, he'd come from Berlin and said that the king[3] had frequently and insistently asked if it was certain that I was going to Berlin, and as I'd not yet come, he then said he was afraid that I wasn't coming. – Ramm got very anxious and tried to reassure him; – to judge from this, things shouldn't go too badly for me. – I'm now taking the prince[4] to meet Duschek, who's waiting for us, and at 9 o'clock we're leaving for Dresden, where we'll arrive tomorrow evening. – My dear little wife, I long so much for news of you – perhaps I'll find a letter waiting for me in Dresden! O God! make my wishes come true! On receiving this letter you must write to me *poste restante* in Leipzig, you understand; adieu, my dear, I must close, otherwise the post will leave without me. – I kiss our Carl a thousand times and kiss you with all my heart. I am ever your faithful

Mozart

1. Major General Johann Joseph Philipp Pachta von Rayhofen (c. 1723–1822).
2. This opera commission from theatre impresario Domenico Guardasoni (c. 1731–1806) was not realized.
3. Frederick William II of Prussia (1744–97) had succeeded his father Frederick the Great in 1786.
4. Karl Lichnowsky.

P. S.: All conceivable good wishes to Herr and Frau von Puchberg, I'll have to wait till I get to Berlin to write and thank him. – Adieu, *aimez moi et gardez votre santé si chère et précieuse à votre époux.*[5]

166. Mozart to his wife, 16 April 1789, Dresden

Half past 11 at night

Dearest and most beloved little wife,

What? – Still in Dresden? – Yes, my dear; – I'll explain it all in every last detail; – on Monday the 13th, after we'd had breakfast at Neumann's, we all went to the court chapel, the mass was by Naumann,[1] he conducted it himself – very mediocre; – we were in an oratory opposite the musicians; – Neumann suddenly nudged me and introduced me to Herr von König, who's *Directeur des Plaisirs* – the doleful pleasures of the elector;[2] – he was exceptionally civil and when he asked if I'd like His Highness to hear me, I replied that it would be a great honour but that I wasn't my own master, I couldn't stay – and that's how we left it; – my princely travelling companion invited the Neumanns and Frau Duschek to lunch: – while we were at table, a message arrived to say that I was to play at court the following day, Tuesday the 14th, at half past 5 in the evening. – This is something quite exceptional here, where it's otherwise very difficult to obtain an audience; and you know that I'd absolutely no thought of doing so here. – We'd arranged a quartet at the Hôtel de Pologne.[3] – We played it in the chapel with Anton Teyber – who, as you know, is the organist here – and Herr Kraft – who's Prince Esterházy's

---

5. 'love me and look after your health, which is so dear and precious to your husband.' Constanze was frequently ill at this time, probably with complications arising from her numerous pregnancies.

1. Johann Gottlieb Naumann (1741–1801), music director to the elector of Saxony.

2. Friedrich August III, Elector of Saxony (1750–1827), whose court was at Dresden.

3. Where Mozart was lodging.

cellist and who's here with his son;[4] among the works I played at this little concert was the trio[5] I wrote for Herr von Puchberg – it received a really quite commendable performance – and Frau Duschek sang a whole number of things from Figaro and Don Juan;[6] – the next day, at court, I played the new concerto in D;[7] and the following morning – Wednesday the 15th – I received a very beautiful snuffbox; – we then had lunch at the Russian ambassador's,[8] where I played a lot. – After lunch we decided to go off in search of an organ. – It was 4 o'clock by the time we got there – Naumann was there too; – I should add that a certain Hässler[9] – he's the organist at Erfurt – is here; he too was there; – he's a pupil of a pupil of Bach. – His forte is the organ and the clavichord – well, the people here think that because I come from Vienna, I don't know anything about their taste in music and style of playing. – So I sat down at the organ and played. – Prince Lichnowsky – because he knows Hässler very well – persuaded him to play too, though it required a great effort to get him to do so; – Hässler's forte on the organ is his footwork, which, since the pedals here are graded, doesn't require much skill; also, he's merely learnt by heart old Sebastian Bach's harmony and modulations and is incapable of playing a fugue properly – he has no solid technique – as a result, he's far from being an Albrechtsberger.[10] – After this we decided to go back to the Russian ambassador's so that Hässler could hear me on the fortepiano; – Hässler played too. – On the fortepiano I think Fräulein Auernhammer is just as proficient; so you can imagine that he's sunk considerably in my estimation. – After that we went to the opera, which was truly awful; – do you know

---

4. Anton Kraft (1749–1820), violoncellist in the service of Joseph Haydn's employer, Prince Nikolaus Esterházy (1714–90); his son Nikolaus Kraft (1778–1853), also a violoncellist.

5. Presumably K563, for violin, viola and violoncello.

6. That is, *Don Giovanni*.

7. K537.

8. Alexander Michailovich, Prince Beloselski-Beloserki (1757–1809), Russian ambassador at Dresden from 1780 to 1790.

9. Johann Wilhelm Hässler (1747–1822).

10. Johann Georg Albrechtsberger (1736–1809), composer and organist at the Viennese court.

who one of the singers was? – Rosa Manservisi, – you can imagine her delight at seeing me there. – But the leading singer, Allegranti, is in fact much better than Ferrarese – not that that's saying much.[11] – We returned home after the opera; now comes the happiest moment for me; I found a letter from you, my dearest, my beloved, something I'd been longing for so very much! – Frau Duschek and the Neumanns were still with me, I immediately went off to my room in triumph, kissed the letter countless times before breaking it open – and then devoured it rather than read it. – I remained in my room for quite a while as I couldn't read it often enough or kiss it often enough. When I rejoined the company, the Neumanns asked me if I'd received a letter and when I said yes they all congratulated me sincerely as every day I'd been complaining that I'd not had any news; – the Neumanns are delightful people; – now for your kind letter; my account of my stay here up to the time of my departure will be continued in my next letter.

Dear little wife, I've a whole series of favours to ask of you; –

1) please don't be sad;

2) *take care of your health* and *don't trust* the spring air.

3) don't go out walking alone – best of all, don't *go walking* at all

4) be assured of my love; – I've not written a single letter to you without placing your dear portrait in front of me.

6) *et ultimo* please go into greater detail in your letters. – I'd like to know if my brother-in-law, Hofer, called the day after I left; does he come often, as he promised he would; – do the Langes come occasionally? – Is any more work being done on your portrait?[12] – What sort of a life are you leading? – These are all things that naturally interest me very much. –

– 5) please pay proper heed not only to *your own honour* and *mine*

---

11. The opera was *Le trame deluse ovvero I raggiri scoperti* by Domenico Cimarosa (1749–1801); Manservisi had sung the role of Sandrina at the premiere of *La finta giardiniera* (Munich 1775); Maddalena Allegranti (1754–after 1801), soprano; Adriana Ferrarese del Bene (1759–after 1803) later sang the role of Susanna in the Vienna revival of *Le nozze di Figaro* (1789) and created that of Fiordiligi in *Così fan tutte* (Vienna 1790).

12. It is uncertain what portrait Mozart refers to here.

in your conduct, but also to *appearances*. – Don't be cross with me for asking this. – You should love me even more for setting such store by honour.

Now farewell, my dearest, most beloved little wife! – Remember that each night before going to bed I talk to your portrait for a good half hour and do so again when I wake up. – We're leaving the day after tomorrow, the 18th; – *from now on you should always write to Berlin poste restante.*

O Stru! Stri! – I kiss and squeeze you 1095060437082 times – here you can practise your pronunciation. I am ever

Your most faithful husband and friend
W. A. Mozart

I'll finish off my account of our stay in Dresden next time. – Good night! –

167. Mozart to his wife, 23 May 1789, Berlin

Dearest, most beloved, most precious little wife, –

It was with extraordinary pleasure that I received your kind letter of the 13th; – but I've only just this minute received your previous one of the 9th as it had to make its way back to Berlin from Leipzig. – First, I must list all the letters that I've written to you, and then the ones that I've received from you. – I wrote to you

on 8 April from the post-stage at Budwitz. –
on the 10th from Prague.
on the 13th and on the 17th from Dresden.
on the 22nd (in French) from Leipzig.
on the 28th and 5 May from Potsdam
on the 9th and 16th from Leipzig.
on the 19th from Berlin
and now the 23rd – that makes 11 letters.

I received your letter of 8th April on 15th April in Dresden.

of 13th – on the 21st in Leipzig.
of 24th – on 8th May in Leipzig.
of 5th May – on 14th – in Leipzig.   on my return.
of 13th – on the 20th in Berlin.
and that of the 9th – on the 22nd in Berlin.

That makes 6 letters.[1]

As you can see, there's a gap between 13 and 24 April, when one of your letters must have gone missing, and so I had to survive for 17 days without a letter from you! – If you too had to contend with a similar situation for 17 days, then one of my letters, too, must have gone missing; – praise be to God, we shall soon have survived these calamities; – and *with my arms round your neck*, I'll be able to tell you exactly how things have gone for me! – But – you know how much I love you! – Where do you think I'm writing this? – In my room at the inn? – No; – in a public house in the Tiergarten[2] – in a summer-house with a beautiful view – where I had lunch today *all on my own*, in order to be able to devote myself entirely to you; – the queen[3] wants to hear me on Tuesday; *but there's not much to be made there.* I simply announced my arrival, as that's the custom here and they'd have taken it amiss if I'd not. – My dearest little wife, when I return you must look forward to seeing *me*, rather than to any *money*. – 100 friedrichs d'or aren't 900 florins, but 700; – at least that's what I've been told. – 2nd, Lichnowsky was in a hurry and had to leave early, so that I have to support myself in Potsdam,[4] which is an expensive place; – 3rd, I had to lend him 100 florins as he was running out of money – I couldn't really refuse, you know why.[5] – 4th, the concert in Leipzig turned out badly, as I always said it would, so that I went

---

1. Of Mozart's letters, four have gone missing: those of 22 and 28 April and of 5 and 9 May; none of Constanze Mozart's letters survives.
2. The Tiergarten in Berlin, formerly a royal hunting reserve, became a public park in the eighteenth century.
3. Friederike of Prussia (1751–1805).
4. The summer residence of the kings of Prussia, southwest of Berlin.
5. Mozart's meaning is unclear here.

32 miles[6] – plus the return journey – for virtually nothing; for this, Lichnowsky is entirely to blame, as he wouldn't leave me in peace but insisted on my returning to Leipzig. – But – more on this in person; – here, there is, *1st*, not much to be made from a concert and, *2nd*, the king wouldn't be keen on it. – You must be content, *as I am*, with the fact that I'm fortunate to enjoy the king's favour; – what I've written here is between ourselves. – I'll be leaving for Dresden on Thursday the 28th and shall spend the night there. On 1 June I'll be sleeping in Prague, and on the 4th – the 4th? – *with my dearest little wife*; – tidy up your lovely little nest for me as my little knave certainly deserves it, he's been behaving himself and wants only to possess your most beautiful . . . . Just imagine the rascal: even while I'm writing, he's creeping up on to the table and looking at me questioningly, but I won't stand for this and give a quick slap – but the lad is simply . . . . . The rogue is now even more on fire and I can hardly restrain him any longer. I hope you'll drive out to the first post-stage to meet me? – I'll be arriving there at midday on the 4th; – I hope that Hofer – whom I embrace 1000 times – will be there too; – if Herr and Frau von Puchberg come too, then everyone will be there whom I'd like to see. And don't forget Carl. – But, most important of all, you must bring with you someone who can be trusted – Satmann or someone like that – who can drive off to the customs with my luggage so that *I* don't have to deal with this unnecessary *seccatura* but can drive home with you dear people. – Most certainly! –

Adieu for now – I kiss you millions of time and am ever your most faithful husband

W. A. Mozart

Mozart arrived back in Vienna on 4 June. He was in financial difficulties once again and planned to give subscription concerts but was unable to

---

6. A German mile in the eighteenth century varied between 7 and 9 km; the distance from Leipzig to Berlin and back is about 290 km, so Mozart is approximately correct.

find any patrons other than Baron van Swieten. Constanze, who was pregnant for the fifth time, was ill, and in August made a visit for her health to Baden, a spa not far from Vienna.

168. Mozart to Michael Puchberg, 12 July 1789, Vienna

Dearest, most beloved friend
and most worthy B. O.,

My God, I'm in a situation that I wouldn't wish on my worst enemy; and if you, my dearest friend and brother, abandon me, I and my poor sick wife and child will *unfortunately* be lost *through no fault of my own.* – When I was with you recently, I wanted to open my heart to you – but I didn't have the heart to do so! – and even now I dare only write, and I tremble as I do so – indeed, I wouldn't even dare to write if I didn't know that you know me and that you're familiar with my circumstances and are entirely convinced that I'm *innocent* as far as my unfortunate and extremely sad situation is concerned. O God! Instead of words of gratitude, I'm coming to you with more requests! – Instead of settling up, I'm demanding more. If you really know my heart, you're bound to feel my anguish at this; I probably don't need to repeat that this unfortunate illness has prevented me from earning any money; but I must tell you that in spite of my wretched condition I decided to give my subscription concerts at home in order to be able to meet my present expenses, which are currently so great and so frequent, as I was convinced that you'd be kind enough to wait; but in this, too, I was unsuccessful; – my fate, unfortunately, is so much against me – *albeit only in Vienna* – that I can't earn anything even when I want to; 2 weeks ago I sent round a list for subscribers, and the only name on it is *Swieten's*! – As of today (the 13th) it seems that my dear little wife is slowly getting better, so that I would have been able to work, if this blow, this heavy blow, hadn't struck; – at least people are comforting us by saying that things are improving – although yesterday evening she again reduced me to a state of dismay and despair, as she was in so much pain – and I with her, but tonight (the 14th) she slept so well and things have been so much easier all this morning that I'm extremely hopeful; and I'm again starting to feel like work – but at the same time I see misfortune facing me from another quarter – even if only for the moment! – Dearest, most beloved friend and brother – you know *my present circumstances*, but you're also aware of *my prospects*; things will remain as we agreed; like *this* or like *this*, you understand; – meanwhile I'm writing 6 easy keyboard sonatas for Princess Friederike and 6 quartets for the king,[1] all of which I'll have Koželuch engrave at my expense; in addition the 2 dedications will earn me something; in a couple of months my fate must be decided in *every last detail*, and so you, my most beloved friend, will not be risking anything; so it depends solely on you, my only friend, as to whether you are willing or able to lend me a further 500 florins. – Until my affairs are sorted out, I'd be grateful if I could repay you at a rate of 10 florins a month; and then – in a few months' time at the very most – I'll repay the whole sum with whatever interest you like and at the same time declare myself your debtor for life, which I shall unfortunately always have to remain, as I'll never be in a position to thank you sufficiently for your friendship and love; – praise be to God, it's done; you now know everything; please don't take it amiss that I've confided in you but bear in mind that without your support, the honour, peace of mind and perhaps even the life of your friend and brother will be destroyed; ever your most grateful servant, true friend and brother

W. A. Mozart

At home, 14 July 1789.
Oh God! – I can hardly bring myself to post this letter! – And yet I've no choice! – If it hadn't been for this illness, I'd not have been forced to behave so shamelessly towards my only friend; – and yet I hope that you'll forgive me as you know what is good and *bad about*

1. It is unclear whether these works were commissioned or whether Mozart merely intended to dedicate them to the king of Prussia and his daughter, Princess Friederike (1767–1820) – and thereby receive a royal gift. In the event, Mozart only wrote three more quartets (see letter 174, n. 1).

my situation. The bad will soon pass, but the good will certainly last if only the present evil can be alleviated. – Adieu! – Forgive me in God's name, I beg you to forgive me! – – and – adieu! – – – – – –

169. Mozart to his wife, mid-August 1789, Vienna

My darling little wife, –

I was delighted to receive your dear letter[1] – I hope you received my 2nd letter yesterday, together with the decoction, the electuaries and the ants' eggs.[2] – I'll be setting sail at 5 in the morning – if it weren't simply for the pleasure of seeing you and holding you in my arms again, I'd not drive out just yet as they'll shortly be performing Figaro,[3] for which I have to make a number of changes, so I'm needed at the rehearsals – I'll probably have to be back here by the 19th – but it would be impossible for me to remain here until the 19th *without you*; – dear little wife! – I want to speak to you very candidly, – you've absolutely no reason to be sad – you have a husband who loves you and who does everything he can for you – as for your leg, you just need to be patient, it's bound to get better; – of course, I'm pleased when you have some fun – most certainly I am – I just wish that you wouldn't sometimes make yourself so cheap – in my view you're too free and easy with N. N.[4] . . . also with N. N. when he was in Baden, – remember that N. N. are not as coarse in their dealings with other women – whom they may well know better than

1. Constanze was then at Baden.
2. Medicaments of various kinds; ants' eggs may refer to a preparation made from the dried pupae of red ants, though they may have been intended as food for a pet bird.
3. *Le nozze di Figaro* was revived at the Burgtheater on 29 August. For this production Mozart replaced Susanna's aria 'Deh vieni non tardar' with the rondo 'Al desio di chi t'adora' K577 and additionally composed for her the aria 'Un moto di gioia' K579.
4. Unidentified. Names have been obliterated from several of the letters Mozart wrote at this time and made anonymous with the letters 'N. N.' It is unclear who made these changes, or when.

they know you – as they are with you, even N. N., who is otherwise well-behaved and particularly respectful towards women, must have been misled by you into writing the most terrible and foul-mouthed *sottises* in his letter – a woman must always ensure that she's respected – otherwise people start to gossip – my love! – forgive me for being so candid, but my peace of mind demands it as much as our mutual happiness – remember only that you yourself once admitted that you were too *indulgent* – you know the consequences of this – remember, too, the promise that you made me – oh God! – just try, my love! – be happy and contented and ready to please me – don't torment yourself and me with needless jealousy – trust in my love, after all you have proof of it! – and you'll see how contented we can be, believe me that only if a wife behaves prudently will she bind her husband to her – adieu – tomorrow I'll kiss you with all my heart.

Mozart

In September Mozart composed the clarinet quintet K581. Wolfgang and Constanze's fifth child, Anna Maria, was born on 16 November but died the same day. At the time, Mozart was hard at work on a new opera, Così fan tutte ('Women are all the same'), which premiered at the Burgtheater on 26 January 1790. After six performances the opera's successful run was interrupted by the death of Emperor Joseph II on 20 February.

170. Mozart to Michael Puchberg, late March or early April 1790, Vienna

Herewith, my dearest friend, I'm sending you the life of Handel.[1] – When I got home after my last visit to see you, I found the enclosed

1. Presumably Johann Mattheson, *Georg Friedrich Händels Lebensbeschreibung* (Hamburg, 1761).

note from Baron Swieten. You'll see from it, as I did, that my prospects are now better than ever. – I'm now standing on the very threshold of my own good fortune[2] – but I'll lose it for ever if I can't take advantage of it this time. My present circumstances, however, are such that, no matter how agreeable my prospects, I must abandon for ever all hope of future prosperity unless I have the help of a true friend; – for some time now you'll have noticed that I've been constantly sad – and only the inordinate number of kindnesses that you've shown me have persuaded me to remain silent; but now, in my hour of utmost need, when the whole of my future happiness will be decided, I call upon you once again, and for the last time, fully trusting in the friendship and brotherly love that you've shown me, to stand by me to the best of your abilities. You know how my present circumstances would harm my application to the court if they were to become known – and how necessary it is that they remain a secret; for at court they judge not by circumstances but, unfortunately, only by appearances. You know and, I'm sure, are entirely convinced that if my application succeeds, as I now hope it will, you yourself will certainly not be the loser – with what pleasure I shall repay my debts to you! – With what pleasure I shall thank you – and, moreover, acknowledge myself for ever in your debt! – What an agreeable sensation it is finally to reach one's goal! – What a blissful sensation to have helped someone else do so – my tears prevent me from completing the picture – in short! – the whole of my future happiness lies in your hands – act according to the dictates of your noble heart – do what you can and remember that you're dealing with an honest and eternally grateful man whose situation is a source of such anguish to himself more on your account than on his own! –

Mozart

[*Note added by Michael Puchberg*]
Sent 150 florins.

2. Mozart was hoping for a position as court Kapellmeister under the new emperor; see next letter.

171. Mozart to Archduke Franz of Austria, first half of May 1790, Vienna[1]

Your Royal Highness,

I make so bold as to beg your R. H. in all reverence most graciously to intercede on my behalf with H. M. the emperor in respect of my most humble petition to H. M. – A desire for fame, a love of work and a belief in my own abilities prompt me to venture to apply for the post of second Kapellmeister, especially as Salieri, although very well qualified as a Kapellmeister, has never devoted himself to church music, whereas I have made this style entirely my own from my youth onwards. The scant reputation that the world has accorded me for my playing on the pianoforte has encouraged me to ask H. M. to grant me the favour of most graciously entrusting me with the royal family's musical education. –

In the sure conviction that I have applied to the worthiest mediator, who looks on me with particular favour, I am fully confident and shall strive to the best of my abilities to convince[2]

172. Mozart to his wife, about 2 June 1790, Vienna

Wednesday
Dearest little wife,

I hope you received my letter; – I'm bound to be a little cross with you, my love! – Even if it's not possible for you to receive a letter from me, you could still write – does it have to be just a *reply*? – I was fully expecting a letter from my dear little wife – but unfortunately I was wrong – I advise you to make amends, otherwise I'll not forgive you as long as I live – yesterday I was at the second part of *Cosa*

1. This is a draft. It is not known if Mozart sent such a letter to Archduke Franz (the future Emperor Francis II), or petitioned Leopold II directly for a position; if he did, it was to no avail.
2. The draft breaks off here.

rara[1] – but I didn't like it as much as the Antons.[2] – If you drive back on Saturday, you'll be able to stay here for part of Sunday – we're invited to a service and to lunch at *Schwechat*[3] – adieu – look after yourself – by the way, N. N. you know who I mean – is an absolute scoundrel – he's perfectly pleasant to my face but is publicly rude about Figaro – and has caused me appalling harm here in the matter that you know about – *I know this for certain* –

Your husband, who loves you with all his heart,

Mozart

On 23 September, Mozart and his brother-in-law Franz de Paula Hofer set out for Frankfurt am Main to attend the coronation of Leopold II as Holy Roman Emperor in October. They were not part of the official entourage of court musicians, and made the journey at their own expense.

173. Mozart to his wife, 28 September 1790, Frankfurt am Main

Dearest, most beloved little wife whom I love with all my heart,

We've just arrived – it's 1 o'clock lunchtime – so it took us only 6 days – the journey would have been even quicker if we hadn't stopped 3 times during the night to rest a little. – We've just arrived at an inn in the suburb of Sachsenhausen, indescribably pleased to have managed to get a room at all – at present we don't know what

1. *Der Fall ist noch weit seltener* by Emanuel Schikaneder and Benedikt Schack (1758–1826), tenor and composer, was a sequel to *Una cosa rara* by Vicente Martín y Soler (1754–1806), premiered at Vienna in 1786. *Der Fall* was first performed at the Freihaus-Theater on 10 May 1790.
2. *Der dumme Gärtner aus dem Gebirge oder Die zween Anton*, a comic opera by Schikaneder, Schack and the bass singer and composer Franz Xaver Gerl. Mozart wrote variations on a song from *Der dumme Gärtner*, 'Ein Weib ist das herrlichste Ding' (K613) in March or April 1791.
3. An eastern suburb of Vienna.

our fate will be – whether we'll stay together or be separated. – If I can't find a room for nothing and if I find that the inn isn't too expensive, I'll certainly stay. I hope you received my letter from Efferding. I couldn't write to you again as we stopped so infrequently and only long enough to rest. – It was a very pleasant journey. – The weather was fine except for one day; – and even this didn't cause us any inconvenience as my carriage – I'd like to give it a kiss – is wonderful. – At Regensburg we lunched magnificently, we had some divine table music, angelic service and a glorious Mosel wine. We had breakfast in Nuremberg – a hideous town. – In Würzburg – a beautiful, magnificent town – we fortified our precious stomachs with coffee. – The food everywhere was tolerable – only at Aschaffenburg, 2½ stages from here, was the landlord kind enough to fleece us quite shamefully.

I'm longing for news of you – of your health, our affairs etc. – I'm now firmly resolved to do as best I can here and am already looking forward to seeing you again – what splendid lives we'll then lead! – I mean to work – work so hard that never again am I reduced by unforeseen circumstances to such desperate straits. – I'd be grateful if you could ask Stadler[1] to send along N. N. to discuss all this. – His last suggestion was that someone should advance the money on Hoffmeister's draft alone.[2] – 1000 florins in cash – the rest in cloth. – In this way everything could be paid off, still leaving something over, and on my return I'd only have to work. – The whole matter could be settled by a friend with carte blanche from me. – Adieu – I kiss you 1000 times.

Ever your Mzt

1. Anton Stadler.
2. Franz Anton Hoffmeister (1754–1812), composer and publisher; among other works, he published the first editions of Mozart's piano quartet K478, the piano trio K496, the so-called 'Hoffmeister' quartet K499, and the sonatas for keyboard with violin accompaniment K481 and K526. The draft referred to here is almost certainly a promissory note that Hoffmeister may have endorsed. The note, pre-signed by Mozart, was dated in Vienna on 1 October. It suggests that Mozart had pawned his furniture to pay for his journey to Frankfurt.

174. Mozart to his wife, 8 October 1790, Frankfurt am Main

Dearest, most beloved little wife, –

I've now received 3 letters from you, my love. – The one dated
28 Sept. has just this minute arrived. The one you sent with Herr von
Alt hasn't arrived, but I'll make enquiries at once with Le Noble. –
By now you should have received 4 letters from me. This is the 5th.
– You won't be able to write to me again as I'll probably not be here
by the time you read this: I'm intending to give my concert on
Wednesday or Thursday and think that my best plan is then to fly
away on Friday – tschiri tschitschi. – Dearest little wife! I hope you'll
have seen to the matter I mentioned in my recent letter – or that
you're still seeing to it; – I'll certainly not make enough here to be
in a position to repay 800 or 1000 florins on my return – but if the
business with Hoffmeister has at least reached the point at which all
that is missing is *my presence*, then, after taking account of *gross*
interest at 20 percent, I'll have 1600 out of 2000 florins. – I can then pay
out 1000 florins – and I'll have 600 florins left. – During Advent I shall
in any case begin a subscription for quartets[1] – I'll also take on some
pupils – I need never repay the sum as I'm writing for *H*[2]– as a result
everything will be in order. – But if you want me to return, please sort
things out with *H.* – If only you could see into my heart – the desire
and longing to see you again and to embrace you contends with the
desire to bring home lots of money. – I've often thought of *continuing*
my travels, but whenever I forced myself to take a decision, it again
occurred to me how much I'd regret it if I were to be parted for so long
from my dear wife for such *uncertain* and possibly *fruitless* ends – I feel
as though it's years since I last saw you – believe me, my love – if you
were with me, I might find it easier to make up my mind – but – I've
grown far too accustomed to you – I love you too much to be able to be

1. Presumably these are the quartets Mozart had originally intended for Frederick
William II of Prussia; see letter 168. Mozart had, in the meantime, written the
quartets K575 (June 1789), 589 (May 1790) and 590 (June 1790); they were published
by Artaria in 1791 without a dedication.
2. Hoffmeister.

separated from you for long – also, what people say about these imperial cities is all mere bluster. – It's true that I'm celebrated, admired and loved here, but the people are even more guilty of penny-pinching than in Vienna. – If the concert turns out at all well, it will be thanks to my *name* – and also to Countess Hatzfeld and the Schweitzer family, who have taken a great interest in me.[3] – But I'll be glad when it's all over. – Once I'm working hard in Vienna and have some pupils, we'll be able to live very contentedly; and nothing can dissuade me from this plan apart from a *good engagement* at a *court*. –

Have words with *Redcurrant Face*[4] or *someone else* and try to *sort things out with Hoffmeister*, and also *spread the word* that I'm planning to accept pupils; then we'll surely want for nothing. Adieu – my love – you'll be receiving some more letters from me, whereas I, unfortunately, can't receive any more from you. – Love me for ever, your

Mozart

The coronation is tomorrow. –

Look after yourself – and be careful when you go out *walking*. – *Adieu*.

275. *Mozart to his wife, 15 October 1790, Frankfurt am Main*

Dearest little wife whom I love with all my heart,

I've still not received any word from you in reply to my letters from Frankfurt, which makes me not a little uneasy – my concert was today at 11 o'clock, in terms of my honour it turned out magnificently, but with regard to the money the outcome was meagre.[1] –

---

3. Probably Sophie, Countess Hatzfeld, later Coudenhoven; Franz Maria Schweitzer, a dealer in silks and fashionable goods, and his wife Paula Maria.
4. Unidentified.
1. The programme for this concert included a symphony, two concertos (usually assumed to be K459 and K537), a scena sung by Ceccarelli, a duet and an improvisation. Owing to the length of the concert, the concluding symphony was not given. See Deutsch, *Documentary Biography*, 375.

Unfortunately some prince or other was giving a big dinner and there were major manoeuvres by the Hessian troops – but there's been some hindrance every day that I've been here. You can't imagine – – – – in spite of all this I was in such a good mood and people enjoyed it so much that they begged me to give another concert next Sunday[2] – I'll then leave on the Monday. – – I must stop now, otherwise I'll miss the post. – I see from your letters that you've not yet received any letters from me from Frankfurt, although I've written 4 – also, I think I detect a tendency on your part to doubt my punctiliousness or, rather, my eagerness to write to you, something that pains me very much. You should know me better than that – oh God! Love me only half as much as I love you and I'll be content.

Ever your
Mozart

Mozart left Frankfurt on 16 October, travelling by way of Mainz (where he gave a concert on 20 October), Mannheim (where he heard Le nozze di Figaro*), Augsburg and Munich (where he performed for Elector Karl Theodor on 4 or 5 November), arriving back at Vienna about 10 November. In March 1791 he composed the clockwork fantasy K608 and gave a symphony at the Lent concerts of the Tonkünstler-Sozietät on 16 and 17 April.*

176. Mozart to the Municipal Council of Vienna, before 28 April 1791, Vienna[1]

Most worthy
Most wise Members of the Municipal Council of Vienna

2. Nothing came of this plan.
1. The address on this letter reads: 'Municipal Council! Humble request from Wolfgang Amadè Mozart Imperial and Royal Court Composer to be appointed assistant to the Kapellmeister of St Stephen's Cathedral.'

Dear Sirs,

When Kapellmeister Hofmann[2] was ill, I was on the point of taking the liberty of applying for his post as my musical talents and works, together with my skill in composition, are well known abroad, my name is everywhere honoured and respected and I myself have for several years had the privilege of being employed as composer to the court here; and so I hoped that I was not unworthy of this post and that I deserved to be favourably regarded by a most learned municipal council.

But Kapellmeister Hofmann recovered, and in the circumstances – as I genuinely wish him a long life – I thought that I might perhaps be of service to the cathedral and of benefit to yourselves if I were to be appointed unpaid assistant to the now somewhat elderly Kapellmeister and in that way have the opportunity to lend a helping hand to this worthy man, thus earning the approval of a most learned municipal council by actually performing duties that I regard myself as being peculiarly fitted to carry out on the strength of my knowledge of – among others – the ecclesiastical style.[3]

Your most humble servant
Wolfgang Amadé Mozart
Imperial and Royal Court Composer

Constanze was pregnant, for the sixth time in eight years, and was frequently in Baden throughout the summer of 1791. Mozart was at work on Die Zauberflöte *('The Magic Flute') to a text by his friend the impresario Emanuel Schikaneder. The most successful singspiel of its time,* Die Zauberflöte *dramatizes the quest for emotional fulfilment and enlightened knowledge.*

2. Leopold Hofmann (1738–93), Kapellmeister at St Stephen's, Vienna; the post was an important and remunerative one.
3. Mozart's petition was granted, but Hofmann outlived him by fifteen months, until 17 March 1793.

177. Mozart to his wife, 11 June 1791, Vienna

Ma très chère Epouse,

Criez avec moi contre mon mauvais sort! – Mlle Kirchgässner ne donne pas son Académie Lundi! – par conséquent j'aurais pu vous posséder, ma chère, tout ce jour de Dimanche – mercredi je viendrai sûrement.[1] –

I must hurry[2] as it's already a ¼ to 7 – and the coach leaves at 7 – – mind you don't fall when you take a bath and never stay in alone – – and if I were you, I'd miss out a day in order not to overdo things. I hope that you weren't alone all last night. – I can't tell you what I'd not give to be with you in Baden instead of being stuck here. – Out of sheer boredom I've written an aria for my opera[3] today – I was already up by half past 4 – amazingly I've managed to open my watch; – but – because I didn't have a key, I couldn't, unfortunately, wind it up, isn't that sad? – Schumbla! – Another word to think about – I wound up the *big clock* instead. – Adieu – my love! – I'm having lunch with Puchberg today – I kiss you 1000 times and say to you in my thoughts: Death and despair were his reward! –

Ever your loving husband

W. A. Mozart

See that Carl behaves himself, kiss him for me.

(Take some electuaries if you're costive – but not otherwise.)

(Take care of yourself in the morning and evening if it's cool.)

1. 'Curse my bad luck! – Mlle Kirchgässner is not giving her concert on Monday and so I could have possessed you all day Sunday – I'll definitely be coming on Wednesday.' Maria Anna (Marianne) Antonia Kirchgässner (1769–1808) was a blind virtuosa on the glass harmonica. The programme of her first concert in Vienna, on 10 June, is not known. At her second concert, on 19 August, she performed Mozart's adagio and rondo K617 for glass harmonica, flute, oboe, viola and violoncello.
2. Mozart was on his way to hear the opera *Kaspar der Fagottist oder Die Zauberzither* ('Kaspar the Bassoonist or the Magic Zither') by Wenzel Müller (1759–1835). The text, by Joachim Perinet, was based on Christoph Martin Wieland's *Dschinnistan oder auserlesene Feen- und Geistermährchen*, published between 1786 and 1789, which also served, in part, as the basis for Mozart and Schikaneder's *Die Zauberflöte*.
3. *Die Zauberflöte.*

178. Mozart to his wife, 12 June 1791, Vienna

Dearest, most beloved little wife,

Why didn't I receive a letter from you yesterday evening? – Is it to keep me worried even longer about your bath? – This and something else ruined the whole of yesterday for me; – I went to see N. N. in the morning and he promised me *parole d'honneur*[1] to come and see me between 12 and 1 in order to sort everything out.[2] As a result I was unable to have lunch with Puchberg but had to wait in, – I waited – by now it was half past 2, – he still hadn't come, so I wrote a note and got the servant to take it to his father, – meanwhile I went to the Crown of Hungary as it was too late to eat anywhere else – even there I had to eat *on my own* as the other guests had already left – you can imagine my lunch, anxious as I was about you and annoyed with N. N. – if only I'd had a single soul to console me a little. – It's not good for me to be on my own when I've got things on my mind, – I was back home by half past 3 – the servant wasn't back yet – I waited – and waited – she arrived with a note at half past 6. – Waiting is always disagreeable, of course, – but even more disagreeable when the result isn't what you expect – it was nothing but excuses, saying he'd not been able to find out anything definite, and nothing but assurances that he'd certainly not forget me and most certainly keep his word, – in order to cheer myself up I then went to see Kasperl[3] in the new opera, *Der Fagottist*, that's been causing such a stir – but which is nothing to write home about. – As I was passing, I called in at the coffee-house to see if Loibel was there – but he wasn't. – In the evening I again ate at the Crown (simply in order not to be alone) – I at least had a chance to talk – then went straight to bed – I was up again at 5 the next morning – got dressed straightaway – went to see Montecuculi[4] – whom I found at home – then to N. N., but he'd

1. 'on his word of honour'.
2. The nature of this affair is unknown.
3. Kaspar.
4. Franz Ludwig, Margrave Montecuculi had earlier been a subscriber to Mozart's concerts.

already fled – I'm only sorry that I couldn't write to you this morning because of all this *unfinished business* – I so much wanted to write! –

I'm now going out to the Rechbergs[5] and the great *banquet they're giving for their friends* – if I'd not given them my solemn word and if it hadn't been so discourteous to stay away, I'd not be going there now – but what good would that do me? – Well, I'll be driving out to see you tomorrow! – If only my affairs were in order! – Who'll keep prodding N. N. if I don't? – If he's not prodded, he loses interest. I've called on him every morning, otherwise he wouldn't even have done as much as he *has* done, – please don't go to the Casino today, even if Frau Schwingenschuh drives out to see you. – Save it up till I'm with you. – If only I had news of you! – It's now half past 10, and lunch is at 12! It's now striking 11! I can't wait any longer! Adieu, dear little wife, love me as I love you, I kiss you 2000 times in my thoughts.

Ever your

Mozart

179. Mozart to his wife, 2 July 1791, Vienna

Ma très chère Epouse, –

I hope you're well; – it occurs to me that you've *rarely* been unwell[1] during any of your pregnancies! – Do you think the baths are making you too loose? – I wouldn't like to wait for *proof*, that would be too depressing; – my advice would be for you to stop now! – I'd then feel reassured. – Today is the day you should have stopped the treatment, but I bet my little wife has been to the baths as usual? – *Seriously* – I'd rather you delayed it till the autumn! – I hope you received my first brief note.

Please tell that dimwitted knave Süssmayr[2] to send me my score

5. See letter 146, n. 13.
1. Mozart probably means Constanze had not had morning sickness.
2. Mozart's student and amanuensis, Franz Xaver Süssmayr, see List.

of the first act[3] from the introduction to the *finale*, so that I can instrument it. It would be good if he could put it together today so that it can come with the first coach tomorrow, in that way I'll get it by midday. – A couple of Englishmen have just been here, they refused to leave Vienna without meeting me – no, that's not true – it was that Great Man Süssmayr whom they wanted to meet, and they came here only to ask where he's living as they'd heard that I had the good fortune to count for something in his eyes. – I told them they should go to the Crown of Hungary and wait for him there till he gets back from Baden![4] – Snai! – They want to employ him as a lamp cleaner.

I'm longing for news of you; it's now half past 12 and I've still not received anything; – I'll wait a bit longer before sealing this. – Nothing's come, I must close now! – Farewell, dearest, most beloved little wife! – Look after yourself, for even if everything else goes awry, I don't care as long as you're well – and good to *me*. – Follow the advice I gave you at the beginning of this letter, and farewell. – Adieu. A thousand kisses, and a thousand boxes on the ear for Lacci Bacci.[5] Ever your

Mozart

180. Mozart to his wife, 6 July 1791, Vienna

Dearest, most beloved little wife, –

I can't tell you how pleased I was to receive the news that the money has arrived safely;[1] – I don't remember telling you to settle up *everything*! As a sensible creature, how could I ever have said that? – If I did, I must have been completely bound up in my own thoughts – which is quite possible as I've so many important things on my mind at present. – My intention was that you should pay *only* for the

---

3. Of *Die Zauberflöte*.
4. Süssmayr had accompanied Constanze to Baden.
5. Presumably a joking reference to Süssmayr.
1. Mozart had sent Constanze 25 florins the previous day.

baths. – The rest is for your own use – – Everything else that still has to be paid for and that I've already worked out for myself I'll sort out when I get back. – Even as I write these lines, Blanchard will either *go up* – or else he'll fool the Viennese for a 3rd time![2] –

All this to-do with Blanchard is most unwelcome to me today – it's preventing me from finishing off my business. – N. N. promised to come and see me before driving out there – but he didn't come – perhaps he'll come when the fun is over – I'll wait till 2 – then I'll throw some food down inside me – and then set off in search of him. – How unpleasant life can be! – Patience! Things will get better – I'll then rest in your arms! –

I'm grateful to you for your advice not to rely entirely on N. N. – But in such cases one *has* to deal with just *one* person – if you turn to 2 or 3 and if the deal gets out – others, with whom you can't then negotiate, take you for a fool or at least someone who can't be relied on.

– But for now you can give me no greater pleasure than to be contented and cheerful – for if I *know for certain* that you want for *nothing* – all my labours are welcome and acceptable; – for even the most disastrous and complicated situation in which I might find myself becomes a mere trifle if only I know that you're *well* and *cheerful*. – And now farewell – make good use of your table fool – think of me and talk about me often – love me for ever as I love you and always be my Stanzi Marini, just as I shall always be your

Stu! – Knaller Paller –

Schnip – Schnap – Schnur –

Schnepeperl.

Snai! –

Give N. N.[3] a box on the ears and say you had to swat a fly that I'd seen! – Adieu.

Catch them – catch them – – bi – bi – bi

3 kisses, as sweet as sugar, are flying your way! –

---

2. The French balloonist François Blanchard (1753–1809) had made two unsuccessful attempts, on 9 March and 29 April 1791, to ascend over Vienna in a hot air balloon; he was successful at his third attempt on 6 July. Mozart parodied his exploits in *Die Zauberflöte*, in the scene where the three boys descend in a balloon.

3. In this instance, probably Süssmayr.

In mid-July Mozart was commissioned by Domenico Guardasoni to write the opera La clemenza di Tito *('The clemency of Titus') to celebrate the coronation of Leopold II as king of Bohemia and Hungary in Prague; the commission had first been offered to Salieri, who had refused it. Mozart appears to have taken about six weeks to compose the score, to a libretto adapted from Metastasio's. At about the same time he was anonymously commissioned by Count Franz von Walsegg-Stuppach (1763–1827) to compose a Requiem in memory of his wife, Anna, who had died on 14 February 1791. The Mozarts' sixth, and second surviving, child, Franz Xaver Wolfgang (1791–1844), was born on 26 July. A month later, Mozart, Constanze and Süssmayr travelled to Prague, arriving on 28 August.* Don Giovanni *was performed on 2 September and* La clemenza di Tito *on 6 September. Mozart returned to Vienna about mid-September and completed* Die Zauberflöte, *which was premiered on 30 September at Schikaneder's Freihaus Theater auf der Wieden. Constanze was once again in Baden.*

181. Mozart to his wife, 7 and 8 October 1791, Vienna

Friday at half past 10 at night.

Dearest, most beloved little Wife, –

I've just got back from the opera;[1] – it was as full as ever. – The duet *Mann und Weib* etc. and the glockenspiel[2] in the first act were encored at usual – also the boys' trio in the 2nd act[3] – but what I like most of all is the *silent approval*! – You can really see how much this opera continues to rise in people's estimation. Now for an account of what I've been doing; – as soon as you'd sailed off, I played 2 games of billiards with Herr von Mozart, who wrote the opera for Schikaneder. – I then sold my nag for 14 ducats. – I then got Joseph[4]

---

1. *Die Zauberflöte.*
2. 'Das klinget so herrlich'.
3. 'Seid uns zum zweitenmal willkommen'.
4. Presumably Joseph Deiner, a waiter at the inn 'Zur silbernen Schlange'. He is thought to be the author of a memoir of Mozart's last days, published in the Viennese *Morgen-Post* in 1856; see Deutsch, *Documentary Biography*, 563–6.

to call *Primus* and fetch me some black coffee, over which I smoked a splendid pipe of tobacco; then I instrumented almost the whole of Stadler's rondo.[5] Meanwhile I've received a letter from Stadler in Prague; – the Duscheks are all well; – I don't think she can have received any of your letters, hard though it is to believe! – Enough – they've all heard of the wonderful reception of my German opera. –

The strangest thing is that on the very evening that my new opera was being performed for the first time to such acclaim, Tito was being performed for the last time in Prague, also to extraordinary acclaim. – All the numbers were applauded. – Bedini[6] sang better than ever. – The little duet in A[7] that the 2 girls sing was repeated – and if they hadn't spared Marchetti,[8] they'd also have repeated the rondo.[9] – People called out bravo to *Stodla*[10] from the stalls and even from the orchestra – O Bohemian miracle! he writes – but I really made an *effort*, he writes; – *Stodla* also wrote that [...][11] and I can now see that he's an ass – [...] you understand, not Stodla – – who's only a bit of an ass – whereas [...] well, he's a *real* ass. –

I went out by the *Stubenthor* at half past 5 and took my favourite walk to the theatre – what do I see? – What do I smell? – – Don Primus with the pork cutlets! – *Che gusto* – I'm now eating to your health – it's just gone 11; – perhaps you're still asleep? – Sh! Sh! Sh! – I shan't wake you! –

Saturday the 8th. – You should have seen me at supper yesterday! – I couldn't find the old tableware, so I got out a white one decorated with snowdrops – and placed the double candlestick with wax candles in front of me! – According to the letter from [...] the Italians are

5. The finale of the clarinet concerto K622, composed for Anton Stadler.
6. Domenico Bedini, who sang the role of Sesto.
7. 'Ah perdona al primo affetto'.
8. Maria Marchetti-Fantozzi (1767–1807) sang the role of Vitellia.
9. 'Deh per questo istante solo'.
10. Anton Stadler, who played the demanding first clarinet part in the opera.
11. A number of deletions have been made in this and the following letter, possibly by Constanze Mozart's second husband, Georg Nikolaus Nissen, when he prepared the correspondence for publication in the 1820s. The deletions are indicated by ellipses.

said to be finished here – also, Frau Duschek must have received at least *one* letter from you as he writes: The [. . .] was very pleased with Mathies' postscript, she said she likes the ASS – or ASS – just as he is. – Do encourage [. . .] to write for [. . .] as he's been on at me to see to this. – Even as I write this, I expect you're having a good swim. – The hairdresser came at six on the dot – Primus had already lit the fire at half past 5 and woke me at a ¼ to. – Why does it have to be raining? – I was so hoping that you'd have good weather! – Just keep nice and warm so that you don't catch a cold; I hope the baths will keep you well throughout the winter – it was only this wish to see you well again that persuaded me to pack you off to Baden. – How I miss you – I predicted that this would happen. – If I hadn't been so busy, I'd have set off at once to spend the week with you; – but *out there* it's simply not *convenient* to work; and as far as possible I'd prefer to avoid getting into *difficulties*; there's nothing more agreeable than to live in relative peace and quiet, and for that one has to work hard, which I like doing. –

Give [. . .]¹² a good box on the ears in my name, and also get [. . .], whom I kiss 1000 times, to give him a couple – for heaven's sake don't let him go short! – The last thing I want is for him to reproach you, today or tomorrow, for not having treated him properly and looked after him – – give him too many blows rather than too few –

It would also be good if you could tweak his nose and knock out one of his eyes or cause him some other visible injury, so that the fellow can't deny having received something from you; – adieu, my dear little wife! – The coach is about to leave. – I hope to receive something from you today, and in this sweet hope I kiss you 1000 times. I am ever your loving husband

W. A. Mozart

12. Possibly Süssmayr.

182. Mozart to his wife, 8 and 9 October 1791, Vienna

Saturday evening at ½ past 10 –
Dearest, most beloved little wife, –

It was with immense pleasure and feelings of joy that I found your letter on my return from the opera; – even though Saturday is post day and therefore a bad day, the opera was again performed to a full house, with the usual applause and encores; – it's being given again tomorrow, but there'll be no performance on Monday – as a result Süssmayr will have to bring Stoll[1] in on *Tuesday*, when it will be given again *for the first time* – I say *for the first time* as it will probably then be given several times in succession; – I've just eaten a delicious piece of sturgeon that my faithful valet Don Primus brought – and as I'm feeling fairly hungry today, I've sent him out for some more, if he can find it. – Meanwhile I'll continue writing to you. – This morning I worked so hard that I didn't notice what time it was until 1/2 past 1 – so I then ran as fast as I could to Hofer's[2] – simply so that I wouldn't have to eat on my own – and found Mama[3] there too. Straight after lunch I returned home and wrote till it was time to go to the opera. Leutgeb[4] asked me to take him again, so I did. – Tomorrow I'll be taking *Mama*; – Hofer has already given her the wordbook to read. – In Mama's case it's no doubt a question of her *watching* the opera rather than *hearing* it. – [. . .] had a box today. – [. . .] applauded *everything*, but he, the know-all, revealed himself to be such a thoroughgoing *Bavarian* that I couldn't stay, otherwise I'd have ended up calling him an ass; – unfortunately I was there at the start of the 2nd act, in other words, during a solemn scene. – He laughed at everything; to begin with I was patient enough to draw his attention to some of the speeches, but – he just laughed at

1. Anton Stoll (1747–1805), music director at Baden; Mozart composed the motet *Ave verum corpus* K618 (17 June 1791) for him.
2. Mozart's brother-in-law Franz Hofer.
3. His mother-in-law, Maria Cäcilia Weber.
4. The former Salzburg horn player Joseph Leutgeb; after moving to Vienna in 1777 he became a cheesemonger.

everything as before; – it got too much for me – I called him *Papageno* and left – but I don't think the fool understood me. – So I went into another box where *Flamm*[5] and his wife were sitting; I was happy to be there and stayed to the end. – But I went onstage during Papageno's aria with the glockenspiel as I felt such an urge to play it myself today. – As a joke I played an arpeggio at a point where Schikaneder[6] has a rest – he was startled – he looked into the wings and saw me – the 2nd time round I didn't play anything – this time he stopped and refused to go on – I guessed what he was thinking and again played a chord – he then hit the glockenspiel and said *shut up* – everyone laughed then – it was because of this joke, I think, that many people discovered for the first time that he wasn't playing the instrument himself. – Incidentally, you've no idea how delightful the music sounds from a box close to the orchestra – much better than from the gallery; – as soon as you're back, you must try this for yourself. –

Sunday, 7 in the morning. – I slept very well and hope that you'll have slept well, too. – I really enjoyed the half of a capon that friend Primus brought back with him. – At 10 I'm off to the service at the Piarists[7] as Leutgeb has told me that I can then speak to the *director*. – I'll also stay for lunch.

Primus told me yesterday that lots of people in Baden are ill, is that true? – Do take care and don't trust the weather. – Well, Primus has just got back with the beastly news that the coach left before 7 this morning and there won't be another one till this afternoon – as a result, I've been wasting my time writing all this at night and in the early morning as you won't receive my letter till this evening, which annoys me greatly. – I'll definitely be coming out to see you next Sunday – we'll then go to the Casino together and return home together on Monday –

Lechleitner was again at the opera; – even though he's no con-

5. Franz Xaver Flamm (1739–1811), later an agent in connection with the taxes attached to Mozart's estate.
6. He was singing the role of Papageno.
7. Mozart was making arrangements for his son Carl to attend the school run by the Piarist Fathers in the Josefstadt suburb of Vienna.

noisseur, he's still a genuine music lover, something that [. . .] isn't
– he's a real *nonentity*. – He'd much prefer a dinner. – Farewell, my
love! – I kiss you millions of time and am ever your

Mozart

P. S.: Give Sophie[8] a kiss for me. Perhaps you'll *pull* Süssmayr's *nose*
for him and give his *hair* a good *tug*. A thousand good wishes to
Stoll. Adieu – the hour has struck – – 'lebt wohl, auf Wiedersehn!'[9] –

N. B.: You presumably sent the 2 pairs of yellow winter breeches
that go with the boots to the laundry as Joseph and I have looked for
them in vain. – Adieu –

183. Mozart to his wife, 14 [and 15] October 1791, Vienna

Dearest, most beloved wife,

Yesterday, Thursday the 13th, Hofer drove out with me to see
Carl,[1] we had lunch out there, then drove home, at 6 I picked up
Salieri and Mme Cavalieri in my carriage and drove them to my box
– I then hurried off to collect Mama and Carl, whom I'd left in the
meantime with Hofer. – You can't imagine how kind they[2] were –
and how much they liked not only my music but also the libretto and
everything else. – They both said it was a grand opera worthy of
being performed at the grandest festivities and before the greatest
monarch and that they'd certainly be seeing it more than once as
they'd never seen a more beautiful or delightful spectacle. – He
listened and watched with the utmost attentiveness, and from the
overture to the final chorus there wasn't a single number that didn't

8. Constanze's younger sister.
9. 'farewell! – We'll meet again', sung by Tamino, Papageno and the Three Ladies
in act 1, scene 8 of *Die Zauberflöte*.
1. Carl, then aged seven, was at a boarding school in Perchtoldsdorf bei Wien run
by Wenzel Bernhard Heeger.
2. That is, Salieri and Cavalieri.

call forth a *bravo* or a *bello* from him, and they could barely thank me enough for my kindness. They'd always intended to go to the opera yesterday. But they'd have needed to have been in their seats by 4 – as it was, they saw and heard everything in comfort. – After the show I drove them home and had supper with Carl at Hofer's. – I then drove home with him and we both had a good night's sleep. It was no small treat for Carl to be taken to the opera. – He's looking splendid – in terms of his health he couldn't be in a better place, but everything else there is unfortunately wretched! – No doubt they can turn out good peasants! – But enough of this, his serious studies – God have mercy on him! – don't start till Monday and so I've asked to keep him till after lunch on Sunday; I said you'd like to see him – tomorrow, Sunday, I'll drive out with him to see you – you can then keep him, or else I'll drive him back to Heeger's after lunch on Sunday; – think it over, a month can't do him much harm, I think! – meanwhile we may be able to sort something out with the Piarists – I'm working on this. – I should add that although he's no worse, nor is he in the least bit better. He's still got the same bad habits, still enjoys making trouble and is *almost less inclined* to study than before but, as he himself admits, merely wanders around in the garden for 5 hours in the morning and 5 hours after lunch, in a word the children do nothing but eat, drink, sleep and go for walks, Leutgeb and Hofer have just arrived; – the former is staying to eat, I've just sent my faithful comrade Primus to fetch something to eat from the Bürgerspital; – I'm very pleased with the fellow he's let me down only once, when I was forced to sleep at Hofer's, which annoyed me a lot as they sleep far too long for my liking, I prefer to be at home as I'm used to my own routine. This one occasion put me in a really bad mood. Yesterday the whole day was taken up with my trip to Perchtoldsdorf, so that I couldn't write to you – but it's unforgivable of you not to have written for 2 days, I hope I'll have news from you today. And tomorrow I'll speak to you in person and kiss you with all my heart.

Farewell, ever your

Mozart

I kiss Sophie a thousand times, with N. N. you can do as you like. Adieu.

Mozart fetched Constanze back from Baden on 17 October and on 17 November his Kleine Freimaurer-Kantate K623 was performed at the Masonic lodge 'Zur neugekrönten Hoffnung'. On 20 November he became ill and was attended by Dr Thomas Franz Closset and Dr Mathias von Sallaba (1764–97). Mozart's condition deteriorated rapidly and he died at five minutes to one on the morning of 5 December. Possibly the most accurate account of Mozart's last days, at least with respect to the medical attention he received and the suddenness of his death, probably from rheumatic inflammatory fever, comes in a letter of 7 April 1825[3] written thirty-four years after his death by his sister-in-law Sophie.

184. Sophie Haibel (née Weber) to Georg Nikolaus Nissen, 7 April 1825, Salzburg

. . . when Mozart fell ill, we[1] both made him a night-shirt which he could put on from the front, for he could not turn over because of the swelling; and as we did not know how very ill he was, we also made him a quilted dressing-gown (for all of which his good wife, my dear sister, gave us the material) so that he would be well protected when he got up, and so we visited him diligently; he made it plain that he was greatly delighted by the dressing-gown. I went to visit him in the city every day, and once when I went in on a Saturday, M. said to me, 'Now, dear Sophie, tell Mama that I am getting on very well, and that I will be coming out to her in the octave of her name day to give her my congratulations.' Whose joy could be greater than mine when I brought my mother such glad tidings, after she

3. Deutsch, *Documentary Biography*, 524–5.
1. Sophie and her mother.

could scarcely expect the news; so I hurried home to calm her fears, after he had really seemed to me to be cheerful and well. The next day was a Sunday, then; I was still young and, I admit it, vain – and I liked dressing up, but I never liked walking from our suburb into the town in my best clothes, and I had not the money for going by carriage; so I said to our good mother, 'Dear Mama, I shan't go in to Mozart today – he was so well yesterday, so he'll be better still today, and one day more or less will make no difference.' She then said, 'I'll tell you what, make me a cup of coffee, and then I'll tell you what you can do.' She was rather concerned to keep me at home, for my sister knows how much she always wanted me to be with her. So I went into the kitchen. The fire had gone out; I had to light a taper and kindle the fire. But Mozart was still constantly on my mind. My coffee was ready, and my candle was still burning. I then saw how wasteful I had been to have burnt so much of my candle. The candle was still burning brightly, and I stared straight at my candle and thought, 'I wonder how Mozart is?', and as I was thinking this, and looking at my candle, the candle went out, it went out as if it had never been alight. Not even a spark remained on the big wick, there was no draught, to that I can swear; I shuddered, ran to our mother, and told her. She said, 'All right, hurry up and take those clothes off and go in, but come and tell me straight away how he is. Now don't be long.' I hurried as fast as I could. My God! how frightened I was when my sister, half demented yet trying to control herself, came to meet me and said, 'Thank God you've come, dear Sophie; he was so bad last night that I never thought he would survive this day. Stay with me today, for if he gets bad again today, he will die in the night. Go in to him for a little and see how he is.' I tried to control myself and went up to his bed, when he called to me at once, 'Ah, dear Sophie, it is good of you to come. You must stay here tonight, you must see me die.' I tried to be strong and to dissuade him, but he answered to all my attempts, 'I have the taste of death on my tongue already', and 'Who will look after my dearest Constanze if you don't stay?' – 'Yes, dear Mozart, but I must first just go and tell our mother that you would like me with you tonight, or she will think some misfortune has happened.' – 'Yes, do that, but come back soon.' – God, how awful I felt. My poor sister came after me and begged me for heavens' sake to go to the priests at St Peter's and ask the priests to come, as if on a chance visit. That I also did, though the priests hesitated a long time and I had great difficulty in persuading one of these inhuman priests to do it. – – Then I hurried to our mother, who was anxiously awaiting me; it was already dark. How frightened the poor dear was. I persuaded her to go and spend the night with her eldest daughter, Hofer, who is now dead, and so it was; and I ran back as fast as I could to my inconsolable sister. Süssmayr was there at M's bedside; and the well-known Requiem lay on the coverlet, and Mozart was explaining to him how he thought he should finish it after his death. Then he commanded his wife to keep his death a secret until she had informed Albrechtsberger[2] of it; for the post was his by right in the eyes of God and the world. There was a long search for Closset, the doctor, who was found in the theatre; but he had to wait until the play was over – then he came and prescribed *cold* compresses on his burning head, and these gave him such a shock that he did not regain consciousness before he passed away. The last thing he did was to try and mouth the sound of the timpani in his Requiem; I can still hear it now.

2. Albrechtsberger succeeded Mozart as assistant Kapellmeister at St Stephen's, Vienna.

List of Letters

List of Principal Correspondents

Numbers after the name indicate the letter.

Index of Mozart's Works by Genre

VOCAL MUSIC

Masses

Miscellaneous church music

Music for plays and ballets

Arias and ensembles

Songs with keyboard accompaniment

Miscellaneous secular vocal music

INSTRUMENTAL MUSIC

Symphonies

Serenades, divertimentos and cassations for orchestra

String quartets

Trios with keyboard

Miscellaneous chamber music

Sonatas and variations for keyboard and violin

Sonatas for keyboard four-hands or two keyboards

Sonatas for keyboard

Variations for keyboard

Miscellaneous keyboard works

Index of Mozart's Works by Köchel Numbers

General Index

Numbers in **bold** indicate an entry in the 'List of Important People' on pp. xxiii–xxxvi.